A HISTORY OF
SPAIN

Rafael Altamira

A HISTORY OF SPAIN

FROM THE BEGINNINGS TO THE PRESENT DAY

by

RAFAEL ALTAMIRA

Translated by
MUNA LEE

SIXTH PRINTING

D. VAN NOSTRAND COMPANY, INC.

PRINCETON, NEW JERSEY

TORONTO   LONDON

NEW YORK

D. VAN NOSTRAND COMPANY, INC.

120 Alexander St., Princeton, New Jersey (*Principal office*)
24 West 40 Street, New York 18, New York

D. VAN NOSTRAND COMPANY, LTD.
358, Kensington High Street, London, W.14, England

D. VAN NOSTRAND COMPANY (Canada), LTD.
25 Hollinger Road, Toronto 16, Canada

FIRST EDITION

A translation of the Second Edition (Spanish)
of *A History of Spain* by Rafael Altamira

First Published October 1949
Reprinted March 1952
Reprinted October 1955
Reprinted May 1958
Reprinted September 1962
Reprinted February 1966

Rafael Altamira

"SPANIARDS have always loved history's difficult discipline," Rafael Altamira remarks in Chapter XIII of the present volume, "with its twofold aspect of art and of science." Dr. Altamira himself, internationally renowned as historian, as educator, and as jurist, is one of the best exemplars of that predilection. As J. B. Trend has said, "A history of Spain which should also be a history of Spanish civilization might almost be said to be an invention of Professor Altamira himself."

Rafael Altamira, born at Alicante in 1866, took his degree in law at the University of Valencia and became Doctor of Law of the University of Madrid at the age of twenty-one. In the capital he first turned his attention to journalism and later was successively a professor of the *Institución Libre de Enseñanza*, editor of the Republican newspaper *La Justicia*, and Secretary of the National Pedagogic Museum, winning distinction also as orator, art critic, and historian. After participation in various international congresses on education, history, archeology, and American institutions, in 1897 he competed successfully for the professorship of the History of Spanish Law at the University of Oviedo. Twelve years later that University sent him on a cultural mission to the western hemisphere, during which he lectured in South America, and Cuba, and participated in the conference of the American Historical Society at New York.

Professor Altamira's professorship was marked among other things by his attention to social problems, and he was frequently called upon to arbitrate labor disputes. The university extension courses that he inaugurated at Oviedo were largely attended by working men in Asturias and Santander. After service as Director General of Elementary Education, he was appointed to the Diplomatic and Consular Institute as Professor of the History of Modern Colonization and of Modern Political History in America. In 1914 the University of Madrid ap-

v

pointed him to the newly created Chair of the Civil and Political Institutions of America.

In 1919-20, Dr. Altamira acted as Spanish arbitrator on the International Commission of Mining Disputes in America. For seven years (1916-23) he served as Senator in the *Cortes,* representing the University of Valencia.

Because of his active interest in comparative law and his wide experience in international arbitration, Rafael Altamira was a natural choice as one of the ten jurists whom the Council of the League of Nations in 1920 invited "to prepare plans for the Permanent Court of International Justice." After that august body had been created, in 1921, and again in 1930, Dr. Altamira was elected Judge of the Court. He is an associate member of the Institute of International Law; doctor *honoris causa* of the Universities of Paris, Cambridge, and Bordeaux, among others; and past president of the Section on Comparative History of Law of the International Academy of Comparative Law and of the Ibero-American Institute of Comparative Law. He has served as corresponding editor of the *Revue Historique* of Paris, has been a correspondent also of *The Athenaeum* of London, and has directed publication of a collection of works on modern comparative law, several volumes of which are devoted to the Permanent Court of International Justice and its decisions. Besides some novels early in his career, Dr. Altamira has published various critical works on art, as well as personal reminiscences and legal and historical studies.

Clarity, objectivity, and scrupulous adherence to the historic fact characterize Rafael Altamira's attitude as historian. It has been said of him that his books show why Spanish things are as they are—in both Europe and America. They show no less what humane and generous concepts, what rectitudes of criterion and what temperateness of judgment, have made Rafael Altamira an enduring interpreter of the history and the conscience of Spain.

MUNA LEE

1949

Author's Prologue to the Second Spanish Edition

THE present edition is characterized by scrupulous correction of the errata and linear transpositions in the first; by addition of some details that seem to me essential for understanding certain facts and of the most important findings of historical research since 1933; and, finally, by recasting of certain passages in order to attain greater clarity and thereby avoid possible misunderstandings as to meaning in the narrative and the accompanying evaluations.

In making these improvements, I have kept in mind and striven not to exceed the limitations on length and content necessitated by a brief history such as this. Those who desire a fuller treatment of subjects in their own special fields of interest, or who believe they find herein gaps to be attributed to the author's inadvertence, should realize that these are deliberate omissions on my part due not only to the concept of the purpose of a brief history as stated in the Prologue to the First Edition, but also to the fact that what is lacking here may be found amply set forth, as I have said, in other works of mine there listed.

The text that readers will find in the following pages was completed in April 1936 for immediate printing. The events in July of that year prevented publication then. The present volume contains in addition to that text the relation of events posterior to the date mentioned.

1946

Author's Prologue to the First Spanish Edition

I. What Is New in This Text

THE present volume is not a mere abridgment of my four-volume *Historia de España y de la civilización española* [History of Spain and of Spanish Civilization] published from 1900 to 1911, the successive editions of which up to and including the third (but not those thereafter) I revised and more or less enlarged. As early as the Prologue to the First Edition I announced my intention to write a Compendium of the two volumes that I then believed would complete the work; but the Compendium that I had in mind in 1898 was planned only as an elementary textbook.

Official and private occupations which since 1911 have altered greatly the direction of my intellectual life, and continue to keep it to some degree out of its original channel, have prevented me from carrying out that intention. The same reasons kept me from publishing a fifth volume of the *Historia* which would have dealt with the nineteenth century in Spain.[1] But despite these hindrances to full development of the project, as the four volumes became known in Spain and in educational circles abroad, the demand became ever more insistent for a one-volume abridgment that could be used in secondary and some university classes.

On different occasions I promised to write this abridgment. Several times I planned it. Finally I began to write; I do not recall exactly when, but undoubtedly before 1920. When the projected work had reached the thirteenth century in the manuscript stage, a new turn in

---

[1] The author has in preparation a specialized History of the Nineteenth and Twentieth Centuries which will complete to date the four volumes published from 1900 to 1911, and will probably be issued in two additional volumes. [Author's note.]

viii

my professional career detained my hand and the book was shelved to await a more propitious moment. But demand for its publication did not cease, nor was there any lessening of the teaching need for such a work which was the basis of the demand. A clear proof of this was the appearance in 1918 of *A History of Spain* which, with my authorization, Professor Charles E. Chapman of the University of California wrote and published. The text of that *History* (except as relates to the nineteenth century) was based on the four volumes of my work, as the author himself states on his title-page ("A History of Spain, Founded on the *Historia de España y de la Civilización Española* of Rafael Altamira." New York, 1918). That is to say, Professor Chapman wrote in English a book similar to the one being asked of me in Spanish.

The propitious occasion for my satisfying this request arrived not long since; but in planning the abridgment anew, instead of taking as a basis the manuscript already begun which I mentioned above, I laid it aside and elected rather to write a new text. Various reasons impelled me: one, the progressive achievements of Spanish historical research during the past ten years; another, the alteration of my own point of view during this time as regards some aspects and periods of our history; and, finally, the fact that I have written recently (1929) a new text for the special History of Spanish Civilization first published many years ago in the series of Soler's Manuals [1] and often re-issued without my intervention; that is to say, without my revising or improving the original edition. That Manual contained the material indicated by its title to the close of the nineteenth century, unlike my History of Spain, published 1900 to 1911, which stopped short at 1808. The new edition of the History of Spanish Civilization, made, as I have said, in 1929—but not for Soler—brought the narrative to 1914. The existence of this book seemed to me to make imperative an important change in the project for a one-volume abridgment or brief history (whether in Spanish or in any other language) to be derived wholly from the four-volume History. That change involved putting the story of Spanish civilization in second place (though without omission of any fundamental data), since a volume of mine on that subject

---

[1] The Manual is titled *Historia de la civilización española*. The first edition, published at Barcelona in 1902, has been followed by many others without revision by the author. A corrected and enlarged authorized edition is scheduled for publication by Espasa-Calpe in Argentina. [Author's note.]

was in print already. At the same time, I was led by several considerations, among them being the intrinsic character of any brief manual, to employ a more familiar, or rather, more popular, style and general treatment of the subject than had characterized the extensive *Historia* of 1900-1911.

These considerations, which seemed to me objectively reasonable and sound, turned out to be furthermore in accordance with the request urged on me not long ago by the editors of the Armand Colin Collection (at the suggestion and through the good offices of Professor Hauser) for a general history of Spain to be published in that series. This request was the occasion to which I have already alluded for my resolving to carry out the project so often postponed. I made the effort; and in spite of the burdens imposed by my official responsibilities, wrote the text of the present volume. This text, however, differs greatly from the one published in the Armand Colin Collection, since the limited number of pages allotted the respective volumes of the series necessitated omission of many pages of the original Spanish. Herewith is the complete text, not cut down by page limitations; though even so, the reader will note that the section on what is called the history of civilization (and particularly on social and juridical institutions) is proportionally less ample than the treatment of the same subject in my History of 1900-1911; this, for the reasons stated above. However, I am planning to publish shortly a History of Civilization new as to range, content, and, not infrequently, as to criterion, wherein the reader so desiring will find amplification of matters here treated in brief; if he be not inclined meanwhile to look up the material in the four volumes already mentioned so often which, though stopping short with 1808, are much more detailed in treatment than the present work.

Moreover, in spite of the differences in content among my several books, those who are acquainted with my first and most complete work and have followed me since through my several historical volumes, arrive perhaps at the conclusion (which seems to me correct) that all respond substantially to the same organic concept of human history, advanced as a theory for the first time in my book on methodology, *La Enseñanza de la Historia* [The Teaching of History, first edition, 1891]. In fact, my History of Spain and Spanish Civilization was merely the attempt to realize in 1900 what I had theorized about nine years earlier with respect to the writing of history, whether universal or national. In my own opinion, the principal service of that work (if it rendered any) consisted not, as a recent critic has said, in collecting "for the first time" the results of modern monographic research on Spanish history, but in presenting a frame of reference, a system of classification and at times of hierarchy for the facts; and of presenting also an integral and organic picture of Spanish life and not merely, as was the current custom, of Spanish political activity. Such, at least, was my aspiration; I am not the one who can say with absolute objectivity if or in what degree I have succeeded. The only thing that I can affirm is that I have hewn to this line ever since, making ever more plain, within the limits of my ability, the organic meaning of history and the psychological root, individual and collective, of the events in the historic process of a people, apart from the influence of the physical environment (which pertains to it in everything at every moment), and especially of those events leaving traces on the life of that people or of humankind in general; the only events, in truth, that merit being known or recorded.

The importance that I continue to give this phase of historiographical writing responds to the very obvious fact that the condensation of the product of new historical research always involves the possibility of its being superseded or even contradicted, since up to the present that is an unavoidable condition of historic science; and may be a condition of it always. However, the organic construction of factual material, in function of concepts and problems of human life, may endure for a long time (aside from the fact of being necessary in any case), helping orient even those who, because they view the historic process and human finalities from a different standpoint, would prefer another and different guide. I believe, nevertheless, that our present knowledge of the subject matter of history and of its tendencies and fundamental movements has already succeeded in fixing definitive elements that are an essential yardstick in understanding human history as a whole. I shall not give up the hope of setting forth in another book the conclusion which I have reached in this respect and of which I gave a preview in my 1923 classes at the Collège de France.[1] In the present volume also my readers will find some manifestations of this conclusion, expressed in the method of selection and presentation of facts

---

1 These lessons are as yet unpublished. [Author's note.]

with reference to Spanish history. In great part this brief history represents conjointly (in measure corresponding to its length and content) the result arrived at today after my long years of endeavor to understand more fully and more deeply my country's history, and, with it, the people making that history: both objectives being less easy and simple of achievement than some suppose and others firmly believe, to judge by the categorical generalizations sometimes formulated, for a real basis of which we should search in vain.

II. What This Book Is

Independently of all the aforesaid, I have tried to make the present brief history conform to certain conditions of exposition which I shall proceed to explain.

In the first place, my purpose has been the utmost brevity possible without sacrifice of matter in my judgment essential. This quality would have seemed to me always meritorious in such a work as this even if only as a reaction against the contrary vice (so usual in Spanish handbooks and abridgments) of excessive detail. In the present instance, brevity has been not so much my primary objective as the natural consequence of the criterion of selection which has guided me above everything else in writing this brief history. What I have desired to write is a compendium of Spanish history reduced to what in my humble opinion represents the minimum of that history with which a Spaniard, or a foreigner, of average culture should be acquainted. And when I say "of average culture," I am thinking of the thousands of men and women who have had no more education in history than is given by our secondary schools and who during the rest of their lives lack time and opportunity to round out the ideas of history thus acquired. Naturally this consideration applies in still greater degree to those millions of fellow-citizens who have received only elementary education, even though some of these in later life may attend one of those liberal arts schools not having secondary training as entrance prerequisite, or may attain, self-taught, a general or a professional cultural training which will in all probability suffer from the gaps due to lack of continuity.

The so-called secondary and even more especially the primary schools require another text than this brief history, because of the

extreme youth of their pupils and of the limited time assigned the subject. That text, though it might be substantially like the present work,
would necessitate in detail and manner of exposition something more,
pedagogically, than a mere abbreviation of the material here presented;
what is needed would be a complete recasting of the subject-matter,
with regard to principles of history-teaching which I have expressed on
other occasions and need not here repeat. I hope that the day will come
when I shall be able to write one or more little books on the history
of Spain in accordance with this criterion and standard just as I think
they should be written and without having to consider any other opinion on the subject. But my purpose in the present volume is distinct.

To return to the criterion of selection according to which I have
determined the material in this brief history, I wish to say that the
very obvious playing down herein of details relating to the political
side of history (that is, of the history of the Spanish State and its
representatives) is due not to the simple desire for restraint but to a
higher exigency which has to do with the relative importance of the
facts themselves as regards one another and in virtue of which I have
most intentionally sacrificed those that do not contribute toward shaping the essential picture of the Spanish historic process. To that category belong, for example, mention of kings who left no useful trace
of their reigns; enumeration of every battle; relation of intrigues by
palace hangers-on or noblemen (in the period when these were possible) which were without substantial consequence in the progress of
the people as a whole; and so on.

I think it advisable to note, at this point, the difference existing
between my own guiding criterion and the pacifist, or anti-war, preoccupation that tends to hide or misrepresent reality by suppressing in
History mention of events that, whether or not we approve them, have
characterized important moments in the life of peoples and, at times,
have deeply influenced their future. Thus, though a convinced and
militant pacifist even as regards the subject-matter in teaching history,
I consider myself authorized as historian neither to erase the war
record from a people's chronicles, since the wars did take place and
wars keep on taking place, nor even to conceal the importance that
men assigned to war in the past and that many continue to assign it
in the present. History must tell "the truth and the whole truth"
about what humankind has done, even though the historians desire

ardently that things be different in the future. Convictions and observations compatible in private individuals may be as incompatible in the special field of history as would be in natural science a naturalist's exact proof of a fact and his personal opinion as to what that fact might or should have been. I have preserved rigorously at every point of our history and with regard to all personages in it that I have deemed it necessary to single out, their own physiognomies; and from that faith-ful portraiture none can infer that this fact or the other seems to me either good or bad from the standpoint of my own doctrinal convictions which, I repeat, in no case would have authorized me to disguise or silence what really occurred.

In another order of considerations, I have tried to emphasize the interweaving of Spanish history with that of other peoples, particularly at its most important moments; and have not been content, therefore, to trace the event and trust the reader to fill in the outlines from a knowledge of world hisory which he may not possess. Rather, I have characterized and explained the foreign event so as to show how and in what direction it has influenced events of our own history, present or past. Undoubtedly there is not much of that kind of thing in this brief history. It, in fact, merely represents an essay toward realization of the idea (which is gaining ground among historians) that the history of the fatherland should be taught as an element in universal history, and even that there might well be a textbook in which both histories are taught at one and the same time, in the proportion exacted by the nationalist point of view. But such teaching remains purely an aspiration which has not, as the phrase has it, found a formula, if, indeed, there be one possible.

Part of the interweaving of the history of Spain with that of other peoples consists in noting reciprocal influences, especially in matter of institutions and cultures; a point of view on which I dwelt in the History of 1900-1911 and which I stressed in the History of Spanish Civilization. In the present abridgment, I have indicated culminating moments of foreign influence on Spain and of Spain on the foreigner, and have adduced some considerations regarding that quality of assimilation which seems to characterize us and which ends by transforming itself into original creativeness; like the power of absorption which the Spanish type has exercised over men of other peoples coming to the Peninsula. I have also given attention to another phase of this interweaving of the national history with the history of other countries; namely, the occasions when Spanish activity, political or otherwise, enters into the channel of universal or of European history and makes our country a factor in international life, unlike those moments in which it isolates itself or reduces the national life to problems exclusively internal.

Another aspect of our own history on which I have placed emphasis because of its implicit importance as to advancement or paralyzation of many fundamentals of living, is the systematic modification of our physical environment by way of making it better satisfy economic necessities.

Finally, I have given especial attention to the relation among the different Spanish States during the so-called Middle Ages and to the way in which the process of unification and vertebration (permit me this once to employ that harsh neologism) was produced among us, beginning with the sixteenth century; this being one of the vital problems of Spanish history not yet solved except in some external aspects.

At the end of the text I have added also chronological tables—material to which little attention is paid in our manuals—that will help the reader place easily in point of time important events and their correlation.

One word more as to the illustrations and particularly the maps. In selecting the former, I have been guided on the one hand by care to include only those that serve to illuminate the text, in which citation of specific monuments, works of art, personages, et cetera, has necessarily been limited to very characteristic objects and individuals; while on the other hand I have felt a compelling desire (not to be satisfied, for reasons obvious without explanation) to revivify in so far as possible the series of illustrations utilized in my former books, offering something new if possible. My readers will find available a comprehensive collection of graphic historical documentation in this and my other volumes.

Regarding the maps, it has been my desire to reduce these to the utmost simplicity possible (apart from the material necessity of not using too many) even to the point of risking a certain vagueness as to detail; a vagueness inevitable when concentration is on the general outlines. Any reader desirous of greater detail will find it in a world atlas or in one of the good modern Spanish atlases of historical geography and in a few specialized maps adorning some modern historical monographs. But in this brief history I have striven above everything else for clarity; a quality which, as we know, is often lost when every smallest detail of a matter is presented.

And now, before broaching the final point that I wish to discuss in this Prologue, let me explain the reason for certain allusions to be found in this book to historic and often debatable acts of other peoples. Sometimes, indeed, I have made a comparison of the conduct of Spaniards or of the Spanish States and that of other human groups or States; not on account of an insensate desire to emphasize things that we do not approve today from the standpoint of our acquired morality, nor of the desire to censure, and still less of the desire to justify my own country by proving that some other country had the same defects. My intention has been simply to indicate the universality of certain human acts or ideas, the better to show how hard it is not to incur in them and how imperative is the duty incumbent on us all to help correct them, instead of confining ourselves to disclosing the errors or cruelties of others. Only thus shall we begin to view history from a general human standpoint and not from a narrow nationalistic angle of vision.

To return to the essential nature of this book as an abridgment, let me say to my readers that without going beyond the limits of my own works, they will find in abundance the detail here deliberately pared down: in the above-cited *Historia de España y de la civilización española;* in my *Felipe II* [Philip the Second]; and, very especially, in the variety and freshness of the data and problems regarding the arts and other manifestations of our spirit in the volumes forming the text of the definitive edition (still unpublished) of the *Historia de la civilización* [History of Civilization] mentioned on page 3. As regards colonization of the Americas, I refer the reader to the collection of documents titled *Textos primitivos de colonización española* [Primitive Texts of Spanish Colonization] which presents, classified and annotated, the legislative sources for the period that we may call that of "establishment" of the regime of dominion, government and economic exploitation of Spain's American and Oceanic territories; and to the series of my *Estudios sobre las fuentes de conocimiento del Derecho Indiano* [Studies of the Sources of Knowledge of Indian Law] in sixteen volumes, in one of the appendices of which the aforesaid

Primitive Texts are included. Many of these studies are not yet published.[1]

Should the reader prefer to seek in other books amplification of the subject matter of the present volume, or should he desire a more specialized treatment, he can consult the classified bibliography in my *Epitome de Historia de España* [Compendium of Spanish History, Madrid, 1924], or in the English translation, by P. Volkov (1930) of my *History of Spanish Civilization;* and, especially as relates to America, the Bibliography accompanying the third edition of my *Programa de Historia de las instituciones políticas y civiles de América* [Program of the History of the Political and Civil Institutions of America, Madrid, 1932].

III. The Readers to Whom I Address Myself

In several of the preceding paragraphs I have referred in passing to the public that I have had in mind while writing this book. I wish to make myself clear on this point.

When, prior to 1889, I began writing my History of Spain, I was impelled, properly speaking, by a desire to teach; but I soon gave that up in order to let myself be guided solely by the single interest of studying, as intensively as I found possible, the vast field of our past and present, without thought as to whether the resultant work would serve any didactic purpose. Similarly, in planning the brief history, as I have said before, my guiding idea at first was to offer the school system a brief, timely textbook such as I was constantly besought to write; but that plan too I gave up. I do not know whether the present volume will be used to meet some of our teaching needs in Spanish schools. Be that as it may, I believe it my duty to say that I have not had that purpose directly in mind while composing it in the form now before the reader. It is true, however, that I have thought of secondary and university classes (of the latter, above all) in other countries, since most of the requests for the work emanate from abroad, and there also my concept and idea of History continue to be accepted and applied.

But I have thought even more—as indicated a few pages back—on the great public, that general public made up of non-specialists and of

---

[1] See the *Bibliografía y Biografío de Altamira* (Mexico, 1946). [Author's note.]

citizens who desire, and need ,an elemental knowledge of Spanish history but have not much time at their disposal for acquiring it. That public, to which I made specific reference in my address in 1923 on entering the Academy of History (*The Social Value of Historical Knowledge*) is precisely the public which most needs to emerge from its present ignorance of our past and present, and above all to set straight all the hearsay of error, anecdote and legend accepted as fact which so often takes the place of sound and fundamental knowledge which, remaining fundamental, keeps within limits that make it easy to read and easy of access. Thinking on that public, I repeat, I have planned and written this brief history as it is. I believe, moreover, that it contains all that a Spanish citizen needs to know about the history of his own people, as well as what should be known by foreigners interested in Spain. If acquaintance with this book spurs its readers to widening and deepening the information acquired from its pages, so much the better; that perhaps would be its greatest success, as happens with a teacher when his pupils thirst for more than he can teach them in the narrow compass of the academic year.

1933

Contents

xix

List of Illustrations

xxi

List of Maps

Foreword

The Geographical Conditions of Spain and Their Influence on Man

THE geographical conditions of a country exercise great influence on its history, because sometimes they facilitate and sometimes they hamper human existence. This holds true both as regards human necessities (food, water supply, land use, et cetera) and as to the relationships among the groups of inhabitants, which may be close, leading toward the speedy union of all, or so slight as to foster separation.

Geographically, Spain has the following characteristics: mountainous country, divided into isolated valleys or great river basins by ranges that cross the Peninsula from East to West; a very extensive coastline, since the peninsula-form is perfect; a narrow strip of coastal lowlands, the limit of which is set, at no great distance from the sea, by mountains and tablelands; high elevation above sea-level of the central plateau (the plains or uplands of Castile and La Mancha, which in consequence are difficult of access from the rest of the country); poor conditions for life in much of the territory in so far as concerns agriculture because of the numerous districts with little rainfall and with terrain making artificial irrigation difficult; general declination of the Peninsula as a whole toward the West (the Atlantic Ocean) in a long gentle slope, while on the other side, the gradient toward the Mediterranean is short and abrupt; as it is also toward the Bay of Biscay. The majority, and the longest, of the rivers, in consequence of that declination flow from East to West and disembogue in the Atlantic; because of the extremely rough country and the mountain ranges along their courses, they are in great part torrential and difficult or impossible to navigate. As a result of all these conditions, Spain offers easy access by sea to foreign countries, which always found in the low-lying maritime zone better living conditions than upon the central plateau, and accordingly settled that zone, with its additional attractions of mining and agricultural resources. This is in part the reason why the inhabitants of the coastal districts were civilized long before those of the interior and of the mountainous regions. On the other hand, geographical conditions have produced a natural tendency in the population groups of the interior to live an independent existence, and to isolate themselves, since many impediments have made communication among them very difficult.

Finally, the subsoil of Spain affords in immense variety and abundance minerals that can be utilized in two ways: by selling them as mined, so that other more progressive peoples may process them profitably; or by effecting this industrial transformation at home, in Spain.

The Action of Man on Nature

But if the conditions of land and climate influence human life in the manner indicated, at times fostering and again more or less paralyzing the welfare of individuals, their civilization, and their formation into great nations, this influence is not always invincible. Man, with his innate intelligence and his close observation of natural causes and effects, comes to control Nature to a great extent, utilizing Nature's forces (water, wind, electricity, and the rest) for his own benefit, and thus modifying adverse conditions. In large part, the peoples of the modern world who are most advanced in material civilization are so because they have learned better than the rest how to control Nature and modify or turn to advantage environmental conditions of soil and climate.

It is well for Spaniards to know, along with the rest of their history, how and to what point they have learned to make the geographical conditions of the land in which they live serve them, what are the difficulties that they have had to face at different periods because of these conditions; and in what degree they have found and put into practice methods of improving them.

But men are all equal neither in their ways of evaluating life nor in the force and subtlety of their minds. Some do certain things better than others; they have a swifter comprehension or a greater aptitude. There are expert and persistent workers, and there are laggards; original minds, and mere imitators. This fact, of which we are daily kept aware as we observe our friends and acquaintances, is equally obvious in the groups of men making up peoples or nations. Verification of those qualities possessed and demonstrated by Spaniards in all epochs is another lesson to be learned from their history.

The Spanish People

However, the Spanish people that we know today, and of which we are a part, is not the same as it was in past centuries; nor does it constitute a pure race; a truism applying with equal force to all other living peoples. Our people formed gradually over a long period, and through amalgamations or replacements by men of widely differing origin, before attaining the present composition in which all the ethnic elements have been fused. These were many and diverse. Some proceeded from invasions and colonizations which we shall discuss hereafter. Others were the result of pacific penetrations such as that of the Jews (a population group that was already looming large in Visigothic times) ; those of the French and Italians who for various reasons flocked into Spain during the so-called Middle Ages; that of the numerous, heterogeneous company of foreigners who have intervened in our economic life and settled on our Peninsula from the time of the discovery of America. Along with such acquisitions have been the repeated instances of removal of inhabitants from one part of the country to another. Some removals were effected by force, at the will of victorious invaders (as was the case with the displacements and deliberate intermingling of Iberian tribes which the Romans carried out). Others were impelled by the movements of other peoples (as in the first Germanic invasions). A third variety was caused by fugitives fleeing a threatened war (as when the Christians in southern Spain fled northward before the Moslem advance and when the inhabitants of a section of Catalonia abandoned that region almost entirely for the same reason). A fourth resulted from shiftings of families or groups because of the need for resettlement during the Reconquest (this happened in the case of the Mozárabes, Christians who had been dwelling among the Moslems, and with people in northern Spain who moved down to settle in the central or southern territory). Finally, we may note removals which were brought about by religious or military considerations (such as the mass change of residence of the Moslems in the sixteenth century).

Thanks to all the foregoing, the present Spanish people is not Iberian, nor Celtic, nor Latin, nor Arab, nor Jew, nor Visigoth; and still less is it the actual perceptible outcropping of any prehistoric race. Physically and mentally we are, as already stated, the result of the interminglings and cross-influences of all the ethnic factors of our history: a new human product which is possessed of originality and abundant distinguishing characteristics in its manner of being, and which has been and continues to be enriched by the sum total of the universal threads woven through the centuries into the fabric of its civilization. Those political and cultural events the occurrence of which has made us essentially the people that we are today will explain to us, as we observe them closely, many peculiarities of our history.

Chapter I

Prehistoric Times

The First Inhabitants of Spain

PROBABLY they came from Africa. Very ignorant still, and clumsy, as were all primitive men, they had no other implements than sticks and stones, especially flint. At first they used the stones just as found in nature. Later they chipped one stone into shape with another, thus procuring almond-shaped pieces that served as axes. With these imperfect instruments they defended themselves and perhaps hunted wild beasts or dug up edible roots and tubers. It is believed that they went naked and were acquainted with fire. They dwelt on the Peninsula probably for thousands of years without advancing very perceptibly in civilization. Their remains (human bones and those stones of theirs) have been found at various places in Spain, such as San Isidro Hill at Madrid and Torralba in Soria.

When these men first came to the Peninsula, the climate here was hot and consequently there were animals that are now native only to Africa and Asia (elephants, hippopotamuses, lions, rhinoceroses), as well as others which still exist in Europe but which at that remote period were much larger than they are today (bears, horses, bisons, deer).

Cromagnon Man

Afterwards other men came to the Peninsula, also perhaps proceeding from Africa; and they introduced improved methods of shaping the axe and initiated the type of small delicate tools; all of which presupposes the passage of considerable time. Long afterwards came another race or population group that modern science calls Cromagnon,

1

a name derived from the site in France where traces of it were first discovered. Cromagnon men were much more robust and better proportioned than their predecessors and knew much more. They fashioned their tools for hunting, fighting and working from stones, bone, and staghorn; but of the stone they shaped only small finely wrought instruments, far more expertly finished than the old-style axes and other tools. We still have some of their knives, arrowheads and lancepoints (of stone and bone), harpoons (of bone), and a sort of truncheon or sceptre of staghorn ornamented with engraved lines and figures of animals.

Cromagnon men used fire, wore clothes made from the skins of wild beasts, and adorned themselves with bracelets and necklaces of mussel and oyster-shells, the teeth of animals, and such like. They lived in caves, in many of which along the Cantabrian coast and in Catalonia, Valencia, the Murcia district, and Andalusia, we have found evidences of their industry.

In the epoch when Cromagnon man established himself in Spain, the climate changed, becoming very cold; so much so that many glaciers were formed in the mountains. Consequently the animals characteristic of the preceding epoch vanished.

The Altamira Paintings

These men were distinguished principally by their art, and in art, by their paintings, of which they left many in several of the northern caves in which they dwelt. The most notable of these caves is the one called Altamira, near Santillana del Mar, in the Province of Santander; its roofs and walls abounding in figures of bisons, horses, boar and deer, painted in red and black. Often the artists took advantage of the natural contours of the rock on which they painted to make the figures three dimensional, thus giving them more life and expressiveness. The paintings at Altamira constitute the most perfect type of pictorial art produced in the world at that time; and in some qualities, such as realism in the drawing of bodies and movement implicit in the attitudes of animals, they are superior to paintings produced many centuries later in Spain and elsewhere. It is estimated that the Altamira paintings were made some 15,000 years before the Christian era. They offer, within their common type, an inner wealth of variety in technique which indicates different periods across many centuries in development of this art. In other caves of northern Spain have been found paintings of wild bulls, mammoths, mountain goats, rhinoceroses, lions, cave-bears, as well as of birds, fish, and serpents, though these latter are less frequent.

Some time ago, other paintings of this same type were found in the Province of Málaga, in the Pilata and Doña Trinidad Caves; and more recently many more were discovered in the Casares and Hoz Caves in Guadalajara and other places of the Peninsula. The Casares and Hoz paintings are of figures and scenes not portrayed previously. Such discoveries, which probably are not the last, seem to indicate the trajectory, or one of the trajectories, of expansion followed by that art down the Peninsula from north to south. In the caves at Guadalajara mentioned above are anthropomorphic figures which include a man fishing and various animals, deeply engraved.

The epoch corresponding to the civilization characterized by the Altamira Cave paintings belongs to the third period of the so-called Upper Palaeolithic Age: the Magdalenian. In the two periods prior to this, stone-carving by the same Cromagnon race and perhaps by others analogous to it, presents variations within the dominant type of delicate finely wrought work.

In the western part of the Cantabrian region, that section of Spain's north coast washed by the Atlantic, as well as in the southern and central regions of the Peninsula, there was flourishing at the same time another civilization exclusively Spanish, though apparently remotely African in origin, which was characterized by the carving of small fragments of stone in geometric forms and the engraving of stone plaques, as well as by paintings of animals, sometimes realistic, again (toward the close of the epoch) in geometric designs such as those found in Sierra Morena. Somewhat later another culture, which appeared from the Miño river to the present Province of Gerona, but principally in Asturias, was characterized by shell heaps or calcareous remains of marine mollusks and by rounded pebbles sharpened at one extremity to a point.

Some scratchings found in both Spanish and French caves belong to the close of this period and of the Magdalenian civilization, or to the transition to the New Stone Age which saw the increasing use of polished stone implements. These scratchings seem to be the beginnings of ideographic writing, which was perhaps the invention of these people of Western Europe.

The Paintings Found in Eastern Spain

To the same general type belonged another people inhabiting the eastern part of the Peninsula from the present Lérida to the present Granada. This people, while as artistic as that in the north, had a very different concept of drawing. The paintings of theirs which we know are for the most part on rock in the open air and, like those at Altamira, they portray animals (deer, bulls, horses, and others) to which is added in profusion the new note of human figures of both sexes. The men are shown hunting, fighting or dancing. Nude as a general rule, in rare instances they are clothed in what seems to be a kind of breeches. Some wear a head-dress of plumes or tufts of feathers; some are bearing a bow and arrows or shooting them. The women are attired in long skirts girdled at the waist. On the cliff-face of Cogul in the Province of Lérida a group of women are depicted surrounding a man in what may be attitudes of a dance; and in the Araña Cave at Bicorp (Valencia) a woman is shown seizing a hive for its honey.

It is characteristic of this rock art that while the drawings of animals are as realistic as were those of the artists at Altamira, the human silhouettes are not. These latter are almost always stylized (sometimes excessively so in case of the men, as may be seen in the warrior figures at Morella la Vella) with modisms of attitude and dynamic gesture reaching exaggeration. Consequently, prehistorians qualify painted-rock art as "expressionist." With all these qualities, this art is very inferior to that at Altamira in use of color. The greatest resemblance to the paintings in the north is in the silhouettes of women, as may be observed in the right hand section of the drawing at Cogul, which also includes the non-stylized figure of a man (a wizard perhaps?) and in the aforesaid engraving in Araña Cave of a woman in a tree gathering honey.

Because of all these differences, among other things, there seems reason to believe not only that Mediterranean Spanish art must belong to people distinct from those of Altamira, but also that it was not contemporaneous with the art of the Cantabrian region and the expansion of the latter to the center and the south. Unique in Europe,

Wild boar in flight, painting from the Cave of Altamira.

these drawings were produced in the Spanish territory which is the same that centuries later was called Iberic, a fact that makes one wonder whether the people that made them were ancestors of the so-called Iberians. The most important examples of these paintings are found at Cogul (Lérida), Valltorta (Castellón), Minateda and Alpera (Albacete). Modern studies of this art, especially of the examples at Minateda, have set forth the hypothesis of a possible relation or influence of the art of Altamira on that of the regions named in eastern Spain. But although, as we have said, rock paintings belong exclusively to Spain as regards the European continent, they have been found also in great number in Africa. Among modern prehistorians (the German and the French, who have studied the regions of Africa where such paintings exist), one, Obermaier, who is also a specialist in Spanish prehistory, has found in his research evidence strongly supporting the theory that it was peoples of that origin and more or less akin who invented and developed on either continent the art that we have been considering.

In the above discussion, I termed the paintings from northern and eastern Spain "artistic." The Abbé Breuil and other prehistorians who have written about them have likewise praised their merit as works of art. Such qualifications do not invalidate the opinion held by the same writers and by other modern commentators, that these pictures were not created with artistic intent *per se,* but for purposes of magic in order to ensure for the chase an abundance of the animals depicted; while in other instances, when the animals pictured were not eaten (lions, hyenas) they perhaps represented totems. I do not believe that these interpretations diminish the artistic worth of the pictures in question—that worth is indisputable—even though the artist's aim was neither art for art's sake nor the plaudits of his fellows, since as a matter of fact he could not count on much public. The pictures seem to have been painted for the most part at the entrances of caves dedicated to magic ceremonies for purposes of obtaining food or to certain rites possibly expressive of very primitive religious beliefs: it is a well-known fact that an artist finds his own sufficient satisfaction in creating his work, apart from its magic or religious import. The two motives, art and magic, with their corresponding ideas, are not incompatible. Medieval artists, who were often monks, felt both the religious fervor impelling them to make pictures, sculptures and edifices for the greater glory of

God and the Saints, and the inspiration of their respective arts instilling the desire to create a perfect work. Why assume that prehistoric man lacked artistic purpose even though his art was motivated primarily by a very different intention? In any case, the creators of the rock pictures, which were usually in the open air and consequently in admiring view of the whole tribe, escaped the handicap of concealment which was the lot of the work of the artists in the north: a fact significant of another difference between the two styles.

In that period the first sculptures appeared also, though they were few. One of them still preserved is the head of a mountain goat carved from staghorn and found at Rascaño in the Province of Santander.

Polished Stone, Agriculture, and the Domestication of Animals

Cromagnon men, or others perhaps who were newcomers to the Peninsula, whence and when we do not know, introduced many new methods and ideas that vastly improved living conditions of the individual and the group.

To the varieties of stone utilized formerly and hammered or chipped into shape, they added porphyry, slate, basalt, and various others that could be polished readily, and that, in fact, these newcomers succeeded in polishing by friction. This supplied them with stronger tools of more diverse uses than had been known before. At this time there appeared also the weaving of vegetable fibres and the art of pottery as represented by simple jars of fired clay shaped by hand, without ornamentation or with mere incisions scratched by the fingernail. Even more important than these forward steps was the cultivation of land by sowing seed, something not practiced by former peoples. Crops produced by this means afforded a surer and more varied diet than had been obtained previously from hunting, fishing, and gathering wild fruits and roots. A new progressive step was the domestication of certain animals; which was the origin of flocks and herds and consequently of cattle-breeding. The first animal to be domesticated was the dog, man's companion and defender from earliest times. The first dogs were tamed wolves. Among the earliest seedcrops cultivated by prehistoric men have now been recognized barley, spelt-wheat, flax, millet, and peas. Rye and oats were utilized later, in the Bronze Age. With all this, man grew accustomed to sedentary life, residing permanently in one place where he was sure of finding close at hand, through his own labor, the means of satisfying his principal needs, without having to seek them dangerously on hunting expeditions that made obligatory a nomadic life, an ever-shifting dwelling-place.

With settlement in one spot, and because the onetime extremely cold climate of the Peninsula grew milder, men built their first homes in the open, in the form of huts constructed of logs, boughs and leaves. Nevertheless, man did not wholly abandon the caves, whether as habitations or as places of burial, as has been proved by many that have been discovered on the Peninsula in Andalusia, Catalonia, Rioja, Portugal, and other regions. In one of these, the Cave of the Bats at Albuñol, has been found a smooth circlet of gold adorning the brow of a mummy surrounded by a dozen other cadavers, probably his servants or slaves.

A handful of huts clustered in a site protected by rocks, stakes tied together, or some similar device, formed the first city or settlement. Remains of such have been found in different localities in the provinces of Guadalajara, Almería, Barcelona and Tarragona.

Arts Contemporaneous with Polished Stone

Men of the Neolithic Age, the age of polished stone, were also artists in other of the plastic arts, though their pictorial art was greatly inferior to the Cromagnon creations. Instead of copying faithfully bodies as they really were, they limited themselves to drawing simple outlines in very imperfect symbolic representation. Some of these are merely engraved or incised; others are colored red or black; and in general they depict men and women; the whole very crude. These forms are accompanied sometimes by linear designs, broken, undulant, or rounded, which are perhaps characters of writing. There are specimens of such drawings and paintings in the Cave of the Jackdaw at Jimena, in Jaen; on the Written Rock, at Ciudad Real; in the Cave of the Writings, at Vélez Blanco in Almería; and at many other places on the Peninsula.

Man in the Polished Stone Age also produced a kind of very imperfect carving on stone plaques (usually slate) or cylinders also of stone; such carvings being effected by incision or engraving and as a rule representing the human figure very crudely and incompletely. The distinctive thing about these figures is that they always have eyes. It is thought that they are religious in character, intended for idols; figures of the gods worshipped by those people. These images have been found chiefly in Andalusia and in Portugal. Occasionally they are carved on boulders or cliff-faces.

Appearance of Copper Objects

Man had lived in this polished stone civilization a long time before appearance of the first use of one of the metals which, because of its abundance and of the facility with which it can be worked, lends itself to the uses of daily life. That metal is copper. The Spanish region that knew it first was Andalusia; the men who dwelt there began to fabricate from copper the tools and weapons that previously they had fashioned of stone or bone. Those men, believed to be ancestors of the so-called Tartessians, of whom we shall speak hereafter, formed—as is inferred from the data regarding them which we possess today—a pacific people, dedicated to agriculture and industry. They dwelt in hamlets of which the huts were surrounded by protective stockades. They were familiar with the handmill for grinding grain, woven cloths of hemp and flax, and other refinements.

The Tartessians properly so named are believed to have lived some 1200 or 1500 years after the period of the dolmens and other megelithic constructions—the latter term meaning "gigantic" and applied to prehistoric monuments such as dolmens and menhirs made from huge stone boulders or megaliths.

The Dolmens

Besides copper, the most notable contribution to the culture of the Peninsula during this epoch was the architectural construction of the sepulchres, or dolmens. Since it is in the Andalusian region that the richest and most varied types of dolmens are found, the supposition has been that this architecture was originated by the Andalusians of the Copper Period; but the prevailing belief today, for which there is some evidence, is that the dolmen civilization toward the close of the preceding Age made its appearance in central and northern Portugal, whence it spread toward Andalusia on one side and on the other to Galicia and the region of the Pyrenees. Moreover, the dolmens were built also elsewhere in Europe and in Asia and Egypt. But if this fact quits Hispanic man of the distinction of having invented the dolmen, it leaves him the considerable importance of his own special form of dolmen which is remarkable for its variety as compared with dolmens not always contemporary with it in other countries. In Spain the dolmens were formed of huge stone slabs set horizontally on other upright slabs. This form has been called, principally because of the opening for entrance or door, the lintel dolmen, since lintel is the term designating the horizontal piece of stone or wood over the top of a door or window. The same people likewise built enclosures—halls or chambers —usually circular in form, approached by a passage, the whole then covered with earth and stones, forming a mound above the slabs. Within these chambers the bodies of the dead were laid out, and interred or merely covered with earth.

The locality where the most characteristic and impressive of these are found is Antequera, in Málaga, near which is the hugest and most admirable of the dolmens, commonly called "the Menga Cave." Its hall is 17 meters long and the passage 8. Likewise important is the dolmen at Soto in Huelva, some 21 meters in length, many of its stone blocks ornamented with engraved human figures. The dolmen at Matarrubilla near Seville is peculiar in that its walls are of rubble work (thin slabs and clay) and its circular chamber has a marble trough which is unique and was probably for funerary ceremonies. It is interesting to note that the men who built the dolmens employed more luxury and art on their tombs than on their habitations, although that after all was not an unusual custom among ancient peoples.

However, not all dolmens found in Spain are of the type described. There are some of which the roof of the sepulchral chamber, instead of being flat, has the form of an incipient dome. The sepulchres of the dolmens and caves at Millares in Almería, Gor in Granada, El Romeral in Antequera, and Castilleja de Guzmán, among others, are like this. These domes seem to be of later date than the flat roofs but they too, of course, are very ancient since the weapons and vessels found in them are of stone and sometimes copper. In any case, they antedate primitive Greek sculptures of the type at Mycenae (about 1400 B.C.) though of identical arrangement as regards the arch.

Chambers with domes more perfectly shaped than those of Andalusia and Algarve are found in the dolmenic constructions of the Balearic Isles called *talayots,* to which we shall refer again. In Basque and Catalonian territory the predominant type is of shallow dolmens open on one side [cistas], exemplified also in the dolmen of Biscar at Jaca in Aragon.

To the same period, or one not far removed, belongs the construction of what is called Cyclopean walls, built of huge stones, usually without mortar, like those of the ancient Greek citadels or acropolises at Mycenae and Tiryns. The most important of such walls in Spain is at Tarragona.

Pottery Contemporaneous with the Use of Copper

The Spanish populations familiar with copper—those of the South (who seem to have discovered or introduced it here) , as well as the other Peninsular populations whom they acquainted with its use— were quite probably the inventors of an art of pottery with two chief characteristics: decoration in pure geometric pattern (straight lines forming bands of parallel stripes and other bands of zigzag lines) and bell-mouth, or campaniform, shape. Though examples of jugs and jars of this kind have been found in France, England, and other countries of Europe, the best and most artistic are from Spain, whence possibly they were exported. Characteristic specimens are the jars discovered at Ciempozuelos and the one from Tardaren Cave in Catalonia.

The Appearance of Bronze

Whether as culmination of this civilization or as the special achievement of a different group, ages later, innovations extremely important to human existence made their appearance in eastern Andalusia, beginning with Granada, and in the southeastern part of the Peninsula in the region of Murcia. These were the almost total abandonment of stone as material for tools and weapons and the substitution for it of copper and of a new metal, bronze, obtained by a mixture, or alloy, of copper and tin, with the resultant product harder than copper and yet flexible. This metal admitted invention of new shapes; among them, a kind of pike or halberd, and swords, in some instances with gold-plated hilts. Silver too was discovered about this time. A most important silver deposit, the first known, at Cuevas de Vera in Almería has been worked ever since that remote epoch.

As tin, an indispensable requisite for making bronze, exists in Europe only in Galicia and in other territory far from our Peninsula, sometimes it has been thought that the invention of bronze also was achieved first on Spanish soil. Though it seems impossible to accept this theory, since there is good reason to believe that bronze is of oriental, Asiatic, origin, it is quite credible that its manufacture was especially developed in Spain. This seems to be evidenced by the fact that some typical forms of bronze weapons and vessels found here are either peculiar to our Peninsula or differ in shape from similar objects known to be from other countries.

The people that manufactured these things no longer buried their dead in sepulchres of dolmen type, but in the ground, in coffins made of stone slabs, or in earthen jars, and sometimes simply in whitewashed holes covered with slabs. In the regions of Cartagena and Almería, we find also ruins of their houses and fortifications, constructed of stone and clay. The most important such ruins are those in the locality called El Argar.

At the same period, it is believed, the inhabitants of the Balearic Isles, which were populated by Spaniards, built the monumental sepulchres of hewn stone in the shape of towers or truncated cones to which we have referred previously and which perhaps derived from the Andalusian dolmens, the *talayots*.

The Epochs of Prehistoric Time

All the ages of time embraced in our narrative up to this point, during which men used stone and bone and became acquainted with and learned to employ the first metals (copper, bronze, silver and gold) are called collectively Prehistoric Time or Prehistory. The reason for this name is found in what is apparently the fact that when man began to make use of iron he began also to write accounts of his life; that is to say, to set down his History. In this meaning of the term *history*, and with relation to it alone, everything that had occurred previously and that we know about today only through the medium of tools, weapons, tombs, dwelling-places, paintings, human bones, et cetera, may in fact be called *prehistoric*. Similarly, the ages that came after the first relations of man's life set down in writing are known as *historic time*.

With respect to prehistoric time, the enormous improvement in human welfare which the discovery of metals and construction of the first metal vessels and weapons represented in comparison with the stone objects used theretofore, justifies making a distinction between two ages in the life of primitive man; each age comprehending thousands of years, with the earlier period immeasurably longer than the later.

Each of these periods is characterized by knowledge and use of one of the two prime materials, stone or metal. Accordingly, the first is called the Stone Age and the second the Age of Metals. We are living in this second period today, while the Stone Age has vanished except for some very backward tribes that still exist in imperfectly civilized regions of Africa, the Americas, and Oceania; though of course all mankind continues to use stone for buildings, ornamentation, and sculpture.

The Stone Age is subdivided into two periods, corresponding to two fundamental methods of working the stone. One is the epoch of hewn stone, which is also called the Old Stone or Paleolithic Age (the latter being the Greek term for "old stone"). The other, the age of polished stone, is called the New Stone or Neolithic Age. Each of these Ages may be subdivided in turn into periods characterized by the differing shapes given the stone tools and weapons, or by some other peculiarity equally important. These are not the only designations used by present-day prehistorians, but in this volume we need not go into such technical details.

It should be noted, however, that the separation in period between hewn and polished stone was not so absolute that when polished stone began to be employed the use of hewn stone was discontinued wholly. On the contrary, hewn stone was still used along with polished and even after the discovery of copper. It was then applied to devising sharp weapons or cutting tools, which had keenest points and edges if made of a stone susceptible of cutting, such as flint or rock crystal. On the other hand, men knew about polishing before they employed it for stone. They polished bone first.

We should also bear in mind the fact that we are only imperfectly acquainted with prehistoric time, a period through which all the human race passed, though not in all parts of the world contemporaneously. In many countries research relating to prehistoric man is still very scant; besides, as regards Spain, there are still many things that we do not know, and our conclusions with respect to others are provisional merely, dependent on future research which conceivably might change our present system of classifying and evaluating known facts.

The Age of Metals includes the epochs of Copper and Bronze and the beginning of that of Iron. But properly speaking, historic time in Spain, in the meaning that we have agreed to give the term, seems to commence with the Iron Age, as the following chapter shows.

Chapter II

The Period of Eastern Colonization

Primitive Colonization

THE VARIOUS peoples that were continually conquering territory in the Peninsula and settling on it found themselves in the situation described at the end of the preceding chapter when suddenly invasions were begun of a very different sort by foreign peoples. They were carried out by men who at that period had already achieved in several parts of Asia and of Europe degrees of civilization much higher than yet existed in Spain, and who came to the Peninsula not with any intention of dwelling there permanently but in order to exploit its natural resources for the benefit of their respective fatherlands. This is what is called *colonizing*.

Phoenician Colonization

The first of whose entrance and colonization in Spain there is certain evidence were the Phoenicians. They came from the Mediterranean coasts of Asia—from Syria, north of Palestine. Dedicated to commerce and navigation, the Phoenicians were rich and prosperous. Tyre and Sidon were their two principal cities. In order to benefit from the products of all countries, the Phoenicians had been scouring the whole of the Mediterranean coast; and thus they came to Spain, attracted beyond doubt by fame of the natural resources there. They found, in fact, on the Spanish mainland and in the adjacent waters, products of great value—cattle, minerals, fruits and fisheries—all of which afforded them good trading. The Phoenicians encouraged commercial development by establishing trading-posts, mostly in the western region of

15

Andalusia then called Tartessos. The most important of these trading posts was Agadir, on the present site of Cadiz. According to ancient tradition, all this was in the eleventh century B.C.

The Phoenicians taught the Spaniards of the south, and later on those of other regions, to extend their commerce, to communicate by writing, to work their mines efficiently, and instructed them in some arts and industries (such as the preservation of fish and extraction of salt). It is not known whether they themselves introduced iron, which had been used in the Orient for centuries, or whether the Spaniards became acquainted with the metal through African tribes.

The writing learned from the Phoenicians by the Tartessians— that is to say, the then inhabitants of the region of Tartessos, one of the most ancient of the western Mediterranean—has come down to us in inscriptions or characters engraved on lead or stone; but we cannot decipher them. From this script apparently originated the writing used later by the peoples in eastern Spain.

Phoenician Objects of Art

As was natural, the Phoenicians brought with them the products of their own art (an art which, though wholly imitative of others, anterior or contemporaneous, achieved some works of positive merit) and also a considerable number of industries from the peoples of Asia and East Africa (Egypt) with whom they traded. These industries produced such objects of oriental art as gold and silver jewelry, ivories, combs, and the like, adorned with carving; ostrich eggs; glass vases in polychrome or solid color; new methods of burial and new sculptures (idols). A magnificent specimen of the glass has been discovered at Aliseda in Cáceres: green, with an engraved hieroglyphic inscription. The most important extant piece of sculpture is the lid of a sepulchre found at Cadiz and representing a human figure in Phoenician dress; very similar to another such lid discovered in Carthaginian territory and preserved in the Lavigérie Museum at Carthage.

The Phoenicians erected a temple at Cadiz famed for its magnificence and wealth of adornment. They also wrote some accounts of their voyages along the coast of Spain, the first such accounts with which we are acquainted, though we have these not at firsthand but through later writers who copied or cited them.

The Phoenician City of Agadir

The great wealth amassed by the Phoenicians is evidenced in the descriptions that we have of the capital of their colonies, Gadir or Agadir. Unfortunately, these descriptions are very brief. They tell of a temple raised there to the god Baal-Melkarte or Hercules of Tyre in which were two lofty bronze columns inscribed with a notation as to the construction costs. The Phoenician sailors, and the Carthaginians after them, doubtless were accustomed, on returning from their voyages, to visit the temple, render homage to those columns, and celebrate rites in honor of Baal.

Gadir's prosperity was great and substantial, continuing into the time of Roman domination. A writer at the end of the first century B.C. says that the boats with which its citizens, the Gaditans, carried on trade in the Mediterranean and the Atlantic were the most numerous craft of the period, and had the greatest tonnage. The city itself was considered to have the largest population of any in the Roman Empire at that time. The region of the Baetis (Guadalquivir) basin was well populated, as is proved among other things by the number of cities there beyond the river.

Another Phoenician city of the south, Malacca (Málaga) was also of commercial importance. The principal traffickers flocking to it were Africans from the opposite coast, the Morocco of today.

Greek Colonization

Some five centuries after the Phoenicians, if the traditions about the founding of Agadir be true—that is to say, toward the sixth century B.C.—there came to our Peninsula the Greeks, a people given to commerce and navigation, who inhabited the Mediterranean coast of Asia Minor and the islands and peninsula composing the territory called Greece. Apparently the Greeks first arrived in Spain at the region called Tartessos, the fame of whose wealth had been spread doubtless by the Phoenicians. The oldest Greek colony in Spain seems to have been Mainake or Menaca, near Málaga.

Since the Greeks and the Phoenicians were rivals with respect to trade and domination of the lands washed by the Mediterranean, they often determined by force of arms which should establish themselves in disputed territory. In Spain the Greeks were successful principally

Talayot of Ciutadella (Minorca).

along the eastern coast, southward from what is now the **Province of Gerona**; although they also founded colonies at other scattered points. Of these cities the one called Emporium or *Emporion* (which means "market-place") ranked first. Among its ruins, discovered in modern times, have been found remains of dwellings, columns, statues, mosaics, pottery, coins, and other objects of great artistic merit. The city of Hemeroskopeion, near the present Denia, was likewise important.

Greek culture, as expressed especially in philosophy (Socrates, Plato, Aristotle), in art (architecture and sculpture), and in literature, was to attain a development and perfection still unexcelled in some respects, including technique and applied sciences. These last found expression in great works of engineering—acqueducts, paved roads, tunnels, water-clocks, bridges. Greek culture was the groundwork, still strong and solid, of what we call European or Western civilization. The arrival and settlement of the Greeks in Spain must have had considerable importance therefore for the advancement of those peninsular peoples reached by their influence; the more so, since the Greeks came to Spain during the chief period of the Hellenic culture of Athens and its later development.

Influence of Greek Art

The Greek influence on Spain was especially marked in the domain of art, as is instanced by the coining of money after the Greek fashion in Lérida and other Iberian cities, and, above all, by the flowering in the southeastern region of a rich and varied sculpture in stone and bronze; of construction (tombs and temples) in which the Greek architectural style of arch falling gradually into a straight line found in the architecture of the dolmens a perfectly adaptable affinity; of gems; of steel swords of a special type, short and sharp, called *falcatas;* and of pottery.

But the most striking thing about the Greek influence was the fact that it did not result in simple copies on the part of the natives of the Peninsula, but in their assimilations and interpretations of Greek models (especially of those from Ionia, a region of Asiatic Greece). Thus the art and imagination of the Spaniards, inspired by the Greek example, produced beautiful original works of art expressive of the native idiosyncrasy. The most perfect of these productions that has come

Madrid: National Archeological Museum

Bull's head from Costix Isle. Mallorca

down to us is the bust which is called the Lady of Elche because it was found in the city of Elche in Alicante Province. A remarkable bas-relief also found in Alicante, at the excavations of Albufereta near the provincial capital, although of disputed derivation, probably should be included in this group of influences.

What Life Was Like in the City of Emporium

We know more details about life in Emporium, the Spanish city or colony of the Greeks already mentioned, than in Gadir. One of the Greek writers in commenting on Emporium says that at first the colonizers settled only the small off-shore island which in that writer's time was called Cíudad Vieja or "Old City." Later the principal establishment was on the mainland and consisted of two distinct cities separated by a wall. The reason for such a division was that in the vicinity of the Emporium settlement lived some Iberian tribesmen called the Indigetes who, in spite of the fact that they were independent of the Greeks, desired for security's sake to possess a precinct in common with the latter. This precinct consisted of the two settlements separated by the wall. Emporium still preserved this peculiarity of form in the year 195 B.C. according to a Roman writer who adds that the Greek part of the city extended along the sea, protected by a wall 400 paces long (equivalent to 1000 feet). The Iberian side for its part was surrounded by another wall much more extensive, 3000 paces in circumference. Considering the fact that the Greek city was thus exposed to attack by sea as well as to attack from the Indigetes, a barbarous and warlike people—as our Greek commentator took pains to note—it is remarkable that its inhabitants lived in safety and preserved their independence. Their safeguard was daily and incessant vigilance with respect to the stronger neighbor. That part of the wall overlooking the countryside was well fortified and had only one gate, always watched by a gate-keeper or sentry who never abandoned his post. At night, one-third of the citizens mounted guard; and it should be remarked that the order that the sentries serve successively in turn and make the rounds was observed rigorously. The Greeks permitted no Iberian to enter the colonized city, nor did they themselves issue forth on the land side without great precautions, though on the sea side they came and went freely. The Greeks never passed through the gate giving on the Iberian city except in considerable number; and as a rule the sally was effected by those who had been on guard the preceding night. The Greeks were forced to these measures by the trade that they carried on with the Iberians who, inexpert in the art of navigation, confined themselves to bartering the products of their land for merchandise brought in by the colonizers; a bond of commercial interest that opened the Iberian city to the Greeks.

That atmosphere of suspicion, which shows how the colonizers began their dealings with the natives, improved with time. The two cities became one, ruled by a mixture of Greek law and native custom. The inhabitants of the town were skilled weavers of linen cloth. Some of the inshore lands that they possessed were extremely fertile; others produced nothing but thistle and swamp-grass, which is the kind of rush least adaptable to basketry.

In Emporium and the other colonies, the Greeks cultivated their own architecture and their own art, as well as those sciences of which they had knowledge. They built theatres that must have presented works of their popular dramatists—Aeschylus, Sophocles, Euripides, Aristophanes, and the rest—which still rank among the world's greatest plays. They also founded schools and academies wherein were read and discussed Greek poets, historians and philosophers. Homer himself, in a passage of *The Odyssey*, apparently refers to the land of Spain.

Greek Accounts of the Spanish Peoples

It is the Greek authors (and voyaging Greek historians) who have handed down to us the first written accounts of Spain and its inhabitants, derived in part, as we have said, from earlier Phoenician chronicles. One of the most ancient of those authors was the first to employ (in the sixth century B.C.) the name *Iberian* to designate the peoples dwelling in the eastern part of the Peninsula, near the mouth of the Ebro, and the coastal regions north and south of the river. Others speak of the western Tartessian region, its cities and its kings; and of the southeastern region (where, as we have seen, Greek civilization exercised so much influence) to which they give the name of *Mastiena*. The accounts of these primitive writers (amplified a few centuries later by further narratives of Greeks and others) are our source of information regarding the degree of civilization attained in those times by inhabitants of the Peninsula after they had come into contact with many other peoples.

What we do not know certainly is the procedence of those Tartessians, Mastienians and Iberians with relation to earlier peoples of the Stone, Copper and Bronze Ages. We are forced to the conclusion that at least some of them must have been direct descendants of these latter.

The Historical Question of the Iberians

It is not really known when and where the Iberians entered Spain, nor with any certainty, whence they came. The opinion generally held today is that they came indirectly perhaps from Mesopotamia, and directly from North Africa. Some modern writers hold that they arrived as far back as the Neolithic Age, in the Age of Metals; among those maintaining this view is the modern prehistorian Bosch Gimpera. The only thing that can be affirmed with certainty is that in the sixth century B.C. the Iberians already inhabited a part of eastern Spain and a considerable portion of southeastern France. We know nothing of their previous history. The Gauls (Celts and Ligurians) drove them out of the latter region at the close of the fifth or beginning of the fourth century B.C. From the third century B.C. the names of tribes undoubtedly Iberian are known in the Mediterranean zone from Catalonia to Valencia. It appears that the Iberians penetrated the central plateau also and later reached the center of what is now Portugal.

Classic authors of the Roman epoch depict them as men of short stature physically, slight and dolichocephalic; and morally noble, hospitable, and religious, though also with the defects of arrogance and sloth.

Aside from all this, it must be borne in mind that the name *Iberian* is of Greek origin and its meaning is of geographical interest solely. We do not know what the Iberians called themselves. We only know, as already stated, the names borne by some of their tribes in the third century before the Christian era; and we should not forget that ancient tribes changed name frequently, or at least were called by different names by the various foreigners who knew them. Perhaps also (as we know occurred in later times) they had more than one name for themselves.

Tarragona. Iberian cyclopean doorway.

The Celts

For a long period, Greeks and Phoenicians divided between themselves the colonization of the Spanish coast and continued producing the multiple effects of their different civilizing influences. But meanwhile the population of the Peninsula had been augmented by a new invasion of foreign tribes: the Celts, who, like the Iberians, settled in Spain to stay.

At the time, the Celts inhabited central Europe, in the region of the Rhine and northern France. Some of them entered Spain toward the year 1000 B.C. by the eastern range of the Pyrenees, occupying the Catalonian zone and the greater part of the Ebro basin. A second and more important invasion took place four centuries later, when Celts entering by the western Pyrenees spread over almost the whole of the Peninsula. Warriors of scant civilization, though acquainted with iron, which they used in fashioning their swords and lances, they fought the Iberians of eastern Spain and then the tribes of the Castilian and northwestern plateau for possession of those territories. The Celtic advance was checked by the Sierra Morena on the south, and by the Iberian mountains separating the Mediterranean zone from the central tableland. Greek writers and others to whom we owe our knowledge of these conflicts say that eventually Spain was divided between Iberians and Celts, except for Andalusia and the Spanish Levant (Valencia and Murcia), and the sites occupied by Phoenicians and Greeks; and that in Aragon and what was to be called much later New Castile, both peoples intermingled to form a racial mixture called Celtiberian. But this term and the explanation of the circumstance giving rise to it are somewhat arbitrary, since it is not a proved fact that the intermixture did take place in all those regions. Some authorities hold that the term Celtiberian meant "Celt from the Ebro." In the mountains of Valencia and Murcia on the east, a Celtic people, the Beribracs, established themselves. The Celtic zones *par excellence,* however, continued to be Galicia and Portugal. Asturias and the Basque region cannot be considered Celtic, though they partook of Celtic civilization.

The Celts, who brought into Spain the central European culture known as Hallstadt, burned their dead (reducing the bodies to ashes by incineration) as the Greeks and Iberians usually did also, unlike the Phoenicians and the other peoples of Spain who buried the bodies

San Martín de Valdeglesias (Madrid). Celt period. The Bulls of Guisando (Avila Province).

(inhumation) in chambers, caves, and trenches. This difference is of great importance in the history of civilization. The large majority of the fortifications [*castros*] and of the walled cities [*citanias*] of which ruins are known, with others frequently discovered, were certainly built and inhabited by the Celts. In these *castros* have been found impressive remains of a form of culture probably initiated in northern Portugal and in Galicia about the fourth century B.C. and later brought to the Castilian zone north of the Duero as far as the section of Avila, all of which is rich in fortifications and burial places (Cogotas, Osera, et cetera), where it developed, creating new types of art. To that culture belong the bulls and boars of stone so abundant in Castile; swords with blades of different shapes, richly inlaid with copper and silver and with magnificent scabbards; belt-clasps in bronze and damascene; hand-wrought pottery dark in color, with engraved ornamentation; and other utensils. Some of the works of art of the Spanish Celts were exported to France, where many surviving examples have been found. Research on this cultural form, begun not long since, may produce surprising and interesting results.

Carthaginian Colonization and Conquest

When things were as we have described them, an event occurred still further complicating the situation in Spain. The Phoenicians at Agadir were attacked in the sixth century B.C., apparently by the Tartessians, and, not deeming themselves strong enough to resist, asked aid of a sister people, the Carthaginians, who were established on the northern shore of Africa in the region that is now Tunis. The capital of this people, Carthage, was a colony that had been founded there centuries before by Phoenicians from Sidon, and had speedily attained great commercial and military importance. The Carthaginians first came to the aid of the colonists at Agadir and then conquered them, absorbing them in their own race.

The Carthaginian colonial regime in Spain was harsher and more militaristic than the Phoenician; but seemingly the Carthaginians were well received in general by the Spaniards in the south. The center of Carthaginian rule was the city that they called New Carthage and that was to be known later as Cartagena. In the third century B.C. the situation changed with the attempt by the generals of the Barca family, then heads of the army and of the Carthaginian military party, to make a conquest by arms of the Peninsula. They succeeded to a considerable degree, penetrating the interior to the Castilian plateau and along the Mediterranean coast to the Ebro. Many Spanish tribes offered resistance; others surrendered and allied themselves with the conquerors. Thereafter numbers of natives of the Peninsula and of the Balearic Isles (which the Carthaginians already controlled in part) fought in Carthaginian armies.

The Civilizing Influence of the Carthaginians

The influence of these new colonizers, like that of their kinsmen the Phoenicians, was principally commercial. They greatly stimulated the coinage of money, which acquired shapes and symbols of African origin; and they are believed to have introduced the swords with undulating blade which are found along with other objects in their tombs. The intensity of the Phoenicio-Carthaginian influence on the customs and general aspect of the settlements where it was longest exercised, seems to be attested by the fact that a Greek geographer, writing long before the dawn of the Christian era, characterized as "Phoenician" the cities of the region then called Turdetani, the ancient Tartesia. It is worthy of note that the Turdetans nevertheless preserved their method of burial which was very different from that of the Carthaginians, who sometimes employed incineration and sometimes inhumation. Recently architectonic remains and other relics of Carthaginian art have been discovered in several places in Alicante Province.

The City of New Carthage

In the land of the Mastienians, the Carthaginians had enlarged their city of New Carthage, making it their military and maritime capital. We have descriptions of it as it was at the time that the Romans conquered it.

New Carthage was by far the most powerful city in the region. Its situation was very favorable for defense. The admirably constructed surrounding wall and the proximity of the several harbors of a lake or basin (the so-called Lesser Sea), and of productive mines, constituted its chief assets. The mines occupied a vast terrain; so much that the Romans after they took them had up to 40,000 men working them. In the vicinity of New Carthage there were also many establishments for salting fish.

Spaniards of the hinterland flocked to the city to provide themselves with merchandise brought in by sea, and foreign traders came there to buy products from the interior of the Peninsula. New Carthage was also the storehouse of money and armaments for the Carthaginian army. Immured in the city were the hostages given by the Spaniards as security against a tribal attack. Besides troops and governing authorities, the population of New Carthage consisted of artisans, mechanics, sailors and fishermen, and merchants in great number. The chief building was a palace erected, as it is thought, for his own dwelling by a general named Hasdrubal. From the military standpoint, the city was so strong that the Carthaginians believed that the Romans would not dare attack it; and in consequence they were careless about taking measures for its defense. As we shall see, General Scipio shrewdly took advantage of that negligence and effected the conquest of New Carthage in a very short time.

The first initiative toward making Spain a unitary State, properly speaking, was taken by the Carthaginians, and this fact should be borne in mind, lest the unification be considered as purely a Roman invention. It was not carried out as fully, however, under the Carthaginians as under the Romans.

Chapter III

Roman Rule

The Coming of the Romans to Spain

The Carthaginians were driven out of Spain by another people, the Romans, established in central Italy in the region of Rome, who were already very powerful in the fourth century B.C., and in the third carried on a conflict with Carthage for possession of the island of Sicily. This conflict is known as the First Punic War (265-241 B.C.). An attack in 219 B.C. by the Carthaginian general Hannibal, an extremely able military leader, against Saguntum, a settlement on the Valencian coast which the Romans asserted was an ally of theirs, provoked a new struggle between Rome and Carthage known as the Second Punic War, and motivated the first entrance of Roman troops into Spain. The victory of the Romans was swift: before the close of the third century B.C. (in 206), they had destroyed Carthaginian power on the Peninsula, notwithstanding the fact that Hannibal, who had invaded Italy in order to attack the Romans on their own territory, won several great victories there. But the Romans knew how to recoup their losses; and after vanquishing the Carthaginians, they extended their own power and dominion over western Europe. Greece also was dominated wholly by them, toward the middle of the second century B.C., in the year 146.

The Conquest of Spain by the Romans

Once they had achieved advantage over the Carthaginians, the Romans, essentially a conquering people ambitious to rule the world, tried to seize the rest of Spain. A large number of the central and

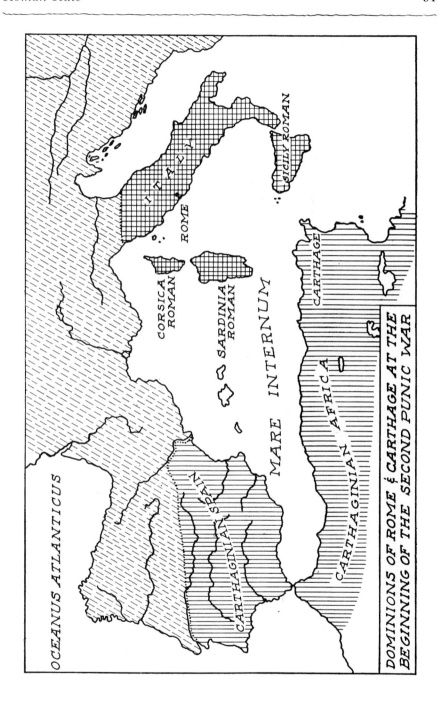

DOMINIONS OF ROME & CARTHAGE AT THE
BEGINNING OF THE SECOND PUNIC WAR

northern tribes tenaciously defended their independence against the
new invader. The Roman struggle to subdue them lasted for almost
two hundred years, from the beginning of the second century B.C.
to the end of the first; and as always happens in such circumstances,
it intensified many innate characteristics of the native fighters: hardihood, devotion, loyalty, heroism, adroitness in deceiving the enemy
and in defending their own lives and property. Thus the deeds of the
Spaniards in the long conflict with the Romans afford very interesting
additions to our information about our ancestors of that period.

Character and Division of the Spanish People

Let us remember that the population of Spain had been in process
of formation through a series of immigrations and foreign conquests.
Even without taking into account the Phoenicians, the Greeks, and
later the Carthaginians (peoples who had their capitals and metropolises outside Spain and for whom Spain was only a place for trading,
for industrial exploitation, for establishment of colonies, and, at most,
for military domination) , the Peninsula was inhabited in the third
century B.C. by elements as varied in origin and in civilization as
the so-called Iberians, the Tartessians, with their kinsmen the Mastienians, and the Celts; not to mention survivals in wild, remote regions
of the Peninsula of other more ancient settlements. It is likely that
these diverse elements had not intermingled except to a very small
extent and among more or less adjacent groups. The dominant facts
were diversity and separation: diversity not only of each group or race
from the rest but internally as well. As a natural consequence, the
tribes lived independently as regards one another, without a common
chief or king even for those akin by blood; much less, for the peoples
of the Peninsula as a whole. Only in especial cases, and then primarily
because of war, some neighboring tribes united in a temporary and
usually rather loose federation. Solely in such circumstances were they
ruled in certain regions, or countries, by a chief in common.

In order to judge that variety of elements which made up the
indigenous Spanish population, nothing could be more helpful than
the general chart of the Spanish people found in the Geography by
Strabo, a Greek writer of the first century B.C. According to him, the
largest and most renowned tribes, or federations, were the following:

Excavations of Ampurias (Emporium).

in the northwest, the *Gallaeci* or Galicians; next to them the *Astures*, who inhabited parts of the modern Asturias and of Leon; beyond them to the northeast, the *Cantabri*, or Cantabrians, between Villaviciosa and Castro Urdiales; in the Basque provinces, Navarre, and part of what was to become Aragon, the *Vascones*, or Basques; the *Cerretani*, *Indigetes*, and others in Catalonia; the *Edetani*, in Valencia and southeastern Aragon; the *Contestani*, in Alicante and Murcia; the *Turdetani* in southern Estremadura and western Andalusia; the *Turduli* in the central and eastern sections of the same reg   the *Lusitani*, or Lusitanians, throughout almost all of central Portugal and a part of Estremadura; the *Celtiberians* in the territory already mentioned; the *Vaccaei* in the northern portion of old Castile; the *Vettones* toward the west, between the Douro and Guadiana rivers; the *Carpetani* in the vicinity of Madrid and Toledo and part of Guadalajara; and the *Oretani* in the region of Cíudad Real. Strabo's chart also shows how in the first century B.C. (and assuredly prior to that) the old names of Tartessians, Mastienians, et cetera, had been replaced by others, and how the primitive localized meaning of the term "Iberian" had been so expanded that the word had become a very general appellation embracing in significance the majority of all the tribes and peoples just enumerated. An erudite modern Spaniard believes that he discerns, amid the variety of tribes and in the geographical zone where the sculptured bulls and boars are found, a single racial stock, to be inferred from surnames and from the names of local or regional gods; a stock that would include the groups denominated as *Vettones, Lusitani, Gallaeci, Cantabri, Antrigones, Caristii, Varduli, Vaccaei,* and *Carpetani.* The supposition refers to the epoch of Romanization.

Their social and geographic division, together with the sturdy individualism, inherent in the majority of Spaniards, caused the tribes that had already struck root in Spanish territory to follow greatly differing lines of conduct when conquerors or invaders such as the Phoenicians or the Carthaginians moved in on them. The Spaniards neither joined as a unit to oppose the invaders, nor merely accepted domination by the latter in exchange for receiving the advantages of a new and in several respects superior civilization. On the contrary, while some tribes fought stubbornly for their independence, others yielded easily to foreign inducements; nor were instances lacking of quick shifts of tribal allegiance from alliance with the invaders to

Barcelona: Archeological Museum

Iberian vase from the burying ground of Archena.

vigorous opposition. Even when the Spaniards did oppose the invaders, as a rule not many tribes united to that end, but each waged battle on its own account. In consequence, and notwithstanding the personal valor of the combatants and many individual acts of heroism, the invaders were sure of victory in the long run, because they themselves were united and well disciplined, obedient to the orders of chiefs and kings. The period of two centuries during which the struggle of the Spanish tribes for independence was carried on, coincides precisely with the greatest expansion of Roman rule. At first a petty kingdom within narrow limits, Rome had come to be by the fifth century B.C. an important Republic, increasing in power until in the first century of the Christian era it formed an Empire dominating the whole of Italy; Greece; the territory embracing modern France, the Netherlands, Britain, and part of Germany and of the Danube basin; as well as many regions in northern Africa and western Asia.

The Resistance to the Roman Conquest

The conquest commenced by the Romans at the beginning of the second century B.C. seemed to change the situation. At least, the many accounts by contemporaneous historians handed down to us give the impression that protest and resistance against domination by the new set of foreigners were both more general and more continuous than had been formerly the case. This may have resulted from the more or less confused awakening, in face of the common danger, of a sense of solidarity not previously existing; it may have been due also to the fact that the Romans, bent on conquering the whole of the Peninsula, penetrated into localities whither previous invaders had never gone, and in consequence clashed with tribes, among the fiercest and the most resolved to maintain their independence, which up to that time had had no contact with foreigners, or had had it only briefly. So avers one Greek historian, commenting on these wars. The fact is that during two hundred years the Romans were compelled to fight almost incessantly in Spain, and that during this time the association of Spanish tribes waging a common war side by side under a single chief was of increasingly frequent occurrence. More frequent also were instances of great heroism, on the part of individuals as well as of cities, in the struggle for independence.

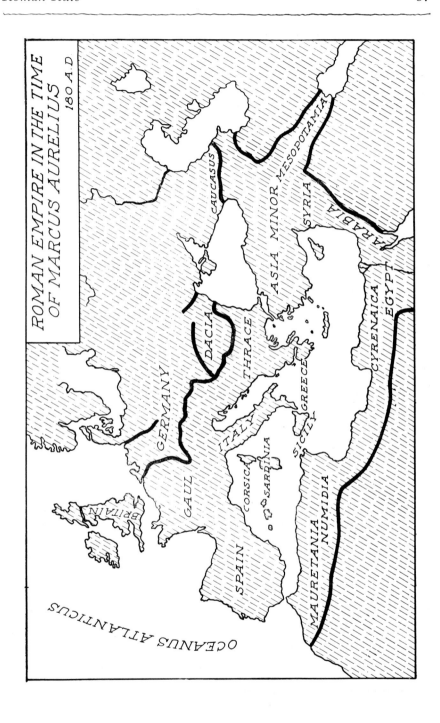

ROMAN EMPIRE IN THE TIME
OF MARCUS AURELIUS
180 A.D

Moreover, until that time the tribes in Spain had never had to fight so strong a power as Rome, nor had they encountered theretofore such firmness and resolution as the Romans possessed. As we have said, the Romans were then the most powerful people in Europe; with the advantage, as regards ambition for dominion, of having formed a well disciplined system of government combining under one central authority all agencies and powers, and continually enlarged by annexation of territories and nations. The Greeks (the other major people of ancient European history) had never succeeded in joining together in a single monarchy or republic. Always separate, and involved in fratricidal wars among Athens, Sparta, and the other city-states of their principal political groups, the Greeks knew unity only (as was to happen later in the case of the Spaniards) under the rule of foreign kings; namely, the kings of Macedonia, a region north of Greece, properly speaking. These were Philip, and in even greater degree his son Alexander the Great, antiquity's most famous and most fortunate conqueror, whose empire (336-332 B.C.) included the whole of southeastern Europe, western Asia to the Indus, and Egypt. On Alexander's premature death in 332, his empire fell apart into several kingdoms, the principal of which was Macedonia (including Greece), Syria, and Egypt where he had founded the great city of Alexandria. Two centuries later, in 146 B.C. as we have said, the Greek territories passed under control of the Romans.

The encounter in Spain of these two ways of life, the Greek and the Roman, so opposite in their concepts of society and its political organization, was inevitably fierce and bloody. We can now have no doubt that victory in the end had to go to the Romans. That victory represented, for the Spanish people, the decisive imposition of a regime of unity and subjection absolutely contrary to their ancient customs; such a regime as the Carthaginians had initiated but had not fully achieved. It also completely changed the course of indigenous Spanish civilization, substituting for it the Roman way which, except in matters of government and legislation, was fundamentally Greek.

Conduct of the Roman Generals—Consul Scipio

The Roman generals, whose official titles were consul, pro-consul, praetor, or legate, were largely to blame for the fact that the war in Spain was so long and so cruel.

Mosaic pavement, from Itálica.

In the beginning, while they were still fighting the Carthaginians, they adopted a very conciliatory attitude toward the Spaniards. Such was the conduct of consul Scipio (209 B.C.) at Tarragona and Cartagena. Regarding Tarragona, a historian of the period relates that when the Iberian tribal king Edecón, one of the most powerful of the region, presented himself before Scipio, asking for the return of his wife and children who had been formerly in the power of the Carthaginians and were by them turned over to the Consul, the latter delivered them to Edecón; and then Scipio, "when he had won, by various ways opened up in the conversations, the regard of the Spaniard, and had waked large hopes in the hearts of his new friends, let them return to their homes." When this story became known generally, "all the folk from the Ebro to Tarragona who had not favored the Romans formerly, joined up with them now by common consent."

Scipio acted similarly at Cartagena, not only toward the Spaniards but toward the inhabitants of the city as well. The latter, who were regarded as prisoners and numbered some 10,000, he separated into two groups: one consisting of the rich, with their wives and children, and the other of artisans. "When this was done," according to the historian cited above, "he exhorted the former to take the part of the Roman people, bearing in mind the benefit to themselves of doing so, and he sent them back to their own residences. As for the artisans, he told them that they were now public serfs (slaves) of the Roman people; but he promised them their freedom if each in his own craft demonstrated love and respect for Rome. This method of dealing with the prisoners won for him and for his country the friendship and loyalty of the citizens; and inspired the artisans with great zeal for serving him, in the hope of gaining their freedom." As for the families of Spaniards whom the Carthaginians had held as hostages, Scipio first ordered that the 300 persons thus held be released to him, and then "passed among them, speaking to each of the children in turn, caressing them, and promising for their consolation that within a few days they should see their parents. He exhorted the rest to be of good spirit and told each to write to his own people, saying that the hostages were safe, that everything was going well, and that the Romans were about to send them home unharmed, always provided that their kinsmen made common cause with the Roman people. When Scipio said all this, he had ready handsome gifts from the booty taken in the siege of the city, which would help along his plan and which he began handing out to the hostages according to sex and age: to the girls, figurines and bracelets; and to the boys, daggers and swords."

Galba

This very humane conduct was rarely imitated by those generals who undertook to conquer the Peninsula after the Carthaginians had been driven out. On the contrary, there were numerous instances of cruelty and of breaches of faith regarding promises and peace terms given the Spaniards. The governor, Galba, afforded a typical example of such perfidy when in order to vanquish the Lusitanians, he pretended to make peace with them; waited for them to come out of their mountain fastnesses and go home to the plains to settle down and work their fields; guaranteed them peaceful possession of their lands; and when he had them thus lulled into a false security, fell upon them, pitilessly putting them to the knife. Naturally, as very often happens in cases of terrorism, Galba's bloodstained strategem, instead of ending the conflict, made it flare up again with renewed fury.

Viriatus

Viriatus among the warriors and Numantia among the cities exemplified Spanish resistance and valor.

Viriatus was a chief, or *caudillo,* of Iberian or Celtic origin who, according to Roman historians, began life as a shepherd. With exceptional talent as a military leader, he united under his authority numerous tribes of central and southern Spain outraged by Galba's cruelty, and thus waged war for many years, making his name a terror to his enemies. The Romans succeeded in ridding themselves of Viriatus only by treasonably plotting his assassination with some of his associates whom the Roman general Caepio suborned for the purpose in 139 B.C.

The War of Numantia

The war against the tribes whose capital was Numantia, on the bank of the Duero above Soria, also lasted a long time. It began about 152 B.C. and did not end until 134 or 132 B.C.; after the

Romans had suffered many defeats and had been forced into several peace pacts with terms humiliating for them. The very name of Numantia came to be dreaded by Roman soldiers, who on repeated occasions refused to take part in the war. This is how a historian contemporary with the event depicts the terror of the Romans: "It was learned in Rome [in the year 151 B.C.] from [the general] Quintus Fulvius and the soldiers who had served in Spain under his orders the preceding year, that they had been forced to have arms in hand practically all the time, since the combats were innumerable, the Roman deaths countless, and the Celtiberians invincible; while Marcellus [another Roman general] was afraid that he would be ordered to carry on the war. Such news caused so much consternation among the young men that their elders declared that they had never seen anything like it at Rome. In short, the aversion toward the voyage to Spain increased to the point that while on other occasions more tribunes [subaltern military leaders] had offered than were needed, none sought the post in this instance. The veteran leaders designated by the consuls to march with the general refused to follow him; and the most deplorable fact of all was that the Roman youth, in spite of being called to arms, did not wish to sign up and in order to avoid enlistment availed themselves of strategems which honor does not permit of examination nor pride of explanation. Such was the multitude of those culpable that punishment was impossible."

How the Celtiberians Made War

The same historian goes on to say that the Romans called the war with the Celtiberians "the war of fire" and that it differed greatly from the kind of warfare waged by the Germans and the Asiatics. These latter conflicts "consist usually of a single battle, rarely of two, and in practically every case the war is decided by the first skirmish, in which all the troops engage. In the [Celtiberian] war to which we refer, the course of events was very different. Ordinarily they fought until nightfall, since both sides bore themselves bravely and, no matter how fatigued, refused to pause for rest. As if regretful that darkness had interrupted the conflict, they would begin fighting afresh at dawn. Winter's cold itself could hardly put an end to this warfare and the scattered fighting." It is evident that in this last phrase the

historian makes especial reference to guerilla warfare, so characteristic
of the Spanish method of fighting in all periods and so fatiguing and
unnerving to armies accustomed to the Roman method of battling in
formation and with large numbers of troops.

The Taking and Destruction of Numantia

However, Rome found the general she needed in Scipio Aemili-
anus, who bore the same name as the conqueror of Cartagena. He
besieged Numantia rigorously in 134 B.C. The inhabitants of the
city lacked both food and water, and received no assistance from
neighboring tribes, less heroic than themselves, who did not dare
oppose Scipio. The Numantians in consequence found it impossible
to continue the struggle. Even so, far from surrendering, they set
fire to their city and decided to fight until killed or to commit suicide
rather than fall alive into the enemy's power. All that Scipio was
able to conquer was a smoking mass of ruins and corpses. These ruins,
recently excavated, have revealed many interesting details of the art
and the customs of the Numantians, as we shall see.

Cantabrians and Astures

The fall of Numantia did not put an end to the war of independence. The final sparks emanating from that conflict were produced
toward the close of the first century B.C. by the formidable resistance
of the Cantabrians and the Astures, and it took the best efforts of the
best general that Rome then had, the Emperor Augustus himself, to
extinguish them. The heroism of the Astures and the Cantabrians
reached such an extreme that they were not intimidated by the terrible
punishments that the Romans inflicted on their prisoners. These included crucifying the bravest young men and selling the rest as slaves;
but these very slaves revolted, started the war again, and kept it up
until 19 B.C. in which year Rome could say at last that she completely
dominated the Iberian Peninsula.

The extraordinary examples of courage and love of liberty which
we have instanced reflect perfectly the mind and character of the
Cantabrians as pictured by writers of that epoch. "We find"—says
one of these—"in the historians and the poets many examples of, I
shall not say the hardihood, but the ferocity, the wild-beast fury, of

the Iberians, those of the north in particular. It is related, for example, that in the Cantabrian war there were mothers who killed their children to keep them from falling into the hands of the Romans. One lad, whose parents and brothers had been bound in chains, beheaded them all by his father's order; and a woman also beheaded her companions in captivity. One prisoner dragged in by some drunken soldiers flung himself into the flames of the campfire. It is said that various prisoners of this race while being crucified by the Romans chanted their song of victory."

The same author recognizes the fact that the Spaniards, who gave these proofs of harsh courage natural to primitive races, were excelled by no people in loyalty to the leaders under whom they served; a loyalty to the death.

Effects of Roman Domination

The fundamental effect of Roman rule and its principal influences on Spanish life and civilization were the following: First, there was *unification* of authority throughout Spain under pressure of a central power (the imperial government of Rome) which increasingly absorbed other peoples. Then, as a natural and immediate consequence came *subordination and discipline of the tribes,* whose previous independence and separation each from the others was completely shattered by Roman rule. As a logical consequence there ensued first *alteration of the pattern* and then *social unification* of the various Spanish peoples through intermingling them, changing the residence of many tribes or forcing their union by other means, including that of concentration in cities. There was likewise *linguistic unification,* through the increasing use of Latin and its imposition as the official and common language. Latin, in fact, the language of the Romans, struck root so deeply in the Peninsula that in time there sprang from it *bable* (the Asturian dialect), Castilian, Galician, Aragonese, Catalan, and Valencian. *Juridical unification* superimposed Roman law on the laws and customs of Iberians, Celts, and the other Peninsular peoples; and brought about a correspondingly *substantial modification* of the concept of the family and of property, laws of inheritance, et cetera, all of which took the Roman forms, abandoning in great part those previously accepted in the Peninsula. Other lasting consequences of

Roman rule were *dissemination of all the manifestations of material civilization* (principally roads, public buildings, commerce, agriculture) , and of the *scientific, literary and artistic culture* of the Romans (such as schools and libraries) as well as of their dress and manners.

The Romans applied to the whole of the Peninsula indiscriminately the names *Iberia* and *Spain* (*Hispania*) but in the long run the latter prevailed. For purposes of government the Romans divided the country into provinces: at first, two (the Hither Province and the Farther Province) , and later five, each under its own Governor.

City Government

The city, center of Roman life, had a government efficiently organized. That organization was called a municipality, a term still in use today. In the beginning the Roman municipality was governed by an assembly of inhabitants, who elected four officers or magistrates, somewhat like mayors: two *duumviri* and two *aediles*. Today we know the names of many highly important Spanish-Roman municipalities; and from some of these (Málaga, Salpensa, Osuna) have come down to our time fragments of the texts of their respective statutes or ordinances engraved on bronze tablets. From these tablets, and from others containing the regulations for organizing the settlements resulting from working the mines (Aljustrel and others) we know in considerable measure not only the general outline of the Roman municipality as regularly organized, but also of many of its variant forms.

The Process of Romanization

The municipality exercised a great influence in the political education of the Spaniards, and was one of the most effective factors in converting them to the Roman way of life and culture. No less important in this respect was the shrewd proceeding of the Roman governors, who at first denying to the conquered peoples participation in the civil rights and citizenship pertaining to inhabitants of Rome and greatly coveted by foreigners, conceded these advantages little by little, until there came a day when all who dwelt in territory of the Roman Empire were deemed equal before the law if they were free men. One of the effects of this gradual participation was that settlements in Spain which because of the tolerance of the Romans, or

Saragossa. Roman Wall.

rather because of considerations of Roman policy, had more or less preserved the native Spanish type of organization, came to abandon this voluntarily in favor of the Roman pattern.

A proceeding in the transformation of Spanish life which was very different from that just indicated, consisted, as previously remarked in passing, in breaking up the interior tribal organization by removing entire tribes from the terrain where they lived and in which they could stir up and carry on rebellions, and thus forcing them to a peaceful and orderly life. To ensure this, the Romans often transported large population groups from one locality to another. They did this with some Lusitanians, transferring them from their own territory north of the Tagus river to another, south of it, which belonged to the *Celtici* as the Romans called them; after Viriatus' death, with a part of his followers, whom they took to the region of Valencia, and assigned lands there; and with the Cantabrians, who were transported, following the first Roman victories, to flat lands far from their native mountains. The Romans also tried to make the Spaniards in general abandon the mountains and give up living in sparsely inhabited communities in order to settle on the plains and accustom themselves to urban life, which is to say, to the city. The Romans founded new cities as well, or enlarged and improved ancient Iberian settlements on the basis of a resident Roman group: sometimes soldiers in service (when it was a question of military posts or encampments); again, soldiers discharged from the army, or civilians. These new cities were commonly called colonies. As was natural, even such as were purely military represented centers disseminating civilization and, of course, pacification. Accordingly, a geographer of the first century B.C. says of an army corps of three legions (regiments) sent by the Emperor Tiberius to the territory of the Cantabrians and neighboring tribes, "the presence of these Romans has done much already not only to pacify but also to civilize a part of these peoples." By this means and by destruction of all the forts and strongholds that the Spaniards possessed, and occasionally of entire cities as well if they offered much resistance, the Romans rendered it impossible for native-born tribes to carry out fresh attacks, and thus accustomed them to living alongside their conquerors and to the habits of peace and the discipline of the State.

Tarragona. Roman wall built on the cyclopean remains, and the Archbishop's Tower.

Apart from these acts of intentional Romanizing policy, the repeated fact that the civil wars which characterized the transition of Rome from Republic to Empire in the first century B.C., were waged in part by Spanish troops and on Spanish soil, influenced the process of Romanization. Such were the armed conflicts between Sertorius and Sulla and between Sulla and Pompey, and not long after, between Pompey and his party and Julius Caesar, the first Roman emperor in point of fact. In these struggles Sertorius and Pompey had the support of many Spanish tribes, especially the former, who succeeded in organizing in Spain a government ruled by a Senate. Although the Spaniards friendly to Sertorius were not given participation in this government, it was a powerful influence in spreading Roman culture and customs among indigenous tribes. In Huesca (Osca), one of his provincial capitals, Sertorius established schools with classes under Greek and Latin teachers which were attended by sons of the leading Spanish families.

Decadence of the Municipalities

From the time of the third century A.D., the absolutism of the Roman Emperors, whose ambition it was to concentrate all power in their own persons, invalidated the oldtime democratic character of the municipality, and exploited both the wealthy and the laboring classes with the main object of gathering wealth by taxation. To assure tax collections, all *decurions,* or members of the municipal council, were made responsible for them; a responsibility that became hereditary, descending from father to son, so that collection of the Emperor's taxes from every family and individual able to pay was thereby guaranteed.

Extent of the Romanization of Spain

The consequence of all the foregoing was that by the beginning of the Christian era, a considerable part of the ancient native peoples of Spain had been Romanized. The Romans called these peoples *Togati,* or The Togaed; the toga, a loose, flowing outer garment being a distinctive article of Roman attire. Thus it is that a historian of the period remarks that the Celtiberians, long famed as the fiercest of the Spaniards, were already *Togati.* Of the Turdetani, especially those living along the banks of the Baetis, he writes that "they have changed over wholly to the Roman way of life, even renouncing the use of their mother-tongue; and furthermore, since many of them have been recompensed by Roman Law [one of the methods of participating in Roman citizenship] and have often received Roman colonies into their cities, it is nothing strange that they themselves are today transformed into Romans. The existence of such colonies as *Pax Augusta,* among the *Celtici, Augusta Emérita* [Mérida] among the Turduli, *Caesar Augusta* [Saragossa] among the Celtiberians, and others similar, demonstrates the change brought about in the country."

Opposition to Romanization

But not all Spanish populations showed the same effects, nor would it be correct to assume that Romanization entirely suppressed the characteristic manifestations of their own civilization such as they had achieved it.

Some of the Galicians, Astures, and Cantabrians in the first century of the Christian era were still recalcitrant to Roman influence. The historian cited above attributes this to the fact that certain mountain tribes were not so completely pacified as others, and were less frequently visited by Romans; and he believes also that a contributing factor was the unproductiveness of the lands that they inhabited and the rigors of the climate. The same conditions held with other tribes in similarly mountainous regions far removed from the large population centers.

Furthermore, and especially during the first centuries of Roman domination, the Spaniards continued to use their native language for inscriptions, especially on tombs (of which we know many today) and to produce objects characteristic of their own art, many of which also are extant, as we shall see. Some local customs were likewise kept up, such as the Cordovan marriage rites, as is attested by a law of the Romans themselves.

Examples of Intense Romanization

Where Romanization was intense, it produced magnificent results described by contemporaneous writers. Let us cite examples.

Turdetania in the first century A.D. had a number of very prosperous Romanized cities. *Corduba* (Córdova) founded by Marcellus was one of the most renowned for its commerce, which was fostered by the fertility and extent of its territory, its situation along the margin of the river, and its mixed Roman and indigenous population, all picked men. Corduba was the first colony established by the Romans in that region. Of prime importance likewise were *Gades* (Cádiz), originally Phoenician; *Arido* or *Aridspi* (Jérez?) which had come to eclipse *Hispalis* (Sevilla), also a Roman colony, as a trading center; *Itálica, Ilipa, Astigis, Munda, Urso* (Osuna), and at least seven others. In them all, as well as in the cities of Lusitania, of the Mediterranean coast, and of other Romanized sections, (the Romans had introduced their monumental style of architecture, their arts, and their refinements. These included lighthouses or beacons along the coast to guide shipping, such as the light at the mouth of the Baetis called the Tower of Cepión.)

All the Turdetan trade was with Italy, and especially with Rome. The Turdetani exported wheat, wine in great quantity, much olive oil, wax, honey, pepper, cochineal (from which scarlet dye was obtained), and cinnabar (a mercury sulphide). They owned and worked many salt-mines, from which they supplied the fish-salting industry so highly esteemed by the Romans. Even more prized was wool of the native sheep; so much so, that a good Turdetan ram sold for a high price at Rome, as did also the fine woven cloth for which the city of Salacia was famous. There was likewise great demand for fish and shellfish from the Turdetan coast, among which the oysters, mussels, snails, eels, congers and tunas were notable for size. Minerals and metals were exported by the Turdetani, including gold dust and nuggets.

The boats that the Turdetani built out of native woods exclusively were the most important of all that thronged the Roman ports. To emphasize this fact, a writer of the time says that they were not inferior in number to the vessels arriving at Libya in Africa, one of the most famed regions of the Mediterranean.

Some sections of what is now Estremadura had been Romanized on a scale equally extensive. Here the principal city was *Emérita Augusta,* which came to occupy tenth place among the seventeen most notable cities of the Roman epoch. The Romanization of central Portugal, called Lusitania, was also intensive. In the eastern section the principal centers of Roman civilization were *Tarraco* (Tarragona) and *Caesar*

Augusta (Saragossa) , besides New Carthage and Saguntum. This last
was rebuilt, and enjoyed great prosperity under the Romans. To the
west, the chief cities were *Astúrica* (Astorga) , *Legio Septima* (León) ,
and *Lucus Augusti* (Lugo) .

Intensity of Cultural Romanization: Public Works, Science, and Literature

The Romans had learned from the Greeks, as we have said, the
substance of Greek culture in science, literature, and art; so that when
Greek culture decayed, the high point of European culture was the
Roman, transmitted continually to Roman-conquered countries. Nevertheless, the Greek root was always discernible in the Roman product,
and Greek influence was kept alive by the continuous presence of
Greeks in literature, the arts, and other intellectual fields of the Roman
world, and by the numerous copies of Greek art, especially of sculpture,
made by the Romans. Some of the copies are of such excellence that
for many centuries they were thought to be the Greek originals; and
they are at the present time the only remaining evidences of several
splendid creations of Hellenic art.

(The Romans, great builders of public works as they were, filled the
Spanish cities with such things; not the larger cities only, but many
others of lesser importance as well. Some of these public works (circuses, amphitheatres, theatres, aqueducts, temples, thermal baths,
arches of triumph, courts of justice, city walls, bridges, richly adorned
tombs, private residences, and various other structures) , have stood
until our own time in more or less ruinous condition; and there have
lasted also a great number of statues, ceramics, mosaics, jewels, and
the like. The same thing is true of all the Roman dominions, not in
Europe alone, but likewise in Asia and in Africa, where ruins have
been found of cities and monuments as imposing as were ever created
by the genius of Rome.)

(In Spain the most striking examples are the circuses at Saguntum,
Calahorra * and Mérida; the amphitheatres at Itálica,† Mérida,‡ and a
portion of the one at Tarragona; the theatres at Saguntum, Clunia
(Coruña del Conde, Burgos) , Ronda, and the magnificent edifice at

---

* The best preserved of all.
† One of the finest known.
‡ Still quite complete.

Roman Aqueduct at Segovia.

Mérida; the majestic aqueducts of Segovia and Mérida; the temples at
Vich (*Ausa*), Evora, on the bridge at Alcántara, the five at Mérida
and scattered or relatively unimportant ruins at Barcelona, Ampurias
(Emporium), Denia, Itálica, Belo, (Bolonia, near Tarifa), Talavera
and elsewhere; the thermal baths, or municipal bath-houses, at Mérida,
Lugo and Alange (*Castrum Colubri*); the monumental triumphal
arches at Bará,§ Martorell, Medinaceli, Alcántara, and Caparra (*Capera,
Cáceres*), analogous in style to that of Caracalla at Tebessa; the sepulchres at Tarragona,¶ Fabara,‖ Sádaba, and the three in the Province of
Gerona; the walls of Lugo, Ampurias, Seville, Coria, León, and other
cities; the bridges at Mérida, Alcántara (Cáceres), Segura (Cáceres),
Salamanca and Lérida; and the numerous but fragmentary ruins of
private dwellings at Ampurias, Numancia, Itálica, Belo, Navatejera
(León), Cuevas de Soria, and elsewhere at many places. A list, even
though abridged and selective, of other remains, and especially of art
objects, furniture, statuary, would be interminable. In many provincial and local museums and in the National Museum of Archeology at
Madrid the best examples of such things are to be found. Surviving
also are ruins of the great highways—the Roman roads—paved or of
rammed earth construction, which were built on the Peninsula. Prolonged contemplation of works of art so numerous and often so magnificent educated the artistic instinct of the Spaniards, who learned
therefrom both the ancient lintel-type of architecture and the use of
arch and dome, characteristics of Roman architecture as distinguished
from Greek. In so learning, however, they turned aside, as we shall see,
from the course whither previous influences had been bearing them,
especially in matters of art. It may be said that by way of compensation Roman public works in Spain as exemplified in highways and
aqueducts (two specialties in which, as in sewers and heating, the
Romans attained technical perfection not excelled until modern
times represent) the first considered and intensive program of modifying the geographical environment of Spain to benefit human welfare.

The Romans adopted a native Spanish method of building stone
walls and mud walls which they themselves had not known theretofore,
but which became general in Roman military architecture; and they

§ The most beautiful of those still standing.
¶ Popularly known as the Tomb of the Scipios.
‖ The best of all.

adopted too the excellent Celtiberian construction method of fabricating iron and steel swords, and the long, slender Iberian javelin.

The Spanish Contribution to Roman Cultur

There has come down to us from the Roman period the name of no architect, sculptor, nor any other artist of Spanish origin. This fact, when taken together with the material evidence offered by archeology, permits us to assume that the impact of Roman art did not wake in the Spanish spirit a creative impulse like that which Greek art had kindled. Perhaps this was because the absorbent character of Romanization killed the original artistic manifestations of the Spaniard.

On the other hand, it has been often said, especially during the past two centuries, that in scientific and literary fields Spain produced, after Romanization had been achieved, notable exponents of philosophy, geography, agriculture, poetry, and oratory; and they have been assumed to be of indigenous Spanish stock or race.

That opinion, which some historians still hold,* is now rejected by the most eminent Latinists of the countries that formerly took the lead in disseminating the theory, principally because in the literary and (to employ the word in its Roman sense) oratorical material, they found reason to criticize caustically the presumptively Spanish contribution, which they presented not as deserving of praise but rather as a blameworthy degeneration of Latin classic style. Each of these conflicting opinions involves an historical error as well as an error of literary and linguistic criticism. Historically, the misconception derived from forgetfulness of the difference existing always in every colonization (and Roman rule in Spain was only a colonization) between the colonists emigrating from the metropolis and their direct descendants, on the one hand, and on the other the native population colonized and more or less assimilated into the conqueror's civilization. As in all dominions of that kind, in Spain a purely Roman population group was being formed, which, persisting on the Peninsula, produced a class that, without losing the essential condition of being Latin-Romans, little by little became characterized with the passage of time by variations in customs, turns of thought, and language, which made them somewhat

---

* The first edition of this History still reflected that view. New research for the fourth volume of my comprehensive *History of Civilization* has resulted in my rectifying what was then said with regard to this and other moot points.

different from the wholly Roman Roman of Rome; as happened similarly later on in the case of the creoles in Spanish colonies of the New World, and of the British colonists in North America before the Revolution. Doubtless no one cares to deny the difference that existed between these population groups and those that continued to live in the respective metropolises. We Spaniards called, and still call, "Americans" those Spaniards who settled in the Americas and spent all or most of their lives there, becoming inevitably changed in some ways by their environment. Likewise, other colonizing nations have used the term "American" and analogous names for men who though resident in the colony belonged by blood to the ruling race (Canada, the one-time British colonies south of the Canadian border, South Africa, the Far East, et cetera). It is not at all surprising therefore that the Romans called their own fellow-citizens on the Peninsula and their descendants "Spaniards."

Moreover, it cannot be denied that the variations arising from the diversity of land and climate affected both the immigrant colonist and the native-born inhabitant; nor that the continued contacts, the long dwelling together of the two classes, in time necessarily had its influence on the traditional way of life brought by the colonists from the homeland to the new country. Naturally, that influence was more considerable in the case of peoples who accepted fraternization and even intermarriage with the nativeborn than it was with those who kept the latter at a distance. An instance in point is the difference between Canada, colonized by the French, and the eastern section of what is today the United States, colonized principally by the British. Another example even more eloquent and more fully developed was afforded by the Spaniard in his American and Oceanic dominions.

The case of the colonization of Spain itself differs from the others here cited in that a great majority of the indigenous Spanish tribes at the beginning of the Christian era embraced the religion of their conquerors, a fact that made their social relations with the latter more intimate, and intermarriage a frequent occurrence. Accordingly—and this is unlike the situation in Anglo-Saxon, British, colonies—transmission to the Latin conquerors of indigenous spiritual traits and ways of life became not only a natural but a logically inevitable consequence. However, such transmissions grew rarer and less direct as Romanization struck deeper root. At any rate, there is ample proof of native Spanish influences on the Latin colonists, as we have already shown by examples cited, along with the contrary effect on the native peoples of loss of many of their own customs, beliefs, and individual and collective ways of life.

On the basis of all these observations, the problem of the supposed racial Hispanism of several great Roman writers of the first and later centuries of the Christian era is easily posed. It is essential above everything else to determine whether they were wholly or in part of Latin nationality or family; which is to say, whether they were immigrant colonists or descendants of immigrant colonists, or were indigenous Spaniards by birth and race. Let us consider the most disputed names. They include philosophers, scientists, orators, and poets: Marcus Annaeus Seneca and his son Lucius Annaeus Seneca, the great moralist, both Cordovans; the two Balbuses, uncle and nephew, orators from Gades (Cádiz); the poets Marcus Annaeus Lucanus of Cordova (Seneca's nephew) and Martial, the epigrammatist, of Calatayud; and Quintilian, orator, critic, and teacher, a native of Calahorra, author of the best treatise on Latin Rhetoric, which for centuries was the accepted text in all countries for both Latinists and less scholarly writers. All these men in different measure established Roman literary standards, and were for a period favorite authors at Rome; and they transmitted to the metropolitan capital their vigor, their originality which to the Romans seemed to have an exotic quality, and the freedom with which they treated rules of rhetoric. In other intellectual fields, several writers of a scientific bent figure among the supposedly Spanish group; for example, Columela of Cádiz, held to be the most learned agronomist of the Roman period, author of a notable treatise on Agriculture; and the geographer Pomponius Mela of Tingentera (a city believed to be Spanish, on the coast of the Strait of Gibraltar), from whom we have a Geography, the outcome of a voyage. Seneca—(Lucius Annaeus Seneca, already mentioned—was the greatest and most influential Latin colonial of the epoch. His ethic, similar to Christian ethics, not only influenced Rome but deeply impregnated the Spanish soul and is still today an austere and noble guide to the character, conduct and doctrines of the Spanish people. Seneca's Moral Epistles continue to be highly esteemed and useful directives for conduct and for the education of the will; and that is their importance in the history of Spanish civilization.)

Unfortunately, however, the known facts regarding the parentage and families of all these authors are few and uncertain; and the more abundant and reliable they become, the more they tend to convince us that these men were of Romanic origin.* The only one of them who because of his own reiterated declaration to that effect presents himself to us as a native Spaniard (Celtiberian or Iberian, he says) is Martial; but at the same time, he asserts repeatedly that his poems are essentially not Spanish but Roman in style and inspiration. In making the most favorable case possible for regarding Martial as artist a Romanized Celtiberian, who preserved characteristic traits of the native race which he declared to be his own, it must be conceded that the absolutely certain meaning of his words is not established. Aragonese intellectuals of our day insist on viewing him as a clear example of the Aragonese backwoodsman at his most realistic and most violent. To be sure this may be an atavistic conclusion, "the voice of the blood" heard across the centuries, which does not constitute proof positive.

Regarding Seneca, the writer whose race most interests us, the information as to his ancestry is vague and fragmentary. Some authors say that his father was "a wealthy gentleman, perhaps a treasury official," and that his mother Helvia was "intelligent, sufficiently cultured, and of lofty character." Others more soberly content themselves with stating that Seneca was "descended from a family of gentlemen"; that his father "made a point of observing the ancient Roman customs,' 'and that his mother was "moderately cultured." This last item seems to receive confirmation in the Epistle (*Consolation*, No. XVII) which Seneca himself dedicates to his mother and in which he attributes the deficiencies in her education to the "old-fashioned severity" of the father. In any case, it is easily deduced from all these things that Seneca belonged to a wholly Roman (or at least Italian) family and not to one of Turdetan or other Spanish origin. If his mother's ancestry had been such, he would not have failed to adduce that circumstance to excuse the lack of culture referred to in the epistle On Consolation. Furthermore, the whole of Seneca's public and private life, from the time that he established himself at Rome, was all a profound expression of his Roman psychology.

---

* The reader will find the argument stated in detail in Volume I of my *Historia de la civilización española*, Second Part, IV, 4 and 5 (as yet unpublished).

Identical or analogous facts (commonly the more convincing for being less ponderous) are found to be true of other writers included by Martial in enumerating a group of Spanish fellow-citizens, and in other cases; as with military politicians and Roman Emperors born in Spain or belonging to Spanish-Roman families: Trajan, Hadrian, Marcus Aurelius, and Theodosius.

On the whole, we must conclude that the theory of Spanish ancestry for Roman writers boils down, in so far as regards the characteristic styles of the group cited, to a case (not unique in history) of great culture on the part of the Romans and Latins who came to colonize or in greater or less degree to govern the Peninsula; a culture which I believe to be a new variant, as regards the classic ideal, and of much intellectual value in itself.

We shall find a somewhat analogous case later on in the Arabs who lived in Spain or were born there during the lengthy term of Arab domination.

A case could be made likewise for existence of a deep intellectual and artistic influence of the native Spanish element on things and tendencies which Romanization did not wipe out, or which the colonizers found to have attractiveness and strength to such degree as to penetrate their Latin classicism. Such a theory, difficult to prove because of lack of data but perhaps veridical, has lost much weight since leading contemporary Latinists have largely disproved the longstanding accusation that "modernisms" introduced into the Latin of that time were created by "Spanish" writers. Recent research shows that these linguistic innovations had many roots and precedents at Rome itself.* The present brief narrative is not the place in which to pursue these questions further. Here it is sufficient to indicate, as we have just done, their present status in historical criticism.

Guilds, Crafts, and Professions

Roman manual laborers generally associated themselves into guilds, usually called "colleges," which included all those engaged in the same labor or employment. Slaves as well as freemen could belong. Tradesmen formed their own organizations in the same way. It is known that in Roman Spain there were guilds of carpenters, workers

---

* See the complete discussion of this question, *op. cit.*

in bronze, fishmongers, masons, shoemakers, firemen, and olive-oil vendors.

These guilds, at first voluntary organizations, in the fourth century were made obligatory by law. Professions were also made hereditary; so that, for example, a carpenter's son could follow no craft but his father's, and individual aptitude and choice counted for nothing.

The Poor

As these disadvantageous changes were effected, the poor and the not very well-to-do middle-class were losing their freedom under ever greater oppression. The reason was that in order to exist, and to protect themselves against those who held authority or power, the poor were forced to work the fields of others on hard conditions, or to seek the protection of more powerful neighbors in exchange for burdensome obligations. Those who cultivated another man's land without opportunity of leaving it were called *colonos* (coloni), who were farmers, but not free men.

The Roman Schools

To disseminate culture, the Romans organized an educational system consisting of three stages: the primary school, which children entered at the age of six or seven; what we may call the high school, for children twelve to fourteen; and the professional schools. These three educational grades were maintained by the municipality, though there were also private schools and tutors.

Wealthy citizens usually employed special tutors for their sons, as had been the custom of the ancient Greeks. Such tutors generally were slaves or ex-slaves, and were known as "pedagogues," which is to say, educators. Among them were well-known writers such as the famous Greek teller of fables, Aesop, whose book is still widely read, and who was imitated by the Roman writer, Phaedrus, son of a slave father.

Field Sports, Circuses, and Amphitheatres

Like the Greeks, the Romans practiced track and field sports enthusiastically—foot races, chariot races, hurling the discus; but their favorite diversion was to watch the blood-stained games of the arena.

These were carried out by professionals and consisted chiefly of combats between armed men, or gladiatorial contests, and struggles of men with wild beasts. Both were marked by extreme cruelty and generally took place in special sites called amphitheatres, distinct from the circuses.

The circus itself was a very long quadrilateral space with rows of seats down both sides and across the rounded ends. There gymnastic sports and chariot races were held. The amphitheatre was elliptic in form, an oval lined with rows of seats. It had a basement or pit where the wild beasts were penned. The punishment of many early Christians was to be thrown to the lions, leopards, bears, bulls, and other fierce beasts that tore them to pieces in the amphitheatre.

Several impressive circuses and amphitheatres were constructed in Spain. There are ruins of these at Mérida, Saguntum, Calahorra, Toledo, and Tarragona. The best preserved circus is at Mérida, the best preserved amphitheatre, at Itálica. The greatest of all amphitheatres was the Coliseum at Rome, much of it still standing.

The Theatre

The Romans, like the Greeks, were addicted to the theatre. Theirs were not roofed like ours today, but open to the sky as the circus was. Ruins of theatres are found at Saguntum, Ronda la Vieja in Málaga, Mérida, Tarragona, and elsewhere. The theatre at Mérida was lavishly adorned with colored marbles and statuary. The seats were of stone, or of brick and mortar.

City Life

In the city, the men spent most of the day outside the house, in the street. The central meeting place was the city square, called the forum, a public park surrounded by important buildings such as the court of justice, the temple or temples, and the markets. Holidays were celebrated in the forum, justice administered there, trading carried on, votes polled, speeches made. A favorite evening meeting-place was the public baths which the Romans used daily and the opening hour of which was announced by ringing a bell. The women and the slaves busied themselves with household duties. However, women could sally forth to the street, attend the baths and the theatres, and so on. Modern commentators assert that never since, not even at the present time, have public baths been built equalling the magnificence of the Roman, nor have there been better heating systems.

Roman Houses

The houses were sometimes one story in height, and again (especially in Rome and the large cities) had several stories for renting. Early houses did not have windows and balconies like ours. The façade was a blind wall unbroken except for the entrance door; or to the left of this entry there might be shops which had no communication with the interior of the building as a whole. The doorway gave on the atrium, rectangular in shape (similar to the patio characteristic of the classic Andalusian and Castilian residence) surrounded by porticoes, with a skylight in the roof. Visitors were received in the atrium; and there were placed the statues of the ancestors. Beyond the portico was what we may call the master's study—the tablium—and the dining-halls; and, finally, there were the family's private quarters: bedrooms, chapel of the household gods, et cetera; and a second columned patio, called the peristyle. Some houses had lateral patios flanking the atrium.

This style of house became generalized in Spain as Romanization spread, especially in the southern and eastern regions of the Peninsula and in towns built along the public highways. Their ruins have been found at Ampurias (Emporium), Itálica, and Bele (Bolonia, near Tarifa). At Mérida are the remains of what is believed to be the oldest Roman house in Spain, one that in the course of time came to be used as a Christian church.

Among the ruins at Numantia are preserved interesting examples of the type of native house continuing in use in other regions. Cellars walled with small stone blocks are characteristic of these Iberian houses. Some had patios with columns (an obvious Greek or Roman influence) and an upper story, reached by a flight of stone steps leading up from the patio.

Country Houses and Public Baths

The Romans liked the country. The well-to-do often had summer houses, called villas, on their farms or rural estates, such as are described in Pliny's Letters and other Roman writings. These villas were tended by slaves and serfs. Ruins of some of them still exist at Constanti in Tarragona, Puig in Valencia, Nava la Tejara in León, Toledo, and Cuevas in Soria. In many of these, and in other places where Romans lived, more or less complete mosaics have been found with geometrical designs or pictures in color of leaves, fruits, animals, men and women and gods. A splendid example of such art which has lasted in Spain for centuries is the polychrome mosaic discovered recently in Portugal, at Arreivo in the parish of Maceira in Leivia township. The Roman Emperor Hadrian, who was born in Spain, encouraged the making and popularization of mosaic. For centuries, throughout the Roman world, the term "villa" was used to designate rural developments and groups of country houses.

Roman baths, already mentioned, also came into general use in Spain. The baths were housed sometimes in luxurious public buildings with numerous halls, swimming pools, and basins of hot and cold water; and they were also in private homes of the wealthy. Ruins of public baths have been discovered in many localities in Spain (Tarragona, Mérida, Itálica, Solsona, the Maragate region, among others). There are traces of private baths in ruined villas at Cuevas and Constanti. The Romans made use of medicinal waters, thermal and otherwise. Many of the present thermal resorts in Spain are built on sites of Roman baths of which the ruins still exist; at Lugo, for example. The Latin inscription on the silver platter found at Otañes in Santander relates to such medicinal springs.

The Indigenous Civilizations and Roman Rule

What has been said here does not imply that the indigenous civilizations, nor the peoples to whom they pertained—the Tartessians, Mastienians, Iberians, et cetera—vanished utterly from the face of the earth. Romanization, and above all the centralizing of Roman government, was extinguishing them little by little over a long period, and paralyzing their creative power; but they preserved for some time, and very visibly, their own character and their own tribal distinctions. We owe our information regarding these matters to writers of the first century of the Christian era; which is to say, after the termination of the Roman military conquest of Spain. At that time, the most civilized and prosperous regions of the Peninsula were still those formerly

known as Tartesia and Mastiena, especially the latter; and neither conforming wholly to the Roman pattern. Next in importance were the
Iberian and Celtiberian sections of central Spain, with respect to which
the excavation of the ruins of Numantia have revealed many evidences
of culture and prosperity. Finally, and a long way behind these in the
arts and other expressions of civilization, were the northeastern territories occupied by the Celts, where Romanization was slow and
inefficient.

Such differences had origin in the pre-Roman centuries, and must
have been due principally to the unequal degree of contact of the several regions of Spain with Phoenician, Greek and Carthaginian colonizers who, in the process of educating the Peninsular peoples in the ways
of their respective civilizations, as they unquestionably did, quickened
the innate faculty of assimilating new ways and making them his own
which has been characteristic of the Spaniard at every epoch of his
existence.

In general, the picture as sketched by first century writers agrees
with modern archeological research which reveals these two fundamental facts: the presence of art objects expressive of an Iberian culture
dating from the fifth century B.C.—that is to say, not long after Greek
colonization and the beginning of Carthaginian rule—and the clear
differentiation of five well-defined regions of culture; namely, Andalusia, Murcia, Albacete, and Alicante; the Valencian and Catalonian
coasts; the lower Ebro basin; and central Spain, to which may be added
a sixth region in Portugal. Over and above this division a marked difference may be noted in the first centuries between the culture of the
coastal territories and those near the sea (Iberian) and the culture of
the interior (Celtic) ; a difference that later on, about the third century B.C., was diminished somewhat by emergence of the Celtiberian
culture, which seems to have had its center in the south, in the region
of Numantia.

Of all these cultures, as we have remarked already on the basis of
first century writings, the most advanced were those of Andalusia and
of the southeastern regions; which is to say, Murcia, Albacete, and Alicante; but the latter proved itself far superior to the former in artistic
achievement and particularly in sculpture (stone and bronze) , pottery
(ornamented with animal figures, more or less stylized floral patterns,

and geometrical designs) and in urban construction, such as the cities, now vanished, of Meca and Minateda in Albacete, and the necropolis or burying ground at Archena in Murcia. Notable examples of the southeastern sculpture, besides the Lady of Elche already mentioned, are the statue of a warrior also found at Elche; the sphinxes of Agost in Alicante; the caryatides and lions at Balazote and Bocairente; the human figures at Cerro de los Santos and the bronzes there and in Murcia at Santuario de la Luz and El Palomar. The finest examples of pottery are found at Elche, Archena and Oliva.

The most striking specimens of the art of the Andalusian region are the lions at Baena and Cordova; the sphinx at Villacarrillo; the bas-reliefs at Osuna and Alcalá la Real; the bronzes of the temples of Despeñaperros and Castellar; the pottery with undulant lines and concentric circles and the alabaster figurine of a woman, found at Galera.

Artistic development in the region of Valencia and Catalonia, like that of the Ebro basin and central plateau, was in general inferior, as is evidenced among other things by the pottery, decorated in relief, and even by the interesting painted ceramics found at Calaceite; by the bronzes (such as those at Castellón) ; and by the bas-reliefs, as at Caspe. The only exception up to the present is the pottery discovered at Liria, which is superior to that at Elche and Archena. Within the regions mentioned here, as in the Andalusian and southeastern zones, different centers and divers periods showing considerable variation are distinguishable. There is no reason to doubt that further discoveries will clarify still further differences, respective evolutions, and chronology.

In the Ebro region the Cabeza de Alcalá de Azaila district is particularly interesting. Ruins of a large city are found there, and a pottery ornamented with geometric designs and figures of people, animals and plants to which only the ceramic of southeastern Spain is comparable artistically. It is now believed that this ceramic belongs to the Roman epoch (the second and first centuries B.C.) and that it represents one of the peaks of indigenous cultural types within the process of Romanization.

The other well-known survival is that of Numantia and its district, as represented in the painted pottery demonstrating an early period of polychrome ornamentation with human figures, quite different from the southeastern ceramic. This pottery, possibly deriving from the close of the third century B.C., and later on to be displaced by a reddish ceramic decorated with painting in black, continued to be manufactured until the destruction of the city in the year 133 B.C., a fact very indicative of the triumph of Romanic over Hispanic culture, since the native Spanish civilizations, as we have said, were turned from the course of their natural development into Roman channels. In the same region, in the province of Avila, an Iberian settlement and fort have been discovered which antedate Romanization. There are similar ruins at Frías in Albarracín.

One point at which both cultures meet, the indigenous and the Roman, each apparently influencing the other, is in the numismatics of the Roman epoch as represented by the coins called *autónomas,* coinage of the Spanish cities that enjoyed a certain degree of autonomy for some length of time under Roman rule. These coins, still abundant, have human, animal, and vegetable designs in relief.

The Portuguese region, where research as yet has not been very extensive, reveals a period of culture different from the Iberian and belonging to the fifth and fourth centuries B.C.; though Andalusian influence is discernible in central and southern Portugal. Other Iberian influences also, proceeding perhaps from the Castilian tableland, seem apparent in north Portugal.

Political and Social Organization of the Native Spaniards

The preceding facts inform us only as to a part of native Spanish civilization for which the source of our knowledge is wholly archeological. For the other sectors of Spanish life during the centuries discussed, Latin and Greek documents complete the picture. They tell us substantially the following story:

The social life of the Spanish people of that time varied in accordance with their degree of civilization. Most of them lived in cities and villages scattered over the countryside, as, for example, did the *Celtici,* who inhabited southern Portugal, the *Gallaeci,* and the *Astures.* In the territory of the *Turdetani* (southeastern Andalusia) abounded large urban communities; that is, fortified cities. This was also true of some settlements of which considerable ruins have been excavated in the central and southern regions; such as Numantia and Calaceite.

The inhabitants of villages and small cities took refuge in case of war in near-by towers and similar fortifications held in common by several tribal groups, or in a fortress pertaining to the capital of an important tribe or to a regional capital.

Among the Iberians and the Celts marriage was generally monogamous, although cases of polygamy were not lacking in some tribes. The wedding ceremonies varied with the locality. Those of certain Lusitanian tribes, according to the classic writers, resembled marriage rites of the Greeks.

Generally speaking, the father was the head of the family; although in the case of the Cantabrians it is believed that the mother was the head, or at least that she and the other women played a very important part in governing the family. Apparently therefore the two systems were then known in Spain, the patriarchal and the matriarchal; forms that, one or the other, for centuries controlled the domestic organization of ancient peoples in different parts of the world.

It was not the family, however, but the gens, that was the most important unit in the social structure of that age. "Gens" is the term used for the group formed by several families, inter-related or recognizing a common ancestral stock. Each gens was ruled by an assembly, or by a chief or patriarch possessing absolute authority, including power of life or death, over its members. These latter were bound one to another by rights and duties. As regards religion, every gens worshipped its special gods who were probably in the beginning its ancestors. Apparently, the families forming a gens dwelt exclusively together in a village and possessed a name of their own. Besides the members of the gens properly speaking, persons outside the family-group received or adopted into it ("clients"), and slaves taken in war or acquired by purchase or otherwise, formed part of the gens.

Free men were divided into patricians and plebeians. The wealthiest and most powerful, and those holding public or military office, were the patricians. The majority of the "clients" seem to have lived under personal protection of the nobles.

The union of several gens formed a higher social entity called a tribe, chiefly political in character. Some were governed by a king or a chief elective or hereditary, and by assemblies; others by institutions of varying structure: by two magistrates, by a council of ten, et cetera. The assemblies were usually dual: one patrician (the Senate), probably made up of the heads of the gens composing the tribe, or of its strong men; the other, popular (the Council).

The names designating the social and political institutions described are those used by Latin writers in referring to them. We do not know of what indigenous terms these were translations or equivalents; but the Latin names merely denote the point of view of the Latin commentators in explaining things to their own people, or the interpretation suggested to them by a foreign ideology. We cannot be certain as to the exactitude of all or even of many such assimilations.

Forms of property varied greatly among Spaniards of that epoch. There is clear evidence in the case of some tribes of individual ownership; for example, the Lusitanians. In others, ownership was collective or communal, including ownership of the fields, so that the crops were consequently also owned in common. Such was the case in the region inhabited by the Spanish people called Vaccali.

Religion and Customs

Besides the particular gods of each gens, there were others: deities special to the various tribes, or worshipped by several tribes in common and having a widespread cult. The Moon seems to have been worshipped in some localities. The Lusitanians sacrificed on their altars animals and men (prisoners of war) whose entrails they examined for auguries. The Romans also practiced such rites and sacrifices, animals usually being the victims. The ancient Jews held these superstitions too, as may be seen in the Old Testament.

The geographer Strabo relates that men of the tribes in northern and northwestern Spain wore black and used as arms of defense breastplates of canvas and mail, and triple-crested leather helmets; and as weapons, lances, daggers and knives. The women liked bright colors. The ordinary diet of these people was acorn-flour bread, butter, and a kind of beer or cider. Meat was the principal food of the Celtiberians. They dressed more luxuriously and lived in greater comfort than did the inhabitants of northern and northwestern Spain. Lusitanians anointed their bodies with oil and essences, let their hair grow long as a woman's, and in battle wore a high head-dress like a kind of mitre.

Also according to Strabo and other ancient writers, the psychological characteristics distinctive of the Spaniards were in general those already indicated: physical hardihood, high courage, lack of discipline, and loyalty leading to the sacrifice of life itself. Their valor and excellent military qualities made them the favorite mercenaries of the period, and in that capacity we find them taking part in the wars in Sicily, Africa, Greece, and later on, Italy. In the Iberian sanctuaries of the Sierra Morena *ex-votos,* or offerings, have been found that represent foot-soldiers armed with the curved sword and helmet, and horsemen with shield and two lances.

The Basques demand a separate paragraph, although they would seem to be included in the comment on the Ibero-Celtic peoples. However, notwithstanding the long-held belief that they belong to the Iberian sector of these, it is historically uncertain that they do so. In fact, the problem of the origin of the Basques is still unsolved. It is true that, as depicted by classic writers, they show certain Iberian characteristics in general culture and customs; but it is no less true that some special characteristics of the Basques differ greatly from Iberian ways. In fact, the most distinctive things about the Basques are their unlikeness to the rest of the Peninsular peoples, and their language which is completely different from the speech of all other Spaniards. Perhaps they are the sole survivors of the prehistoric tribes that inhabited the caves of the Pyrenees and left so many evidences of artistic ability and technical skill.

As the reader will have noted, the information transmitted to us by historians and geographers of the Graeco-Latin epoch, though extremely interesting in itself, relates to only a few sections of the Spanish Peninsula, and leaves great gaps in our knowledge of the manners and customs of numerous native tribes and regions.

Chapter IV

Christianity

The Preaching and Spreading of Christianity

ALMOST coincidentally with the transformation of Spain into a Roman colony—which is to say, in the reign of the Emperor Augustus—occurred an event supremely important in the history of mankind: the birth of the Christian religion.

The various Spanish tribes practiced different religions typical of beliefs held by ancient peoples, and especially by primitive civilizations. Romanization propagated in Spain the Roman creed, Paganism: the worship of numerous gods under the relative superiority of Jupiter. In contradistinction to these, Christianity appeared, preaching the doctrine of one God, Creator of heaven and earth, in Whose sight all men are equal whatever their race or state. At the same time, Christianity established as rules of conduct humility, charity, forgiveness of injuries, and condemnation of violence. There could have been offered no greater contrast to the rules governing such a society as the Roman, in which none of these attributes was regarded as a virtue and in which slavery was a social and economic basis of the social order as it had been likewise in Phoenician, Greek, Carthaginian and indigenous Spanish society.

The preaching of Christianity in Spain began very early. The first to preach it there, as is believed, were St. Paul and some of his disciples. Already in the second century, and still more in the third, there were Christian communities on the Peninsula. In Spain, as elsewhere, they suffered effects of the cruel persecutions by which some Roman Emperors tried to contain the new religion spreading like wildfire. But martyrdom and death could not prevail upon the Christians to give up

70

the living faith to which they clung tenaciously; and many of them died for it at Barcelona, Valencia, Toledo, Saragossa, and other settlements. The cruelest and most rigorous of these persecutions took place in the reign of the Emperor Diocletian (284-305 A.D.). Many Spanish Christians then perished heroically, and some of them have since been canonized: St. Vincent of Valencia, St. Eulalia of Mérida, St. Severus of Barcelona, St. Leocadia of Toledo, and St. Grace and the innumerable Martyrs of Saragossa.

The persecutions did not cease until early in the fourth century, in the year 311, when the Emperor Galerius published an edict tolerating profession of Christian faith and recognizing the right of the Church to local assembly. This beginning reached fruition under the Emperor Constantine, who in 312 handed down another law (Constitution) which prohibited persecution of the Christians, and shortly afterwards a third, granting Christianity the same legal rights as the pagan religion, which until that time had been the official religion at Rome, and ordering the return to the Church and the Christian communities of property that had been confiscated from them.

Organization of the Christian Church

In consequence of these edicts, and of the greatly increased and constantly growing number of professed Christians, Christianity was acquiring rapidly the character of a privileged State religion, and organization of the Church was facilitated thereby. Its supreme head was the Bishop of Rome, who took the name of Pope; a circumstance in itself demonstrating the enormous influence then exercised by the capital of the Empire that ruled a great part of the known world. Immediately under the Pope were the Bishops (heads of provinces and extensive charges) and finally the presbyters, who had smaller charges comprising one or more towns and called parishes. All these and their auxiliaries (deacons) constituted the clergy of the Christian Church. Those Christians not belonging to the clergy were known as the laity.

The clergy met in assemblies called Councils, composed sometimes of the clerics of one bishopric only; again, of those of several. The Council deliberated on matters of Church interest, and issued regulations (canons) fixing the duties, rights and rules of conduct for clergy and laity. Three Councils were held in Spain during the period of

Roman rule: that of Illiberis or Elvira (near Granada) in 306, that of Saragossa in 380, and the First Council of Toledo in 400. The Council of Illiberis was memorable for ruling that priests must be unmarried, a ruling that contributed in great degree to establishment of celibacy as a general rule for all the clergy. That same Council prohibited marriage between Christians and non-Christians. The Council of Toledo took the highly important step of adopting for Spain the Nicene, or Catholic, Creed proclaimed at the Council of Nicaea, whence the Church derived the name Catholic, which means universal.

The clergy did not limit their activities to Church matters. The respect and confidence inspired in all Christians by their zeal and love for their fellow-men were responsible for their being granted the faculty of intervening in many lay matters. Thus, they could act as judges in disputes which the interested parties voluntarily submitted to their decision; and they were often appointed as municipal officers, charged with keeping under observation the public conduct of the authorities and of tax-collectors, and with defending the rights of the people, especially the poor. They were also given the faculty of authorizing the formalities that had to be observed by those clement masters who freed their slaves.

Culture of the Spanish Clergy

Among the Spanish clergy during the first centuries of the Christian era (the Roman epoch), there were men of great worth besides the martyrs already noted. Chief among these was Hosius, Bishop of Córdova, who was largely responsible for the conversion of the Emperor Constantine to Christianity. Hosius was president of the Council of Nicaea, and to him is due in great part the proclamation of the Nicene Creed as profession of Christian faith. In this period also, Spain gave the Church the first Spanish Pope, St. Damasus (fourth century).

Christianity produced famous orators and poets in Spain. Among the latter should be noted Juvencus and Prudentius, both belonging to the fourth century, who wrote beautiful Latin poems extolling the triumphs of the new religion and the heroic faith of its martyrs. Prudentius was born in Calahorra or in Saragossa.

Christianity and Early Christian Customs

It was logical that Christianity, which brought into the world new ideas and new yearnings, should create a way of life and a method in art different from the Roman; although at first, as was natural, the Christians made use of Roman technique and form.

The persecutions suffered by the Christians at the beginning of the fourth century prevented the new religion for the time being from making much outward show of its places of worship, or otherwise calling attention to them. Consequently, little groups of the faithful usually met in private homes, or in the oratories of wealthy believers or at their family tombs or pantheons; a custom which was the beginning and basis of Christian cemeteries.

Christianity did not accept cremation of the dead, a prevalent custom among the Romans, but insisted upon interment of the body in the earth or in open shelves, or niches, in a wall. The latter method was also known among the Romans, who termed it *columbarium*. The increase in the number of believers in time necessitated considerable enlargement of such cemeteries, which was achieved by digging underground galleries that came to constitute subterranean towns of the dead with long passage-ways widening out into small plazas. These underground tunnels were called catacombs. The most famous and most extensive were those at Rome. Probably there were catacombs in Spain also, to judge from some accounts by Christian writers of the period and from the subterranean chapels and crypts in certain ancient churches.

The existence of church or chapel in a private home seems to be equally well attested by the remains of such a chapel at Mérida, near the theatre. Another has been found at Ampurias. Both are of the basilica type.

The First Churches

When at last Christians could practice their religion publicly, they began to build churches conforming to the architectural type that the Romans called a basilica, but with addition of new elements taken from the catacombs. The entrance to these early churches was through a portico giving on a patio, or atrium, with sheltered galleries on the four sides; then a vestibule or hall, and immediately beyond that the

church, generally divided by columns into three parts, called naves:
the right nave was occupied by the men, the left by the women, and
the central nave by the clergy. The altar was at the rear, and in some
instances had been erected above the tomb of a Christian martyr.
Sometimes the basilica roof was sloping, though usually flat and tiled.
Interior walls were adorned with paintings and mosaics.

Another, humbler type was the church with a single nave, sometimes with and sometimes without a vault, such as the one found at
Ampurias. To this type also perhaps belonged certain crypts or underground chapels in some ancient churches of Asturias.

Sepulchres and Christian Symbols

Christian sepulchres were sealed customarily with a slab of stone
or marble on which a simple inscription was carved. There were
paintings or bas-reliefs on the walls. Christian painters imitated the
Roman, but introduced new figures in symbolic representation of elements of their religion. Of most frequent recurrence are Christ as a
shepherd bearing a lamb (the Good Shepherd), or a lamb alone; the
dove, signifying the soul; the fish, representing the name of Christ
with letters transposed in an anagram.

The figure of the fish was engraved on small sepulchral lamps—
lucernarias—usually of clay, which the Christians copied from the
pagans; and on other objects.

The distinctive emblem generally worn by the faithful was a tiny
fish of clay, ivory, or other material, on the order of a scapulary. They
also wore medals with allegorical designs or figures of saints.

In time, decoration became more lavish and of greater artistic merit.
At the end of the Roman epoch, private tombs were richly ornamented
with carved geometric designs (undulant fluting) or with symbolic
figures and representations of Biblical personages. Some forty such
sepulchres have been found in Spain: at Ampurias (this one has the
figure of the Good Shepherd), Tarragona, Layos (Toledo), Berja
(Almería), Saragossa, Gerona, Hellín (Albacete), Valencia, Husillos
(Valencia), Ecija, Puebla Nueva (Toledo), and elsewhere. Their
number and dispersion is additional evidence of the extensive acceptance of Christianity by the Spaniards.

Chapter V

The Visigoth Domination

The German Invasions

IN THE last century of Empire the culture, prosperity and grandeur of Roman life decayed. Invasions by the peoples called Germans (inhabitants of the Scandinavian regions and of what was later to be Germany) had undermined those three qualities; the more so because the wars that supervened and eventually the destruction of government at Rome rendered impossible—or at best, exceedingly difficult—the continuity of institutions. These wars overthrew many of the organizations that upheld the social order, and kept men from devoting their time and talents to science, literature and art, just as it deprived them of the comforts of life previously enjoyed.

A Spanish historian contemporaneous with the first invasion by the Germans (which was carried out by the Suevians, Vandals, and Alani, or Alans) thus describes the turmoil that it caused: "The barbarians who had penetrated into Spain swept everything with fire and sword. The plague, for its part, took as many victims. Famine reached such extremes that men were to be seen devouring human flesh, and even the mothers fed on flesh of their own children whom they themselves had slaughtered. Wild beasts, battening on heaps of starved bodies, war, and the diseases felling even the strongest men, were making an end of the human race."

This first invasion, in the year 409, was followed by that of the Visigoths in 414, which was less cruel than those preceding it. The Visigoths had lived for many years (since 270) on the borders of the eastern provinces of the Roman Empire in intimate contact with Roman civilization, which influenced them greatly. Their conver-

75

sion to Christianity in the early part of the fourth century further modified their customs. A factor contributing greatly to the same educational end was the work of a Bishop named Ulfila who translated the Bible into the Gothic tongue. The Visigoths, who at first were Catholic Christians, were converted to Arianism at the end of the fourth century, conversion being the condition imposed by the Emperor of Constantinople in return for his permitting them to occupy territory of the Empire south of the Danube. We shall see the later effect of this on Spain. The Romanization of the Visigoths was accelerated when they pushed on into Gaul and settled down in the southern part as allies of the Roman Emperor. Meanwhile, other Germanic peoples were occupying divers regions of the Roman Empire and entering into Italy, thus constituting a direct threat to the capital itself which, indeed, they finally seized.

In addition to all this, the wars had become continuous; and were in themselves cause of confusion and turmoil, with destruction of property and insecurity of life. Such was the situation, among other times, in the middle of the fifth century, when Theodoric, King of the Visigoths, fought for possession of Spain with a Suevian King, Rechiarius, and lost to the Suevians, who treated all inhabitants of Roman race with utmost cruelty; enslaving many of them, including the priests, sacking the churches, destroying the altars, and committing other acts of terrorism.

The Conquest of Spain. Euric

The Visigoths established the center of their kingdom in the region of Gaul called Aquitaine, and made Toulouse their capital; sallying from that city to conquer Spanish territory in successive campaigns of 414, 416-18, 456 and later years. They made their first entrance into the Peninsula by way of the northeast (Catalonia). By the second half of the fifth century they were already in possession of all the eastern region (the ancient lands of the Iberians), the southeast, and some sections of Baetica (now Andalusia). The rest of Spain was in power of the Suevians.

The Visigoth king who completed these conquests was called Euric (467-485), and was not only a great warrior but also a man of culture, with talent and ability for governing. In his hands the Visigoth mon-

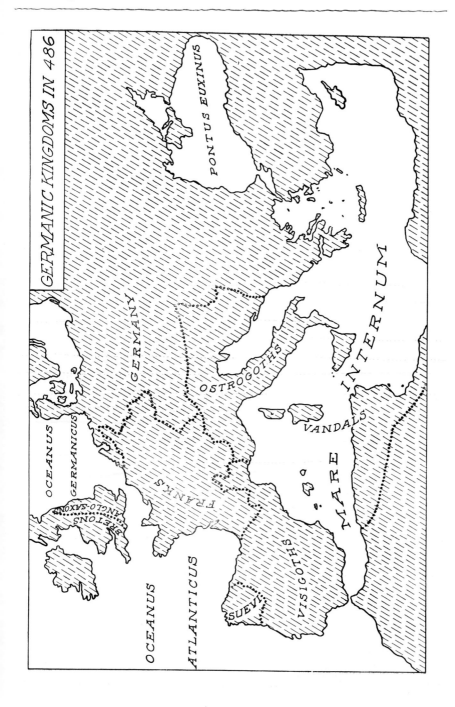

GERMANIC KINGDOMS IN 486

PONTUS EUXINUS

MARE INTERNUM

GERMANY

OSTROGOTHS

VANDALS

OCEANUS GERMANICUS

FRANKS

BRETONS
ANGLO-SAXON

OCEANUS ATLANTICUS

VISIGOTHS

SUEVI

archy became the most influential and powerful in western Europe.
Ambassadors of other kingdoms, including those of the Byzantine
Empire, flocked to his court seeking alliances; as did also envoys of the
other Germanic peoples that were likewise established in various of
the former Roman possessions. Among such were the Franks, the
Saxons, the Herulians, the Burgundians, and the Ostrogoths, who had
occupied provinces both of what would later become France and of
Italy.

In 475 Euric's political situation was strengthened when the Emperor Nepos recognized the independence of his Visigothic kingdom
of Gaul and furthermore ceded to him the region called Auvergne.
One year later the last Roman Emperor in the West was dethroned.
Of that great State, ruler of the western world and of part of the Asiatic
and the African, there were left standing only the territories in the
East, out of which had been formed at the beginning of the sixth
century, in order to keep down the struggles for the throne, a new
Empire, independent of the one having Rome as capital, called the
Eastern Empire. Its own capital was Byzantium, or Constantinople,
the city founded by Constantine in 326.

It was due to Euric's initiative that the Visigoths set down in writing, methodically grouped in the form called a Code, along with laws
of Roman origin, the common law regarding government, the family,
and property which had ruled them heretofore. That Code, to which
Euric's name is given and which is also known as the *Statuta legum*,
was the first which the Visigothic population governed by Euric and his
successors ever had, and it applied to that population exclusively. The
Gallo-Romans and the Hispano-Romans continued to be governed by
the laws of the Roman Emperors collected in another Code (*Roman
Law of the Visigoths*) in 506, during the reign of Alaric II. Euric, an
advocate of social and political union with the Romans and the
Romanized inhabitants of the countries that he ruled, gave important
posts in government and at court to leaders of these groups.

The Visigothic Kingdom of Spain

The Visigothic kingdom of Gaul was conquered not long afterwards by the Franks, a Germanic people like themselves, who, having
established a kingdom in the north of Gaul, in the first third of the

sixth century invaded districts of northern Spain (Cantabria, the Basque country, and the region of Saragossa), from which they were driven out. In consequence very little territory in Gaul remained in possession of the Visigoths, who had to transfer their center of government to Spain. Until the middle of the sixth century they had no fixed capital, but finally settled upon Toledo which accordingly began to assume importance as one of the principal cities in the history of Spain, and which bears to this day cultural imprints of all the successive peoples and kingdoms that have governed it. Remains—not always absolutely authenticated—of Visigothic domination at Toledo include the Church of Christ of the Light and the city walls, the crosses and crowns found near the city at Guarrazar, and the capitals of some columns.

Establishment of the capital at Toledo was the work of King Athanagild, whose ambition for the throne led him to overthrow Ajila, who occupied it, and to ask that auxiliary troops be sent him by the then Emperor of Constantinople, Justinian (554). Justinian acceded; and in the arrival of those auxiliaries is the origin of Byzantine domination of the southern part of the Peninsula, which domination was itself one of the reasons why the civilization of the Eastern Empire exerted influence on the Visigothic world. Justinian's reign was one of the most magnificent periods of that civilization—perhaps the most magnificent; not only in matter of laws (concerning which we shall have more to say) but also as regards industry and the arts. To his reign belong the great Church (or Mosque) of St. Sophia at Constantinople and the magnificent basilicas at Ravenna. Constantinople was then the principal center of Mediterranean commerce and took over from China the monopoly of weaving silk textiles.

Athanagild continued Euric's policy, courting the friendship of Catholic Spaniards. With him began the most brilliant epoch of the Visigoth monarchy in Spain. His brother and successor Leovgild (582-586) consolidated and extended his people's power in the Peninsula, conquering the kingdom of the Suevians and destroying it; subduing various central and western districts that were as a matter of fact independent; and suppressing the rebellious Basques. To maintain vigilance over these last, he constructed a fortified border outpost that he called Victoriano, the origin of present-day Vitoria. Likewise on the side toward the upland region of Alcarria he established another fortress that he called Recópolis, of which hardly a trace remains. Leovgild surrounded himself with all the outward pomp that could enhance his royal prestige, and to that end adopted the ceremonial of the Emperors at Constantinople. He also issued gold coins commemorating his election. Some undated coins of the period, not known theretofore, still exist and are to be found in the Provincial Museum at Alicante.

The Religious Conflict between Hermenegild and Leovgild

In Leovgild's reign occurred the most momentous religious conflict that ever took place in the Visigothic kingdom. One of his sons, Hermenegild, an Arian in religion, like all the rest of the family, married the Catholic Princess Ingunza, of Frankish nationality. The marriage was with Leovgild's complete consent, though he was in general unfriendly to Catholics and had attacked them on several occasions. Soon after, Hermenegild was converted to Catholicism by the influence and counsel of his wife and of St. Leander, Bishop of Seville, one of the most eminent priests of the time. The conversion motivated a general uprising of Catholics in Andalusia, who acclaimed Hermenegild as chief and thus placed themselves in open opposition to his father.

At first Leovgild adopted a tolerant attitude toward his son, striving to win him over, and with him the rebels; but as the rebellion spread and grew more violent, the king decided to attack Hermenegild and his followers directly. Beseiged at Córdova, Hermenegild surrendered to his father, who began by receiving him kindly, merely depriving him of the government posts that he held and exiling him to Valencia. Soon, however, for what reason we do not know, Hermenegild was transferred to Tarragona in custody of Duke Sisberto, who thrust him into a dungeon, demanding insistently that he renounce Catholicism and return to the Arian creed. Loyal to his faith, Hermenegild refused to abjure it, and in 585 he was assassinated, as is believed, by the Duke himself. It is not known whether the Duke was carrying out orders of the King, nor how the latter reacted to news of his son's death. The historians who have done most research on documents of the period incline to believe Leovgild innocent in the murder of Hermenegild, whom the Catholic Church held to be a martyr to the faith and elevated to sainthood. The religious war had lasted six years.

Reccared, and the Approximation of the Two Races

Leovgild's other son, Reccared, who succeeded him on the throne, put into practice the policy of fusion with the Romanized Spaniards, in this respect pursuing a different course from his father's. The outward sign of the change was the conversion to Catholicism of the King and his court (587), by which act he won the friendship of the Spanish Catholics just as the Suevians conquered by Leovgild had won it in their time. The conversion gave rise to conflict, however, between the Catholic majority of the country and those Visigoths who had no desire to be converted and accordingly remained Arians; and who, in order to stir up trouble for Reccared, found support sometimes among the Franks, who were always ready to strike a blow at the Visigothic kings, and again among rebellious nobles. The internal peace of the realm was thus disturbed for a long time.

It seems very probable that it was Reccared also who sponsored the reform of various Visigothic laws to the end of improving relations between the conquering race and the conquered (especially with regard to land ownership) and of granting certain privileges to the Catholic clergy; and in addition to this, he promulgated a new compilation of the Code of Euric, to which he gave the force of common law.

The movement toward approximation was furthered by two other kings, Chindaswinth (642-653) and his son Recceswinth (653-672), who brought about the recasting of the diverse Visigothic and Hispano-Roman laws into a single Code, and at the same time abolished some laws and juridical customs that, when rigorously applied, impeded cordial relations between the two races. This Code, which has come down to us in Latin, just as it was written in Recceswinth's reign, is called the *Liber Iudiciorum*. It was further amended in later years; and the final compilement, with addition of other laws, was promulgated about 654.

King Wamba

The last great Visigothic king was Wamba (672-680). His realm was plunged into continual wars, most of them due to uprisings of the Visigothic nobles. During Wamba's reign, the Arabs, a people of Asiatic origin who dominated northern Africa, tried to make entry into

Spain. Repulsed at that time by Wamba's troops, they made another, more successful, attempt some years later. Wamba, aware of the ills from which the kingdom was suffering and of the grave dangers that were inciting rebellion at every turn, tried to confront all these military perils. Accordingly, he reorganized the army and imposed, with severe penalties for evaders, the general obligation of military service when called up by the king. Wamba also rebuilt the city walls of Toledo, apparently employing for the purpose material taken from the Roman circuses in that city.

Visigoth Decadence and Its Cause

But neither the splendor of former reigns nor Wamba's forceful energy could long maintain the monarchy. Its decadence was swift and brief. There were many contributing causes: but the main reason for its fall was the continuous state of rebellion among the nobles.

Succession to the throne was by election, in accordance with Visigothic custom; a circumstance leaving the way open for any noble of prestige and power to be chosen king. Consequently there was never-ending competition for the election. The violent nature of the Visigoths and their lust for power frequently led the more ambitious to start a rebellion without waiting on the electoral process, and to seize the throne or assassinate the incumbent. The fierce unbridled passions of these men resulted time and again in the murder of brother by brother. Moreover, every king who succeeded in winning the throne by reason of his strength or his military prowess tried to arrange for his sons to succeed him either without formality of election or through pressure on the electors. They tried, in short, to make the crown hereditary without ever succeeding in having it become so under the laws, although some of the kings were upheld in their efforts to this end by the more cultured members of the clergy, who were fully aware of the great danger with which the electoral method was constantly beset.

In addition to these conflicts there was the bitter rivalry between Catholics and Arians already alluded to; while the fusion of the two races, Visigothic and Hispano-Roman, was still incomplete, notwithstanding the great progress made since the end of the sixth century.

In spite of all this, it was a mere thirty years after Wamba's overthrow until the Arabs, in a new attack, vanquished Roderic, the last Visigothic king, and destroyed the monarchy of the Visigoths.

The Councils of Toledo

The period of political splendor already noted (from 562 to 681) was also the high tide of Visigothic civilization. As we have seen, the Catholic clergy constituted its principal element. Apart from the religious, scientific and literary works written by clerics, the culture of the clergy was expressed in the laws which they inspired and which are incorporated in the several Codes. These laws were drawn up at meetings or deliberative assemblies called Councils, which, since they were usually held at Toledo, are also widely known as Councils of Toledo.

The first two Councils, held before Reccared's conversion, were notable for purely religious reasons, and their decisions influenced the discipline of the Church, then in process of formulation. The Third Council was the one of the conversion. At the Fourth, over which St. Isidore presided (633), rules were established for electing the king, in an effort to surround the election with some guarantees, since it was not then possible to change over to the hereditary system. The Fifth, Sixth, and Seventh Councils dealt with the same problem, with especial regard for protection of the persons of the monarch and his family and for the strengthening of royal authority: needful measures, in view of the continuous rebelliousness and disrespect on the part of the nobles, especially of those who had designs on the throne. In the text of these laws are formulated some of the most important governmental principles known to humanity at that time; and they continued to be for several centuries the ideal norm of Spanish monarchy.

The Councils of Toledo were composed of representatives of both clergy and nobility; on which point they differed from the purely religious councils wherein only clerics took part; but until the eighth century none of the enactments were signed by nobles, a seeming indication that the clergy were the prevailing factor in the assemblies, at least until the end of the seventh century.

The king consulted the Council on matters concerning which he thought their advice needful; and the Council, for their part, informed the monarch of the desires or opinions of its two sectors. The result of this collaboration was to transform the Councils, in fact, into the consultative agency of the Visigothic kingdom on matters of legislation. However, it would be an error to believe that the kings were subject to the Council with respect to their own power to legislate, and still less as regards their power to carry out executive acts of government, even though they usually accepted, purely as a formula, the principles and precepts emanating from the clergy. At most, the kings as an almost universal rule proceeded with due concern for their own advantage, sometimes in open contradiction to what the Councils had ordained; as was demonstrated by various instances of usurpation of the throne and by persecutions of the Jews which the great prelates censured.

Writers of the Visigothic Period

The greatest writer of the Visigothic period was St. Isidore, brother of St. Leander and Archbishop of Seville, whose influence had much to do with the conversion of both Prince Hermenegild and King Reccared. St. Isidore, of Byzantine origin, son of the Governor of Cartagena, was born in the middle of the sixth century. His great learning and piety elevated him to the bishopric on St. Leander's death in 596. With a zeal equalling his brother's, Isidore devoted himself to propagation of the Catholic faith and destruction of Arianism, and, at the same time, to studies in science and literature. He wrote several works in historical and other fields; among which his book called *Origins* or *Etymologies,* noteworthy as a kind of encyclopedia or compendium of Greek and Latin learning, long served as a basis for advanced studies, not only in Spain but in other countries as well. In 633, on his deathbed, St. Isidore ordered that his private wealth should be distributed among the poor. Another cleric famed for his culture was Orosius (fifth century), a native of Tarragona and author of the first Universal History, a general historical account of all the peoples then known to the western world, written as an apologia for Christianity. For centuries this History was the most widely used manual in Europe. Together with these two eminent figures, Isidore and Orosius, should be named many other authors of works on religion, morals and history, and also of sacred poetry. Chief among them are Idatius, like Orosius an historian; St. Leander, Archbishop of Seville, poet and moralist, who was born in the region of Cartagena; Juan de Biclara, of Visigothic stock, historian of Leovgild's reign; St. Braulius, Bishop of Saragossa, mystic poet and biographer of saints and martyrs; St. Alphonsus, Visigoth, Archbishop of Seville; and St. Julian, Archbishop of Toledo, author of books on many subjects, among them a history of part of Wamba's reign.

Of non-clerical Goths famed for their culture we know only the Kings Chindaswinth, Recceswinth, and Sisebut, Duke Claudius and Counts Bulgarano and Lorenzo, some of whom were writers or patrons of literature, possessing important libraries.

The Visigothic Catholic clergy applied themselves to learning Hebrew, Chaldean, and Greek; but all the works of the period of which we have any knowledge were written in Latin. From that clergy, and principally from St. Isidore, issue, as we have indicated, the lofty juridical and moral doctrines incorporated in the *Liber Iudiciorum;* for example, the doctrine which subordinates the king's authority to principles of Law in a pithy phrase that may be rendered as "King you will be if you deal justly; and if you deal not justly, you shall not be king." From that same source come the doctrines of tolerance, and of nonviolence as means of conversion to the faith; the latter doctrine having been expounded by a Council (the Fourth of Toledo) and by St. Isidore himself with reference to the Jews. The importance of the scientific and literary movement of the period is shown plainly by the influence of the Visigothic school on other countries of Europe, especially France, after the seventh century; and later, on medieval juridical doctrine.

The Jews

From ancient times, many Jews lived in Spain and in south Gaul. They were characterized by industriousness in manual labor and in trade, and some of them were noted for their culture in religious and other fields. In general, their rights were respected, thanks to the doctrines of the Catholic Church upheld by St. Isidore and the most illustrious Catholic prelates, who counselled that the Jews should be converted to Catholicism only by means of sermons and persuasion, and that in no case should force be utilized to make them change their religion. Some kings (Sisebut, Chintila, Recceswinth, and Egica) flouted this doctrine, though their reasons were sometimes not religious but political; and when they did so, their acts were censured or checked by the Bishop and by the Fourth, Sixth and Seventh Councils of Toledo. When the Visigothic monarchy came to an end, an important Jewish population, in addition to those Jews who had been converted to Catholicism on different occasions, continued to live on the Peninsula.

From the Guarrazar Treasure

Recceswinth's Crown.

Visigothic Art

It is known that Visigothic art was based on the Roman, so abundantly represented in Spain, plus the Byzantine influence. But, to judge from the scanty remains of their architecture and decorative art that have come down to us, the Visigothic artists, while often apparently availing themselves of Roman material and frequently imitating the Byzantines as well, managed to stamp their work with a certain distinctive character, a rudimentary style of their own, which probably lacked time for reaching full development. It was then, of course, that the Gothic cathedral architecture was perfected, with accentuation of those characteristics distinguishing Christian art from pagan which had begun to manifest themselves by the fourth century.

Among remains of Visigothic architecture known to us today are the Church of St. John at Baños, built by Recceswinth in 661; that of Christ of the Light at Toledo, already mentioned; that of San Román de la Hornija (much disfigured by restoration); and those of St. Comba at Bande in Orense; San Pedro de la Nave (Zamora), Elche, St. Felix at Játiva, Palencia (seventh century crypt), Bamba and perhaps Santa María at Palma de Mallorca. Some of these still preserve their basilica plan. Of another type of construction are the Door named the *Puerta de Sevilla* at Córdova and one of the walls of the present Cathedral (which belonged to a Visigothic basilica) as well as other recently discovered architectonic remains in the Court of Oranges; various traces and ruins of structures at Cabeza del Griego, Evora (dating from King Sisebut's time), Mérida, Alcaudete, and Toledo (Wamba's reign); important fragments of houses (at Nueva Carteia and Herrera del Pisuerga); and cemeteries (Carpio del Tajo and Nueva Carteia). At the last-named site, in the Province of Córdova, a skeleton was found. The Visigoths have left us also stones and bricks with bas-reliefs or inscriptions; capitals of columns; sepulchres; earthen jars; a brooch in the shape of an eagle, found at Calatayud; belt buckles made in two pieces showing Ostrogoth influence; mosaic; bronze crosses; coins; and, above all, some magnificent gold crowns and crosses set with precious stones and very Byzantine in type. Several of these are preserved at the Royal Armory at Madrid. Recceswinth's crown and other jewels are in one of the museums at Paris. The Visigothic writers allude to many other contemporaneous works of art

Door jamb, Church of San Miguel de Linio, near Oviedo.

which have now disappeared or been destroyed. Modern art historians advance the theory that Visigothic music may have influenced Spanish music of the era of the Reconquest, and concede merit to certain Visigothic modalities in the plastic arts. In juridical material, we shall see later on the considerable Visigothic contribution after the seventh century.

Customs and Dress of the Visigoths

Roman customs underwent some modification because of influence of the Visigoths. The latter preferred rural to city life, and the force of that preference was such that it took people out into the country instead of concentrating them in cities. It may be said that under the Visigoths there was a marked increase in constructing housing of the Roman villa type, especially by the nobility, many of whom lived on estates or farm lands amongst numerous *colonos,* serfs and dependents forming a kind of court which was at the same time a small army. War was the principal occupation of the Visigoths. The soldiers wore trappings and helmet of leather, with metal shield and coat of mail. Unlike the Hispano-Romans, they let their hair grow long. Such a costume came to be an indication of race; to the degree that a man who cut his hair was thereby incapacitated for public office, especially the office of king, which always had to be held by a Visigoth. It is told of Wamba that the successor who dethroned him, taking advantage of the fact that the king had been drugged, first of all cut his flowing locks.

The weapons of Visigothic soldiers were arrow, lance, sword, and dagger. Military calls were sounded on horns or bugles. The soldiers wore a kind of loose jacket of wool or skins and great lined breeches. Nobles and ordinary civilians little by little laid aside the national dress in favor of Roman styles.

In the field of sports, the games and combats of the arena ceased. On the other hand, according to a contemporaneous account, bull fights were very popular.

Chapter VI

Moslem Domination
The Emirate (711=912)

The New Invaders

THE MOSLEMS who at the beginning of the eighth century destroyed the Visigoth monarchy after having defeated Don Rodrigo in the battle of the Guadalete, or Janda Lake (July, 711), have also been called Arabs. But that name rightly belongs to only one group of Moslems, those born in Arabia. In Spain still another term became general, *Moors,* which properly designates inhabitants of Mogreb or Morocco, who formed the majority of the troops coming to Spain. Moors too were the Almoravides and Almohades who, centuries later, were to repeat the invasions of the eighth century.

Mogreb in that century belonged to the Asiatic Moslem monarchy called the Caliphate which had its origin in a political and religious revolution of certain Arab tribes inhabiting the peninsula called Arabia.

Prior to the seventh century, the Arabs lived as scattered tribes, some sedentary, others nomadic, each with its own chief or sheik; independent as the ancient Spanish tribes had been, and continually clashing with one another, every tribe jealous and suspicious of the rest. The tribal was the only social bond recognized and respected by the Arab; for his tribe and fellow-tribesmen he would dare anything, but to the rest of the world he was indifferent.

The impulse toward unification came to the Arabs from Mohammed, who was at once a religious fanatic and an astute and ambitious politician. His career belongs to the first part of the seventh century. The Arabs professed different shades of religious belief, most of which recognized various gods or idols worshipped at Mecca, a city on that part of Arabia jutting into the Red Sea. There were also some Christian and Jewish tribes among the Arabs. Mohammed began to preach to all these a new religion with ideas taken over from both Christianity and Judaism. He proclaimed the existence of only one God, Allah; the resurrection of the dead; the final Judgment at which the good would ascend to Paradise and the wicked descend to hell; and other beliefs. He decreed for the faithful the obligation of prayer five times daily, of one month of fasting each year, of alms-giving, and of at least one visit in a lifetime to the temple at Mecca which was consecrated to the new faith (this last was the famed pilgrimage to Mecca). All these precepts were set down in a book called the Koran.

The rapidity with which Mohammed's doctrines spread throughout Arabia soon came to constitute a religious bond among the tribes, and inspired them with a militant spirit that was propagated among other peoples of Asia and Africa conquered by Mohammed's successors, who founded a great empire which had as capital first Medina, then Damascus, and later Bagdad. At its height, this empire represented the greatest military power in the world. The dual bond, religious and political, which it gave the peoples submitting to it resulted naturally enough in coinage of a common name to denote all the peoples subjugated by the Arabs. That name was *Moslems*. The Christians used the terms *Mohammedans, Moslems,* and *Saracens* indiscriminately. The chief of the Moslems bore the titles of Emir and Caliph.

The Moslem Empire in the epoch of its greatest territorial expansion and political power embraced extensive regions of Asia, Africa, and Europe. In the last-named area it occupied a part of South Italy, the Balearic Isles, Sicily, Sardinia, and the whole of the Spanish Peninsula. This condition held until in the tenth century the empire began to fall apart, while at the same time the Christian peoples of Spain and Italy were forcing back the northern limits of Moslem domination in their respective territories. Although separation of the Emirate of Spain from the capital at Damascus was to weaken the political power of the empire from the standpoints of Moslem ethnology and Moslem civilization, it was in reality of secondary importance, since Spain continued to be a Moslem dominion and consequently a European expansion of the Moslems, from which emanated oriental influence such as the other Moslems were exerting from Sicily and Italy.

Some fifty years after this political schism of the Spanish Moslems, a Christian empire ruled by Charlemagne was formed north of the Pyrenees in Gaul, which counterbalanced on European ground the Moslem strength in Asia and Africa; although, as we shall see, it had scant influence in checking or repulsing Moslem expansion in southern Europe.

The Conquest of Spain by the Moslems

The Moslems invaded Spain from Mogreb in the eighth century as supporters of one of the factions then disputing the Visigothic crown. That was the party of the sons of Witiza, the king dethroned by Rodrigo. Witiza's followers sought aid from the Arab Governor of Mogreb to overthrow Rodrigo in his turn, but, as had occurred already on other occasions in Spanish history, and was to occur again more than once in later centuries, the Moslems who came as allies remained as conquerors. In the next seven years they seized the entire Peninsula except for a few small, almost inaccessible mountainous districts in the north.

The Spanish population was divided, as it had been in time of the Carthaginians and the Romans. Apparently events shaped themselves as follows: upon news of the first defeats of the Visigothic armies, the majority of city-dwellers fled to the mountains and to places easy to defend, and there withstood the invaders; while strong resistance was offered also by several forts and by various leaders and bands of soldiers in different sections. That was why, though the northward march of the Moslems was swift and their entry and capture of the principal cities relatively easy, the war was long-drawn-out, and in some regions fierce and cruel. At the close of the seven-year-period, the Moslems, sure of their power and desirous of ending the resistance of Visigoths and Hispano-Romans who kept on fighting, tried to appease and win them over by promising to respect their religion, language, and laws, including the officials who governed them; provided that they recognize the supremacy of the Caliph and of the Emir, or Governor, who ruled Spain in his name; which things, to be sure, had been the general policy during the war when occasion was propitious. On this basis, some Visigothic counts yielded (at Orihuela, Tarragona, and else-

Victory Cross, in the Cathedral of Oviedo.

where), and various cities, such as Mérida, surrendered. The consequence of this proceeding was that a great part of the Spanish population returned to live in the territory conquered by the Moslems or, if they had not fled previously, remained there; and, in fact, this class of Spanish Christians in Andalusia and other regions was so numerous that they were called by a special name, the Mozárabes ("Arab Hangers-on" or "Would-be Arabs"). On the other hand, because of the fact that conversion to Mohammedanism freed Christian slaves, and exempted freemen from paying taxes and from other heavy charges, there were also many Spaniards who professed the Moslem religion. These converts were called *Renegados,* or Renegades.

But not all Christians who had fled the cities and the open country fearful of the hazards of war returned optimistic and confident because of the Moslem policy. A considerable number of the fugitives, especially those who belonged to the Catholic clergy, sought refuge beyond the Pyrenees—that is, in Frankish territory—or in the northern extremity of the Peninsula. Many cities, and some Spanish districts, were depopulated in consequence; Catalonia, for example, the northern portion of which was left deserted.

The political result of the Moslem conquest was that Spain came to form a province—an Emirate—dependent on the Moslem Caliphate and governed by an Emir.

The Dependent Emirate

This situation of dependence with respect to the Caliphate of Damascus lasted fifty years. During that time the Spanish Emirate saw its internal peace disturbed by rivalries among the Arab tribes and by the constant fighting of these tribes with Moors or Berbers: clashes resulting frequently in civil warfare of greater or less duration. There was an additional element of disturbance after 740, in which year a Moslem contingent from Syria arrived in Spain to further complicate the factionalism already existing.

The most notable Emir of this period was Abd-er-Rahman el Gafeki (730-732), who gave fresh impulse to the conquest of Gaul undertaken by the Moslems in 716 when already they had felt sure of their control of Spain. At first the invasion of Gaul had been on the whole favorable to the invaders, who, notwithstanding a defeat suffered at Toulouse in 719, were overpowering Narbonne, Carcassonne,

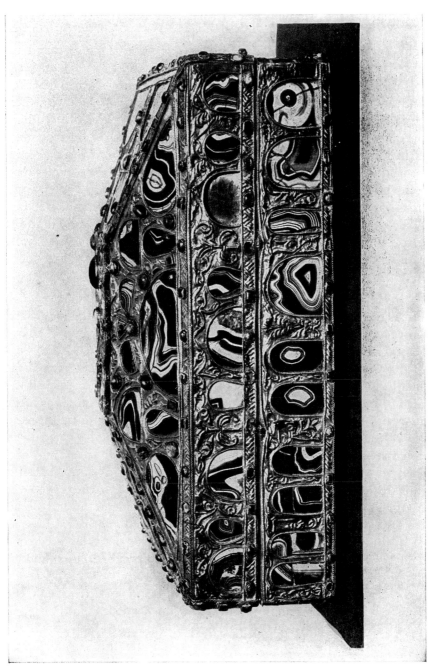

Fruela II's Agate Box, in the Cathedral of Oviedo.

Nîmes, and later (under Abd-er-Rahman's command), Bordeaux.
Thence the Emir's troops marched against Poitiers where in 732 was
fought the memorable battle in which the Moslems were routed utterly. Abd-er-Rahman el Gafeki himself was slain. That victory, the
battle of Poitiers, won by the Frankish leader, Charles Martel, checked
the advance of the Moslems, who had to content themselves with their
conquests in southern France, which, however, they were able to hold
for a few years only. The result of all this was that Moslem domination in western Europe was reduced practically to the Iberian Peninsula, where at that period, as we shall see, the Spanish Reconquest had
already begun. Nevertheless the Moslems continued to menace Europe
from Asia and Africa, constituting a threat to European Christendom
for centuries; until in the fifteenth century, Europe was invaded on the
east from Constantinople by the Turks who, while Moslems also, were
of a different race from the Arabs.

The Independent Emirate

In 756 a Moslem prince named Abd-er-Rahman, of the royal family of the Ommayads which had been deposed at Damascus by the rival
Abbasside family, escaped to Spain as a fugitive from the East. Supported by Ommayad partisans in Spain, by one of the Arab parties (the
Yemenites), and by a considerable number of Berbers, he attacked the
Emir of Córdova, conquering him at the battle of the Alameda on the
outskirts of that city. Entering the capital of the Emirate in triumph,
Abd-er-Rahman promised from the pulpit of the Mosque to deal justice impartially to all, without distinction of race nor party, and pro-
ceeded to found a Moslem monarchy independent of the Abbasside
Caliphate of the East. That monarchy continued to be called the
Emirate during Abd-er-Rahman's lifetime and that of several of his
successors.

But the victory of the Alameda and the peace pact celebrated soon
after at Armilla, near Córdova, with the conquered Emir Jússef and his
general, Somial, did not procure Abd-er-Rahman I a tranquil reign.
On the contrary, he had to keep on fighting against troops of the
Caliph, who tried for some time to regain his Spanish dominions, and
against the Arab and Berber parties that continued to disturb the
public peace. The danger which this last represented was Abd-er-
Rahman's chief anxiety, as it was also that of all his successors. He

understood perfectly that in order to constitute a strong political power it was necessary to reduce to unity, or at least to discipline, the divisionism that was drenching Spain in blood; and that, above all, he must control the egocentric spirit of the Arab and Berber tribes and their racial prejudices. Achievement of this ideal solution was, in fact, the guiding principle of the internal policy of the Spanish Onimayads. To attain it, the new heads of the State of Córdova had to contend not only with the Moslem population but also with some of the Christians who continued to dwell there.

Six Emirs ruled after Abd-er-Rahman I. Two of these are remembered for their urbanization and adornment of Córdova: Hisham I (788-796) who continued work on the great Mosque commenced by his father Abd-er-Rahman I, and Abd-er-Rahman II. Mohammed I (852-866) was notorious for persecutions of the Christian Mozárabes. Abd-er-Rahman II also distinguished himself by his wars against the Christian nucleus-groups of the Reconquest (which we shall discuss hereafter) and against the Normans, a people of the Scandinavian regions who reached Spain (Galicia) for the first time in 844; and thence proceeded southward, arriving by the Tagus and Guadalquivir rivers at Seville, which city they sacked. Although Abd-er-Rahman II defeated them and then made a pact of friendship, they kept on attacking the Spanish coast at Algeciras and on the southeast; but the threat they represented did not go beyond that region and soon came to an end.

Mozárabes and Renegades.
The Reign of Omar-ben-Hafsun

The Mozárabes and Renegades often played a leading part in the civil strife of the Emirate; and there were even occasions when Renegade uprisings constituted a grave danger for the Moslems. The most serious disturbance of the sort, which occurred at the end of the ninth century when Mohammed I was Emir, was headed by the descendant of a Visigothic family, whose Arab name was Omar-ben-Hafsun. For several years this Visigothic Renegade maintained a kind of independent kingdom centered in the Málaga highland. Although Omar ended by abjuring Mohammedanism and becoming a Christian, he incurred in the fatal error of not making a pact with the Christian groups, nuclei of the Reconquest, who had established themselves in the north. Ultimately his Mohammedan followers forsook him; and so ended, in the year 917, the reign of Omar, which might have been the occasion of seriously crippling Mohammedan domination of Spain.

Life of the Mozárabes

The Mozárabes formed a little world of their own in the Moslem cities, with their churches and cloisters of monks and nuns, their own civil authorities (Counts), their judges, their laws (the Visigoth Code), and their language; but none of this kept the Moslems from dealing with them in the affairs of daily life, nor did it prevent the reciprocal influence of each race on the other. Within the limits of their own group the Mozárabes at first continued to speak Latin, though in a vulgarized form; but as time passed, little by little they gave up using it, especially in documents, which they finally wrote in flawless Arabic, as is proved by writings of theirs still extant.

The extent to which Arabic language and Moslem culture influenced their thinking is attested by a Mozárabe, the Cordovan Alvaro, who comments in one of his books (toward the middle of the ninth century) : "Many of my co-religionaries read the poems and tales of the Arabs and study the works of Mohammedan philosophers and theologians, not with the idea of refuting them but of learning how to express themselves in the Arabic tongue with more elegance and correctness. All the young Christians illustrious for their talents are acquainted with the language and literature of the Arabs only; they read and study Arab books zealously; they expend huge sums collecting libraries of such works; and on every occasion they proclaim loudly how admirable this literature is."

Alvaro himself was beheaded at Córdova in the reign of Abd-er-Rahman II, together with a priest named Eulogio and two girls, Flor and María, on the charge of having insulted Mohammed and Allah, an offense punishable by death according to the law. The Church made them saints in virtue of their martyrdom.

Not only among the Mozárabes was use of the Arabic language spreading. Because Moslems and the northern Christians were frequently drawn into close relations, whether of war or of peace, many of the latter, especially those in regions along the frontier, learned Arabic. Such persons were called *cristianos algaraviados;* that is, Chris-

Church of Santa María de Naranco, near Oviedo.

tians who spoke Arabic more or less well. Conversely, there was also a sizable group of Moslems (*moros latinados* or *ladinos,* which is to say, Latinized Moslems) who learned the Latin which was at first spoken by the Christians and which by a gradual process of transformation gave place to the several Romance languages, as we have said. Of course, it is to be supposed that in Arabic as spoken on the Peninsula there were different dialects. This seems to be evidenced by the varying matices of the Arabic words now incorporated into the Spanish language.

The Visigoth Tradition among the Mozárabes

In order to oppose the current described by St. Alvaro of Córdova in the passage quoted, his friend Eulogio tried to foster a renaissance among the Mozárabes of Latin studies in the Visigothic tradition. That he succeeded to some extent is proved by the development of several notable Mozárabic writers in Latin, especially on religious themes, such as the Abbot Speraindeo, Vivencio or Vincent, Samuel, Samson, St. Eulogio himself, and St. Alvaro cited above. A characteristic Mozárabic Bishop was Hostogasis, mentioned by the Abbot Samson. Of St. Eulogio we know that he traveled to northern Spain, returning to Córdova with books in Latin on Christian religion and literature; a fact that indicates not only how well the ancient culture was preserved but also how freely Mozárabes could come and go in Moslem territory and how tolerant the Mohammedans then were. Some of the authors we have mentioned wrote poetry. Further proofs of their culture were translation of the Bible and of the Canonical books; compilation of the Chronicle by the writer who called himself "Anonymous, of Córdova" which gives accounts of many seventh and eighth century events up to 754; and other writings.

The Mozárabes also retained the ways of praying and of saying mass which had been in vogue in Visigothic times, and which were known accordingly as the Mozárabic Rite or Missal.

Beginning of the Reconquest

The rapid conquest of Spain by the Moslems and the progressive strengthening of the Emirate of Córdova from the time of Abd-er-Rahman I, did not keep those Spaniards hostile to the idea of Moslem domination who had taken refuge in the furthest Pyrenees and in the Cantabrian cordillera from soon renewing the offensive in an attempt to recover the territory of the fatherland from the invaders. That purpose, which was tenaciously adhered to during eight centuries, has been given the name of the Reconquest.

The Reconquest was begun in the eighth century by a group of Visigoth nobles and soldiers, aided by natives of the region (Astures), whose eyrie was in the massive heights called the *Picos de Europa—* the Peaks of Europe. Their chief was Pelayo, a Visigoth noble. Their first victory over the Moslems was at Covadonga, at the foot of the Holy Rock (*Peña Santa*), one of the Peaks, on a date still disputed. As a result of that victory the little kingdom of Asturias was formed. Its capital was first Cangas de Onís, then Pravia, and finally, at the end of the eighth century, Oviedo.

About this time other nucleus-groups of reconquerors appeared in Navarre and in the Pyrenees of Aragon; which groups, not so strong as the nucleus in Asturias, were slower in achieving the category of kingdoms for their regions. However, in the eastern sector (later to be called Catalonia) the Franks, whose monarch was then the mighty Emperor Charlemagne, attacked the Moslem masters of the leading cities there (Gerona, Lérida, Barcelona).

Charlemagne, attempting to conquer northern Spain, failed in the Pamplona and Saragossa districts, but not in that of Catalonia where he and his son Ludovic, or Louis the Pious, in the course of relatively few years (785 to 811) took almost all the important cities and organized a Frankish province which they called the Spanish March, placing at its head a high official with the title Marqués, or Marquis. The rapid Frankish advance was then paralyzed until fall of the Caliphate of Córdova.

Progress of the Reconquest until Early Years of the Tenth Century

Events pursued a similar course in the kingdom of Asturias, which, notwithstanding the frequent military expeditions of its Kings Alfonso I and Alfonso II, was unable to extend its borders beyond the cordillera until the middle of the ninth century, except for two districts that they conquered; one on the west (Galicia), and the other, not so large, the origin of Castile, on the border of the present Province of

Santander. Not until after 866 did the Asturian kings advance their frontier to the line of Tuy on the Miño, Astorga, León, and Amaya; and they had to fight continuously to hold what ground they had. At the end of the ninth century they reached Burgos and Castrojeriz on the Castilian side and Lancia, Zamora, Toro, and Simancas in the direction of León; and not before the early years of the tenth century (which is to say, at the beginning of Abd-er-Rahman III's reign, of which more hereafter), when the Christians were at last firmly established in the regions of León and Castile, did Asturias gain control of the Douro frontier, an achievement making it possible for them to carry the war into the territories south of that river.

Let us examine in detail the process of this onward thrust.

Alfonso II and Compostela

The reign of Alfonso II of Asturias is extremely significant in the history of the beginnings of the Reconquest. Apart from his campaigns, which reached the Tagus river and counted some victories in spite of his inability to hold the southern district where these were gained, two capital events occurred in his time. They were the discovery of the tomb of Santiago, with all that that meant, and the thwarted effort to make a pact with Charlemagne. The former is important from the religious standpoint, and the other, as regards the formation of the Spanish spirit, which struggled to preserve its personality even in the early times of the Reconquest when, as we know, the nucleus-groups of Christians were very weak, needing help from anyone who would offer it.

The discovery of the sepulchre and body of the Apostle James—or, to employ his Spanish name, Santiago—in the countryside near the city then called Iria Flavia (now Padrón) caused such great rejoicing among the Christians that the King ordered that a church and a bishop's residence be erected there. So many dwellings were built in the vicinity as soon to form a new city called Compostela, and known also as Santiago de Compostela.

Pilgrimages, which increased steadily in size and frequency, were organized to visit the sepulchre of the Apostle. The pilgrims were not Spaniards only. Foreigners from the most distant parts of Europe made the journey on foot or on horseback from their respective countries.

Thus, for several centuries there was brought about a constant influx of visitors, and at the same time of foreign customs and ideas, into Galicia and many other places in northern Spain, such as Oviedo and León, through which the pilgrims passed and in which they broke their journey. The way they took, which became fixed by tradition into a permanent route, was called "the French road" because most of the pilgrims from other countries crossed France in order to reach Spain. That road, which began at Roncesvalles on the frontier of Navarre, continuing to Rioja (Nájera) and thence to León and Asturias, was one of the communicating links between the port of Spain and the rest of the European world. Hospices and inns for the pilgrims were established at various towns. Those at Oviedo and the one at León (which was the origin of the Monastery of San Marcos) were widely famed, as of course was also the one at Santiago founded by King Fernando I in 1061. Modern criticism holds that among the spiritual fruits of the pilgrimages was the series of legends and songs of the wandering ballad-singers—the minstrels or *juglares*—relating to the Frankish Emperor Charlemagne and his contemporaries and to various real or fictitious Spaniards.

The pilgrims bore a scallop-shell as their emblem, a custom that gave rise to the production for sale to them of relics and amulets of precious metals or of jet, of which some specimens of artistic merit are still extant. These were manufactured not only in the middle ages but also at the beginning of the so-called Modern Era, and found their way to every nook and cranny of Europe.

Spanish devotion to the Apostle Santiago was so intense that it produced many pious legends, among them that of the Apostle's appearance to the Christian armies fighting the Moslems at the battle of Clavijo (which is believed to have taken place in 844), and on other occasions; an apparition that heralded victory. That is why Santiago was named Patron Saint of Spain and particularly of Spanish knighthood, and why "St. James, and close in, Spain!" —*¡Santiago y cierre España!*— became the popular battle-cry against the Moslems. About 1170 a military order of knights was organized, called the Order of Santiago, its emblem a red cross in the form of a sword. The principal mission of the knights of Santiago was to defend the pilgrims (in whose files were often noblemen, princes, and members of the high clery from other

countries) against attack by Moslems and the bandits who frequently
attempted highway robbery.

Spain and Charlemagne

The second most important event of Alfonso II's reign was the
effort to establish an alliance with Charlemagne and the frustration,
or rather, rectification of that effort. As we know, Charlemagne was at
the time the most powerful monarch of western Europe. In natural
consequence of this fact, foreign rulers needing military or other aid
sought his assistance. Charlemagne, for his part, as already noted, several times penetrated into Spain with the object of breaking the Moslem power and mastering part of the country. On one of his first expeditions against the fortress-city of Saragossa, with whose Moslem governor he had a pact, the Emperor suffered a setback, because when his
army came within sight of Saragossa, the city, instead of receiving him
as agreed, closed its gates and prepared for defense. Thereupon, renouncing his project, Charlemagne decided to return to France. He
withdrew through the Pass of Roncesvalles in the Pyrenees of Navarre,
and there the Navarrese natives, or possibly Moslem troops, attacked
the rear-guard of the Franks, almost annihilating them. The date was
August 15, 778. This incident gave rise to the legend of Roland, a
Frankish military leader who in fact was slain in the combat. The
legend has come down to us through different channels; among them,
several French poems of which the most important is known as the
Chanson de Roland, or Song of Roland, composed, in the form we
have it today, a century after the rout at Roncesvalles. Some Castilian
ballads, or *romances,* of much later date than the event also commemo-
rate it.

This defeat was no hindrance to Charlemagne and his son Ludovic
(Louis the Pious) in their conquest not long afterward of the territory in the northwest of the Peninsula which made up the Spanish
March. Nor was it an obstacle to Alfonso II's seeking an alliance with
the Emperor and his son, toward effecting which he undoubtedly
made considerable progress until, for reasons not quite clear to us
now, the Asturian king suddenly changed his mind and broke off
negotiations.

A legend famous in Asturias and León, though transcribed in a
thirteenth century poem long after the time of Alfonso II, seems to

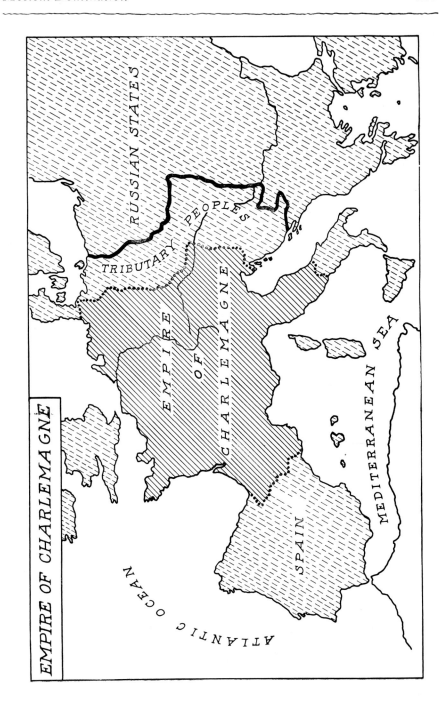

imply, attributing a principal part in the proceedings to an imaginary personage called Bernardo del Carpio, that King Alfonso's change of heart was due to misgivings and opposition on the part of the nobles of the realm who, according to this theory, stood staunchly for rejecting a foreign influence that might endanger the independence of Asturias and the Galician region. Whatever the reason, the fact remains that the projected alliance between Alfonso II and Charlemagne was broken off, and the Asturian monarchy continued with its own unaided efforts the reconquest that Pelayo had begun. Nevertheless, the civilization characteristic of the period of Charlemagne influenced the Asturian kingdom for a long while, as it also influenced the Spanish March. This is shown, among other things, by the architecture of the time, the dissemination of Frankish coins, and some points incorporated in jurisprudence.

The New Kingdom of León

An important step in progress of the Asturian Reconquest was domination of the tableland of León south of the cordillera. Alfonso III—Alfonso Magno, or the Great—had prepared the way by his conquests, but the definitive conqueror was his son Ordoño II (914-924) who gave concrete proof of mastery by removing the Court from Oviedo to León. The transfer of the capital showed Ordoño's confidence in the security of his possession of the Leonese territory. He showed this even more convincingly by re-establishing in the city of León the episcopal see formerly existing there. With this new conquest, the Christian dominions included the districts of Asturias, León, Galicia, on the west; and on the east, Castile and parts of Vasconia (the Basque country) and Navarre. However, strictly speaking, control over these two last, and over Galicia as well, was more nominal than realistic, since the nobles resident there consistently refused to recognize the authority of the Leonese kings. That circumstance apart, the dominions of those monarchs reached Dueñas and Simancas on the south; on the east, up the Duero beyond San Esteban de Gormaz; and on the Castilian side, to the north, they included the district of Burgos (the foundation of which as a fortress is attributed to Alfonso II) toward the mountains. On the west Zamora and Salamanca were already fortresses well able to withstand Moslem attacks. Salamanca was re-settled in 941.

It is thought that Ordoño II's transfer of the capital in 944 was occasion of the first use of the title of "King of León," an initiative attributed to him.

Foundation of the Caliphate of Córdova

The end of the reign of Alfonso III of Asturias coincided, almost point by point, with transformation into a Caliphate of the independent Emirate of Córdova. This change was effected by the Emir Abd-er-Rahman III, who ruled from 912 to 961. Abd-er-Rahman III represents the high-point in that enterprise of peace and of reduction of Hispanic Moslems to homogeneity and social discipline which Abd-er-Rahman I had begun and his successors, of whom we have spoken, had carried on. Abd-er-Rahman III succeeded in quelling the anarchical situation that had made several cities and districts, among them Toledo and Badajoz, independent in fact. Subduing the rebellious and overambitious among his subjects, he assumed the title of Caliph, as if to affirm in the most solemn manner possible the political unity of the monarchy founded by Abd-er-Rahman I, and its category of equality with the Caliphate of the East. Thus commenced the period of great splendor which from that time forward was to be called for more than one hundred years the Caliphate of Córdova. Our next chapter deals with its history.

Interior Organization of the Kingdom of Asturias

The Christian kingdoms of Spain, as well as the Counties of the Spanish March, had to struggle in their early days not only against the Moslem in battle but also against enemies within their gates, in the effort to organize the life of the population flocking in from every side, to unify the common action, and to combat the anarchistic tendency of the upper classes.

Accordingly, the kings and the men of learning who surrounded them could count on only two adaptable elements: the example of social organization and government that had been set by the Visigothic kingdom, and the lessons that were to be derived from the new life of continual warfare and numberless difficulties. Of these two elements, the former, naturally, must have seemed to constitute a natural precedent embodying experience that could be utilized with profit.

Hence, the first organizations that we know about in the kingdom of Asturias, which was the focus of origin, domination, and government of the other northern and northeastern districts, were simply a re-shaping of what existed there prior to the Moslem invasion, though the re-shaping was on the modest scale made necessary by the limited radius of the new monarchy. That the latter should view itself as a continuation of the rule of the last Gothic king was humanly logical; and that it did so is demonstrated by the terms applied in more or less contemporaneous documents to the kings of Asturias, who are sometimes referred to as "of Spain" and again as "of the Goths." For this reason, also, the Court of Alfonso II at Oviedo imitated in part the organization of the old Visigothic Court at Toledo and the same thing was true of his other governmental institutions; although it cannot now be doubted that in the organization of the royal Court in Alfonso II's reign some regulations Frankish in origin were adopted as well, a manifestation at the administrative level of Carlovingian influence. In general, the laws applying in Asturias were those of the Visigothic *Liber Iudiciorum,* along with the new enactments made necessary for repopulation and for organizing defense. At the same time, there was a resurgence of Visigothic customs that the Code of Euric and his successors had not seen fit to recognize legally; and new customs were evolved also to meet the new conditions prevailing. These customs old and new were being set down in part in the documents called the Town Charters—*cartas pueblas*—and the Statute Laws, or *fueros.*

Resettlement and the Town Charters

These town charters, or *cartas pueblas,* were documents granting lands for settlement and cultivation, and for securing means of subsistence for a population forced to defend any special place against Moslem attacks. Accordingly a considerable proportion of the people making up the new Spanish society independent of the Moslems were settling the land. They were of four classes: *Spaniards* (Visigoths or Hispano-Romans), who combined their efforts to bring the new monarchy into being; *vanquished Moslems,* taken in the war and not expelled from the conquered territories, who sometimes remained as prisoners and were enslaved, and again were set free (in which latter case they were called *Mudéjares*); *Mozárabes,* who returned to reintegrate themselves into the Christian world; and *Jews,* who with the

de Naranco, later converted into a church. In all these may be discerned Visigothic influence, with important innovations seemingly of Frankish origin; such innovations becoming still more apparent in the tenth century, though then of different derivation, having been brought by the Mozárabes, as we shall see, to the Castilian and Leonese tablelands.

Also, Spanish culture, no less in those elements that were inherited from Visigoth and Roman than in the already more composite culture of the Mozárabes, exerted influence beyond the Spanish borders. A notable example of this is the work of the Spaniard Theodolphus, of the school of St. Isidore, himself one of the most famous educators at Charlemagne's Court (eighth century); St. Prudentius, Bishop of Troyes (died, 861), distinguished as being one of the most learned prelates of his time, to whom seekers after counsel came from many lands; and Recemund, Bishop of Elvira, who suggested to Liutprand (Bishop of Cremona in Italy, and adviser to the Emperor Otho) the idea of the famous historical work entitled *Antapodion* which narrates the principal events from 886 to 950. Moreover, the doctrines of St. Isidore, including his juridical work, continued to influence the intellectual life of Europe throughout the period called the Middle Ages. In this manner, Spanish culture, while itself being enriched and enlarged by contributions from other countries, began to contribute reciprocally to the intellectual progress of the rest of the world through eminent men of the period such as those already named and through doctrines that had been handed down from former times.

Moslem Domination and Its Influence on Europe

Moslem domination of our Peninsula signified not only a military and political but also a cultural fact. This means that the destroyers of the Visigothic kingdom brought with them a civilization of which the nucleus had been formed in Asia, whence it continued to irradiate over all the far-flung territories of the Caliph's empire of Damascus, even after some of these, as in the case of Spain, had declared themselves politically independent. The period of two hundred years, therefore, which comprehends the Emirate of Córdova before it was converted into the Caliphate, represents the initial step in transmitting that culture to the soil of Spain and is the beginning of its influence on the Christian inhabitants; first, on the Spaniards themselves, and then, in a form that we shall consider later, on those from other European countries.

That transmission in its totality (which is to say, from the eighth century to the fifteenth, but principally in the thirteenth) affected every aspect of civilization; from the contribution to Europe of Eastern fauna, flora, and industrial products not previously known there, to the loftiest peaks of scientific and philosophic thought. The radii of its dissemination from the points of direct contact—Spain and Italy—reached the whole of Europe, though the effect was mainly evident in those two countries, and most especially and most intensely in Spain. The following chapter will show this in greater detail, since it deals with the Caliphate, the most magnificent period of Moslem civilization in Spain; although as regards the spreading of that civilization among the Christians on the Peninsula, the subsequent period (from the eleventh to the fifteenth centuries) was to prove equally fruitful and the facts that we have regarding it are much better substantiated by exact chronological data. To state this is not to imply that the first two centuries were a wasteland. What has been said concerning the Mozárabes is sufficient of itself to disprove any such idea as that.

Chapter VII

The Caliphate of Córdova and Moslem Ascendency

Abd-er-Rahman III and the Christian Kings

THE DYNAMIC personality of Abd-er-Rahman III and his exceptional administrative ability laid what might well have been considered a permanent foundation for the Caliphate. His long reign of forty-nine years gave him time to cement this foundation and bequeath his successors a State which during a considerable period may be said to have lived on the vital energy engendered by this first Caliph. Abd-er-Rahman not only triumphed over lawlessness within the Emirate but increased the strength of the Moslem monarchy of Spain by forming alliances with sheiks of several Moslem tribes. He hoped with their assistance to transform the whole of northwest Africa as far up the coast as Argel into a dependency of Córdova; an ambition that he did in fact make reality for some years. His efforts to that end commenced auspiciously with the taking of Ceuta in 939 and the formal recognition of him as Caliph by the Berber sheik Abu Yezid who conquered Kairouan and made it the center of his own political authority.

All these successes, even though the victory in northwest Africa held only until 947, gave Abd-er-Rahman international fame. His navy was then the most powerful in the Mediterranean and his army the best organized and strongest of the western world. Following the tradition of his predecessors, he intensified city planning and added to the splendid beauty of Córdova, which was so famed in consequence that it became one of the cities most visited by Moslems and Christians alike. At the same time, Abd-er-Rahman made the capital of his Caliphate the center of economic and intellectual life for Mohammedan Spain, another means of attracting to it both his own people and foreigners.

In spite of this grandeur, Abd-er-Rahman's work did not long endure. His Caliphate was to survive only seventy years after his own death in 961; and during fifty-five of those years the royal authority, as we shall see, was actually in a period of decadence, even though for this length of time the Spanish Caliphate's military and political predominance was maintained.

However, it would be erroneous to believe that during the forty-nine years of Abd-er-Rahman III's reign and the fifty-five immediately succeeding it, the advance of the Reconquest undertaken by the Christian kingdoms of Spain was kept at a standstill and that their armies experienced nothing but defeat. The fact is that the tenth century—with the early years of which Abd-er-Rahman's reign commenced (in 912) and the close of which saw the beginning of the end of Almansor's military supremacy (which we are about to discuss) — witnessed a positive strengthening and at times a very appreciable extension of the Christian frontiers; and it is no less the fact that during the century the Spanish kings achieved some notable victories, even over Abd-er-Rahman.

Until 951, there was at most an ebb-and-flow of power with respect to the Christians and the Moslems of the frontier districts; but after Almansor's death in 1002, the balance inclined in favor of the Christians. The apparent contradiction in what is said here as regards Moslem military power is due to two important facts: first, the aforesaid progress achieved by the Christian States both in their internal conditions and in their territorial extent, normally protected on the southern front; and second, the nature of the Moslem campaigns, of which even the most hard-fought were only a *raz*—a raid or foray; sudden onslaughts with intent to keep the enemy in check, divert his forces, take prisoners and booty, and lay waste such property as could not be carried off; without, however, incorporating into the Caliphate the territory victoriously over-run.

The rhythm and range of the increasing power of the Christian kingdoms will be explained in detail a little further on. At this point, it is sufficient to say that Abd-er-Rahman's reign (912-961) was coincidental in its early years with that of Ordoño II of León (913-925), whose conquests we have noted; and in its later period with that of Ramiro II of León (930-950) and the command of Fernán González, Sovereign Count of Castile (950-970), who like those monarchs was famed for his wars against the Moslems. A few years after Abd-er-Rahman's death, Navarre under Sancho Garcés III—Sancho the Great— became the strongest Christian kingdom of Spain.

As for the ebb-and-flow of victory and defeat, it is evidenced by the fact that while Abd-er-Rahman's troops in 916 won the battle of Mutonia, and were in general successful in the campaign of 920, especially at the battle of Valdejunquera and in the 924 campaign when the Cathedral of Pamplona was burned and Navarrese territory otherwise terrorized; in the 934 campaign, during which Abd-er-Rahman destroyed the city of Burgos and seized the monastery of Cardeña; and in that of 936, which saw the conquest of Calatayud and the beheading of that city's Alavese garrison: it is equally the fact that Ordoño II of León in 914 advanced as far as Mérida; that in 917 the Moslems were defeated at San Esteban de Gormaz; that not long after the 920 campaign, Nájera and Viguera were regained by Christian arms and it is believed that Ordoño II led his troops very near to Córdova; that in 932 Ramiro II took Madrid; that in 933, this same Leonese king conquered the Moslems near Osma, and conquered them again in 939 at Simancas and Alhandega, the latter victory so overwhelming that Abd-er-Rahman himself had to flee lest he be taken prisoner; and that in 951 Ramiro II triumphed once more, this time at Talavera. But when all was said and done, the superior strength was still that of the Caliphate.

The minority of the Navarrese King García Sánchez, whose mother, Tota, was his regent, made that kingdom after 937 a tributary dependency of Córdova. The death of Ramiro II, together with internal dissensions in his realm between Leonese and Castilians, left the way almost completely open for Abd-er-Rahman's military excursions. Fearful of them, Ordoño III asked for and signed a peace pact. When his successor and half-brother, Sancho the Fat, ascended the throne, the situation worsened. The nobles disliked the new king: he tried to stamp out their rebelliousness and they ended by dethroning him. They alleged as pretext an inglorious defeat suffered by Sancho in war against the Moslems and his extreme fatness which made it impossible for him to mount a horse and caused him to be a laughing-stock.

Sancho sought refuge at Pamplona with his grandmother, Queen Tota, and despatched a plea for assistance to Abd-er-Rahman III, who promptly acceded, sending not only troops but a Jewish physician as well, whose ministrations successfully reduced the royal avoirdupois. This Moslem alliance, through which Sancho in 960 regained the throne of León, placed his kingdom at the Caliph's mercy.

Abd-er-Rahman's Successors. Almansor

The situation did not improve substantially during the reign of Abd-er-Rahman's immediate successor, Hakem II (961-976), who achieved victory after victory over the Christians. The latter, nevertheless, seized every opportunity of shaking off the influence and political pressure of Córdova. The Caliphate, however, continued to be the strongest State in Spain, maintaining its world-wide prestige; while Hakem because of his intense personal interest in cultural development, fostered scientific and literary work and founded schools and libraries.

Conditions might have changed, perhaps, during the reign of Hakem's son, Hisham II, had it not been for an extraordinary general, Almansor. Hisham was a minor twelve years old when his father died, and at first the Caliphate was ruled by his mother, Aurora (who was of Basque origin), and by the Prime Minister, Mohammed-ben-Abdullah, later known, because of his victories, as Almansor—"aided of God." A favorite of the Sultana Aurora, who was then in fact head of the Moslem State, Almansor soon took over all authority from her and her son.

To Almansor was due creation of the first regular army that the Caliphate ever had. It was formed of mercenaries, differing in race and nationality, among whom were many Spanish Christians. One of the principal effects of this army was to relegate to secondary importance the militia of the several tribes, which had often been hard to control because of internecine rivalries and the anarchical spirit of the sheiks. Almansor led his army on different campaigns by which he captured Christian strongholds as far off as León, Astorga, Santiago de Galicia, and Barcelona; but notwithstanding the great losses inflicted on Leonese, Galicians, and Catalans by these victories, the Count of Barcelona and the King of León very quickly recovered and repopulated those cities because of the fact that Almansor did not establish permanent dominion over them and the surrounding region, but soon withdrew to the frontiers of the Caliphate, of which one of the first military strongholds was Medinaceli, south of the province of Soria, eleven kilometers northeast of Sigüenza.

It was at Medinaceli that Almansor died in 1002, whereupon the military power that he had built up vanished rapidly; since, though his son Abdul Malik maintained it for six years longer, after the latter's brief reign there was anarchy in Córdova; anarchy ending in 1031 when Hisham III was dethroned and the Caliphate split into several independent kingdoms known as kingdoms of *Taifas,* a word that means "band" or "faction."

The Kingdom of León during the Caliphate of Córdova

We have related already the principal events of the reigns of Ordoño II and Ramiro II of León, and the decadence of that kingdom in confronting the Moslem threat, a decadence caused by dynastic wars and very especially by Sancho the Fat's submission to Abd-er-Rahman. His policy was duplicated years afterward when Ramiro III and his cousin Bermudo II were disputing the Crown. Bermudo accepted Almansor's support in exchange for a political subjection that Bermudo himself later on, by successive revolts, tried in vain to end. The only effect of his attempts at rebellion was to produce a new series of victorious campaigns for Almansor, 987-88 and 995-97. It was during the first of these that the Moslems seized León and Coimbra; on the second that they took Astorga and Santiago.

Bermudo II's son and successor in León, Alfonso V (999-1027). found himself better situated than his father had been for throwing off the Cordovan protectorate. Two years after Alfonso ascended the throne, Almansor died and the Christian king was emboldened to repopulate and restore the city of León, where he again installed his Court. Alfonso V gave León a special statute law, or *fuero,* regulating, among other things, the internal government of the city and its market. It was adopted at a session of the Court (*Curia regia*) held in 1020. Alfonso V conquered numerous settlements over toward what would later be Portugal, and he gave much thought to bringing more inhabitants into his kingdom, as Alfonso II had done before him, encouraging Mozárabic immigration from the Caliphate's territories.

The New Kingdom of Castile

The birth of the kingdom of Castile is one of the events expressive of the spirit of independence which characterized the nobles of those centuries; and it is no less expressive of the spirit of individualism which was developing throughout the region. It is believed today that the principal source of that Castilian individualistic pride and of the temperamental difference between Castilians and Leonese had origin in the fundamental differences between their populations. The lands of León were repopulated chiefly with Mozárabes; the Castilian lands, with mountaineers or Cantabrians.

As has been mentioned, the kings of Asturias and León had possessed for many years the territories of the Burgos district and those adjacent, lying toward Navarre and the Basque provinces. The first capital—that is, the most important settlement—in these territories was the city of Amaya which is thought to have been founded in the ninth century by a Count Rodrigo. Burgos was founded later, as we have shown. The whole region, anciently called Bardulia, later acquired the name of Castiella (Castile) because of the numerous forts or castles that had to be erected for its defense. It was divided into small limited areas, or counties (such as Alava, Lauratón, Cerezo, Burgos), with chiefs or Counts appointed by the Kings.

The Counts governing Castile, like most of those of the other Christian territories, were much inclined to look to their own advantage and pay as little heed as possible to the King. The distance between León and Burgos, the difficulties of communication (heightened by unremitting warfare), and the civil strife that harassed and weakened the monarchs, perhaps contributed toward making independence *de facto,* even though not *de jure,* more feasible in Castile than in other parts of the realm. The Castilians finally achieved their independence about the middle of the tenth century (which is to say, a little after the death of Ordoño II, King of León) through the valor and ability of a Count called Fernán González who united under his single command all the other Castilian Counties, enlarged the territorial extent of Castile, and established for his family hereditary possession of the region, which signified practically complete independence, since it annulled the King of León's previous appointive powers with regard to Castilian governmental officials. Hence, although, as we shall see, Castile did not legally acquire the name of kingdom until

1032, it functioned as such in practice from the time of Fernán González.

The figure of Fernán Gonzáles, regarded as the champion of Castilian independence and famed as a mighty warrior against the Moslems, was exalted and extolled with all the broidery of anecdote and heroic legend in a thirteenth-century poem written in Spanish, probably by a monk in the monastery of Arlanza, near Burgos. This poem, undoubtedly incorporating the popular tales current in Castile, describes Fernán González as follows: *

> By the name Fernando was the first Count dight;
> Never in the world was there such another knight.
> Ever to the Moslems a cause of mortal plight,
> They called him Killer Vulture for his prowess in the fight.

The new kingdom, segregating its own territory from what had up to that time belonged to León, left the latter still relatively extensive, with limits approximately as follows: the boundary began on the northeast at the Deva river (the present line of demarcation between Asturias and Santander) ; swung to the west along the Galician coast to the mouth of the Duero; followed the right bank of that river, then dropped to the so-called Cliff of France—Peña de Francia—south of Salamanca; turned to the northeast by lands of Avila and Segovia; again crossed the Duero by way of the present Province of Valladolid; veered northward more or less along the boundaries of the provinces of Palencia and Burgos, and closed the circuit at the mouth of the Deva river.

But the kingdom of Castile, created *de facto* by Fernán González, preserved its independence for a few years only, since in 1028 (which is to say, fifty-eight years after death of its founder) Sancho the Great, King of Navarre, conquered it and annexed it to his throne.

Birth and Apogee of the Kingdom of Navarre

Until the beginning of the tenth century (905) , there are no trustworthy accounts of the Kingdom of Navarre, part of whose territories

---

* Hubo nombre Fernando el conde de primero,
nunca fué en el mundo otro tal caballero,
éste fue de los moros un mortal homicero,
decianle por sus lides el buitre carnicero.

on the west and in the Basque provinces were dominated, as we have said, by the Kings of Asturias and León, although at that period their rule was more in law than in fact. By the end of the eleventh century, in the time of Alfonso III of Asturias, Navarre must have acquired already a certain importance because that monarch contracted marriage with a daughter of García Iñiguez, then presumably the Navarrese King. Not long after, another King of Navarre, Sancho Garcés, fought alongside the King of León at the battle of San Esteban de Gormaz, already cited.

That Sancho Garcés is the first Navarrese monarch for whom we possess authentic dates: 905 to 925. He extended the territories of Navarre as far as Nájera, Tudela, and Valtierra—that is, south of the Ebro river; and although new Moslem attacks (especially in Almansor's reign) later endangered Navarrese independence, particularly during the regency of Queen Tota, Navarre in the early years of the eleventh century, under King Sancho Garcés III called the Great (1000-1035), came to be strongest and most important of the Spanish Christian kingdoms. Its domains then stretched from beyond the Pyrenees, in what is now the French Basque region, to the western frontier of the Catalonian Counties, extending to the ancient territory of Sobrarbe, as well as that of Ribagorza and Pallars, ruled by the Franks since the end of the eighth century. For a considerable period Navarre also embraced the new kingdom of Castile, as already noted, and the region between the Pisuerga and the Cea which had belonged formerly to León. That region, as well as the lands of Rioja and Bureba, frontiers from that time forward between Castile and Navarre, were the objective, during many years, of struggles between the two kingdoms, which disputed definitive possession; and then followed wars to the same end between Aragón and Castile; such a situation not being uncommon in border states.

On Sancho the Great's death in 1035, his extensive domains were split up, because he restored independence to Castile, bequeathing it as a kingdom to his son Ferdinand; gave part of the territories on the east to another son, Ramiro, with the title of King of Aragón, and part (Sobrarbe and Ribagorza) to a third son, Gonzalo, though not granting him the title of King but simply that of Lord; and the Crown of Navarre he left to his firstborn, García. Accordingly, and without taking into consideration the counties of Catalonia, the following

Spanish Christian kingdoms were in existence in the first third of the eleventh century: León (including also Galicia and Asturias), Castile, Navarre, and Aragón, in addition to the mentioned seignorial holdings of Sobrarbe and Ribagorza.

The Spanish March of the Franks

After the Franks conquered Barcelona in 801, they continued the design of extending their dominions in northeastern Spain. In 811 they made tributary the Moslem city of Tortosa. Charlemagne's son Ludovic, or Louis the Pious, annexed his Spanish territorial possessions (the so-called Spanish March) to his holdings on the other side of the Pyrenees called Septimania (part of Roussillon, Narbonne, Carcassonne, and up to Nîmes on the northeast), terming the whole the Marquisate de Gotha. First Marquis of the new marquisate was a Count of Barcelona named Besa. Other counties than that of Barcelona were carved from the Spanish part of Gotha; among them, Ampurias, Gerona, Urgel, and also Pallars and Ribagorza, both of which last, as we have seen, belonged for a time to Navarre though they were later Frankish dependencies until made independent (seemingly, at the end of the ninth century) when Ramón I, brother-in-law of Garviá Jiménez of Navarre, was Count.

The Marquisate lasted until 865, in which year it was reduced to the territorial limits of the Spanish March; that is, to the Hispanic or Cis-Alpine district.

A few years later the Count of Barcelona, and of Urgel as well, was Guifré, or Wifredo, nicknamed the Shaggy or Hairy, who joined to these two counties those of Sardinia and Gerona also. Consequently, toward the close of the ninth century, he thus became the most powerful of the Lords of the March. At his death in 898, however, the counties were again divided, and passed to his sons.

Independence of the Spanish March and its Territorial Gains

To this Wifredo has been attributed the legendary independence of the Spanish March in relation to the Frankish Emperors; but any such attribution belongs to the realm of fable. In reality, taking advantage of the conflict existing in France, from the end of the ninth century onward, between the successors of Charlemagne and the noble family of Eudes (descendants of a Count of Paris, Robert the Strong), the Counts of Barcelona continued to intensify their *de facto* independence, and, though not yet daring an open break with the Frankish Kings, to oppose Frankish demands by passive resistance. At the same time, the Counts of Barcelona let pass no opportunity of expanding their territories at Moslem expense.

Count Borrell IV (940[?]-992) by refusing to recognize as sovereign the Frankish King Hugh Capet who had just ascended the throne, affirmed his autonomy in fact. From that time forward, ever more fully and freely, the Counts of Barcelona and the other Counts of the Spanish March acted with positive independence, while the Frankish Kings did not attempt to interfere. Meanwhile, as the power of the Counts of Barcelona increased, that of the other Counts was becoming subordinate to it. A contributory cause was the fact that through marriages and otherwise the Counts of Barcelona joined to their own territory that of various neighboring counties, while at the same time establishing family ties with several Frankish Counts on the other side of the Pyrenees—the Counts of Auvergne, Toulouse, Carcassonne, and Gascony.

Ramón Borrell and Berenguer Ramón I

The two Counts of Barcelona of this period most notable for their personal qualities, their military prowess, and their achievements in government and social organization, were Ramón Borrell (992-1018) and his son Berenguer Ramón I (1018-1035). Ramón Borrell maintained relations with the Court of the Caliph of Córdova and carried out two important military expeditions: the first in aid of one Moslem prince against another, an undertaking climaxed by the hardfought battle of Acbatalbacar in 1010; and the second a forward thrust that reached the rivers Segre and Ebro. The fame attained by Ramón Borrell is expressed with remarkable poignance in the extant funeral chant, written in Latin.

Berenguer Ramón I was characterized in particular by his untiring effort to ensure for himself and his house dominion over his County, and his resultant organization of frontier defenses, and for the laws he promulgated in favor of the citizens of Barcelona. In his time (1032) the basilica of Ripoll was inaugurated. Almost at the same time, Count Wifredo of Sardinia founded the famous Monastery of St. Martin of

Canigou, of which the glories have been sung by the modern poet Verdaguer. Another monastery of the March, greatly celebrated in the tenth century and the early years of the eleventh, was that of Guixá in Sardinia, headed for some time by the Abbot Guari or Gari, in which many eminent Italians took their vows, including the Venetians Duke Paolo Urseolo (later canonized), Giovanni Gradenico, Marino and Giovanni Morosini, and he who was to become St. Romuald.

The year of Berenguer Ramón I's death—1035—was also that of the dethronement of the last Caliph of Córdova and of the birth of the new Christian Kingdom of Aragón with which Catalonia was soon to be united.

The Moslem Culture of the Caliphate

Not for its military strength only was the Caliphate of Córdova great. The Moslem people loved learning, and were zealous in encouragement of education. A proof of this was their establishing in Spain primary schools with a curriculum that included reading and writing with the Koran as text, poetry, letter-writing, and grammar. In the higher schools, which we today would call universities, were studied, the religious traditions and commentary of the Koran, grammar, medicine, philosophy, law or jurisprudence, and literature, the latter course including history. The foundation stones of Moslem learning were the Greek and Roman works, especially the former, translated by Arab scholars of Syria and Persia, and in some instances by Nestorian Christians [of the sect of Nestor, a fifth century patriarch banished from Constantinople on account of his heretical teaching that the divine and human elements were not merged into one personality in Christ]. Thus the Moslems came to be the upholders and transmitters of classic culture; of the Hellenic culture properly so termed and of the Alexandrine Hellenism (third century B.C.). This was especially true of them from the seventh to the thirteenth centuries of our era; which is to say, when St. Isidore's example in this respect was losing force in Spain, and the other countries of Europe, bent on selfish ends of political power and conquest, had largely forgotten the cultural tradition of the Roman world which, when the Roman Empire ended, incorporated both Mediterranean and Eastern culture. Moreover, the Moslems embodied in their own culture the scientific and artistic elements that they found in peoples of western Asia, India, and China. They did not limit themselves to duplicating and assimilating foreign forms, but produced as well an original, vigorous scientific and literary movement of their own. Thus they transformed themselves into the most cultured people of Europe, in the dual sense of being, as goes without saying, preservers of the classic and importers of the eastern Asiatic learning, and at the same time contributors of new ideas and discoveries. Hence, from a very early period and from many of the Christian peoples of Europe, scholars came to Spain to study there in erudite Moslem circles branches of learning which could not be acquired elsewhere. A notable trip of the kind was that of the French monk Gerbert of Auvergne who in mid-tenth century came to Spain as companion of Borrell II, Count of Barcelona, visiting that city and Córdova and in the latter capital studying geometry, mechanics, astronomy, and other sciences. To him is attributed, as a result of what he learned in Moslem schools, the introduction into northeastern Spain and France of the Arabic numerals that we employ today and of the clock with weights. Gerbert, renowned for his wisdom and his learning, became Archbishop of Ravenna and later Pope, under the name Sylvester II (999-1003). Elsewhere in these pages we shall consider more fully the penetrations of Moslem science into Europe. At this point we need add merely that in the tenth century and well into the eleventh the Monastery of Ripoll was the center from which irradiated Arabic science, especially mathematics.

The library of the Caliph of Córdova came to number 600,000 volumes, and in Andalusia 50 public libraries were established. The Caliph Hakem employed agents to purchase or copy for his collection ancient and modern books in principal cities throughout the world. In consequence of all this, education was very general throughout the Caliphate, with a low percentage of illiteracy.

Arabic was the language in which Moslem authors and scholars wrote their works; but there coexisted with the written language a vulgar tongue—that is to say, the speech of the masses of the people—which was interlarded with Latin words and, later on, also with neo-Latin, or Romance, expressions, and which was employed even in official documents. The Spanish Moslems were particularly fond of folk poetry. Folk songs with musical accompaniment were extremely popular; and, rendered by wandering singers on street corners and in the public plazas, and in villages and throughout the countryside, they greatly influenced similar compositions in the Spanish Christian king-doms and in foreign countries; an influence not limited to verse form and content but extending to the music as well.

It is only just to state that, if Spanish Moslems by virtue of their culture contributed notably to the science and letters of their time, not all this contribution was originally their own. As we have pointed out, the Moslem world of the East was also a great focus of culture, and the Spanish Moslems maintained contact with it through frequent voy-ages that continually transmitted to the Peninsula influences of eastern Asia and of Egypt, enriching the technique and stimulating the crea-tive power of the Occidentals. That creative genius came to produce, as following pages will show, cultural modalities which are Spanish, properly speaking, and which markedly differentiate Western literature, art and even philosophy, from Eastern.

The Jews in Spain, who at that time were to be found chiefly in the Moslem territories, likewise distinguished themselves in cultivation of poetry, philosophy, and medicine. In practice of this last they enjoyed great prestige and were often consulted by Christians themselves.

Moslem Arts

The great culture of the Spanish Moors and Arabs was manifested with equal impressiveness in the arts. Although in this field too they were disciples of the ancient Asiatic peoples (Chaldeans, Assyrians, Persians) and of the Byzantine Romans, they could invent new and characteristic forms as is shown, above all, in their architecture and decorative arts. Accordingly, the well-founded theory has been ad-vanced by a recent historian of Hispano-Moresque art that that art in its evolution constitutes an original achievement, distinct from the Moslem art of the East. This originality had Spain as point of depar-ture, produced strongly derivative examples in the architecture of North Africa, and influenced construction not only in Spanish Chris-tian cities but in some in France as well.

The principal edifice of Arab or Moslem architecture was the build-ing dedicated to the Mohammedan religion, the mosque. Usually it had an entrance court; one or more naves, separated by columns con-nected one with another by horseshoe arches; what we might term an altar, a kind of vaulted niche or recess which the Arabs call a *mihrab* and which, though holding neither image nor statue, is always ori-

Mosque of Córdova: *Plaques of marble fretwork in floral design, in the door of the Mihrab.*

ented toward Mecca, the holy city of the Moslem; and, finally the towers or minarets (one or several for each mosque) from which a special functionary, the muezzin, announces in a ringing voice the hours of prayer (the Moslems make no use of bells, leaving them to the Christians). The roof of the mosque is vaulted, usually with a cupola. Most famous of Spanish mosques is the one at Córdova, representative of the first period of Moslem art in Spain, the building of which continued from the eighth to the tenth century. In its construction the Arabian architects utilized much material from former Roman and Visigothic buildings, especially the Roman columns and capitals; but they also contributed very important structural innovations which were greatly to influence Christian architecture. Among the most conspicuous are solution of the problem of balancing and safely carrying huge architectural masses on slight supports, often simply columns; and the intercrossing, both an artistic and a technical achievement, of the arches (horseshoe, ogive, and lobed) and the interlaced mouldings of the dome in which Arabic art anticipated Gothic. These three innovations may still be observed in the Mosque, especially in three of its sections: the *mihrab;* the *lucernario,* or skylight designed to give light from without to buildings of great size; and the *maesura* (an enclosure reserved for the caliph, the imán, or public prayer-leader, or for the sepulchre of a personage deemed worthy of sainthood). All three architectural inventions seemingly are owed to a Moslem architect summoned by the Cordovan Caliph Hakem II to work on the Mosque of Córdova from 961 to 969. As for towers or minarets, the one at Seville called the Giralda is a model of soaring grace; but the Arab part of it was built in the twelfth century, after the fall of the Caliphate of Córdova.

In decoration of buildings the Arabs used principally the form to which they have given their name, arabesques—plaques of marble or plaster carved in lacy fretwork with geometrical or floral designs on red or blue ground, and in the more luxurious buildings, with gilded relief; glass mosaics, of which a good extant example is the anteroom of the *mihrab* at Córdova; and *azulejos,* or glazed tiles in relief that ornament the *zócalos* (flat square members under the base of pedestals), of which many have survived to the present.

The most remarkable and splendid civil edifices of the period of which remains exist are the Palaces of Medina Azzahra and of Alamiria,

Ivory Jar, from the Cathedral of Zamora.

both on the outskirts of Córdova and both built in the reign of Abd-er-Rahman III.

In industrial arts the Moslems excelled principally in ceramics (tableware painted in colors in metallic lustre, jars of different sizes and uses, and the *azulejos*); the work of their gold- and silver-smiths (lamps, sword-hilts and scabbards, jewel chests with plaques of precious metals and carved marble, jars and jugs); and textiles (cloths of silk and wool, and tapestries, for which the chief production centers were Almería, Málaga, Murcia, and other cities). Among textiles of the period of which we have specimens today should be mentioned a late tenth century tissue of gold interwoven with silver which bears the name of the Caliph Hisham. All these industrial arts were imitated by the Christians and from them were derived in great part those of the same type which flourished later in the Spanish Christian kingdoms.

Moslem Wealth

This admirable development of the scientific, literary and artistic culture of the Spanish Moslems rested on a sound foundation of general prosperity. Agriculture was very advanced, and extremely productive, thanks to improvement in the condition of the working class, which was made up principally of Mozárabes; the introduction of new crops (rice, sugarcane, cotton) and of new orchard fruits (peach, apricot, fig, date, pomegranate); and to extension and regularization of artificial irrigation.

The Moslems also encouraged mining and stock-raising; and they established, stimulated, and enlarged the wool and silk textile industry mentioned; the production of paper from plant fibers to replace parchment; plain tanned and stamped leathers (the famous *guadameciles* or Cordovan leathers processed in that city); carved marble; glass, crystal, and other tableware. The manufacture of paper, an industry imported from China by the Moslems of western Asia, was established at Játiva by the tenth century; it is known to have existed at Toledo in the eleventh century, since we have from that city some eleventh century documents such as the Mozarabic missal of Silos, written on paper. Yet the production of paper, which was so greatly to influence the development of culture, was for several centuries exclusive to Spain among countries of western Europe; it did not begin to be known until the thirteenth century in the regions beyond the Pyrenees, whither apparently it was carried about 1300 by master-workmen from Spain and northern Italy; though before that time Spanish paper must have been exported there just as paper from Játiva was exported to the Orient. Correlated with this industrial and agricultural activity was very brisk commerce, especially in the Mediterranean. The Moslem merchant marine was the largest of the period, and its principal ports of loading and unloading were Seville, Málaga, and Almería. Trade was chiefly with North Africa (Morocco) and with Egypt, Constantinople, the coasts of the Black Sea (by which means the merchants communicated with Central Asia and India) and of western Asia (Palestine). Money was abundant in Moslem Spain. Among the several varieties of gold, silver, and copper coins the most important were the *dinar* (gold) and the *dirhem* (silver), both later imitated in the Christian kingdoms.

Prosperity of Moslem Life. The Great Cities

All this wealth and activity was reflected in the general comforts of life and in the luxury of the wealthy. Naturally, Córdova was the topmost expression of that prosperity. At its zenith, in the ninth and tenth centuries, it had 200,000 residences, 600 mosques, and 900 public baths patronized by all social classes; and was then one of the largest and richest cities in the world. Its streets were paved; piped water was supplied to its citizens. The houses, with blank façades pierced only here and there by a window, showed by a coat of whitewash, always fresh because often renewed (as is still the custom in Andalusia, the garden section of Valencia, and other districts) how highly cleanliness was esteemed. Interior walls were whitewashed too; and fountains, airy and sunlit patios, and decorations in vivid color made home-life pleasant. The palaces of the caliphs, the nobles, and the great merchants and landowners were sumptuous, as were the mosques. The Great Mosque at Córdova had 21 doors and 1200 columns of marble and jasper with gilded capitals. The pulpit was of marble and exotic woods, lighted by hundreds of lamps, many of them of silver.

On a less extensive scale than at Córdova but similarly expressive of wellbeing and vitality, were such other Spanish Moslem towns as

Seville, Málaga, Granada, Almería, Toledo, Murcia, and Saragossa. Their fame and that of Moslem culture attracted numbers of travelers, not only Moslems from Africa and Asia but also Christians from France, Italy and other countries, as well as visitors from the nearby Spanish kingdoms. Gerbert's has been mentioned as a typical case. Thanks to the religious tolerance already noted, it was not unusual to see in Córdova foreign monks who lodged in the several monasteries on the city's outskirts. Spanish monks and clerics also traveled through other European countries. Instances in point are Recesmund, Bishop of Elvira, sent by Abd-er-Rahman as Ambassador to the Court of Otto the Great (Germany) and some monks and abbots of the Spanish March who visited Italy time and again, especially in the lifetime of Gerbert both before and after he became Pope. Such contacts of Spanish and foreign Christians with the Cordovan focus of culture, like those effected by way of Italy with other Moslem populations, were (together with the pilgrimages to Santiago de Compostela of which we have further to say) the means by which in Spain, and in the rest of Europe, the inventions and discoveries made by the Arabs were being broadcast: Arabic numerals, the compass, windmills, Greek medicine as well as the new Moslem medical lore and other branches of science, oriental literature, and all the different elements of non-Christian civilization. The intensiveness of such assimilations was exemplified by the medical school of Salerno, in Italy, which, inaugurated in the tenth century, by the eleventh was already a vastly important center of research and experiment on the basis of books translated from Arabic. We have mentioned already the center at Ripoll in Spain, likewise dating from the tenth century.

The Mozárabes and Their Influence

The principal medium for transmission of these influences to Christian Spain was the Mozárabes who, since they dwelt among the Moslems, learned and took over much from the latter, even while because of their religious and juridical freedom and their loyalty to the Visigoth traditions (already cited), they preserved not a few elements of the former culture, among them the *Liber Iudiciorum* and the Latin language. They represented in consequence a cultural factor within the Caliphate itself as well as in the Christian kingdoms to which they journeyea on the emigrations of which we have spoken, or into which they were incorporated with the onward surge of the Reconquest.

We still find today expressions of this culture, especially as regards the central and western part of the Peninsula; in the monumental art and architecture built on the Duero tableland and in other districts after the beginning of the tenth century (San Miguel de Escalada, San Baudel de Berlanga, Santa María de Melque, Lebeña, Peñalba, Celanova, San Salvador de Palat, Sahelices del Río, and others), which are in contrast to the modest proportions of those that had been constructed previously in the kingdom of Asturias. These Mozárabic architectural monuments reflect the Moslem art of the Caliphate, including the architectonic innovations of the Mosque of Córdova, and their style soon spread northward; while at the same time it was reproduced in Spanish territories under Moslem domination and influenced contemporaneous monuments of architecture and those of later centuries in various regions of Italy as well as in western France, England, and Moslem lands of Asia and Africa.

In the field of economics it should be noted that the monies circulating at that period in the Spanish Christian kingdoms were for the most part Moslem; a condition that continued for some time thereafter.

The Mudéjares

Moslem influence in the Christian territories was exerted also by the Mohammedan populations who yielded as the Reconquest advanced and who, unlike the prisoners of war, were respected in their rights by the Christian Kings with regard to freedom, religion, and special laws. These Moslems were known as *Mudéjares,* and they represented in Christian Spain the same principle of tolerance in living together which the Mozárabes had represented in the Caliphate. The number of Mudéjares increased decidedly after the beginning of the eleventh century. The continuous daily contact of Moslem and Christian caused many Arabic words to be adopted by the Spaniards in common usage, and often these words are integrated fully into modern Spanish. On the other hand the frequent journeys to Córdova made by Christians—including many Kings of Castile and Aragón and Counts of Barcelona—and the mixed marriages then deemed valid between members of the two races, were strengthening these influences constantly.

Relations between Christians and Moslems during the
First Centuries of the Reconquest

The war of the Reconquest had a very special character in its first centuries. Though it lasted for eight hundred years, it was not absolutely continuous. As we have said, the military expeditions as a general rule were seasonal; made at certain periods of the year only. In the intervals of peace, Christians and Moslems communicated with each other and on many occasions lent reciprocal aid. It was frequently the case, therefore, that Moslem kings (after the disappearance of the Caliphate) sought in their conflicts with one another assistance from the Christian kings with whom they were allied or whom they regarded as friendly, or strove to enlist the support of renowned Spanish captains. For their part, the Christian kings and nobles in their own civil wars sought aid of the Moslems; and when forced to flee into exile or when pursued by their enemies, took refuge in Moslem cities. Among refugees of this sort were Sancho I the Fat of León and his grandmother Queen Tota, and later on Alfonso VI of Castile and others.

Mixed marriages were of frequent occurrence. As is natural, only in the case of notable personages have accounts of such marriages been preserved, but it is highly probable that there were many in all social classes. Among the first were the weddings of a daughter of the Moslem chief of Aragón, called Muza, with a Count García; of Doña Sancha, daughter of the Aragonese Count Asnar Galindo, with the Moorish King of Huesca; of Muza, offspring of the above-mentioned marriage, with a daughter of the Navarrese King Jimen Garcés; of a noble Christian lady with the Cordovan Prince Abdullah (they became grandparents of Abd-er-Rahman III) ; of the Caliphate's famous General Almansor with a Christian princess believed to be daughter of King Sancho II of Navarre; of Alfonso VI with Isabel (Zaida) , daughter of the Moslem King of Toledo; and there were many other such alliances. One curious thing about these unions is the fact that, although according to Koranic law the Christian woman was not obliged to change her religion in order to contract marriage with a Moslem, some of the brides became Mohammedans nevertheless. Almansor's wife is known to have done so.

Most assuredly, these cordial relations, which by no means prevented resumption at every opportune occasion of the struggle for the

Reconquest, must have been strongest between Christians living in Moslem territory—the Mozárabes—and their rulers. As regards Córdova, we know that some Christian holidays, such as St. John's Day and the first day of the year, were celebrated by Moslems and Christians jointly. In Almansor's reign, the troops (among whom, as we know, were many Christians) had Sunday as a general holiday. There were cases of mutual tolerance reaching such a point as to countenance use of separate sections of the same building as mosque and church respectively.

Naturally, these friendly interchanges decreased in proportion as the territory under Moslem control was whittled down, the Christian kingdoms widened their borders to include greater numbers of Mozárabes, and Christian power grew along with Christian military prestige. Nor did friendly relations when existent exclude (especially in the last centuries of the Reconquest) the fervent and ceaseless work of Catholic proselytism among Moslem populations in Christian territories, nor silence public polemics, religious in nature, which had the same purpose. In other words, the tolerance was rather a political measure which was not carried over in the long run (though during the first centuries it was) into religious matters, not even into social respect for another man's creed such as is the rule today. The same thing held true with regard to the Jews, who were esteemed in Christian territories chiefly for their culture and their propensity for work, which fact was no bar to the religious controversies often stirred up by the preaching of Catholicism.

Population and Culture in Reconquered Territory

On the other hand, the slowness of the advance of the Reconquest during the first three centuries, from the beginning of the eighth to the beginning of the eleventh, was not wholly due to Moslem military superiority and unified strength. The Moslems had additionally in their favor the fact that they were in possession of the richest and most densely populated regions of Spain, which afforded them abundant resources for sustenance and prosperity. The Spanish groups that started the Reconquest, on the contrary, for a long period of time had nothing but mountainous lands, poor and hard to cultivate. The first extension of their frontiers brought them only unpopulated areas and untilled terrain, as was the case with the Asturians when they descended from their peaks to the tableland of León which ever since the Moslem conquest in the seventh century had been evacuated—for no ascertainable reason—as far as the Duero river. The Franks encountered the same situation, as we have seen, when, penetrating into Spanish territory, they found themselves on the similarly desolate and abandoned soil of northern Catalonia.

In these circumstances, the most pressing need of the new kingdoms was, as already stated, to settle the land and cultivate subsistence crops. The Christian kings gave their best efforts to this twofold task. Accordingly, on expeditions against Moslem-controlled territory that they could not conquer definitively, they carried off as many of the inhabitants as they could; sometimes Mozárabes, who preferred to return to live among Christians, and again Moslem prisoners whom they enslaved. Voluntary immigration of Mozárabes who flocked to the Christian kingdoms as they observed the progress of the Reconquest also helped solve the problem of population.

With regard to breaking the ground of terrain previously uncultivated, as the settlers were doing in their own interest, the monks, especially those of the Order of St. Benedict, who founded many monasteries and were dedicated to agriculture, were both an aid and an example. The principal monasteries, both in early and later centuries of the Reconquest, were those of Sahagún, Escalada, Mazote, Castañeda, and Vime, in the region of León; all these were established by religious who proceeded from Moslem territory, preferring to dwell among Christians, and are apart from other Orders of later foundation, such as those of Cluny and Cister. In the region of Castile, the most important monasteries of the time were at Silos, Oña, and Arlanza. Contemporaneous monasteries in Catalonia have been noted already.

By these several means, many localities of Galicia, Asturias, León, Aragón, and the Spanish March were being resettled. Every new group of pioneers and every league of earth brought into production augmented the strength of the nascent kingdoms and heightened their economic and military resources for the Reconquest. When the Caliphate ceased to exist, at the beginning of the eleventh century, the disappearance of so formidable an enemy coincided with the increase achieved by the Spaniards in wealth and in the number of troops they could muster. The conjunction of all these favorable circumstances made possible the extremely important advance effected later on, which we shall discuss in due course. The terms of the problem were now reversed: the Moslems, though secure in possession of the most fertile regions (Andalusia, the valleys of Aragón, the Mediterranean littoral of Murcia and Tarragona), were already weak militarily because they were divided; the Christians, however, were strong and could turn to advantage the division and rivalries that had set the Moslems to wrangling among themselves.

How Villages and Cities Were Governed

When an abandoned village or city was resettled or a new one was founded, the inhabitants (aside from the authority of the Count, in representations of the King or of the particular Lord) adopted measures for keeping local government in their own hands in accordance with their common interests, as has always been the way of humankind in such cases. The title of "Count," which dated from Visigothic times, was applied during centuries of the Reconquest, and thereafter, as much to some of the nobles who were functionaries of the King's Court as to the Governors entrusted by the monarchs, as we have just said, with direction of the districts or variously denominated sections (*Mandationes, Condados* or Counties) into which their territory was divided. A very curious late tenth century document gives us the form of one such grant, as follows: "Alfonso, King [it was Alfonso IV]. To our cousin Don Gutierre. By this our most serene precept and mandate, we name you to govern the County of Carioca, Castelión, the half of Laura, Saliniano, Joserio and Ortigueira, in such manner that all these towns obey you for our benefit and that they comply with and without exception execute whatsoever may be commanded and ordained by us. And we shall permit and tolerate none to disturb you in the least."

The counties were not all equal in size and importance. Large and small, they must have been many, to judge from the names of those we know. These names show too that some counties had an important population as center (León, Astorga, Lugo, Burgos); and others, small towns or more or less sizable districts (Liebana, Bureba, Deza, Oca, Alava, Asturias de Santillana).

There were also Counts who, while not Governors, ruled sections that were their own private property, their relation to the settlers on it being that of landowner to whom rather than to the King the tillers of the soil paid tribute; but we are not sure what degree of dependence or independence these counties maintained with respect to the monarch. It is probable that normally the Count paid the King tribute or rendered him stated services in exchange for being left to do as he pleased in all other matters.

The prevailing moral condition of the population in those days and the economic dependence of even the most important cities on agriculture and stockraising, were responsible for the fact that the common interests of the group lay chiefly in fields and herds. Consequently, their assemblies or *juntas* touched only on matters relating to such things, as had likewise been the case in the villages of Visigothic times.

The Councils or Assemblies

Tenth century documents call these *juntas,* or meetings, councils or *concilios,* employing the Latin word that means any kind of assembly, congress, or meeting. From it is derived the Spanish word, *concejo,* which we still use. In those times *concilio* also meant the tribunal or juridical assembly for each of the districts (*Mandation* or County) that the free men of the region were forming from territory ruled by the Count, or sometimes by the Bishop if there were one in the locality. However, what is most helpful to us in visualizing life as it was lived in the *villas* and villages is the non-judicial *concilio.*

The matters with which that *concilio* dealt (which, as we have remarked, were the general interests of the neighborhood) were the grazing lands and woodlands held in common and used for the flocks and herds of all the men of the township; the juridical relations among landowners with regard to right of way for livestock, horsemen and pedestrians, or for apportionment of water from irrigation canals where such existed; the sale of lands whenever the case arose; the setting of wages for field labor and of prices for produce brought to market, as well as establishment of standard weights and measures with penalties for violation; in short, those practical interests of the neighborhood which were the basis of its material existence and were therefore logically held to be matters of prime importance. Such was the *concilio* of the villages in the vicinity of León, to which were being extended a large part of the *fuero* or grant of rights given to that city in 1020.

Nevertheless, the difference between the capital and the villages was already noticeable by the beginning of the eleventh century and later resulted in different attributes as regards their respective *concilios.* On the other hand, the dependence of town on country, already noted, continued to be evidenced, among other things, by the very fact of territorial division.

What a Tenth-Century Christian City Was Like

We may picture to ourselves the general arrangement of a city of the period and its government by taking León as an example. What we now call a municipality [or county], whether León or another, in those days included several townships. Each had its own *concilio,* with one inclusive *concilio* at the capital, general for all the territory. The city consisted of the following: in the center, the core of the population, with homes and gardens and fenced hay-fields; beyond, the fields and meadows under private ownerships; and yet beyond these, the *ejidos (exiti* or *exidos)* —pastures, forests, and other communal holdings.

The main importance of the city proceeded from its having more population, greater wealth, and better housing, and from the facts that the official authorities lived there and it was more strongly fortified; surrounded, that is, by walls and towers, a highly advantageous feature in those times of continual warfare. Today it is hard for us to realize how advantageous it was, accustomed as we are to the great security normally surrounding us and to the protection afforded by civil authorities, the police, and the like. But from the eighth to the eleventh century, and even later, city walls and watchtowers were a great benefit. Men have always set store by peace and tranquillity, even in those periods when strife was most usual. The Kings and the Catholic Church bent their efforts toward securing those two requirements in so far as possible, given the turbulent condition of the ruling classes and the rancors and jealousies that continually flared up into armed conflicts. The city walls and the separate fortresses—the castles— were of very material assistance in warding off some of the ever present dangers.

In the realm of morals, another means was invented, known as "the peace and truce of God"; initiated, it is believed, about the middle of the eleventh century (in 1041) at the *concilio* of Toulonges, a French *villa* near Perpignan (if identification of that place with *Tuluges* be correct) and soon thereafter introduced into Catalonia, whence probably it spread throughout all Spain. The truce of God was prohibition of any fighting, unless against the Moslems, on certain days of the week —from Wednesday night until Monday morning—and on important holidays. In order to have the truce duly observed, the nobles (who were the principal instigators of civil warfare because of their disputes one with another and their frequent depredations on merchants and on the houses, lands and treasure of prosperous lower-class working-men) were threatened for infractions of it with fines and with penance imposed by the Church; such penance then being greatly dreaded because of the people's profound religious faith. Tribunals were also formed which were known as Peace Tribunals.

Everything that has been said above, especially with reference to León and Castile, is also true in general of the other Christian kingdoms. The differences among them are differences in detail and emphasis; now one of the social and political factors (king, landed nobility, clergy, municipalities) and now another being in the ascendant; and sometimes there is a chronological difference—that is, a variation as to priority of date for institutions or events. But the fundamental problems and basic needs were the same in all the kingdoms.

Chapter VIII

The Great Christian Advance from the Eleventh to the Thirteenth Century and the Beginning of Cultures Properly Termed Spanish

General Characteristics of the Period

THE PERIOD extending from the fall of the Caliphate of Córdova in 1031 to almost the middle of the thirteenth century was of capital importance in every aspect of Spanish history. Three great events characterized it: first, the remarkable advance of the Christian Reconquest, which progressed from the line of the Duero river reached in the tenth century to the Guadalquivir on the South and the Mediterranean littoral on the southeast (Valencia, Alicante, Murcia); second, the concentration of the various political centers constituted at the beginning of the eighth century (kingdoms of Asturias-León, Navarre, Castile, Aragón; counties of Catalonia absorbed by the County of Barcelona; Basque Provinces) into two large units (Kingdom of León and Castile, with two of the Basque districts; kingdom of Aragón, with Catalonia), besides the little realm of Navarre; third, appearance and development of the Romance languages (Galician, Castilian, Catalán and its derivatives), and, correlatively, commencement of the respective cultures in which were already perceptible the characteristics belonging to the Spanish genius and to its regional variants.

140

We shall proceed to examine the three events in detail, and with them another, which should be considered along with the second of these—that is to say, the general movement toward concentration and union—not on account of its conformity to the prevailing pattern but of its departure from it. This last event is the dismemberment of territory in the western part of the Peninsula, from the river Miño on down, with subsequent affirmation of itself politically and nationalistically as an entity separate from the other Hispanic groups: birth pangs, in other words, of the kingdom of Portugal.

Commencement of the New Territorial Advance

In 1035, four years after the fall of the Caliphate of Córdova, Ferdinand I, son of Sancho the Great of Navarre, mounted the throne of Castile. Two years later (1037), victorious in war against the King of León, Bermudo or Vermudo III, Alfonso V's son and successor, he united both kingdoms under his single mandate; and in another, later war against his brother García, King of Navarre, the same Ferdinand recovered the territories of Rioja and Bureba which Sancho the Great had won by conquest years before. Thanks to Ferdinand, the eastern frontier of Castile in this section was to be from that time forward the river Ebro.

A born warrior, Ferdinand I was fired with the idea of Reconquest. Circumstances favorable to its being carried out in great part were concurrence of the splitting up of the Caliphate of Córdova and of the growth in population and wealth represented by union of the Christian kingdoms of León and Castile. Ferdinand knew how to utilize every possible advantage in these factors, directing his campaign chiefly toward the south in order to attain the banks of the Tagus; and on the west attacking the central region of the ancient Lusitania, below the Duero river.

Campaigning toward the Tagus, he conquered the northern part of the Moslem kingdom of Toledo in 1062, thus establishing the Castilian frontier very close to that river. In the Lusitanian undertaking, he took Viseo, Lamego, and Coimbra, advancing Christian borders to the Mondego river, a little north of the Estrella sierra (1057-1064). In western Soria he took San Esteban de Gormaz on the Duero, southwest of Osuna, and also made an invasion toward Valencia which because

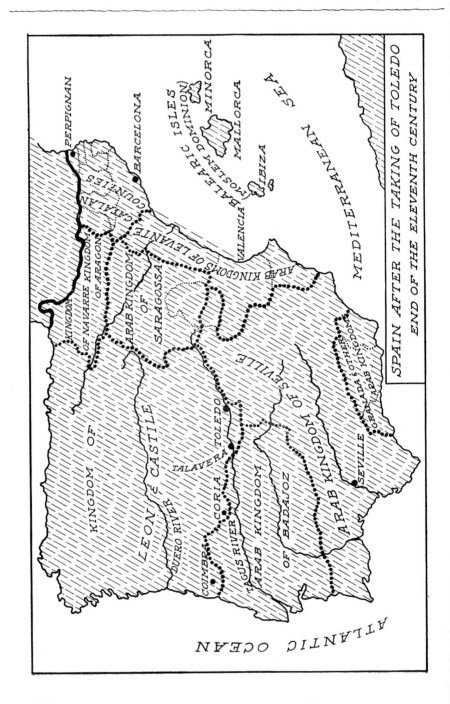

SPAIN AFTER THE TAKING OF TOLEDO
END OF THE ELEVENTH CENTURY

of his illness (he died soon after) produced only a single victory over the Moslems, at Paterna.

Aside from the territorial acquisitions noted, Ferdinand, because of the moral effect of these and of his fame as a warrior, succeeded in making the Moslem Kings of the *taifas* of Saragossa, Badajoz, Seville and Toledo declare themselves his tributaries; that is to say, bind themselves to pay him fixed sums annually in recognition of his superiority, and also with the practical purpose of not merely insuring themselves against attacks by him but actually obtaining his protection and assistance in case of need. The contribution thus paid was called *parias* at that time; but the system did not last long, because as a general rule the Christian Kings who followed Ferdinand I preferred to take outright possession of conquered Moslem forts and lands.

The Conquests of Alfonso VI

Ferdinand I, with a lack of discretion not unusual in monarchs of those days, which was inherent in their patrimonial attitude toward monarchy and which his own political experience was not great enough to overcome, instead of seeing to it that the political unity achieved by himself should endure, divided his kingdom into three parts—Castile, León, and Galicía—in order to satisfy his three sons. But the rivalries and clashing ambitions of the three very quickly provoked fratricidal conflicts that, after various permutations, ended by Alfonso VI's making himself master of the three Crowns with all their territories.

Two armed incursions into the region of Seville, whose Moslem King, Motamid, saved his throne for the time being by paying double tribute, and intervention in Toledo, where Alfonso aided the petty king, Cádir, to whom he owed personal favors, in recovering the crown, constituted the prelude to the principal military achievement of Alfonso VI. That was the taking of Toledo, a fortified city of considerable strategical importance because it dominated the Tagus river border and also because of its local topography. Hence, this conquest, effected in 1085, represents a decisive moment in the change in the respective positions of Moslem and Christian power.

The army that Alfonso VI collected for conquering Toledo was large and various, made up of Spaniards from diverse regions: Castilians, Leonese, Galicians, Asturians, Biscayans, Navarrese, and Ara-

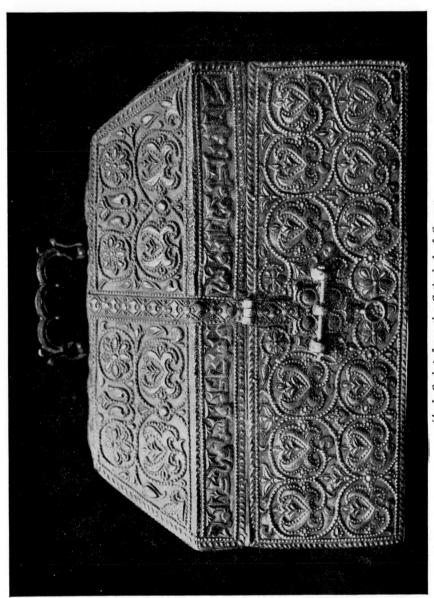

Arab Casket, from the Cathedral of Gerona.

gonese, these last being led by their own King, Don Sancho. There were also foreigners among them, including many Frenchmen and some soldiers from Italy and Germany; which fact was very soon to bear consequences of fundamental importance in Peninsular politics. The population of Toledo, for its part, like many others in the ancient Caliphate, was composed of Mozárabes, Moslems (a large number of whom were Renegades) and Jews. Upon the surrender of the city, King Alfonso promised the Moslems who wished to remain there that he would respect their lives and property, permit them to preserve their own laws and judges, impose no new tributes, and let them continue to celebrate their religious rites in the principal Mosque. These were the conditions usually granted the Mudéjares. Accordingly, though many Moslems left Toledo to follow their King, who was afforded safe conduct to Valencia, others remained in the conquered city. The importance of the loss of Toledo, with its strategic situation dominating the Tagus valley, greatly affected Moslem morale, and contributed considerably therefore to speedy reconquest of many other cities in the same zone, from Talavera on the west to Uclés and Cuenca on the east. That conquest also permitted resettlement on a permanent basis of such other cities and districts in the rear as Salamanca, Avila, Arévalo, Olmedo, Medina, Segovia, and Cuéllar.

Population and Government of Toledo

The Castilian King, either because he wished to keep the Moslems under observation by and subjection to a Christian majority, or because the city and outlying districts as a whole were underpopulated, issued a call to all men who desired to go to Toledo, encouraging them to do so by offer of houses and lands. He made the same offer to the foreigners who had taken part in conquest of the town, and to other auxiliary troops; and as compliance with these promises gave Toledo an extremely heterogeneous population with a hodgepodge of nationalities. Each national group was granted its own special law or *fuero*. There were four such *fueros:* one for the Moslems now transformed into Mudéjares; another for the Jews; a third for the foreigners, Frenchmen for the most part, and consequently called inclusively "the Franks"; and the fourth for the Castilians. Each of these groups had its own judges and chiefs and its own law different from the rest, including the groups that, while both Spanish and Christian, were of different regional origins. Thus the Mozárabes continued to be ruled strictly by the Visigothic *Liber Iudiciorum,* which about a century and a half later came to be called, in the Castilian Romance tongue, the *Fuero Juzgo;* and the Castilians observed the laws of their own kingdom which differed in much from those of the *Fuero Juzgo.* For the general government of the city the King set up two mayors, one Mozárabic and the other Castilian, but he gave the former a certain degree of supremacy.

The case of Toledo should be regarded as a typical example of the method followed with regard to most of the towns of the time that were being reconquered from Moslems and resettled by Christians.

The Mosque of Toledo and Archbishop Bernard

Queen Doña Constance, Alfonso VI's second wife, was French by birth and naturally cherished an affection for her fellow-countrymen. Among the many Frenchmen who had come to Toledo was Bernard, a monk of the Order of Cluny, Abbot of Sahagún. The King had him made Archbishop of Toledo, and, in order to add authority and lustre to the Archbishopric, bestowed on it many *villas* and villages and several castles, as well as farms, mills, and numerous houses and shops or markets; so that with the income from all this property, the Cathedral and its services were richly endowed. Because of this, and of the confirmation of the rank of "Primate of Spain" assigned the Archbishop by Pope Urban III, the mitre of Toledo became one of the wealthiest, if not the wealthiest, in Spain, and its prelate the highest-ranking Spanish cleric. This Archbishopric was to be held later by many of the priests who have loomed largest in Spanish history, influencing it not only in the realm of religion but also politically and culturally.

The Archbishop Don Bernard, as a foreigner, was not much acquainted with the sentiments and ideas of Spaniards, and apparently did not understand the tolerant community life that Spaniards lived alongside Mudéjares and Jews. So either on that account or because of the strict ideas characteristic of the monks of Cluny, the Archbishop, in complete accordance with the French-born Queen but disregarding the concessions granted by the King, had a squadron of soldiers take over the principal Mosque in a surprise attack and convert it into a Christian church. The Mudéjares rioted against this abuse of their

Madrid: *National Archeological Museum*

Ivory Cross, from San Isidoro de León.

law and *fuero;* and King Alfonso, who was away on a trip when he received news of the occurrence, hastened back to Toledo, greatly upset and determined upon punishing the guilty and returning the Mosque to the Moslems. The latter, whether from generosity or prudence, asked the King to pardon the offense. He replied that the insult had been not to them only, but to him as well, since the King's was the highest authority, to which all subjects owed obedience and respect. But the Moors insisted, stressing the argument that to punish the guilty would mean to make all Moslems suffer the consequences of stored-up resentment as soon as Alfonso himself should die. Accordingly, they renewed their plea to the monarch that he pardon the Queen and the Archbishop, but make sure that thereafter the other Moslem rights should be respected. Alfonso VI let himself be persuaded in the end, and thereby avoided plunging Toledo into mourning.

The Cathedral of Toledo

The edifice of the ancient Mosque, thus transformed into a Catholic Cathedral, was replaced two centuries later by the present Cathedral, Gothic in style, the cornerstone of which was laid August 12, 1227, when León Ferdinand III reigned in Castile and Don Rodrigo de Rada occupied the Archbishopric of Toledo. It was more than two hundred years in building, and was added to in later centuries. Among the sculptured figures adorning the chancel, or high altar, is one of the Moor Abu Walid, the Mudéjar *alfaquí* or savant, who was spokesman for the Moslems when they urged King Alfonso VI not to inflict punishment on the despoilers of the Mosque.

The Mozárabic Missal

Toledo was also site of another important episode in the religious history of Spain, one that originated in great part, as had the incident of the Cathedral, with the brethren of Cluny.

The Mozárabes owned several churches in Toledo wherein they observed the prayer service, manner of saying mass, and other rites of the Church according to the forms that had been established in Visigothic times, some Visigothic prelates having been personally concerned with their composition. But in Rome other rules, and another way of saying prayers and the mass, had been evolving; and the time

Tapestry depicting the Creation, from the Cathedral of Gerona.

arrived when the Popes, strongly supported by the monks of Cluny, claimed that the Roman rules (the "Roman rite" or "missal") were the only ones valid in the Catholic Church. The Roman rite was adhered to in Aragón in 1071, and in 1077-78 in Castile; and received sanction in 1085 from the Council of Burgos, which abolished the "Mozárabic rite" or "liturgy" throughout the realm.

When Toledo was conquered, the question of the rites surged up again, with respect to the churches there owned by the Mozárabes. Recalcitrant to giving up what they revered as a glorious tradition handed down from the time of St. Isidore, the Mozárabes resisted any such idea. It was finally agreed to let the matter be decided by certain means expressive of beliefs then prevalent as to the nature of Divine intervention in determining matters of human justice. Two such measures, or "judgments of God," were invoked in this instance: the judicial duel between a defender of the Mozárabic and a defender of the Roman rite; and the so-called "test by fire." The latter consisted of throwing into a bonfire the object under dispute, which if it did not burn was held to be innocent, with the right on its side. Accordingly, a great fire was laid in Toledo and when it blazed up, a copy of the Mozárabic missal and one of the Roman were flung upon the flames. The huge audience of townspeople crowding about the bonfire were praying aloud for a miracle to save the Mozárabic missal from burning. As a matter of fact, that is what happened, while the Roman missal was consumed to ashes. The judicial duel likewise resulted in favor of the Mozárabic missal. Such is the local tradition as set down two centuries later by an Archbishop of that city who wrote a History of Toledo. These events are supposed to have occurred in 1090.

The King, however, yielding to pressure of the Pope and of the monks of Cluny, commanded that the Mozárabic rite be abolished in Toledo also; although he conceded the special privilege of continuing it to six of the churches then existing in the city. The Mozárabes who still lived in Moslem territory also preserved their ancient rite. At least, we know that this was true of Valencia when Jaime I conquered it in 1238.

The Cid

One of the nobles of the Court of King Alfonso VI was Ruy, or Rodrigo, Díaz of Vivar, the Cid Campeador as the Moslems called

Barcelona: Museum of Art and Archeology

Apse, Sant Climent de Tarill.

him—"the Warrior Lord." A native of the city of Burgos or the neighboring village of Vivar, he was already a conspicuous figure at Court in Ferdinand I's reign (1035-1065), and later, serving in Sancho II's army (1065-1077), was at the siege of Zamora with that King when the latter was assassinated treasonably by a Zamoran called, so tradition says, Bellido Dolfos. The Cid witnessed the murder from afar, but, since his horse was not saddled and he was not spurred, could not reach Sancho in time to save him or punish his assassin. This incident, real or imaginary, gave rise to one of the most beautiful of the ballads, or *romances,* relating the poetic legend of the Cid; a legend that finds its highest expression in the *Poema,* or *Gesta, del Mio Cid,* written about the middle of the twelfth century. By means of this poem, generations have been enabled to see the figure of that great Castilian warrior, prototype of the Spanish captains who waged the mighty battle of Reconquest. The *Poema,* or Poem, however, is not a biographical account of the Cid, even when narrating actual occurrences; although in other ways and from other sources we can today reconstruct the life-story of that typical Castilian.

King Alfonso VI, Sancho II's successor, during the first years of his reign held Ruy (or Rodrigo) in high esteem and gave proof of this fact by marrying him to Jimena Díaz, daughter of the Count of Oviedo and niece of the King. Another evidence of regard was sending the Cid to Seville to receive in the King's name the tribute owed by the Sevillian Moslem monarch. Apparently this mission gave rise to one of the chief reasons for the estrangement that soon, and for many years thereafter, was to distance Alfonso VI from the Cid. The root of the matter was very typical of the epoch. The King of Seville was at war with the King of Granada, who was supported by several Castilian nobles, among them the very powerful Count García Ordóñez; but since the King of Seville was himself an ally of Alfonso VI, the Cid believed it his duty to aid that Moorish monarch and in one battle vanquished the soldiery of the other Moor, King of Granada, taking as prisoner his own Castilian countrymen and friends. From that time forth, Count García Ordóñez was one of the Cid's bitterest enemies, indefatigable in trying to turn King Alfonso against him.

The first occasion of real discord between Alfonso and the Cid, however, was the fact that the latter without the monarch's consent attacked the Moslem King of Toledo who, like the Moslem King of

Seville, was an ally of Alfonso VI. The latter was angered to the point of exiling the Cid in 1081—which is to say, of forcing him to leave Castile.

The Cid's Exile and Its Consequences

The fact of exile in that period meant the breaking of every legal tie of interdependence between the exiled noble and his king, so that the former was left free to offer his services as a warrior wherever he chose. The Cid elected to serve under the Moorish King of Saragossa with whom he was allied thereafter for many years and whose right arm in battle he became; the confidence thus shown him evidencing both the personal prestige of the Cid and the strength of the troops he commanded, made up for the most part of Castilian knights who were his friends and kinsmen. At the time, the King of Saragossa was at war with the King of Lérida, who, though likewise a Moslem, had the aid of the Christian King of Aragón and of the Count of Barcelona. In consequence, the Cid had to fight in defense of a Moslem kingdom not only against the Moslem troops of Lérida but also against Aragonese and Catalans. During that campaign (1082) he vanquished and took prisoner the Count of Barcelona. This feat was duplicated some years later in 1089 at which time the Cid, newly exiled by his King, had to fight once more as ally of the King of Saragossa against the Count of Barcelona. In this second war, as in the first, Ruy Díaz manifested chivalry and clemency, remarkable qualities in an age when it was not customary to show mercy to the vanquished.

The Cid's moment of crowning glory, culmination of his part in the Reconquest, was the taking of the city of Valencia and most of the Moslem kingdom of the same name, which since the fall of Toledo had been a dependency of the Crown of Castile. This state of dependency had origin in Alfonso's naming as King of Valencia in 1086 Cádir, who, as will be recalled, was erstwhile King of Toledo. When in 1092 Cádir was dethroned and put to death by an uprising of his own subjects, the Cid, desirous of avenging him, laid siege to Valencia and entered the town, making it a Christian seignory, or dominion, which recognized sovereignty of the monarch of Castile. In Valencia the Cid made his residence, living, in fact, as if he were king, until his death in 1099. He was always greatly beloved by his soldiers, and, in spite of the persistent animosity of Alfonso VI, honored by the Christian kings.

The Cid's daughters made brilliant marriages: María became the wife of Ramón Berenguer III, Count of Barcelona; Cristina, of the Aragonese Prince Ramiro. Jimena, widow of the Cid, continued to be a powerful personage in Valencia until in 1102 she abandoned the city on advice of the Castilian King, who believed that the town could be held no longer against Moorish attacks. Jimena bore the body of the Cid with her, interring it anew in the Church of St. Peter of Cardeña at Burgos. Ruy Diaz de Vivar nobly personified the purest and loftiest type of the warrior nobility of his time, as well as the general aspiration for Reconquest.

The Almoravides and the Almohades

In the beginning there were seven of the *taifa* kingdoms of the Moslems, founded when the Caliphate came to an end: Seville, Granada, Murcia, Toledo, Badajoz, Saragossa, and Valencia. Their divisionism and rivalries not only facilitated advance of the Reconquest for the Christian kings, but prevented union of Moslem forces to resist that advance. However, after the capture of Toledo and Valencia with ensuent political consequences, those kings of *taifa* States who still preserved their thrones became extremely apprehensive about losing them and invoked the aid of the Moors of Morocco, called Almoravides, who had established there a very powerful Moslem empire.

The Almoravide Emperor Yusuf-ben-Taxfin gave the *taifa* kings the assistance they asked. He entered Andalusia at the head of Moroccan troops, and together with the Kings of Seville, Granada, Almería and Badajoz, proceeded toward Toledo to do battle with Alfonso VI who at the time was besieging Saragossa. Alfonso, augmenting his army with Aragonese and Catalan soldiers and some from the south of France, hastened to the fray. The two armies, the Moslem and the Christian, clashed at Sagrajas, or Zalaca (Badajoz) in October, 1086, and the Christians were completely routed. Yusuf, however, did not know how to press his advantage. Instead, he returned to Morocco. The *taifa* kings likewise were either ignorant of how to make the most of a positive advantage or unable to do so. In 1090 Yusuf returned to besiege the Castle of Aledo, a very strong Christian strategic outpost between Murcia and Lorca. Although unable to take it, he shattered the fortifications to such an extent that the Castilians abandoned the place, firing it as they retired.

Yusuf had something more in mind than merely fighting Christians. Repeating the occurrence of 711 some three centuries previous, he transformed himself from ally into master, annexing to his empire the lands of the *taifa* kingdoms (1090-91). Thereupon Moslem Spain became a dependency of the Almoravides of Morocco. But none of Yusuf's successors, notwithstanding their continual attacks on León, Castile, and Aragón, were able to push back the frontiers already attained by these realms, in spite of the taking of Valencia by the Almoravides, the defeat at Uclés in 1168, and other Christian reverses. Quite the contrary, the frontier of Aragón broadened southward with the conquest of Saragossa by Alfonso I in 1118.

A revolution mainly religious in character, provoked in North Africa by the Atlas mountaineers who had been incited by the sermons of the Mahdí Ben Tumrut, founder of the unitarian Almohade sect, dethroned the Almoravide Emperors of Morocco in 1122. The then Almoravide leader, Ali-ben-Yusuf, who was at the time resident in Spain, hastened to Morocco with his troops in order to put down the uprising, and the kings of the *taifa* kingdoms took advantage of his absence to declare themselves again independent. After a quarter of a century's fighting between Almoravides and Almohades in Morocco, the latter were victorious in the end and thereupon turned their attention to Spain, crossing in 1146 to the Peninsula, where the fact that a general religious discontent with the Almoravides was simmering in the Moslem kingdoms facilitated further victory. By 1172 the Almohades were in control of all Moslem territories on the Peninsula, and to these they added the Island of Mallorca in the early years of the thirteenth century.

However, the Almohades were not equally fortunate with regard to the Christian territories over which Alfonso VII was then reigning. In the series of campaigns that they directed against Castile and Aragón with alternate victories and defeats, the Almohades marked only an ephemeral advance after the great battle of Alarcos in 1195, which enabled them to occupy places as far north, in relation to Moslem domains, as Madrid, Guadalajara, and Uclés; but the Christian victories of Navas de Tolosa in 1212 and Fabraegen in 1213 forced them to withdraw south of the Sierra Morena again. That ended forever all hope of overturning the military power of the Christian kingdoms of Spain. To complete the Almohade disaster, Spanish Moslems rebelled so violently against their new masters that when the Almohades were dethroned in Morocco, the *taifa* kingdoms in Spain once more split up along the old lines and set to warring among themselves until the great thirteenth-century Castilian and Aragonese conquest (soon to be related) left Moslem territory reduced to the Kingdom of Granada, founded by Alhamar of the Nazarita family. This Kingdom of Granada, so termed because in 1238 Alhamar made the city of that name his capital, included at the time of its origin (about the middle of the thirteenth century) the territories of Granada, Málaga, and Almería, the southern part of Jáen, and also the southern portion of the Province of Cádiz.

The Union of Aragón and Catalonia

The first of the two great political concentrations (achievement of which has been noted as being one of the characteristic events of the epoch) was the union of Aragón with what was called the Principality of Catalonia, which is to say, the territories that were then hereditary property of the Counts of Barcelona. This union was due initially to the marriage, celebrated in 1137, of the Aragonese Princess Petronilla, only daughter of King Ramiro II, with Ramón Berenguer IV, Count of Barcelona. The two realms were not combined into one as immediate consequence of the marriage, although Ramón Berenguer, as a man, played a considerable part in the public life of his wife's kingdom; but their son, first called Ramón and later Alfonso (the Second of Aragón) inherited the dominions of both his mother and his father. Thus commenced the personal union of Aragón and Catalonia which thereafter formed a single monarchy.

The Counts of Barcelona, sovereign princes of Catalonia, contributed to this monarchy the extensive possessions that they had acquired piece by piece, principally through inheritance, in the south of France. These acquisitions gave rise to rivalries and wars with the French kings but also created a political strength that was to produce very important international consequences for Spain and for Europe. In 1076 such French possessions included the Counties of Toulouse, Carcassonne, Manerbes, Narbonne, Sabert and Foix, to which were later added, as we shall see, those of Sardinia and Provence. The last-named territory extended eastward to Nice.

On the Spanish side of the Pyrenees, little territorial advance was marked under the two Counts who ruled from the time of Ramón Berenguer's death in 1076 to Ramón Berenguer IV's accession fifty-five years later—that is, Berenguer Ramón II (1076-96) and Ramón Berenguer III called the Great (1096-1131). It is believed that Berenguer Ramón II conquered Tarragona in 1091. As for Ramón Berenguer III, in 1106, in alliance with the Count of Urgel, he seized the *villa* of Balaguer, in northeastern Lérida, which even so late as that time was still in power of the Moslems. He also made armed incursions against the city of Tortosa and into Valencian territory; and with aid of Italian sailors from Pisa, rendered tributary the islands of Mallorca and Ibiza. By voluntarily declaring himself vassal, the Count of Ampurias in 1123 brought about what amounted substantially to the incorporation of his domains into territory of the Barcelonese State.

The Conquests of the Kingdom of Aragón

For its part, the Kingdom of Aragón had succeeded in greatly enlarging its territories since its establishment as a monarchy in 1035. At that date it included one exiguous area: the strip extending from the valley of the Roncal on the west to that of the Gistain on the east. A little later, in 1037, the King acquired by inheritance from his brother Gonzalo the districts of Sobrarbe and Ribagorza which extended his eastern frontiers. The second King of Aragón, Sancho Ramírez (1064-1094) made the first important thrust of the Reconquest into territories further south held by Moslems of the kingdom of Saragossa. He fortified the southwestern border (Marcuello, Loarre, and Alquezar) and from that vantage attacked and took the fortified towns of Barbastro (1065) and Monzón (1089), and reached Montaragón (1091) and Huesca. It was at the siege of Huesca in 1094 that Sancho Ramírez was slain by an arrow.

His successor, Pedro I (1094-1104) succeeded in conquering Huesca in 1096, and five years later recaptured Barbastro, which had been lost not long before, as well as other towns and castles. Alfonso I the Battler who next ascended the throne (1104-1134) advanced the frontiers of Aragón considerably by conquests of Ejea (1110), Saragossa (1118?), Tudela, Borja, Tarazona, Calatayud (1120), Ariza and Daroca; that is to say, practically the whole of the present Provinces of Huesca and Saragossa. With the taking of Montreal del Campo, north of the Sierra

Museum, Vic

Romanesque frontal, from Ripoll.

Palomera and south of Calamocha, the frontier of Aragón was made contiguous to the district of Teruel. A *rábida,* or hermitage, was established there; a religio-military institute of frontier knights analogous to what Calatrava and Montresa represented in the Kingdom of Castile. The climactic episode of Alfonso I's campaign was the taking of Mequinenza (1133) in the southeastern part of the province of Saragossa. In some of these military undertakings he was aided by knights from the French territories of Gascony and Bearne. We shall examine later Alfonso I's conquests in Castile and León.

In 1125 and 1126 he had carried out an expedition which was more brilliant than effective in territories of Valencia, Murcia, and Andalusia, as far as the coast of Salobreña south of Motril; but the only benefit that this gave him was the not unimportant one of enabling him to take back from the districts through which he passed some 14,000 Mozárabes with whom he resettled part of Aragón.

After a brief reign by Ramiro II, the Kingdom of Aragón was governed by Ramón Berenguer IV, Count of Barcelona, already mentioned as husband of Ramiro's daughter, Doña Petronilla of Aragón. He made considerable territorial acquisitions, taking the fortified towns of Tortosa (1145) which meant command of the mouth of the Ebro and consequently of upstream navigation, Lérida (1149), Fraga, and, later on, the mountain district of Pradas between Tortosa and Tarragona.

Alfonso II, eldest son of Ramón Berenguer and Petronilla, inherited the County of Barcelona from his father and the Kingdom of Aragón from his mother, as we have said; and from this time on, both States had a common monarch whose title was King of Aragón. By inheritance from a cousin, Alfonso II obtained also the Duchy of Provence in 1166, and later that of Roussillon (1172). This gave him as vassals the Counts of Bearne and Bizorna while his younger brother Pedro, who was also his feudatory, maintained (in representation of the family holding of the County of Barcelona and by inheritance from their father Ramón Berenguer IV), the County of Sardinia, the Seignory of Carcassonne, and rights over Narbonne. Consequently, the territorial possessions and influence of the Kingdom of Aragón extended very considerably on both sides of the Pyrenees.

Alfonso II augmented the Spanish portion of his realm by his campaigns in the district of Teruel, the capital of which he conquered

Marble plaques adorning the San Félix Chest, from San Millán de la Cogolla.

Madrid: National Archeological Museum

and settled in 1171, making it his outpost against the Kingdom of Valencia. In 1102, three years after the death of the Cid, Valencia had fallen into Moslem hands again.

Pedro II and Loss of the Catalán-Aragonese Hegemony in Southeastern France

Pedro II, son of Alfonso II, continued the Reconquest in the region of Valencia and planned an expedition to Mallorca. He was forced to give up all idea of such an undertaking, however, because of matters touching on his possessions in southern France where the situation was decidedly critical because of the Albigensian heresy widespread among both upper and lower classes in the County of Toulouse and adjacent regions. [The Albigenses believed that a good spirit created the spiritual world, an evil spirit the material world, and that in consequence Christ could not have been incarnated in a human body which was a creation of the evil spirit. They also recommended suicide and condemned marriage.] Since the Albigensians, whom the Spanish friar St. Domingo de Guzmán tried to convert, constituted a threat not only to the established Church but to the social order, the Pope declared a Crusade against them. Thus the Count of Toulouse, Pedro II's brother-in-law, and the Viscount of Béziers and Carcassonne, his vassal, saw themselves directly endangered. French knights commanded by the famous Simon de Montfort composed the Crusade. The repression of the heresy which they were charged with putting down was marked by episodes of such cruelty in assaults on the settlements of Béziers and Carcassonne in 1209 as to cause St. Domingo de Guzmán himself to protest. Simon de Montfort was not content merely with achieving the punitive religious objective of the Crusade, but possessed himself of the vanquished towns and districts, an act that Pedro II consented to recognize. But fresh excesses of cruelty on de Montfort's part caused the Aragonese King, with good reason, to sally forth in defense of his French vassals. The expedition fared so badly, however, that in the first battle—that of Muret in 1213—Pedro was routed and slain. As premium of victory, Simon de Montfort received from the Council of Letrán (1215) almost all the Count of Toulouse's holdings and tried to obtain others in territories of Bizorne. The Crown of Aragón, in consequence of all this, lost the hegemony that it had enjoyed up to that time in southern France.

The Crown itself was inherited by the son of Pedro II and Marie de Montpelier, Jaime I, who in 1213 was still a minor. His extraordinary natural ability and intelligence caused him to triumph over the lawlessness that had broken out at his father's death, and won the respect of his subjects. He and Ferdinand III of Castile were the heroes of the strongest advance movement of the Reconquest that characterized the military picture in the thirteenth century.

Castile. Alfonso VII

While these events were taking place in Catalonia and Aragón, the Kingdom of Castile, after various vicissitudes of internal politics, continued its struggle with the Moslems and, as we shall see, advanced the Reconquest in so far as it could.

The death of Alfonso VI in 1109 ushered in a period of civil warfare in León and Castile, complicated by the matrimonial discord of his heiress, Queen Urraca, with her second husband, King Alfonso I of Aragón, discord giving rise to serious conflicts between the two kingdoms, in which state of things the most conspicuous figure was that of the Bishop of Santiago de Compostela, Don Diego Gelmírez, who typified the political-minded, fighting prelates of the period and was also an illustrious representative of the influence exercised in Spain by the monks of Cluny.

Alfonso I took advantage of the opportunity offered him as King Consort, and of the vagaries of Doña Urraca, to seize all Castile and almost the whole of León, and of Toledo as well; so that the Queen was left with practically no territory but Galicia, of which—not without resistance on her part—Prince Alfonso, her son by her first marriage with Don Raymond of Burgundy, was crowned King in 1111. After various ups and downs, mother and son were reconciled through Bishop Gelmírez' influence, whereupon both turned against Alfonso I of Aragón, their first objective being to recover the territories of León, Castile, and Toledo. Since Alfonso of Galicia was successful in this enterprise, he soon became King of León and Castile as Alfonso VII, being crowned as such in 1126. On the death of his stepfather, Alfonso I of Aragón, he became pretender to the Crown of that Kingdom too, but desisted from an attempt at its conquest after having invaded Aragonese territory, reconquered the districts adjacent to Nájera which had been annexed by Alfonso I, and entered into Saragossa in 1134, of which realm he was for a while titled King by cession of the then monarch of Aragón, Ramiro II.

Alfonso VII's campaigns against the Moslems were important. They helped to break Moslem power and to strengthen the force of Leonese and Castilian arms, but were, however, ineffective with regard to permanent territorial enlargement. A characteristic episode was the siege of Almería and taking of the town by assault, with participation of troops from all the Spanish kingdoms and of Catalán and Italian ships; but the fortress remained in Alfonso VII's power a mere ten years, from 1147 to 1157. His victory was equally inconclusive at Córdova, conquered in 1146 and lost in 1149. Not long before, Alfonso VII had taken the powerful fortress of Coria.

In another field, the elevation of Santiago de Compostela into a metropolitan archbishopric was due to Alfonso. Gelmírez continued as its prelate (1120) and the dioceses of Braga, Mérida, Salamanca, and Coimbra came to be its dependencies.

At his death in 1157, eleven years after entry of the Almohades into Spain, Alfonso VII incurred in the final error (more than once repeated by other monarchs during the Reconquest) of dividing his realm between his two sons, Sancho III, to whom he bequeathed the Kingdom of Castile, and Ferdinand II, to whom he left León.

Alfonso VIII of Castile; the Crusades and the Battle of
Navas de Tolosa

Sancho III reigned for a single year and was succeeded by his son Alfonso VIII. After a long and turbulent minority (he was only three years old when his father died), during which the rivalry of the two great noble houses of Castile, the Castros and the Laras, drenched the land in blood, Alfonso VIII began reigning at the age of fourteen. He soon distinguished himself as one of the most war-minded of the Christian monarchs and one of the most determined to push ahead with the Reconquest. Victories of his were the taking of Cuenca, a city of great military importance, in 1177, and the battle of Navas de Tolosa which he won over the Almohade Caliph in 1212.

That 1212 campaign took on the aspect of a Crusade, the name then generically applied to expeditions against the peoples called infidels. The kingdoms of Europe at that time were circled on the East and the South by Moslem peoples and States: those of Syria and Egypt

Cloister, Monastery of Sant Cugat del Vallès.

and those of Spain and northwest Africa. The former dominated the
territory of Palestine—that is to say, what was to the Christians the
Holy Land—and various other regions in Asia. The military expeditions termed Crusades were initiated toward the close of the eleventh
century with the object of seizing the Holy Land from the Moslems
and of converting the latter to Christianity. There were eight such
Crusades; the last took place in the twelfth century and was led by
King Louis IX, St. Louis of France. Different kings and countries participated in the Crusades: French, Belgian, Italian, German. The
Spaniards did not take part in them because they, as a matter of fact,
had been in perpetual crusade against the Moslems ever since the
eighth century, although they did not give that name to their campaigns of Reconquest nor did their soldiers wear the cross on the left
shoulder which was the Crusader's distinctive emblem. Hence, when
the Spaniards were once twitted for not joining with other peoples of
Europe on a Crusade in the East, a Spanish king, overhearing, replied
with simple truth, "We are always on Crusade!"

But Alfonso VIII wanted to publicize the 1212 campaign to check
the Moslem advance as a Crusade so that popular enthusiasm for it
would bring many volunteers to his army. Consequently he sent the
then Archbishop of Toledo, Don Rodrigo Ximénez de Rada, to
Rome to ask that the Pope grant indulgence to all those wearing a
distinctive cross or emblem who enlisted to fight the Moslems at their
own expense. Alfonso also notified the other Spanish Kings and the
Count of Portugal, laying before them the gravity of the situation,
since there was imminent the attack of a strong Almohade army commanded by its own Emperor. By virtue of these steps, many Spaniards
and foreigners gathered in Toledo, though almost all the latter soon
deserted, perhaps because they were exhausted by the heat and hard-
ships on the march toward Sierra Morena. Only the Archbishop of
Navarre, a native of Castile, with his troops remained, and the noble
Theobald de Poitiers with his. Among the Spaniards were the Kings
of Aragón and Castile.

With the Christian victory of 1212 at Navas de Tolosa in the
province of Jaen, Ubeda, Baeza, and other fortresses fell into power of
Alfonso VIII. Not long after, the victory of Fabraegen gave the Castilians temporary possession also of fortresses as important as Cáceres

Façade, Monastery of Sant Cugat del Vallès.

and Mérida, and later on (in 1229) of Badajoz and others that made sure their control over Estremadura.

The Frontier with Aragón in 1179

Another notable event of Alfonso VIII's reign was the celebration of a treaty (Cazorla, 1179) which initiated the series of treaties, terminating in the time of Jaime I, by means of which limits were fixed for the respective conquests of Castile and Aragón in Moslem territory. In accordance with this treaty, Aragonese conquests were to stop short at a line passing through the port of Biar in the present Province of Alicante, thus leaving to the Kingdom of Castile the remainder of the region of Alicante and Murcia, together with that of Albacete and Cuenca, conquered not long previous, as well as an open road to reconquering Andalusia.

The foundation and construction of the monastery of Huelgas at Burgos and of the center of General Study or University of Palencia date from the time of Alfonso VIII.

The Kingdom of León from 1157 to 1230

The new separation of León from Castile resulting from Alfonso VII's testament lasted only 73 years. During this period two Leonese Kings occupied the throne: Ferdinand II, who, as we know, was Alfonso VII's son, and Alfonso IX. The Kingdom of León then consisted not only of its traditional territory but also lands of Asturias and Galicia and regions of Estremadura bordering on Portugal.

Ferdinand II distinguished himself by his campaigns against the Moslems which won him the fortified towns of Jelves and Alcántara and brief occupation of Cáceres.

Alfonso IX took definitive possession of Cáceres and also of Mérida, Badajoz, and Elvas, thereby greatly advancing the frontier toward the south. These gains by Alfonso in the great enterprise of Reconquest were darkened by his wars against Castile, in the course of which he made alliance with the Moslems of Estremadura, though not without having the Pope threaten him with excommunication on that account. These family conflicts ended in 1197 with the marriage of Alfonso IX of León to one of the daughters of Alfonso VIII of Castile, Doña Berenguela. The son of this marriage was to become Ferdinand III— Saint Ferdinand, or San Fernando Rey.

The Lasting Union of Castile and León

That same event made possible the definitive union of Castile and León in 1230. On the death of Alfonso VIII of Castile in 1214, the Crown was inherited by his son Enrique I. Enrique became the ward of his sister, Doña Berenguela, who had been separated from her husband, Alfonso IX of León, by order of the Pope on the score of consanguinity. She retained her post as guardian very briefly, being obliged to yield it to one of the Castilian nobles of the Lara family; an occurrence that brought on fresh civil conflict such as had raged during the minority of Alfonso VIII and of other kings. But Enrique I, the new monarch, died prematurely in 1217 while still a minor, so that the Crown was inherited by Doña Berenguela who ceded it to her son, Ferdinand III. Alfonso IX of León opposed her doing so, notwithstanding the fact that he was Ferdinand's father, and invaded Castile for the purpose of preventing his son's accession to the throne. Alfonso of León's hostility toward the branch of his own family reigning in Castile was so great that when he died in 1230, he bequeathed the Crown of León to his two daughters by his first wife, who were therefore Ferdinand III's half-sisters. In consequence of Alfonso's action, the separation between the two kingdoms might have become permanent, had Ferdinand not been able to negotiate transfer of the Crown to himself, a solution accepted by his half-sisters in return for rich dowries.

Thus the two kingdoms, first separated in the tenth century and more than once at war with each other, came to be united permanently. Their former unions had been little lasting because some of the kings had lacked the political insight (of which other neighboring monarchs had full share) that would have made them increase their territory and thereby population and wealth, instead of diminishing it by slicing their realms into portions that as a general rule produced nothing but family quarrels.

The County and New Kingdom of Portugal

Among the notable events of the twelfth century was the formation of a new realm on the Peninsula: the Kingdom of Portugal. Its extraordinary importance arises from the fact that it was the means of breaking the geographical unity of the Iberian Peninsula and thus of influencing basically the life of the peninsular peoples. Broken as well was that *national unity* which the Romans had discerned as a possibility and had tried to bring about, considering the peninsula of *Hispania,* or Spain, as an integral whole. The formation, separately from the other Christian monarchies, of a Portuguese monarchy that from the beginning resisted union with the sister-States of which it was an off-shoot, was an event that originated in the first instance simply from the ambition of a French Count, a Spanish royal Princess, and their son; but instead of finding some such satisfactory settlement as had been arrived at by creation of Castile, in this case a State was evolved that held itself aloof from the others of the Peninsula, withdrew into itself, and eventually created a people and a national spirit ever more vigorous and more individualized, deeming itself utterly distinct from its elder sister-peoples, that is, the Galicians, the Leonese, and the rest who had been settling a large part of the territory of ancient Lusitania in proportion as the Kings of Asturias and León conquered it. The nascent *Portuguese people,* thus come into being, retained the Galician language spoken by the first inhabitants of the new realm, and by thus preserving that tongue from absorption into Castilian, made it the source of the Portuguese language which, while still at the present day revealing traces of its derivation, has acquired with the passage of time original forms and characteristics expressed in a great literature of its own.

The Kingdom of Portugal was formed in the following fashion. Alfonso VI was so grateful for the aid lent him by some French nobles in the conquest of Toledo that he not only gave his eldest daughter, Urraca, in marriage to Raymond of Burgundy but also wed his other daughter, Teresa, to Count Henry of Lorraine, to whom he granted lands between the Miño and Tagus rivers from which was formed a County including the cities of Braga, Oporto, Coimbra, Viseo, and Lamego. That County was called *Portucalense* (soon transformed into *Portugal*) and Henry of Lorraine received it as a vassal of the King of Castile, with obligation to pay the latter a fixed annual tribute and to supply 300 knights for Alfonso's army in the war against the Moslems. But Don Henry was ambitious, as were all men of his rank in that day and age, and the tumultuous state of affairs in Castile at the time afforded him an opportunity of giving his ambition free rein. He recruited soldiers in France for his undertaking, and made an alliance with his sister-in-law, Queen Urraca, Alfonso VI's daughter and successor, aiding her in the war against her husband, the King of Aragón. It is believed that she promised Don Henry in exchange additional territories north of the Miño and eastward toward Valladolid.

Don Henry of Lorraine died young in 1114; but his wife Teresa continued his ambitious projects. Striving to achieve them, sometimes with and sometimes against her sister, Queen Urraca, she seized every opportunity afforded her by the anarchic conditions in Castile. Thus, in 1119 Doña Teresa succeeded in gaining possession of the districts of Tuy and Orense until, when her troops had been defeated by the combined forces of Urraca and the latter's son, Alfonso VII, a peace pact was arrived at by terms of which Teresa obtained confirmation of the status as a kingdom of her County of Portucalense; a recognition given by Alfonso VII at a conference with Doña Teresa's son, Alfonso Henríquez, which was held at Zamora in 1143 and which assigned Portucalense additional territories in southern León and Castile. Such was the earliest origin of what came to be later the Kingdom of Portugal, first affirmed as such, on a date not certainly established, by Alfonso Henríquez over the King of Castile's protest. What can be stated definitely and substantiated is that Alfonso Henríquez called himself King on April 10, 1140, three years in advance of the Castilian King's formal recognition of the title. Portuguese historians, in order to explain their country's formation as a nation, add an ethnic factor that gave political strength to the Counts of Lorraine, proceeding from the Lusitanian population; a theory deserving of close study.

Consolidation of the new State's independence came later when it was recognized officially by Alfonso VIII of Castile. Alfonso X ratified this recognition approximately one hundred years later and was aided by the King of Portugal in conquering from the Moslems by Castilian arms the district called Algarve, which later on became part of Portugal.

The Kingdom of Navarre from 1035 to the End of the Fifteenth Century

Sancho the Great's division of the realms belonging to the Crown was most prejudicial to Navarre. It brought on rivalries between that monarch's sons and a series of struggles over domination of frontier territory or on account of personal enmity between the Navarrese

Kings of Castile and of Aragón. The result was that Navarre lost the districts of Rioja and Bureba and part of the lowlands of the territory properly Navarrese, and that the policy of its kings and lords oscillated between alliance with Castile against Aragón and alliance with Aragón against Castile. The prevailing tendency was to favor Aragón, which both in its people and in its land was closer to Navarre than was Castile; and that is why the Navarrese and Aragonese Kingdoms were for a while united under a single King through free choice of the Navarrese (1076-1134). Moreover, proximity to France had brought about in the Navarrese royal family, just as it had in the ruling house of the County of Barcelona, matrimonial alliances with the nobility on the other side of the Pyrenees; and in the final analysis the balance of Navarrese political life inclined toward France. The decisive event in this respect was accession to the throne of Navarre in 1234 of Theobald of Champagne, son of Count Theobald IV of Champagne and of Doña Blanca of Navarre, sister of the last Spanish king of that period, Sancho the Strong.

For many years thereafter—except for a brief fifteenth century interlude during which King Juan II of Aragón was King Consort of Navarre—the latter country was governed by kings of French origin belonging to the houses or dynasties of Champagne (1231-1305), Evreux (1328-1479), and Foix (1479-1512) and to the royal house of France itself (1307-1327). Because of this Navarre was out of the central current of Spanish life for about one hundred years, notwithstanding the Spanish roots of its people.

Incorporation into Castile of the Basque Provinces

In the reign of Alfonso VIII of Castile the Basque regions or provinces of Alava and Guipúzcoa were incorporated under his Crown.

Alava seems to have been linked politically with Asturias from the earliest times of the Asturian monarchy, although neither the measure nor the political scope of its dependence is quite clear. Later, we find mention of some Counts of Alava who apparently more or less governed the country. But the first clear-cut political position is manifested in the testament of Sancho the Great of Navarre who, considering Alava to be one of his own dominions, included it in the territory of his kingdom and consequently in the inheritance bequeathed his son García.

Prior to this, the Alavese territory, seized from Navarre by Alfonso VI of Castile, had passed back to Navarre some years thereafter before its definitive and final conquest by Alfonso VIII and incorporation into Castile in 1200. Alfonso, however, had respected local government organization, which consisted of a mixed assembly of nobles and clergy called *Cofradía de Arriaga*. Governors who were first titled Counts and later *Adelantados* represented the sovereignty of the Castilian king.

Guipúzcoa seems to have been in the beginning under the influence of Navarre and continued in more or less effective subjection to the Navarrese king until the close of the twelfth century, with only an interval during the reign of Alfonso VII of Castile when it is known to have been ruled by a Castilian governor, or royal judge, named by that monarch. While Alfonso VIII was occupied with the siege of the capital of Alava in 1200, the Guipuzcoans addressed themselves to him, asserting their readiness to separate from Navarre and recognize the sovereignty of the Crown of Castile. And so it came to pass.

Biscay, however, where there had been the same alternating influence of Castile and of Navarre during the first centuries of the Reconquest, was not incorporated into Castile until almost two centuries later, in 1379; but from the twelfth century onward, the political life of the Lords of Biscay had been closely interknit with that of the royal house of Castile.

Moreover the preponderance of Castilian influence in the three Basque provinces is shown strikingly in Basque legislation of the Reconquest period, which, besides the grounding in its own traditions, is based on the extension to this region of some of the *Fueros* that were properly Castilian, mingled with others Navarrese in origin.

The Great Thirteenth Century Conquests

During the first third of the thirteenth century when, as we have seen, the last Moslem drive, spearheaded by the Almohade invasion, had been overcome and the southern frontiers of Aragón and Castile had been extended greatly, every indication pointed to a swift and successful conclusion of the Reconquest. The coincidence in point of time of the reigns of a King of León and Castile—Ferdinand III—and of a King of Aragón—Jaime I—both of whom were inspired by the same zeal for completing the Reconquest and both of whom had the military and the executive ability essential for the enterprise, made possible, if not the total success so long sought, at least considerable progress toward that end, of which the details are as follows.

Ferdinand III's Conquest

The conquests by Ferdinand III included all of northern and western Andalusia, with the two great capitals, Córdova (1236) and Seville (1248), and the important city of Jaén (1246) as bases. Seville was taken after a siege lasting more than a year, for which the Castilian King employed a strong army with troops from every region of Spain and some foreigners, together with an improvised squadron of ships from the maritime settlements of the Cantabrian coast as well as other vessels built expressly for himself. This squadron—embryo of the not yet developed Castilian navy—which attacked by the Guadalquivir, was commanded by Don Ramón Bonifaz, Burgos-born, the first Admiral of Castile.

Each of the above-mentioned conquests brought in its train possession of many *villas* and villages in the respective regions. In particular, the victory at Seville meant the surrender of Jerez, Medina Sidonia, Lebrija, Rota, San Lúcar, and other towns. Shortly before, in 1244, Ferdinand III had captured Arjona and advanced onto the plains of Granada, thereby forcing the Moslem king of that land to declare himself tributary of the monarch of Castile and to aid the latter in besieging Seville.

Almost at the same time, Castilian troops commanded by Ferdinand III's son, Don Alfonso (later King Alfonso the Wise) occupied the Moslem Kingdom of Murcia which had declared itself vassal of Castile in exchange for the Christian monarch's protection. Don Alfonso advanced from this region toward Alicante with the object of anticipating in so far as possible extension of the conquests being made by Jaime I of Aragón in the northern part of the Alicante region as he descended from Valencia with his troops. Fortunately this concurrence in the same territory of the armies of the two Christian kings did not result in war between them but in a pact, the Treaty of Almizra (May 26, 1244), closing the series of conventions among Castile, Aragón and Catalonia by which they had been bringing to peaceful settlement the boundary problems that arose from their respective reconquests. The Treaty of Almizra established the frontier between the Aragonese

Kingdom of Valencia and the Castilian Kingdom of Murcia along a winding line that started at the junction of the rivers Júcar and Cabriel (southwestern limit of the present Province of Valencia), passed through the port of Biar and turned northward at Alcoy to cut across the garden-lands of Alicante to Denia.

Jaime I's Conquests

Contemporaneously with Ferdinand III, as already noted, King Jaime I of Aragón made two great conquests: the Balearic Isles and Valencia. He attacked the Islands with the agglomeration of troops, vessels and money collected for the purpose by various lay and ecclesiastical Lords of Catalonia and cities of that region and of the French Midi. The conquest of Mallorca was effected swiftly in 1229, and there the monarch assigned lands to the chiefs and soldiers who had aided him. He appointed an official called the King's Deputy to govern the Island. In 1233 Minorca was made vassal, and in 1235 several lords conquered Ibiza, with which crowning victory the Balearic Isles were incorporated into the Kingdom of Aragón. The great majority of the Christians who went to settle the Islands were Cataláns, especially from the Ampurdán region, who spread throughout the Balearics their own language, culture, and customs.

The conquest of the Moorish Kingdom of Valencia, which followed up the Balearic achievement, was begun by an Aragonese noble named Blasco de Alagón; but Jaime I opposed his continuance in the undertaking which the monarch himself took over as an exclusive enterprise of the Crown. The King prosecuted the campaign successfully and in 1238, after having captured the most important castles and cities of the region, laid siege to the capital. Many lords, cities, and *villas* of Aragón participated in this siege, with the Aragonese and western Catalán element predominating. In September of the same year the city surrendered, thus returning definitely into power of the Christians, 144 years after the Cid had conquered it and 136 since Jimena had had to abandon it. The Moors surrendered Valencia on condition that the Moslem King, Zaen, and all those who wished to follow him, together with whatever clothing and other personal effects they wished to take with them, should be given safe conduct from the town.

These previous victories were consolidated by conquest in subsequent years of cities and *villas* in southern Valencia, some of them very important, such as Xátiba (Játiva), Alcira, and still further south, in the present Province of Alicante, Biar (1253). The lands of Valencia and its district were distributed, as had been the case in the Balearic Isles, among lords who aided in the conquest. A considerable Moslem population stayed on, part slave and part free.

Since, in spite of Alfonso's conquests in the Kingdom of Murcia, some cities and *villas* of that region were still in Moslem possession (even though in vassalage to the Castilian King) Jaime I undertook to conquer them once and for all, with the aid of various Aragonese and Catalán nobles. He began by taking Alicante and Elche, and soon after, in 1266, the city of Murcia itself which surrendered, according to the treaty agreement, to the then King of Castile, Alfonso X. The Treaty of Almizra was complied with also as regards Elche and Alicante. The concurrence of Castilian, Aragonese, and Catalán elements in these conquests is reflected, among other things, in the linguistic heterogeneity of that part of Spain—a mixture of the Castilian Romance tongue with influences of High Aragonese and of a softened Catalán similar to the Valencian dialect but less pure.

Results of These Conquests

The victories of Jaime I and of Ferdinand III produced two far-reaching results apart from the tremendous advance of the Reconquest which they represented. One was the reduction of Moslem dominions to the Kingdom of Granada and some small territorial holdings toward Huelva. The Kingdom itself had been formed only a short while previous, on the basis of the Arjona district, at the time of the uprising against Almohade domination. The petty king of Arjona, Alhamar, in 1232 seized Jaén and was later recognized as chief of the populations of Baza, Guadix, and Granada. He established his Court in the last-named city in 1238 and thus founded a new Granadine realm with territory including the Sierra Nevada Valley (north and south) and all the coast from Almería to Gibraltar. If Ferdinand III's successors had continued his policy even for a short time, the work of the Reconquest would have been soon completed in southern Spain. But—as we shall find out—this was not to be. On that account, and also because of the fact that part of its terrain was wild and rugged, the Kingdom of

Granada was able to survive for another two centuries and a half, not only maintaining its original frontiers but even extending them on occasion (though not for long), thanks to assistance from African Moslems. Ferdinand III was well aware of this danger always threatening from Africa; and with the passage of time other Spanish monarchs came to perceive it too. After taking Seville, Ferdinand planned to send a large expedition of troops into North Africa, but he died in 1252 before the plan could be carried out.

Because of Ferdinand III's unimpeachable piety and religious zeal, he was canonized by the Catholic Church; and is therefore known as St. Ferdinand King of Spain—San Fernando Rey.

The second of the two significant results of his victories and Jaime I's was paralyzation of the activity in the Reconquest theretofore shown by the Kingdom of Aragón. In fact, the great drive toward Reconquest launched at the beginning of the eleventh century by the kings and warriors of Castile had been steadily reducing, because of the very fact that it had covered so much ground successfully, the area of expansion in Moslem territories permitted to the Principality of Catalonia and the Kingdom of Aragón. The Treaty of Cazorla is an honest recognition of this fact, which Ferdinand III's initiative, with his son Alfonso's cooperation, had affirmed shortly before in the thirteenth century. Jaime I strove with utmost tact and integrity to prevent the encounter of the two armies in the eastern district of the Kingdom of Murcia from giving rise to a clash of arms. Castile, for its part, when Valencia was again taken by Jaime I, did not invoke any right that might have been derived from the Cid's long past domination of the city. In that epoch of violence, such sensible and fairminded proceedings were all too few.

But the result, as we have said, was that Aragón came to regard its part in the work of Reconquest as ended. What remained of Moslem possessions in Spain was left to Castile to conquer. Any territorial expansion that Aragón might contemplate later on would have to be sought outside the Peninsula, in the zone already clearly indicated by the acquisition made as we have noted by the ruling house of the County of Barcelona. The possibilities in Italy were to become apparent later. Nevertheless, until the beginning of the fourteenth century, the Aragonese did not wholly cease to cooperate in campaigns of conquest in southern Spain. Nor can it be doubted that Jaime I felt an incentive toward recovery of the Peninsula, and, in general, toward fighting Moslems. His two last armed undertakings—each a failure, though for very different reasons—demonstrated both attitudes.

One was his Crusade against the Mohammedans in Palestine. Jaime gathered troops from Castile, Aragón, and Catalonia and from the military Orders of Santiago and of St. John of Jerusalem, or the Knights Hospitalers; but a terrific gale scattered the squadron transporting these forces, so that the enterprise suffered almost total disaster (1269). Jaime's final military project was an expedition against the Spanish Moors, in union with Alfonso X of Castile (1273); but the Catalán nobles refused to follow their King, alleging that they were not obliged to serve the Castilian monarch. This made strongly apparent, on the part of the people who had formerly constituted the mighty Aragón-Catalonian axis, their withdrawal from the traditional struggle for Reconquest.

Another event of great international significance brought about by Jaime I was the Treaty of Corbeil in 1255 with Louis IX—St. Louis of France. By this treaty the French monarch renounced all claims to any sovereignty that might have been his over the ancient Spanish March, and Jaime I made similar renunciation of any claims relative to the County of Foix and Languedoc, excepting Narbonne. This agreement lopped off a large portion of the rights in southern France long held by the ruling house of the County of Barcelona.

The Municipalities and the Christian Middle Class

It would be erroneous to believe that the great mid-thirteenth century advance of the Reconquest was due solely to the personal ability and martial spirit of kings and nobles, together with the military strength acquired by the Christian kingdoms. True, these factors—especially the aptitude and zest for fighting—were very strong motivating causes, not only because even an undertaking expressive of a collective ideal requires strong personal leadership (a condition very necessary in the proceedings of such a public collectivity as was the patrimonial monarchy) but also because of the nature of warfare in that period, when hand-to-hand combat and individual valor were of first importance. But we must not forget that the military strength that could be mustered depended, then as now, on social conditions. Such were the increase of wealth in the Christian kingdoms, fruit of terri-

Cloister, Monastery of St. Domingo de Silos.

torial and population gains, and the ever greater security of life and property in districts that ceased to be "the border"; while the expanding frontiers contributed in marked degree to birth and development of new social classes and correlatively of political institutions denoting their importance.

On the other hand, the life and general prosperity of the Spanish peoples was not derived solely from victories over the Moslems and advance of the Reconquest. Two other conditions of an entirely different kind were equally responsible: interior order, and discipline. The principal enemy of both these, as we have indicated hitherto, was the nobility; and this was as true in Castile as in Aragón and in the different regions bordering on the two Kingdoms. The disturbing element injected by the nobility was not only political, through their ambitious intermeddling in dynastic questions such as regencies during a minority and seizures of royal power, but social as well, because of the continual abuses committed by many nobles with regard to the common people (laborers, tradesmen), among such being invasion of the farmlands to demand tribute or to pillage the caravans that carried on trade between one locality and another. All the kings, and especially those most largely endowed with a mind and a will of their own, strove to control the disorderly element of the nobility. In that struggle they found (more or less solidly according to the region and the time) important support in the municipalities and the middle class.

With the initial work of resettlement and of founding towns under way, and in view of the advantages accorded settlers by the *Cartas-pueblas,* or People's Charters, the municipalities and the middle class were becoming stronger and widening their scope as the Reconquest was extended. In proportion as the number of inhabitants in the Christian territories increased, so did the wealth and well-being of the communities. The first effect of the new importance acquired by the common people (whether in town or country) was the creation, as a natural consequence of its mode of life, of a numerous free population; that is to say, of people who were not serfs and who were acquiring means of their own independently of the lord; sometimes in agriculture and again in trade and industry. Thus, confronting the great wealth in landed property held by the lords and by the monasteries and churches, possessors of vast holdings in land (examples of this in León and Castile were the noble families of Lara, Castro, Haro, and the monastery of Sahagún, the church of Santiago de Compostela), another form of wealth was taking shape and waxing greater which had its principal source in labor and thrift; and taking form and dimension along with it was the so-called middle class or bourgeoisie (the latter term comes from *burgo,* which means a tower or castle, and, more remotely, a small population dependent on another, larger one). The great importance that commerce thus acquired was made clear when in the eleventh century the Christian countries of Europe could renew free relations with the Orient by way of the north Mediterranean, thus making possible for them the export trade which before that time the Moslems had monopolized or restricted.

We have seen that residents of cities and of rural areas were organizing themselves under authority of the kings and the count-governors, with judicial functionaries appointed by the former directly or through the *juntas* or judicial assemblies presided over by the count. Little by little, the councils acquired the faculty conceded by the Crown, and sometimes by the regional lords, of electing their own judges (in addition to those appointed by the king) to decide their lawsuits and resolve questions of general interest for the neighborhood. We do not find well attested manifestation of this new procedure before the twelfth century in the Kingdom of León and Castile; but after that time it came to be the general custom. It gave the municipal councils, or *municipios,* a greater sense of democracy than they had possessed formerly, and an increasing awareness of their gradually extending power and influence. Along with this, the municipal councils were obtaining other advantages and privileges relating to tributes and services due (as in the ancient People's Charters) to king or lord, and also with regard to penal legislation and other matters. Concurrently, the fundamental principles of individual rights were being formulated in municipal legislation; that is, recognition of the inviolability of domicile, respect for human life, protection against abuse of power by those holding it (and this occurred often, even in the administration of justice), right of trial for infractions of the law.

The Municipal FUEROS *and Feudal Legislation*

The documents in which all these innovations were being set down and which consequently fixed the pattern of social and mercantile life for the middle class, are the *Fueros,* the origins of which we have already discussed, together with certain seignorial or feudal laws.

The juridical basis of the *Fueros* is found, on the one hand, in the ancient Visigothic customs maintained by tradition in the Spanish population of that stock, and on the other, in the new forms of trade arising from current needs; although the kings exerted every effort to implant as the ultimate law of the land the code of the ancient *Liber Iudiciorum,* later known (as we have said) as the *Fuero Juzgo.* The latter, which is the Castilian appellation, is derived not from the former, which is the seventh century Latin title, but from the variant appearing centuries after in manuscript copies, *Liber Judicum,* and sometimes, *Forum Judicum.*

The number of *fueros* granted, principally by the kings, during this period from the eleventh to the thirteenth centuries was very great in Castile as well as in Aragón and in the County of Barcelona and other Catalonian counties before Barcelona absorbed them. Some of the *fueros* are marked by extension of their privileges and by the new regulations that they establish relating to almost all matters of interest to the municipalities and their inhabitants. Typical of such *fueros* are those of León, Longroño, Benavente, Toledo, Soria, Escalona, Burgos, Cuenca, Jaca, Saragossa, Tudela, Teruel, Agramunt, Barcelona, and Valencia; this last, in consequence of Jaime I's conquest.

The people esteemed their civil rights so highly that they often petitioned the king to have these confirmed and amplified, and constituted into definitive, inalterable laws. They kept a jealous close watch as to whether there was full observance of laws thus enacted. However, it was not always by normal and peaceful means that the municipalities obtained concession or amplification of their *fueros.* Sometimes (and more especially in the case of populations dependent on lords, whether lay or ecclesiastical) civil rights were won by the method of revolution. Notable instances of this are the outbreaks at Santiago in the time of Bishop Gelmírez; at Sahagún on several occasions (one was in 1117) ; and in other episcopal seignories, such as Lugo and Orense.

The feudal type of legislation was exemplified chiefly in Catalonia. In León and Castile the Order of the monks of Cluny tried to implant it in the territories and seignories granted them; but these attempts

Church of San Pedro de Olite.

met strong resistance, as instanced by some of the uprisings mentioned above, which were followed by civil rights reforms.

The documents in which the Catalán legislation cited is set forth are: first, the laws emanating from the Frankish Kings in the period of the Marquisate de Gotha (*Capitulares francas*) and, in the second half of the eleventh century, a codification of customary practices under the expressive name of *Usatici*—"Usages"—in the time of Ramón Berenguer I. These *Usatici*, of which we do not have the earliest text, were augmented not long after and are most generally known by the Catalán title, *Usatges*. Other similar codifications were also made in Catalonia though not before the thirteenth century. Of these, the collection of the statutes of Lérida (1228) is apparently the most ancient. It contains an interesting enumeration of the sources of Catalán law, which it lists as: grants and privileges of the rulers; customs, written and unwritten; Gothic and Roman law and practice. These two last elements, which in part figured already in the *Liber Iudiciorum,* or *Fuero Juzgo,* and which continued to be manifest in the municipal *fueros,* very soon, as we shall see, gave rise to a juridical conflict of immense importance to Spain.

As capital of Catalonia, Barcelona enjoyed special legislation, important in both the public and the private aspect. It was initiated to a certain extent by the charter of settlement which Count Berenguer Ramón granted the municipality in 1025 and which began by confirming franchises and freedoms previously conceded; but its principal development was during the thirteenth century, sometimes by means of codes of a private character which later obtained official sanction (such as the *Consuetudinem Cathaloniae,* or *Commemoraciones,* of Pedro Albert and the *Ordinacions* of Santacilia) ; again, by compilations of privileges and ancient customs, such as the so-called Privilege of *Recognoverunt proceres* presented to the King by the Municipal Assembly of Barcelona and approved by the Cortes in 1283.

Inception of the Elements of Legislative Unification

Civil rights or municipal legislation, along with feudal legislation, contributed to a state of legislative diversification. Every locality, and each social class as well, had in those times its own special law, which we shall evaluate juridically later on. But notwithstanding the preponderance of such extreme juridical individualism, forces toward unification were at work within the system itself; or, if not toward absolute unity, at least toward reduction of the multiplicity of special laws. There were two main causes for this. On the one hand was the continuing prestige in Spanish territories of the Visigothic *Liber Iudiciorum*, still in force in Asturias, León, Castile, Aragón, and Catalonia. We have seen already that in the Asturias-Leonese monarchy that code played the highly important part of royal legislation, setting the pattern for appeals.

The other element of influence correlative with this factor of established usage was a very natural psychological motive: the spirit of imitation, or rather the human desire to have a share in what is best and most advantageous. Thus, whenever and wherever a *fuero* important because of the number and nature of its concessions and forms appeared, all other cities and *villas* sought to obtain one like it, or to have it extended over an ever larger geographical area. Consequently, even though the individualized form of the text and of its local application should persist, the existence of different *fueros* did not always indicate a real variance in legislative content. Through these imitations and extensions in application of the best municipal laws, a store of enactments common to many localities was being built up which counteracted the absolute isolationism of the early days.

This was brought about very strikingly in Catalonia by application to a great part of the territory—and as time passed, to all of it—of the privileges and customs that in the beginning had been especially for Barcelona. Also, what we today call *citizenship,* the conjunction of public and private rights enjoyed by residents of Barcelona, was being granted to other cities and *villas* and formed a new nucleus of unification.

By these various means the way was being prepared for what modern jurists term the conversion of municipal laws into territorial laws. Very soon (as regards Castile, in the reign of Alfonso X) that movement found itself reinforced by the Crown's energetic initiative, of which Ferdinand III's reign had shown the prelude, and by reiterated and persistent attempts to introduce Roman legislation of Byzantine type; based, that is, on the Justinian Code. In Aragón and Catalonia a movement to that end is already clearly discernible during the reign of Jaime I. In Castile the new legislation is represented principally in the code (which was rather a juridical encyclopedia) of Alfonso X, *Las Siete Partidas.*

The Hermandades, or Federations

Municipal political life was not limited to the aspects expressed in the *fueros* and the functioning of the assembly and of popular justice. The municipalities supported, because it was to their own interest to do so, the anti-nobility policy of the kings; these, in turn, favored the middle class in that regard, especially during the periods of intensest conflict with the anarchic nobility, making use of middle class strength to this end. For their part, the municipalities adopted their own means of defense, now against the nobles, now for general security, which was often threatened by the bandits and free lance adventurers drawn thither by the wars. Consequently, federations, fraternities, or leagues —*hermandades*—were formed, of which we know twelfth and thirteenth century instances. The basis of action of these brotherhoods was the militia of the municipality alongside which they went to war when convoked by the king.

On the other hand, the brotherhoods also met a need arising from inadequacy of the means of protection on which the kings could count. Consequently there were brotherhoods that did not confine themselves to the union of forces of the municipal middle class against the nobles but rather included all social classes. These facts demonstrate the broad application of the term *brotherhoods,* or *hermandades,* of which the most powerful examples at that time were the brotherhoods established by maritime *villas* along the Cantabrian coast (from Bayonne in France to Bayona in Galicia), principally the one formed by the four *villas* of Castro Urdiales, Santander, Laredo, and San Vicente de la Barquera. The autonomy enjoyed by this brotherhood, whose privileges Ferdinand III recognized, are evidenced by the fact that it made alliances with foreign kings and that its fleet aided the English in their wars against the Kings of France, from whom they conquered territory in Gascony and elsewhere. In Aragón the brotherhoods were called *comunidades,* or communities. There they could not be constituted without the king's consent and other considerations of a political nature.

The Privileged Character of Civil Rights and of Class Rights

These manifestations of solidarity are especially interesting because they show the birth of sentiments and ideas which in the future were to change the meaning and scope of the rights achieved by the middle class and by the common people or laboring class in the municipalities. These rights then had, properly speaking, the significance and meaning of privileges, as we have said. Each population sought them for itself and tried always to augment them, without caring whether the other populations had them and even with intention of outdoing the others. In consequence, a *fuero* would apply to the group of citizens to whom it had been granted but not to those of another township. The modern idea that all men are equal before the law and the modern belief in the individual value of the human being whatever his rank or origin, existed then only in the theoretic and purely moral view which Christianity had been introducing into the ideology of Christians as a whole, but which was not carried over into the statutes of law nor which, even as a theory, was adhered to by any except persons of great culture.

What happened as regards the municipalities occurred also with respect to social classes. Each class sought to accumulate privileges for itself but not to extend them to the others; rather, on the contrary, striving to make its privileges exclusively its own. Obviously this very struggle conduced in fact (by increasing extension of the privileges of every municipality and of every class) to creating a common store of personal rights shared by an ever greater number; and thus, though slowly, the way was being prepared for recognition of the equality of all men before the law, the achievement of which was to cost so many centuries of struggle. The gradual liberation of the servile classes, together with the active contribution of the municipalities, helped foster this sense of equality.

Liberation of the Servile Classes

Ever since the first period of the Roman Empire, there had been a tendency to make the tillers of the soil, whether simple peons or laborers or small landowners, dependents of the wealthy landlords with large agricultural holdings. The same thing held true when, as the Reconquest of Spanish territory began and in proportion to its advance, there arose as we have seen the prime necessity of settling and cultivating the land. Consequently, the rural population that worked in the fields, and some of the mechanics and craftsmen in the towns (not to mention the Moslem slaves taken in war) were for several centuries folk who lived in what amounted to servitude, or, at least, in a state of very strict personal dependence, with respect to the proprietor or lord of the land and at times with respect to the land itself, since when it was sold their services were sold along with it. Even in cases when the lord freed the serf, the latter continued to be bound to his former master through obligations greatly curtailing his freedom of action.

With different names for this state of things, and in circumstances of greater or less subjection, thousands of Christian men lived thus in all the Spanish kingdoms. Such conditions underwent changes varying with the regions which cannot here be related in detail. The main point is that from the twelfth century on, in the Leonese-Castilian kingdom (and with different dates in the others), an improvement began to come about in the situation of those serfs and semi-serfs, and a preparation for the eventual liberation that would later transform them into free laborers, with condition analogous in fact, if not in law, to that of renters on the land; or that would lead up to this.

For that gradual and not always uniform process of liberation the several districts afforded different causes of political, social, or economic nature. The last-named were principally the development of agriculture and the increased production, together with the lesson taught by experience that free labor produces more than slave labor. Sometimes the liberalization or improvement in labor conditions, and the lessened subjection to the lord, resulted from uprisings of the serfs themselves, in those cities or seignories where they were numerous. A conspicuous example has been cited already from Sahagún, where the monks owned extensive lands and had the monopoly of certain industries. For one reason and another, by the close of the twelfth century and in the territory of the Leonese-Castilian kingdom, the serfs and *colonos* had obtained generally the following advantages: exact definition of the work that they had to perform in benefit of their lords; abolition of the custom of selling the serf's services along with the land, against which practice a Council had declared early in the eleventh century; and recognition of the validity of marriage even when effected without the lord's consent. Pope Adrian IV (1154-1159) was

very influential in obtaining these important improvements in existing conditions. A law issued soon after, in 1215, by Alfonso IX of
León at the instance of the Archbishop of Santiago, completed them;
according to its provisions, the *colonos*—called *foreros* or *juniores de
heredad*—on the royal *villas* could thenceforward change domicile
without loss of the property that they personally owned in their place
of residence, provided that they continued to pay the corresponding
rental. This law, which at first benefited only the *foreros* on the *villas*
of León and those of the seignory of Santiago (following the method
of granting privileges then in vogue) was extended later, one after
another, to all others of the same class.

Contrariwise, it seems that there was a backward step, or more
accurately, a restriction, as to the extent of the right of asylum for serfs
who fled to municipal territory, and also a deterioration in the condition of a certain class of families, constituting the so-called *behetrías,*
or free towns, which class was subject to a lord for a considerable series
of tributes. The deterioration seems to have consisted in the fact that
the ancient freedom that some of these *behetrías* enjoyed, of selecting
their lord by their own free choice, was lost (if not by all of them, by
the majority), so that thereafter they were obliged to elect the lord
from some specific noble family.

Situation of the Social Classes in Catalonia and Aragón

In Catalonia, the ancient nobility together with the wealthy allo-
dial (or non-feudal) lords and the monasteries and churches owned almost all the land. Dependent upon these lords were various classes of
laborers in the fields or in the crafts, whose inferior or less free condition was that of the serf *colonos* (there called *payeses*), burdened with
obligatory tributes and services to be rendered. These serfs, like some of
the Leonese and Castilian, were forbidden to abandon the land except
in the case (which exception must have come about little by little) that
they redeemed themselves by payment of money. That is why the Catalán *colonos* were called *payeses de redención*—"redemption payers," a
term appearing in documents as early as the twelfth century.

While such was the way of life in the rural areas, the middle class
was shaping up strongly in the Catalán cities, where the importance
and the privileges accorded it varied in proportion to its wealth. That

is why the middle class in Barcelona was the strongest of all, and the most favored by legislation, so that Barcelona through development of its trade and industries came to exercise a veritable economic and social hegemony throughout Catalonian territory.

In Aragón the nobility was divided into two classes, the first and most powerful being called simply *ricoshombres* (the rich men). They enjoyed greater authority in their dominions than the Castilian and the Catalán lords had in theirs. It is now believed that before the thirteenth century the serfs or *colonos—vasalles de parada—*could change domicile freely; but after that time the bad features of their situation seem to have been aggravated, the rights of the lords over them reaching such a point as to be sanctioned by law in the hard phrase "to slay them by hunger, thirst, or cold." So declared the *Cortes* of Huesca in 1245; which is to say, during the reign of Jaime I.

The middle class, not so important in Aragón at that time as in Castile and Catalonia, also formed itself into associations called *universidades* in the municipalities, and was so markedly privileged in its *fueros* as often to make common cause with the nobles against the king.

Valencia, Mallorca, and Navarre

In Valencia (constituted by Jaime I into a kingdom with the King of Aragón as its titulary monarch) there was no servile Christian laboring class but rather one made up of Moslem slaves and *colonos* handed over by King Jaime to those conquerors whom he favored with grants of land. Since these latter were for the most part Aragonese nobles, rural life in Valencia was dominated by the lords and regulated by the laws and customs of Aragón. Conversely, the middle class and the free lower class element were dominant in the cities and important *villas,* and gave the Valencian municipalities a distinctly democratic character, authorized by the *fuero* which Jaime I granted the capital and which is a model of thirteenth century municipal and social legislation, setting an example soon to be followed at Tarragona.

The history of social classes in Mallorca greatly resembles that of Catalonia with the difference that the seignorial element was represented on the Island not by nobles and the clerics but by the bourgeoisie or rich citizenry of the capital, who were the principal landowners. The exploitation by them of the country people—the *forenses* —produced a ferment of protest and rebellion which a century later was to degenerate into red-handed revolt.

In Navarre the situation was very like that in Aragón; inequality before the law and servitude in benefit of nobility and clergy continued to be the rule there for a long time.

The CORTES *of León and Castile*

The greatest innovation of a political character produced during the period from the eleventh century to the thirteenth was appearance of an institution of government unknown in previous centuries; namely, the parliamentary institution—the *Cortes*—which was initiated in Spain before it was in the other countries of Europe.

The *Cortes* were assemblies generally made up of elements from the three powerful social classes of the period: the nobles, the ecclesiastics and the middle class, the last-named being represented by the municipalities. In Castile, where apparently one of these assemblies was already functioning in 1188, the essential thing about it was the presence of deputies (*personeros, procuradores*) from the municipalities. The meeting of nobles and ecclesiastics with a king did not make a *Cortes,* but that name was applied for a long time to both the parliamentary institution and the judicial or governmental assemblies that the monarch continued to convoke according to ancient custom, with attendance of the more important members of the nobility (especially those forming the Palace Court) and the clergy.

It should be understood that none of those summoned to attend the *Cortes* were called because of any inherent right of their own to take part, but simply at the king's will, so that for a long while the personages and councils concurring in the *Cortes* varied from time to time. Later, with regard to the municipalities, the privilege of being always summoned was gradually allotted specified cities and *villas.*

The characteristic function of the *Cortes* was voting the imposts or taxes requested by the king to defray costs of war and other expenses. Since ordinarily the only social class that paid taxes—or at least, paid far the greater part—was the commonalty (the middle class and the more or less free agricultural and industrial workers) the presence in the *Cortes* of representatives of the cities and *villas* was both logical and necessary. But the cities and *villas* acquired also, indirectly, a certain legislative faculty through the right granted them by the king of petitioning for a new law to be adopted, an old law to be reformed, or stated measures of government to be taken. The kings often acceded to such petitions, sometimes by reason of deeming them just and again because of the force of circumstances making it the part of wisdom to gratify or yield to special social and political elements. Thus, the municipalities, whenever they represented for the Crown a useful or important force in the struggle with the nobility or for any public purpose, had no difficulty in obtaining favorable legislation. One of the most interesting pieces of such legislation in parliamentary history was granted by several monarchs in the form of a promise to convoke the *Cortes* regularly for fixed periods annually, or every two or three years; but these promises were never kept.

Aside from the petitions, the *Cortes* intervened under certain conditions in ratification of the transmission of the Crown by inheritance, or by election if the case arose; in formation of the councils of regency, if the king were a minor; and in other political matters. On taking possession of the throne, the king swore before the *Cortes* to maintain the laws and *fueros* of the country.

Accepting 1188 as the date of the first meeting of the *Cortes* of León makes that the kingdom which inaugurated in Spain—and consequently in Europe—the parliamentary regime of medieval type. In Castile the first meeting of the *Cortes* of which we have a verified account occurred toward the end of the period under discussion, in 1250.

The Cortes in Aragón and Catalonia

We do not know just when the *Cortes* in Aragón began meeting. Some historians believe that it was in 1163; others, in 1274; which is to say, two years before the death of Jaime I. That it did not meet there sooner was due to the little importance of municipalities in Aragón up to that time. In Catalonia, the first occasion that the syndics, or deputies, of the municipalities attended the *Cortes* was in 1218 at Villafranca, with Jaime I presiding; but the complete constitution and parliamentary function of the Catalonian *Cortes* came somewhat later. In Navarre the *Cortes* seems to have had no certain existence until the subsequent period, very late in the thirteenth century or at the beginning of the fourteenth. Notwithstanding the fact that Aragón and the

Principality of Barcelona belonged to the same kingdom, each of the
two regions always had independent *Cortes,* save in exceptional cases.
The faculties and functions of the Aragonese and Catalán *Cortes* show
the notable attribute of what was called *greuges,* or damages; that is
to say, presentation of the complaints that the municipalities and other
social elements participating in the sessions brought against the king
or his officers for flouting the laws. These *Cortes* with the passage of
time came to enjoy also a somewhat greater intervention than did those
of León and Castile in formulation of the laws themselves. The origin
of this enlarged faculty seems to have been not previous to 1263, which
was during the reign of Jaime III's successor, Pedro III.

Unanimity was required for passage of a measure; and it should be
noted that the principal cities had several votes while those of lesser
importance had only one. Saragossa and Barcelona had five votes each.

When the death of a king without an heir meant extinction of a
family which had hereditary right to the throne, and a new monarch
had therefore to be elected, the *Cortes* held a special session called a
Parlamento, or Parliament. That term was also applied to other kinds
of assemblies or meetings. While the *Cortes* were closed, there functioned a *Junta,* appointed by the *Cortes,* which in Aragón was called
the General Deputation or *Diputación general,* and in Catalonia by an
analogous name, the *Diputación del general,* which is to say, the Deputation of the *Cortes* or Community. But the formal existence of that
organism corresponds to the following period, or fourteenth century.
Navarre and Valencia also adopted it later on. The function of this
Junta was to watch narrowly as to whether the laws were observed and
as to how public funds were invested.

The Administration of Justice

The great social inequality, the system of privileges (by means of
which it was sometimes attempted to decrease and again to augment
that inequality), the lawlessness of the nobility and in general of all
persons in high places, and the abuses committed by government
officials themselves, united to make life and property insecure; and, as
is natural, these were least secure for the weakest. Not even the condition of living under protection of a strong lord, as many of the weak
did, was in itself sufficient to prevent violation of personal and prop-

erty rights; since the continuous struggles among the lords and also among the different jurisdictions that had been created by grants of privileges, as well as the abuse of power by those holding official posts, were felt most keenly by serfs and humble persons even though they might have a patron. There was only one effective remedy for all this: organization of a strict system of public justice and possession by the authorities charged with making it respected—beginning with the king—of enough power and prestige to make the law apply to everybody and to force every man to show respect for the rights of the rest. Men in that age saw the necessity for this clearly enough.

Those whose rights were most frequently trodden under foot or most constantly endangered proclaimed that fact by complaints and petitions. The kings, and such members of the nobility as supported their policy, also demonstrated repeatedly their understanding of what was the efficient method to employ, by concerning themselves with protection of the weak through honest administration of justice. In fact, humanity has always realized that justice—which is to say, the application of the law to all men alike, without privilege and without distinction—is one of the firm foundations of society and of the internal peace of nations.

The administration of justice included not only the subordination of every man, no matter how high-placed nor powerful, to the authority of tribunals of law, but also the protection of the judges themselves, so that they should not be hindered from doing justice nor impelled to yield to pressure, however strong. It likewise implied stamping out the abuses which might (and often did) involve the authorities delegated by the king or the lords. Consequently at every step there may be noted the efforts of the monarchs, and of the social elements most concerned about social order and discipline, to strengthen and perfect the administration of justice.

Working against such efforts were, primarily, the causes already enumerated, and also the much-discussed resurgence of certain Germanic [or Visigothic] customs in accordance with which transgressions of the law were not in most cases questions to be settled by recourse to the courts but rather between the individuals concerned, the complainant and the defendant; sometimes by duels (such as the judicial duels or judgments of God invoked in the matter of the Mozárabic missal) whereby decisions as to which was the rightful or lawful side depended on the valor or personal skill of the combatants; and sometimes by a mixed system of private vengeance recognized as legitimate and of indemnification in money or kind. Again, the decision as to the matter in dispute or the damage caused was arrived at by considering evidence completely apart from any legal relevance to the case, as we saw exemplified during the reconquest of Toledo. In this category were the trials that consisted of plunging the hand of the accused into boiling water or bringing it into contact with redhot iron, and declared him innocent if he were unharmed and guilty if his hand were injured; or the cold water trial, which meant throwing the accused, tied hand and foot, into a great vat and deeming him innocent or guilty according to whether or not he remained afloat; and the trial by fire, when such objects as books, furniture, or the like were held to be blameless and innocent if when cast into the flames they were not consumed. Needless to say, none of these proceedings contributed toward the triumph of justice.

Consequences of the great concern as to the necessity of doing away with such imperfections were not only the increasing number of appointments of royal judges throughout the realm in each of the Christian kingdoms, charged with hearing cases in litigation and with giving support to those who had suffered abuses, but likewise the creation of juridical organisms and methods that would better arrive at the truth by replacing the former penal system by the method of examination or direct justice. Examples of the new approach are the following:

The king himself administered justice personally (sometimes through his representative) in his tribunal (the *Corte,* or *Cort*) which functioned in the palace or whatever was for the time being the royal residence. This *Cort* had to do not only with civil and criminal suits but also with those adopting the outworn extravagant practices of judicial duels and trials by fire and water. Notable instances in the eleventh century of such jurisdiction by the royal *Cort* were the tests already cited of trial by fire and the judicial duel, employed at Toledo not long after Alfonso VI conquered the city, to decide whether the Mozárabic or the new Roman missal—also called the missal of Cluny—should be maintained in the churches of Spain; in the twelfth century, the duel between the princes of Carrión and the followers of the Cid, which, even though it may be a fiction invented by the author of the

Poema, adheres closely to fact in describing the manner of carrying out such ceremonies.

The custom of a direct plea to the king for justice, which might be made by even the humblest of his subjects, the justice being administered by the monarch in person, endured for centuries. Many sixteenth and seventeenth century dramatists made use of this theme in their plays; Lope de Vega and Calderón de la Barca among others.

A judicial authority still higher than that of the king's *Cort* was established to pass upon appeals or claims arising from the *Cort's* decisions. That authority was the Judge of the Book (the "Book" being the *Liber Iudiciorum* or *Fuero Juzgo*), the origin of which post we do not know, although its existence in León as early as the mid-tenth century is attested by a document of the period. In the thirteenth century the office of Judge of the Book was still in force, and was filled by a prebendary of the cathedral. The site of the judgment was the cathedral cloister or the bishop's palace. An inscription testifying to existence of the same institution is preserved in the Cathedral of Oviedo.

Another special judgeship was the one in Aragón, pretty well attested from the time of Alfonso II's reign, under the generic name of the *Justicia,* or Justice. This justice, appointed by the king, had jurisdiction over cases relating to violation of privileges by any person whatsoever and to complaints formulated against officials for infractions or floutings of the law. The nobles tried to deprive the king of his faculty of appointing the justice; and finding themselves unable to do this, they maneuvered to convert some of his functions as judge, all of which were delegated to him by the king, into individual or exclusive authority to be exercised by the justice in his own right. They succeeded in making Jaime I accede to this in 1265. Among the functions that thus became the justice's own was that of acting as judge in suits between the nobles and the king himself; an attribution responsible for the long-current belief that the justice was a kind of intermediary power, or mediator, between nobility and royalty. Later we shall note some of the vicissitudes encountered by that judicial authority.

Finally, in their function of peace, the Truce of God and the Peace of God, both of which we have already discussed, should be included among the auxiliary and complementary institutions of the administration of justice.

Capitular Hall, Monastery of Las Huelgas.

The Monarchy and the Empire

Some Spanish kings of the realm that was first Asturian and later Leonese received along with their natural title of "King" that of "Emperor" as well. We have proof of this in historiographical though non-official documents from the time of Alfonso III to that of Alfonso VI; except in the case of Ramiro III whose status as Emperor appears in a diploma with his seal and arms; that is to say, in a document emanating from the Royal Chancellery and signed by the King. The title of Emperor as applied to Ferdinand is found not only in chronicles but in words uttered by his brother and contemporaneous monarch, the first King of Aragón. With reference to the same Ferdinand I and to Ramiro III, the title of *Magneus Basileus,* previously used by Charlemagne, was also employed. None other of the Christian kings of Spain, excepting only Sancho the Great of Navarre and Alfonso I of Aragón, called himself—or was called by others—by either of these two titles. In Sancho's case, his title of Emperor appears in the texts of historians and on the coins that he minted. Alfonso I adjudicated the title of Emperor to himself when he seized the territories of León and the capital. Many documents of Alfonso VI of Castile are extant wherein he is termed "Emperor" or "Emperor of all Spain" and the like; as well as documents not his own in which the title is applied to him with such variants as "Emperor of Toledo," among others.

The first Leonese-Castilian king who is known to have been crowned and been recognized officially as emperor by other Spanish monarchs is Alfonso VII. The coronation took place at León in 1135, and King García of Navarre demonstrated his conformity by attending the ceremony. Contemporaneous chronicles state that the Counts of Barcelona and Toulouse and various others from Gascony and neighboring districts of France were likewise Alfonso VII's vassals; as was also the Moslem petty king Zafadola, Lord of Rota. Alfonso VII received the imperial crown from the hands of the Archbishop of Toledo, in which city, it seems, he was crowned a second time, thus ratifying his authority.

Whatever might have been the cause or purpose for assigning to the Asturian and Leonese kings imperial rank, or whatever their own motives in accepting and proclaiming it—and this was perhaps their conviction that they were direct successors of the Visigothic monarchy that had been mistress of all Spain; or a nationalistic reaction of inde-

Burgos Cathedral: Puerta del Sarmental.

pendence against Charlemagne's attempts at rule in Spain; or the intention of each to proclaim his own monarchy as chief of Spanish Christian kingdoms and to force its recognition as such; or the motive might have been explicit recognition of the common objective of all the Christian kingdoms with regard to the Reconquest—whatever the underlying motive was, the fact is that it had little effect on the political reality of the Peninsula. In the case of Alfonso VII himself, his coronation was very soon protested by the King of Navarre and the Count of Portugal. No other Leonese or Castilian monarch ever again used the title of Emperor, although Ferdinand III made an unsuccessful attempt to do so. On the other hand, while it is true that Leonese or Castilian kings sometimes aided other Spanish monarchs who were in military or political difficulties (which military fact has been interpreted by some modern commentators as an evidence of overlordship), it is no less true that these monarchs were themselves aided in many instances; and that while on occasion all or the majority of the Christian kings perceived the common Moslem peril and the necessity of meeting it with a united front (as in 1212), the case was also usual of their refusing to cooperate at times when the path of the Reconquest was hard beset.

These mutually contradictory facts explain why, as we said above, the unitary intention manifested by those kings of León and Castile who saw themselves as emperors had little effect. A contributory consideration is the fact that in the end they did not achieve, in spite of the vassalage recognized in Alfonso VII's reign, even the political union of the Peninsula into a confederation or voluntary association of the Spanish Christian kingdoms under an Emperor likewise Spanish. The condition essential for carrying out the idea was lacking; since, although various political leaders during those centuries recognized the desirability of such a union, there militated against it both the jealousies and rivalries prevailing among the Christian kings and the affirmation of its own individual personality on the part not only of each monarchy but of every district of each. Even granting that the kings of León and Asturias felt a firm conviction that they were successors of the Visigothic monarchs, granting too their desire to make this conviction of theirs a political reality by restoring the unity of the Spanish State, we cannot believe them to have been oblivious of the fact ever more apparent, that other Spanish kingdoms were ready to defend their own sovereignties tenaciously and would be, to say the least, very hard to conquer.

At any rate, between the Spanish Christian empire as its creation was projected and logically attempted, and the general European empire that in mid-tenth century was in the hands of the German kings, there existed an essential difference of concept and of political objective. We shall see this clearly when we consider Alfonso X who was for a short while legally (that is, in law and in fact) Emperor of Germany.

As for the relationship borne by the imperial aspirations of the Castilian and Leonese kings to the idea of Spanish unity, our present knowledge of the existence and nature of that idea after the period of Roman unity is not sufficient to authorize our arriving at an historical conclusion. It is true that we find the idea of unity expressed by some eminent personages of the Visigothic period and of the epoch of the Reconquest. Among them was St. Isidore of Seville in his eulogy of "Mother Spain"—*Mater Spania*—who was author of the ninth century Albeldensian Chronicle, as well as Alfonso III of Oviedo, and possibly others. Independently, however, of the exact force that the expressions which they employed may have had in their own minds and of the motives behind them, the fact always remains that the great majority of men, and especially of those who then had part and influence in the political life of Spain (and not merely in that of León and Castile) seem not to have accepted the idea, but rather the contrary. Whether or not it appeals to us today, and whether or not it would have redounded to the greater benefit of Spain, are questions outside the province of history. The only unity that was achieved was, as we have seen, ecclesiastical unity, the concept of which was undoubtedly bound up with the ideas of Leonese and Castilian political aspiration.

The Industrial Populations

Growth of the collective wealth and development of the political power of the Christian kingdoms promoted increased production, agricultural as well as manufacturing, and stimulated decorative and constructive arts. These last were applied chiefly to objects of the most common domestic use and made extremely important the work of not only illustrious artists who distinguished themselves in these fields but also of all the innumerable craftsmen and laborers whose tasks in greater or less degree were influenced by the fine arts. Special circumstances, such as the devotion for certain saints or religious sites, contributed to the same end. Of the latter, the most important was Santiago de Compostela, by reason of the pilgrimages thither during several centuries, as we have already noted from another point of view. Especially during the period from the eighth to the eleventh century, Santiago came to have the most highly developed commerce and industry of northwestern Spain. The numerous pilgrims representing every social class who wended their way to that city made necessary the construction of inns and hospices, establishments for changing foreign money, and crafts for manufacturing the metal shells worn as emblems by the pilgrims, and the crosses, medals, jet ornaments, and other objects of devotion.

At the same time, Barcelona in eastern Spain was becoming an important port, thanks to Catalán commerce in the Mediterranean, and, in the beginning, especially with Italy. Later it was extended to Barbary, Egypt, and the coasts of Palestine and Syria, thereby greatly increasing its mercantile activity and its wealth. A striking manifestation of both these aspects was the creation of the post of commercial representatives, called *consuls,* at various foreign points. The custom of appointing consuls abroad spread to the other Spanish districts carrying on trade with foreign nations, as did Castile, the Basque Provinces, and Aragón, which traded with various North European countries, including France, and Flanders.

Although not reintegrated into the Christian community until almost the end of the period under discussion, Valencia speedily became a principal center of trade and industry. That was also true of Mallorca, whose commercial importance, due chiefly to her Italian trade, has been made plain by recent research.

Seville, a great capital under the kings of the *taifa* States, continued to have considerable importance after the Reconquest, particularly in the fields of commerce and industry.

Guilds and Cofradías

Mechanics and craftsmen, merchants, sailors, laborers, and even the artists, formed themselves into corporations called *gremios,* or guilds. In the early years of the development of Santiago de Compostela in Galicia, guilds of shoemakers, carpenters, stonecutters, butchers, tanners, bakers, merchants, goldsmiths and silversmiths were already in existence. Similar guilds were being established in all the other cities of the Christian kingdom as they were resettled. Each guild owned a common house or guildhall, and had its own treasury, seal, flag, and patron saint. There were three ranks in the guild: apprentice, craftsman, and master-craftsman; terms still employed. Apprenticeship was longer or shorter according to the nature of the work, and usually the apprentice paid a fee similarly variable in amount to the master-craftsman under whom he learned. Craftsmen lived with the master-craftsman like members of one family and did their work under his roof. Wages were small, because the limited scope of such a home industry did not permit of anything else; but there was the major consideration of the craftsmen's always being sure of food and lodging. For workers to advance from the category of craftsman to that of master-craftsman, an examination was held of which the principal feature was an evaluation of each man's individual skill and accomplishment. Decent living and honesty were required of the workmen. Each guild imported a set of inspectors—*alcaldes*—to keep the workshops under observance so as to prevent the sale of inferior goods, to settle differences that arose among the various crafts, and to defend any of the crafts against which suit was brought. It was customary for the industrial workers of each guild or craft to live in the same part of the city or on the same street with his fellow-craftsmen; which is why there are still to be found in many Spanish cities a Street of the Silversmiths, a Street of the Locksmiths, a Street of the Wool-dressers, a Street of the Silk-weavers, and the like.

The Prosperity and Influence of the Guilds

Under protection of the municipalities and their *fueros,* and of the kings as well, the guilds, continuing to increase in importance, came to be highly influential social elements in the life of the Spanish towns. The mechanics and craftsmen made a practice of forming also, apart from the guilds, *cofradías* and brotherhoods, established as mutual benefit or religious associations, for such purposes as financial assistance and nursing care for the sick, the holding of banquets and celebration of holidays at appointed times, the worship of a saint. After the fifteenth century in particular, the kings issued general laws for regulating not only the internal life of the guilds but also such matters as the daily wage, the length of the work-day, the requirements to be met by the product of each craft. Such legislation tended to lay ever greater stress on economic and professional objectives, to make guild membership obligatory, and to generalize the examinations; but it also comprised a margin of differentiation with respect to the working hours and wages corresponding to particular requirements of the various crafts and districts. That margin of differentiation, which modified the tendency toward uniformity in the laws, was adopted later in other kinds of juridical regulations.

On several Spanish municipal councils, or *Ayuntamientos*—those of Barcelona, Valencia, and others—the most important guilds had representation. The sense of privilege or of monopoly which the guilds acquired in increasing degree, and the prohibitions against permitting any worker not a guild-member to work at his trade, provoked in the course of time, and in proportion as increasing wealth augmented the demand for labor, an anti-guild movement favoring individual freedom of choice for the worker.

Laborers in the fields, much less favored than city workers, founded *cofradías,* or brotherhoods, in some districts, as we have seen. Some of these *cofradías* owned land communally which the members, or *cofrades,* worked in common and the products of which were assigned for the common costs, distribution among the *cofrades,* or for benefits and charities.

The Religious Faith of the Spanish People

The deep-held religious faith of the Spanish people throughout the period of the Reconquest was shown principally in three ways: by the foundation of numerous churches and monasteries; by the evolution of many pious legends; and by the number and the fame of Spanish saints.

The foundation of the churches, whether cathedrals or of lesser category, and of the monasteries as well, was accompanied by donations of immense tracts of land. In the case of the Cathedral at Santiago de Compostela, the land thus given extended for twenty-four miles; and in that of the Archbishopric of Toledo, the properties granted by Alfonso VI included many farmlands, houses, shops, and mills in the city and in the nine neighboring towns of Rodiles, Canales, Cabañas, Coneja, Barcides, Alcolea, Melgar, Almonacid, and Alpobrega.

The clergy was granted personal immunity, which was the right not to be tried in the ordinary tribunals of the king, and royal immunity, which was exemption from fiscal taxes. Both rights began as special privileges and were later made general in spite of many laws and many petitions of *Cortes* which tried to set limits on tax exemptions.

The special importance of the monasteries did not derive solely from their religious aspect (though it derived chiefly from this), but also, as we know, from the great stimulation that they gave to cultivation of the land, resettlement, and in consequence of both, to the wealth of the country. These facts explain, too, why the monasteries were often very rich: they possessed broad acres, houses, mills, and the like on the scale of great landowners; and not infrequently in fact were themselves the greatest landowners. The cultivation of those lands, occupancy of those houses, and utilization of those mills attracted numerous farm laborers and mechanics, thus creating a population that increased the influence and social importance of the monasteries. A greater or lesser number of the field-hands and household servants of the monks were Christian and Moorish serfs, which fact was in conformity with ideas and customs of the age. With all this, the monasteries constituted one of the principal elements in the society of the period. The richest of them came to enjoy a position in the social structure and an authority over the persons living on their domains like that of the nobles. Those faculties were granted and often amplified by the kings with the intention of counteracting the power of the nobility, a class naturally more unruly and more likely to disturb public tranquility than were the monks. In return, the monks with their dependants were obligated to take part in war if called on by the king; and this they did, the abbots sometimes commanding the troops made up of serfs, *colonos,* and others under their protection, and again handing them over to a nonecclesiastical leader. In this way the monasteries were at one and the same time a factor in the country's resettlement and agricultural prosperity, a factor of order and of support to the monarchy against the nobility, and a military factor in the Reconquest. The same services, especially these two last, were rendered by the great churches, especially those attached to the bishoprics and archbishoprics. Notable examples of these and of the monasteries were Santiago de Compostela, Lugo, Sahagún, Escalada, Mazote, Castañeda, Vime, Toledo, in Galicia, León and Castile; and Gerona, Pala-

Cathedral of Santiago de Compostela: Portico of Glory.

frugell, La Bisbal, Urgel, in Catalonia. In other instances, the monasteries were chiefly centers of culture and religious life; such were Ripoll, Roda, and San Cugat, in Catalonia; Oña, Silos, Arlanza, Santa María de Huerta (the most important Cistercian monastery in Spain) and San Millán, in Castile; San Juan de la Peña, among others, in Aragón. As for Navarre, mention should be made of Leyre.

Considering the monastic institution as a whole, it should be said that the steadily growing prosperity of the Christian districts may be reckoned from the number of monasteries existing in each. Therefore, quite as well as by taking the dates of victories and Christian conquests as guide, the progress of the Reconquest and the increasing wealth of the several kingdoms may be followed century by century on a map showing the monasteries during the successive periods. Spanish districts that lost their importance when the center of life and authority shifted rapidly toward central Spain and thence southward, and that are overshadowed today by the brilliance of great modern cities, were thus, in the first centuries of the Reconquest, important abodes of civilization and of social and economic activity; the most conspicuous proof of this fact being the number and power of their monasteries. For example: at the commencement of the independent existence of Castile, the region of Burgos and the eastern part of Rioja; at the beginning of the Spanish March, northern Catalonia; in the early days of the resettlement of Galicia, the districts of Santiago and Lugo; in the initial period of Navarre and Aragón, the zone of the Pyrenees.

Spanish Ecclesiastical Unification

In this period from the eleventh century to the thirteenth occurred important events that brought about unification of Spanish ecclesiastical life, in the sense that they caused all Peninsular bishoprics to recognize a common Metropolitan, or superior regional authority. To some of these events we have referred already; namely, those relating to elevation of the ecclesiastical hierarchy of Toledo during Alfonso VI's reign and those pertaining to submission of the northwestern bishoprics to the Archbishopric of Toledo in the reign of Alfonso VII. Let us here add the incorporation of the Catalán bishoprics (and later of the Aragonese and Navarrese), which previously had been dependencies of Narbonne in Gaul, into the ancient ecclesiastical province of Tarragona (Sancho I's reign, 956-966); an incorporation negotiated in the

Leonese Court in 959 and achieved in spite of opposition by Aragón and by Catalán prelates. At that time the center of attraction was Santiago de Compostela ,and in consequence, politically speaking, the Kingdom of León. But afterwards, as we have seen, Toledo, under which Tarragona was placed, became more powerful. Separation later on of the County of Porto, converted into the Kingdom of Portugal, removed the Portuguese dioceses from that Peninsular unity.

Sacred Legends and Spanish Saints

The culture of the monks in those times—like the culture that had characterized them in the Visigothic period when the high clergy usually came from the monasteries—made them collectors and narrators of accounts of remarkable occurrences and of the legends that sprang up regarding them; on occasion, in all probability, even made them creators of such legends. Accordingly, some of the earliest Castilian poems (Castile being a region in which this kind of poetry flourishes) were written by monks before the *juglares,* or *jongleurs—*ballad-singers of foreign race and their Spanish disciples and imitators in the various kingdoms—invaded the land.

The Spanish genius was as prolific of heroic legends about kings and warriors as of sacred legends relating to the Virgin and the Saints and the memorable incidents in their lives. Some of these were put into verse (St. Domingo, the *Cantigas* of the Virgin) and others were handed down in tale and story which are often moving and beautiful.

A strong foundation for development of this sacred literature was afforded by the number of clerics who because of their piety, charitable works, or other endowments—and sometimes in the Moslem kingdoms by reason of martyrdom—acquired the stature of saints. Some among these are especially celebrated; for instance, St. Alvaro and St. Eulogius of Córdova (already cited) , St. Domingo de la Calzada, St. Domingo de Guzmán, St. Raymond de Peñafort, St. Oleguer or Olegarius; St. Peter Nolasco; and, later on, St. Vincent Ferrer.

New Religious Orders. The Inquisition

In this same period there were created in other European countries or in Spain, and soon spread throughout the Peninsula in addition to the French Order of the monks of Cluny several times referred to, two new religious Orders which were for many centuries among the most powerful and influential. One was the Franciscan Order, founded in 1215 by the Italian monk St. Francis of Assisi, among the greatest figures of the medieval Catholic Church; the other was the Dominicans—the Order of Preachers, or Black Friars—established by St. Domingo de Guzmán, native son of Calahorra. Along with the latter was created a specific tribunal for investigation, trial and punishment of heresy; a tribunal that speedily acquired very far-reaching activity and public notice: the Tribunal of the Inquisition. A product alike of the great disquiet that some important heresies of the time had sown in the minds of the faithful and of the Church, and of steps taken by Bishops and Popes, especially Pope Gregory IX, the Tribunal of the Inquisition took form in the Bulls of the latter (1233) and the first Spanish Inquisition was constituted in the Kingdom of Aragón as a special tribunal, independent of the Bishop. It was entrusted to the Dominican Order which had been founded at Barcelona in 1219. The first instruction to inquisitors for Spain, drafted by the monk Raymond de Peñafort (later canonized) was published in 1235 by the Bishop of Tarragona. St. Raymond was a very eminent personage, a trusted adviser of Pope Gregory IX. He compiled the latter's Decrees; that is, made a collection of his pontifical decisions.

Moslem Civilization and Influence after the Caliphate

Although during the period of the *taifa* kingdoms political and military hegemony passed, as we have seen, from a Moslem State to the Christian States, this was not true of the hegemony of culture. In that field supremacy for some time continued to belong to the Mohammedan element, as it did to the Jewish in the fields of science and letters. In the arts, while Moslem influence continued strong, the originality of the Spanish spirit and the introduction of styles proceeding from other Christian countries (France and Italy) produced important stylistic deviations in architecture and sculpture.

In fact, the fall of the Caliphate did not on the whole diminish the prosperity and culture of the Moslem Spanish world. It was damaging to Córdova and other cities, but, in exchange, favored Seville, Granada, and some of the rest. Moreover, the religious intransigence of Almoravides and Almohades forced many Moslem and Jewish savants and artists among those who lent lustre to the *taifa* kingdoms and to the eleventh and twelfth century African empires, to emigrate to the Christian kingdoms where they were not only welcomed but were signally favored by the kings, especially by Alfonso VI and, later, Alfonso VII. During part of the twelfth and thirteenth centuries, Toledo occupied the post in the world of science held formerly by Córdova: that of a center to which recurred intellectuals from other countries and which was a kind of international clearing-house for translation of Jewish and Arabic works, especially those relating to philosophy and the sciences. Also, as we have noted already, in Aragón and Catalonia some Moslem and Jewish educators had been influential in the cultural life of native-born inhabitants of that country ever since a period preceding the one in Castile just referred to. Thus, at Saragossa in the early years of Moorish domination, there flourished the famous philosopher Avempace; at Barcelona, among others the Jewish poet Isaac ben Reuben, the philosophers of the same race, Judah ben Barzilai and Hardai Cresques, the theologian Solomon ben Adret (the most eminent religious authority among European Jews at the close of the thirteenth century), and the mathematician Abraham-bar-Hiya; at Tortosa, the Moslem savant Ibn Abi Randaga. Barcelona represented besides, in the times of Ramón Berenguer III, a center for oriental translations analogous to Ripoll and Toledo and concerned principally with works on astronomy and mathematics.

Considering together the Christian kingdoms and the Arabian and Jewish influences upon them, it may be said that the writers of those races who enjoyed greatest prestige and whose teachings insofar as possible were most intimately incorporated into Christian learning were, in philosophy, Algazel, Abenhazam, Averroës, and the Murcian, Mohidin; in medicine, Avicena, who, while he was neither Spanish nor even visited Spain, attained in Spain his extraordinary renown as physician and philosopher. In the former character he is cited by Abentofail.

In the field of architecture and the decorative arts allied with it, Moslem influence produced a new style called *Mudéjar* which spread throughout almost all Spain. We shall return to it later for discussion. Some Arabic architectural monuments in Andalusia, such as the Giralda tower of the Mosque at Seville, belonged to this period. Besides the Mudéjar art that then made appearance and mingled with its immediate predecessor, the Mozárabic, the early Arabic influence emanating from the Mosque of Córdova and other structures of the

Caliphate continued to be exercised in the Christian territories and was evidenced in a large amount of the construction, both religious and lay, during the eleventh, twelfth, and thirteenth centuries. We shall find that the influence was carried over into centuries later still.

Another influence likewise Arabic in origin was that of textiles, an industry perpetuated and further developed in the territories being conquered by the Christians. Thus, in the thirteenth century, silk-worms were raised in many towns and villages of Jaén, and there were 6,000 looms at Seville. Such Moslem textiles as tissues and velvets continued to be produced in the new Castilian and Aragonese dominions after the conquests of Andalusia, Murcia, and Valencia in the thirteenth century.

Archbishop Don Roderick

In Castile, the representative figure in the realm of culture during this period of intense and transcendental intellectual activity was Don Rodrigo (or Roderick) Ximénez de Rada, Archbishop of Toledo (1170 or 1180-1247). Through his fostering and inspiring influence, translations were made into the Castilian Romance language and into Latin of the great Greek writings (Aristotle, Euclid, Galen), edited and annotated by Moslems, and original works were produced by Arabic and Jewish savants. The most important collaborators in the Archbishop's cultural program were Canon Marco, Archdeacon Domingo González, or Gundisalvo, and Juan Hispalense. Gundisalvo also wrote in Latin several original philosophic works that show strong influences of oriental science. In addition to all these, some of the foreigners who, as we have said, were drawn to Toledo in great numbers by its fame as a cultural center, made translations in their turn, or had them made. Of these we may instance, as highly meritorious, Gerard of Cremona, Adelard of Bath, the two Hermanns (the Dalmatian and the German), Michael Scotus, and Albert de Retines. This work was continued in the thirteenth and subsequent centuries, as we shall see, by other translators, mostly Jews. Thus, by means of this great mass of translations produced at Toledo at the initiative of Spanish kings and prelates, there was disseminated throughout Europe the influence of Eastern science, not only Moslem but also the Greek and that deriving from the Greek, in the fields of Astronomy, Medicine, Alchemy,

Mathematics, Physics, Logic, Morals, Politics, and other branches of learning.

Archbishop Don Roderick was himself author of a book that is the first general history of Spain and at the same time the first work of the kind utilizing not only Christian chronicles and popular legends but Arabic sources as well. This volume, written originally in Latin, was translated into Castilian by the author, who called it *Historia de los godos*—History of the Goths—although as a matter of fact it embraced all the ages from the creation of the world to the year 1243. Don Roderick, a typical and illustrious example of the prelates of the time— soldier, politician, scientist, and man-of-letters—stands first in the memorable series of Archbishops of Toledo who were to exercise so great an influence in Spanish public affairs. Besides the accomplishments already noted, we owe to him the founding of the first university, the *Estudio general de Castilla*, as well as great contributions in promoting the definitive union of León and Castile. He was one of the staunchest champions of the effort to make the nobility observe law and order, and for this reason has been called a forerunner of Cisneros, another of the great Toledan Archbishops. Don Roderick also contributed in large measure to the building of the Cathedral of Toledo, which was begun in 1227.

Other Cultural Influences

Along with Jewish and Moslem influences, others, proceeding, as we have said, from various European countries—but chiefly from France and Italy and next in order, Flanders—began to be felt in the Christian Spanish territories. The media for spreading and implementing these were on the one hand the monks of Cluny, belonging to the French Benedictine Order established at Cluny, which appeared in Spain in the eleventh century and acquired great power, especially in León and Castile; the Cistercians (the Order of St. Bernard, also French) ; and other Benedictine groups who in monasteries at Silos and elsewhere represented important centers of culture: and on the other hand, the adventurers who came in throngs to take part in the war against the Moors and in civil strife within the Christian kingdoms; and also, of course, the innumerable pilgrims who visited Santiago de Compostela in Galicia. A more specific contribution to the same end was made by the poets and wandering minstrels—the *juglares* and troubadours—

who came from France and other countries; the foreign professors whose cooperation helped Castilian and Aragonese kings of the twelfth and thirteenth centuries to found the first universities; the Spanish students who went in great numbers to pursue their studies in Italy and France; and the merchants, Cataláns and Valencians as well as Castilians, who carried on an active foreign trade, the former in the Mediterranean, principally with Italy, and the latter in the Atlantic, chiefly with Flanders.

Invigorated by all these influences, the Spanish spirit, that had already in former times given so many evidences of creative power, now with the social life of the Christian realms thus enriched and growing steadily more powerful, produced a magnificent outflowering of science, letters and art. This productivity was especially noticeable after the beginning of the eleventh century; and at the same time the formation, development, and general use of the new Romance languages was ever on the increase.

The two forms in which that native intellectual activity properly called Spanish was demonstrated were original literary and scientific works and the desire to acquire foreign culture. This latter ambition was evidenced on the Peninsula principally by the translation centers already mentioned and by creation of universities and libraries.

We have noted hitherto the foundation of the *Estudio general,* or University of Palencia, which took place in 1212 or 1214. The Universities of Salamanca and Valladolid were next established, with the assistance of Spanish professors and of others summoned from France and Italy; and it is worthwhile to note that the University of Salamanca, which speedily was to achieve European renown and which in the beginning offered no course in Theology, was the first in the world to include Music in the curriculum. For their part, studious Spaniards frequented foreign schools and universities. An example in point is the research carried out by Archbishop Don Roderick at Bologna and Paris.

In proportion as the previously established libraries at convents and cathedrals as well as the royal libraries increased the number of their volumes, there was a corresponding increase of love for books. These could be both preserved and distributed because of the numerous manuscript copies made. Such manuscripts were sometimes very beautiful, enhanced by jewel-like illuminated miniatures showing great perfection of detail. Splendid specimens of these are the *Libro de los Testamentos*—Book of the Testaments—at Oviedo; the Bibles of the monk Beatus (St. Beatus of Liébana) and his *Commentary on the Apocalypse,* of which there are copies in León; the Bible of the Monastery of St. Peter de Roda and that of the Abbey of Farfán, which apparently was made at Ripoll. The illuminated miniatures in these and similar manuscripts reflect the Carlovingian (Frankish) influence chiefly, though sometimes they show traces of Moslem art (as in the manuscript at Silos) and of Visigothic tradition; in fact, the text of the manuscripts of St. Beatus make express acknowledgment of this tradition.

On the other hand, intellectual culture began to leave off being the exclusive patrimony of the clergy; and there were notable examples of this both among the nobility and in royal palaces.

An Authentically Spanish Culture

Results of all this cultural activity are to be seen in every field of intellectual interest, but most of all in literature. A contributory consideration was that this was the epoch in which Latin was no longer the everyday speech nor was it used at all by the mass of the people. Instead, the modern languages of Spain made their appearance: *Castilian,* in the tenth century, already very widely used by the twelfth; and, correlatively, *Galician* and *Aragonese* (which latter did not long survive as a tongue distinct from Castilian) ; *Catalán,* at about the same time, and *Valencian* and *Mallorcan* after Jaime I's conquests.

Ot de Moncada, the first Catalán poet of whom we have notice, belonged to the eleventh century; and the earliest known literary text in Catalán was written at the end of the twelfth. Of the same century was the poet Arnau de Mont, educated in the school of the Monastery of Ripoll. In the twelfth century Castile also produced her first literary works in her own language, principally heroic poems or *Gestas* of chivalry, of which the highest example is the *Poema de mio Cid;* ballads or *romances,* brief narrative poems derived largely from the *Gestas;* and devotional poetry; as well as other kinds in lesser degree. The leading authors whose names are known are Gonzalo de Berceo, who was born probably toward the close of the twelfth century, and Juan Lorenzo de Segura. It is a disputed question today whether prior to the *Crónica,* or Chronicle, of Jaime I, written by that King himself,

there were epic poets in the Catalán language. The matter has not yet
been decided definitely. Provençal influence was slight in Castile but
stronger in Galicia, where it adopted the regional speech; while in
Aragón and Catalonia it attained great popularity. The principal poets
of that region showing Provençal influence in their work were King
Alfonso II, the first Peninsular troubadour; Berenguer de Palol (1136-
1170) ; Guillén de Bergadá; Gureau de Cabrera; Vidal de Besalú; and
Cerverí de Gerona. The last-named was also the last of the troubadours as well as one of the most popular (1250-1280). Catalán prose
(apart from twelfth century ecclesiastical writings) was represented by
the *Chronicle* of Jaime I already mentioned, and by a translation of
Don Rodrigo Ximénez de Roda's *History*.

The Fine Arts.   Romanesque Architecture

Perhaps the most eloquent testimony to general progress in the
Christian kingdoms, and to the increase of public wealth as well, is
supplied by Fine Arts, especially Architecture and the related arts.
The different foreign influences that met in Spain can be traced in
these, and along with them, the modifications and innovations that at
times expressed the inventive genius of the Spanish artist.

Construction which, generally speaking, had been relatively meager
in previous centuries, increased from the eleventh onward, and was
enriched in every phase; great churches and palaces were erected and
adorned with statues, bas-reliefs, and paintings. In both types of building, lay and ecclesiastical, a new style was evident, which some time
before had sprung up to replace the architectural style called Carlovingian because it had its flowering in the reign of Charlemagne and his
successors. (The preceding chapter dealt with its influence in Spain.)
The creative centers for this new art were France and Italy. The
Benedictine monks were in large part responsible both for its creation
and its dissemination. This style has been called *Romanesque* just as
the new languages were termed *Romance,* because basically Romanesque architecture is a new version of the Roman, a perennial model
for all the peoples proceeding from the Roman Empire.

In France one of the most important centers of Romanesque art
was Provence, whence it invaded Spain through the medium of artists
of the region. It left on the Peninsula numerous examples of the two
variants which reflect the spiritual divergence between the two Bene-

Pedro Berruguete: *Auto de fe presided over by St. Domingo de Guzmán.*

dictine Orders, that of Cluny and that of Cister (the Cistercians), far apart despite their common origin. The Cluny form of architecture is rich in ornamentation. The Cistercian by its sobriety and simplicity expresses the utter austerity of its spirit. And on both, the Spanish artists who contributed to construction of the buildings left the imprint of their own aesthetic and their own technique. This may be well observed in structures that at first sight might have been regarded as pure expressions of the French or Italian Romanesque.

The most important Romanesque monument of Spain, on which apparently Provençal artists worked, is the Cathedral of Santiago de Compostela, begun in the first third of the twelfth century. The sculptures for the Door of the Silversmiths were six years in execution, from 1137 to 1143; the lintels of the Portico of Glory were laid in 1188, and the Church as a whole, completed, was consecrated in 1211. Analogous to it, but much less imposing, are the churches at Lugo, Zamora, and Túy.

Romanesque art spread throughout Spain, except for Andalusia where Moslem influence kept the ascendency, though acquiring certain adaptations that we shall discuss later; but the type of churches built in Castile, Navarre, Aragón and Catalonia are not like those erected in Galicia, nor indeed are they like one another. Each region had its own distinctive architectural characteristics. In Castile, for example, there was the spherical exterior dome of which the old Cathedral of Salamanca, commonly called the Tower of the Cock, presents an original example; in Catalonia, the Lombard (Italian) influence, instances of which in the purely architectonic field are the Cathedral of Urgel, dating from the first half of the eleventh century, and in that of the decorative arts, the remarkably profuse wealth of bas-reliefs adorning the door of the basilica of Ripoll, mausoleum of the Counts of Barcelona, consecrated in 1032. To list the Romanesque architectural monuments would be a lengthy process even if merely the principal examples in each region were included. To those already mentioned, we shall add only the door and the royal mausoleum of the Cathedral of St. Isidore in León where Ferdinand I interred the remains of St. Isidore of Seville and where the King himself is buried; the monastery of Segre in Navarre; that of Poblet, an example of Cistercian influence, and that of Silos; the Cathedrals of Lérida and Tarragona; the Palace of Carracedo (which has almost wholly disappeared),

Toledo: Puerta del Sol.

and many cloisters and doors in Catalonia, Aragón, and Valencia. As example of the military architecture of the period the walls of Avila should be noted, a city whose Cathedral is the most complete Spanish example of the church-fortress (eleventh century) in its central arch, as is that of Sigüenza, built a little later, in its façade and towers; both structures being a mixture of the religious and the military, which was fitting in those times made turbulent by civil wars.

In the other arts, characteristics of Romanesque style were reflected in sculpture in stone (decoration of churches; religious images), in marble, and in wood; admirable examples of which are the crucifix of Ferdinand I, in León; the Virgin in the cloisters of Solsona; the capitals and the carvings in relief of the cloister of Silos; those of the Cathedral of Tarragona, of the portico of Santiago de Compostela, and of the door at Ripoll already mentioned; and those on an arch in San Millán de la Cogolla.

Romanesque art in working gold and silver found expression in chalices, crosses, crowns, and coffers for relics, and sometimes in sacred images. Striking examples are the chalice of St. Isidore at León, the Holy Coffer at Oviedo, and the small chest of St. Leocadia in the same Cathedral; and the Virgin of the Mead (in enamelled silver) at Salamanca (possibly an imported French piece). There are also important Romanesque sculptures in marble, such as the ceremonial chair at Roda.

Among all these arts, the one most expressive of an originality rightly to be called Spanish is sculpture, which by the twelfth century had already achieved such great expressions as the works cited at Silos, "the most typical series in all Spain" at that time. This budding originality was checked somewhat in the thirteenth century by the influence of French sculpture.

As for painting, the native Spanish touch appears on the one hand in the frescoes of many Leonese, Asturian, Castilian, Aragonese, and Catalán churches; and in Valencian also after the thirteenth century; and on the other, in the illuminated miniatures already described and in paintings on wood which constituted one of the elements of decoration of the altar, such as the frontals (front panels) of which many examples have been found in Catalonia. These paintings have a strongly indigenous character differentiating them from the French.

Noteworthy examples of these various types are the paintings in the churches at Pedret, Fenullar, San Miguel de la Seo, Tabull, Gigena,

Liria, and San Isidoro at León, and the frontals of Vich and others in Catalonia. The miniatures have been instanced.

As regards the textiles of the period, they are all Arabic and Byzantine in design and in manufacture. Very often the bodies of saints and holy relics were wrapped in these cloths. It is known that Archbishop Roderick Ximénez de Rada, of whom we have spoken several times, was shrouded for burial in a cloth woven by Moslem labor; that King Ferdinand III used both silks and arms of Moslem manufacture; and that in the tomb of Doña Leonór de Castro (Vidalcázar de Sirga) was found a fabric of silk and gold that was Moslem too.

Gothic Architecture: The Ogive, or Pointed Arch

But in Romanesque construction as early as the thirteenth century (such as the examples cited from Santiago de Compostela, Lérida, Tarragona, Santas Creus, and Poblet) there were already to be seen modifications indicating the advent of a new style. It was the ogival style, taking its name from the ogive, or pointed arch, which characterizes it, although, as we have seen, that arch itself was of much earlier date. Ogive art originated apparently in France whence it spread to Spain.

The epoch of ogive art—more generally called Gothic art in English—corresponded in Spain to the period of building the great cathedrals and the castle-palaces, or chateaux-forts—of the kings and wealthy lords. On the Peninsula, however, few examples are to be found of the magnificent municipal buildings (guild halls or town halls) which are so often met with in France, Germany, and other countries. The only Spanish construction of this type was for commercial purposes (*lonjas*, or bourses), with now and again a public building such as the Town Hall and the Custom House at Barcelona and the house of Bishop Gelmírez at Santiago. Apart from this, the most notable specimens of Gothic architecture in Spain, as to churches, are the Cathedrals of León, Cuenca, Burgos, Toledo, Barcelona, and Mallorca, although several of these were constructed or completed in centuries following the thirteenth. The cloisters of some of the Cathedrals mentioned, and of others, as well as those constructed at the monasteries of Santas Creus and Poblet, are very beautiful and are typically Gothic. The same observation should be made regarding the towers (León, Burgos, and others). Among civil edifices we should note the Palace

Interior, Synagogue of Santa María la Blanca, at Toledo.

of the Infantado at Guadalajara; the Miraflores Palace at Burgos; the so-called *Casa de los Picos,* or House of the Peaks at Segovia and *Casa de las Conchas,* or House of the Shells, at Salamanca; the Lonjas, or Bourses, at Barcelona and Valencia (the latter built 1482-1498) ; the castle-palaces of Solivella, Palafolls, Peralada, and Requeséns in Catalonia, and of Bellver in Mallorca.

Since the cathedrals were the most important of all the monuments of architecture in size and grandeur and were in natural consequence a long time building, they often reveal a mixture of the two styles, Romanesque and Gothic. Some, begun in Romanesque style, had Gothic elements superimposed to such extent as to become predominant while not, however, obliterating all traces of Romanesque; as may be observed in the old Cathedral of Salamanca, in the Cathedrals of Burgos and Valencia, in the Monasteries of Poblet and Santas Creus, and in many other edifices. Two churches meriting especial mention because of their mingling of the two styles and their brick construction are Santa María de la Mejorada at Olmedo and Nuestra Señora de la Lugareja at Arévalo. Again, there are churches that present a pure or unmixed architectural style (saving some details or additions of much later date than that which now occupies our attention) , as occurs in the case of the Cathedrals of Santiago (the primitive part) and León, the former being Romanesque and the latter Gothic; and of the Monastery of Ripoll.

The Lesser Gothic Arts

The new style, as was natural, left its mark not only on architecture but also on the other arts concerned with the decoration of buildings and lesser constructions (such as altars and monumental fireplaces), and on styles in furniture. Thus, sculpture produced beautiful work for the adornment of doors, tombs, and retables; and also in the form of the wayside crosses erected to mark the entrance into a municipality, and the so-called *rollos,* or Columns of Justice, generally to be found in city plazas. The art of the goldsmith and the silversmith excelled in monstrances, which at times were of extraordinary richness; crosses to be borne in processions; coffers for relics; pax or image plates; and other articles used in the religious rites which then acquired great importance. Also in the grill-work of altars and chapels. Wood carving reached a high state of perfection, especially on choir stalls and some pieces of household furniture such as the *bargueños,* or desk-chests, so typically Castilian. The art of the worker in ivory created exquisitely carved images of saints and plaques for coffers. Ceramics was still influenced preferentially by Moslem art, the Moslem method maintaining its types in such diverse Spanish localities as Valencia (Manises, Paterna), Talavera, and elsewhere. But the majority of the notable works of this kind produced in Spain belong, as we shall see, to a later period.

Mudéjar Art

While the foreign influences noted were invading the Peninsula and spreading widely first the Romanesque manner in art and then the Gothic, oriental or Moslem art (which by that time might well be called Spanish, in spite of its remote foreign origin) continued fruitful, producing new forms as a result of the ever more intimate contact of the two civilizations. It was not the Moslems themselves—nor was it, as had been the case some centuries previous, the Mozárabes—who created the indigenous, peninsular type of art which was called *Mudéjar* because of its origin, and of which we have made mention hitherto. This is the product of a combination of Arabic and Gothic elements which, intermingled, made something original in aspect. Its architecture is characterized by exterior use of bare brick, with which ornamentation was traced on the walls; blind arcading (covered or enclosed, that is), purely decorative in intent; slender arched windows centered by a dividing column of *azulejos,* or glazed tiles; and horseshoe arches employed as both decorative and functional elements. There are admirable specimens of Mudéjar architecture at Toledo (the Puerta del Sol and the old Puerta de Bisagra which is an expression of popular art very close in date to the conquest; the Synagogues of Santa María la Blanca and the Tránsito, and other buildings); at Tordesillas (the Palace of Alfonso XI); at Burgos (the Cistercian monastery of Las Huelgas—Santa María de las Huelgas); at Seville (the Alcázar); at Saragossa (the New Leaning Tower); at Calatayud (the bell-tower of Santa María); at Teruel (the Tower of San Martín); et cetera. The most ancient monument showing Spanish Romanesque architecture pervaded by the influence of Mudéjar art is the Church of San Lorenzo at Sahagún, which dates from the close of the twelfth century or beginning of the thirteenth. Mudéjar art—or *Mudejarismo*—is expressed also in beautiful carved and painted panelling (Santa María la Blanca, Cathedral of Teruel, Court Chamber and hall of the Bourse at Valencia, House of the Dueñas at Seville); in pediments and ornamentation of plaster and glazed tile; in the work in ceramics already instanced; in book bindings with geometrical designs patterned after the decorations on buildings and on the *azulejos;* in some details of sepulchral statues and of the tombs themselves; and in the illuminated miniature paintings until these became wholly Gothic in type.

Chivalry and Tournaments

In the field of the physical exercises that we today call sports, typical diversions of the age were the contests on horse or on foot with arms so blunted as not to inflict a fatal nor a serious wound. These contests, strictly an upper class sport, were termed jousts and tournaments. Developed through influence of those Frenchmen who at the end of the eleventh century came in numbers to fight the battle of Reconquest, the tournaments served—aside from any other consideration—to implant in Spain the ideas and customs of what was then called chivalry, an institution characteristic of the centuries termed medieval.

Chivalry held arms to be the essential profession and decreed that the following virtues should adorn it: indomitable hardihood or valor; honorable dealing with all men, even with enemies; dignity, such that the knight could permit none to doubt his word, his courage, nor the beauty and chastity of the lady he served, much less offer them insult or injury. In each of these cases, should occasion arise, the knight had to avenge his offended honor and fight with the offender, and was under obligation also to champion all weak and defenseless persons who sought his protection.

These ideas, which were carried throughout the world by various poems of the period, mostly French though a few Italian, gave rise later to tales or novels called the books of chivalry. They were the tomes that Don Quixote de la Mancha read so assiduously and that impelled him to transform himself also into "a knight like that." The first Spanish book of chivalry, *Historia del caballero . . . Sífar*—

History of the Knight Sífar—was written in the late thirteenth century; the period, that is, immediately subsequent to the one that we are now considering.

No one, not even though of royal blood, could be deemed a knight until he had spent a term of apprenticeship, serving as a squire. At the end of this service he received from the hands of a dubbed knight, with special attendant ceremonies, arms and the right to bear the coveted title himself: this was his knighting, or the ceremony of knighthood.

The reign of Juan II, with which we shall deal in the following chapter, was the apogee of the tournament in Castile.

Chapter IX

End of the Reconquest and Beginning of the Political Unity of Spain (1252-1516)

General Character of the Period

THE PERIOD included between the second half of the thirteenth century (Ferdinand III died in 1252; Jaime I a quarter-century later, in 1276) and the beginning of the sixteenth, is characterized by four general circumstances. First was paralyzation of the Reconquest, which after 1349 was reduced to sporadic campaigns until the *Reyes Católicos,* or Catholic Kings—Ferdinand and Isabella—undertook the conquest of Granada. The other circumstances were tapering off of the military power of the Granadine Moslem kingdom, a neighbor which, though sometimes troublesome and again submissive, no longer represented any real danger, though it did embody a strong resistance; intensification in the Christian kingdoms of civil strife (dynastic struggles, and disputes among the nobles, or of one social class with another) resulting in outbreaks of violence; aggravation of the political conflict between the unifying and disciplinary principle of the monarchy and the unsettling and separatist principle of the nobility; a conflict on this political issue that brought moments of utmost humiliation to the Kings of both Aragón and Castile, but that terminated in both kingdoms, though not simultaneously, with triumph of the royal authority and consolidation of the hereditary absolute monarchy. So much for the political and social life of the time.

In the cultural field, the period was marked by the ever more emphatic affirmation of the creative activity of the Spanish people with its own original genius; an originality which, in spite of the constant influx of very diverse foreign influences, was to make a firm foundation for the magnificent blossoming two centuries later.

Human nature being what it is, some of the reigns of the epoch, in Castile as well as in Aragón, were a typical dual expression as much of the individual personality of the Kings themselves (Alfonso X, Juan II, Alfonso V) as of the collective mind in the two fundamental aspects already indicated: the political—civil conflict and the opposition of royalty and nobility—and the cultural.

Alfonso X of León and Castile

Fernando III was succeeded by his son Alfonso X whose reign, politically speaking, was marked by two prime factors: the struggle, already noted, with the nobles who were in a practically continuous state of rebellion, and his own aspirations to the imperial throne of Germany which came very near to success, and which, if successful, would have anticipated by three centuries the principal event of the reign of Charles I of Spain who was likewise Charles V of the Holy Roman Empire; although of course we cannot say that it would necessarily have had analogous consequences.

For both these factors Alfonso X lacked the essential element: strength of character. He was a man of thought rather than a man of action (though a valiant warrior); and his political work, while well-planned in theory as is shown by his juridical writings and especially his great book *Las Siete Partidas* (The Seven Divisions) —which we have mentioned previously—suffered from indecisiveness at critical moments and regarding matters of consequence, and so weakened his own ideology of government, which was inspired on the one hand by the absolutist Justinian Code and by the patrimonial concept of monarchy on the other. In Alfonso X's mind both these influences were tempered, though only theoretically so, by the democratic doctrine of royalty which had been characteristic of Spanish thinking since the epoch of the Visigoths. It is scarcely necessary to note that the term "democratic" used in connection with those times has a meaning very different from its significance today.

Various events showed plainly Alfonso X's personal and absolutist sense of royalty, and as a natural consequence gave rise, in the distrustful and insubordinate circle of the nobility, to their evincing anew an independent attitude. As to Alfonso's absolutist ideas, the only

Tower of Giralda, at Seville.

critically acceptable evidence would seem to be in regard to his renunciation of the rights pertaining to the Castilian Crown with respect to the duchy of Gascony (1254), received as dowry by the wife of Alfonso X's grandfather, Alfonso VIII. The suppositious cession of Algarve to the King of Portugal has no bearing; the only basis in fact for that legendary cession was the temporary agreement of the Portuguese King Alfonso III to lend military aid in conquering that region.

Aside from this misconception, which must have been exploited politically during Alfonso X's reign, the nobles judged the two matters as showing an abuse of authority on the monarch's part, and seized upon them as pretext for starting a series of revolts in which the leading figures were the Lords of Biscay, the Counts of Haro, and the *Infantes,* or Royal Princes, Don Enrique and Don Fadrique. The King tried to put an end to the civil war both by making concessions to the nobles and by executing some of the instigators of the rebellion; but both measures had limited effectiveness and that for a short time only.

Alfonso X and the Holy Roman Empire

Nor was Alfonso X more fortunate in his logical ambition to wear the imperial crown of Germany as head of the Holy Roman Empire. We have had occasion more than once to mention that imperial dignity which was very different from the imperial rank in part aspired to and in part attained—though more in name than in fact—by some kings of Asturias, León and Castile.

The institution of Empire, as the reader knows, arose from the Roman tradition and became generalized in the political life of Europe. The prestige of the Roman Emperors and of their rule over almost all European countries and some in Asia and Africa persisted even after the Germanic tribes invaded the Roman provinces, settling in many of them and penetrating into Italy. That prestige and the superiority of Roman civilization over German motivated the adoption by almost all the invading peoples of the customs, laws and political structure of the Roman Empire with respect to the Royal Court and its ceremonial. When Augustulus, the last Roman Emperor, was dethroned in 476, the title of Emperor vanished from the Western world. The heads of the Eastern Roman State, or Byzantine Empire, with Constantinople

Cloister, Monastery of Pedralbes, Barcelona.

as their capital, continued to employ it; but it lapsed in the West until the Emperor Justinian (527-565) conquered a large part of Italy and of the ancient Roman provinces of Africa, and added the title of Emperor of Rome to that of Emperor of Constantinople.

The Roman Empire then, though less extensive than in the time of Augustus, achieved a restoration of political power acknowledged by all the contemporaneous kings. Constantinople was regarded as the capital of the world. But the dependence of the Western sector of this Empire on the Eastern was to continue briefly; and in fact the throne in the West remained long empty. It was filled in 800 in the person of Charlemagne, King of the Franks, who was crowned as Emperor at Rome. His son Ludovic, or Louis the Pious, inherited his title. The Empire at that time deemed itself to be the supreme civil power of Europe, independent of the ecclesiastical power, which belonged to the Pope, though allied to and closely associated with the latter, whom the Emperor had to protect with his military strength. The segments of the Empire in Europe continued to be joined together at the accession of Charlemagne's heirs, who, however, divided the territories belonging to them in such way that the imperial title, on the death of Louis the Pious, passed from the branch then ruling in France to the branch inheriting the Germanic realms; and German monarchs—or those from that part of Europe—continued to hold it for centuries. In the early years of the fifteenth century the Emperor was Philip, Duke of Swabia, whose daughter Beatrice married King Ferdinand III of Castile. This union was one of the results of the political prestige won by several twelfth and thirteenth century Spanish kings, by virtue of which they had established direct personal relations with the Emperors of Germany. Prior to this, Alfonso VII had allied himself (1152?) with the German imperial house by his marriage to a niece of the Emperor Barbarossa, or Frederick I, who in his turn had married the heiress of the House of Burgundy, a House that centuries later was to have a far more direct intervention in the political history of Spain. Castile's claim to the Basque province of Gascony, dowry of the wife of Alfonso VIII, was renounced to England by Alfonso X when the latter's sister, Eleanor of Castile, married Prince Edward, later to become Edward I of England. (When his greatly beloved Queen died, Edward erected thirteen crosses at the places where her body rested when brought from Lincoln to Westminster. The name, Charing Cross, commemorates one of these resting places.)

Alfonso X was the son of Ferdinand III of Castile and Beatrice of Swabia; and in that fact lies the justification for his claims to first the duchy of Swabia; and later the Empire. The immediate basis for the latter ambition was the initiative of the Republic of Pisa in recognizing him as Emperor in 1256. Richard of Cornwall, brother of Henry III of England, presented himself as opposition candidate; but Alfonso soon procured by bribery (an argument then much in vogue and one, we may add, that Richard likewise employed) the support of four of the most important Electors of the Imperial Crown, a number assuring him the majority of the votes. Consequently the election, held April 1, 1257, was won by the King of Castile, who received at Burgos several months later the German embassy that came to tender him the Crown of the Holy Roman Empire.

Far from being pleased by the high honor thus bestowed on their King, Castilian public opinion viewed it with disfavor. It is known that this opposition was due in part to the huge sums spent by Alfonso to buy the election and to entertain the embassy, both of which expenditures were in painful contrast to the current hard times. The economic situation was so unfavorable as to have impelled the King to adopt, among other risky measures, that of devaluating the money. But it is very likely that one influential factor in the attitude of the Castilian public was the spontaneous repugnance for any foreign venture which was felt by the elements that then had most weight in Castilian policy. It may be also that Castile at this period lacked a clear conception of the importance of the Holy Roman Empire in European politics—though centuries later, each in his own manner, Charles I and Philip II were to understand this very plainly.

The antagonism at home made Alfonso hesitate and, at times, act with a dangerous degree of dissimulation with regard to questions relating to his new dignity; but if this was detrimental to his interests as Emperor, even more so was the lively and almost unremitting opposition of Pope Alexander IV, Pope Clement IV, and all their successors up to and including Pope Gregory X; each of whom, for different reasons connected with papal policy in Italy, supported some other candidate. That opposition on the part of the Popes delayed inordinately the final solution of the controversy, and resulted in Alfonso X's renunciation of the Imperial throne in 1275 under pressure from Pope Gregory X. The entry of Castile onto the general European political scene, with the possible consequences thereof, was thus frustrated.

The Question of the Succession to the Throne

In that same year 1275, the eldest son of Alfonso X, the Crown Prince Don Ferdinand de la Cerda, died. His death stirred up a new controversy for the King, giving rise to further, and fatal, indecisiveness on his part. Alfonso, ever zealous to embody juridical principles in concrete legislation, had established for the first time in the Castilian legislation, as one of the laws of his *Siete Partidas,* the order of succession to the crown. It made this succession hereditary, in accordance with the custom by that time frankly prevalent in Castile, and in conformity also with the Roman civil law of representation by virtue of which the eldest son transmitted the hereditary right to his own sons. Application of that law on the death of Prince Ferdinand de la Cerda made it necessary to proclaim his first-born, Don Ferdinand, as heir apparent to the throne; but Alfonso's second son Sancho opposed this, and the consequence was civil warfare and a series of successive changes in Alfonso's will and testament. Shameful episodes ensued, as when King Alfonso X himself was deposed in 1282 by the *Cortes* held at Valladolid which was packed with Sancho's partisans. Alfonso died before the dynastic tangle could be straightened out.

To offset such political calamities can be adduced only some gains made by Alfonso X in the course of the Reconquest. These were the capture of the district of Cádiz from Morón to Medina Sidonia and Rota; of Niebla and part of Algarve; and of the fortress of Cartagena; which victories narrowed on the west and the east the former coastal frontiers of the Kingdom of Granada.

Alfonso X and Cultural Life

The unhappy picture offered, apart from these military victories, by the politics of Alfonso X's reign, finds compensation in the monarch's own scientific and literary importance and in his considerable influence on Spanish culture. He was a great patron and disseminator of the scientific knowledge of his time (as had been Alfonso VI and Alfonso VII before him), seeking it out where it was then chiefly to

Initial miniature, Cantigas de Alfonso el Sabio, with portrait of Alfonso the Sage.

be found, among Moslems and Jews. His educational achievements include creation of the university courses in Latin and Arabic at Seville, and of the mixed School or University of Murcia with a faculty representing the three races: Spanish Christian, Spanish Moslem, and Jew. He attempted to create at Seville also chairs of the natural sciences for the physicists who came from foreign countries, just as he established chairs of medicine, surgery, music, and plain song at Salamanca. Contemporaneously with Alfonso X, the regular and secular clergy organized for priests and monks special instruction which included the Arabic language and literature, grammar and logic, theology, and the Holy Scriptures. On the King's own initiative, the very comprehensive juridical encyclopedia called *Las Siete Partidas* (already mentioned) was written. The *Partidas* is not only a book of Law which summed up the juridical knowledge of its time and introduced vigorously into juridical practice (and later into legislation proper) important elements of Justinian Law, but it constitutes as well one of the literary monuments of the Castilian language. By that time Castilian had already acquired much of the vigor of expression and richness of words which made it capable of producing the great literature of a somewhat later period. The *Partidas* was read far and wide and translated into other tongues. Fragments are extant of what were probably two Portuguese translations, made in the fourteenth century or perhaps earlier.

The savants who surrounded Don Alfonso also wrote, at his behest, works on cosmography, astronomy, and chemistry; corrected the astronomical tables then used to measure time; edited the so-called *Crónica general de España,* or General Chronicle of Spain, which ends with the reign of Ferdinand III and the original text of which we do not possess but merely fourteenth and fifteenth century copies; and rendered other important scientific services. Moreover, the King himself was a poet, and he bequeathed us, together with their musical accompaniments, an enchanting collection of his songs to the Virgin, in the Galician tongue, known as the *Cantigas de Santa María.* He also left other poems satirical in style. In recognition of all this he was called *Alfonso el Sabio*—Alfonso the Sage.

Although, as we have just noted, Alfonso wrote poetry in Galician, he employed in prose both scientific and political (public documents), and had others employ, Castilian instead of Latin; thus contributing

Painting on wood, Collection of Don Román Vicente, Saragossa

The Virgin of Tobed, Adored by King Don Enrique II of Castile, Queen Doña Juana Manuel, Prince Don Juan and Princess Doña Leonor.

greatly to the development, and much extending the use, of that Romance language of central Spain, the *lengua castellana,* or "Castilian." "Spanish" as the name for the language is much more modern.

The Successors of Alfonso X to Alfonso XI

The reign of Sancho IV, who ultimately emerged as victor from the dynastic struggle with Crown Prince Ferdinand de la Cerda's sons, afforded little that was new in the way of internal politics. However, there were two very important innovations in foreign policy. One was the peace pact with Aragón, which under Alfonso III (1285-1291) had been at war with Castile in consequence of Aragonese support of de la Cerda's sons against Sancho IV. Also on Alfonso III's death, the Castilian monarch, seeking to reach an agreement with the successor to the Aragonese throne, Jaime II, obtained the latter's signature to a treaty according to which the two Kings divided the territories of North Africa between them; Castile reserving the western portion from the Muluya to the Atlantic (in reality, the Sultanate of Morocco), and Aragón the eastern part, from the Muluya to Bujía and Tunis, this last having been an Aragonese protectorate since 1280. The first step on Castile's part toward carrying out this arrangement was a campaign against the extreme southern part of the Cádiz district which resulted in capture of the important fortress of Tarifa in 1292. It was then garrisoned by troops of Benimerines from Morocco, successors of the Almohades and constant allies of the Kings of Granada. Years later, in one of the episodes of the dynastic struggle, Sancho IV again had to fight the Benimerines, auxiliaries in that instance of the *Infante* Don Juan, brother of the King and himself pretender to the throne. In this latter campaign, Sancho destroyed the squadron that the Benimerines had gathered at Tangiers to transport their troops to Spain; while the Governor of Tarifa, Guzmán the Good, defended the fortress against the attacking Moslems. Possession of this stronghold, which the King of Granada also coveted, gave Castile the military key of the Strait against African invasions.

The minority of Sancho IV's son and heir, Ferdinand IV, produced a new period of lawlessness such as had prevailed during Alfonso VIII's minority. The situation was saved in great part by the admirable political sagacity and great personal endowments of Doña María de Molina. mother of the child king. The problem was the more pressing because there were not only internal enemies to fight but also Aragón, Portugal, Granada, and France; all of which severally tried to turn the situation to their own advantage. When the crisis had been surmounted and Ferdinand IV had become of age, he made peace with Portugal and Aragón and pacted with the Aragonese King to carry out a conjoint campaign against the Moors of Granada and the Benimerines of Morocco, provided that Aragón cede the district of Almería to Castile (Pact of Alcalá, 1309).

Ferdinand besieged the fortified town of Algeciras and the Aragonese King Jaime II laid siege to Almería, but neither achieved his objective. However, the united forces of Castile and Aragón succeeded in overpowering the fortress of Gibraltar, an achievement due principally to Guzmán the Good. That occasion was the last on which Aragón took part in the Reconquest in the Andalusian sector.

Alfonso XI

The reign of Alfonso XI (1312-1350), son and successor of Ferdinand IV, was especially remarkable from the point of view of the war against the Moslems of Spain and Africa. After a minority even more turbulent and unruly than that of Ferdinand IV, its difficulties aggravated by defeats suffered in war with the Kingdom of Granada and consequent loss of several fortresses along the southeastern frontier— among them that of Baza, in 1324—the new King, declared of age in 1325, proved to have extraordinary ability as an administrator and as a military commander in the struggle with the Moslems. He subdued the internal disturbances, punishing and reducing to submission the rebel lords; fostered the civil liberties and political authority of the municipalities; built up the public treasury; and by means of improvements and guarantees in the administration of justice, he bent his efforts toward protecting the common people and the weak against abuses by those in power.

In strife with the Moslems he demonstrated great tenacity of purpose and a firm determination to destroy the continual menace of the Benimerines. Misfortune beset his first campaigns. In 1333 he lost Gibraltar, and in 1340 the Castilian squadron was routed at Algeciras by the Benimerines who laid seige anew to Tarifa. Without losing heart, Alfonso XI hurled his troops against them, and in two battles— Salado in 1340 and the Palmones river in 1343—defeated the Moroccans, who were aided by the Granadines, and eventually in 1344 he conquered Algeciras. In this last feat of arms Alfonso XI had the aid of Philip de Evreux, King of Navarre; Gascon troops from the Counties of Foix and Castiellon; and English and German knights.

Five years later, in 1349, Alfonso XI renewed the effort to recapture Gibraltar. He did not succeed in doing so, because the plague (one of the many epidemics that devastated Europe during the Middle Ages) brought death to the great King himself, whose valor and steadfastness had rid Spain of the threat of the Benimerines and had diminished further still the military importance of the Granadines. By reason of this, the battles of Salado and Palmones river may be said to have been as decisive in the history of the Reconquest as had been the battle of Navas which in 1212 turned back the Almohade invasion.

From Pedro I to Enrique IV (1350-1474)

The century and a quarter—or, to be exact, the one hundred and twenty-four years—from the accession to the throne in 1350 of Pedro I, son of Alfonso XI, to the death of Enrique IV in 1474, were a dark and dismal epoch in the political life of the Kingdom of León and Castile; except for brief intervals that were without effectiveness in remedying the serious ills from which the internal constitution of those lands was suffering.

A dynastic struggle that was paramount throughout almost the whole of Pedro I's reign (1350-1369), terminated with his assassination by his bastard brother, Enrique de Trastamara, who seized the throne. A conflict of this new King was waged with Portugal, Navarre, Aragón, England, Granada, and the followers of Pedro I, who were faithful to the latter's memory and upheld the rights of his sons; a conflict that the bastard King brought to a close by a great display of military strength and by means of money grants—*mercedes*—to the nobles which seriously undermined the income of the Crown. In the brief reign of Enrique de Trastamara's son, Juan I (1379-1390), the two most noteworthy events were a frustrated attempt to unite the Crowns of Castile and Portugal under a single King, an attempt that met with violent opposition from the Portuguese. The reconciliation of the Trastamara branch with the legitimate heirs of Pedro I was brought about by marriage of the *Infante* Enrique, Juan I's son, with Pedro I's granddaughter; the daughter of John of Gaunt, Duke of Lancaster,

Thereupon the young Prince took the title of Prince of Asturias, which had not theretofore been used but from that time forward was to be the title of the heir-apparent to the throne. The regency during the minority of this Enrique III was as turbulent as previous minorities had been, which state of lawlessness Enrique brought under control on attaining his majority in 1399, by punishing several nobles and revoking many of the money grants made by both his grandfather and his father—acts on his part which gave the Crown momentarily a semblance of energy that found expression in international affairs by a naval expedition against Tetuan resulting in destruction of that city in 1400 and by the aid given by the Castilian King in the conquest of the Canary Islands, begun in 1402 by the Spaniard Rubín de Bracamonte and the Frenchman Jean de Bethencourt. Another reign humiliating for the Crown was that of Juan II (1406-1454), a monarch deficient in will-power who paid slight attention to the requirements of government, whereupon a fresh outbreak of rebellion among the nobility proved too strong even for the dynamic energy and customary fortune in arms of the King's Minister and favorite, Don Alvaro de Luna, who was to be the final victim of the clash between the clique of nobles and the Court intrigues. Ultimately, there ensued an epilogue of royal debility as represented by the reign of Enrique IV (1454-1474) who was deposed of his crown by the nobles and was submissive to their affronts to such degree as tacitly to admit that he was in fact not the father of his presumptive daughter and only child, Juana ("Juana la Beltraneja" she was nicknamed by those who believed her to be the daughter of the King's favorite, Beltrán de la Cueva), though Enrique was later to name her heiress to the Crown. Such, substantially, was the picture of the internal life of Castile from the middle of the fourteenth century to the close of the fifteenth.

King and Nobles in the Aragonese Monarchy

The political crisis was as violent and ill-starred in Aragón as in Castile but found a more rapid conclusion there with the victory, though it was only relatively speaking a victory, of the monarchy.

Jaime I, as we know, had to muster all his courage and energy to control the nobles who several times rebelled against him. History repeated itself in the reign of his son and successor Pedro III. The principal threat to the Crown came from a kind of association of

Aragonese nobles called the Union, which was joined by some of the cities and *villas* less democratic in feeling and less opposed to the nobility, but also less royalist, than those of León and Castile. In 1238 this Union presented to Pedro III (who at the moment was overburdened with other political problems) a long list of petitions and grievances which he had to accept with fair promises that were not, however, fulfilled. The sum total of the privileges thus promised by the King was called the *Privilegio general,* or General Privilege. It consisted chiefly of the preservation of the *fueros,* privileges, and ancient customs by the nobility and the bourgeoisie. In that total, while there was recognition of some rights and there were general guarantees against outrages on the part of the powerful and abuse of authority, the special privileges of the nobility, which far exceeded those of any other class, were also perpetuated and intensified. Consequently there was likewise continued and strengthened the tendency of the nobility to evade the State's judicial discipline which was mainly in the hands of the king's representatives.

Alfonso III, Pedro III's successor, less energetic and resolute than his father, was more yielding, and in 1287 granted to the coalition of nobles and municipalities a new privilege, known as the *Privilege of the Union,* one of the clauses of which empowered the *Cortes* to depose the king if he failed to fulfil any of the privileges conceded. Strife burst forth again, hotter than ever, in the reign of Pedro IV (1335). That monarch was the last man in the world to be complaisant with anybody. In addition to holding rigid convictions as to royal authority, Pedro IV was by temperament arrogant and violent, bold and obstinate in all circumstances, and little scrupulous with regard to measures for reaching his objectives.

The conflict was soon raging high. A pretext for it was afforded by the attempt of Pedro, who had no male heirs, to have his daughter Constanza sworn as his heiress in prejudice of what the Aragonese and Valencian nobles held to be the right of Jaime, who was Pedro's brother. For the time being, the King had to give in to these nobles because he had only the Catalán nobility on his side; but he cherished the determination of revenging himself upon them at the first possible moment. This revenge Pedro tried to achieve in 1348 against the Unionists of Valencia; but he failed of his purpose. A new effort in the same year, directed against the Aragonese, defeated them overwhelmingly at Epila. Thereupon Pedro IV entered Saragossa in triumph, abolished the privileges of the Union, and sentenced many of the rebels to death. Shortly after, he repeated this performance in Valencia.

As evidence of the ferocity of the conflicts of the time, the fact is cited that the King inflicted hideous tortures on the Valencian Unionists, such as forcing down their throats the molten metal of the bell that had summoned them to meetings of the Union. It is related also that with his own poignard Pedro IV scraped the text of the Privileges from the parchment whereon they were written, and that he did so with such fury as to wound himself in the hand. That was the origin of his Valencian nickname, *En Pere del Punyalet*—Don Pedro of the Little Poignard.

Abolition of the Privilege went no further than doing away with the special concessions that had been written into it. Consequently, the rights recognized by the common law of the realm in favor of both nobility and municipalities remained intact; which proves that Pedro IV did not proceed against the political organization of Aragón and Valencia in its fundamentals but rather against the exaggerated grants to the nobility and to the municipalities allying themselves with the nobles. Thus ended for the time being the struggle between the two forces, monarchy and aristocracy.

The Foreign Conquests of the Kings of Aragón. Pedro III

Jaime I had divided the realms under his crown into two kingdoms independent one of the other: Aragón and Mallorca. By doing so he was continuing the patrimonial tendency of the Spanish kings which had ascendency in their minds over their understanding of the general interests of the State and over the accumulated experience that should have shown them that strength (such as then and for centuries after they understood strength to be) resided in the cohesion and territorial extent of the realm, which were the foundation of resources and of power. Jaime gave Aragón, with Catalonia and Valencia (which were constituted into the kingdom but subordinated to the Aragonese sector) to his eldest son, Pedro III, whom we have considered in another connection. The Kingdom of Mallorca, with the Counties of Roussillon and Sardinia and the Seignory of Montpelier he gave to his second son, whose name was also Jaime. In 1278 the latter declared himself feudatory of his brother; an act which, demonstrating the superior importance of the Aragonese kingdom, soon brought on conflicts that in the final analysis made the new Kingdom of Mallorca independent.

This political mis-step on Jaime I's part found a certain compensation in that it led to the marriage of his son Pedro with Constance of Swabia, daughter of Manfred, King of Sicily. It was from this marriage that the Kings of Aragón derived their rights to the southern part of Italy and the Island of Sicily. It was Jaime I's intention to counteract by means of the alliance the danger to the traditional influence of Aragón and Catalonia in Provence which was represented by the recent marriage of the Countess of Provence to Charles of Anjou, who belonged to the French royal house which was the perennial rival in southern France of the Counts of Barcelona and the Kings of Aragón.

The first action with international consequences effected by Pedro III was his intervention in Tunis. Jaime I had been allied with the Moslem King of Tunis, El-Mostansir, who paid tribute to the Aragonese crown. On El-Mostansir's death, the Tunisian throne was usurped by one of his sons, in defiance of the legitimate heir's rights. Pedro III took advantage of the occasion to send a military expedition into Tunis in 1280 under command of a Sicilian mariner, Coral or Conrad de Llansa, who was in the service of Aragón. The result was to establish in that Moslem kingdom a sort of Aragonese protectorate, the advantage of which for Pedro III were those of collecting both direct tribute and half the wine-tax; establishing consuls at two points in Tunis; and having an _alcalde,_ or justice, in the person of an Aragonese or Catalán knight, for the protection of Christians resident there. In such fashion began Spanish influence in north central Africa. It is thought that Pedro III's chief concern in this was with regard to possible developments in the neighboring Kingdom of Sicily, which at that time belonged to the German imperial house and was ruled by Pedro III's father-in-law, Manfred. The Popes coveted the Neapolitan kingdom that belonged to Manfred, jointly with the Island of Sicily. In order to acquire more or less direct possession of these territories, the Popes had need to break the Imperial power with which they had long been in conflict over the question of investiture (appointment by the Emperor of ecclesiastical authorities) and other matters concerning Italy. It seemed to the Pope that a good way of achieving his object would be to concede the Kingdom of Sicily to Charles of Anjou on condition that he redeem it from power of the Germans and declare himself feudatory of the Church. In 1264, agreeing to this proposal, Charles conquered Sicily after a brief campaign in which both Manfred and his young nephew Conrad perished. Thus in Sicily and Naples commenced the rule of the Angevine house of France: the Anjous.

But neither the conquest nor the Pope's concession of the kingdoms in expectation of great returns could invalidate the lawful rights of the House of Swabia. On the deaths of Manfred and Conrad, the surviving representative of these rights was Pedro III of Aragón who therefore became the only hope of the Sicilian Ghibellines (partisans of the Empire, belonging for the most part to the nobility), who in consequence were harassed more than ever by the papal Guelphs, consisting in the main of merchants and burghers. Although it cannot be stated definitely at just what moment the Aragonese King really began to take an active interest in the opportunity that offered, it may be said that he did not long delay negotiations with the Ghibellines through the medium of the Sicilian knight, Juan de Prócide, or Próxida. The purpose of those negotiations was to concert a League against Charles of Anjou, composed of the Kings of Aragón and Castile, the Emperor of Byzantium, many Sicilian knights and the Pope himself (at that time Nicholas III), who is supposed to have desired establishment in Italy of two kingdoms, Lombardy and Tuscany, for two of his nephews; in carrying out which project the Angevine domination was a hindrance. Nicholas III's death in 1280, and election of the French Pope Martin V, frustrated all hopes of the proposed League.

None of this, however, discouraged Pedro III nor the Sicilian Ghibellines from their purposes. The King prepared for the probable war, trying to straighten out the internal problems of his kingdom and seeking an alliance with Sancho IV of Castile, while at the same time he pushed naval preparations with the apparent object of sending an expedition to Constantina, in Argel, whose Bey had sought Pedro's aid against the Sultan. In June 1283 the squadron, 140 vessels strong with 15,000 men, did in fact set sail for the Barbary coast, where the Aragonese troops seized the fortress of Alcoyll. Shortly before, in March, had occurred the uprising in Sicily against the Angevines which is known as the Sicilian Vespers. In consequence of its success a Sicilian embassy was sent to Pedro III to tender him the Crown of Sicily in recognition of his embodiment of the rights of the House of Swabia. Pedro III accepted, not without opposition from many of the nobles who accompanied him; and on August 30, 1283, he arrived at Trapani with his fleet and army. His victory was swift and decisive, both on the Island of Sicily and in the mainland territory of Naples. The most dashing figure of that campaign was the King's Admiral, Roger de Lauria, who routed the Angevine fleet at Malta and at Naples in June, 1284, and took prisoner Charles d'Anjou's son, known as Charles the Lame.

Charles of Anjou died in January 1285, leaving the Angevine cause without a leader in Italy, a fact greatly facilitating the Aragonese conquest. But the Pope, Martin IV, had interposed new and very serious obstacles to this conquest by excommunicating Pedro III and declaring him deprived of his realms, which were conceded by the Papal verdict to Charles de Valois, third son of the King of France (May, 1284). In order to give these decisions the stamp of legality, the Pope based them on the infeudation of the Aragonese kingdom made by Pedro II, father of Jaime I, although that act of Pedro II's had been repudiated repeatedly by Jaime and by Pedro III, and had been completely and unanimously rejected by Aragonese public opinion as well.

The Pope's action encouraged Charles de Valois and his father, the French King, to invade the territories of the Aragonese Crown, an invasion which in the circumstances took on the character of a Crusade preached by the Holy See. The invaders were supported by the King of Mallorca, brother of Pedro III and Lord of Roussillon; and when they penetrated into Catalonia they also found cooperation among the Catalán nobles and ecclesiastics and in various municipalities of Ampurdán. Roger de Lauria, urgently summoned to counteract the initial victories of the French troops who were laying siege to Gerona, won a naval victory—the battle of the Fornigas Islands—which, together with an epidemic that spread through the French army, then led by King Philip the Bold himself, decided the campaign. Philip withdrew into France, not without first suffering the severe defeat of his army at the port or *coll* of Panissars; but the war continued for some time in Roussillon, while Aragonese rule was strengthened in Sicily and Naples.

Nevertheless, Pope Martin IV's purpose was on the verge of achievement, since Pedro III, on his deathbed, November 11, 1285, beseeching the Archbishop of Tarragona to absolve him from the excommunication inflicted by the Pope, declared that he then and there returned to the Holy See the Kingdom of Sicily.

The New Kingdom of Sicily

However, this deathbed decision by Pedro III was accepted neither by his eldest son, Alfonso III, heir to the Crown of Aragón, nor by his second son, Jaime, who during his father's lifetime had been sworn as heir to the Crown of Sicily. By agreement between the two brothers, Jaime had himself crowned King of Sicily in 1286; an event which made that kingdom definitely independent of Aragón though ruled by a member of the Aragonese royal house, and which even while substantially in opposition to the Papal claims and those of the French, facilitated bringing about a compromise between Alfonso III and his political enemies. This compromise took shape in the Peace of Canfranc in 1288, the principal conditions of which with respect to Sicily and Aragón were the following: recognition of Jaime's possession of the Kingdom of Sicily; revocation of the Pope's investiture of the Kingdom of Aragón in favor of Charles of Valois; recognition of the lordship of the Aragonese kings over Mallorca and Roussillon, territories which Alfonso III had seized as punishment for the disloyalty of his uncle, Jaime, King of Mallorca, in giving aid to the French; liberation (though indemnities and additional ransom were demanded) of Charles the Lame, who had remained a prisoner since June 1284.

Once Charles the Lame was put at liberty, however, neither the King of France nor the Pope would carry out the other measures agreed upon at Canfranc, so the war continued in Sicily and Calabria. A new peace treaty signed at Tarascon in 1291 was equally ineffectual, although Alfonso III obligated himself by it to pay the Holy See the quit-rent promised by Pedro II with all overdue back payments, and to ask his brother Jaime to fulfil Pedro III's dying wishes by returning the Kingdom of Sicily to the Pope. But the Treaty of Tarascon was not to be put into effect. Alfonso III died soon after signing it, and the Crown of Aragón, Catalonia and Valencia was inherited by his brother Jaime II who, abandoning Sicily in order to receive his new States, left as sovereign of that island his brother Fadrique, Pedro

III's third son. The inevitable result of this was renewed warfare with France. Jaime II was able to check the conflict by negotiating a third treaty, that of Agnani (June 5, 1295), which reaffirmed Pedro III's promise with respect to Sicily, though adding the stipulation that Aragón receive the islands of Corsica and Sardinia, which the Pope ceded to the Aragonese King on condition the latter conquer them on his own account and pay quit-rent to the Holy See.

Fadrique, pursuing a line of conduct like his brother Jaime's with regard to the Treaty of Tarascon, did not wish to recognize its validity, nor did Sicilian public opinion favor doing so. Consequently, the singular spectacle ensued of the King of Aragón and the French King fighting as allies to deprive an Aragonese Prince of his dominion, a kingdom that had been conquered by another King of Aragón. But the war lasted only a few years. In 1302, in a new peace treaty, Charles d'Anjou recognized Don Fadrique as King of Sicily, although only on condition that the latter marry Doña Leonor, Charles' daughter, and that on Fadrique's death the Sicilian Crown should pass to France. But that final stipulation was no more to be complied with than had been some clauses in former treaties; on the contrary, the Kingdom of Sicily was long to continue in the power of the royal house of Aragón.

The Expedition to the Near East by Cataláns, Aragonese and Navarrese; and the Duchy of Athens

The end of the Sicilian war brought one unexpected result which, within the military customs and venturesome spirit of the times, may be (and has been) described as glorious.

The peace pact of 1302 left thousands of men jobless in Sicily, since the only work that they had learned to do was fighting. King Fadrique, well aware that the existence of so many unemployed was a threat to the internal peace of his realm, looked about for a means of uprooting this menace and found it in suggesting to one of the leaders of those idle soldiers, Roger de Flor of Brindisi, that the troops go to the aid of Andronicus, Emperor of Constantinople, at the time hard-pressed by the attacking Turks—a very war-minded people—who had already made themselves master of all the Byzantine possessions in Asia Minor. Roger de Flor welcomed the suggestion, and in 1303 set sail on ships facilitated by Fadrique with a mixed army, infantry and cavalry, of 6500 men. The Emperor Andronicus received them joyfully; in token of gratitude he bestowed the title of Megaduke on Roger de Flor, and gave him the King of Bulgaria's daughter for wife. With the launching of the campaign against the Turks in Asia Minor, Roger and his followers very soon gained great victories. As news of them spread, other Catalán, Aragonese and Navarrese adventurers hastened to enlist, and carried out new expeditions under command of Berenguer de Rocafort and Berenguer de Entenza. The Emperor of Byzantium, in recompense for the success of the campaign which quickly liberated him from the Turks, awarded Roger de Flor the title of Caesar and transferred that of Megaduke to Entenza. He also ceded them in 1305 the whole of Anatolia, to be partitioned among the knights of their respective troops.

Such extraordinary marks of favor, well-deserved though they were, excited the envy of the imperial courtiers and of the heir-apparent, Prince Michael. The consequence was a conspiracy culminating in the assassination at a banquet of Roger de Flor and many of his officers, together with 1300 of his followers. Other groups of Cataláns and Aragonese, at Constantinople and Gallipoli, were similarly assassinated. The expeditionary force was reduced thereby to some 3300 infantry and 200 cavalry. Burning with rage, and determined on revenge, these survivors in their turn attacked the Byzantines, whom they defeated in several skirmishes, and put some towns to the torch. When the King of Sicily learned all this, he sent Prince Ferdinand as his plenipotentiary in the crisis from which obviously there might arise very grave consequences. But the disputes that flared up among the leaders of different divisions of the troops (as often happens with heterogeneous masses in which the several component units are accustomed to operate independently), neutralized the advantages attained and gave a new direction to the military activities of the Catalán, Aragonese, and Navarrese warriors. It was brought about by a call made to them by the Duke of Athens, who, under attack from political enemies, besought them to come to his aid. This they did, with brilliant success crowning their arms; but once again their reward was treason and ingratitude. Reacting toward treachery in Greece as they had in Byzantium, the Spanish soldiers took the city of Athens by assault, establishing themselves there and placing themselves under protection and sovereignty of King Fadrique of Sicily. He accepted the role of protector, and sent his second son Manfred to head the new

Interior, Maritime Exchange, Palma de Mallorca.

State. Thus in 1326 the Sicilian duchy of Athens (and indirectly, the Crown of Aragón) was born, to last some sixty-odd years until 1387 or 1388; and in this normal manner terminated the derring-do of those soldiers of fortune who bore the standards of Aragón and Catalonia in triumph through Greece and Asia Minor. As always happens in such cases, that political domination brought in its train an influence of Hispanic civilization on the Near East and especially on Greece, and affected too the literature of chivalry, as is obvious in the work of the fifteenth century and early sixteenth century Italian poets Bojardo and Ariosto.

The Conquest of Minorca and Sardinia

It was not in the Near East only that dominions of the royal house of Aragón were extended in the late thirteenth and early fourteenth century. In the western Mediterranean likewise its domains were augmented, first by conquest in 1286 of the island of Minorca, which, though it had been subject to vassalage since the time of Jaime I, was in possession of the Moslems; and second by conquest of Sardinia. This latter achievement was effected in 1223-24, when Jaime II's son, who was later to ascend the throne as Alfonso II, was still heir-apparent. Pisa, the Italian maritime city-republic that had possessed Sardinia prior to that time, defended the island most tenaciously, thus greatly delaying the establishment there of a stable Aragonese foothold. In Sardinia also the influence of Catalán civilization was strongly dominant.

Not long before this, in 1312, the dispute pending with the Crown of France over dominion of the Valley of Arán in the Pyrenees was settled by a judicial decision. The documentation in the case presented by the Aragonese Crown fully demonstrated that by right Arán belonged to sovereignty of Aragón.

The Kingdom of Mallorca

For the decade from 1285 to 1295 the Kingdom of Mallorca lost its sovereignty, which had been incorporated into that of the Aragonese Crown in punishment for Jaime II's disloyalty. This measure, as we have seen, was recognized and sanctioned by the Treaty of Canfranc. Returned to Jaime II in 1295 on his declaring himself Aragón's feudatory, Mallorca enjoyed internal peace during his reign and that of his son Sancho; and the island prospered economically and culturally. The Castle of Almudaina, the Castle of Bellver, and the Convent of St. Francis at Palma belong to this period. When Sancho died childless in 1325, a dispute regarding the succession to the throne arose between his nephew, Jaime III of Mallorca, and King Jaime II of Aragón; a dispute temporarily silenced by Jaime III's marriage to a granddaughter of King Jaime II of Aragón, the daughter of the deceased Alfonso IV. Then in 1329 the Kingdom of Mallorca declared itself a new feudatory of the Aragonese Crown.

A few years later, in 1343, Alfonso IV's successor, Pedro IV, put an end to Mallorcan independence by conquering that island, and Minorca and Ibiza as well. The following year he conquered Roussillon, meeting stronger resistance there from Jaime II's followers. The latter tried to recover his kingdom by force, but his troops were vanquished at Lluchmayor, Mallorca, in 1349. In this battle Jaime III of Mallorca himself perished. His son, Jaime IV, who had the title of king but no kingdom, made another attempt to recoup his losses in 1374, but without avail. With his death the aspirations of the ephemeral Mallorcan royal house, those ill-starred descendants of the great Jaime I of Aragón, were at an end.

From Pedro IV to Martín I

Without delaying over the brief and unimportant reign of Alfonso IV of Aragón (1327-1336), we shall consider some aspects of that of his successor, Pedro IV, whose struggles with the Union and ultimate victory over it we have already discussed.

The early years of Pedro IV's reign were taken up with the war against the Benimerines and the Moors of Granada and of Mallorca. The preceding paragraphs took note of the latter conflict and its consequences. Mention was made of the former in relating the campaigns of Alfonso XI of Castile, with whom Pedro IV collaborated. The strife in Sardinia preoccupied Pedro IV as fully as had these earlier conflicts; popular uprisings were being continually fomented by the Republic of Genoa, acting with the Republic of Pisa and other Italian elements. Pedro IV resolved to end this state of affairs once and for all, formed an alliance with the Seignory of Venice, availing himself of the age-old animosity of Venetians against Genoese, and

Cloister, Cathedral of Barcelona.

declared war on Genoa. The combined Aragonese and Venetian fleets twice defeated the Genoese squadron; but since this of itself was not sufficient to subdue the island of Sardinia, in 1354 Pedro IV disembarked there in person with a strong army, taking possession of several important Sardinian towns. Although these victories made Aragonese control considerably stronger than it had been theretofore, they did not avail to suppress wholly the uprisings of the always unruly Sardinians.

A compensation for this uncomfortable state of disquiet was the tender of the Duchy of Athens, offered Pedro IV in 1381 by the Catalán and Aragonese elements in Greece who up to that time had been dependents of the Crown of Sicily. Pedro accepted the dukedom, and in return granted Athens the same city-charter of privileges enjoyed by Barcelona, the most autonomous municipality of Catalonia, superior in its chartered rights, as we have seen, to all the rest.

The two kings who followed Pedro IV, his sons Juan I (1387-1395) and Martín I (1396-1409) are little worthy of note. During the reign of the former, disturbed by rebellion in Sardinia and in Sicily, Aragón lost the Duchy of Athens which was promptly conquered in 1388 by the Florentine banker Nerio Acciajuoli, Lord of Corinth. Although the Cataláns, Aragonese, and Navarrese resident in Athens defended themselves with great courage, lack of aid from Aragón forced them to yield. The Navarrese, in alliance with the Republic of Venice, tried to recapture the Duchy and did succeed in taking Nerio prisoner in 1389. The King of Sicily also made attempts to recover Athens; but neither Sicily nor the Navarrese achieved definite success. The Turks seized part of the territory in the Spanish zone of influence, and the city of Athens remained in power of Venice.

Martín I, who during Juan I's reign was already King of Sicily, succeeded the latter on the throne of Aragón, and the two Crowns were thus again united in 1409; but Martín's premature death without a testament that could apply (since the only one extant named as his heir a son who had predeceased him by several months), left the question of the inheritance of the kingdoms very much involved.

As a matter of fact, such a state of affairs was nothing new in the dynastic history of Aragón. Similar conditions had prevailed more than once in former centuries. The situation brought about by Martín I's death, however, resulted in one of the most important political and judicial events in the history not only of Spain but of Europe. This was the pact known as the Compromise of Caspe.

The Compromise of Caspe

The two principal pretenders to the Crowns of Aragón and Sicily were Don Ferdinand of Antequera, son of a sister of the deceased King Martín I, and Don Jaime, Count of Urgell, son of a cousin of that monarch and thus grandnephew of Pedro IV. Public opinion in the two kingdoms and in the region of the ancient County of Barcelona was very much divided. The chief reason for the unpopularity of the candidacy of Ferdinand of Antequera, Prince of the Castilian royal house, among the majority of the Cataláns and Valencians and with some Aragonese, was the mere fact of his being "a foreigner"—that is, one who by nationality belonged to none of the regions governed by the King of Aragón. After two years of uncertainty and conflict, the Catalán *Cortes* took the initiative of meeting in 1410, upon convocation by a Governor of the region, in order to try to find a solution to the dispute by legal means instead of violence. The advocates of the two claimants appeared before this *Cortes* to argue the rights of their respective clients to the royal heritage. In 1412 both Aragonese and Valencians expressed willingness to abide by the decision; and it was agreed to name a mixed Commission to investigate and decide the question. Mallorca, Sicily and Sardinia were not represented among the nine Commissioners, three of whom were from Aragón, three from Catalonia, and three from Valencia. One of the most eminent members was Fray Vincent Ferrer, the Valencian preacher later to be canonized, whose prestige was very great. The Commission, meeting at the *villa* of Caspe, functioned in reality as a tribunal, examining the case from the standpoint of the law, and considering it particularly in the light of the laws of civil inheritance which had been adopted by Alfonso X in *Las Siete Partidas* to regulate the succession to the throne; in other words, the case was handled as a lawsuit between relatives and not as a political problem, which latter would have required an evaluation not so much of the degrees of kinship as of the candidates' respective qualifications, with due regard for tradition and public opinion. But it is certain that the final decision was influenced by these last-mentioned circumstances and by the personal qualities of Don Ferdinand, who was renowned in Castile for the fair-mindedness and the generous spirit which he had shown as regent during young King Juan II's minority, and for his military successes against the Moors, from whom he won various fortresses, Antequera among them.

One thing is sure: the Castilian Prince was elected by the votes of St. Vincent Ferrer (who was motivated, says an ancient Aragonese historian, by "justice, according to God and his conscience"), the Bishop of Huesca, the Prior General of the Carthusian Order, the advocates Bardaxi (Aragonese) and Gualbes (Catalán), and the Aragonese Francés de Aranda. The Archbishop of Tarragona opined that it would be "more useful" (which is to say, more diplomatic) to elect Don Ferdinand, although he believed that both the Count of Urgell and the Duke of Gandía had better legal right. The Catalán advocate Vallseca was definitely of the same opinion. The statement of the decision, set forth with due solemnity in notarized minutes on June 28, 1412, was welcomed in Aragón, but received with some reservations in Valencia and with many in Catalonia, where the majority opinion seemed to favor the Count of Urgell. Nevertheless, the Catalán Parliament, meeting at Barcelona, sent an embassy to the King-elect, who was at the time in Castile, to make formal acknowledgment of his authority and to request a general amnesty, principally applicable to the Count of Urgell but stipulating that the latter should respect the Caspe decision.

Don Ferdinand granted the petition of the Catalán Parliament with good grace; and himself seconded it to the extent of proposing to the Count (who sent his advocates to the new King to offer his obedience and leave a memorandum regarding his claims) that the Count's daughter marry Don Ferdinand's own third son, Prince Don Enrique, Grand Master of the Order of the Knights of Santiago. Ferdinand further offered the Count the dukedom of Montblanch and a considerable grant of money. But the Count of Urgell, ill advised by his mother and by Don Antonio de Luna, Lord of Loarre, instead of making the best of the matter and accepting the condition imposed by the Catalán Parliament, started a civil war, aided by English, Gascon, and Navarrese knights and soldiers, and with the moral support of the Duke of Clarence, one of the sons of the King of England. Don Ferdinand quickly obtained the victory, with the Aragonese and Castilian troops come to his aid. The Count of Urgell surrendered at

Balaguer October 31, 1413, on condition that his life be spared, which Ferdinand agreed to. The Count remained under detention in the Castle of Ureña, near the Mota del Marqués in Valladolid, but with permission to keep his own servants, receive visitors, and enjoy other concessions. With the surrender soon thereafter of the Lord of Loarre, and imprisonment in a castle of the Count's mother, who was suspected of conspiracy, the civil war was at an end.

Ferdinand I and the Catalán FUEROS

One section of Catalán opinion, nevertheless, continued hostile to the new King, because of the doctrines of absolutism which he was believed to hold, a deduction drawn principally from the fact that he was a Castilian. The deduction evidently had little foundation, since the Aragonese kings, especially those posterior to the union with Catalonia, aspired no less than the Castilians to strengthen the prestige and authority of the Crown; an aspiration equally inherent in all the contemporaneous monarchies of Europe and but the more emphasized with the passage of time.

Perhaps Don Ferdinand, in general so discreet, did not fully appreciate how much it would advantage him to dissipate that prejudice, by leaning over backward if need be in showing his respect for every traditional right and custom which did not conflict directly with the king's sovereignty, as had been the case in time past with the Privilege of the Union which Pedro IV had sternly abolished and punished. The conjunction of that lack of understanding on Ferdinand's part and of an excessively zealous determination on the part of some Cataláns to maintain the general and the local *fueros* resulted in friction on several occasions during the reign of Ferdinand I of Aragón. One such was the action of the *Cortes* of Montblanch in 1414 at Tarragona, when it denied the King a subsidy that he had requested and also chided him for having employed as "mediators"—or lobbyists—at the *Cortes* some Castilian knights whom the common law of the time regarded as foreigners. Another clash occurred at Barcelona. On that occasion the King refused to pay a general tax, alleging that the monarch should by right be exempt from such obligations, a doctrine which in modern times was to triumph in political law; but the Barcelona municipal council-member, Juan Fivaller, whom the King summoned to hear the reason for the royal refusal, replied that the city's charter of rights had to be complied with and that the citizens of Barcelona weie prepared to defend their *fueros* with their lives. Public opinion on the question was at white heat. The King gave in, and paid the tax. About two centuries later, Philip II, more diplomatic than Ferdinand I—or perhaps adept at taking warning from this and similar instances—made formal request, even in regard to such a minor matter as his bringing in some effects for personal use that he had ordered from Venice, that he be relieved of paying import duty; a request that the Aragonese civil rights authorities promptly granted.

Ferdinand I and the Western Schism

For a long while—since 1378—the question of the papal succession had been beset by great difficulties, giving rise to the dual papacy or Western Schism, two separate candidates each having been elected with full canonical legality, one of them residing at Rome and the other at Avignon. In the series of the Popes of Avignon, the post of High Pontiff was then held by Benedict XIII, later to be called the Anti-Pope Luna (he belonged to the Luna family of Aragón). In the dispute over the throne of Aragón, Benedict XIII had favored the cause of Ferdinand I; but Ferdinand, urged by the Emperor of Germany, who was in agreement with Popes John XXII and Gregory XII that the Schism should be ended by their own resignation and the election of a sole Pontiff, kept insisting that Benedict XIII should facilitate this solution of the problem by likewise renouncing his Mitre. In this matter Ferdinand I acted in consonance with St. Vincent Ferrer. However, Benedict XIII refused to resign, taking his stand on canonical reasons that modern writers incline to deem justified; although it is possible that the Schism had reached a stage where it could no longer be solved by principles of law but only by considerations of general welfare. Steadfast in his decision, Benedict XIII immured himself in his Castle of Peñíscola and continued to call himself Pope up to his death in 1423. The Western Schism, however, did not end until the death in 1449 of Felix V, the last Anti-Pope; at which time Nicholas V, elected in 1447, survived as the one and only Pope in law and in fact.

Alfonso V and the Kingdom of Naples

Ferdinand I, on ascending the throne, had sent his son Juan to Sicily as his deputy. The Sicilians, who were dissatisfied with annexa-

tion to the Aragonese Crown, attempted to form an independent kingdom once more, and tried to elect Prince Juan himself as monarch.
When King Ferdinand died prematurely in 1416 at the age of thirty-
seven, his eldest son, Alfonso V, inherited the united Kingdoms of
Aragón, Mallorca, Valencia and Sicily. Fearful of the Sicilians, Alfonso
called back to Spain his brother Juan who by his marriage in 1419 to
Doña Blanca, daughter of the Navarrese King Carlos III (1387-1485),
was to become after some years King Consort of Navarre.

Feeling more at ease with respect to Sicily, Alfonso V directed his
efforts against the Genoese, in order to bring to a conclusion, if possible, the long drawn out and vexatious question of Sardinia and Corsica, always in dispute between Genoa and Pisa. Once he was in Sardinia, Alfonso received an embassy from Doña Juana, Queen of Naples
(which then formed a monarchy separate from that of Sicily). She
asked the Aragonese King's aid against her enemies, who were various, offering to make him Duke of Calabria and to name him as heir
to the Neapolitan throne upon her death. That throne had been disputed years before by Louis II of Anjou and Ladislao Duras, Juana's
brother whom she succeeded. In 1417 Louis III of Anjou had renewed
the claims of his father, Louis II.

Alfonso V accepted Juana's offer, sent out a squadron that put to
flight the fleet of Anjou, and then appeared in person at Naples and
seized the Castle of Cena, near the city. Queen Juana, changing attitude completely, broke her word, and withdrew recognition of Alfonso
as her heir, bestowing that honor instead upon Louis d'Anjou himself,
thereby setting off a new war between the Crown of Aragón and the
House of Anjou (1423). The death of the Queen of Naples a dozen
years later, in 1435, leaving Renato of Anjou as her successor, further
complicated the situation and decided Alfonso V to conquer that
kingdom. At first the campaign to this end went against him, since
Renato was aided by a Genoese fleet which in that same year 1435
took prisoner the King of Aragón himself, his brother the King of
Navarre, and many of their knights. However, with a complete right
about face typical of politicians and would-be leaders of that epoch (and
of most modern epochs as well), Renato freed Alfonso in 1436 and
formed an alliance with him. The fighting started again, soon to be
ended by the total victory of the Aragonese King, who entered Naples
February 16, 1443, in a manner which, in accordance with Renaissance
tastes, was reminiscent of the triumphal entries of the Roman Emper-

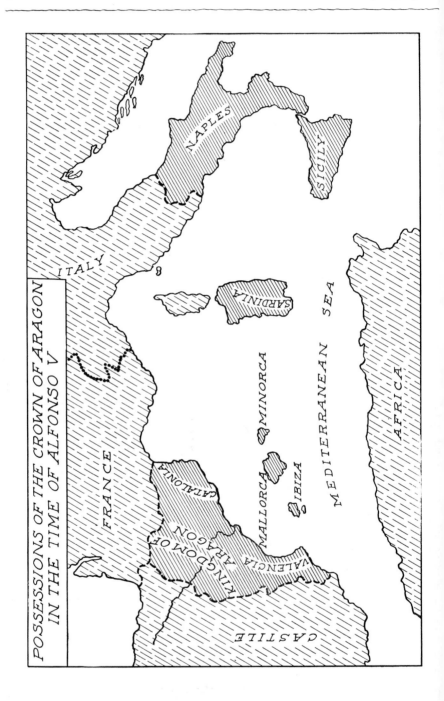

POSSESSIONS OF THE CROWN OF ARAGON
IN THE TIME OF ALFONSO V

ors. That victory facilitated Alfonso's settlement of the question pending with the Duke of Milan who recognized Alfonso as heir of his States.

Thenceforward Alfonso V resided in Naples, turning a deaf ear to the continual messages from Queen Doña María, Governor of Aragón during his absence, and from the influential personages of that realm, all of whom insisted upon his returning to Spain. Italian matters were of more interest to Alfonso than were those of his Spanish dominions, and he was greatly attracted by the Renaissance way of life and by the light that in those times played upon Princes who became patrons of art and letters. He made Naples one of the literary Courts of the period, which was contemporaneous with Juan II's reign in Castile. We shall have more to say about both later on.

Juan II and the Prince of Viana

Upon Alfonso V's death in 1458, he bequeathed his States as follows: the original realms of the Crowns of Aragón and Mallorca, with the islands of Sicily and Sardinia, to his brother Juan who, as we know, was already King of Navarre; and the Kingdom of Naples to his natural son Ferdinand, whom the Pope had legitimatized. Queen Doña Blanca of Navarre had died in 1442, leaving Juan II a widower. The heir to the Navarrese throne was their son Carlos, Prince of Viana, on whom his grandfather Carlos III had imposed the condition that he should not take the title of King during the lifetime of his father Juan II.

Since Juan II paid more attention to the political affairs of Castile (the struggles between the monarchy and the nobility and in especial against Don Alvaro de Luna) and to those of Naples than to matters relating to his kingdom of Navarre, his son Don Carlos governed that monarchy on several occasions as his father's deputy during the latter's absence. Don Juan's remarriage in 1447, the bride this time being Doña Juana Enríquez, daughter of the Admiral of Castile (one of Don Alvaro de Luna's enemies), brought about discord between father and son which soon intensified into conflict that drenched the realm in blood.

The immediate occasion of this was an attempt by Don Alvaro de Luna himself to make peace and form an alliance with the Prince of Viana. The Prince accepted his offers, while public opinion in Navarre was divided into two camps whose respective political doctrines in reality voiced the mutual antagonism of two great noble houses of Navarre—the Agramonts and the Beamonts—as well as the prevailingly anarchical sentiments of the Navarrese ruling class. The party of Prince Carlos and his policy called themselves Beamontese, since the Beamonts were his supporters, and the party of King Juan (who was urged by his wife to persist in his long-standing opposition to Don Alvaro), Agramontese, since they had backing of the Agramonts. The course of the ensuing civil war was mainly unfavorable to the Prince, whose disinheritance was proposed by his father Juan II in a pact celebrated with Count Gaston de Foix, husband of that same monarch's daughter Leonor who was the Prince of Viana's sister. The Prince himself became a refugee in Italy, where he found sympathy for his cause, in so far as regarded his right of succession to the throne of Navarre, on the part of both the Pope and Alfonso V, King of Aragón; but the latter's premature death (as we have noted) made Juan II monarch of both kingdoms, Aragón as well as Navarre, and deprived the Prince of Viana of his best chance of success. No sooner had he returned to Spain than he was imprisoned on his father's orders. The Catalán public thereupon demanded Don Carlos' release so vociferously that Juan II was forced to yield and to sign the so-called Agreement of Villafranca (June 21, 1461) which recognized the Prince of Viana as heir to the throne. The compact was not to have force for long. Three months after it was signed Don Carlos died suddenly, and the general public attributed his death to poison administered by his stepmother or one of her agents. Civil war flared up again in consequence, supported chiefly by a sector of Catalán opinion. The following year, Juan II and his wife Doña Juana Enríquez were declared public enemies of Catalonia by the *Diputación General* and were expelled from the territory. The *Diputación* itself sought a new King to aid it in its struggle with Juan II, and after several fruitless attempts to interest Enrique IV of Castile and the Constable of Portugal, the rebellious Cataláns, forgetting the centuries of quarreling with French Kings and particularly those of the House of Anjou, named Renato of Anjou to be Count of Barcelona—an act signifying the separation of the County from the Crown of Aragón.

This period of turmoil ended with the peace negotiated amicably by Juan II in 1472. Ten years previous, he had ceded to France Rousillon, which was, as we know, an integral part of the domains of the

Crown of Mallorca reincorporated into that of Aragón by Pedro IV. Although Juan II speedily had attempted himself to recover Roussillon by force of arms, he had not succeeded. As for the Kingdom of Navarre, which was inherited on Juan II's death by his daughter Leonor, who, as stated, was married to the Count of Foix, it fell once again under French influence, which had been exercised there since 1234.

The Royal Consorts of Aragón and Castile. Mutual Prospects

King Juan II died January 19, 1479, and was succeeded on the throne of Aragón, Catalonia, Valencia, and Mallorca by Ferdinand II, son of his second wife, Doña Juana Enríquez. While still a Prince, Don Ferdinand had married Princess Isabella of Castile, sister of Enrique IV, who had become Queen in 1474. Thus, after 1479, the two great monarchies of Spain were ruled by two royal consorts who are called generally *los Reyes Católicos,* the Catholic Kings, or the Catholic Monarchs. The term "the Catholic Kings" belongs especially to Ferdinand and Isabella, though ever since their time the King of Spain has been referred to as "His Catholic Majesty." This dual role and dual rule of Ferdinand and Isabella made possible the future union of both Crowns in a single monarch, a consequence which, while in 1479 neither foreseen nor apparently sought, was in the final analysis logical and perhaps inevitable.

The Period of the Catholic Kings

Although the vacillating character of Enrique IV, already noted, made the succession to the Crown a vexed question, the civil war between partisans of Juana, Enrique IV's daughter and legal heiress, and that monarch's sister Isabella, which followed on his death, lasted only five years. The fact that it lasted even so long as that was due to intervention in the conflict by King Alfonso V of Portugal, whose marriage to Juana was proposed by Castilian nobles defending her cause. But many important figures of León and Castile ranged themselves on Isabella's side. Moreover, the accusation of illegitimacy of birth which had been launched against Juana (an accusation in which, as we saw, Enrique IV himself tacitly concurred) was believed by the people although apparently refuted by the fact that the presumptive lover of Juana's mother, the Palace Mayordomo Don Beltrán de la

Cueva, adhered to the party of Isabella and fought against Juana and her supporters. Two victories by Isabella's troops, at Toro and Albuera, decided the war and resulted in the signing of a peace treaty at Trujillo in 1479, in accordance with the terms of which Alfonso V of Portugal withdrew from the dynastic struggle, abandoned also his claim to dominion over the Canary Islands and recognized Castile's right to navigate the west coast of Africa. With this last concession, the Castilian projects regarding Morocco, which had been initiated in the treaties with Aragón, received affirmation.

It was proposed to Princess Juana by way of compensation that she marry Prince Don Juan, eldest son of Ferdinand of Aragón and Isabella of Castile; but Juana elected rather to retire to a convent without renouncing the title of Queen of Castile which to the end of her life she deemed rightfully hers.

Thus a single year—1479—witnessed the twin events of Isabella's full and peaceful recognition as sovereign of Castile and her husband Ferdinand's elevation to the throne of Aragón. That year marks the beginning of the era properly called the Period of the Catholic Kings; one during which some of the great social and political problems of Castile and Aragón finally found solution and which produced two achievements of utmost importance in the history of Spain: the victorious termination of the Reconquest and the discovery of America, both occurring in the same year, 1492.

Political Reforms in Castile. The Diarchy

The Articles of Marriage of Isabella and Ferdinand had foreseen and stipulated against the possible inclination of the Aragonese Prince to intervene overmuch in the government of Castile when Isabella should become its Queen; a tendency that, it was likewise anticipated, might receive fresh impetus on the day that Ferdinand inherited the throne of Aragón. The precaution was not superfluous. Its wisdom became apparent when, upon Enrique IV's death in 1474, Ferdinand, supported by Aragonese public opinion and by some Castilian nobles, himself became pretender to the throne of Castile, basing his claim on the fact that he was the nearest male descendant of the dynasty of Trastamara and on the established Aragonese custom which, though it did not formally exclude females from the throne, in practice gave preference to the husband when the wife inherited; as had occurred in the case of Doña Petronilla. Isabella's followers bruskly rejected the claim of Isabella's husband; and an arrangement was then agreed upon, by virtue of which there was regularly established in Castile a diarchy; which is to say, a joint government by two monarchs. In fact, according to the terms of the agreement proposed by the arbitrators appointed (the Cardinal of Spain and the Archbishop of Toledo), justice was to be administered by Isabella and Ferdinand jointly, if they were in the same place at the same time, and individually and independently, if they acted while separated one from the other; royal ordinances were to be signed by both; money was to be stamped with the busts or figures of both; and the royal seals were to bear conjointly the arms of Aragón and of Castile. Only the administrative duties relating to Castile were to remain privy to Isabella.

Although at first Ferdinand declined to consent to this arrangement, which appeared to diminish his authority, he ended by accepting it. The well-known saying, *"Tanto monta monta tanto / Isabel como Fernando"*—To stand as high, as high to stand, / Isabella as Ferdinand —expressed the equality that, generally speaking, existed between husband and wife with regard to the Crown's government of Castile. That co-participation was in no wise reflected in the government of Aragón, which was exclusively Ferdinand's prerogative.

The most serious political and social problem in Castile was the nobility's utter disregard for the law, as had been evidenced so emphatically in the preceding reigns of Juan II and Enrique IV. The Catholic Kings solved it by taking strong and forthright measures, annulling through laws of the *Cortes* the special privileges imprudently granted the nobles by former monarchs or wrested from the weak hands of some kings. At the same time the Catholic Kings attempted, with considerable success, to transform the nobility into a class of courtiers whose political influence would depend wholly on the monarch's favor and good will. By various means the nobles were persuaded away from their habit of permanent residence on their estates and in their castles (one consequence of this change being that it brought about the first form of absentee landlordism in rural life). Among the persuasions used was the grant of honorary posts at Court and invitation to service in the Palace Guard, which was created in 1512 with the name of "Corps of Gentlemen of the King's House and Guard." These gentlemen (two hundred picked men from

Antoni Cloperos: *St. George*. Key of the dome of the Cloister of the Cathedral of Barcelona.

the most aristocratic families of Castile, Aragón and Sicily), received a salary in addition to the honor which their preferment represented and which was greatly coveted; and from this arrangement was traced the initial plan for the permanent army that Cardinal Cisneros was to perfect somewhat later. The military Orders, until then directed by nobles, were incorporated indirectly under the Crown by attribution to the king of their administration (1487-1494). The nobles who did not transfer their residence to the Court or to other principal cities, continued living in obscurity and in ever greater isolation on their inherited estates, unable to finance rebellions because they had no part in public office nor the public treasury. With the Castilian nobles thus under control, and allured moreover by the advantages offering in wars against the Moors and against Italy (to which we shall refer again), the political threat until that time inherent in the nobility was vanquished at last. In order to strengthen individual security and public order throughout the land, the monarchs created the *Santa Hermandad*—the Holy Brotherhood—the first form of gendarmerie or civil militia in Castile.

At the same time the Catholic Kings tried to centralize local political life, intervening very decidedly in the municipalities through the medium of *corregidores,* or magistrates, *veedores de cuentas,* or accountants, and other representatives of the Crown, and through the reduction of the occasions for meetings of the *Cortes.* Ferdinand and Isabella initiated too the series of specialized royal Councils which were speedily to lay the cornerstone of the bureaucratic government that Charles I and Philip III would later bring to its highest development.

Political Reforms in Aragón and Catalonia

Ferdinand introduced this last innovation into Aragón also, although he dared not embark upon direct measures of greater consequence. More important were those applied to Catalonia, where the King intervened forcibly in organization of the municipality of Barcelona, reforming it on his own initiative. The reforms consisted in the direct appointment by the Crown of the *concelleres,* or members of the Municipal Council (1490), and, later on, in the imposition of a system of balloting on or drawing by lot names for municipal offices. Ferdinand also reformed the Council of One Hundred, increasing the

representation of Barcelona's plutocracy on it (1493). With reference to social legislation, we shall observe hereafter the favorable
treatment for rural laborers which was obtained by the King's personal intervention; these advantages, however, applied in Catalonia
only.

Social Reforms

It is not known with certainty what were the positive results of
the changes noted above in the political actuation of the nobles in so
far as relates to their power as large landholders, nor in the social condition of the tillers of the soil. The economic importance of the nobility—its importance as capitalists—continued to be exceedingly great in
spite of the fact that some of its grants of special privileges had been
annulled and many others diminished. The data that we possess today
respecting the wealth of the noble houses of Castile and the extent of
their landed estates are good proof of this fact. The sanctioning, in
what is known as the Toro Laws, promulgated by the Catholic Kings
in 1505, of the institution of *mayorazgo* or entailment—by which the
eldest son was in general the favored heir of family property—facilitated building up and handing down from one generation to another
the great patrimonial possessions of the aristocracy; although a way
was also opened for the middle class. On the other hand, we should
not overlook two things characteristic of fifteenth century Castile's
attitude toward the juridico-economic condition of the rural laboring
class. One is the lack of obligatory general regulations applying
throughout the whole region to the semi-servile group still existing
among that class. The other is the existence of many abuses and extra-
limitations on the part of the lords, as attested by various contemporaneous documents, complaints, and appeals before the *Cortes*. It
seems an authenticated fact, nevertheless, that there was a general
movement for the emancipation of tillers of the soil and their conversion into free renters according to the various forms assumed by
that system of agricultural production and development. We are still
ignorant, however, of the several steps taken in bringing this tendency
to concrete realization, nor do we know at what moment it could first
be said that this emancipation was a general fact throughout the Kingdom of Castile.

Luis Dalmau: *The Virgin and the Councillors.*

The Catholic Kings contributed toward hastening and assuring that evolution by means of a law of October 28, 1480, which confirmed the extensive application of the license of 1285 conceding to field laborers in the Castilian realm the faculty of changing residence (that is, of leaving a seignory) and taking with them all their chattels, livestock, and farm produce. This law must not have been very fully complied with, however, to judge from the recorded instances of violations; particularly, to be sure, on farmlands belonging to the seignories. We cannot therefore make a simple inclusive statement to the effect that by the end of the fifteenth century all field laborers had achieved *de facto* a situation comparable to that of renters on the land (in cases where they did not own the plots they cultivated) or of proprietors tilling their own fields. The fact is that uprisings among the rural laborers steadily decreased in number—and these had been frequent in previous centuries. Conflicts of this kind as serious as those taking place in Aragón, Catalonia, Valencia and Mallorca, never occurred in Castile in the fifteenth century nor the sixteenth; which in itself is a powerful indication that in territories of the Castilian monarchy the question of the agricultural laborer's freedom was not as problematical as it was in the realm of Aragón; but more than this we cannot affirm with certainty. On the other hand, the alteration effected throughout practically the whole of Europe in the respective values of landed and of personal property and the comparative values of free and of servile labor, was a purely economic compulsion even more effective than juridical enactments in furthering the liberation of the working classes. Nor did the slave class, properly so termed, which existed in conformity with the law, wholly disappear. The slaves were for the most part Moorish prisoners of war who continued to be bought and sold like merchandise, with several *fueros* of the period from 1252 to 1516 giving evidence of the harsh treatment that they received. This condition of slavery lasted for some time after the epoch of the Catholic Kings.

The Servile Classes in Aragón and Catalonia

In Aragón the problem was very serious, as was proved by the frequency of rural uprisings toward the close of the fifteenth century and at the beginning of the sixteenth. Ferdinand the Catholic tried to remedy this troublesome state of things by setting a limitation to the rights of the lords and most particularly to their excessive demands on the dependent servile classes for labor and tribute; but he encountered such strong opposition from the nobles that he had to desist from his purpose.

In Catalonia, on the contrary, after a formidable revolt of the *payeses de remensa** which lasted for some time and was accompanied by great turbulence and bloodshed, the King was named as arbitrator to settle the question. This Ferdinand the Catholic did by what is called the Decision of Guadalupe after the site where he pronounced it, the Monastery of the Virgin of Guadalupe in Estremadura. The decision was favorable to the *payeses* in that it freed them from some of the tributes and labor which they owed the lords and which were generally called by the name *malos usos*—or bad customs. One benefit thus achieved by the *payeses* was the right to purchase their own freedom with a cash payment. In consequence, a rural or country middle-class evolved which acquired importance in the social pattern of the sixteenth and seventeenth centuries.

The End of the Reconquest

The Catholic Kings Ferdinand and Isabella, no less well oriented and soundly based in international policy than in internal, planned to complete the Reconquest by conquering the Moorish Kingdom of Granada. The occasion was propitious. Not long previous, while Enrique IV was still on the throne, Ismail III, King of Granada, had handed over to Castile the fortress of Gibraltar (which had again come into possession of the Moors), at the same time obligating himself to pay tribute; both of which occurrences show the military decadence of the Granadine kingdom and its fear of Castilian strength. In 1466 Ismail was succeeded by Abul Hassan Ali, also known as Mulay-Hacen, who refused to continue paying the tribute to Castile and in 1481 began hostilities by a surprise attack on the Castle of Zahara. Months later, the Castilians responded to that aggression by an assault on Alhama, a stronghold about seven leagues west of the capital city of Granada. With these two armed clashes the War of Granada was fully launched. It was to last for eleven years, affording abundant opportu-

---

* *Payese de remensa* was the term applied in Catalonia and the Balearic Isles to the laborers who were able to redeem themselves from their ancient subjection to the owners of the land.

ITALY IN 1494

SWITZERLAND

TYROL

DUCHY OF MILAN

VENICE

GENOA

MANTUA FERRARA

MODENA

OTTOMAN

EMPIRE

DALMATIA

FLORENCE

KINGDOM OF SAN MARINO

ADRIATIC SEA

SIENNA

UMBRIA

PAPAL STATES

CORSICA

ROME

SICILIES

SARDINIA

TYRRHENIAN SEA

MEDITERRANEAN

TWO

SEA

AFRICA

nity for deeds of utmost heroism on the part of both Christians and Moslems which have been recorded in innumerable legends enshrined in the *romances* called *moriscos,* or Moorish songs, and *romances de frontera,* or border ballads.

The main difficulty that had to be overcome by Spanish Christian arms in this conflict arose from the military prowess of Granadine Moors and from the flaming patriotism of many of them. In counteracting this dual difficulty, the family dissensions of the Granadine reigning house, especially the animosity between Abul Hassan and his son Boabdil and between the latter and his uncle the *Zagal Abou* Abdullah Mohammed, worked decidedly to the advantage of the Christian Spaniards. The Catholic Kings knew how to make the most of these dissensions, which motivated a civil and dynastic war amongst the Granadines, with vicissitudes that we need not here recount.

Toward the close of the year 1489, when the Christians had already mastered all the important fortresses and cities of this last Moslem kingdom in Spain—some of them taken by force of arms, others yielded up (in consequence of the surrender of Baza which brought about the rendition of Guadix) by the *Zagal,* who thereupon admitted himself to be conquered—there remained to Abul Hassan's son Boabdil only the city of Granada itself, capital of his vanished realm. The siege of Granada was to continue for several months; but from that date the eventual result could be foretold. After the city capitulated, the Catholic Kings entered the Alhambra January 2, 1492. The principal terms of the surrender, similar to those that had been made for other cities of the Granadine kingdom, were protection for Moslem life and property; religious freedom for the Moslems and application of their own law in lawsuits; freedom for all Moors to remain in their homes in Granada or to emigrate to Africa, taking their valuables and the money received from sale of their property in Spain; and liberation of prisoners. In accordance with these conditions the Granadine Moslems remained in substantially the same juridical and social situation as that of the Mudéjares before the conquest of Granada.

Failure to Comply with the Terms of the Surrender of Granada

However, while at first the Christian authorities (the Crown of Castile but not that of Aragón, in accordance with the thirteenth century treaties already cited) complied with the terms of surrender, and did so in such degree that the principal civil offices of Granada were filled by Moslems, an excess of zeal on the part of Cardinal Cisneros in striving to convert the inhabitants of Granada to Christianity soon shattered the promised religious tolerance. This infraction of the peace treaty resulted in a general uprising of the Moors in the city .and in the districts of Alpujarra, Baza, Guadix, Ronda and the sierra of Filambres. It was like a second War of Granada, lasting several years and costing many lives; but instead of rectifying that policy of conversion by force which had provoked the revolt, the victory of the Christian troops served to intensify the intolerance, utterly changing the principle of the traditional policy of Catholic Spain toward the Mudéjares. In fact, a royal ordinance of February 11, 1502, required all Moslems in Castile and León either to abjure Mohammedansim and become Christians or to depart from Spain, and produced violent repercussions in the Basque provinces and some districts of Teruel and Valencia. In Aragón the King Don Ferdinand, on petition of the lords who had Moorish vassals and of the *Cortes,* preserved in general these traditional privileges of the Mudéjares and prohibited the Inquisition from trying to convert them.

The Danger from Africa and from the Turks

Queen Isabella's ardent desire to conquer the Kingdom of Granada was not due solely to ambition for completing the Reconquest; which is to say, of putting an end to the rule of a foreign, non-Christian people on the Spanish peninsula. If that had been her only motive, her purpose would have been achieved with the Granadine conquest itself and consequent dethronement of the last remaining Moorish king. But the Queen knew, and may have learned from the previous history of Spain, that unless the onset of further African invasions were forestalled, the Peninsula would be in constant peril. Therefore she tried to dominate likewise the part of North Africa where many of the Moslems leaving Spain took refuge and where there was always a popular disposition to renew efforts to regain the lost Spanish possessions. The Queen's conviction on this point was so strong that in her last will and testament she expressly recommended that the matter be not lost sight of. King Ferdinand and Cardinal Cisneros thought as she did on this.

The latter himself organized and directed expeditions to Morocco and Argel to establish outposts there which would assure the defense of Spain.

With the same object, treaties were celebrated with the Portuguese who for some time past had been likewise attempting to safeguard their own frontiers by capturing African strongholds. For themselves they wanted the western part of Africa, where they waged war and made discoveries of new territories on voyages skirting Morocco and continuing toward the south and the Canary Islands. These treaties, which confirmed and extended the pact of 1478, had as their purpose establishment of the limits for Portuguese and Spanish conquests respectively, assigning the Spaniards a zone of northern Africa in which to carry out Isabella's intention, and recognizing her dominion over the Canaries.

The fortress of Melilla was conquered for Spain in 1497 by Don Pedro Estopiñán, with ships belonging to the Duke of Medina Sidonia. The Canary Islands were definitely mastered—after the last lords, descendants of the first conquerors, had renounced their rights in favor of the Crown of Castile (1477) —by Captain Pedro de Vera, Don Alonso Fernández de Lugo, and the *Guanches* (or indigenous Canary) petty kings or *monceys,* Guanarteme and Añarterve de Güimar, both converts to Christianity and both in high favor with the Catholic Kings. The Hispanization of these islands was rapid; and it was carried out with the same feeling of equality as between the natives (in this instance, the *Guanches*) and the Spaniards, and with the same earnest desire for complete mutual understanding culturally and juridically, which, with sound and realistic variations, was to characterize the normal official conduct of Spaniards in the colonization of the Americas.

This whole African policy became more exigent than ever because to the age-old requirements for the defense of Spain was added the need for protection against the Turkish peril as well. The Turks; who had been for a long time rulers of the ancient Caliphate of Syria, by the fifteenth century had come not only to dominate the Moslem territories of North Africa but to make an entry into Europe, destroying the Byzantine Empire (1453) and constituting a threat to all the Christian monarchs everywhere. Consequently "the Turkish peril" was, quite naturally, a constant preoccupation of the Christian kings who succeeded Isabella I and was the motivation of many wars on land and sea waged by the Spanish in Europe and Africa, regarding which we shall have more to say.

The War in Italy

Except for this problem, dual in appearance but single in reality—the problem of the African Moors and the Turks—the Crown of Castile by the close of the fifteenth century was confronted by no other pressing international question: except that of America, which suddenly loomed up.

Aragón, however, did have such problems, in the south of France and in Italy, as we have seen. Both the one and the other derived politically from the age-old rivalry between the respective royal houses of France and Aragón; in the case of the latter it was chiefly a quarrel acquired by inheriting it along with other rights and claims of the Counts of Barcelona. It might have seemed in 1493 that the long-standing rivalry would be appeased by the Treaty of Barcelona signed in that year, according to which Charles VIII of France returned to the Crown of Aragón the domains of Roussillon and Sardinia which had been unwisely ceded not long previous by Juan II of Aragón. For his part, Ferdinand the Catholic obligated himself not to favor the enemies of the royal house of France, unless the enemy were the Pope, and to ally his house by marriage neither with the royal houses of England and Naples nor with the imperial house of Hapsburg. Charles VIII interpreted this treaty as giving him a free hand with respect to Naples, the domination of which, so much disputed in the thirteenth century, had not been renounced by the French monarchs. Ferdinand the Catholic, however, protested vigorously against any such interpretation, alleging that since the Kingdom of Naples was a fief of the Pope, it was included in the exception taken in the Treaty of Barcelona. This argument did not alter Charles VIII's attitude in the slightest; on the contrary, seizing Naples by force, he had himself crowned there in February, 1495. Thereupon Ferdinand made a pact of alliance with the Pope (who was then Roderick de Borgia, Alexander VI) ; with the dethroned King of Naples, bastard great-grandson of Alfonso V of Aragón; and with Germany, the Duchy of Milan, and the Seignory of Venice. This league was called the Holy Alliance.

The war provoked by the conflict over Naples was carried out in two campaigns. In the first, the army of the Alliance, of which the main nucleus was composed of Spanish troops (not only Aragonese but also a large number of Castilians) vanquished the French and reconquered Naples together with Calabria (1495-98). When hostilities were thereupon suspended, Ferdinand the Catholic, taking advantage of the fact that King Ferdinand II of Naples had died in the meantime and been succeeded by his uncle Fadrique, negotiated with Charles VIII (continuing the negotiations, after the latter's death, with Louis XII) a settlement of the differences by means of a secret treaty (the Treaty of Granada, 1500) which provided for dethronement of King Fadrique and division of the Kingdom of Naples between France and Aragón. The partition would give the Aragonese monarch Apulia and Calabria, while Naples itself with the Abruzzi and the so-called Land of Work would pass under dominion of France. The Pope and Venice signified their approval of such division.

Carrying out this treaty gave rise to the second campaign in Italy which, while at first carried on in conformity with the Granada treaty and with triumphs for both French and Spanish arms, soon degenerated into a new conflict between these erstwhile allies. This state of affairs was brought about by the dispute as to which should receive the districts called the Capitanate, the Basilicate and the Principate. Again the Spanish troops won the definitive advantage, after the land victories of Seminara, Ceriñola and Garellano and the naval victory of Otranto, all four in the year 1503. In consequence the whole of the Kingdom of Naples came under Spanish rule.

The greatest military prestige of the two campaigns belonged to General Gonzalo Fernández de Córdoba (1453-1515), who had previously won distinction in the Wars of Granada and whom Ferdinand the Catholic's allies nicknamed "the Great Captain"—by which name he was generally known thereafter. He was notable for his concept of strategy, evidenced chiefly in opportune and carefully planned troop movements and in new and perspicacious combination of the three branches of the armies of the period (infantry, cavalry and artillery) and most particularly in that employment of infantry which was mainly responsible for what was to be during a century and a half his international fame as a military leader. The Great Captain was also renowned for his sagacious choice of battlefields. His collaborators were Artillery General Pedro Navarro, Fernando de Andrade, García de Paredes, Zamurio, Villalba, Don Diego de Mendoza, Pizarro (father of the Conquistador of Peru), and other captains and soldiers, some of whom were veterans of the Moorish wars and some new to the service but soon to distinguish themselves in the war in Flanders or in the conquest of the Americas. Gonzalo de Córdoba, in addition to being an extraordinary soldier, was the coordinator of Spanish possessions in the zone of southern Italy.

The Discovery of America

While the ancient dominion of Aragón was thus being strengthened in Italy, and the foundations were being laid of future territorial aggrandizement, and also of new wars with France, the Popes, and the Italian seignories, there occurred an unforeseen event of utmost importance: the discovery of America.

It is profitless to mull over the biography of Christopher Columbus, which in reality has slight bearing on the geographical achievement that made him famous. Most authorities accept his own statement (which is proof enough, so long as it is not contradicted by other evidence of greater force and more certain historical value) as to his Genoese nationality; but it cannot be doubted that this fact—important to Columbus personally and perhaps, though not inevitably, contributory to the shaping of his thought—is of no real importance with respect to the Discovery itself. It is very probable, to say the least, that Columbus would not have been the one to make the Discovery if that Genoese sailor, who knocked in vain for so long at the doors of the Courts of Portugal, England and France, had failed to win for his project the interest of the Queen of Castile and the King of Aragón; not to mention the fact that Columbus himself did not suspect the existence of the double Continent that stretched across the path leading toward the Spice Islands of the Ocean Sea and the Asiatic East.

The voyage of discovery proposed by Columbus was based on commercial needs. At that period, trade with India and China was a chief economic interest for Europeans, because from those regions they obtained, among other merchandise, the spices (cinnamon, cloves, pepper, and the like) which were then esteemed so highly and sold so dear; and which consequently gave large profits to European merchants. This trade for many years had been in the hands of the Italians (Genoese and others), and it had been carried on by sending vessels to the coasts of Syria and Palestine to pick up the merchandise brought thither by Moslem traders who obtained it in their turn from India and elsewhere in Asia. When the Turks conquered western Asia, they first hindered this trade, and finally by conquest of Constantinople rendered it impossible for the Christian Europeans. Then there was utmost need of finding a way to trade on the other side— toward the west—without running into Turks. The Portuguese believed that they could achieve this by sailing south along the western coast of Africa, since they thought (and were right in thinking) that they would thus reach a point marking the ultimate limit of the African continent which their ships could round, and then sail once again northward to reach India by the other sea. Some European mariners and geographers, however, held that the voyage to India could be made without having to sail around the whole of Africa but merely by navigating directly west, since if, as was supposed, the world was round, by this method also a ship would have to arrive at India. Columbus was one of those who believed this; and he was convinced moreover that such a westward voyage would be much shorter than the route around Africa proposed by the Portuguese; partly because he thought the diameter of the earth to be much less than it really is and partly on account of other geographical considerations.

When as we know, Columbus found that the Courts of Portugal, England and France rejected his proposals, he came to Spain to present them to the Catholic Kings. There some members of the clergy and some nobles saw the point and encouraged him to persist until he succeeded finally in interesting King Ferdinand and Queen Isabella in the project of the westward voyage. At last, after various vacillations, the monarchs and Columbus signed a contract, a document immeasurably important in world history, since it was the cause of America's being discovered at that time. This contract is called *Capitulaciones de Santa Fe*—the Articles of Santa Fe—and it was signed April 17, 1491, some eight and one-half months before the city of Granada surrendered. Santa Fe was the name of the encampment that the Catholic Kings had had built near the besieged Moslem city. The persons who were most helpful to Columbus in persuading Ferdinand and Isabella to approve the voyage were Alonso de Quintanilla, the Queen's Auditor; Fray Diego Deza; Fray Antonio de Marchena; the Catalán pilot Jaime Ferrer de Blanes; the Duke of Medinaceli; Fray Juan Pérez, prior of the

Monastery of La Rábida; the Andalusian pilot, Martín Alonso Pinzón; the King's Chamberlain, Juan Cabrero; and the scribe Luis de San-tángel—names, all of these, that deserve to be held in grateful remem-brance forever. The Catholic Kings ordered the Mayor of the port of Palos, in Huelva, to place at Columbus' disposition two vessels of the type then called caravels, and to make available to him at a fair price, tax-exempt, whatever he needed in the way of provisions, lumber, and the like. Since this was easier said than done, the ships, and perhaps part of the money for the voyage, were supplied by Martín and Vincent Alonso Pinzón. It is not known with certainty what was the source of the rest of the funds for financing the expedition.

So Columbus sailed from Palos, not with two caravels but with three: the *Santa María* (or St. Mary), the *Pinta* (or Painted Woman), and the *Niña* (or Girl), directed by Spanish captains and pilots—among them the two just mentioned, Martín Alonso Pinzón and his brother Vincent, and Juan de la Cosa, who owned the *Santa María*—and with a crew made up of Spanish sailors. The sailing was on August 3, 1492, a memorable date; and on October 12 of the same year, after a long and arduous voyage, the ships made the first new-world landfall at the Island of Guanahani in the archipelago of the Lucayas, or Ba-hamas, which Columbus believed to be off the coast of India. They then proceeded to discover islands of the Antilles, including Cuba (the northern coast) and Haiti, which Columbus named Española; and on January 4, 1493, they began the return voyage to Spain. Some time later it was ascertained that Columbus had not in fact achieved his purpose of reaching Asia, but instead had found islands situated at the entrance of the Gulf of Mexico—which, practically, was to discover the American continent. The positive discovery of the mainland was effected by means of the three succeeding voyages of Columbus, the last of these being 1502-1504, and by those of other Spanish mariners.

On his second voyage (1493-1496), Columbus discovered most of the lesser Antilles and the island of Borinquen, or Puerto Rico. On the third (1498-1500), besides finding other islands, he touched at the northeastern coast of the mainland of South America at the mouth of the Orinoco and traversed the Gulf of Paria between northeastern Venezuela and the island of Trinidad. On his fourth voyage Columbus visited several islands of the Antilles, and reached the cape of Hon-duras, and the places named Porto Bello, Nombre de Dios, Basti-

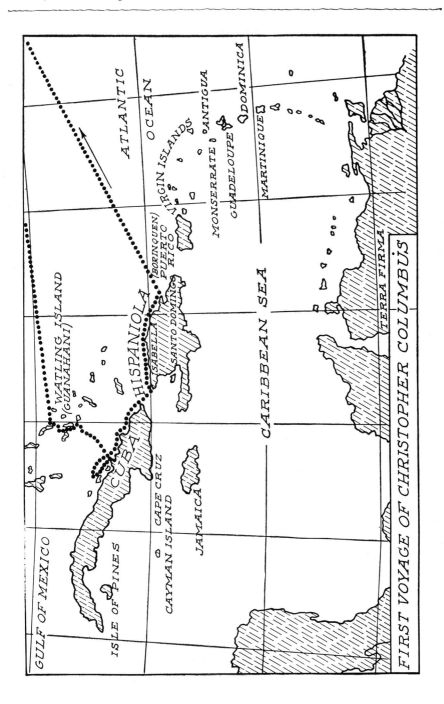

FIRST VOYAGE OF CHRISTOPHER COLUMBUS

mento, Retrete and Belén; which is to say, the northeastern coast of what was soon to be called Castilla del Oro, and later on, Central America. But none of these discoveries led him to believe that he was viewing a new part of the world, an unknown continent. He kept on thinking that he had arrived at eastern Asia—the island of Cipango, or Japan, and adjacent regions; and to the last he had his mind set on finding a passage to the peninsula of Malacca, which ancient writers called the Golden Chersonese.

It was Spanish pilots, such as Juan de la Cosa and others, or pilots in the service of Spain, such as the Italian Amerigo Vespucci, who accompanied Columbus on some of his voyages, themselves made others independently, and were thus enabled to rectify the Discoverer's error and proclaim to Spain and the world that a new continent had been discovered in the west, lying betwixt Europe and Asia. With the first of these expeditions, which was made in 1499 (when Columbus had already begun his own third voyage) by Alonso de Ojeda, or Hojeda, together with Juan de la Cosa and Amerigo Vespucci, there began the most tremendous series of geographical discoveries, in number, results, and display of fortitude and courage, ever produced in the history of the world before or since by the work of one single country. During these voyages almost the whole of the American continent and the Pacific Ocean and its islands were discovered; and moreover Asia was reached by sailing westward just as Columbus had prophesied it would be.

Yet nothing of this availed to give a Spanish name to the vast expanses of territory thus revealed by Spain to mankind. Vespucci's narrative account of four of his voyages, published in 1504, which attributed to the author priority over Columbus in discovery of the continent, had a great repercussion; and soon thereafter, in 1507, a German geographer, Waldsee Müller, proposed that the newly discovered region be given the name *America,* in honor of Vespucci, instead of *Columbia* or some other name more directly related to the Spanish voyages of discovery. The suggestion was received with favor, and the name "America," popularized in Europe, was adopted, and has endured. In Spain the designation favored for the American dominions was "the Indies," in line with Columbus' idea that he had reached India. However, it should be stated that what Vespucci himself discovered was the greater part of the Atlantic seaboard of South

Gothic Gallery, Palace of the Generalidad of Catalonia, Barcelona.

America (Brazil, and territories as far south perhaps as the Falkland Islands or Patagonia). It is true that the German editor Müller in suggesting the name "America" intended it only for that region discovered by Vespucci and not for the lands to northward; but all these came to be called inclusively, America.

Contemporaneously with Columbus' third voyage, the Portuguese (captained by Vasco de Gama) doubled the Cape of Good Hope and reached Asia ("the Indies") by sailing East (1497-1499). In 1500 the Portuguese took possession of the Brazilian coast in South America.

With the discovery of America and the voyages on the Atlantic and the Pacific, the age of the sailing vessel was ushered in. Sailing ships, which were constantly being improved and brought nearer to perfection, came to displace the vessel with oars of which the highest type was the galley, though the latter continued to be used in naval warfare into the sixteenth century.

International Consequences of the Discovery

These New World discoveries greatly stirred the peoples of Europe, firing their imagination and throwing into sharp relief the political importance of Spain, which the European world was already beginning to regard as a political unit notwithstanding the fact that the two independent kingdoms of Castile and Aragón persisted as such until 1516. The reason for this concept of Spanish unity is to be found, first and foremost, in the concerted action of the two Catholic Kings and of national elements in both kingdoms, in relation to problems that specifically concerned only one of their two realms; as, for example, in the cases of the conquest of Granada (a political undertaking by Castile) and of the wars in Italy (which were, strictly speaking, the affair of Aragón). The solidarity of Isabella and Ferdinand with regard to the government of Castile, in conformity with the arrangement agreed upon on Enrique IV's death, must have contributed no less to the concept of Spain as a unit; and another important factor in formation of this unitary image of Spain was, perhaps, the real preponderance which by that time had already been achieved throughout the Peninsula by a single language—Castilian—and the culture springing from it.

It is quite understandable that a necessarily decisive element in the value assigned the international power of both, according to the judgment of other European States, was the experience that those States had

had with regard to the positive union of the forces upon which Ferdinand and Isabella relied for the solution of all political problems and conflicts. The unexpected addition to the strength of the Catholic Kings of everything that America was believed to be, increased instantaneously, immensely, and most naturally, foreign estimates of that strength.

The discovery of America had other consequences as well. In the international field there was a transient conflict with Portugal, whose mariners had discovered the Madeira Islands at the beginning of the fourteenth century and had undertaken later on, with the approval and under the direction of the Portuguese monarchy, a series of coastal expeditions along the western littoral of Africa in search (as we have shown) of communication with India by encirclement of that continent. Columbus' first voyage alarmed the Portuguese, as well it might, with regard to the success of their own expedition to India. The intervention of Pope Alexander VI, to whom the Catholic Kings had addressed themselves also in order to augment the authority of their imminent dominion over the lands already discovered in 1493 and those that might be discovered later, solved in principle the conflict between Spain and Portugal by means of four famous Bulls, especially the Bull of May 4, 1493, in which the Pope fixed a line of demarcation from north pole to south between then existing and future dominions of Spain and of Portugal. This imaginary line was drawn one hundred leagues west of the Azores, or Cape Verde Islands, with all the lands lying east of it assigned to Portugal and all on the west to Spain. The indefiniteness of the line, and the ambition of the King of Portugal, who aspired to something more, created diplomatic difficulties that for the time being found solution in the Treaty of Tordesillas (July 7, 1494). The line established by this treaty passed 370 leagues west of the Cape Verde Islands for future discoveries, and 250 for everything that had been discovered by Castile up to June 20, 1494.

Effects on Castilian Jurisprudence of the Discovery of America

In the field of internal Castilian law, the discovery of America brought other problems. The most immediate, and first to become apparent, was that of the status before the law of the indigenous inhabitants of America—the Amerinds, as they are often called today, though from the time of the Discovery they were mistakenly termed Indians.

Lateral Façade, Customhouse, Barcelona.

It was then believed, by Christians the world over, that it was lawful and just to enslave barbarous or savage peoples who were furthermore not Christian. The Portuguese accordingly had enslaved the Negro tribes that they had discovered in Africa, whom they sold into servitude in Europe. Columbus tried to follow the same practice with regard to the Indians of the Americas, but the great heart and lofty sense of justice of Queen Isabella prevented him from doing so. The Queen felt scruples lest those tribes, whose conversion to Christianity was from the beginning one of her deepest desires, should be made slaves by the whites; and after consulting upon the matter with eminent personages who doubtless shared her scruples, she ordered Columbus to set free all the Indians whom he had brought to Spain to sell. The Queen's order was issued June 20, 1500, a date that the world should keep in mind because it marks the first recognition ever made of the respect due the dignity and freedom of all men no matter how uncultured and primitive they might be; a principle which no law had ever proclaimed before that time nor much less had any nation ever practiced. That measure was soon ratified and amplified by others, followed from 1512 to 1542 by laws in which all the Indians were declared to be free men—*hombres libres*—and which were the basis for a policy of protection for the Indians which was the special and unique characteristic of the rule of Spain in the Americas and of which the glorious originator was Isabella I.

The Queen's last will and testament lays stress on her recommendation that this protection of the Indians should never be relaxed. Seven years after Isabella I's death, there was commenced in America itself (as we shall see), by Father Antonio Montesinos in 1511 and Fray Bartolomé de las Casas in 1515, the noble campaign waged energetically against the abuses by which some Spanish colonizers nullified in practice the principles set forth by Spanish law.

Indirectly, the juridical recognition of the personal freedom of the indigenous American peoples brought about the introduction into the Americas of Negro slavery which was already being carried on by the Portuguese and which was permitted and exploited by the other European countries, some of whom disputed among themselves over which should be permitted to take cargoes of African slaves to the Spanish colonies in the New World. There were jurists and theologians in Spain, conscientious men who opposed Negro slavery as much as Indian slavery—Francisco de Vitoria, the creator in Catholic Spain of the new international law; Las Casas and his predecessors in the Americas; Soto; Sepúlveda himself; Melchor Cano; the Viceroy Luis de Velasco; Martín de Rada; Bishop Salazar; Benavides; Father Valdivia; Avendaño; Albornoz; Claver; Sandoval—but they did not succeed in changing the prevalent opinion with regard to the former.

The problem as to the juridical title by virtue of which the Spanish monarchs had a legal right to occupy lands which prior to discovery had been owned by indigenous American tribes, was more difficult for the Powers of that epoch to understand; established as these Powers were on the basis of the patrimonial principle of government and of the free right of conquest, application of which depended (both for inferior races and for the civilized peoples of Europe) on superiority of military force and on the characteristics of the respective States. The Bulls of Alexander VI contained the more or less explicit statement of a legal title respected by Christian nations (that is, the papal concession), which kings found useful to accept and bring forth in all cases where it might advantage them to do so. Notwithstanding this, the highminded spirit of Spanish theologians and jurists of the period, not satisfied with prevailing beliefs, planted this problem of legal right for the first time in the world's history, and raised the question regarding it, only a few years after Isabella's death. It should be noted that for those jurists and theologians, the only basis for Spain's legal title to occupy the new-found lands was moral and humane in nature, and that they did not deem the papal grant sufficient of itself to justify conquest of the Americas.

The Expulsion of the Jews and the New Inquisition

From the fourteenth century onward, the tolerance toward the Jews expressed juridically in Royal laws and in pacts, turned into intolerance and often into violent persecution. We have already remarked that that tolerance, as well as the tolerance shown the Moslem Mudéjares, had never wholly excluded the conflict inherent in Catholic proselytization for conversion of both Jew and Moslem. The theological arguments, in sessions often open to the public, which were carried on by ministers of the three religions, afforded eloquent examples of this proselytization. Both intolerance and proselytization were intensified from the thirteenth century on. It seems accurate to say that in

Madrid: Prado Museum

The Virgin of the Catholic Kings.

particular the dwelling together of Jews and Christian Spaniards in the same community had been motivated for centuries by the expediency of utilizing Jewish skills and industrial and commercial astuteness, rather than by a relaxing of opinion with regard to beliefs or by such friendliness as may reasonably be assumed to have existed on the part of Christian Spaniards for the Mudéjares. But what is quite certain is that the Jews benefited legally from that attitude and, up to the time mentioned, had the protection of the laws without fear of infringement. Then a wave of aggressive intolerance and terrorism swept through the people, stirred up by vulgar prejudice and by the preaching of some Catholic clerics. The same phenomenon occurred in other countries of Europe, with local variations; in some instances it was mob frenzy rather than incitements of the clergy which was responsible for the persecution of the Jews and the damage to their homes and the neighborhoods in which they lived; and again there were such violent, insensate and inexplicable manifestations as that of the French mob of so-called "shepherds" that invaded districts of southern France and were punished by civil and ecclesiastical authorities alike who had been horrified by that murderous frenzy.

Although the Catholic Kings tried to prevent this kind of explosion, and generally speaking maintained protective legislation for the Jews, prejudice against the latter was widespread and increasing, and the religious and social gulf between Christians and Jews became even deeper than that existing between Christians and Moslems. The Catholic Kings were keenly aware of this prevalent antagonism and of the dangers that it engendered. On the other hand, they clung to the ideal of the religious unity of Spain. Both aspects of the royal thinking led logically to the conclusion that brought about the order to expel the Jews from Andalusia and from Aragón (1483[?]-1486)—which order was not carried out—and the one of March 31, 1492, which forced Jewish inhabitants of the realms of Castile and Aragón to be baptized as Catholics or, in default of that, to leave Spain within four months. We do not know the exact number of families nor of individuals who rejected this forced conversion and expatriated themselves. The figures given by historians more or less near the time of the event range from 35,000 families (which, counting six to a family, would mean 210,000 persons) to 500,000 individuals; but whatever their number, it was sufficient to undermine seriously the national economic life. The

Spanish Jews thus expelled were the ancestors of the Sephardic Jews of eastern Europe, northern Africa, and some nations of western Europe (France, Holland, etc.), who preserve to this day as their own language the Castilian idiom of the fifteenth century and who have not lost their love for the Iberian homeland of their forefathers.

Other Jews, and here again we do not know certainly how many, were baptized. But that did not solve their religious problem. Public opinion and the clergy distrusted these converts with the natural doubts attendant on conversions by force, which are seldom the product of sincere conviction. Such suspicions were confirmed by discovery of some real cases of religious disloyalty on the part of the converts which constituted the offense of heresy; Christians who change their religion or preach against it being called heretics, while those who profess other faiths and have never been baptized are termed infidels or pagans.

Chiefly for the purpose of putting an end to that heresy, the Catholic Kings established in Castile the Tribunal of the Inquisition which, as we have said, had been in existence in Aragón ever since the thirteenth century but which up to this time had been unknown in Castile, where matters concerning religious offenses were wholly under the regular jurisdiction of the bishops, seconded by penal legislation of the State which in Spanish codes of the period was very clear on this point. The Inquisition thus created, first by a royal Act published at Seville in 1477 and later by several Bulls of Pope Sixtus V (in 1478, 1480, and 1483), was at the time rightly called the New Inquisition, because it differed from the Aragonese Inquisition in its total independence of the bishops, in its more intimate relationship with the Monarchs, and in its more firmly integrated and more rigid organization and regulations. The first two Inquisitors were appointed by the Catholic Kings; the third, Fray Tomás de Torquemada, by the Pope. In 1507 the Inquisitor was Cardinal Cisneros, to whose policy in Granada we have already referred. It was in 1483 that the Supreme Council of the Inquisition was created by papal Bull.

The New Inquisition was implanted in Aragón also, not without some resistance, in 1484; three years later, against greater opposition, in Catalonia; and in 1490 in Mallorca. The first general Instructions, which modified the early ordinances of the Inquisition, were drafted by Torquemada and went into effect in 1488.

Mural painting in the Mozarabic Chapel of the Cathedral of Toledo
Juan de Borgoña: *Landing of the troops of Cardinal Cisneros on the Coast of Africa.*

The Dynastic Alliances

Ferdinand and Isabella had five children: one son, Juan, their second-born, and four daughters—Isabella, Juana, María and Catalina. Catalina is known in English history as Queen Katherine, first wife of King Henry VIII of England, by whom she was divorced after 18 years of marriage during which she bore him five children. (Katherine, or Catalina, had been wed first to the English Crown Prince, Arthur; and after his death to Henry.) The Catholic Monarchs had a carefully planned policy of marrying their children into foreign reigning houses where such a bond would contribute most to the international security of Spain and the future greatness of their own dynasty. The success that they achieved in these dynastic alliances is further proof of the prestige enjoyed by the Spanish kingdoms, the ultimate union of which into one monarchy was foreseen by the other European rulers. Only in the case of Navarre were Ferdinand and Isabella's proposals regarding an international marriage frustrated; and Navarre refused two such from the Catholic Kings, in both instances because of difficulties raised by the Queen Mother, the Countess of Foix.

The eldest child of Ferdinand and Isabella, the Princess Isabella, first married Don Alfonso, Prince of Portugal, and after his death, the Portuguese King, Don Manuel, an alliance not only ensuring the friendship for Castile and Aragón of the Peninsula's third kingdom, which by interventions before that time had caused major political difficulties in Castile, but also preparing the way for unification of the three realms. As a matter of fact, Miguel, only child of the Princess Isabella's second marriage, in 1498 and 1499 was sworn heir of the Crowns of Portugal, Castile, and Aragón. The Catholic Kings had hoped for their own two kingdoms to be inherited by their son Prince Don Juan, whose general education and policy they guided with loving care, and whom they married to Margaret of Austria, daughter of the Emperor Maximilian of Germany; but Don Juan's premature death in 1497 blighted that hope. The plans which Ferdinand and Isabella then based on their grandson Prince Miguel were likewise frustrated, for he was only two years old when he died. The little Portuguese Prince's death left to carry on their dynasty only the possible children of the marriages of the Princesses Juana and Katharine. The former married Philip the Fair, Archduke of Austria (son and natural successor of Maximilian, Emperor of Germany, founder of the House of

Sepuchre of Prince Juan, son of Ferdinand and Isabella. Work of the Florentine sculptor
Domenici di Alessandro Fancelli di Settignano.

Austria which for centuries ruled the Holy Roman Empire) and Duke of Burgundy. We have already noted the Princess Catalina's, or Katharine's, marriages first to Crown Prince Arthur and then to Henry VIII of England. It was not Katharine's union with Henry of England, however, but Juana's with Philip of Austria which decided the future political destiny of Spain, inclining it toward solidarity with the Houses of Austria and Burgundy and with the Holy Roman Empire; a foreign solidarity that eventually was to prove fatal to the internal greatness of the Spanish nation, the foundations for which had been laid so well at the end of the fifteenth century.

Castile and Aragón after the Deaths of Isabella I and Ferdinand II

The Catholic Queen died November 24, 1504. Don Ferdinand survived her by twelve years, dying in 1516. If events had developed normally during those dozen years, the two Crowns, Aragón and Castile would have continued their differential existence to a considerable degree and perhaps for a long time, although there would have been the possibility of their uniting into a single monarchy on Ferdinand's death. But the misfortune that seemed to pursue the Catholic Kings in the persons of their children actively beset their daughter Doña Juana, next in line of succession to the throne of Castile. By that time Doña Juana's mental instability had become obvious, a circumstance rendering necessary a political guardianship in the form of a more or less disguised regency. The Catholic Queen, who had foreseen this, named Doña Juana as her successor but stipulated in her will that if Juana should be incapacitated, Ferdinand should exercise the regency. In 1505 the *Cortes* of Toro recognized his authority in this respect; but Juana's husband, Philip the Fair of Austria and Burgundy (who as King Consort, was called Philip I of Castile), avid for power and utterly tactless with respect to the Spanish traditions and customs with which his inherited Burgundian ideas and manners were constantly clashing, raised difficulties in the way of carrying out the provisions of his royal mother-in-law's will. In short, he wanted to rule over Castile. Since Philip had formed an alliance with Louis XII of France, Ferdinand, not daring openly to oppose him, relinquished the regency but lost no time in himself making a pact with Louis XII (October 12, 1506) according to which the French King transmitted to his niece

Germaine de Foix, a descendant of the Cid and member of the royal house of Navarre, all his rights with respect to Naples, and Ferdinand married Germaine, agreeing that the Crown of Naples should be inherited by offspring of the marriage, if any. Philip the Fair, when he learned of all this, decided that it was the part of wisdom to come to terms with his father-in-law. The existing difficulties were apparently settled by a pact between Philip and Ferdinand; but the practical result was that the latter resigned the regency and retired to his kingdom of Aragón, and that Doña Juana—"Joanna the Mad"—was declared incapable of ruling. Consequently Philip I acted as King *de facto*, although he was thus to reign for a short time only, since in the very year of his arrival in Spain with Doña Juana—1506—Philip died, a young man. His death, together with the increasing insanity of the Queen, who was thrown into a state of frenzy by the loss of her husband whom she passionately loved, made urgently necessary a provisional regency of Castilian nobles of whom Cardinal Cisneros was one; and also made advisable Ferdinand's return as regent. The old-time factions and turmoil among the nobility broke out afresh. Don Ferdinand took vigorous measures to restore order, exercising the regency from 1507 until his death in 1516.

During that decade, the principal political events were the conquest of Navarre, the new wars in Italy, and the continuation of the North African expeditions and conquests begun during Isabella's lifetime.

The Conquest of Navarre

The conquest of Navarre was a consequence of the perfidy of the rulers of that monarchy, Catalina and Juan de Albret, who on the one hand pretended to form an alliance with Ferdinand, and on the other made a pact with the King of France. The critical moment of this two-faced political policy was represented in the Treaty of Blois in July, 1512, by which the monarchs of Navarre obligated themselves to Louis XII of France, on his promise to respect their domains of Foix and Bearn, and not permit passage of Spanish troops through Navarrese territory; a maneuver that might prove useful to Ferdinand in his war with the French King. When Ferdinand of Aragón learned about this pact, he brought the matter to an issue immediately by requesting permission for the Spanish army to pass through Navarre. Refusal of the request provoked a war which ended in little more than three months with the victory Ferdinand's. Juan de Albret fled to France, whence he sent a letter throwing himself on the mercy of Ferdinand, whose first proposal was to occupy Navarre so long as his war with the French King lasted and then return the kingdom to its former sovereigns. Ferdinand added to this a further proposal that the then Prince of Viana, heir to the Navarrese throne, should marry a princess of the Spanish royal house on condition that the monarchs of Navarre should not lend aid to the King of France; but Catalina and Albret, instead of receiving courteously the Spanish Ambassador who came with these offers, took him prisoner and handed him over to the French. That incident made Ferdinand determine to consolidate his occupation of Navarre and incorporate the kingdom into his own Spanish realms, bringing it once more into the peninsular political society of countries. An attempt on the part of Louis XII and de Albret to recover Navarrese territory by armed force was an utter failure. As regards the special laws and institutions of Navarre, including its *Cortes,* Ferdinand the Catholic respected them wholly.

Prior to entry of the Spanish troops into Navarre in July, 1512, Pope Julius II had issued a Bull on the twenty-first day of that same month in which he excommunicated the Navarrese monarchs Catalina and Juan de Albret, depriving them of their kingdom, possessions and titles. A second Bull on January 18, 1513, ratified the first with regard to dispossession of the Kingdom and recognized the property rights therein as pertaining to whoever should conquer it, a conquest which when the Bull was issued Ferdinand had already effected. Soon afterward, on Ferdinand's order, the Salamancan jurist Palacios Rubios wrote and published a treatise on *La justicia y el derecho de la adquisición y retención del reino de Navarra*—The Justice and Legal Right of the Acquisition and Retention of the Kingdom of Navarre—the first edition of which was issued at Salamanca in 1514. The reasoning on which Palacios Rubios based his proofs was almost exclusively religious in character (the schism of some Cardinals, supported by the King of France, against Pope Julius II) ; but there can be no doubt that the real motives inspiring Ferdinand were political. By declaration made in the *Cortes* of Burgos in 1515, the King ceded Navarre to his daughter Juana and grandson Charles and the latter's successors, thereby incorporating that kingdom "into the Crown of the said Kings of Castile."

New Wars in Italy

The political reasons noted above relate, as we have indicated, to a new episode in the age-old conflict between the Aragonese and the French monarchies. From motives of general policy in Italy, Pope Julius II had formed in 1508 a new league called the League of Cambrai and consisting of Ferdinand the Catholic, King Louis XII of France, the Emperor of Germany, and other monarchs and lords. This League was aimed against the Seignory of Venice.

But since the principal activating passion in all these pacts of political alignment and in most of the wars of the time was mutual rivalry and distrust among the Chiefs of State (Popes, Monarchs, or Lords of Republics), Pope Julius grew envious of the success achieved by Louis XII's troops, and accordingly sponsored another Holy Alliance (1511) into which, with the self-seeking bad faith prevalent in those days, Venice entered along with the Argonese King and others, while the Emperor of Germany joined forces with France. The campaign, in the beginning favorable to the French, ended with victory for the countries of the Alliance, a victory due chiefly to Swiss troops and won at Novara in 1513. In consequence of it, Louis XII had to withdraw from Milanese territory. The dual factors of this withdrawal and of dissension within the Alliance greatly strengthened Spain's political situation in Italy. Louis XII therefore in December, 1513, arranged with Ferdinand the Catholic a truce on the Italian question.

Conquests in Africa

The third series of important events during the period under discussion consists of the conquests in North Africa. The animating spirit of these was Cardinal Cisneros, who not only inspired the King to undertake them but intervened in them personally and paid out of his own purse the costs of one such expedition. The sum total of the results was the taking of the Rock of Gomera (1508), of Orán (1509), of Bugía (1510), and of Tripoli (1511), all of these victories being achieved under the military command of Count Pedro Navarro. Cisneros was present to witness the capture of Orán. The fall of Bugía brought about the surrender of Argel and recognition of vassalage to Spain on the part of the Kings of Tunis and Tremecen. But a tremendous defeat suffered by Spanish troops in August 1511 on the Island of Gelbes paralyzed the African conquest for a number of years.

The conquest of Orán was immortalized in art by the paintings of Juan of Burgundy which adorn one of the inner walls of the Mozárabic Chapel of the Cathedral of Toledo, of which diocese, as we know, Cisneros was Archbishop.

Death and Heritage of Ferdinand the Catholic

Ferdinand the Catholic died in February, 1516, naming as his successor on the throne of Aragón Charles of Ghent, eldest son of Juana the Mad and Philip the Fair, and appointing Cardinal Cisneros as regent of Castile, León, Granada and Navarre. This latter appointment, although Don Ferdinand had no authority in law to make it, was necessitated by the mental incapacity of Queen Juana. The new King of Aragón, who was soon to be King of Castile as well, approved the appointment of Cisneros. But the face of things very soon changed aspect radically.

Spanish Civilization, 1250-1500. The Epoch of Alfonso X

The period of two and one-half centuries which we have just been considering was not only the preparation for, and toward its close the achievement of, the political dominion and monarchical unity of the Spanish Christian States (with the exception of Portugal, which stubbornly held out against union, except briefly during King Don Manuel's reign); but was also a time of flowering for Spanish culture, especially in the fields of science, literature, and art. Its two high points were the appearance of the originality of the Spanish spirit, emerging full and clear from amid the strong and complicated foreign influences surrounding it, and the supremacy achieved by the language, literature, and thought of Castile over those of the rest of Spain. The first of these two points is merely reiteration of a trait which we remarked upon while discussing the Iberians and which seems to be one of the most constant factors in Spanish psychology; namely, the ability to assimilate foreign influences and fuse them in such a way as to extract from the fusion an original, a truly Spanish, creation. That quality manifests itself not only in the manner just indicated, but inversely as well; which is to say, in the power of absorption which these indigenous Spanish creations and tendencies have often exercised even over artists who themselves have come to do their own work in

Principal Façade, Church of San Pablo, Valladolid.

Spain. Perhaps the loftiest expression of this activating influence of the Spanish spirit is represented by El Greco, whose work is discussed in the next chapter; but in the fifteenth century when Spain, and Castile perhaps most of all, was invaded by foreign artists (John of Burgundy, Siloe, Roderick Alemán, Copin, Mercadante, and many others), the architecture and the sculpture produced on the Peninsula by those artists show modalities that are clearly Spanish in type. A conspicuous instance of this is afforded by the interior of the church of San Juan de los Reyes, built at Toledo during the reign of the Catholic Kings.

As for the second point—supremacy of the Castilian spirit—we shall observe later on how that found expression.

The culminating moment of the cultural process here indicated was, at the beginning of the period that we are considering, the reign of Alfonso X of Castile, regarding which we have already stated the principal facts connected with the personal achievements of the King himself. But it would be erroneous to believe that even at that early date the literary and scientific activity of Spain was confined to the Castilian Court and its cultural centers.

Throughout the whole of Europe the second half of the thirteenth century was a period of great intellectual productivity, philosophical, juridical, and of every kind. In philosophy there were such surpassing talents as the Italian, St. Thomas of Aquinas (1127-1274), author of the famous *Summa Totius Theologicae,* an encyclopedic summation of scholastic thinking, which for centuries has been the guiding text of Catholic philosophy; and the Mallorcan Ramón Lull, or Raymund Lully (1235-1315), likewise a Catholic philosopher and evangelizer whose work is still read and cherished. It should not be forgotten that the works of both the Italian and the Mallorcan reflect influences of Arabic origin, a fact which is nothing to wonder at when we recall how widely read the great Moslem authors then were, in Spain and elsewhere. It is a well-know fact that as late as the end of the fifteenth century, these authors were being studied in European universities and new editions of their works were being issued. Raymond Lully was not the only exponent of Spanish philosophy in that age; on the contrary, work in this field was extensive, as much in theology (which was, in fact, the preferred branch) as in philosophy proper and in morals, and also in the realms of mathematics and the physical sciences. In this latter connection, special mention should be made, because of their influence on the fifteenth century geographical discoveries, of the Mallorcan and Catalán cosmographers and geographers who, like the Italian and the Portuguese, enriched and helped develop those studies, which were influenced also by contemporaneous Arabic writers. One of these latter, author of a famous ruttier, *Instrucciones náuticas* (1489-1490), accompanied Vasco de Gama on his voyage to India.

The Period of Alfonso V of Aragón and Juan II of Castile. The Renaissance

Another period of high intellectual achievement fostered by the stimulating patronage given to science and letters by the kings was the first half of the fifteenth century at the Courts of Alfonso V of Aragón (1343-1359) and Juan II of Castile (1419-1454). The substantial difference between Alfonso X and Alfonso V arose from the fact that the former brought to Castilian culture, and thereby to the rest of the Peninsula, influences both of the Moslem East and of the Justinian Code of Roman Law; while the latter held his Court at Naples in a center of Renaissance culture that was fundamentally classical.

In the time of Alfonso V, Italy was one of the great European centers of world culture, ranking high in both the quality and the quantity of literary and scientific production. It was in Italy that there was launched the tide of ideas concerning literature, art, philosophy, and life in general known as the Renaissance. That amplitude of ideological content—later on to be still further extended by new factors and direct consequences of the inaugural impulses—makes it very hard to say just when and where the Renaissance began. The truth is that its various aspects, far from appearing simultaneously, or in a single country, or amid one group only, came to birth in different places and at different moments. Precisely because of the variety of its factors, the great figures who seem most truly representative of the Renaissance very rarely express it as an integrated whole, notwithstanding the fact that one of the characteristics of the Renaissance movement was its encyclopedism, which is to say, its inclusiveness, its thirst to savour everything. The Renaissance ideal was the rounded culture that made an individual, if he had the innate qualities demanded for it, cultivate multiple fields of knowledge, and some-

Retable, Carthusian Monastery of Miraflores, Burgos.

times prove to be a creative artist in several; an ideal not infrequently attained also in the fifteenth century and the sixteenth. An example of fragmentary, or partial, participation in the Renaissance was Dante (1265-1321), who, though he belongs to Renaissance literature, was in philosophic and religious thinking, and also in his general concept of life and conduct, closer akin to St. Thomas Aquinas than to fourteenth and fifteenth century Italian writers. Leonardo da Vinci, on the other hand, also an Italian but a little later than Dante (1452-1519), was almost the complete expression of encyclopedism.

While it is true that Italy, taken as a whole, saw the inauguration of the Renaissance in the fields of law, literature relating to the Greek and Latin classic writers, and the plastic arts, and also in an ample sense of the scope of human life, it is no less true that Italy's participation was slight indeed in the geographical discoveries of the fifteenth and sixteenth centuries (except for the bare fact of the nationality of Columbus and of Vespucci, both of whom made their discoveries in the service of Spain), and even less in the religious Reformation—Protestantism—and in the realms of historical and philosophical criticism; which latter were produced principally in Spain and Portugal, in Germany and Holland, in England and France.

Furthermore, "Renaissance" is in itself a highly specialized descriptive term referring to the revival of the reading and direct study of what are called the classic authors—Greek and Latin—and to contemplation and imitation of the art of those great ancient peoples whom for several centuries after the fall of the Roman Empire western Europe knew only at second hand; that is, through medium of the Moslems. An exception to this general rule was the fact that some Latin authors continued to be studied in the centuries intervening between the Visigothic invasion and the year 1300. But that literary and artistic concept of the term *Renaissance* (more concretely known by the denomination *Humanism*) does not cover all the rich variety and complexity which the movement represents historically and to which we alluded above. Still less does it suppose that all those who accepted that part of the movement and promoted it with tireless zeal, accepted likewise the rest of the doctrines and the other aspects of the Renaissance. Thus, to cite an example from Spain, Cardinal Cisneros enthusiastically supported Renaissance ideas regarding the classical languages and literatures—as he proved by founding the University of

Alcalá and its bilingual College, and by ordering and supervising preparation of the *Biblia complutense,* or polyglot Bible—but in everything else Cisneros was anti-Renaissance. A similar situation occurred some years later in the case of the Jesuits. Our great Spanish philosopher, Luis Vives, also in the same fifteenth century and the early years of the sixteenth, was a much fuller and more comprehensive representative of the Renaissance, and was not limited merely to its philological and literary interests. Two further characteristics of the Renaissance, the concept of the State as a work of art and that of sublimation (more or less noble or selfish according to the specific circumstance) of the individual as a human person, were either not known to the Spaniards or not accepted by them. This is true in especial of the second mentioned concept, except when it crops out—along with that doctrine of gathering rosebuds while you may which asceticism was soon to stifle—in some writers, mostly novelists, toward the end of the fifteenth century and in the sixteenth and early seventeenth.

The modern idea of the State, which we may discern to a certain degree in Philip II, is wholly divergent from the concept of the State held by the Italian Princes and *condottieri.*

The first extension of the Italian Renaissance into other countries was through the medium of its literature and of the study of classic authors and artists, with their corresponding influence. In the former aspect, two of the most representative Renaissance figures, Petrarch (1304-1375) and Boccaccio (1313-1375), very quickly entered into the consciousness of cultured Spaniards, as we shall see; and in Spain Juan II, Alfonso V, and the Catholic Kings Ferdinand and Isabella repeated that open-hearted and ardent patronage of the movement which was given in Italy by the great aristocratic families—the Medici, among them Lorenzo the Magnificent, for instance, in Florence—and by the Popes.

The Literary Court of Juan II of Castile (1419-1454)

Earlier by several years than the Court of Alfonso V of Aragón at Naples, Juan II's Court in Castile was predominantly a literary group; and it united to its love of letters a decided taste for merrymaking and for the sports of strength and skill characteristic of chivalry. At the Court of Juan II, accordingly, poetry was held in highest esteem. Precisely at this time, poetry was at a period of crisis as betwixt the Gali-

Coca Castle.

cian influence theretofore dominant (which had reached its culmination in the thirteenth century) and the strengthening Castilian; moreover, Italian influence had already become important, not only in matters of technique and general taste but also in the specific work of such more or less contemporaneous writers as Dante, Petrarch and Boccaccio and of the Latin classics, especially Virgil; this all interfused still with the final pulsations of Provençal poetry. Prior to Juan II's reign, Spanish literature had been lifted already to great heights by such original and distinctive artists as Juan Ruiz, the Archpriest of Hita (1283[?]-1350[?]) ; Prince Don Juan Manuel, author, among other works, of a collection of tales and fables called *Libro de Petronio, o Conde Lucanor,* the first real example of prose-style in Castilian and predecessor by thirteen years of Boccaccio's *Decameron;* the Chancellor López de Ayala; and King Alfonso XI himself. The influence of oriental literature is easily discernible in some of these authors, especially in tales, legends, and other imaginative fiction.

Belonging to Juan II's time were the so-called Marquis de Villena (1348-1434), translator of Latin and Italian writers and author of moral treatises and other works; the Marquis de Santillana, poet, literary historian, and collector of Castilian proverbs; Juan de Mena, likewise a poet; Juan Alfonso Baena, to whom we owe the first *Cancionero,* an anthology of poems in Castilian and Galician which was dedicated to Juan II and includes the work of poets flourishing from the reign of Enrique II to Juan II's minority; the author, or authors, of the excellent *Crónica*—or Chronicle—of Juan II; Fernán Pérez de Guzmán, biographical historian of the reigns of both Juan II and Enrique III; Martínez de Toledo (Archpriest of Talavera) ; Alfonso de la Torre; the novelist Juan Rodríguez de la Cámara; and other illustrious writers. A poet of the time who was a direct representative of Italian influence was the Genoese Francisco Imperial, who popularized in Castile and Andalusia the works of Dante and other Italian Renaissance writers. Don Alvaro de Luna, writer as well as statesman, shows the influence of Boccaccio in one of his books. By Juan II's time, intellectual production was no longer the work of the clergy alone but of the nobles and the kings as well, a broadening of the field that had begun in the preceding period.

This literary movement was continued in the reign of Enrique IV, both by successive compilations of the *Cancioneros,* of which there were several, and of lyrical and satirical poetry, historical prose, and moral works. The principal poets were Gómez Manrique; his nephew, Jorge Manrique (author of the beautiful elegy on the death of his father which Longfellow translated into English) ; Garcia Sánchez de Badajoz, Rodrigo Cota, Antón de Montoro, Juan Alvarez Gato, and others, some of them convert Jews. At the same time a type of satirical poetry developed which was political and social in intent and, as a rule, tart and realistic in expression, and of which the principal examples were the so-called *Coplas del Provincial*—Verses of the Provincial —and the stanzas, *Mingo Revulgo* or, in the idiom of our own time "John Q. Public."

Notable prosewriters of the period include Diego de Valera, Fernández de Palencia, Hernando del Pulgar, Enríquez del Castillo, Almella, most of whom are historians. It should be noted that others flourished alongside these, historians likewise, who returned to the old custom of writing their books in Latin, undoubtedly in consequence of the influence of Renaissance classicism. At that time a didactic *genre* also fluorished, sometimes moralistic and again political in theme, which was to be continued into the sixteenth and seventeenth centuries and which, during the period that we are now considering, reflects to considerable extent Arabic sources of similar tenor, among which mention should be made of a book that was perhaps Syriac (or ancient Syrian) which Juan Hispalense in the twelfth century translated into Latin and which in that language is entitled *Secretum Secretorum*.

This literary productivity dovetailed with that of the reign of the Catholic Kings.

The Renaissance Court of Alfonso V at Naples

Alfonso V of Aragón, like Alfonso the Sage of Castile, was a man of intellectual interests, and was consequently very speedily and completely intoxicated by the great intellectual ferment in Italy. Accordingly, and coincidentally with the first years of Lorenzo the Magnificent at Florence, Alfonso made his own Court at Naples a meeting-place for Italian philosophers and men-of-letters and of such cultured Spaniards as Juan García and Fernando de Córdoba. At that Court, Latin works of great importance (those of the Cordoban philosopher Seneca among them) were translated into Catalán and Castilian. King

Alfonso V—whose palace was like an academy or a university thronged daily with philosophers, physicians, jurists, theologians, grammarians, and the like—also intervened personally more than once in the scientific discussions that went on there, and on such occasions he demonstrated his great learning, especially on philosophical and religious topics. The Court entertainments also introduced such Spanish elements as the masked ball from Castile and *Morisco* dances.

At Naples Alfonso founded a free primary school and the Alphonsine Library which was well staffed, and well stocked with books that the King had brought in from all countries. He gave due attention also to public works, extending and improving the city and the port of Naples and constructing there walls, towers, castles, parks, streets, and such public buildings as the Custom House, one section of what is called the New Castle (which was the royal palace), and the Arch of Triumph adjoining it. On all of these works, some of which are still standing, Spaniards—architects, sculptors, carpenters, and others—worked alongside Italian artists and artisans, thus introducing an original Spanish influence into Neapolitan territory; while Aragón and Catalonia were receiving a reciprocal Italian influence, which made itself felt principally in literature and philosophy. Belonging to this period are the Catalán writers Jordi de Sant Jordi, Alfonso V's Chamberlain; Andrew Febrer, translator of *The Divine Comedy;* Bernart Metje; Lorenzo Mallol; and the Valencian poet, disciple of Petrarch, Ausias March. A drama in the Valencian language was presented at the Royal Palace of Valencia in 1394; its title was *L'hom enamorat y la fembra satifesteta*—Man Makes Love and Woman Complies—and the author seems to have been Domingo Mascó, Counselor of Juan I of Aragón. In devotional literature, St. Vincent Ferrer was renowned for his writings and famous throughout Europe for his eloquence as a preacher. The many facetted theologico-political Franciscan writer Francisco Eximinis (or Jiménez), Bishop of Elna, belongs to the same period.

The foundation of the Spanish College at Bologna by Cardinal Albornoz in 1364 was an expression both of the Spanish Renaissance and of Spanish penetration into the cultural life of Italy.

Spanish Culture during the Period of the Catholic Kings

Anterior cultural processes reached their culmination in the period of Ferdinand and Isabella. The Catholic Kings were themselves cultured, fully conscious of the value of culture to society and the individual. Both tried to attract to the Court persons of great merit, either to add to their own knowledge (as in the case of Doña Beatriz Galindo, who directed the Queen's Latin studies) or to contribute to the education of their children, Prince Don Juan and Princess Doña Juana. In order to make the success of such instruction more certain, Ferdinand and Isabella brought foreign professors also to Castile. The nobles for their part followed the same practice; and consequently many excellent teachers and writers were attracted to Spain who together with native-born Spaniards helped shape Spanish universities. For the encouragement of culture, a law was promulgated in 1480 ordering free entry, exempt from import duty, of all books needed for study; an exemption that was extended a few years later—in 1548—by the Emperor Don Carlos, or Charles I, to the West Indies; and was ratified in 1591 for all Spain's American possessions by the Book of Excise Rates.

These cultural objectives were helped on greatly by an invention that had been made some years previous, it is not known by whom nor where, and that was perfected about 1439 by a German named Gutenberg: the invention of the printing press. Before that time, books had been in manuscript form, so that having duplicate copies made, especially in the case of long works, was a very costly and tedious proceeding. Nevertheless, the love of learning had given a great impetus to the art of copying, first on parchment and later on paper (which, as we know, had been introduced into Spain by the Arabs); and culture was being widely disseminated therefore in spite of difficulties. There were excellent copyists in Spain, and some admirable manuscripts of theirs are still extant. Many of these are adorned with ornamental margins, decorative initial letters, and the jewel-like paintings in miniature already described, whch are often exquisite, constituting a highly special art in themselves.

The printing press aided enormously in the popularization of books and greatly cheapened production. German and Italian merchants resident on the Peninsula introduced the press into Spain. It is believed that the first book printed here appeared at Valencia in 1474; that is to say, in the same year that Isabella the Catholic ascended the throne. This book was a collection of poems in praise of the Virgin.

The use of the printing press was extended rapidly to almost all of the important Spanish cities and also to monasteries such as those of Miramar in Mallorca and Montserrat in Catalonia. The Catholic Kings aided in spreading this new art, and ruled that printers need not pay taxes. Both facts attest the love for culture that Spain then cherished. Expressions of it were the writings of the great philosopher and teacher, Juan Luis Vives, and of Juan de Lucena, Alonso de Palencia, Fray Antonio Montesino, Juan del Encina (one of the earliest of Spanish playwrights, "father of Spanish comedy"), Rodrigo Cota, Diego de San Pedro, Diego de Valera, Hernando del Pulgar (already cited), Antonio de Lebrixa or Lebrija; the anonymous compilers of the Castilian text of *Amadis de Gaula,* most famous of the books of chivalry; and the unknown author (Fernando de Rojas?) of *La Celestina, o Tragicomedia de Calisto y Melibea,* a book which exemplifies more than any other work the profound Renaissance influence on the concept of human life, expression of which had however been to some degree anticipated a century earlier by the Archpriest of Hita. Because of this quality, *La Celestina* is one of the first books truly universal in feeling produced by Spanish genius, and it was the forerunner of the picaresque novel.

Most of the writers mentioned wrote in Castilian; although in Catalonia and the other Spanish Mediterranean countries use of the regional languages, and of Latin, persisted. One expression of this usage was the creation at Barcelona in 1393 of the *Gaya Ciencia,* or Art of Poetry, and of the *Juegos Florales,* or Floral Games, in imitation of those already established at Toulouse in France. Leading writers of regional literature in Catalán and Valencian included the poets Johannot Martorell and Johan de Galba; the unknown author of the famous novel of chivalry, *Tirant lo Blanch* (1490); Boades and Tomich, Catalán historians; the Valencian poets Joan Roix de Corella (1430-1500) and Joan Roig (1400-1478), and the author of a more or less picaresque novel called *El Spill.*

Changes in Social Classes

While Spanish intellectual life was thus being transformed and was finding expression for its new ideals, the social structure also was undergoing change; or, better said, a change was taking place in the actuation and the components of the various elements, or social classes, in both public and private life.

That does not mean that the nobles and the ecclesiastics lost their position of preeminence. This they continued to hold for a long time, especially in the high political and administrative offices of public life. But members of the middle class began to share in these posts of distinction, and moreover were looming much more important in the economic field, thanks to the growth of industry and commerce, to the steadily increasing value of property acquired through these means, and particularly to the rapid expansion of trade and the increased money exchange to which the new American possessions overseas contributed enormously toward the end of this period. Notwithstanding these new trends, the nobility for a considerable time continued to be possessed of great wealth, as is proved in the case of Castile by the data that we have regarding the fortunes and luxurious living of the great houses of Medina Sidonia, Mendoza, and Haro, among others. The same can be said with respect to several Archbishops—the Archbishop of Toledo, for example—and to the religious Orders.

Both because of the political advantages that might ensue and because of the genuine and well-nigh universal esteem for culture, the Catholic Kings made a special point of showing favor to the middle class in the persons of the *letrados,* which is to say, the holders of law degrees from the universities, almost all of whom were members of the bourgeoisie or of the lesser nobility. From their ranks were made most of the appointments not only for the Courts of Justice—as was logical, in view of their specialized training in law—but also for the Royal Councils and public offices, which were gradually being organized by a previously non-existent specialization of the different administrative branches of government. The *letrados,* and the *legistas,* or legists, naturally felt flattered by such distinction. Moreover, the class to which they belonged was usually royalist in its sympathies at that period, not so much because it favored the monarchy as because it opposed the nobility, as we have observed. For their part, the *letrados* received at the universities a juridical education based chiefly on the Byzantine or Justinian Roman Law, the theory of which was extremely monarchical; and this training inclined them toward the royal policy of leveling out class distinctions while at the same time strengthening the authority of the monarch, centralizing therein those faculties of government that had formerly been dispersed. With this goal in view, the *letrados* felt that satisfactory immediate progress was being made toward secur- ing that triumph of law and order over disorder and lawlessness for which their training in Law had determined them to strive. But it was both natural and inevitable, considering how the anarchical nobility had succeeded very often in making over public order into public disorder, that all this aided in establishment of a monarchical regime tending toward becoming increasingly absolute. This tendency was markedly developed and strengthened in the reigns of the rulers fol- lowing the Catholic Kings.

Decadence of the Municipalities and the CORTES

The advantages gained by the *letrados* in the manner just de- scribed, and consequently indirectly by the middle class to which they mostly belonged, were not carried over, however, into corresponding advantages for that municipal institution in which democracy, as it was then understood, had been evolved and through which it had found expression. We have seen already how the Municipal Councils had been achieving the faculty of electing their judges and justices; but that did not mean, as we pointed out, that these faculties of the Coun- cils excluded those of the monarchs, who retained and almost invari- ably exercised the faculty of naming their own judges. Thus, in the fifteenth century, all the important cities of the realm (Burgos, Seville, Córdoba, Jaén, Murcia, Alicante, León) had the King's justices or judges, along with and without opposition from the Council's judges; and it was almost always the former who convoked and presided over municipal meetings. In addition to this uninterrupted practice, the townships themselves often petitioned that the king send them chief justices, or *alcaldes mayores,* who about that time began to be called *corregidores.* The result was that almost as soon as municpal auton- omy in the election of municipal officers came into being, it was para- lyzed or neutralized by the great importance assigned to officers ap- pointed by the Crown.

One innovation, which is attested by documents of Alfonso XI's reign relating to the district of León, contributed toward preventing the municipality from attaining the maximum independence possible. This was the replacement of the general Assembly consisting of heads of families—the Open Council, an institution that had been carried over from the villages to the cities—by a Municipal Commission or Council, later to be called the *Ayuntamiento* or *Cabildo* which was charged with the functions previously pertaining to the Assembly. In effect, the disappearance of the latter (which was due largely to the increase in population), and consequently of the corresponding personal participation in public affairs by all the citizens, placed municipal authority in the hands of a few, rendered abuses of power more easy, and kindled ambitions for holding the offices on which the Council's life depended.

The frequent civil wars and periods of lawlessness recurring from the time of Alfonso X throughout the fourteenth and fifteenth centuries, created an environment propitious to such ambitions; by reason of class struggles in the municipalities (the common people against the nobles in the cities and large *villas,* or the merchants against the *letrados*) as well as of the conflict of individual with individual, family with family, and, finally, township with township.

Toward the close of the reign of Enrique IV, and in the early years of that of the Catholic Kings, complaints from the *Cortes* and from many municipalities against such a state of things abounded. A law of the *Cortes* held at Madrigal in 1476 alludes to the reprisals taken by some townships against others with consequent "violence and damages," and to the public scandals that "the justices (*alcaldes*) of the locality" did not avail to remedy. There is much other evidence of similar disturbances in the internal life of the municipalities. The Catholic Kings took several measures to correct these conditions, including the following: frequent appointment of *corregidores* who were, however, made subject to what was called "an inquiry in residence"— an investigation, that is—making them answerable for any abuses that they might commit; the sending out of special judges—*pesquesidores,* or examiners—when the *alcaldes,* or justices, of a locality were unable to decide the questions brought before them, and of inspectors— *veedores*—to audit the accounts and review the use to which municipal property was put; suppression in some municipalities of the method of filling posts on the Council by election, in order to avoid such riots as had occurred at Cáceres; and regulation of the elective system where continued, by making it a general practice to limit the right to be elected to *caballeros,* or knights, members of the lower rank of the nobility of whom there were great numbers in the cities and *villas.*

To these measures, occasioned by the lawlessness and conflicts noted, the Catholic Kings added a direct attack against the more autonomous forms practiced in some municipalities or by their federations or brotherhoods (the *Hermandades*). This occurred in the case of the *Hermandad de las villas del mar*—Brotherhood of the *Villas* of the Sea—which from that time forward steadily declined in influence.

In consequence of all this, the political importance of the middle class, properly speaking, in its natural sphere of municipal life, was considerably undermined; the evolution of the municipal regime toward a more complete autonomy was cut short as well, and its authority, like the nobility's, was subjected strictly to the throne's. The institution of the *Cortes* itself, the most flourishing period of which was from the end of the thirteenth century to the end of the fifteenth, suffered effects of the triumph of the monarchical principle. The Catholic Kings ceased to convoke the *Cortes* as soon as they made use of that institution to carry out internal reforms, especially with respect to the nobility, notwithstanding the matters of extraordinary importance that arose in Castilian public life. From 1482 to 1498, the *Cortes* were not convoked, which fact is proof that the Catholic Kings did not consider them, or did not wish to recognize them, as a basic element of government. Between 1498 and 1502 they were convoked five times.

The *Cortes* in the other ancient kingdoms of Spain continued to meet frequently; and in the Basque provinces, Don Ferdinand the Catholic himself solemnly swore to maintain the functions of the regional *Cortes*, which consisted chiefly in specialized measures of administration. Notable examples of these were afforded by the *Junta* of Guernica, and analogous bodies.

The Codes and General Laws

Also in this period the movement (which had been initiated in the preceding) in favor of unification of the laws, or at least of forming new nuclei of laws, common severally throughout all the territory of each kingdom, was continued and emphasized.

As already noted, general legislation applying throughout the Kingdom of León and Castile was not represented, until Ferdinand II's death, except by some laws on particular points which the monarchs had issued or which had been brought about by petitions from the *Cortes* and by extension to a wider area of certain municipal *Fueros* and even of the *Liber Iudiciorum* in Castilian translation (*Fuero Juzgo*).

But it seems to have been Ferdinand III of Castile and León himself, to judge by the information on the matter which has been handed down to us from the early thirteenth century, who conceived the idea of making a code or compilation of laws, for the purpose of having it apply throughout his realm; and it is even believed that work on this code, called *Setanario* because it was divided into seven parts, was begun during his reign. However, no such project was carried out in the lifetime of King St. Ferdinand. Not long thereafter, Alfonso X gave a general *fuero*, known as the Royal *Fuero*, derived from that of Soria which in turn was based on the *Fuero* of Cuenca and the civil rights established in the *Juzgo*. The *Fuero Real*, or Royal *Fuero*, was granted individually to various cities, but was not promulgated as a law common to all.

A similar tendency, though more limited in scope that the project attributed to Ferdinand, showed in Aragón and Catalonia. In Aragón it resulted in the drawing up in 1247 of a so-called General *Fuero*, the Compilation of Huesca, which is in reality a collection of procedures general throughout the kingdom. This compilation nullified none of the municipal *fueros*, and was considered to be merely laws supplementing them, and applying to appeals before the King's tribunal. During Alfonso V's reign a further compilation of general practices was made; under the title *Observancias*, or Observances, it was divided into nine books.

In another field, there was an important compilation of maritime juridical procedures which was called *Libro del Consulado del Mar* (Book of the Consulate of the Sea); which is to say, the book of the centers established at Valencia in 1283, at Mallorca in 1343, and at Barcelona in 1347, to be used as a legal directive for sailors and maritime traders.

In 1283, or not long before, this Book was issued at Barcelona. It speedily acquired celebrity on the Mediterranean littoral. The institution of the Consulate of the Sea was soon extended to Castile, Aragón and the Basque provinces. All this shows how greatly commerce had developed during those centuries and how steadily it continued to increase in importance, thanks to the close relations with Italy and other regions in southern Europe, and to the industrial and mercantile activity of the great maritime cities belonging to the Crown of Aragón, especially Barcelona, Valencia and Palma de Mallorca. Mallorca, indeed, kept up extensive trade with Italy; and there were at the time numerous Italian merchants in the Canaries also, as well as at Valencia. As we have observed already, they grew to be strong competitors of Barcelona.

Canonical Law and Roman Law

Along with this legislative development which, as may be seen, was based principally on the *fueros* and on custom, a tendency to incorporate into legislation of the Christian kingdoms of Spain the principles of Canonical Law (that is, law given out by the Catholic Church at its Councils and by the Popes) and of Roman Law, or the Justinian Code, began to become evident as early as the twelfth century.

The Roman tradition, represented in part by the Visigothic *Liber Iudiciorum* in all of the territories in which the latter continued in force (although in conflict with municipal *fueros* and feudal customs), and in Catalonia by other elements, was greatly strengthened by the newly acquired popularity in leading European universities, especially those of Italy and southern France, of the study of the ancient laws of the Roman Empire, known as the Justinian Code because compiled in the sixth century during the reign of the Emperor Justinian. These Justinian compilations, forgotten in western Europe for centuries, were discovered anew in Italy and studied in the universities mentioned, where there were many Spanish students who, returning home, introduced into the Peninsula the doctrines of the Justinian Code, which differed in many respects from those incorporated in Visigothic Roman Law.

But tentative efforts along this line were cut short for a considerable period by opposition from those who preferred the Spanish laws and customs which had come to birth during the Reconquest and were contained in the *Fuero Juzgo*. Thus we see that in Jaime's I's reign the *Cortes* of Alcañiz in 1250 and in 1251 opposed having Roman laws— that is, laws from the Justinian Code—recognized by the Tribunals of Justice; and they took the same stand with regard to Canonical Law; as did the Catalán *Cortes* in 1243. Nevertheless, it is now an established fact that toward the end of the twelfth century (in the year 1173), Roman Law was made applicable in Catalonia as a supplementary authority. In some volumes or compilations of ordinances and customs in certain localities such as Perpignan (1175) and Lérida (1229) there were to be found already regulations deriving from Roman Law. But resistance against making such adoption of foreign law general was kept up for a long time in the Kingdom of Aragón as well as in Castile.

In the latter realm, the supporters of Roman Law received strong backing from Alfonso X. This found expression in his book called *Las Siete Partidas* (The Seven Divisions) which we have considered several times already from different points of view. Juridically, *Las Siete Partidas*, which is rather an encyclopedia than a code—in spite of the fact that much of its text is divided into sections entitled "Laws"—reflects the Justinian Code only in part, and whenever it does so, usually transmits Justinian doctrines without modification. On the other hand, *Las Siete Partidas* reveals plainly the multiple sources from which it is derived, among these being the Castilian *fueros* and laws. Unquestionably, the Roman part in it is considerable, and emanates as much from the Justinian laws themselves as from the interpretations made by commentators on that code—the *glosadores,* or glossers—at foreign universities; but, as we have said, *Las Siete Partidas* did sometimes modify the Justinian intention, as, for example, in the case of the caesarist or absolute conception of monarchy, which is very much watered down in the encyclopedia of Alfonso the Sage.

Although *Las Siete Partidas* was not promulgated as law, its prestige and authority spread over the whole of the Peninsula and influenced all the jurists and tribunals of justice. In the universities—Castilian, Catalonian, and Portuguese—the work was used as a class-room text. In 1348, Alfonso XI made *Las Siete Partidas* the general supplemental legislation, and thereafter the way was open to imposing its innovations and through them unifying a good part of the law of the land. Likewise in the fourteenth century this Justinian influence was increased by the great prestige which Bartolo (1313[?]-1357), Commentator on Roman Law and Professor at Bologna, Pisa and Perugia, acquired throughout all Europe. His teachings paved the way (and were sometimes, as in Portugal, preferred to the text itself) for Justinian's code and compilations. The Catholic Kings shared the general esteem for Bartolo and testified to it—as well as to their regard for other foreign commentators—by the group of laws which they promulgated at Toro in 1505 and which introduced, chiefly in the field of civil law, principles derived from both Roman and Canonical Law.

That is how the juridical influence of the Renaissance entered into Spain.

Fine Arts and Industrial Arts

While in the various regions of Spain intellectual life was bringing forth the creative genius that produced literary masterpieces, Spanish artists—architects, sculptors, painters, and the rest—trained in the French, Italian and Flemish schools of art, were demonstrating their own innate endowments and affirming the individuality and original-ity of Spanish art by admirable work in building and adorning cathe-drals, churches, universities and palaces.

To this period belong the Cathedrals of León (begun in the twelfth century), with construction continuing in the thirteenth, four-teenth, and fifteenth), Cuenca, Toledo (most Spanish of all in type: thirteenth century), Burgos (fourteenth and fifteenth century), Bar-celona, Mallorca, and many more; as well as the cloisters of innumer-able monasteries, castles, and royal and seignorial palaces which in their varied settings of town and country show the transition, during this period and the early sixteenth century, from the ogive arch of Gothic architecture to the Renaissance manner.

At the same time, Mudéjar art in all its striking originality contin-ued to be brilliantly realized not only in public buildings but in pri-vate residences at Toledo. (Among the latter the one called the Mesa house, with its splendid Mudéjar salon, should be noted; and among the ecclesiastical buildings, the triforium of the Cathedral, of which there are other magnificent examples at Saragossa, Seville, and else-where.) Similar luxuriousness and beauty are to be found in the cas-tles (Manzanares; the upper gallery of the Castle of Bellver; and others) and—on a different plane—in ceramics, panelling, fretwork, *azulejos,* bookbinding.

Spanish sculpture in marble and stone as early as the eleventh and twelfth centuries had surpassed contemporaneous work in other Chris-tian countries, and in the second half of the thirteenth was excelled only by the French, as may be observed in the sculptures of the Cathe-drals of Burgos, León, Toledo, and (fourteenth century) Pamplona. Spanish artists were sometimes called abroad to execute original work;

for instance, the Aragonese Juan de la Huerta designed and constructed the sepulcher of the kings at Dijon, France. In Catalonia, Pedro Juan de Vallfogona carved the St. George in the Palace of the Deputation of Barcelona and part of the greater retable at Tarragona.

The fifteenth century produced sculpture in rich variety. The most impressive groups, at Burgos, Toledo, Seville, and León, were executed by Spanish and foreign artists working together. Their inspiration and technical skill gave birth to admirable work in religious statuary, Gothic as well as Renaissance in type; the latter style having been imported by the Italian sculptors. Among other works then produced were beautiful doors and ornamentation for churches; such mortuary sculpture as the Doncel tomb at Sigüenza; that of Don Alvaro de Luna and his wife at Toledo; those of Don Juan II, Queen Isabella, and Prince Don Alfonso at Miraflores; and that of the first Marquis and Marchioness de Poza at Palencia, perhaps the earliest of all the Renaissance sepulchers; as well as retables such as those of the Cathedrals of Seville, Toledo, the Carthusian Cathedral at Miraflores, the Churches of San Nicolás, Santa Ana, and many others.

In the diverse application of carving to furniture, objects of religious use, et cetera, there was some remarkably beautiful work in such things as choir stalls (for instance, the magnificent specimen in the Cathedral of Toledo, with carvings in part portraying the Wars of Granada); bargueños; small coffers for relics; portapaces, or image plates (sometimes enamelled); fine monstrances in gold or silver; processional crosses and custodias which were occasionally also of precious metals and gems, such as may be seen in the Cathedrals of Toledo, Córdoba, and Barcelona, and in many fifteenth century churches; and jet ornaments of the period from Santiago de Compostela.

We have from this period too some of the finest examples of grillwork in iron (and at times in silver), still to be admired at Toledo, Burgos and Pamplona, as well as many other objects representing great diversity and fertility of inventiveness, which for many centuries before the splendid culminative outflowering in the sixteenth century, made Spain one of the regions of the world most abounding in works of art.

As for painting, it should be remembered that in the fourteenth and fifteenth centuries (and principally in Italy) the Renaissance stimulated the development of schools rich and splendid in diverse manifestations. To this period belong the illustrious names of Giotto, Orcagna, the Lippis, Massaccio, Botticelli, Signorelli, Perugino, Mantegna, Leonardo da Vinci, and Raphael (who was late fifteenth century: 1483-1520). All of these had more or less direct influence on Spanish artists, as did also the French and the Flemish painters; an influence exercised most immediately through artists of those countries who came to Spain to paint. Spanish painters in the different regions show varying preferences with respect to these foreign influences, and at times reflect a happy commingling of two of them, as may be observed in the famous painting by the Catalán Luis Dalmau, Alfonso V's Court painter, *La Virgen de los Concelleres*—The Virgin and the Councillors. Mention should be made also of the *Virgen de la Piedad* by the Cordoban Bartolomé Bermejo in the Chapter Hall at Barcelona. Bartolomé was the first Spanish painter to employ oils, which he used extensively but not exclusively. Velázquez, a century later, was to be the first Spaniard who painted only in oils. Before that time Spanish painting was in tempera, a method that Dalmau still employed also, although the Flemish painter Van Dyck, whose work had great vogue in Spain, had already popularized oil painting to a considerable degree.

But the really important thing in Spanish art at that time was the appearance in ever-increasing number of artists of purely Spanish stock, whose originality freed itself of foreign excrescences and shone with the light of its own genius. They included, among others, under the name Bartolomé de Cárdenas, Bermejo, mentioned above; the Maestro Alfonso, called Maestro de la Sisla; Pedro Berruguete, in the opinion of many critics the most Spanish painter of his time; and various anonymous artists.

The First Renaissance Architecture and the Isabelline Style

The influence of Renaissance architecture (furthered in Italy by imitation of Roman monuments and application of the theories of the first-century architect, Vitrubius) though later than that of sculpture, commenced to become noticeable in Spain toward the close of the fifteenth century.

Gothic architecture had struck such deep root in Spanish earth, alongside the eastern, or Mudéjar, that the Renaissance type was long in displacing it. However, the intermixture of Gothic and Renaissance produced a new architectural style known as Plateresque because its

The Alhambra: Hall of the Ambassadors.

exuberant ornamentation was reminiscent of the filagree work of the *plateros,* or silversmiths. There were excellent typical examples of Plateresque as early as the reign of the Catholic Kings, such as the façade of San Pablo, the College of San Gregorio at Valladolid, and the façade of San Esteban at Salamanca. Plateresque architecture was still flourishing in the epoch of Charles I.

Together with this new tendency, and at times blending with it, appeared another, more national type, resulting from the fusion of Gothic, Renaissance, and in very marked degree, Mudéjar: a type that modern art critics call Isabelline, because it belongs to the period of Isabella I. One of its typical expressions is the Vélez Chapel of the Cathedral of Murcia; just as the interior of San Juan de la Penitencia at Toledo, demonstrating another phase of the fusion, and belonging to what may be called the Cisneros group of churches, is likewise very typical of the period.

The Final Period of Moslem Arts, Architecture

To make the artistic panorama of the period complete, something should be said about the Moslem art of the time. Moslem architecture was then marked by lavishness of ornamentation, which was more abundant than in preceding periods and not surpassed by any people nor by any art. The interior walls of the Moslem buildings (mosques, palaces, or whatever) were sheathed with plaster panelling carved in relief; the arches were diversified in form, some of simple horseshoe shape, others slender-lobed, and so on; the capitals of columns were "cushioned," and covered with decoration; the domed ceilings dripped magnificent pendants, or "stalactites"; the socles, or flat square members underneath the bases of pedestals, were patterned colorfully in minute bits of stone (*alicatado* mosaic) or in large square glazed tile (*azulejos*). The decorative designs also made extensive use of human figures and animal sculptures.

The building, or rather the group of buildings, at Granada known as the Alhambra is not only the sole structure preserved practically complete from that period, but is also the one embodying with greatest richness and variety the characteristics just noted.

The exterior of the Alhambra shows the surrounding and defending belt of walls and towers, a magnificent example of Moslem fortifications of the time. In the interior, beauty of structure and wealth of ornamentation characterize the patio called the Court of the Lions; the halls (*miradores*), such as that of Lindaraja; the *agimeces,* or windows, like the one in the Captive's Tower; and the gardens with trees and flowers corresponding to the banks of windows in each wing of the structure. The Mosque of the Alhambra, no longer in existence, was, in the words of a fourteenth century Arab writer, a monument of architecture, magnificent "for the richness of its decoration, the grandeur of its pillars or columns adorned with bases and capitals of silver, and the beauty of its design." Though we may take some of this with a grain of salt, the eulogy in general denotes the impressiveness of the Alhambra and the loveliness of its patterning in gilt and silver.

The gardens of the Generalife, adjoining the Alhambra, are likewise an extremely beautiful exemplification of the Granadine art that irradiated its influence to several regions in Africa just as the art of the Caliphate of Córdoba continued to influence various European nations.

Industrial Arts

Spanish Moslems achieved eminence not only in architecture and the adornment of buildings, but also in ceramics, characteristic and enduringly beautiful examples of which are their platters (especially those in gold lustre) ; their urns (of which we have some examples from the Granadine period) ; their *azulejos,* or tiles glazed in color. Splendid examples of their metal work include lamps in silver, bronze, and other media; hilts and scabbards for swords and daggers, finely wrought in gold and silver, those in filagree being especially remarkable; jewel caskets inlaid with plaques of precious metals and ivory, carved and engraved. Equally noteworthy were their wool and silk textiles for wearing apparel, or for rugs and tapestries; their decorations in leather—Cordoban stamped leather or Guadamacil leather patterned in gilt; and their inlays of wood—*taraceas*—or of metal—damascene. All these exquisite creations were disseminated among the Christians by the Mudéjares, and they are perpetuated in some of our characteristic Spanish arts, such as ceramics (Manises) and certain designs in silver.

Blue and gold porcelain jar from the Hall of the Two Sisters, Alhambra.

The Spanish Middle Ages

For a long while now, the historians of all countries have been calling the period included between the fifth century Visigothic invasion and the mid-fifteenth century by the collective designation of the Middle Ages, or Medieval Times.

Some Spanish and foreign writers have been protesting for more than fifty years against the employment of any such terms; but these continue to be used, and have, in fact, became household words. Consequently this terminology has to be taken into account if most of today's history books are to be comprehensible to the reader.

The obvious relativity of any such term as "middle ages" or "medieval times" is in itself authorization to modify their application somewhat with respect to the particular history of each people; so that we could with some justification say that the Spanish Middle Ages, which may be considered as beginning with the Germanic or Visigothic invasions of the fifth century, lasted until the end of the reign of the Catholic Kings, at which time a completely new political life opened up for Spain. It seems also apparent that if we should take the ideological rather than the political point of view as criterion, giving our attention to the great change in ideas brought about in Europe by the appearance and triumph of the Renaissance, the close of the reign of the Catholic Kings would still mark the end of the Spanish Middle Ages. However, the fact must be recognized that—since mankind's changes of ideology (and even more, the conduct consequent on such changes) are never effected all of a sudden, but gradually, step by step— while it may be stated that the Renaissance by the end of the fifteenth century was already influencing and modifying Spanish life and thought, it is no less true that alongside this new factor many characteristics of the Middle Ages survived— and continued to survive for a long time. This observation is equally applicable to all the rest of Europe. And that is why a modern historian has justly observed that it is impossible to say precisely when the Middle Ages left off and the Renaissance began, since exact limits can be set neither for the one nor for the other.

Be that as it may, in Spanish history we can divide the so-called Middle Ages into two great parts, though they are unequal in length of time. One extends from the fifth century to the beginning of the eighth, and corresponds to the Visigothic domination; and the other, from the eighth century to the end of the fifteenth, which is the period of the Reconquest. Regarding this latter, it could be said with equal foundation that it represents the period of evolution of the new Spain, the Spain that during that period created its political territory, its languages, its culture, and all the faculties that caused it to become later on a prime factor in the process of universal civilization. That period was our veritable Spanish Middle Ages, if we wish to maintain this illogical classification currently in use. The period from the first century to the eighth was no more than the last Act of the great Tragedy of the Roman Empire, which had fallen into clutching hands of the Germanic tribes and yet in substance had not been utterly destroyed: it was the period definitely marking the end of so-called Ancient History.

Chapter X

The Period of Spain's Ascendancy and its Conclusion (1516=1700)

Cisneros' Regency and the Beginning of Charles I's Reign

THE REGENCY of Cisneros was brief. It began in January 1516 and ended in November 1517. During those months he had to confront three grave difficulties; the continued absence in Flanders of Charles of Ghent who, in addition to being Ferdinand II's successor on the throne of Aragón, had now become King of Castile *de facto,* even though Queen Doña Juana was living still; the renewed efforts of some Castilian nobles to acquire for themselves a condition of independence verging on anarchy; and even a struggle lasting for some time between the two sons of Doña Juana and Philip the Fair: Charles himself and Ferdinand.

Charles had been born in 1500 at Ghent, where his parents then resided. In accordance with the express desire of his paternal grandfather, the Emperor Maximilian of Germany, and contrary to the wishes of his maternal grandfather, King Ferdinand of Aragón, Charles was educated in Flanders, with the natural result that the shaping of his thought was essentially Flemish. This was true particularly of his concepts of power, relations among the social classes, and customs. His younger brother, Prince Ferdinand, on the contrary, had been born at Alcalá and educated in Castile. Ferdinand the Catholic, believing for that reason that the grandson who was his namesake was logically fitted to govern Spain, thought first of him in the matter of the succession to the Crown of Aragón and Castile; a thought that was incorporated in his first will, dated 1515. The exertions by Charles and his Council of Flanders, where he had been ruling since January of that same year (1515), as well as the opinion of some of Ferdinand the Catholic's own advisers, caused the latter to reconsider; and so he drew up a new will making Charles heir of the Spanish States. This decision was on the point of causing Prince Ferdinand's followers to start a civil war, but the resourcefulness and energy of Cisneros succeeded in preventing the outbreak. Perhaps that change in his will was the greatest mistake ever made by King Ferdinand and his advisers.

Charles of Ghent never recognized how much he owed Cisneros. Since Charles was determined to be proclaimed King of Castile forthwith, and his courtiers from Ghent were eager to participate in and control the government of Spain, the lot of them, including Charles, kept Cisneros surrounded by a cortege of ambassadors and a bevy of spies who created endless difficulties for him. Some Castilian nobles jealous of the Regent did their part in contributing to these difficulties. But Cisneros himself, immovable in his loyalty to the monarchy and not to be swayed from consistent action in affairs of state, did everything in his power to uproot from public opinion in Aragón and Castile every trace of opposition to Charles, and carried out the latter's wishes by having him proclaimed King of Castile to rule jointly with his mother, Queen Doña Juana. The consequence was to make him the only monarch in fact. The ceremony to that end was held at Valladolid in April 1516, and at Madrid the following month. With this moot-point settled and the incipient civil war thwarted, Cisneros devoted himself to controlling the nobles with a strong hand. Although they had become very much emboldened by the monarch's absence, he did control them.

Both in order to cope with these internal dangers and to meet Spain's further military requirements, Cisneros, fired with the same ideas that had brought about initial formation of a permanent army in the reign of the Catholic Kings, created the national militia called *Gente de la Ordenanza*—"the Ordinance Boys," as the idiom of our own time might phrase it—which was authorized officially May 27, 1516, and speedily became an army corps of more than 30,000 footsoldiers.

Learning in the summer of 1517 that Charles was setting things in
readiness to come to Spain, Cisneros prepared to receive him and hand
over the reins of government. With that end in view, he undertook
the journey to northern Spain, leaving Madrid in August. Charles set
sail from Flanders September 7, and reached Villaviciosa in Asturias ten
days later, with a numerous company of Flemish gentlemen. When
these latter were informed that Cardinal Cisneros was desperately ill,
they tried to delay the King in resuming the journey to meet his Regent, and thus prevent an interview between them if possible. They
were successful; for Charles decided to go on to Valladolid (against
the advice of Cisneros, who wrote to him several times) ; and so the
Cardinal Regent died at Roca on November 8 without having seen
his sovereign. As a result the Flemings and those Castilians who had
been Cisneros' enemies were left in possession of the field.

The "Personal" Union of the Spanish Kingdoms

With the proclamation of 1515 the political union of the ancient
Spanish Kingdoms in the person of Charles I had become a legal fact,
since Queen Juana—"mad Queen Joanna"—was incapacitated for ruling. Therefore, although it could be said that until Doña Juana's
death on April 11, 1555, there were two monarchs in Castile and only
one in Aragón and Navarre, the fact is that Charles was sole ruler of
the Spanish Kingdoms.

Thus it was that the ideal which some have believed to be implicit
in the imperial title assumed by several former Kings of León and
Castile was converted into a reality; though in a form different from
what had been presupposed by that terminology, since Charles I, being
the only king in Spain, could never hear himself called "Emperor" by
any other Spanish king.

That unity of the Spanish State came, then, by paths far removed
from any such origin as the expressed will of all or any of the Spanish
peoples; or a feeling of Peninsular unification originating in the desirability of uniting the various States born during the Reconquest in
order to constitute a strong homogeneous entity with ideals common
to all. Neither of these sentiments existed in Spain on the date when
Charles became sole King by inheriting a patrimonial monarchy,
through family interest, at a very early age.

The Reconquest had operated, as we know, as a factor of separation among the diverse Christian groups, because of the circumstance that the struggle against the Moslems had sprung up independently, not always at the same time, at different points on the Peninsula, widely separated, and inhabited by distinct elements of population. Geography also played a great part in maintaining these groups isolated during a long period. In the case of the Spanish March, the interposition of a foreign political power (that of the French kings of the Carlovingian dynasty) helped about the same end.

Once the Christian monarchies had been created—first, two kingdoms (the Asturian and the Navarrese) plus the Spanish March; later, four (the Asturian-Leonese, the Castilian, the Navarrese, and the Argonese, as well as the County of Barcelona) —the fact that they were distinct political entities necessarily tended to divide the peoples of each of these States from their neighbors, since their leaders were in frequent conflict over possession of the frontier regions and fought sometimes for the Crown itself, for total annexation of the adjacent kingdom, or for any other reason there might be; not to mention the conflicts arising from political passions inherent in high office: envy, jealousy, ambition, and pride of place. The division of States noted (to which, it is well to repeat, the rugged mountain ranges of our Peninsula and the diversity of the races populating it during the early period of our history naturally conduced) was favorable to formation of special ways of life, government, institutions, and customs in each of the Kingdoms and in the territories of the County of Barcelona. It favored as well, in the process of transformation of Latin which had already become highly differentiated in eighth century regional popular speech, the expression of the individuality of each of these Spanish groups through development of its own language, different one from another though all of Latin derivation and hence all Romance tongues; with parallel variants in art and literature. These last were in part manifestation of the differing genius of the several regions and of the way in which the ethnic elements of each had been developed; and in part, also, they were the result of the different foreign influences brought to bear upon them or of the varying intensity of these influences. Such was the root of the fruitful variety produced in Spanish life and thought for centuries past, and still to be observed today.

On the other hand, Moslem domination and the effort to throw it off influenced other aspects of Spanish life and was, if not a unifying influence, an element that tended at least to create a common fund of thought and opinion. On the one hand, these opposing forces progressively strengthened the Christian faith of the Spaniards because of a natural reaction against the religion of their enemies and because of the prejudices that wars engender. From these and concomitant causes emanated the rich flowering of Christian religious literature, and of the pious legends, which we have discussed already; while the religious bond, notwithstanding the tolerance toward Moslems and Jews, the underlying causes of which we have noted, continued to draw the various elements of the Christian Spanish population ever closer and to create a fund of public opinion held by them all. The war of the Reconquest aided this ideological rapprochement in other ways also. *In general,* because danger and suffering experienced in common draw men together, as does mutual endeavor toward the same objective, which in that case was that of expelling the Asiatic and African invaders; and this in spite of the frequency with which the kings delayed the main objective by their personal quarrels and rivalries. The cause *in particular,* was that over a long period and to a great degree this devotion to a common cause with all that it meant of shared peril and privation was evinced in the mountainous areas of northern Spain which were precisely the regions that up to the time of the wars of Reconquest had been the most isolated of the Peninsula and, in comparison with the central and southern regions, the most refractory to both Roman and Visigothic domination (the Basques, for example, were in a continuous state of revolt from the fifth century to the eighth); consequently, the northern areas had been those least influenced by the culture of the Romans and Visigoths.

Allied to these facts are the following. Fortunately, the political position of the kings with respect to one another neither resulted in the irreducible separation of their peoples nor rendered it impossible for general interests to develop, held in common. The War of the Reconquest was one such interest; and we have noted several instances of concerted action by the different monarchs, directed toward checking new Moslem assaults or toward progress in reconquering territory. Besides these cases of cooperation, it is evident that the mere thought of war against the Moslems made all Spanish hearts beat in unison, whether Leonese, Galician, Cantabrian, Castilian, Navarrese, Aragonese, Catalán, or any of the rest. On the other hand, the problems of reconstruction by means of reconquest and resettlement were identical in all regions, and inevitably were solved in ways which, while differing in certain details or tendencies, were in many substantial things identical or very similar.

For their part, the influences of Moslem and Jewish civilization, as well as those of the other Christian European countries, were exerted conjointly over all the regions of the Peninsula. The great currents and manifestations of science, letters and art, produced in the European world from the eighth century to the fifteenth, inundated all the lands of Spain and reached every group of Spaniards. Carlovingian culture; Roman art; Gothic art; Provençal culture; the Italian influence; the Flemish; the Renaissance. All that the various elements of these cultural contributions connote for the whole life of a people were disseminated over Spain; and in spite of the different ways in which they were interpreted and applied in the various regions (the facets or special aspects revealed by these influences in each section of the Spanish Peninsula) their essential characteristics must have acted with equal force wherever distributed, leaving their own stamp on the Spanish mind. A similar function was effected by the essential factors in forming the body of Spanish jurisprudence; that is, the Visigothic customs (the Germanic element) and the uninterrupted influence of western Roman Law, reinforced from the twelfth century on by renascence of the Justinian Code, as we know, and by the new mercantile and monetary laws which were a creation of the Middle Ages.

In this manner, and commensurably with the progress of the centuries, two parallel movements were being produced in Spanish cultural life. One was common and uniform, with its essential qualities proceeding from the circumstances themselves and from the foreign influences affecting all Spain; and the other was individual and varied, product of the differing effects produced by these same influences upon the originality and personality of each group, and of the strength and scope of that personality and of the individualist sentiment that is concomitant with the existence of independent States.

How the Single Monarchy Settled the Traditional Duality

The opposition of these two (the movement toward unity and the movement toward variety) could have been settled by the greater pressure of the one or the other, with the corresponding triumph of the more powerful. It should not be forgotten that this fact of duality was not special to Spain in the centuries of the so-called Middle Ages. All other European countries shared it, though in varying degrees and for longer or shorter time. It was not solved by all in the same fashion. In France, for example, after surmounting the great crisis of the Hundred Years War fought with England in order to recover much French territory, King Louis XI (contemporaneous with the Catholic Kings) succeeded, by measures analogous to those employed by Ferdinand and Isabella in Castile, in dominating the high nobility and building up a strong monarchy, politically homogeneous in sentiment and progressively more firmly established. It is true that in this political achievement Louis XI had had a notable and indefatigable precursor in his grandmother Queen Yolande of Anjou, of Aragonese ancestry (daughter of King Juan I), whose influence over the Dauphin Charles at a time when the monarchy was in great difficulties had been a powerful factor in initiating reconstruction of the French State. The unity and homogeneity achieved by Louis XI became, in the hands of Francis I who was a contemporary of Charles I of Spain, the major means of French resistance in a crisis of the national life. In Italy, on the contrary, it was not homogeneity but variety that triumphed, with continuance of the division into various republics that almost always were governed by oligarchies and were in constant strife with one another; a combination of circumstances largely responsible for the fact that not until the nineteenth century could Italy be transformed into a great State and nation.

Spain found solution of the problem in a middle way between homogeneity and unity. In the field of culture, the progressive hegemony of the Castilian personality increased century by century after the beginning of the thirteenth, spontaneously and naturally, without any resort to violence nor any political imposition over the other regions. As the Castilian language developed in forcefulness, variety, flexibility, and beauty, creating a literature ever more vigorous, it absorbed and overshadowed the Peninsular importance of the other, kindred tongues that had been evolved in Asturias, Galicia, León, Aragón, and the non-Basque section of Navarre; although some of these regional idioms—Galician, for instance—enjoyed for a considerable period an active literary life. Castilian penetrated even into the Basque Provinces, and was adopted by a portion of the inhabitants. Catalán, Valencian, and Mallorcan were more resistant to the rising tide of Castilian, and, as we have pointed out, bore rich fruits in science and literature; but in the end, Castilian gained ascendancy over them as the language of intellectual life and as expression of the larger Spanish ideology.

On the other hand, factors very different in kind from the anterior contributed to the effective preponderance of the Castilian element in the realm of Spanish thought. Castile, last of the kingdoms created in the central and western regions of the Peninsula, was the one that acquired by far the most territory. Under Ferdinand I Castile conquered a great part of what was later to be Portugal, and invaded the Moslem Kingdoms of Toledo and Seville; under Ferdinand III it made all central and western Andalusia Castilian; under Isabella the Catholic it dislodged the Moors from Granada. Although a well-known couplet asserts

> *A Castilla y a León,*
> *nuevo mundo dió Colón*

(Gift to León and to Castile, / Columbus did a new world reveal), America was considered officially to be the conquest of the Crown of Castile, so that mention of León was superfluous.

As for the Basque Provinces, after having yielded for some time to the allurement of Navarre, they entered decidedly into the sphere of Castilian influence: Alava and Guipúzcoa from the beginning of the thirteenth century, and Vizcaya, or Biscay, at the end of the fourteenth, came to form part of the realm of the Crown of Castile, as we have said. Although because of Jaime I's conquests the Kingdom of Aragón (except for the brief duration of Mallorcan independence) occupied extensive territories both on the Peninsula and lying near its borders, and although further conquests by Pedro III incorporated very important domains first of Italy and later of Greece, nevertheless, at the end of the fifteenth century, the total territory belonging to Castile was greater than that of any other kingdom in Spain, and it was plain to be seen that the influence of the center and the west counted for more on the Peninsula than that of the east.

Nevertheless, when at the beginning of the sixteenth century the Crown of the two great Peninsular kingdoms and that of Navarre fell to the lot of a single individual, the union of government which that fact signified served undoubtedly to strengthen the spiritual unity already achieved by the Castilian spirit which was penetrating and dominating in consonance with the spread of spoken Castilian and of books in that language; but all this did not modify essentially the internal political situation of the States inherited by Charles I. Under his sole authority, there persisted the distinctive characteristics which the different kingdoms and regions of Castile had possessed at the close of the fifteenth century; that is to say, after the reforms made by Ferdinand the Catholic. Aragón, Catalonia, Valencia, Mallorca, Navarre, and the Basque Provinces retained their own special laws; the regional language (when such existed) continued to be employed in daily life and sometimes in literature as well; and many of the essential political institutions—the *Cortes* among them—persisted; and this state of things lasted, substantially as indicated, throughout the enire period of the rule of the House of Austria. Until the constitutional government of the nineteenth century there was no over-all Spanish *Cortes*—no single Parliament, that is to say, for the whole of the Spanish monarchy. However, each region kept up its own customs, its folk art, its typical dress, and its own unmistakable character which today still personalizes each, setting it apart from the rest. These individual differences were maintained not only as between Castile and the other kingdoms but also in the various districts of the realm of Castile. All of these things make it evident that the superiority demonstrably attained by Castile from the thirteenth to the close of the fifteenth century and later, was not produced by imposition of force nor was it a well-laid plan for annulling the personality of the other Spanish kingdoms. It was the natural consequence of those special qualities possessed by the Castilian mind which made themselves felt because of their own weight and of the driving force of Castilian culture, which was dominant by reason of its genius.

It would therefore not be in accordance with the facts of history to believe that Charles I, once he had become the sole King of Spain, viewed the problem of the political heterogeneity of the old Peninsular States as we would view it now, and that he solved it on the conscious basis of any such concept. There is extant no contemporaneous evidence that permits us even to assume that any of the monarchs of the House of Austria envisaged that problem as it is seen by modern historians and statesmen whose point of view is also modern. Those monarchs were content to leave things as they found them, feeling no need of changing what seemed to them a natural state of affairs. Only the Count-Duke of Olivares, as we shall soon note, seems to have regarded the political problem of total unification as a statesman might regard it today. The problem tangent to that, which the centralizing idea of the absolute monarchy implanted, struck at regional autonomy from another angle, although in the final analysis it arrived at conclusions contrary to political diversity.

In fact, the attack of the monarchy of the House of Austria on the autonomies that escaped their patrimonial and absolutist concept was made, not with the object of suppressing them as survivals of ancient independent sovereignties, but in order to reduce the political liberties that the Middle Ages were creating; and the attack therefore extended not only to the Crown of Aragón but also, and more strongly because it was more accessible, to that of Castile which was first to give in to this new conception of the monarchic State.

A problem of a different nature was the application of the absolute theory of monarchy—that of the divine right of kings—to the internal life of each country. In Spain, as we shall see, it was Castile that underwent it first and most intensely. As for the other bonds, *effective political unification* and *abolition of the* FUEROS, doubtless they corresponded to the same program and reasoning on the part of the absolute monarchy; but they came much later. On the other hand, these occurrences were general throughout Europe, not only in Spain. They were very different from those events that were essentially responsible for the spiritual unification attained in the sixteenth century on the basis of a preponderant Castilianism. Nor were they a natural product of the existence of only one king for the whole of Spain. They sprang rather from the political orientation of the entire world, which, in all likelihood, would have made itself felt in Spain as it did everywhere else regardless of whether there were two kings or three or one.

For the time being, the political pattern of unity of the State such as Charles I and his successors represented, did not produce constitutional unity nor even, strictly speaking, a centralization erasing the autonomous boundary of the ancient kingdoms. The contrary was rather the predominant fact during the sixteenth and seventeenth centuries. There were merely some internal reforms in Aragón and Catalonia, to be detailed hereafter.

In fact, the different kingdoms united in the person of Charles I did not consider themselves by mere virtue of that fact to be fused and molded into a single political entity and a single nation. The only homogeneous group which seems to have felt an aspiration for such a Peninsular solidarity was Castile, comprehending the territories that belonged to Isabella I's kingdom. The rest, although recognizing one King over them all, were very far from feeling nationalistic or political aspirations in common with Castile nor with any other one realm. Not only did Navarre, Aragón, Catalonia, Valencia, and Mallorca continue to possess their organisms of internal government, as we have stated already, but they retained also the separatist spirit evinced in former centuries. On a lesser scale than these ancient States, the Basque Provinces had legislation and customs different from those of Castile in matters of administration and civil law.

The spirit of dissociation, or separatist tendency, mentioned above, was transmuted into the firm determination to perpetuate the privileges and *fueros* that contributed to making impossible the union of all. The principles of these *fueros,* politically speaking, were the following: refusal to admit into their respective territories foreign troops (the Castilian troops being included in that category) ; refusal to permit public office to be held by any persons not of the region or realm (only Argonese could hold office in Aragón, Cataláns in Catalonia, and so on) ; refusal to participate in or be concerned about anything which in their opinion did not affect them directly. Hence the Aragonese did not consider themselves under any obligation to defend the frontiers of Castile even when these were attacked by French or other non-Peninsular troops, and on that account Aragón was very resistant to lending aid against the French invasions that took place in the Fuenterrabian region. Several analogous examples could be cited. It is not to be doubted that those differing *fueros* caused difficulties in the process of government and affected adversely the defense against common enemies of all Spain, and that they lent themselves to continuous conflict even when efforts were made to avoid this. The bad effect of such consequences was intensified of course when tact was lacking in pre-

The Alhambra: Patio of the Lions.

serving a duly respectful attitude toward the *fueros* and toward the regionalist sentiment of separatism, even though these things should be deemed hindrances to the unity of Spanish action.

On the other hand, the regionalist sentiment demonstrated lack of comprehension of or indifference toward the international policy undertaken by the House of Austria (and by all the other royal houses of Europe) ; even though in so far as regarded France and Italy, that policy proceeded neither from the House of Austria nor the House of Burgundy, but from the traditional attitude of Catalonia and the Aragonese kings toward those two realms.

Let us now examine the first results of Charles I's arrival in Spain.

The First Clash with Castilian Public Opinion

The first clashes of the King with Spanish public opinion were caused by the Flemings. Charles, as we have observed, had not received the training that would have enabled him to understand, of himself, the psychology of the people that he had come to govern; and he was slow in acquiring that strength of personality and independence of character which years later were to distinguish him historically as a king taking in unusual and extraordinary degree a personal part in government of his realm. When Charles came first to Spain, he did not even speak the Castilian language which he afterwards lauded so highly and loved so greatly.

On the other hand, his Flemish friend and chief adviser, Guillaume de Croix, Seigneur de Chièvres, tried by every possible means, in order to maintain his influence over Charles, to keep the latter isolated from the Spanish nobility and high clergy, who naturally were important figures at the Castilian Court. The Flemings, considering themselves to be in a conquered country, and giving the King to understand that he could fill public offices at his pleasure, allotted to themselves the most lucrative and honored posts, including the Archbishopric of Toledo which was bestowed on a nephew of Chièvres who did not even come to Spain to preside over his diocese. Charles was so indiscreet as to hand over the presidency of the first Castilian *Cortes* that he convoked (at Valladolid in 1518) to one of his Flemings; an act which justly angered the public. Castilian dignity and forthrightness, no whit less than those of the Cataláns when they refused to be dominated by Ferdinand II, were demonstrated in that *Cortes* by indignant expul-

The Alhambra: Comares Patio, or Patio of the Pool.

sion of the Fleming from the hall of sessions, and by the integrity with which several members—especially Zumel, of Burgos, deputy for Valladolid—asked Charles I to show respect for the laws of the realm, to appoint no foreigners to office, and to learn the Castilian language "in order that Your Majesty better understand your subjects and be better understood by them." It was Charles who implanted in Spain the pomp and ceremony of the Burgundian Court, to the distaste of the Castilians and of Prince Philip as well; but that innovation completed the submission of the nobility to the Court which had been initiated by the Catholic Queen.

Charles I of Spain Becomes Emperor of Germany. Consequences of This

Very soon an event no less unexpected than momentous, and from one point of view bringing confusion to Spain, made matters worse. That was the accession of Charles of Ghent—Charles I of Spain—to the Imperial throne of Germany on the death of his maternal grandfather, the Emperor Maximilian, in January 1529. Rival contendants for the Emperor's Crown were Francis I of France, Henry VIII of England, and up to a certain point Frederick of Saxony. Frederick in fact was elected Emperor, whereupon he renounced his rights in favor of Charles, who had paved the way for this outcome through the very shrewd negotiations of his favorite, the Seigneur de Chièvres, and the expenditure of a great deal of money. Charles was the fifth of that name to be elevated to the rank of Emperor, so he is commonly called Charles I of Spain and V of Germany; and since at the same time he inherited the Archduchy of Austria from his paternal grandfather, Charles' family or dynasty is known as the House of Austria, though it might more properly be called the House of Burgundy, or better still, the House of Hapsburg, for Maximilian belonged to the Hapsburg family which ruled the Empire for a long period.

But in Spain, and especially in Castile, news of that election was very unwelcome; on the one hand, because from the viewpoint of the independence of the Peninsular kingdoms, the fact that their King should at one and the same time be Emperor as well, inspired distrust; and on the other, because Spanish public opinion feared that the attention and care given by the King to foreign affairs would diminish his interest in Peninsular matters. And public opinion did not err.

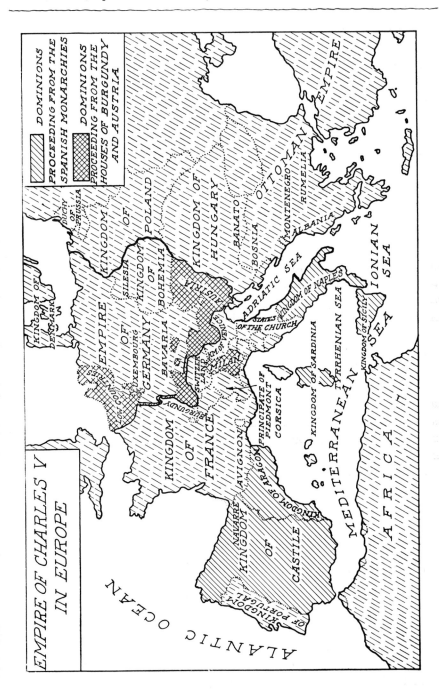

EMPIRE OF CHARLES V IN EUROPE

DOMINIONS PROCEEDING FROM THE SPANISH MONARCHIES

DOMINIONS PROCEEDING FROM THE HOUSES OF BURGUNDY AND AUSTRIA

With inheritance of the two Spanish Kingdoms, the States of the House of Burgundy, the Empire, and the Archduchy of Austria in his possession, Charles I became the most powerful monarch of Europe; but he became also, by the same token, the head and ruler of vast, widely separated territorial possessions scattered throughout Europe, America, and Africa. Naturally, this made inevitable the dispersion of attention and strength. Furthermore, speaking generally, the affairs of his other States in Europe absorbed more of Charles' interest than did those of Spain; a fact easy to understand, because he had been acquainted longer with them than with Spanish affairs and they constituted the traditional preoccupation of the Hapsburg family to which he belonged on his father's side and in the environment of which he had been reared; and also because they were of greater weight and gravity. Consequently, the Crown of Spain in the beginning meant to Charles only a contributing factor—for it increased his power and his material resources—toward achieving his principal objective, the Crown of Emperor, in which function he believed, as he himself declared, that he acted as representative or temporal Vicar of the Christian Church.

The Spaniards were justifiably annoyed by this predominant fixation on matters alien to Spain. They did not at first realize the importance nor even the significance of the European imperial problem. Naturally also, they were much more in favor of conserving and increasing their own country's strength than of encouraging foreign expansion or power. For some time, this difference in point of view gave rise to discord between Charles and his Spanish subjects. All of them, and especially the Castilians, repeatedly besought the King to put an end to wars in France, Germany, and Italy, and to devote himself exclusively to the affairs of Spain. Similar manifestations in regard to the war with France were made in 1536 by Francisco de Vitoria, the Constable Pedro Fernández de Velasco, and many of the nobles. At first Charles did not understand these petitions. Later, taking into account the divergence in interests between the two sectors of his realm, he tried to conciliate them in a common purpose. Failure of this attempt, which was basically impracticable, was one of the things that embittered his life.

A considerable part of the Spanish upper classes, however, finally came to understand the imperial objective with respect to the community of the Christian States ruled by the Emperor; an idea that with different coloration was expressed by many jurists of the period and of the seventeenth century. By virtue of this understanding, and perhaps also because of the attraction which war and so-called military glory then held for that part of the Spanish people, they enthusiastically furthered Charles I's European policy. During that and subsequent reigns until the end of the seventeenth century, the practical result, as regards spilling the blood and treasure of the Peninsular peoples, was that Spain had to expend a great part of her resources of man-power and money to settle questions and uphold causes that, notwith-standing their intrinsic importance, left in abeyance measures for solving internal problems that were therefore paralyzed or delayed.

To these causes wholly political in nature were added soon an-other, religious in character: the starting up in 1517 of the religious revolution generally called the Reformation, or Protestantism, of which we shall have more to say hereafter. The forces resisting it would very likely have won the support of the Spanish kings, with or without the Empire, but unquestionably it engaged their attention the sooner and more forcibly (and first and foremost, naturally, that of Charles I), be-cause of the fact, highly important to them, that the dissension broke out and made greatest inroads in the territories of the Empire and of the House of Burgundy. The Reformation dragged Spain into long drawn out wars far exceeding in scope and cost any that Spanish mon-archs presumably would have fought with those of other countries for any strictly political reasons.

Spain and International Affairs

At the same time, the Empire, with all its train of political and religious consequences and with Charles as its head, produced in Spain (especially during the period of its greatest military strength), a ruling class intensely aware of current European problems and wholly conversant with them. Since the beginning of Isabella I's reign, the Castilian monarchy had had a political horizon strictly circumscribed by the boundaries of the Peninsula. Even the struggle against the Moslem invasion of Europe acquired in Spain the character and limi-tations of an internal struggle, which fact, as we have noted, explains the scant participation of Spanish forces in the great general enterprise of the Crusades. The territorial conflicts between the Aragonese monarchy and the French, and the commercial rivalry in the Mediterranean of Cataláns and Valencians with the Italian republics, did not go beyond the common field and current of the imperialist disputes between neighboring States or over antagonistic interests; and they did not constitute human problems with universal bearing. On the contrary, the question of Empire and the question of the religious Reformation, with all the concomitant questions regarding liberty of conscience, the relation of Church and State, and other analogous points, did have universal bearing. Automatically, and in consequence of the universality that Spanish policy thus acquired, the Moslem problem also, which by that time had practically ceased to exist on the Peninsula itself, acquired for Spaniards a universal character and was transformed into a foreign crusade against the Turks in the Mediterranean and in western Europe; a crusade that represented (in the reigns of Charles I and Philip II, principally) one of the strongest motives for Spanish military action.

To all of these causes, in juxtaposition with former Spanish ideology, there was added, with the same effect of universalizing the political activities of the Castilian-Aragonese monarchy, the discovery, conquest, and colonization of America: events independent of the Empire and understood from the very first by the Spanish kings and jurists as being something far more than simple occupation of more or less uninhabited territories and incorporation of these into the occupying State, or than an unforeseen opportunity propitious for opening up a current of emigration, which was in itself a new experience for Spain. From the beginning, everything relating to the Americas took on in the Spanish mind a character human, juridical, and cultural, with full and logical universal transcendancy. And it is clear that for these reasons, and for others geographical, ethnological, and economic in nature, the action of Spain upon America and of America upon Spain reached proportions and attained results that went far beyond the confines of national interests. But the attention concentrated by the Spanish monarchy upon grave European problems was prejudicial to Spanish orientation in the Americas, and prevented full and free attention to universal problems inherent there.

But though one section of Spanish thought (the best) understood readily and in the manner indicated the program that should be planned and carried out in the Americas, there was, as we have said already, no analogous comprehension of the action consequent upon the Empire and the political conflicts of which the House of Burgundy had sown the seeds in Europe before the time of Charles I. Let us now see how the sharpest conflict between the King's political ideology and Castilian public opinion was brought about.

The Castilian Cortes and King Charles I

The gulf between the King's ideas and those of the Castilians; the mistakes committed by Charles personally because of his lack of experience in Spanish affairs; and the abuses of authority of which the Flemish nobles were guilty: all these soon led to a violent clash. This is how it started: When Charles was elected Emperor, he considered it essential to proceed to Germany for his Coronation; moreover, he felt that the religious problem there demanded his presence pressingly. He needed funds for travel and other expenses, all the more because he had had to borrow the money expended on his election as Emperor from the famous German banker Fugger, whom the Spaniards called Fúcar. In order to obtain from Castile the funds that he deemed neces-sary, Charles convoked the *Cortes* at Santiago de Compostela in 1520, and asked it for an appropriation of 400,000 ducats, which at that time was a very large sum, equal in amount to the regular appropriation made every two years. The two-year period for which the preceding appropriation was made had not yet expired, however. Some of the representatives of cities and *villas* attending the *Cortes* refused to vote the new appropriation. The King, impatient to receive the money and begin the journey, resorted to the dangerous and ignoble expedient of persuading some delegates by grants of special favors; and after trans-ferring the *Cortes* from Santiago to La Coruña, he succeeded in having his request granted by the bare majority of one vote. Public opinion and that of the representatives in the *Cortes* itself viewed this proceeding on the King's part as an outrage, aggravated by his additional imprudence in leaving as Governor of Castile in his absence—against the very explicit decision of the *Cortes*—not a Spaniard, but the Flem-ing Adrian de Utrecht, dean of St. Peter's at Louvain, and Charles I's former preceptor at Ghent.

The Revolt of the Comuneros

The results of all this were not slow in becoming manifest. First was the attitude of the city of Toledo, where the general reasons for discontent arising from the King's policy were heightened by his offensive appointment of Chièvres' nephew as Archbishop. Therefore, in the letter addressed by the citizens of Toledo on November 7, 1519, to the other cities of the Castilian realm, for the purpose of promoting conjoint action, it was proposed that the King be sent a petition on the following bases: that the monarch should not absent himself from Spain; that he should not give public office to foreigners; and that he should not take money out of the Kingdom. As may be observed, in this petition there were not as yet adduced reasons connected substantially with the municipal *fueros*. The allegation referred either to general principles of law practiced in all the Spanish States (such as that of nationality as a qualification for public office, whether lay or ecclesiastical) or to considerations of economic and political advisability with regard to the national welfare, respecting which there might be dispute. The central and culminating reason for the protest was still the Castilians' repugnance to the thought of their King's leaving Spain, since they viewed such absence from the country as an abandonment detrimental to the Spanish realm in benefit of Charles I's other States. The direction of the Toledan movement was centered in the Municipal Council, or *Ayuntamiento*, and at first it was headed by members of the city's high nobility, especially Juan de Padilla. The Cathedral Chapter joined it in February 1520, and after that, all the clergy, the monks as well as the parish priests, carried on even from the pulpit active and ardent propaganda against the King and in favor of the stand taken by the *Ayuntamiento*. Part of the Castilian nobility was also in sympathy with the Toledan movement. Such important personages as the Constable of Castile and Cardinal Adrian, the Flemish Governor ruling the kingdom as representative of the King during the latter's absence, opined that the rebels were right on certain points.

The rebellion was not slow in spreading to other cities, particularly after the disastrous ending of the *Cortes* of Santiago-Coruña. In July 1520 representatives of the 15 Castilian cities and *villas* adhering to the movement, which now included elements of the masses of the people, met at Avila and named a committee called the *Santa Junta* with Pedro Lasso de la Vega as its chairman. From the first, the proceedings of this *Junta* were frankly revolutionary, in the sense that it took it upon itself to solve problems pertaining to the Throne or to persons to whom the Throne had delegated the authority. The *Junta* revoked appointments made by Charles, imprisoned members of the Council, and addressed to the King a letter which, after avowing loyalty to the Crown, formulated a sweeping political program. It included—along with new provisions without precedent in the *fueros*, privileges and general laws—affirmations and guarantees favoring the norms of central and municipal government already in effect and censuring the arbitrary acts and inefficiency of some officials. In addition to all this there were, of course, the demands that no foreigners be given public office and that no money be taken out of the country. In the main, the other documents (manifestos, letters, instructions) which the *Junta* and the municipalities later drew up and circulated widely were re-statements of what was set forth in this preliminary letter. But this Toledan movement, which at first was very favorably received because of the convincing force of its arguments, began to lose ground in consequence of the excesses, including murder and destruction of property, during outbreaks of violence in several cities. Besides, the movement was being transformed, with increasing popular support, into a revolution of the lower classes against the lords: that is to say, into a war of classes, or social conflict. Throughout Europe the epoch was propitious for such conflicts. The principal effect of this new development in Spain was to cause withdrawal from the movement of many municipalities that had supported it in the beginning, and to augment the King's party.

Ultimately war was formally declared on October 31, 1520. It is called the War of the *Comunidades,* or Communities, using the word in its meaning as "municipalities." The communal leaders demonstrated little ability in its management, one indication of this being their failure to make use of the principles of the program that had been formulated, which could be common to all and affect the interests and ideas of all social classes, by which procedure they could have transformed what was originally a municipal movement, practically confined to one region of central Spain, into a nation-wide operation; and so would have prevented, or checked, the incipient class struggle. The *Comuneros,* or partisans of the *Comunidades,* thus not only alienated the high nobility of Castile and other elements of Castilian opinion, but committed additional mistakes as well, by reason of which the military aspect of the revolution was brief, hapless, and for the most part inglorious, aside from the personal heroism of some of the rebels. A single battle (that of Villalar, in April 1521) sufficed to defeat and scatter the army of the *Comunidades*. Some of their leaders—Padilla of Toledo, Juan Bravo of Segovia, and Pedro Maldonado of Salamanca—were beheaded the following day. The rebellious cities were subdued easily, except for Toledo, which held out for some months. Thus was rendered almost wholly ineffective, to detriment of the country as a whole, that outburst of protest which was quite justified in its original criticism of the errors of judgment and the foreign point of view characterizing the early years of Charles I's conduct in his kingdoms of Spain.

The Brotherhoods of Valencia and Mallorca

Contemporaneously with the War of the *Comunidades*, rebellions occurred in both Valencia and Mallorca which are called the Revolutions of the *Germanías*, or Brotherhoods. (The Catalán and Valencian word *germans* is equivalent to the Castilian word *hermanos*, or *brothers*, and related to the English word *germane*.) The Wars of the *Germanías*, to an even greater degree than the War of the *Comunidades* in its final phase, were social revolts of lower class against nobles and bourgeoisie. The feeling of class against class ran high in Valencia. It was strengthened by the general conviction as to the immorality of the upper classes, especially with regard to the administration of justice, which the people believed to be subject to pressure from the nobility and the wealthy. The first *Germanía* organized at Valencia had as its head a laborer, the wool carder Juan Lorenzo, and as members of its *Junta*, or executive committee, Guillén Sorolla, weaver; Onofre Peris, shoemaker (he made peasant sandals) ; Vicente Mocholi, field laborer; and two sailors. This *Junta* presented to the King a Memorandum of grievances against the nobles, who, it said, treated the common people like slaves and murdered members of the working classes and abused their families on any pretext. The complainants asked that this state of things be remedied by appointment of two *Jurados*, or magistrates (one of the municipal offices) from the ranks of the workers. The King did not grant this petition, and a furious class conflict broke out, reaching extremes of violence and hatred. It lasted more than two years (1520-1522) , ending with defeat of the Brotherhoods and the death of their principal leader.

The rebellion of the Mallorcan *Germanía* or Brotherhood was organized in February 1521 by workmen at Palma de Mallorca in protest against tax rates; but it quickly spread beyond the city limits to the countryside and was heightened by the same class feeling that had been injected into the movement of the *Comunidades*. Until March 1523 this revolt could not be controlled; and in the end, very harsh measures were taken in the trial and punishment following on the defeat of the united mechanics and *payeses*.

The revolt of the Valencian *Germanía* or Brotherhood brought the further consequence of application of a very restrictive policy in respect to the *Mudéjares*, who were farm workers and serfs of the Valencian nobility; a policy that so aroused those social classes as to cause in the end a rebellion that required considerable time and money to put down.

These social conflicts were not exclusive to Spain. During the same years similar, and very sanguinary, conflicts occurred in southern Germany and in Flanders.

The Foreign Wars of Charles I

The foreign wars of Charles I belong for the most part rather to the general history of Europe than to the national history of Spain. Substantially, they may be classified in three groups: religious and political wars in Germany; wars of rivalry with the French monarchy and its King, Francis I, Italy being the principal battlefield; and wars against the Turks. All these offered occasion for adding to the prestige that Spanish arms had already attained in the time of the Great Captain, and they strengthened and extended the possessions in Italy, but did not directly serve Spanish interests, which were rooted in Spanish earth and—by extension—in America's newfound lands. We shall therefore pass over the details usually related with regard to these wars, which are beside the point in the present volume. Let us record merely the events of greatest repercussion which are still cited and discussed.

Among these was the battle of Pavia on February 24, 1525, one of the greatest and most famous engagements of modern history, which was won by the troops of Charles I, who captured the King of France and carried him off to Madrid where he remained a prisoner for some time. This occurrence, not usual in warfare, satisfied the *amour propre* of the Spanish people for the time being, and contributed toward reconciling some of them to the sacrifices that Charles I's policy was imposing on the country; but it did not put an end to the rivalry and warfare between the two monarchs. The war, in fact, after Francis I's death in 1547, continued to be waged against his son Henry II. A memorable episode was the siege of Rome and seizure of the city by one of Charles I's armies under the command of Charles de Montpensier, Constable of Bourbon (a French ally of the Emperor's) and the German general Frundesberg. The siege was motivated by the fact of Pope Clement VII's having entered into an alliance with Francis I to dislodge the Spaniards from northern Italy; which pact was another case of history repeating itself. When the Pope refused to accede to Charles' efforts to have the alliance broken off, the troops of the latter—whose religious sentiments drew a sharp line of demarcation between acknowledgment of the Pope as spiritual head of the Church and the policies that the Pope carried out as a temporal sovereign—took the capital of the Holy See by assault and sacked it frightfully, taking Clement VII prisoner. Practically all of the troops participating in this action were foreign mercenaries and not Spaniards. Charles did not himself approve of the act of his generals.

The reason for Charles I's wars against the Turks was twofold: on the one hand, the attack by the Turks on the southeastern territories of his Empire and up to the very gates of Vienna, a matter of direct concern to Charles both as Emperor and as Archduke of Austria; and on the other, need to maintain in North Africa the policy previously carried out there by the Catholic Kings and Cardinal Cisneros. Spanish possessions in that region—and indirectly, the coasts of Spain—were then being menaced by the Turks, one of whose generals, the notorious pirate Haradín (Barbarossa, or Redbeard) by arrangement with the Sultan of Constantinople had seized Tunis and part of Argelia. The most important of Charles I's campaigns in consequence of this was the one against Tunis, which was crowned with success by the taking of the Fort of Golita at the entrance to the port of Tunis and conquest of the city itself. Some superb tapestries of the period bear the testimony of art to this feat of arms.

The Religious Wars in Germany and Their Repercussion in Spain

At two different moments of time the Emperor had two utterly distinct attitudes with regard to the religious and political problem posed in Germany by the Reformation, the religious movement of dissidence from the Roman Catholic Church which the Augustinian monk Luther had initiated. The immediate cause of the dissidence was the protest of Luther (who in this was representative of a state of opinion widespread in Germany, especially among the humanists) against abuse of the sale of indulgences by the Catholic clergy; but the underlying reasons were more substantial. They were partly due to the disillusioning impression received by Luther on a visit to Rome where he was greeted by the spectacle of unconcealed vices and defects on the part of not a few clerics and even at the Papal Court. These misdemeanors had long been perceived by many Catholics, and by the most consecrated and devout members of the clergy, who held that a reform in the discipline and customs of the Church had become necessary; a reform that had been already made in part by Cisneros with regard to the priesthood and the monastic Orders in Spain. But Luther, reflecting a very marked tendency of the Renaissance as that movement was understood in Germany, especially by many of the humanists, came to have also very strong ideological views differing from those of the Catholic Church. Among them were the doctrine of Grace, holding that a Christian was saved not by works (piety, charity, et cetera) but by faith alone; denial of the efficacy of all but three of the Catholic sacraments; the ·doctrine that a Christian needs no other intermediary with God than reading and meditating on the Bible; and other doctrines of lesser importance. The theses expressing those differences, presented by Luther in 1517, were condemned by the Holy See in June 1520; but Luther, instead of being deterred by this, on December 10 of that year publicly burned the Bull condemning him, along with a collection of canonical laws, and thereby broke with the Church. From different motives (some wholly religious and others political, or arising from a covetous concern about ecclesiastical property), many German bishops and a considerable part of German public opinion ranged themselves on Luther's side. The conflict was very serious, and naturally claimed the Emperor's attention. He dealt with the matter initially at the first Imperial Assembly, or Diet, at Worms in 1521, on the agenda of which was a consideration of the measures that should be adopted with regard to Luther.

Principal Façade, Alcázar of Seville.

At first Charles wished, and tried, to temporize. Then, in view of the progressive growth of the Lutheran movement and the political threat that it held for the Empire, he opposed it resolutely. Thereupon the religious war sustained by Luther's followers broke out. They called themselves Protestants and their new doctrine Protestantism or the Reformation. It spread from Germany to other countries; first to Sweden, whose King, followed by all his people, embraced Protestantism (1529) ; then to France, where it encountered strong opposition but acquired many converts (the Huguenots) and was soon tolerated; and to Geneva and its district, where a Frenchman, John Calvin, preached and established a Protestant sect—Calvinism—differing from Luther's, which took root in Holland and Scotland. As for England, the then King, Henry VIII, did not wish to accept the Reformation; but because of a dispute with the Pope he declared in 1535 that, separating from the Church of Rome, he would himself be head of the national Church of England, also called the Anglican Church. After Henry VIII's death many of the English were converted to Protestantism, a fact that gave rise to persecutions and to internal strife.

The religious war in Germany ended in 1555, and it was won— principally in consequence of the treason of Maurice of Saxony, one of the Emperor's generals—by King Henri II of France, who for wholly political reasons related to his conflict with Charles was at that time siding with the Protestants. The pact known as the Peace of Augsburg, which terminated the war, gave the Lutherans religious freedom and equal rights with the Catholics, who continued to be numerous in Germany in spite of the great popular appeal of the Reformation.

Protestantism made some proselytes in Spain; not many, but a chosen few, such as some of those who had succeeded in escaping the persecutions of the Inquisition. Among them were the brothers Alfonso and Juan Valdés, admirable writers both, the latter becoming a propagandist at Naples for Protestantism and there forming into a group some 3,000 converts who spread Luther's doctrines throughout Italy; Francisco de Encinas, great philologist and stylist and most important of the Spanish Protestant men-of-letters; Casiodoro de Reina, translator of the Bible into Castilian; Antonio del Corro, a professor at Oxford University; and Cipriano de Valera, who corrected Reina's translation of the Bible and himself translated Calvin's Catechism.

It is not the historian's province to inquire how widespread Protestism might have become in Spain had it not been swiftly and sternly suppressed; but it is a reasonable supposition that the mass of the Spanish people were too profoundly Catholic for the Reformation to have found as easy acceptance in their country as elsewhere. Moreover, the Renaissance in Spain had not made headway as freely as in Germany and other northern countries in the fields of philosophy and religion, but only in literature and the classics (the humanities). As we have seen, this, together with the artistic aspect, also characterized the movement in Italy.

However, it is a fact that the ideas of one of the great humanists of the period, Erasmus of Rotterdam, were accepted readily in Spain by men of science and of deep religious conviction, such as Luis Vives; the savant Nuñez Coronel; Juan de Vergara, professor at Alcalá, and his brother Francisco; Archbishops Fonseca and Manrique (the latter Inquisitor General); Francisco de Vitoria; Juan Maldonado, Vicar General of the Archbishopric of Burgos; the great Benedictine preacher, Alfonso de Virués; Miguel Servet (or Michael Servetus), heterodox physician and theologian, in Switzerland; and many other eminent persons. It is true that most of them esteemed and read Erasmus (translations of whose works into Spanish were already circulating in 1520) because of his indubitable authoritativeness as humanist, philosopher, and editor of religious texts, and true also that he acquired adherents in Spain by reason of his criticism of certain of Luther's ideas; but it is no less the fact that Erasmus, independent in his thinking, was not a Catholic. He proclaimed a Christianity that might perhaps have taken the place of Luther's and of that preached by other Protestants and have prevented the widening of the religious rift and the armed strife among Christians. Erasmus himself expressed the independence of his mind, declaring that what he sought was the truth, which was to be found sometimes with the Catholics and sometimes with the Protestants. Fundamentally, what Erasmus taught was the reform of mankind through education, which would do away with ignorance, the worst of dangers for the mind. After several initially fruitless efforts to that end on the part of the clergy, Spanish Erasmists were persecuted and the Inquisition prohibited the reading of the Spanish translations of Erasmus.

The Counter-Reformation

King Charles I and the Spanish clergy, who in this had the general opinion of the country on their side, did not confine themselves to defending the Catholic Church throughout the Empire and to persecuting the Protestants in Spain. Strictly speaking, Spain was the cradle of what is called the Counter-Reformation, which is to say, the Catholic offensive in reaction against the dissidence dividing Christianity into two great parts. Fundamental expressions of that offensive were the Council of Trent (1545-1563) and the Society of Jesus (1536).

The Council of Trent, which took its name from the place where it held its sessions, represents, for the one part, the carrying out of the cherished desires of many good Catholics that the discipline and customs of the priesthood and the monastic clergy should be reformed, and that abuse of authority by the ecclesiastic tribunal (particularly at Rome) should be corrected; and for the other part, the defense of the Catholic articles of faith and the adoption of regulations and measures by which the homogeneity and solidarity of Catholic elements and interests should be tightened, and norms conforming to the meaning of what was held to be orthodox doctrine should be introduced into the general life of the Catholic Church and its communicants. Charles I was the most constant and indefatigable proponent of the Council. Also strongly in favor of its being held were Cardinal Adrian of Utrecht, later to be Pope (1522-1523), who died more than two decades before the Council finally met; the Cardinal-Dean Carvajal, a Spaniard; Egidio de Viterbo, General of the Augustinian Order; and other illustrious prelates. With stubborn patience, the Emperor kept wearing down the opposition of other sectors of the clergy and of more than one Pope; striving first to have the Council meet and then for it to continue its deliberations once they had begun; and in the end he achieved his purpose, ably assisted by the Spaniards in the Council and by his Ambassador Hurtado de Mendoza. In that great assembly of the Catholic Church the Spaniards were especially unyielding and outspoken on questions of discipline and customs, such as those relating to residence of bishops, incumbency of parishes, and also on the subject of correction of the abuses of the Roman ecclesiastical tribunal. The canons, or canonical laws, enacted by the Council of Trent, were adopted in Spain two years later (in 1565), with some

Patio of the Damosels, Alcázar of Seville.

reservations, and they caused modification of certain parts of our civil legislation, such as, for example, those relating to marriage.

The Society of Jesus was a religious Order born of the mind and dynamic will-power of the Guipuzcoan knight Ignatius de Loyola, later canonized as St. Ignatius. Its effective foundation was in 1539, and it was approved by a Papal Bull of September 27, 1540, which confirmed the name, the Society of Jesus (given, it is believed, by the founder himself in 1537), and took the organization under protection of the Holy See. The new Order introduced various innovations all its own. Chief among these was absolute submission (except in case of sin) to the Pope, and, within the Society itself, unquestioning obedience of its members ("as if they were cadavers that let themselves be moved hither and yon and dealt with at will") to their superiors. The Society's submission to the Pope proved of utmost importance and significance in those times when the Protestants were attacking the Papacy and when the Roman ecclesiastical tribunal, as we have seen, was meeting with much opposition from Catholics who desired its reformation and a limitation of its authority. No less new and remarkable was the concept of the Company of Jesus as being a militia, with the character of shock-troops, as we would say today. The founder himself wrote in explanation of this concept that he did not consider that he had given up military service, but rather that he had consecrated it to God. The war that this militia planned to undertake, and in fact did wage, was against heresy in all its forms, and against every enemy of the Papacy. As a tactical measure directed toward making this military concept effective, Loyola, instead of immuring the members of the Company of Jesus in monasteries, sent them forth into human society so that, mingling with other men, they might win souls through the psychological approach. Because of all these attributes, the Company of Jesus was the axis of the Counter-Reformation, especially in so far as regards the significance of that movement in checking the advance of Protestantism and in opposition to the latter's becoming deeprooted and widespread throughout Europe.

In these ways, then, a considerable part of Spanish thought contributed to orienting Catholic action in the world; although it was not the same way in which Spain, centuries before, had contributed to formation of the Nicene Creed and of the canons adopted at the first Councils of Toledo.

Another sector of Spanish thought deemed compatible with these fundamental principles an aspiration to withdraw from violence, in so far as the essentially violent atmosphere of Europe at the time would permit, and to find inner solace not unlike that which had been taught long before by great figures of the Visigothic Catholic clergy. Thus a nineteenth century Spaniard,* too little known for his work in this field, could say: "In the fullness of the grandeur that we then achieved, those virile spirits, glory and crown of Catholicism, the Luises, the Teresas, the Carranzas and the Hernández de Talaveras, the Hurtado de Mendozas, Sigüenzas, Nebrijas, Bracenses, Arias Montanos, and Marianas, the saints and the savants, one and all, foresaw the necessity of unifying our [Spanish] character, correcting its divisionism, and establishing a life veritably religious and Christian." And in another paragraph he returns to those lofty spirits who "preferred to save humanity by charity and persuasion," citing also "St. Ignatius de Loyola whose noble designs laid the foundations of a religious life more in conformity with human nature and with its various finalities, and stood then for an ideal in every way sounder, more realistic, and loftier than that of the supporters of that terrible institution." (This last reference is to the Inquisition.)

But those generous aspirations were overcome by the ruling spirit of the time and also, to some extent, by the violence, intolerance and exaggeration which are among the characteristic tendencies of our own people.

Spanish Intolerance and the Inqusition

The Inquisition participated intensively in the religious conflicts of the time, both in Spain and in the other dominions of the Spanish kings, European and American, wherein it was introduced and applied to all heretics and not to Protestants only. In persecution and punishment of the latter the Inquisition was very severe, to such a degree indeed as to rouse protest from officials and private individuals important in Spanish life. Nevertheless, the Inquisition was not an exclusively Spanish institution, nor, as we have seen, had it been exclusively

---

* He was the famous jurist and educator, Francisco Giner de los Ríos, professor of the graduate school of the University of Madrid (1860-1915), and founder of the *Institución Libre de Enseñanza* discussed in Chapter XII.—*Author's Note.*

Cathedral of Burgos.

Spanish in origin; neither was intolerance toward those not belonging to their Church an attribute confined to Spanish Catholics. That sentiment of intolerance was then to be found in all Christian countries and was common to men of the time, whatever their beliefs. Intolerance as a state of mind, and the Inquisition or some analogous form of persecution and punishment as its instrument, acted with substantially the same rigor, though with varying modalities, against all *heresies;* a qualification of which the meaning had broadened by force of circumstance so that it had come to be appropriated by all creeds. Thus the anti-Protestant was considered to be a heretic by those professing Protestantism in whatever of the new church or creeds into which it had split; just as for the Catholics a heretic was anyone who had been baptized into the Catholic faith and had left it. Protestantism in its early days frequently demonstrated the same intransigence that was shown toward it by the organisms of the Catholic Church and by monarchs Catholic in religion.

Accordingly, in not a few regions where the population was Lutheran, Calvinist, Anglican, or otherwise Protestant, Catholics had their rights trampled upon, as did also those who, while not Catholic, were refractory to or had failed to accept some of the new beliefs triumphant in that locality. And thus it was that numerous distinguished men and religious groups might be cited that were prosecuted and found guilty, and cases could be adduced of many who were burned at the stake or otherwise executed. Italy contributed to the list the great astronomer and physicist Galileo (1633) and the philosopher Giordano Bruno (1600). In France, the Protestants of Provence were persecuted and Louis de Berguin, translator of Erasmus, was burned (1529) in the reign of Francis I, while in that of Charles IX occurred the Massacre of St. Bartholomew's Day .and other violent outbreaks against the Huguenots in 1572 and 1676. In Calvinist Geneva, the Spanish physician Miguel Servet—to whom reference has already been made—first to report upon the circulation of the blood, was burned at the stake, and the Catholics were victims of terrorism at Basle (1528). In Holland the Arminians, a Protestant sect, suffered violent persecution in 1619, as did at various times members of analogous minority groups not adhering to the type of Protestantism predominant there. In England, there was persecution not only of Catholics but also of **Puri-**

House of the Shells, Salamanca.

tans, Quakers and other sects of dissidents from Anglicanism; while in the English colonies in America, where some of these dissenters sought refuge, they themselves, once established there, persecuted members of other creeds or refused to let them live in the colony. Very few men of any land preached and practiced tolerance in those days. Among the few who did were the Italian Socinians or Unitarians; the Anabaptists; the Arminians of Holland; the Catholics of the English colony of Maryland in its beginnings and the Baptists of Rhode Island. Prior to the Reformation, the same kind of persecution had been carried on with no voice raised against it, except one here and there advocating tolerance or at least the renunciation of violence as a method of conversion, which renunciation had been preached by the Visigothic bishops. To cite only a few cases, there were the massacres of the Albigenses (in southern France and northern Italy) in the thirteenth century and of the Jews in Provence in 1487; the strangling and burning of Savonarola at Florence in 1498; and the execution of John Huss at Constance in 1415, followed by the crusade against his followers in Bohemia (1419-1431). The difference from country to country in intransigent action and terrorism, therefore, in Europe at the time was only a difference as to the degree and the duration of persecution, factors that depended, sometimes exclusively, on the political situation or on the zeal—which often reached extremes—of the authorities charged with carrying out the repressive measures. In other words, instances of bloodshed caused by intolerance abounded in all countries, as did restrictions on not only religious but also scientific freedom of thought.

The Spanish Inquisition was extremely harsh and prone to suspiciousness in the sixteenth and seventeenth centuries, even to the point of persecuting (or at least of interfering with) on very ill-founded motives, such persons of unquestionable religious faith as Bishop Carranza, the great poet Fray Luis de León, Fray Luis de Granada, the Venerable Juan de Avila, St. Teresa, Sister María de Aguda, Father Sigüenza, Arias Montano, Nebrija, and Ignatius de Loyola himself.

A most important episode in the course of the religious housecleaning in Spain was the order issued by Charles I in 1526 that all *Mudéjares* should be baptized, on pain of expulsion from the realm. That measure was again taken in Philip II's reign and completed eighty-three years later—in 1609—by Philip III, with a further order that all *Moriscos* (which was, as we have said, the name given to baptized *Mudéjares*) regarding whose faith and religious practices there was any doubt (a doubt often well founded), should likewise be expelled from Spain. It should be said that into the expulsion of the *Moriscos* entered not only the religious factor in circumstances similar to those that had brought about the expulsion of the Jews 117 years earlier, but a political factor as well, since the *Moriscos* time and again showed an inclination to favor and further the plans that were being hatched by the Moslems of Africa and the Turks for recovering dominions from Spain. A supplementary consideration was the damage to settlements and enterprises of the Spanish maritime regions occasioned by frequent attacks and landings by the Moslems whenever they could elude the vigilance of the Spanish watchtowers and warships along the coasts.

Exploration and Conquests in America and Oceania

When the explorations of Columbus on his last voyages, which were contemporaneous with those of Amerigo Vespucci in the coastal zones of South America, demonstrated that what the Discoverer had found was not eastern Asia but an unknown part of the world, the Spanish monarchs and their advisers in these matters, without giving up their original purpose embodied in the unrelenting determination to find a strait or passage to the Far East, directed their principal activities toward exploration and conquest of the newfound lands. When the actuation of the Spanish with relation to the Americas and the East Indies is compared with that of the Dutch and the English, it is immediately obvious that the purpose of the latter two countries from the first was chiefly commercial in character, on the basis of mercantile companies that were thinking first and foremost about exploitation of natural resources and not about conquests. Thereby Holland and England differentiated themselves from the political character (dominion and colonization under government control) and the action by individuals which conjointly were highly important in the Spanish system, as we shall proceed to explain.

Almost the whole of the task of conquest was achieved during the reign of Charles I. Among the many who greatly distinguished themselves by their military achievements in carrying it out were Hernán

Cortés, Pizarro, Almagro, Valdivia, Alvarado, Montejo. The conquest, properly speaking, was effected over many regions of the vast number making up the immensities of the dual American continent. This was by reason of the fact that the Spaniards overcame strong nuclei of resistance among the indigenous populations which were made up for the most part of scattered, relatively small tribes, or of tribes with peaceful customs and rudimentary political and social organization. The first English and French colonists in North America likewise encountered such tribes as these, so that there was no occasion for the military conquest made necessary in Mexico and Peru by the opposition of strong organized States; quite apart from the determinant mercantile objectives of the English and Dutch.

In those regions of America explored by the Spaniards, the only centers which at that time were both strong and well-organized were the Aztec Empire of Mexico and the Inca Empire of Peru. Hernán Cortés was the Conquistador, or conqueror, of the former (1519-1521) ; Pizarro and Almagro of the latter (1532-1533). Valdivia completed this second conquest as regards Chile. Alvarado conquered the regions of Costa Rica and Guatemala (south of Mexico) ; and Montejo, Yucatán, a Mexican district on the southeast. The second chapter of the conquest of Chile was the war with the Araucanian Indians who inhabited what is, practically, the whole of the present Republic of Chile, and whose heroic valor was sung eloquently in his poem *La Araucana* by a Spanish Basque poet, Alonso de Ercilla, who himself took part in the wars against the Araucanians. The military successes of Hernán Cortés and Pizarro resulted in the absolute disappearance of the two empires, the Aztec and the Inca, whose civilizations, very advanced in certain fields of artistic and social life (especially in Peru, as regards the latter) and very inchoate and backward in others, were absorbed quickly by Spain's work of assimilation; that is to say, by European civilization in its Spanish modality, as we shall soon see.

The work of exploration and discovery, naturally much more important and far vaster than that of conquest, was also carried out by Spaniards and by a few foreigners under orders of the Kings of Spain, and always with Spanish barks and crews. Among the Spaniards especially deserving of mention were Nuñez de Balboa, discoverer of the Pacific Ocean at the Isthmus of Panama; Orellana, who found and explored the Amazon; Mendoza, who with Irala and Ayolas penetrated and dominated the eastern region from the River Plate to the Paraguay River; Nuñez Cabeza de Vaca, who traversed these same regions and had journeyed previously from Florida along the northern coast of the Gulf of Mexico westward to California; Coronado, who reached the Colorado and Missouri Rivers; and many others.

To Charles I's reign belongs also the expedition of Ferdinand Magellan, a Portuguese mariner in the service of Spain, and the Basques Elcano and Legaspi who, seeking by way of South America the long desired western passage to the Orient, found what was called the Strait of Magellan (running for 350 miles between the southernmost point of South America and Tierra del Fuego, and connecting the Atlantic Ocean with the Pacific), and who discovered—thereby arriving at regions of India such as Columbus sought—among other Pacific islands, the groups to which they gave the names Marianas and Philippines. On one of these islands (Zebu in the Philippines), several members of the expeditionary force, including Magellan himself, were slain by the natives. Elcano continued with Legaspi the return voyage to Spain in the vessel *Victoria,* and, doubling the Cape of Good Hope, became the first to circumnavigate the world. Soon after that commenced the Spanish explorations in the Pacific Ocean, giving rise to many geographical discoveries; but Spain made permanent occupation only of the Philippine Islands and some small archipelagoes lying near them. The Philippines were speedily transformed into an important center of Spanish commerce and culture.

The Abdication of Charles I

A sick man, worn out in mind and body by the continuous conflicts and unremitting anxieties that gave him no respite during the thirty-nine years of his reign, Charles I in 1556 abdicated the Crown of Spain in favor of his son Philip II. He also adjudged to Philip the Kingdom of Naples, the Duchy of Milan (proceeding from possessions of the German Empire in Italy), Flanders (northern and southern) with the Franche Comté (an ancient province of France), and Luxembourg: the domains, that is to say, pertaining to the House of Burgundy. This last concession, together with the marriage that Charles himself negotiated between his son Philip and Mary Tudor, future Queen of England (daughter of Henry VIII and Katharine of Aragón, and granddaughter therefore of Ferdinand and Isabella), were the two

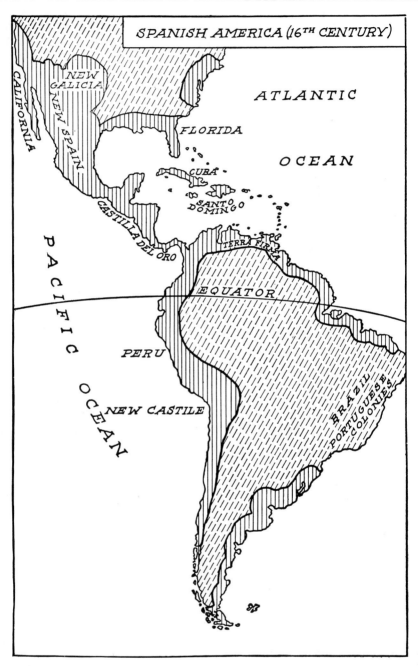

The striped portion indicates approximately the area of effective domination in the sixteenth century; but as a matter of fact the continental penetration in many regions of South America was much greater than thus appears; as, for example, in the zone which on the interior connected Peru with the territories that were to become the Viceroyalty of Río de la Plata.

great culminating mistakes—from the point of view of Spain's national interests—committed by Charles I. Philip would have preferred to inherit, in addition to the Crown of Spain, the Imperial dominions in Italy, which possessed a long Spanish tradition, unlike the domains of the House of Burgundy which bore no relation whatever to the interests of the Spanish Crown. He had to resign himself, nevertheless, to the decision of his father, whose mind was also set on the matrimonial alliance with the English royal family.

The first of these errors resulted in perpetuating and increasing the burden that had weighed on Spain ever since Philip the Fair's death had brought about incorporation into that kingdom of the States pertaining to the Houses of Burgundy and Austria. Not only were parts of these States coveted by the French Kings, but religious difficulties were soon to kindle in them a war that, logically enough, sparked the national sentiment of independence in those countries. The second error soon brought about another conflict, also religious in origin, because of the fact that Mary Tudor, a Catholic, persecuted the Protestants; a proceeding on her part disapproved by her husband Philip II, who thereupon recommended a conciliatory attitude of preaching and persuasion toward the English Protestants. In Flanders this latter tactic was soon replaced by violence, as we shall see when we turn our attention to that country.

But Charles I's imperialist ambitions made his point of view in these matters different from Philip's. Charles' imperialism, which was like that of most European monarchs of his time, is understandable according to the political ideology of the period; but that fact is neither palliation nor excuse for the consequences to Spain's future internal development which were consequent on his actions.

The succession to the Crown as Emperor, Charles decided in favor of his brother Ferdinand, who in March, 1558, was recognized as Emperor of Germany by the Prince Electors meeting in the Diet of Frankfort. Six months later Charles I of Spain and V of Germany died at the Monastery of Yuste in Estremadura, to which he had retired in search of rest for body and mind.

Philip II

From the Spanish national point of view, the most important of the Kings of the House of Austria, and the most Spanish, was Philip II.

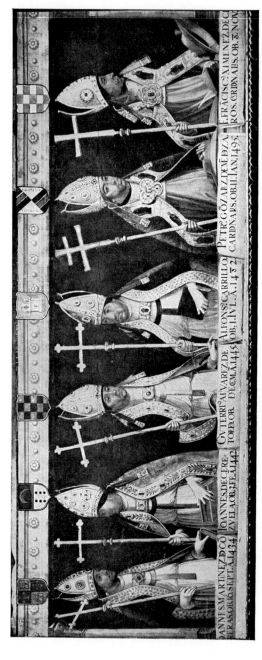

Mural painting in the Capitular Hall, Cathedral of Toledo; at the extreme right, a portrait of Cardinal Cisneros.

The volume and influence of his action in government were as great in the sixteenth century as had been those of Ferdinand and Isabella in the fifteenth. But the principal problems that Philip II had to confront differed from those solved by the Catholic Kings (and from those of Isabella in especial) by being for the most part problems that were essentially foreign to Spain and that arose from relations good or bad with other countries. Open attacks and overt threats by monarchs hostile to the House of Austria and to its power in Europe contributed not a little to this state of things. More than once, in order to preserve the independence and defend the national interests of Spain, Philip II found it necessary to fight enemies banded together. But the fact also had weight that Philip II, although he did not inherit the Empire, continued to strive resolutely for the objectives characteristically imperial, which, to his thinking, had been virtually transmitted to him along with the Spanish Crown. The difference between his imperialist criterion and that of Charles II was that Charles looked on the Empire from the standpoint of an Austrian and a Hapsburg, while Philip II's point of view was that of a Catholic, for whom the supreme necessity was to save the world (not Spain alone) from the heresy triumphant in northern and part of central Europe. This perhaps was Philip's chief political error with respect to Spanish interests; notwithstanding the general humane sentiment of his purpose, within the ideology of the era. It is open to question, however, whether (apart from reasons of religion and of supporting the Imperial family) Philip II was capable of understanding wherein lay the interests of that realm which he had inherited through his father from Isabella of Castile and Ferdinand of Aragón. The only aspects of that national interest which Philip seems properly to have understood in their every phase were Spanish cultural life and the economic necessity of increasing land use in Spain through improving the physiographical environment. Philip's efforts to harmonize what he regarded as his international obligations with the duties of a Spanish King at that period, constituted both his most serious political error and his major inner tragedy.

Philip had been carefully educated to rule by his father, Charles I, and by various persons of culture and experience who surrounded him in his youth. With the purpose of completing that education and of becoming acquainted at first hand with the European countries pertaining to his Empire, Charles had had Philip visit Italy, Flanders, and Germany. Not long afterward, in consequence of his marriage to Mary Tudor, Philip resided for some time in England.

With all this, he became personally acquainted with the men and the problems that were then stirring Europe, and he acquired very markedly a high sense of his own responsibility as ruler, within the absolutist concept. That sense of responsibility was brought to bear in two ways characteristic of Philip II's method of government: one was his direct personal intervention in all administrative questions; the other, his tenacious defense of the interests of the monarchy against all its enemies, including the Pope when the latter mixed in matters affecting the dominions of the Spanish Crown or its sovereignty.

Philip's personal and direct intervention, symptomatic of his independence of character and zeal for his functions as king, was evidenced in that he never delegated the solution of problems to anyone else, not even to those in whom he had most complete confidence—his secretaries—but studied and solved them himself. That method of procedure, in part deserving of praise, had its disadvantages. By centralizing government down to its last details in himself, he took away initiative from all officials lower in rank than the king, and left them powerless to make decisions even on pressing occasions when there was no time for delay. Moreover, taking into consideration the inevitable slowness of communication in those days, the necessity of awaiting direct instructions from the King resulted often in receiving his orders too late for achieving the desired result. Added to this were Philip's innate vacillations and slowness, which, whatever the psychological explanation, constituted what practically amounted to an inferiority complex on his part when confronted by the dynamic energy demonstrated by his enemies, in particular Queen Elizabeth of England and Catherine de Medici, Queen Mother and Regent of France. The only exception to this bureaucratic technique that Philip employed was the system of legislative autonomies, at times very ample, which he applied in Spain's American and Oceanic colonies. This was the origin of abundant legislation in code and custom which in practice modified in not a few respects the laws dictated from Spain.

Another of Philip II's characteristics, already referred to in passing, was his sense of juridical responsibility regarding application of

St. George Frontal, Generalidad of Catalonia, Barcelona.

and respect for the laws. At first glance it is not easy to understand why that particular monarch had that particular good trait, which is seemingly contradictory to, for example, his dealings with his secretary Antonio Pérez, the punishment he meted out for the uprisings at Saragossa, and similar incidents to be considered in due course. But if we set against these missteps other of Philip's actions and attitudes, such as the respect that he showed for the Aragonese *fuero* in relation to the appointment of the new Viceroy; his refusal to let the vanquished *Moriscos* be expelled; his renunciation of all ownership in a house which he had thought to be his own property, when a woman of the working class disputed his title and convinced him that she had the better claim; his acceptance of the Aragonese import tax *fuero,* invoked with respect to some articles imported by Philip for his own personal use; and many other analogous incidents: all these make one hesitate to say what was Philip's basic characteristic. Was it the underlying impulse that often causes men to sin, repent, and perform good works by way of amends without feeling constrained therefor to sin no more? Or were these apparent contradictions not contradictions in basic doctrine, but rather differences of criteria, arising perhaps from different circumstances of the cases in point regarding, sometimes, observance of the laws and, again, the king's right to inflict punishment? This possible explanation is not rendered inacceptable by exceptions to it such as Acevedo's assassination, which was an act of injustice for which no extenuation can be offered.

Another criterion must be brought to bear, because it was within the political ethic of the period (to which I shall return), on the inflexible severity with which Philip II acted in religious matters, in affairs related to "reasons of State," and in all things affecting his personal sovereignty; so that he felt no hesitation in having a presumed critic poisoned and might have thrown a fagot with his own hands on the flames consuming a heretic even though the heretic had been his son. Philip saw in all this only just and faithful application of the law applying in each case. To acts of this category belongs also his conduct with regard to the religious question in Flanders and the Netherlands; an expression of which was his instructions to successive Governors there, warning them that they could yield on some points but never on any that was "in detriment to our Holy Catholic Faith, because I shall never consent to the slightest weakening in this, not even though these dominions be lost thereby." *

The Struggle with Protestantism and Its Political Consequences

The resolute determination to crush Protestantism which characterized Philip II led him to come to an understanding with the Catholic parties in France, England, Ireland, and Scotland, and to aid them in their struggle against adherents of the Reformation in their respective countries. Because of this he had to keep up warfare more or less related to the politically motivated wars to which we have referred previously and which influenced these latter greatly.

So it was in the Netherlands, which Philip had inherited from the House of Burgundy. These domains held little interest for him. He entrusted their government first to his natural sister, Margaret, Duchess of Parma, and a council composed of William, Prince of Orange and Count of Nassau, known as William the Silent; Counts Egmont and Horn; and other eminent personages of the country. In addition to this Council, Philip placed at Margaret's side as Prime Minister Cardinal Granvelle, a learned man but stiff-necked and hard-headed. This appointment was very unwelcome to the Flemings and the Dutch, because Granvelle, a native of the Franche-Comté, was a foreigner. Bad feeling was engendered by the changes which Philip introduced in the two bishoprics and which were regarded as fore-runners of the Inquisition, and gave rise to the deduction that persecution of Calvinists and other Protestants would be intensified. After several embassies of the high Flemish nobility demanding government reform, Philip acceded to Granvelle's dismissal, but he could not bring himself to slacken his persecution of non-Catholics. In one of the King's personal letters to his sister, he told her that he was ready to burn 60,000 or 70,000 persons, if need be, in order to wipe out heresy in Flanders.

Then commenced the resistance, which Margaret checked by suspending the trials of Protestants. Philip himself made some conces-

---

* This psychological complexity in Philip II, never probed to its depths by his biographers (whether those who extol him beyond reason or those who see in him only a moral monster), I have attempted to portray with the greatest possible equanimity in my own study of that monarch; a study as yet unpublished except for a summary of several of its chapters printed in the three-volume work in French, *Hommes d'État.* —*Author's Note.*

Titian: *The Emperor Charles V.* (*Charles I of Spain*)

sions: suppression of the Inquisition was among them. One sector of Dutch and Flemish opinion deemed these concessions insufficient, and its opposition set off an insurrection that sacked Catholic churches in spite of the fact that Lutherans and other persons of weight in the community opposed such acts of violence. Philip responded to the attack by implanting a system of harsh repression. Accordingly, he sent the Duke of Alba with instructions to put down not only the heresy but every movement favorable to the traditional autonomy of those regions or even merely representative of opposition to the royal policy of a strong central government. Alba carried out these instructions with utmost severity, even going beyond the King's order in this respect. The result was to set in operation simultaneously in the minds of the Flemish and the Dutch the two principal mainsprings of action when peoples rebel against governments: national freedom and religious freedom. War broke out, under leadership of William the Silent and his brother Louis (1568), and Alba condemned to death Count Egmont and Count Horn and other personages. With the situation thus dominated by terrorism, war flared up again in 1572, and was then waged by the Low Countries (Holland, Zeeland, Gelderland, Overijssel, Utrecht). It lasted until 1597, and brought in its train many vicissitudes, victories, defeats, and much heroism on both sides. Philip II, disheartened and near to death, ceded the low countries of the North—though retaining Spain's protectorate over them—to Archduke Albert of Austria to whom he married his daughter the Princess Isabella Clara Eugenia (August, 1597). Philip provided, however, that if their marriage were without issue, in case of the death of either those States should revert to the Crown of Spain. But he failed of his purpose, because later on these lands were again to burden Spain's strength and there was renewal of the strife which terminated only with Dutch independence.

The only satisfaction that remained to Philip II was that of seeing that the southern regions of Flanders (corresponding in part to what is now Belgium) remained Catholic for the most part. As regards the religious struggles in France, Philip also found relative compensation in the fact that King Henri IV (1594-1610), although a Protestant in religion, had to be converted to Catholicism in order to be able to control the political situation and conquer the united forces of the King of Spain and of the French Catholics.

Hernán Cortès (from an old engraving).

The wars with England had an unhappy ending for Spain. Philip planned the invasion of the British Isles so that he could fight on their own ground the English Protestants and Elizabeth their Queen, who consistently favored the rebellious Dutch and Philip's Portuguese enemies, and who were also attacking his possessions in the West Indies. For the invasion he outfitted a large fleet which he called the *Armada Invencible*—the Invincible Armada; but it was as a matter of fact badly equipped, much of its personnel was incompetent, and its commander, the Duke of Medina Sidonia, lacked naval experience. The fleet was shattered by storm and then overcome by English vessels (swifter and better armed than the Spanish ships), notwithstanding the heroism of many Spanish captains (1588). Although soon after this the Spanish obtained several victories over the English, they could not carry out their purpose of invasion, and the destruction of the Invincible Armada not only struck a heavy blow at Spanish morale, but gave rise abroad (especially in England) to a conviction that Spain lacked ability in naval warfare. As for Philip II, he received news of the disaster serenely, and expressed his reaction to it by saying (and therewith touching upon only part of the facts), "I did not send my ships to fight the tempest."

The Spanish Army

These many wars added to the fame of the Spanish army, principally because of the achievements of its infantry, which owed its strength to excellent organization and skilled tactics. We have already shown how the foundations of that organization were laid in the time of the Catholic Kings and how it was brought to completion by the Great Captain, Gonzalo de Córdoba.

An army at that epoch differed greatly from an army today. It was made up of volunteers, convicts (who were utilized principally in the navy, which depended on sail and oar), forced recruits, and some troops whose wages were paid by the rich nobles. The volunteers, who made up far the largest group of soldiers, were of two classes: Spaniards and foreigners, all receiving pay. In Philip II's reign the volunteers were very numerous, comprising the "old soldiers" or veterans, who were the ablest and best disciplined troops. Among them were many sons of the lower nobility—the *hidalgos*—to whom a military career opened the way to improving their economic condition. On the other hand, the foreigners (Germans, Italians, and others) whom it was necessary to hire because continuous and far-flung wars called for many men, were an unruly lot who mutinied often and committed many depredations in assaults on cities and in other circumstances in which the military code of the times sanctioned sacking, or violent seizure of private property.

Instead of regiments, which were created later, the army then was composed of what were called *tercios,* or "thirds," consisting of several companies—12 or 15—with a total number of soldiers varying from 3,000 to 4,500. Each "third" was commanded by a *Maestre de Campo,* or Camp Master, and each company by a Captain. The latter title was already in use in the time of the Catholic Kings, whose army had been divided into *Capitanías,* or Captaincies, and *Lances,* while the commanders of any one arm (as, for example, Infantry) were called always Captains General; a title also given at times to the Governors of territories, such as the Navarrese frontier.

The companies bore vari-colored banners. The Royal Ensign was red, with the monarch's shield and sacred figures. Some of the soldiers carried pikes, others firearms—arquebuses or muskets. These last, which were constantly being improved, ultimately displaced the pikes. There were cavalry and artillery troops also. The cannon, which were of bronze, fired stone and iron balls. Spain was the first country of modern Europe to establish field hospitals for soldiers, a Roman practice that had fallen into disuse during the Middle Ages.

These excellent conditions of the Spanish army, which at that time was commanded almost invariably by generals of highest ability, some of whom were nationals and others foreigners, were very often counteracted by lack of money for paying the troops and buying provisions, munitions, and other essential war materials. Time and again that lack of money produced serious uprisings of the soldiery (as we have remarked) which brought the fighting to a standstill. More than once, too, it resulted in bringing about a peace simply because of the impossibility of longer sustaining the costs of war: an indirect means of imposing pacifism on the period's belligerent monarchs. The huge sums expended on military operations justified the frequent petition of the *Cortes* that wars should cease, and explain in great part the impoverishment of a country that had to sustain such costs.

Episodes of the Wars

Among the many memorable victories won by Spanish arms in Philip II's reign is the naval battle of Lepanto (October 7, 1571) in which the King of Spain and the Republic of Venice, allied with the Pope, vanquished the Turks. The expedition was commanded by a Spanish general, Don Juan of Austria, generally known to the English-speaking world as Don John of Austria, illegitimate son of Charles I. Miguel de Cervantes fought as soldier in the ranks at Lepanto, and had his left hand shattered by a musket-ball. That victory, and one achieved not long previous (in 1565) at Malta during the siege by the Turks, freed Italy and Spain from that time forward of any serious or imminent Turkish threat. No less famous, though not so important as to results, were the battle of St. Quentin, a French city that Spanish troops took in 1557, thereby opening the way (though they did not follow through) to the capture of Paris; and the battle of Gravelines, where the French, menacing Brussels, were again defeated in 1558. One episode in this war with France, which was terminated in 1559 by the peace of Chateau Cambrésis, was the attack by Spanish troops under command of the Duke of Alba (1557) on the dominions of Pope Paul IV, enemy of Spanish supremacy in Italy and ally on that account of the French King Henri II. By this attack Philip II demonstrated that he was as adept as his father Charles I in combining fervent religious faith and adherence to the Pope as spiritual lord with defense of his own political interests if the Pope acted against them in his quality of temporal lord or head of an Italian Seignory.

This same point of view, which was fundamentally political, was responsible in ideology of the Spanish absolute monarchs for the so-called Regalism which caused them to insist upon and practice intervention in ecclesiastical affairs, defend the supremacy of civil over ecclesiastical jurisdiction in various matters, and reserve to themselves the granting of permission—*pase regio*—for publishing in Spain Papal Bulls and Briefs. The Crown often intervened also in the Spanish Inquisition.

Philip II, King of Portugal

In the closing years of Philip II's reign, the vast territories of his monarchy were augmented by those pertaining to the Crown of Portugal. The Cardinal Enrique, who was without direct heir, had been sovereign of that kingdom since 1578. As had always occurred—and continues to occur—in such cases, diverse pretenders to the Throne presented themselves, basing their several claims on their kinship to the Cardinal King. Philip II's claim was strongest, since he was the legitimate grandson of the great Portuguese King Emanuel I (1495-1521), from whom descended in direct line the monarchs anterior to Cardinal Enrique. Philip's superiority in degree of blood-relationship was recognized in the Portuguese *Cortes* at Almeirin in 1580 by the nobility and the clergy represented in it. Consequently, when Don Enrique died, Philip II should have inherited his throne.

But Don Antonio, Prior of Ocrato and natural grandson of Manual I, was very popular among the masses of the Portuguese people. When Enrique died, Don Antonio's followers prepared armed resistance to Philip II's perfectly legal accession to the throne. In this fashion they were expressing the feeling of independence and of separateness from Spain (and especially from the kings and peoples of León and Castile) which in spite of their remote Spanish origin, the Portuguese had felt and had demonstrated for centuries; sentiments that have in their favor all the arguments adduced by our present-day ideology in justification of the independence of well defined and long established national and political groups. But this ideology was not prevalent in the sixteenth century, nor could ruling classes and kings of the period have understood it. Philip II therefore proceeded legally and logically to defend the rights that the *Cortes* of Almeirin had recognized as his. Nobody in Europe at that time—except the Portuguese followers of Don Antonio—would have comprehended Philip's reasoning if he had done anything else.

To counteract the opposition of the Prior's followers, Philip II sent to Portugal troops commanded by one of his best generals, the Duke of Alba. A brief three-months campaign cleared the way. Don Antonio fled to France; and although some of his party continued resistance in the Azores with support from the Kings of England and France, the Spanish squadron, under one of its greatest Admirals, the Marquis of Santa Cruz, defeated them and routed the French squadron that had come to their aid.

Philip II was again recognized as lawful King in the Portuguese *Cortes* at Thomar in April, 1581, which thus ratified the judgment of the *Cortes* of Almeirin. The new King, with praiseworthy prudence and tact, showed utmost respect for Portuguese laws and institutions; and carried this so far as not to appoint a single Spaniard to office, thus avoiding the mistakes that his father Charles I had made in Castile. During the war itself, the Duke of Alba carried out the orders of his King by severely punishing depredations (which could not be wholly prevented, the custom of the times and the composition of the armies being what they were) committed by some soldiers and officers against Portuguese peasants and their property at Montemor and in other localities, and also against the monasteries of friars who were adherents of Don Antonio. That severity in punishing such misdemeanors was, to be sure, something theretofore unheard-of; and it is convincing evidence of the pains taken by Philip II in order not to afford any legitimate cause for discontent and protest in Portugal.

The Uprising of the Moriscos *and the Insurrection at Saragossa*

In the field of internal politics, Philip II's reign witnessed two very considerable disturbances.

The first in point of time, and the most serious, was a new uprising of the Moriscos, provoked by the publication in 1567 of an Edict increasing the number of religious and social restrictions established by the Decree of 1526. The Moriscos were exasperated beyond endurance by the steadily increasing pressure to which they had been subjected ever since the time of Cisneros and by the growing harshness of the Inquisition. This Edict of 1567 was disapproved by such important and religiously impeccable personages as the Marquis of Mondéjar, Captain General of Granada; the Duke of Alba; the Commander of the monastic-military Order of Alcántara; and others of eminence. Pedro de Deza himself, president of the Chancellory, or *Audiencia,* of Granada and member of the Supreme Council of the Inquisition, expressed the opinion that the terms of the new law should be softened. However, the opinions that prevailed were instead those held inflexibly by Philip II's secretary, Diego de Espinosa, and the Archbishop Guerrero; and so the Edict went into effect. Insurrection followed almost immediately. Its first sparks shot up in April 1568. It was led at first by Don Hernando de Córdoba y de Valor (Aben Humeya), a descendant of the Ommayad Caliphs, and later on by the *Morisco* Adalá Abenabó. With various vicissitudes, in which mutually contradictory parts were played by Captain General Mondéjar's policy of persuasion and benevolence and by Deza's harshness, the war lasted until 1571 with great expenditure of effort and much bloodshed. Once the rebels had been subdued, the surviving *Moriscos,* even those who had taken no part in the conflict, suffered mass deportation from Granada and were distributed in different regions of Estremadura, León, Galicia, Castile, and the province of Seville. The *Moriscos* of Albaicín (some 3500 men and many more women) had been deported previously. There was a body of opinion in favor of their expulsion, but the King himself was opposed to it.

The insurrection at Saragossa sprang from causes very different from those of the *Morisco* uprising. One of Philip II's secretaries, Antonio Pérez, had been tried in a court of law; first, because of rancorous disputes with another secretary, Vázquez; second, because of his excessively luxurious style of living and his immoral relations with the Princess de Eboli; and, finally, because of suspicion that he had brought about the assassination of Don John of Austria's secretary, Escobedo. Antonio Pérez escaped from prison in 1590 and fled to Saragossa, where he asked aid of the Chief Justice, Don Juan de Lanuza. The latter, availing himself of one of his judicial prerogatives, immured Pérez in what was called the Jail of Declared Prisoners. This was sufficient to ensure that Pérez would not be molested in any way during his trial; and that when he should have been tried and sentenced, he would be handed over to the Judge competent to enforce the Court's decision. In other words, confinement in that particular prison was up to a certain point tantamount to right of asylum; it practically removed the accused from the range of direct action of the royal jurisdiction. The King responded to this shrewd maneuver on the part of his secretary by sentencing him to death. Pérez, not once showing himself outside the protective walls of his prisonhouse, wrote a Memorial in which he accused Philip II—and produced letters of the King's to support the charge—of having himself issued the order for Escobedo's assassination. This complicated the affair considerably. Antonio Pérez was thereupon accused of heresy and removed from the Jail of Declared Prisoners to the one reserved for heretics. The people of Saragossa, who viewed this proceeding as an act violating one of their *fueros,* mutinied against it (1591), and Pérez and his friends took advantage of the insurrection to circulate propaganda linking his personal fate with defense of the liberties of Aragón. When Philip sent troops to put down the revolt, Antonio Pérez fled to France and tried to stir up interest there in fostering a general uprising of the Kingdom of Aragón. Majority opinion in Aragón was not with him, however. Saragossa opposed no resistance to the royal troops. By promises of clemency, Philip succeeded in causing the return to Saragossa of the Chief Justice and some nobles involved in the rebellion who had fled the city; but as soon as he could lay hands on them, he had them haled into court. The result was that Chief Justice Lanuza was beheaded, several nobles died mysteriously in prison, and 69 Aragonese citizens were condemned by the Inquisition to be burned at the stake, although the sentence was carried out only in the case of six of them.

So far as public order was concerned, that settled the matter. Antonio Pérez, who took to drifting from Royal Court to Royal Court all over Europe, made several attempts (always in vain) to reconcile himself with Philip II. At the same time, he never let slip an opportunity of making accusations against the King. Many of his defamatory stories were false; but when he said that Philip himself had issued the order for Escobedo's assassination, Pérez told the truth.

Philip II and Prince Don Carlos

Another most lamentable episode—this time within the family circle—troubled the current of the King's life. It had to do with his firstborn son, Prince Don Carlos. The facts relating to this tragic incident have been not only often exaggerated, but sometimes supplanted by stories utterly without historical proof, or by facile hypotheses maliciously accepted as truth. In the first place, Philip II's affection for his children, as revealed by his letters, would never authorize *a priori* supposition of any spontaneous and unjustified severity on his part toward Prince Carlos.

What can be stated, on the basis of actual testimony of extant authentic documents, is, in the first place, that Don Carlos' mind was unbalanced and that his mental instability increased progressively as he grew older. It happened therefore that he frequently committed insensate actions of which he himself was first to suffer the consequences, and which not seldom affected his father and persons of high standing at Court. It is not straining a point to assume that this mental unbalance was at the root of his attempt to flee and join the Dutch who were rebelling against the rule of the King of Spain. Whatever the circumstantial justification there might be for his wanting to do such a thing, from the standpoint of personal judgments by men today, who take into consideration certain aspirations and acts that do not look the same from every point of view, the indubitable certainty is that that design of the Prince's was totally irreconcilable from the standpoint of the Spanish State with his condition as Prince and heir presumptive to the Spanish throne. In no Court of the world, nor in any reigning family, would such an attitude as his have been tolerated in that epoch; and if it had been evidenced, harsh repressive measures would have been taken. Such was Philip II's procedure in ordering that the Prince be taken into custody and kept in seclusion in rooms of the Royal Palace.

Although the document in which the King officially communicated this news to various groups and corporations (among them, the Municipal Council of Madrid) does not state in so many words the reason for his decision, it says with utmost clarity, and over and over again—in different forms but always with the same meaning—that there were "very just causes and considerations which concern the service of God and the public welfare of these Kingdoms" and were "of just foundation and purpose."

Six months later the Prince died at the Palace in consequence of the imprudences and eccentricities that his illness and his own violent nature impelled him to commit. We know of no evidence affording any basis for a supposition that either his father the King or the Inquisition had a hand in his death.

Measures for Economic Protection

Philip II was a warrior king for the reasons and in the ways that we have shown, but he was not a war lord only. He was also deeply concerned for the cultural and the material welfare of Spain; and more for the former than for the latter, since the enormous expenditures that the wars demanded, as we have seen, left little money on hand for meeting the multiple requirements of agriculture, industry, commerce, and public works, and, very especially, the building of roads. It is clear, nonetheless, that the King and his advisers on these matters felt the necessity of doing something to ameliorate Spain's unfavorable physiographic and climatic conditions in order to better, in so far as was at that time within the scope of action by the State, the welfare of the people and economic conditions in general.

With that end in view, various highways were built or improved, as were many bridges (300 were designed from 1592 to 1596), some of them of great importance; and the task of making the principal rivers navigable was undertaken, a project presented to Philip II by the engineer Antonelli. Of this over-all project, the plans for the Tagus River were carried out, so that for some time the textiles manufactured at Toledo and at Talavera de la Reina, as well as other merchandise, were shipped downstream to Portugal and goods landed at Lisbon were carried upstream by ship as far as Toledo, Aranjuez, and other towns of Castile. Thus the reign of Philip II marked the first moment—after the Roman achievement many centuries earlier—at which public authority in Spain developed a policy of modifying the physical environment by making advantageous use of the good features and systematically attempting to improve the bad.* Even though confined to one special need (to be sure, a highly important one) — that of supplying internal means of communication in the country —that policy was wise and beneficial. It is just to say that in the matter of land transportation (highways and bridges), improvements that the *Cortes* had demanded repeatdly during the sixteenth century, the work was initiated and carried out by the central government only in cases of military necessity or travels of the Royal Court. For the rest, it was the municipalities, and sometimes the merchants, who planned and executed these public works.

Something was also done to improve the harbors, by opening up those of Cartagena, Málaga, Bilbao, San Sebastián, Motrico, Gijón, Mahón, Ceuta, Gibraltar, Valencia, Cádiz, Pasajes, and others. The Port of Barcelona, controlled by the Council of One Hundred and by a *Junta*, or Commission, received important improvements. More was planned than accomplished with respect to artificial irrigation, which was acutely needed in many districts. A half-completed project was the Imperial Canal of Aragón, dug no further than the Jalón River (1538 or 1540); and two projects fully completed were the Col-

---

* Cf. in the *Foreword* to this book the section on *The Geographical Conditions of Spain and Their Influence on Man*.

menar Canal draining from the Tagus and the Cherta Canal from the Ebro. Several irrigation reservoirs were constructed, including the artificial lake at Tibi to supply water for the Alicante truck-farms, and the Almansa reservoir. The *Cortes* asked for intensive action along these lines; but it encountered an obstacle in the ignorance and prejudices of the rural masses, such as the opposition a little later to deepening the channels of the Tagus and the Manzanares because "if God had intended them to be navigable he would have made them so just by a *fiat.*"

Related to all the foregoing measures were the steps initiated in Philip II's reign to establish settlers in some districts and to take a census of the population. As regards the former, the most considerable undertaking was resettlement of localities left deserted by removal of the *Moriscos* from the Kingdom of Granada. It prepared the way for confiscation of the property of those who had been expelled, which was made in benefit of the Public Treasury; but the lack of settlers and consequently of tillers of the soil over an extensive region cried out for remedy in interest of the national economy. The remedy took the form of distribution of plots of land among Christians who would come to settle it in accordance with a carefully worked out plan (Orders and Instructions of 1571 to 1595). Unhappily, because of deficiencies in judgment and common sense on the part of those encharged with carrying out the land distribution, it did not produce all the expected results, although the resettlement was effected.

As for the census of population, it was begun in 1574 with the so-called *Relaciones topográficas,* or Topographical Reports, which are veritable descriptions of the towns of Spain compiled from most comprehensive and well-planned questionnaires intended to supply data for drawing up the population map of the country which the cosmographer Esquivel began in 1566, employing for the purpose very advanced methods of triangulating the Peninsula. As we now know, 636 towns of the 13,000 queried answered the questionnaires. The replies taken as a whole reveal depopulated or underpopulated areas in many regions, a state of things which many contemporaneous documents deplored. The energy necessary to correct it was not brought to bear, not even to the extent of employing the indirect measures that would have tended to auto-correction in so far as feasible.

Encouragement of Culture

Philip II also gave great encouragement to cultural developments, his interest finding expression not only in the support given the universities and other instruments of study and research, but also in the development of libraries and in the aid amply granted to workers in the fields of the plastic arts, music, and the sciences. Among the educational foundations established by Philip II were the Academy of Sciences, which functioned in the Royal Palace itself with sessions attended by nobles and officers of the armed services; the Academy of Mathematics, the first director of which was the architect-engineer Herrera, designer of the Escorial, and in which were studied hydraulics, architecture, cosmography, navigation, artillery, and the construction of forts and city walls; the specialized library of this latter Academy for which books were procured from all over Europe, and its great collection of machines and instruments for use in experiments; the Botanical Garden at Aranjuez; the magnificent Library of the Escorial; the Spanish Archives at Rome and at Simancas; the scientific expedition to the Americas led by Dr. Francisco Hernández, which was fitted out with everything to be had in the way of equipment and facilities for such an undertaking and which resulted in great botanical and pharmaceutical discoveries; the preservation and classification of the botanical collections coming from the New World, a task that the King confided to the eminent naturalist Antonio Nardo; et cetera. The scientific importance of the Academies mentioned was far-reaching; one of the many reasons for this being the fact that they very usefully supplemented the teaching of the Universities which had come to be deficient in scientific branches. Thus, while such university courses were declining, especially in the disciplines being renovated by the Renaissance, the Academies kept more in step with European progress. A Spanish historian commenting upon them opines that the closing later on of some of the Academies was the principal cause of the decadence of certain studies in seventeenth century Spain. About this same time (1645), the English created their Royal Society, the leading scientific association in Great Britain.

Philip II was also originator of the project for establishing a monopoly of the publication of religious books, for which purpose he obtained a license from the Pope and gave large subsidies to several presses. The most important of these was the Plantín Press where the

Madrid: Prado Museum

Titian: *Religion Succoured by Spain.*

erudite Spaniard Arias Montano supervised printing of the Polyglot Bible with the original text and its translations into several languages printed in parallel columns for purposes of comparison, a monumental edition unique except for the Complutensian Polyglot Bible (published in Spain in 1522), from which it is quite distinct. The building where the Plantín Press was installed may still be visited at Antwerp.

To Philip II's time belong some of the most illustrious Spanish scientists, artists, and men-of-letters, who, lending lustre to what has been called the Age of Gold and famous in their own time, are not all forgotten, since much of their work is still a living force today.

The reigns of Charles I and Philip II coincided also with the great period of the Spanish universities, of which Salamanca was the most famous.

It is an interesting fact that the multiplicity of heterogeneous matters demanding attention and action by the King and by public officials made necessary the making of many laws and the publication of a new Code of Spanish internal Law. That Code, repeatedly requested by the *Cortes* in petitions concerned with the confusion among the Castilian Crown's ancient juridical sources, which confusion had been augmented since the reign of the Catholic Kings by the new legislation, was promulgated in 1567 under the title *Nueva Recopilación,* or New Code. Many efforts were made, as we shall see, to publish colonial legislation separately.

Industrial Prosperity and National Wealth

Philip II's reign likewise coincided with the moment of Spain's greatest industrial prosperity, due in part to the measures taken first by the Catholic Kings and later by Charles I, and in part to the increase of national wealth because of trade with the Americas. The following figures show the proportions of that prosperity: In 1564 in Seville there were some 3,000 looms with 30,000 operatives. The city's Alcaicería section (the term is Arabic and means Silk district) was described in 1587 by a writer who said that that part of town was full of the shops of silversmiths, jewelers, and dealers in silks and linens, adding that Seville was purveyor "to the whole world" of raw silk, wool, hides, flax, and other products. The silk looms of Toledo numbered about 50,000 and the looms for other textiles, there and in La

Mancha, were more than 38,000. The wealth of the Toledan guild of makers of fine felt caps (the *bonetes* used by clergymen, collegians, and university faculty members), was so great that on one occasion no less than 564 of its master-craftsmen marched before Philip II, arrayed in satin and velvet embroidered in silks and gold and silver thread. Many other Spanish capitals were equally flourishing—Granada, Segovia, Valladolid, Saragossa, Valencia, Cuenca among them—as were also places of lesser importance, such as Ocaña, famed all over Europe for the manufacture of gloves, which it exported in large quantities.

The prosperity of the textile industries rested in great part on that of the sheep-raising industry; not only on the size of the flocks but even more especially on the high quality of the wool produced by the species known as merino, native to and typical of Spain, and the origin of most breeds the world over raised for wool at the present day. The livestock industry was directed and administered by a corporation of sheep-and-cattle-raisers called the *Concejo de la Mesta,* or Council of Sheep and Cattle Owners, which enjoyed the special protection of the kings. In 1556 the *Mesta* owned some seven million sheep. As of interest in indicating the great production and sale of Spanish wool, we may cite the figures jotted down in 1545 by a foreign writer who reported that the city of Brussels (one of many buying our wools) received from Spain annually from 36,000 to 40,000 bales or fardels of wool, each of which produced two and one-half lengths of woolen cloth. Thus it could be said in 1573 that when the trade in silk and wool was in existence, "there was no man nor woman who lacked a way of earning enough to eat and to aid one another, so much so that it was wonderful to travel over the uplands of Segovia and Cuenca and see how everybody was employed and that nobody of any age, male or female, was idle, but all were busily working in wool, some within their own homes and others in the house of someone else, because there was not enough room at Toledo for all the looms, and the places nearby were overflowing and in every one of them people were hard at work, skilled, prosperous, and contented; and not the native-born inhabitants of those regions only, but also an infinite number of foreigners." Typical expressions of that prosperity were the fairs held at the important commercial centers, that of Medina del Campo being especially famed.

Another conspicuous and lasting manifestation of that state of prosperity may be observed even today on a visit to the towns of Castile —Estremadura, La Mancha, and, in fact, Spanish towns generally— where one may see the great public and private buildings, in a better or worse state of preservation, all of which (except some that we shall speak of hereafter, constructed in the eighteenth century) belonged to the period of Spain's great industrial and commercial activity, when money flowed freely for all. It is worth noting that the wealth proceeding from the Americas contributed to this by stimulating private enterprise. Many other industries flourished in consonance with those mentioned: tanning, artcrafts, ceramics, salt-mining, silkworm raising, manufacture of arms and armor, cabinet-working, soapmaking, to name only a few.

All this wealth very soon melted away, chiefly in consequence of the wars. Accordingly, not long after Philip II's death, and most particularly at the close of the seventeenth century, a condition of industrial decline and poverty was brought about which was in sad contrast to former prosperity. That recession was due largely to the expulsion of the *Moriscos*, a hard working and highly skilled people, which was ordered by Philip III and against which many of the noble landholders whose properties were inhabited by the oldtime *Mudéjares* protested. The ensuant poverty was called then and continued to be called until modern times the *Spanish decadence*. It was in fact not a decadence confined to the dwindling of the public treasury (already much weakened in Charles I's day, as he himself had owned), but a decline likewise of the body politic. Spaniards could not even fight as well as they had done theretofore; but the worst feature of all was that they lost confidence in themselves and so came to lack that sense of well-being which makes men happy and nerves them for large undertakings. The overwhelming burden that weighed upon the country during a century and a half was almost more than human strength could bear, and inevitably it resulted in exhaustion of economic opportunities. Add to this the lack of leadership. The great personalities who had been at the helm to pilot Spain amid the previous reefs and shoals had not been succeeded in the seventeenth century by others whose capacities were equal to the country's needs nor whose abilities could solve the problem of organization presented by the heterogeneous territories under Spanish rule. By and large, the down-

Titian: *Marqués del Vasto Addressing His Soldiers.*

fall of Spanish hegemony (which was fundamentally the downfall of the House of Austria) was only one example more of the inevitable awakening that awaits every imperialistic dream in the world of politics.

The Rapid Process of Internal and International Political Decadence

We have just pointed out some of the essential underlying causes that brought about destruction of the ascendancy enjoyed by the Spanish monarchy throughout Europe during the reigns of Charles I and Philip II. With these causes, which had to produce their natural effect sooner or later, was combined the temperamental disability of Philip III and Philip IV (Philip II's immediate successors), both of whom lacked that zeal and keen interest in government which had characterized their forebears. The decadence was precipitated by the fact that these later Philips entrusted the direction of public affairs to Ministerial favorites (the Duke of Lerma, the Duke of Uceda, and others) who were as a rule unwisely chosen, ill prepared for such high functions, and more intent on intrigues to keep themselves in power than on affairs of State. The most conspicuous external expressions of the decline were military defeats and the abandonment of enterprises great in themselves but not in the best interests of Spain, such as retention of the Low Countries of northern Europe (Holland). In European opinion of the time, the date marking Spain's loss of military preponderance and prestige on the continent was that of the battle of Rocroy, May 19, 1643, which took place after Philip IV's accession to the throne. In the Americas the force and fame of Spanish arms was maintained somewhat longer; one proof of which fact was the defeat suffered in 1665 at Santo Domingo by the strongest fleet ever sent out by England against the Spanish possessions, carrying a powerful landing force and made up, according to contemporaneous documents, of picked and proved English soldiers. And although Spanish military strength declined in Europe, the fact remains that in the New World, throughout the entire period of the House of Austria, Spain retained all her vast overseas possessions in spite of the repeated attacks launched against them by other European powers.

With regard to Holland, we have seen already how Philip II had tried to rid himself of that problem by ceding the territory (which, it must be repeated, was not a conquest by Spain but an inheritance of the House of Burgundy and Austria which Spain was forced to keep up) to his daughter Isabella Clara Eugenia who was married to Albert, another Archduke of Austria. But that cession did not appease the Dutch party fighting for independence. The Kings of Spain in consequence had to come to the aid of the Archduke and Archduchess —just as, generally speaking, the Spanish Crown felt that it was its duty to aid the German Emperors in all their wars—and the strife was renewed. Although Spanish arms still proved strong enough to win important victories in this conflict, it was to end (1609) with a truce in which there were clauses recognizing the independence *de facto* of the Dutch Netherlands, and agreeing to Dutch free trade in the ports of Europe. But when this truce terminated in 1621, war started up afresh and was carried by the Dutch to the Portuguese colonies of Brazil, while new strife broke out with France and with England. Although in Holland the Spanish won such brilliant victories as the taking of Breda (1624) —which is the subject of Velázquez' magnificent painting, *Surrender at Breda,* with its pattern of lances against the sky —and though in Brazil the Dutch were dislodged from the fortified town of Bahia after they had taken it, while the English were repulsed in their attack against Cadiz in 1625, it was already evident that the Spanish forces could not much prolong such continuous and dispersed efforts.

From 1640 to 1646, three new conflicts greatly aggravated the situation: the revolution of Portugal, which kingdom was demanding independence; the revolution of Catalonia, the immediate cause of which was the quartering there of troops (a very frequent practice at the time throughout Europe and on the part of all armies) that in this instance had been sent to the defense of Roussillon, under attack by the French; and the revolutions of Sicily and Naples (Masaniello, 1667), sponsored by France. The Government of Spain was headed at the time by Philip IV's favorite, the Count-Duke of Olivares, a Minister much superior to his immediate predecessors, but one whose good qualities and sagacity in respect to some important questions of internal policy were, unhappily, often counterbalanced by his defects. Olivares had to face the three serious problems at a time when the European religious conflict known as the Thirty Years War, which commenced in 1618, continued to involve Spain's military strength in behalf of the House of Austria. The defeat of Spanish infantry at the battle of Rocroy already mentioned, an occurrence which had great moral effect in Europe and of course in Spain, belongs to this period.

The ultimate result of these multiple contemporaneous struggles was that at the close of the seventeenth century Spain had lost the following dominions: the Low Countries of the North, or Dutch Netherlands; part of the Low Countries of the South (Flanders); Luxembourg, Artois, the Franche Comté, Roussillon (Treaty of the Pyrenees, 1659); Cerdegne; some of the African possessions; and the Kingdom of Portugal. The losses comprised all the territories of western Europe which proceeded from the heritage of Philip the Fair, part of Catalonia's ancient acquisitions in France, and part of the territory acquired in Africa during the reigns of the Catholic Kings and Charles I, besides the Portuguese inheritance of Philip II. Those disasters were influenced to some extent by the egotism of the Hapsburg Imperial House which, forgetful of all that Spain had done for it, sacrificed Spain in 1648 to its own selfish interests by terms of the Peace of Westphalia terminating the Thirty Years War. But the major part of all these losses resulted from the treaties known as the Peace of the Pyrenees (1659), the Peace of Nimiguen (1678), and the Truce of Ratisbon (1684).

The Uprising in Catalonia

The clashes that resulted from the quartering of troops in Catalonia (referred to above) were only the immediate occasion—or better still, the pretext—for the conflict. Tension was deliberately increased by widespread propaganda, especially among the rural population, defaming the Spanish troops that had arrived to save from French aggression a territory belonging to the Kingdom of Aragón and united by age-old ties to the expanding frontiers envisaged by the House of the Counts of Barcelona. The Catalán country-people were led to believe that the Spanish soldiers were heretics and that a rebellion would soon break out in the Ampurdán district. Nothwithstanding the seriousness of these surface events at the moment, the fundamental, underlying reason for the opposition, which was maintained by one sector of Catalán opinion, was distrust of the absolutism of the kings of the House of Austria and of their policy of a strong central government which, it was feared, might result in abolition or abridgment of the ancient civil rights *fueros* and privileges of Catalonia, especially of

Barcelona. A fervent desire to preserve and even amplify that margin of autonomy also had its weight. Such suspicion was rooted in the distant past, as we know, since it had been manifested as far back as the Compromise of Caspe, when the question of succession to the Crown of Aragón was decided in favor of Ferdinand of Antequera. To that long-standing, chronic cause of discontent which had never been uprooted from the consciousness of part of the Catalonian people was added in the middle of the seventeenth century dissatisfaction with the policy of the Count-Duke of Olivares which favored obtaining greater homogeneity—financial, military, and otherwise—among the different Peninsular territories belonging to the Spanish Crown.

The first outbreak of violence was the uprising of the Ampurdán district, followed by flare-ups and tension in different sections, with terrorism of every variety. Official lack of restraint added fuel to the flames; and after a riot with much bloodshed in the capital itself (on Corpus Christi Day, June 7, 1640), which was engineered principally by the agricultural laborers, or *payeses,* the struggle became general. The Catalán party in opposition to the monarchy of the House of Austria sought the support of the French Throne, which at first accepted proclamation of a Catalán Republic that would be a French protectorate, but soon issued Louis XIII's proclamation declaring himself to be Count of Barcelona. Civil war was thus complicated by an international war in which there was at stake the retention for Spain or the loss to France of an extensive Peninsular region.

The war had its ups and downs, with the battle at times favoring Cataláns and French, and again the troops of Philip IV. Some of the Catalán public very soon reacted against France because of the fact (a not unusual experience) that French soldiers and officers not merely occasioned but aggravated the reasons for discontent that had set off the explosion at Ampurdán in the first place. It all ended in victory for Philip's, or the Spanish, party and the rendition of Barcelona in October 1652. As a result, almost the whole of Catalonia yielded, and Philip IV was newly recognized as King by the Catalán General Deputation. That fact did not prevent the loss by Spain soon afterwards of Roussillon and Cerdegne in accordance with the Peace of the Pyrenees which in 1659—as we have said—terminated the War with France.

Philip IV, instead of taking reprisals for the Catalán rebellion and alliance with the French, as the Cataláns had feared that he would do, confirmed all the *fueros* and privileges of Catalonia on January 3, 1653.

The Loss of Portugal

Notwithstanding the liberal policy with respect to the customs and institutions of Portugal implanted by Philip II and continued by his successors, public opinion in that country persistently opposed union with Spain; the principal elements in forming that opinion being the lower clergy and the religious Orders, especially the Jesuits. During Philip II's reign these elements found a motive for stirring up animus against Spain in some enactments by the Duke of Lerma, Spanish Prime Minister, in favor of the Jews. To this argument was added resentment against the imposition of new taxes collectible in 1635 and thereafter; and thus was supplied motivation for a first uprising, which broke out at Evora in 1637 and spread rapidly over Portugal. In the beginning neither the nobility nor the middle class, nor the Duke of Braganza himself (who belonged to the old Portuguese Royal House), was in sympathy with the rebels; but some errors in government committed by the Count-Duke of Olivares, together with the ambitions of the Duchess of Braganza (who was Spanish by birth, of the House of Medina Sidonia) brought about a change of heart. The revolt in Catalonia offered a good opportunity to those who were fostering the movement for Portuguese independence, the outbreak of which occurred December 1, 1640. The rebels elected the Duke of Braganza King of Portugal with the title of Juan IV, and sought alliance with France, Holland, and England, all determined enemies of the House of Austria in its every branch. The lack of Spanish troops and resources sufficient for carrying on the war energetically, along with the other causes noted, resulted in its virtually coming to an end in 1665 with the defeat of the Spanish troops at Villaviciosa. In that same year Philip IV died. His successor, accepting the accomplished fact and the intervention of England, on February 13, 1668, recognized the independence of Portugal which has never been again united with Spain. The only fortified city of Portuguese procedence left to the Spanish Crown was Ceuta in Morocco, opposite Gibraltar.

The End of the Spanish Branch of the House of Austria

The political decadence, international and national, coupled with the economic decadence, reached its nadir in the reign of Charles II, Philip IV's son and successor and last Spanish monarch of the dynasty of Austria. The fact that Charles II inherited the throne in infancy (at the age of four), together with his ill health and limited intelligence, added to the profound depression and pessimism which preyed upon the Spanish ruling classes after the disasters closing Philip IV's reign (1665), combined to form an environment little propitious for stimulating national political life. In those dismal circumstances, the French monarchy, victorious in the mid-seventeenth century European wars, could exert pressure not to be withstood. The opposing influence of England and of Holland, enemies of Louis XIV and of his policy of imperialism, counteracted in part, and in favor of Spain, the effect of the French monarch's hegemony.

When Charles II attained marriageable age, he took as wife, in response to French indications, Marie Louise of Orleans (1679). She died ten years later, in 1689, and the Austrian party at the Spanish Court, led by the Queen Mother María Ana, herself of the House of Austria, succeeded in having the King take as his second wife that same year an Austrian Princess, Mariana of Neuburg. But it was a matter of public knowledge that Charles could not expect to have a child; and this fact gave rise to numerous intrigues for having him name as his heir a member of one or the other party. The French party won out in the end, persuading Charles to make a will in favor of Philip, Duke of Anjou, grandson of Louis XIV and of Charles II's sister, María Teresa. Thus, by bequest—one of the clearest and most definite acts of the absolute monarchy, which in natural consequence of being absolute, considered itself to be patrimonial as well, with the succession a family property—Spain's political fate was transferred from the direct descendants of Philip the Fair and Juana the Mad, all of whom after Charles I had been Spanish in nationality, to the Royal House of France, which at that time was the House of Bourbon. Charles II died on November 1, 1700, and the Duke of Anjou was proclaimed King of Spain as Philip V.

As for Europe, the continent as a whole gained nothing by the disappearance of the Spanish hegemony, nor by that of the House of Austria, which occurred soon after. The imperialistic and militaristic policy of both was continued by the French Bourbons with intensity equal to theirs, or greater; and French imperialism in its turn had to contend with the distrust and envy of the English kings and of other European monarchs, which brought on wars and all the evils to which wars give rise.

New Decadence of the Castilian CORTES

Because of the definite triumph of absolute monarchy in Castile after the curtailment of the nobility's power brought about by Queen Isabella, and its triumph in the rest of the Peninsula likewise because of the personal prestige and executive ability of Charles I and Philip II, absolutist principles were necessarily reflected in all governmental institutions. This was notably true of the Castilian *Cortes*.

What had occurred in the case of Charles I and the *Cortes* of Santiago-Coruña in 1520 was evidence enough that thenceforward the opinion and authority of the King would be predominant, taking away the independence of action of the *Cortes* comprehended in its faculty and sovereign function of deciding whether or not to grant the kings the taxes that they asked. The defeat of the *Comunidades*, or Brotherhoods, influenced greatly in hastening that result. The increasing disunity of the social classes contributed toward the same end, as did also the unscrupulous conduct of the representatives of the Municipalities, who let themselves be controlled increasingly by the Royal Court's bedazzlements and bribes. The King for his part tried to widen still further the gulf between the social elements concurring in the *Cortes,* and on several occasions convoked these different elements separately. His purpose in this met with strong opposition from the nobles, who objected to being considered as really a part, or branch, of the *Cortes,* since their admission of any such status would be equivalent to placing themselves on the same level as the common people in the matter regarding which the nobility was most recalcitrant; namely, the payment of taxes.

Although the kings continued to convoke the *Cortes* in Castile (and did so 44 times during the reigns of Charles I and the three Philips, a total of 146 years) in which *Cortes,* aside from the principal purpose of obtaining money from the Municipalities, petitions for laws and administrative reforms were made, public interest in the *Cortes* as an institution, as well as confidence in its beneficial effects on the government of the country, were on the wane. The most conspicuous example of this fact was that the Municipal representatives themselves, who had been either elected by vote or chosen by lot, were acquiring the custom of yielding their posts, sometimes in return for money, to persons who were not members of the *Ayuntamiento,* or Town Council, and who at the time were not even residents of the city or *villa,* but— as a document of the period puts it—were "powerful personages who sought procurement for their private purposes and not in benefit of the realm nor even of the cities" that they represented. Although an attempt was made to correct these corrupt practices by a decree issued by King Philip IV in July 1660, it accomplished little. At the same time, the number of cases increased in which the representative or delegate of the Municipalities was chosen not by election but by royal appointment. Finally, in September 1665, a decree of Austrian-born Queen Doña María Ana, regent of the kingdom during the minority of her son Charles II, tranferred to the *Ayuntamientos* the faculty of granting the taxes requested by the king; and so rendered unnecessary the meetings of the *Cortes.* In fact, the *Cortes* of Castile were not once convoked during the reign of Charles II, 1665 to 1700. And thus died out that basic political institution, victimized not only by royal absolutism but by the indifference of the mass of the Castilian people as well.

The CORTES *of the Other Regions*

The Decree of 1665 applied only to Castile; so that in the other regions that had *Cortes* (Aragón, Catalonia, Valencia, and Navarre), sessions continued to be held. Difficulties in the way of these meetings likewise continued; since, as was natural, each region wished for its *Cortes* to be presided over by the king and to be held in its own territory; both of which circumstances required travels by the Royal Court which considerations of time, cost, and conditions sometimes made impracticable. Nevertheless, during the approximate two centuries that the Austrian dynasty ruled Spain, the *Cortes* of Aragón met 17 times; that of Catalonia, 13; of Valencia, 14; and of Navarre, 73. The truth is that the meetings produced no great results, especially for the Crown, because these *Cortes* severally put up a strong resistance against imposing new taxes; and when they did accede to doing so (and that not until threats and other recourses had been employed in order to bring about a favorable vote), it was with such parsimony as almost never to help the monarchy out of its monetary straits. Sometimes, indeed, the amounts granted barely paid for the travel of the King and his courtiers to and from the meetings.

Nature of Royal Absolutism in Spain.
Royal Concept of Contemporaneous Jurisprudence.

What happened with respect to the *Cortes,* and especially the *Cortes* of Castile, is not enough of itself to give a complete and exact idea of what the absolute monarchy in Spain was like. We have already observed the important fact of the centralization of certain powers and the very great degree of personal intervention in government decisions practiced most particularly by Charles I and Philip II; but these things did not signify, in the Spanish juridical concept (the principles of which the great Spanish jurist Suárez synthesized in 1613), the exclusive sovereignty of the king's arbitrary will, nor did they result in reduction to a single type and form of the varying regional methods of administration.

It is true that both Charles I and Philip II held that the sovereign will of the monarch was above everything else; but the men of the period who specialized in the study of political law and set down their conclusions, neither believed nor ever taught that the monarch could with impunity fail to comply with the law nor proceed in any other manner than in accordance with the requirements and interests of the country. Thus a very definite distinction was made between *absolute* authority—which is to say, authority single and unshared—and *tyrannical* authority, proceeding capriciously from the monarch's whim without regard to law and justice. That same distinction is found in the work of dramatists of the period (Lope de Vega, Calderón de la Barca, and others), some of whose most famous plays exalt in fact the upright king who forces fulfillment of the law of the land and whose sense of justice causes him to pardon those delinquents whose offenses were provoked by some great injustice (examples: *El Alcalde de Zalamea, El Comendador de Ocaña, Fuente Ovejuna, El mejor alcalde, el rey*). Thus sixteenth and seventeenth century ideas regarding the monarchy and the manner in which kings should exercise their authority reaffirmed the concepts held by St. Isidore and other writers of the Visigothic epoch and the doctrines of the *Fuero Juzgo.*

What has just been said incorporates the prevalent ideal of cultured Spanish opinion and of the Spanish public. But in practice, many arbitrary acts were committed in spite of those principles, because of the very human facility with which absolute power frequently falls into tyranny by absorption; especially if there is also involved the patrimonial feeling with regard to the head of the State. Accordingly, abuses and injustices took place in the time of Charles I and Philip II, though not always at instance of the Kings themselves, who, however, as we have seen, were guilty of some. We should also bear in mind the fact that what was then considered just is not always in accordance with our modern ideology. Arbitrariness and injustice became still more frequent when the kings who followed Philip II left the government in the hands of Ministers (generally, of one Minister incorporating all ministerial responsibilities in himself), who enjoyed the complete confidence of the king and were therefore commonly called "favorites." Arbitrariness is not, of course, a fault exclusive to any one form of government but can and does occur in all regimes, even in those that seem to come closest to perfection. The chief preventive to strict application of the juridical concept explained above was, unquestionably, the destruction of the effectiveness of the *Cortes* (in part, the result of absolutism) and the growing indifference of the old-time political classes (aristocracy and municipal bourgeoisie) which had come to be dominated by blindly selfish motives or by an equally blind sentiment of unquestioning submission and loyalty to the monarch.

If we wish to understand events fully, we must not forget that the ideology then predominant in Europe was concomitant with the abuses of power to which absolute authority inclines when it is not held in check by a deep and scrupulous sense of justice. Early in the sixteenth century appeared the famous book of the Italian Machiavelli, *The Prince,* which elevated to the category of principles of statesmanship the wholly unscrupulous governmental practices which the contemporaneous kings and oligarchies of republics practiced at home and abroad. That political unscrupulousness was termed in the period's juridical phraseology "reasons of State," a euphemism that has been evoked in justification of abuses against law and loyalty from that time to this. Machiavelli's book (against which an abundant literature was published in Spain then and later) was widely read by contemporaneous rulers. It is said of Charles I that he kept it always at hand; and some written commentaries upon it have been attributed to Philip II.

The cited transgressions in the practice of government and in fulfilment of the duties of citizenship are not sufficient, nevertheless, to annul the ideal value of the political concept held by our Spanish jurists, theologians, and men of culture, even though in practice it was set aside repeatedly. That concept shines out like a star from that age, nor was it the only one in the ideology of our men of learning, as we have seen already when considering the Counter Reformation and the attitude toward violent intolerance.

On a par with it, in the field of international policy, were not only the ideas of Francisco de Vitoria, his disciples, and here and there a predecessor of his, respecting war and conquest (with which question we have dealt already), but also the concept of international society as a community of States. Our Spanish theologian and jurist Francisco Suárez (1548-1617) is principal exponent of that doctrine, according to which "humankind, although divided into peoples and States, constitutes in a certain sense a political and moral unity dominated by the natural law of love and charity extended to all men, including foreigners no matter what the people to whom they belong. Although each State forms a completely distinct entity, it is at the same time and with relation to the human race, a member of the great community. Because from the point of view of service, as well as that of ethics, the States need one another and cannot do without mutual support, reciprocal influence, and constant cooperation. While the law which in this respect rules the States has numerous roots in natural logic, that is not the only source from which it proceeds. The customs of the countries supplement natural logic; man's law has its basis in the indispensable cooperation and mutual action of States."

With regard to the special legislation of the ancient Kingdoms other than Castile (Aragón and Catalonia, Valencia, Navarre, Mallorca), we have noted that in general it was maintained, although Charles I tried to modify the laws of Aragón in certain particulars. Philip II, as we have said, notwithstanding the rebellion of the Saragossans during his reign (the case of Antonio Pérez) did not make any fundamental change in the old form of the Aragonese *Cortes* nor that Kingdom's *fueros,* in spite of the fact that there then existed in Castile a strong body of opinion favoring abolition of the latter. Nor did he do away with the office of Chief Justice of Aragón. Furthermore, Philip spontaneously renounced the idea of naming a foreign—that is, a non-Aragonese—Viceroy. He limited himself to taking away from the office of Chief Justice the life tenure that it then involved, and to making the length of term dependent upon the monarch's will, as had formerly been the case. The attacks on constituted law and traditional institutions were carried out, therefore, independently of the external and apparent structure of the State, which remained unchanged in form; and, as we have remarked before and shall explain more fully hereafter, such attacks modified only a few activities in political life.

In the general government of the territories of the Crown, Charles I and his successors amply developed the bureaucratic system which had its beginnings in the King's Secretariats and in the Royal Councils for different administrative matters and for the various dominions (Italy, the Americas, et cetera) united under the Crown of Spain. Thus the way was prepared for the multilateral bureaucracy which is one of the characteristics of the modern State, the intellectual concept of which had already begun to make itself felt and to displace the unilateral idea of a personal monarchy. This was true notwithstanding, and over and above, the absolutism invoked by the caesarists or absolutists and practiced in some instances by the King's Ministers.

The Government of the Americas

Just as soon as the magnitude of the discoveries made by Columbus and the Spanish explorers was understood, steps were taken forthwith to organize a government in the New World and implant colonization overseas. The work of Spain in achieving this dual purpose was admirable, quite apart from the freedom and protection afforded the Indians, already commented upon.

From the beginning, the task of discovery, exploration, and occupation of the American lands was performed under the King's direction. He issued the licenses for undertaking and maintaining expeditions and conquests, even though these were carried out by private enterprise and not by troops of the regular Spanish army. In order to aid the King in these matters, what was called the *Consejo de Indias*—or Council of the Indies—was created speedily; as were also the *Casa de Contratación* (house of Trade) , which was charged with principal direction of voyages to the Americas and American trade and with settlement of lawsuits arising from those activities, and the *Consulado,* or *Universidad, de cargadores* (the collective tribunal of the shippers to the New World), which was patterned in part on the organizations already in existence for the European trade and soon extended to various localities in the Americas. There should be noted also the official establishment of a system of detailed reports on the countries discovered, which were made obligatory for pilots and chiefs of expedition. From these were compiled what were called the *Relaciones de Indias,* or Reports on the Indies, commenced in 1501. In 1512 the *Padrón de Indias,* or Register of the Indies, was established. In 1571 the order was issued to compile a book descriptive of all the Indian provinces; and similar descriptions dating from the sixteenth and seventeenth centuries, analogous to the Topographical Relations of the Peninsula, are still extant.

In measure as the new territories were occupied, they were organized into regions governed, in accordance with their importance, by Viceroys, Governors, Captains General, and, sometimes, by *Audiencias,* or Courts of Judicature. There were only two Vice-Royalties at first: Mexico, or New Spain, and Peru. Alongside the Viceroys and Governors, the *Audiencias,* composed of jurists, functioned principally as courts of appeal for the administration of justice. They were also given sufficiently ample intervention in the political government in order to ensure that the principles of justice and respect for human rights be properly observed.

Of equal importance was the introduction into the Western Hemisphere of the Spanish type of municipality, which became both cradle and nucleus of future political developments. The Spanish municipality in the New World was governed in accordance with the *Ordenanzas de cabildos* (Ordinances of Town Corporations) which was drawn up in 1574 by the Oidor ("Hearer," or Judge of *Audiencia*), Alonso de Cáceres, and was regarded then and is still regarded as one of the most nearly perfect municipal codes in the world at that time. The aggregate of Spanish colonial laws of Peninsula procedence is to be found, although not integrally, in the *Recopilación de las leyes de Indias*—Code of Laws of the Indies—promulgated in 1680, which represents the legislation denoted as being then in force, but does not show the process of its formulation and modification since 1492; **nor** much less does it include the sum total of colonial legislation since the Discovery. Besides this class of laws, a considerable number of others was being produced in consequence of the autonomy granted to different categories of colonial authorities, beginning with the Viceroys. That mass of new legislation was nowhere codified completely, and in some regions was not codified at all. Its enactment and observance, together with the juridical customs created in the colonies and very often recognized or acquiesced in by the Spanish kings, constituted a portion of the Law in force in the Americas, which in the aggregate was as impressive in volume as was the body of laws prevailing in Spain, and as a rule was more efficient. It is interesting to note that a part of that American-made legislation, and especially the ordinances and other regulations that could be handed down by the Viceroys and such lesser authorities as had relevant jurisdiction, included or sanctioned customs of the indigenous Indian inhabitants; as may be observed, for example, in the ordinances of the Viceroy Toledo at Lima, and in those given out some time later for Chile.

The Philippine Islands—the most important Spanish possession in Oceania—were governed and colonized in accordance with the same regulations as the Americas; and an active trade was carried on from Mexico (New Spain) with the Philippines and some countries of eastern Asia.

It is just to add in relation of the foregoing that Charles I and the three Philips who succeeded him interested themselves in the problem of good government for the New World colonies, and deserve credit for some of the best laws of the Americas. While Charles II's reign was less fruitful in this respect, it did see publication of the *Recopilación,* or Code, of 1680, the selective collection of the laws of the Americas which the three Philips had been unable to complete.*

Spain's Purpose in America

But the Crown, as well as the Council of the Indies and the other groups or individuals who were concerned with American affairs, also held from the beginning that what was involved therein was not a

---

* To further document this legislation (laws and customs) , see my *Estudios Sobre las Fuentes del Derecho Indiano* (an eighteen-volume work consisting of an Introductory volume, twelve parts or sections in 14 volumes, and 3 additional volumes of documentary Appendices). Consult also my *Historia de las Municipalidades Coloniales* soon to appear in Spanish and in English.—*Author's Note.*

Façade of Charles V's Palace, Granada.

problem of conquest merely, but a great work of colonization with these two main purposes: populating the newfound lands, and developing whatever natural resources might be found there, not for the benefit of the Administration alone, but of the nation as a whole; that is, of Spanish agriculturists, industrialists, and merchants. With respect to civilizing influence, the great twin objectives that Spain strove resolutely to achieve were the evangelization of the native Indian inhabitants (their conversion to Christianity), and the extension over the Americas, for both white colonists and Indians, of all the cultural media that Spain then possessed and employed. In pursuing these dual objectives, especially the former, the missionary friars of the different religious Orders, the Franciscans and Jesuits in particular, took a leading part. The men who waged a tireless campaign in protection of the rights of the Indians of the New World were—to name only a few among the many who could be cited—Father Avendaño, initiator of the movement in behalf of the Indians; Fray Bartolomé de las Casas (at the beginning of the sixteenth century), **Motolinia** (Fray Toribio de Benavente), and Father Junípero Serra (eighteenth century). Advocates of the indigenous inhabitants of the Philippines were Father Martín de Rada; Father Domingo de Salazar, first Bishop of Manila; and Miguel de Benavides. In the sphere of government, as well, the New World natives had staunch defenders, among whom were Queen Isabella and Kings Philip II and Philip III, and the Viceroy Luis de Velasco who was called "Father of the Indians." Protective legislation for the Indians, which had been developed very extensively in the period preceding the Laws of Burgos (1512) was emphasized in the regulations progressively more favorable included in the new Ordinances of 1523, 1526, and 1545.

The anti-militaristic sentiments of some of the missionaries should be noted too. They were embodied especially and very remarkably, with reference to Chile, in Father Luis de Valdivia, belonging to the close of the sixteenth century and beginning of the seventeenth. Since notwithstanding the general protection afforded the Indians by legislation for the Americas, it was permitted as an exception to the rule to enslave them in case of war, Father Valdivia and other members of the clergy tried to have abolished or modified the application of that provision, which was responsible for many unjust and unauthorized

Titian: *Portrait of Philip II.*

practices. The high-principled scrupulousness brought to bear in this matter came to be so great that a Royal Cédula of the sixteenth century declared that the Crown would renounce further exploitation of the American pearl fisheries rather than consent to this industry's costing human lives.

But paralleling such humanitarianism on the part of kings, clergy, and not a few government officials, was the selfishness of other Spaniards and of foreigners colonizing the Americas who were actuated by motives wholly different. Thus the history of our Spanish colonization of the New World had as one of its most characteristic aspects the incessant struggle between, on the one hand, a State which was desirous of giving full protection to the Indian and was aided in this by all who shared the ideas which the legal norms expressed, and, on the other, those greedy individuals who put their own private fortunes above everything else and sacrificed to personal pecuniary gain Indian liberties and Indian lives. That primary reason of dissension was accompanied by another which in some instances, perhaps, signified a purely intellectual conviction without self-seeking admixture: the divergence of opinion, which from the first was manifest among the men who influenced Spanish policy toward the Indians and which is reflected in the official texts themselves, regarding the Indian's capacity to receive the civilization that Spain proffered him.

To the same class of ideas favorable to the indigenous inhabitants of the New World, and with an interest which was in high degree both idealistic and practical, belong the different experiments in completely pacific penetration and colonization which were carried out in the sixteenth and seventeenth centuries. The best known and perhaps the most representative of such during this period was that of Las Casas at Cumaná on the island of Hispaniola. Closely allied with these efforts was the placement of Indians who evidenced an aptitude therefor in the same conditions of agricultural and civil life as were enjoyed by Spanish farm workers themselves; the object being to try the Indian out and thus ascertain if he possessed the qualities necessary to make his own way in the world, given the opportunity, with no tutelage whatever. That experiment of tossing him into the stream to find out whether he would sink or swim was called at the time "the Indian experiment."

Colonization, Properly Speaking

In order to achieve colonization most effectively, an effort was made on the one hand to send to the Americas—"the Indies"—men skilled in agriculture and industry who could establish both in the New World (farm laborers, ditch diggers and canal-builders, mechanics, mining experts, and the like) ; and on the other hand, to keep colonists supplied through regular shipments with seeds, plants, working tools, and species of livestock previously unknown in the Western Hemisphere. All this was done on a large scale; so that in the vegetable kingdom alone about 170 species were introduced by the Spaniards, among them some which today constitute the principal sources of agricultural income in the Americas (including the United States, of course). No less economically important was the livestock introduced by the Spaniards—horses, cattle, asses, goats, sheep, chickens— the rapid increase of which on the rich and virgin soil of the Americas soon made stock-raising one of the principal sources of wealth, especially in the regions particularly adapted to it, among them the River Plate section, and Mexico, or New Spain.*

Although the fact that ownership of gold and silver was considered the most worthwhile source of wealth lent a special allure to the search for those precious metals, it was not by mining developments alone that the Spaniards gave economic value to the Americas. In the first place, not all the newfound lands were mining regions. On the contrary, there were vast expanses of territory which held no deposits of gold or silver, or in which they had not yet been discovered. In such regions the immigrant Spaniards had to develop the elements of wealth afforded by the locality; and that explains the establishment of great agricultural and stock-raising industries; sugar production in Cuba and elsewhere affording notable examples of the former. This industrial progress is reflected in the writings of numerous foreign travelers who visited the Americas in the eighteenth and nineteenth centuries.

A similar experience befell the English colonists on the Atlantic coasts of North America. They devoted themselves to farming, hunting, and fishing, since there were no mines along the northeastern seaboard. If there had been, the English would have exploited them as

---

* See my monograph on *The Share of Spain in the History of the Pacific Ocean* in the work on *The Pacific Ocean in History*, published by Macmillan (New York, 1915-17) .—*Author's Note.*

intensively and as enthusiastically as the Spaniards did in Peru and certain parts of Mexico; as, in fact, the "Forty-niners" did centuries later when gold was discovered in California, and other treasure seekers later still in Alaska and elsewhere in North America.

The efforts of the Spanish colonists to make their farmlands in the Americas productive, and the governmental trade policy (which was protectionist, like that of all contemporaneous States) met very detrimental opposition by way of frequent attacks on merchant vessels and on the colonial territories themselves, carried out by English, French, and Dutch pirates and corsairs who occupied many small islands of the Lesser Antilles and were aided more or less openly by the Governments of their respective countries. The active contraband emanating from these nations contributed to the same result. The financial and commercial importance of this contraband, in which were often implicated Spanish merchants and private citizens, including some individual members of religious Orders, diminished the benefits of colonization and had its influence on the economic decadence of Spain, to which we referred in a preceding section.

Emigration to the Americas

Looking to the best means of developing American lands by manpower, and with the general purpose of screening the colonizers, the Spanish laws on the subject were so framed as to place difficulties in the way of passage to the New World for persons undesirable on account of either lack of morals or lack of skill; but on the one hand the Herculean task of keeping close watch on emigration, and on the other the great facility of access to the Americas by clandestine means often rendered those precautions useless.

Among the legal impediments to clearance for the trip was the question of religion. The unity of religious practice which had been brought about in Spain by actuation first of the Catholic Kings and later of Philip III, naturally was sought with especial vigilance in the Americas in order to facilitate the Christianizing of great masses of Indians. The religious requirement applied to foreigners (that is, non-Spanish Europeans) , who were not permitted to make the trip to Spanish possessions overseas unless they were Catholics. Foreigners who were Catholics could not only receive a license (which Spaniards also had to have) to voyage to the New World, together with any other requisite formality, but could also trade there or carry on, from headquarters in Spain, trade with Spanish overseas colonies. Foreign merchants did both throughout the whole period of Spanish dominion in the Americas.

As we have stated, the English colonizers of the eastern part of North America followed, in general, the same line of conduct in religious matters as that of the Spanish State; at times prohibiting any who were not Christian from settling in their colonies (thus keeping out Jews, Moslems, and those—such as Indians—deemed to be idolaters), and in some cases prohibiting Catholic settlers as well; again, expelling from the colony or disqualifying for public office Catholics and members of Protestant sects distinct from the Church of England or whatever other creed was dominant in a particular colony. Although the English did not establish the Inquisition as a specialized tribunal for heresies, the result, in so far as regards freedom of conscience, was similar to that in the Spanish colonies; save in some exceptional cases. In the Spanish colonies of America, the Indians were exempted from the jurisdiction of the Inquisition; and there were even cases, the documentation concerning which is still extant, of permitting Indians to take oath in Court proceedings in accordance with the tenets of their own indigenous religion. It is known that Philip II also ordered that the personal liberty of the Moslems in the Philippines be respected (Instructions to Legazpi).

Emigration to the Americas was relatively numerous, although it was not so great as has been sometimes stated in order that this factor might thereupon be alleged as a main contributing influence to the Spanish decadence of the late sixteenth and the seventeenth century. Sufficient research has not yet been made in this matter, regarding which there must always be taken into account the fact that immigration varied greatly in accordance with circumstances and the various periods of Spanish colonization. The most reliable method of getting at the figures would be to plot the immigration curve in each region of the Americas and in those of Oceania. That of New Spain (Mexico) shows some 7,000 European settlers in 1550 (only 63 of whom were non-Spanish); in 1574, the geographer López de Velasco gave the number as 7,067 Spaniards and in the last years of the eighteenth and first of the nineteenth century, the known population figures fluctuated from 5,200,000 to 6,000,000, including both Spanish and indigenous inhabitants, with 1,097,928 Spaniards reported in 1810. To be sure, those statistics included all Spaniards then living in Mexico, the majority of whom were creoles, which is to say, persons born in Mexico who were children, grandchildren, great-grandchildren, and great-great-grandchildren of immigrants from Spain. It is interesting to note that the great majority of these immigrants were males. Spanish women in the New World were few, especially in the early years of conquest and colonization; but as yet we do not have verified figures on the various groups of women coming to the New World at different periods. It seems to be a fact that for a considerable time the marriages of Spaniards with Indian women were very numerous, so that the creoles inherited biologically some of the spiritual qualities of the Indians along with others from the Spanish colonists.

Spanish Cultural Policy in the Americas

As we have pointed out, culture in relation to the Americas was understood by the Spaniards with the liberalism to which they had been obligated by their recognition of the Indian's status as that of a free man. Consequently, the media of culture—general and professional schools, the printing press, and all the rest—were extended to the Indians and not restricted to European colonists, whether Spanish or of other nationality, as was the rule in colonizations carried out in the New World by men from other lands than Spain. In accordance with this liberal criterion, Spain even brought to the Americas our institutions of higher learning—the Universities—and advanced methods of scientific work and research, whether employed for such industries as mining or applied to unselfish labor in the field of the natural sciences; in which field, as we shall show later on, our Spanish naturalists, chemists, cosmographers, mathematicians, and others, greatly distinguished themselves. The first printing press of the Western Hemisphere was founded by Spaniards in Mexico one hundred years before the first English book to be printed in America was issued at Boston in 1640.

The education of the Indians was effected by the official or private establishment of special schools, and most particularly those created by the religious missions (Franciscans, Jesuits, and those of other Orders) which in some districts formed model communities of peaceful, civilized living or of agricultural or other activity; such as was done, for example, in Paraguay and California.

Spanish Culture during the Reign of the House of Austria. The Two Centuries of the Golden Age

Throughout the two centuries during which the House of Austria occupied the Spanish Throne, Spain, excepting for the final years of the seventeenth century, had greater glory and influence in the world through the genius of her writers, artists, and men of science than on account of the martial achievements of her kings and armies. The already splendid flowering of Spanish culture during the time of the Catholic Kings increased magnificently during the reigns of Charles I and the Philips (1517 to 1665), sponsored and stimulated by those Kings and especially, as we have seen, by Philip II. This period has been called the Siglo de Oro, or Century of Gold—the Golden Age— of Spanish literature; an inaccurate denomination, be it said, not only because the period lasted for more than a century and a half, but also because some of our great Spanish writers, artists, and men of science, as well as of many others who, without possessing great genius, pro- duced important work nevertheless, did not cease in their labors when the House of Austria came to an end in Spain, but continued to pro- duce after 1665.

The great creative achievement of the Spanish period during those two centuries may be outlined as follows:

In Literature:—The Novel, principally in what is called the pica- resque *genre:* a portrayal of the impoverished, the underprivileged, and the delinquent, which *genre* was initiated with *La Celestina* and in which Spanish writers preceded and surpassed those of the rest of the world; *The Theatre,* in both comedies and tragedies and in moral- ity plays, or *autos sacramentales*—all of which, taken together, formed one of the richest and greatest theatres of all time; *The Romances,* or ballads, initiated in other countries by contemporaneous writers and brilliantly continued by sixteenth and seventeenth century poets, and in both form and content very characteristic of Spanish genius and Spanish history.

Among the picaresque novelists, mention should be made of Mateo Alemán, Espinel, Delicado, and Quevedo; among the dramatists, of Lope de Vega, Calderón de la Barca, Tirso de Molina, Alarcón, and Moreto; among the authors of *romances,* of Lope de Vega and Que- vedo (both already cited as dramatists) and Góngora. And there were many others. Above all the rest towers the colossal figure of Miguel de Cervantes, author of the unsurpassed picaresque novels known as the *Novelas ejemplares* and of *Don Quixote—Historia del ingenioso hidalgo Don Quijote de la Mancha*—universally acknowledged as a crowning peak in the realm of the novel, and as one of the loftiest and most profound expressions of the human spirit.

In the Humanities:—*Catholic Theology,* which produced one of its most characteristic manifestations in Spain as an instrument in the conflict with Protestantism, mysticism, of which the Spanish Catholic literature ranks with the greatest and most original expressions of the philosophy of religion; *International Law,* Colonial, Public, and Private, in which, as stated hitherto, the ideas of Spaniards opened up new paths of scientific investigation and implanted theories that have been reëxamined and evaluated in our own time; *Geography* and *Physics,* fields in which our Spanish mariners, mathematicians, and discoverers of unknown lands and seas distinguished themselves as authoritative writers and in which they made notable inventions; *Natural History,* which the Spaniards enriched considerably in all its branches, especially through study of the flora, fauna, and minerals of the American continent, which they published to the world; *Medicine* and *Pharmacy,* in both of which the Spaniards made momentous contributions, among them being Servet's pioneer work in discovery of the circulation of the blood, the invention of spectacles by the ophthalmologist Daza de Valdés, and the treatment of many grave diseases; *Chemistry,* greatly advanced by Spanish research, especially in connection with mining; *Economics* and the *Science of Commerce,* which the requirements and the experience of mercantile relations with the Americas intensified, and in which the Spaniard Salgado de Somoza expounded ideas still regarded today as fundamental; the *Science of Education,* wherein such writers and teachers as Luis Vives (famed throughout Europe for his learning, and tutor of Mary Tudor who became Queen of England), Pedro Ponce de León (the Benedictine monk who in the sixteenth century invented a method of teaching the deaf), Juan de Castro, Ramírez de Carrión, Bonet (Ponce de León's contemporary who also did valuable work on the education of the deaf), and Simón Abril made progressive and productive contributions to man's knowledge; *Philosophy,* which in its very typical and highly individual Spanish expression produced profoundly original works that were studied by scholars and summarized for use as textbooks by

Protestants and Catholics alike in the sixteenth and seventeenth centuries; *Psychology*, proceeding from observance of man and society, which had in the Jesuit Baltasar Gracián one of its most penetrating commentators, as regards both the individual and the group (the psychology of the Spanish people), as well as a stylist whose patterned prose is always temperate, polished, discriminating, and eloquent; *History*, to which a new method was contributed, especially by those "chroniclers of the Indies" who set down first hand accounts of conquest and colonization of the Americas, as well as a great mass of new data on events, customs, social organization, and creeds of the indigenous peoples of the New World, all completely unlike anything previously known to Europeans; the *Grammar* of the American Indian languages, studied and transmitted by the Spanish missionaries in vocabularies, translations, and the like, which form the basis of our present knowledge of the subject.

In the Plastic Arts:—The sixteenth and seventeenth centuries, during which the great Italian, Flemish, and Dutch painters flourished—Michael Angelo, Titian, Rubens, Rembrandt, Frans Hals, and others—were also the triumphant period of Spain's original genius in painting and sculpture. This originality showed at first, except for exceptions already noted, commingled with and partially obscured by Italian and Flemish influences, then blazed free and clear in the works of El Greco ("the Greek," Domenico Theotocopuli), Velázquez, Murillo, Zurbarán, Rivera, and many others in painting; Ordoñez, Zaya, Berruguete, Forment, Siloe, Hernández, Montañés, Cano, Mena, and others in sculpture, especially in woodcarving and in clay. There was a similar flowering of industrial or decorative arts, particularly in ceramics (plates and jars from Manises, Triana, Paterna, Toledo, Teruel, Daroca, Talavera); iron-work (grills for presbyteries, choirs, chapels and private homes); gold and silver work (especially monstrances, crosses, and other ecclesiastical objects); ornamental vaulting; cabinet-work; embroideries; textiles (examples of which are the many magnificent tapestries collected by the Spanish kings in Spain, in addition to those imported from Flanders and elsewhere). The list might be much extended. Even in *Architecture,* in which the general tendency of European art was felt everywhere, Spanish genius succeeded in introducing modalities and interpretations that characterize distinctive styles. Thus, besides the Isabeline, Plateresque, and *Mudéjar* styles

Toledo in Storm, by El Greco.

which we have discussed already, and all of which were of Peninsular creation, when the full triumphal progress of the Renaissance had almost wholly displaced Gothic art, which by that time had come to be looked on as barbarous, such typical and magnificent buildings were constructed in Spain as the monastery of the Escorial and many of the royal palaces—the Alcázar at Toledo, the Palace of Charles I in the Alhambra—as well as splendid private dwellings that have stood through the centuries as monuments of architecture. And when that art degenerated, breaking geometrical regularity of line and overdoing ornamentation which often became as over-elaborate and fussy as a too-lavishly-frosted wedding-cake, Spanish artists created their Baroque architecture (also called Churrigueresque, after the architect and sculptor José Churriguera), which differed from the French and produced original works of great artistic merit. Both these styles when extended to the colonial dominions acquired modalities (and this is especially true of the Baroque) that emphasized their deep-rooted Spanish origin, which bore new fruit in America on being crossed with the rich variants of indigenous New World art, thereby producing forms differing from and revitalizing plastic arts of Spanish procedence to such extent that it may well be said that the colonial Baroque includes constructions and decorations that cannot be explained by European Baroque.

Those indigenous influences were extended to other artistic styles as well, and even succeeded in introducing modifications into Spanish architecture on the Peninsula, with results that, according to some modern critics, left their imprint in particular upon certain districts of Andalusia.

The Baroque art that flourished so vigorously in Italy and France has been described likewise by a modern art historian as being a characteristic expression of the Catholic Counter Reformation. That it was contemporaneous with the latter and its relative triumph is evident, as is also the fact that Baroque art continued to be produced on a large scale in the eighteenth century, when the intellectual environment of a great part of Europe was already in many aspects rather anti-Catholic (e.g., the Encyclopedists) ; but perhaps the fact is less evident that innovations brought by Baroque art to Renaissance architecture and decorative arts correspond to the spiritual traits characteristic of the Counter Reformation and are derived from the same ideological source.

In Music:—In Music also Spanish genius produced ends and means that were its distinguishing characteristics in the Age of Gold. The Spanish music of the period was marked by its tendencies and vigorous expression and by its cultivation and adaptation of folk songs and *romances,* which are sometimes introduced into the work of the master composers. In the field of devotional music famous composers of the time include Victoria, Salinas, Cabezón, and Guerrero; in profane music, besides several of those just mentioned, Milán, Juan del Encina, Escobar, Valderrábano, Mudarra, Pisador, Fuenllana, Blas, A. de los Rios, Durango, Literas, Timoneda, Sabonera, Hidalgo, and some others little known or of secondary importance. In the theatre, music was heard on concert programs or in musical comedy, *eglogas* (ecologues or pastoral poems which were sung or chanted), and opera. In the operatic pieces the libretto was by such illustrious poet-dramatists as Lope de Vega, Calderón de la Barca, and others of recognized genius. The seventeenth century opera of which most music is still extant is *Celos aún del aire matan;* Juan Hidalgo composed the music and Calderón de la Barca was librettist. Calderón also wrote the words for Delgado's *La púrpura de la rosa.* Spanish music, like the Spanish plastic arts, was introduced into the Americas and was studied in New World universities. The construction of musical instruments became common in the Spanish colonies overseas. A notable instance was the building of the great seventeenth century organ by a native-born Indian artisan in the Church of San Francisco at Quito, Ecuador.

The Influence of Spanish Civilization Abroad

Even in the event that this massive and richly various creative work (of which innumerable additional examples could be adduced) had never gone beyond the Spanish frontiers, it would have lost none of its intrinsic worth. But such was not the case, particularly with respect to literature, the several branches of science, and music. The works of Spanish novelists and dramatists were translated into all languages and had their imitators in all countries, especially in France, where, during the reigns of Louis XIV and Louis XV, both tragedy and comedy (Corneille, Racine, Molière) were indebted to Castilian models. The picaresque novel was imitated likewise, one good example of this being Le Sage's *Gil Blas.* It is unnecessary to say that the work of Cervantes—his *Quixote,* of course, above all the rest—became as soon as published part of the inalienable cultural heritage of the world. The Castilian language, which by that time had come to be considered the official and representative tongue of the whole of Spain, was fashionable in foreign capitals, and was taught far and wide, competing in popularity with Latin, even though the fifteenth century use of Latin as a universal, or international, language, continued during much of the sixteenth. Latin continued too to be the preferred vehicle of most great European writers, although by that time it had to contend with the growing use of the national Romance tongues. Numerous examples might be instanced of the Peninsula support given the use of Castilian as a substitute for Latin. Many Portuguese writers of the Golden Age made Castilian their medium, and regarded it as their own language. Because both of such prestige and of the vast geographical extent of the dominions of the Spanish Royal House, Spanish books were printed not only in Spain but in other countries: at Antwerp, Venice, Amsterdam, and elsewhere.

What has been said regarding literature applies to the sciences and the other humanities as well. The important works of our Spanish theologians, philosophers, cosmographers, mathematicians, and botanists were read everywhere and translated into many languages, so that their ideas and inventions were internationally current; and they are in fact reflected in the enduring scientific methods and achievements of other nations. That is true of music also, especially of Spanish devotional music, which was held in high esteem at Rome and influenced the reform of the art initiated there by musicians of the Vatican.

As for our other Spanish arts—such as architecture, painting, sculpture—while they did not exercise contemporaneous influence on the other countries of Europe, they were widespread throughout the Americas, as we have seen, and created there new forms based on the Spanish schools of art, which proved to be seedbeds of art education for those peoples in formative process in territorial dominions from which in the course of time the Hispanic American Republics would emerge. This was in addition to the specific influence which the great Spanish painters of the Golden Age—Velázquez, El Greco, Ribera, and the rest— were to exercise, and which is still felt.

In these many ways Spain made ample contribution to the common treasure-house of human culture, and returned to the world a rich harvest from those alien seeds that our country had received and nurtured.

Bridge over the Tagus, Ronda.

Chapter XI

The Eighteenth Century and the House of Bourbon

The War of the Spanish Succession and Its Consequences

THE VICTORY obtained by French diplomacy in the designation of Philip V as King of Spain produced what was at one and the same time, a civil war and an international conflict. It is known as the War of the Spanish Succession. A section of Spanish opinion in Aragón, Valencia, Mallorca, and especially Catalonia, notwithstanding the political stand taken by the last-named in 1640, declared in favor of continuance on the throne of the House of Austria, then represented in the person of Archduke Charles, son of the Holy Roman Emperor, Leopold. In strict accordance with the tenets of patrimonial monarchy, Charles was in fact closer kin to Philip IV than was Philip, Duke of Anjou; Charles was the nephew of the Spanish king, son of his sister Margaret, while Philip was merely the grandson of another sister, María Teresa, who had married Louis XIV of France. England and Holland, jealous of French preponderance, supported the claims of Charles and naturally enough they were joined in this by Austria and the Imperial Diet of Ratisbon, obligatory defenders of the dynasty of the House of Austria. The war commenced in 1702, and for the first two years was waged almost exclusively in Italy, Flanders and the Americas. In May, 1704, Archduke Charles entered Lisbon with English and Dutch troops. He was there proclaimed King of Spain; and Portugal declared herself to be an ally and entered the war alongside the enemies of France. In 1705 the Archduke's partisans in Catalonia revolted against Philip V, and their representatives signed at Genoa a treaty of alliance with England. Thenceforward the Peninsula was the center of the War, which continued until 1714 with great vicissitudes for the cause of Philip V, whose troops (French and Spanish) were victorious at the battles of Almansa and Lérida in 1707 and of Brihuega and Villaviciosa in 1710, but were routed in the latter year at Almenara and Saragossa. The accession of Charles of Austria to the imperial throne as Charles VI of the Holy Roman Empire, together with reasons of internal policy, moved England to seek peace with France toward the close of 1710. In 1712 Holland, Portugal, Savoy, and Prussia followed suit; and in 1713 at Utrecht they signed a peace treaty with France which was followed up by peace treaties with Spain (1713-14 and 1715). This left as partisans of the Archduke-Emperor—in addition to his own House of Austria—only some German princes and an important minority of Spaniards (especially in Catalonia) who remained hostile to Philip V. Accordingly, the war continued; but on September 12, 1714 Barcelona capitulated, followed shortly after by Minorca, which had also opposed the new dynasty.

The succession of the French House of Bourbon to the Spanish throne, thus achieved, cost Spain thirteen years of strife, huge losses in men and treasure, and the consequent delays in development of national enterprises. The territorial losses were no less important. By the Peace of Utrecht (1713), Philip V ceded to England the Island of Minorca and granted important advantages in the Americas, in addition to relinquishing the Island of Sicily to his father-in-law, Victor Amadeo of Savoy. By the peace of Rastatt with the Holy Roman Empire (1714), Philip had to cede to the Empire the Spanish possessions in Italy, as well as Sardinia, Luxembourg, and Flanders. Thus was lost not only the remnant of the Burgundian heritage then pertaining to the Spanish Crown, but all the conquests that had been won by the Crown of Aragón as well. Of these latter, however, the Kingdom of the Two Sicilies—that is, Naples and the Island of Sicily—was briefly recovered while Philip was still on the throne, being retaken in 1734 by Spanish troops aided by those of the Pope, and adjudged to Prince Charles, later King Charles III of Spain.

The War of the Spanish Succession produced still further consequences in Spanish internal politics. Philip V, enraged by the tenacious resistance of districts in the realm of Aragón, waited only until he had won the conflict to abolish their *fueros;* doing away with them wholly

Monastery of the Escorial.

in Valencia and Mallorca and partially in Catalonia and Aragón. In lieu of the dispositions abolished, the *fueros* of Castile were extended to those districts. Such was one of the first steps toward uniformity of Law—principally of Public Law—throughout Spain. There were also certain modifications, chiefly in the direction of stronger centralized government, made also by Philip V in the *fueros* of the Basque provinces. Philip's successors tried to whittle down, and even abolish, the remaining *fueros,* but failed in the attempt.

Philip V, Louis XIV, and the French Influence

The first fifteen years of the eighteenth century—a period including the War of the Spanish Succession (1701-1714)—was marked not only by military and diplomatic fluctuations in the relations of Philip V with the Allied Powers and with partisans of the dynasty of Austria, but also by his variable relations with Louis XIV. In fact, although dynastic interest led France and Spain to fight side by side, there was no lack of vicissitudes arising from personal and political differences between grandfather and grandson.

Philip V was seventeen years old when he became King of Spain. Although valiant in battle, as he proved repeatedly, he was weak in character, hesitant and irresolute: qualities far from desirable in a chief of State. "He had few defects and few virtues," comments a historian of the time: "he cared only for hunting and praying." Philip was born to be ruled by someone else; and so indeed he was, throughout his life. At the end of his first six months in Spain, his fellow-countryman and confidant, the Frenchman Louville, said of him that he would never really rule. Philip was wholly devout and conscientious, as regards his religion, but his immoralities were nonetheless such as to cause, among other neurotic manifestations, melancholia and eccentricities of action that bordered on madness. Though much of this was not obvious until later, Louis XIV must have been aware of the vacillating nature of his grandson; and since it favored Louis' own secret ambition to control the Spanish Government (notwithstanding his original formal declaration that he desired that Spain should rule herself) and his innate sense of personal authority, he was not slow in establishing himself as King Philip's mentor. The facts should be recognized, however, that many Spaniards encouraged Louis in this, and

Philip willingly let himself be guided by his grandfather. Among the political recommendations which the latter made his grandson was never to forget that he was French; and in order that Philip not forget, Louis XIV saw to it that a flock of French guardians and advisers was ever on hand at the Spanish Court. Prominent among these were the Marquis of Louville and the Princesse des Ursins; the former brought to Spain by Philip himself; the latter sent by Louis XIV as principal lady-in-waiting, or *camarera mayor,* of Queen María Luisa of Savoy, Philip's first wife. Louville did not last long at Court, because he lacked discretion and speedily antagonized first the Spaniards and then his own fellow-countrymen. His attitude toward the King was despotic and humiliating for both the latter and the Queen; as was also that of the Cardinal and Abbé d'Estrées in the years 1703 and 1704. The widowed Mme. des Ursins because of her ability and knowledge of the world, united to an acquaintance with Spanish customs acquired during her marriage to a Spanish Grandee, soon became a dominant influence over the young Queen. The latter, who had married Philip in 1701 when she was not yet fourteen, was possessed of excellent qualities, with a gift for ruling and for making friends. Mme. des Ursins' influence was exercised suavely and discreetly; she was careful not to let it be obvious, which was the reason probably that she retained it longer than did any other of the royal advisers. It is a moot point among historians whether she had a hand in political affairs also; but there is no question of her personal ascendancy with both Philip V and María Luisa, nor of the latter's affection for her. Nor can it be doubted that Mme. des Ursins had much to do with fostering the spread of French culture in Spain, and with the shaping of the Spanish State after the French pattern. Nevertheless, though she had been sent to Madrid as Louis XIV's emissary, she did not abuse her power in prejudice to the young King and Queen. She always took Philip's part in the many controversies with his grandfather, heartening him with her own optimism, even at moments when there was reason to hesitate and fear, and advising him staunchly against abdicating or exchanging the Crown of Spain for some other—as Louis XIV insisted in the end.

In 1704, however, Mme. des Ursins was relieved of her post by the order of Louis XIV, who had been informed by the French Ambassador, Cardinal d'Estrées, and by the Military Attaché that she was responsible for the existing excitation at Court, and had made the monarchs practically "her prisoners." However, Louis soon became convinced that it was impossible to rule Spain without Mme. des Ursins, for whose return, moreover, María Luisa pled ardently. A special envoy sent to Madrid to investigate the matter added his word in favor, and so Mme. des Ursins was reinstated at Court in spite of some secret opposition from Philip V himself who had become jealous of her influence over the Queen. After returning, Mme. des Ursins developed a possessive ambition not formerly in evidence, which led eventually to her downfall.

Among other influential Frenchmen at Madrid were the Ministers Orry and Amelot, and several of the King's confessors; as well as Louis XIV's Ambassadors and the Generals sent on special missions.

However, notwithstanding all this tremendous pressure upon him, and his inborn inclination to yield, Philip V sometimes rebelled against his grandfather's tutelage and clung to his own point of view. Louis XIV, who found that the question of the Spanish succession had involved him in a war full of complications and of military setbacks, tried once more to lighten his load as King of France by sacrificing his grandson and the Spanish State. Accordingly in 1706, wishful of peace, and seeing that France was being bled white by the costs of the war, Louis XIV made overtures for peace to Holland and the Empire, with the proviso that Philip V retain his possessions in Italy. But Philip, with unexpected vehemence, rejected any such arrangement, declaring that he "would not consent to the dismemberment of his States before having known the joy of really possessing them." Not so much Philip's protests as the excessive territorial demands made by Holland caused the negotiations to be broken off. Louis XIV then persuaded Philip to surrender the Spanish possessions in the Low Countries and Italy, and to renounce all claim to the throne of France, while the Duke of Orleans made a corresponding renunciation of any claim to the Spanish throne. However, as regarded his throne of Spain, Philip stood firm, writing to his grandfather on August 6, 1708: "I hope that you will do me the justice to believe that I shall take leave of Spain only when I take leave of life. . . . I prefer to die at the head of my troops, defending my States, rather than to abandon them cravenly."

In all his trials and tribulations, Philip was upheld by the courageous spirit of the Queen, whose devotion to Spain won the love of the Spanish people. When María Luisa's own father, the Duke of Savoy, joined the allies against France and Spain in the War of the Succession, she showed consummate tact and sagacity, not breaking with her family, but voluntarily acquainting Louis XIV with the contents of all her letters to them, and never wavering in steadfast loyalty to the Spanish cause. Unhappily for Philip, María Luisa, whose influence over him was always good and decisive, died in 1714. In December of the same year Philip married Isabella Farnese, Duchess of Parma.

Isabella Farnese, Alberoni, and the Italian Influence

In bringing about the King's remarriage, the paramount influence had been Mme. des Ursins, who believed that she could control Isabella Farnese as she had controlled María Luisa; but in her first interview with the new Queen—who had no intention of being ruled by anyone and who had received many warnings against Mme. des Ursins—the latter was dismissed from Court, with Philip acquiescing.

Isabella Farnese had a far stronger nature than Philip. Endowed with social charms and graces, in spite of her iron will she would make any sacrifice for power and position. She endured all Philip's eccentricities and caprices—which in his frenzies sometimes descended to blows—so long as she could guide his policy and secure the future of her children. Her chief agent and abettor was the Italian Abbé Alberoni who had originally influenced Mme. des Ursins to propose to Philip the marriage with Isabella Farnese. The new policy of the Spanish Court came to be the rupture of close ties with France and the recovery of the lost Italian territories, with the further object of expelling the Austrians from Italy. These were policies that plunged Spain into new wars which the nation seemed little able to carry on; yet such were the talents of Alberoni and the Queen that some slight territorial gains resulted.

The break with France was, in truth, more Philip V's work than Alberoni's. The King, although he had formally renounced his claims on the throne of France, had not relinquished all hope of possessing it. He kept referring to the fact that the renunciation had been forced from him under pressure by Louis XIV and the allied powers. However, when Louis XIV died in September 1715, his will named the

Duke of Orleans as regent for Louis XV, a sickly lad who, far from dying soon as was generally expected, was to reign more than half a century.

By the Treaty of Utrecht, as we have seen, Spain had ceded to England Gibraltar and the Balearic Isle of Minorca, along with the monopoly on importation of Negro slaves into the American colonies. In January 1717 France, England, and Holland made a triple alliance with the main objective of effective maintenance of the Treaty of Utrecht and support of the Royal Houses of England and France.

In order to assure the peace of Europe, it was necessary to secure the adhesion of Philip V of Spain and of the Holy Roman Emperor, Charles VI, who had not made peace with each other and, while not engaged in hostilities, were technically at war. Philip V, averse to the treaty, prepared to fight, but with such secrecy as to deceive the French Regent and the British. Charles VI himself afforded a pretext for the conflict by sending his troops into Genoese territory, negotiating with the Duke of Savoy to exchange Sicily for Sardinia, and harassing at Milan the Spanish inquisitor Molinés. The surprise of the other powers approached stupefaction on August 22, 1717, when they became aware that a strong Spanish expeditionary force which had left Barcelona in July had landed on Sardinia and had the situation well in hand. England, as guarantor of the peace of Italy, made immediate protest, and English and French emissaries asked that hostilities be suspended. They promised Philip the Emperor's renunciation of his claims to the Spanish throne, and offered him the duchies of Parma and Tuscany, and even—though in somewhat vaguer terms—the return to Spain of Minorca and Gibraltar. Alberoni vetoed these proposals, and ordered a second expeditionary force against Sicily (then ruled by the Duke of Savoy) where the Spanish troops, when they landed, were enthusiastically received by the Sicilians, and took possession of the country with the aid of the fleet and of the citizens of Palermo and other towns.

The Triple Alliance of 1717 became Quadruple in 1718 by Austria's entry into it. A treaty of that date established the putative bases of a peace between Philip and the Empire: Spain to return Sardinia and renounce all the Italian States (including Sicily) and the Low Countries; with the Emperor in exchange to renounce his pretensions to the throne of Spain and to Spain's American empire, and to recognize Prince Don Carlos, son of Philip and Isabella Farnese, as heir to

Parma, Placentia, and Tuscany. Philip rejected this proposal, in spite of further intimations by the English Ambassador Stanhope, regarding the possible return to Spain of Minorca and Gibraltar. England thereupon sent a squadron to Sicily with the ostensible purpose of defending the States then belonging to Austria in case peace negotiations should fall through and they should be attacked by the Spaniards. But the secret orders which Admiral John Byng carried were to attack the Spanish fleet in such manner as to make it bear apparent responsibility for the clash. And so, on August 11, while Ambassador Stanhope was still carrying on conversations at Madrid, Byng, without any prior declaration of war, attacked the Spanish navy, destroying it at Cape Passaro near Syracuse, and then landed Austrian troops in Sicily so that they should continue the war. Not content with this, the English Government urged the French Regent to fight Spain. Discovery of a plot by the Spanish Ambassador at Paris to overthrow the Regency was a decisive factor in the French declaration of war against Spain, though this was delayed until January, 1719. England's formal declaration of war had been made on December 28, 1718. Hostilities began in April, with great success for the French who celebrated their victory by burning the arsenal, warehouses and warships at Santoña and Pasajes, with the announced intention of "destroying the Spanish navy in its home port." Spain was outnumbered on every hand. In spite of heroic resistance, she lost Messina to the imperial troops; and the English landed at Vigo, taking the town, though they soon had to abandon it. Unsuccessfully Alberoni sought aid from Russia and Sweden; and his power at Madrid waned as the allies made his dismissal one of the conditions for peace. He left the Ministry, and Spain, in December, 1719. In the peace treaty of January 20, 1720, Philip V declared his adhesion to the Quadruple Alliance.

Reconciliation with France, Abdication of Philip V, and Reign of Luis I

The questions pending between the powers, especially between the King of Spain and the Holy Roman Emperor, as a matter of fact were not settled by simple conformity to the Quadruple Alliance. Other negotiations were necessary to put into effect what the Alliance proposed, and these were slated for discussion at a congress to meet at Cambrai in October of the same year. Meanwhile, France and Spain resumed relations; and a new triple alliance was established of those two powers and England. The Spanish-French treaty was signed March 27, 1721; and the Spanish-French-English, June 13. By the latter England bound herself to restore Gibraltar to Spain; and it was agreed, at Philip V's instance, that the latter's eldest son, Luis, should marry the daughter of the French Regent (Mademoiselle de Montpensier, Louise Isabelle of Orleans), and that Philip's only daughter, María Ana Victoria, should marry King Louis XV of France. By means of these two marriages—and the expected inheritance by Prince Carlos of the promised territories in Italy—the King of Spain felt that he had made sure the future of his descendants and was at length free to realize his deepest desire, the abdication of his throne. In consequence, on July 27, 1720, Philip V and his Queen Isabella Farnese—who interposed no objections at all to his decision—solemnly abjured the throne and were succeeded by their son, Luis I. The double abjuration was repeated after holy communion, at the foot of the altars, on August 15 of the same year and again on August 25, 1721.

Luis I and Louise Isabelle—who became Queen Luisa Isabella—were married early in 1722. Since Luis' little sister, betrothed to the French King, was only four years old, she was sent to France to be educated for her future queendom. Louis XV himself was a lad of twelve.

Philip V's abdication astonished Europe, especially France, where apparently there was considerable doubt as to its sincerity. Some suspected a political motivation. It was in fact hard to believe that the strong-willed, ambitious Queen would have submitted unprotestingly to a life that promised to remain forever devoid of pomp and power. Furthermore Philip's tenacious insistence years earlier, recently repeated, that his own renunciation of claims to the French throne had been a renunciation in words only, gave color to the supposition that some thought in that respect was brewing in his mind. The step down from the Spanish throne might be a step toward the French. Modern historians are still discussing these points at length from opposing camps.

However, Luis I's reign was of brief duration. On August 31, 1724—less than eight months after his accession—he died of smallpox. A few days before his death he made restitution of the throne to his father. Court, clergy, the French Ambassador and Isabella Farnese, all besought Philip V to accept the Crown, which he did reluctantly, his scruples overborne by the decision of a theological commission which declared his vow of abjuration not to be binding, and by the Council of Castile.

The New Agreement with France and the Italian Conquests

Philip V's second reign lasted for twenty-two years, from 1724 to 1746. Queen Isabella Farnese's ambitions with regard to the Italian territories and Philip's with regard to the French sprang up anew. Those two irreducible ambitions, especially the former, together with the conflicting interests of the European powers, explain all that happened during those years.

Philip's return to the throne revived the Queen's ascendancy, which was soon evident in diplomatic relations. Alberoni's place as Isabella Farnese's agent had been taken by Baron Ripperdá, the complete adventurer, who lied and intrigued with easy audacity. He first appeared at the Spanish Court as a Dutch Protestant, Minister from the Low Countries, but soon embraced Catholicism and became a Grandee of Spain. Still later, after having been Premier, only to lose his post when his lies found him out, he was to flee to Africa and become a Moslem. Meanwhile, though Philip had been warned against him, Ripperdá's boldness and perfect *sang-froid,* and the Queen's confidence in him, kept him in power for some years. However, great as were Ripperdá's talents for intrigue, they were unequal to the task that Isabella Farnese set him: to go to Vienna and effect an alliance of Spain with the Emperor, in the interest of furthering Spanish conquests in Italy. In particular, Ripperdá was to bring about the betrothal of the Emperor Charles VI's two daughters with the two sons of Philip and Isabella Farnese. Unable to fulfil any part of his mission, Ripperdá lied magnificently to all concerned. He assured Charles that Philip acceded to all Charles' requests, and pledged Philip that Charles met Philip's every demand. This could not have kept up very long, in the normal course of events; but a new turn of affairs prolonged Ripperdá's reputed diplomatic triumphs.

The incoming Regent of France, the Duke of Bourbon, fearful that the frail Louis XV would die before leaving an heir, and that the French throne would pass in consequence to the House of Orleans, decided to put an end to Louis XV's betrothal to the little Spanish princess María Ana Victoria—who in 1725 was not eight years old. Therefore in March of that year she was returned to her parents, the King and Queen of Spain, so that Louis XV might find a wife of marriageable age. This meant the breaking of relations with Spain, and in natural consequence Philip's representatives abandoned the Congress of Cambrai, and Philip and Charles VI in April 1725 negotiated a treaty of peace and alliance, based on the London pact of 1718 and the Treaty of Utrecht. As a reward for all that he said that he had done, Ripperdá was raised to the rank of official Ambassador to Vienna, and the importance of the treaty made the question of the betrothals a secondary consideration. In a second treaty signed the same day, the Emperor bound himself to employ all his good offices, and to mediate, if the parties so desired, to have England fulfil her pledge to return Gibraltar and Minorca to Spain; while the King of Spain granted free trading rights to Austrian vessels, and both sovereigns pledged mutual defense if either were attacked by a third. There was a further treaty on commerce and navigation even more advantageous to Austria and especially to the Austrian Low Countries. These treaties—which, once their provisions were fully known, caused great discontent in Spain— woke suspicions in other powers; a fact that only served to strengthen relations between Spain and Austria. Ripperdá continued to carry on negotiations for Prince Carlos' marriage to the Austrian Archduchess, continued to be unsuccessful, and continued to inform Philip that all was going well. Another secret treaty of friendship and alliance forbade either the Spanish or the Austrian Royal House to intermarry with the French Bourbons, and ratified the mutual armed defense pact, while Philip V gave extensive trading rights in Spain and the Americas to the Ostend East Indies Company, established in the Austrian Netherlands.

These treaties of 1725 with Austria had important results. On the Peninsula, some Catalán patriots, defrauded of their hopes to have their *fueros* included in the documents, attempted a new uprising, which failed. Among the European powers, the approximation of Spain and Austria brought about a special alliance of France, England, and Prussia which Holland, Sweden, and Denmark soon joined. Those treaties signed at Vienna implied, in fact, a danger for the future balance of power in Europe (because of the possible future union of the Austrian and Spanish Crowns) as well as a special threat to France, whose trade was killed in favor of the Ostend Company, and to England, on account of the unsettled dispute over Gibraltar and Minorca and of the damage to English commerce because of the special trading privileges granted Austria.

The War of Jenkins' Ear; the War with Austria; and the Peace of Aquisgram

Peace did not last for long in Spain. Disputes with England were continuous, especially those arising from English contraband trade in Spanish colonies in America. A treaty looking toward settlement of these differences was signed between the two countries in January 1739, with Spain obligating herself to pay England an indemnity of 95,000 pounds sterling; and it was agreed to hold a conference at Madrid to settle pending complaints and boundary questions. But when the Spanish Government insisted that the English in their turn should pay an indemnity because of the smuggling carried on under cover of the *asiento* treaty, which gave the English the monopoly on importing slaves into the Americas, England responded by threatening war. Walpole, Prime Minister at the time, was opposed to the war-mongering, but his opposition was overborne by public opinion, which had been excited by the propaganda of the merchants who were growing rich on the profits of the West Indian trade, by the exaggerated tales told by the English corsairs about the cruelty of the Spaniards in tracking down smugglers, and by the fiery opposition of Pitt in the House of Commons. A scare-story gave rise to what is called in English (but not in Spanish) history the War of Jenkins' Ear. Robert Jenkins, a one-eared master mariner, appeared before a committee of the House of Commons with what he declared to be his other ear, cut off by Spanish Captain Frandino who was searching Jenkins' ship at Havana for contraband. William Pitt and other imperialists brought about a rapid bombardment of diplomatic notes and threats of reprisals which finally resulted in a declaration of war by England in October 1739. Incidentally, it was proved (and is so duly recorded in English histories) that while Jenkins undoubtedly had suffered the loss of his ear by Spanish steel, it was a pirate who cut it off and the Spanish Government at Havana had punished the pirate.

On November 28, Spain countered with her own declaration of war against England, companioned by a manifesto that recapitulated the innumerable acts of piracy and inhumanity committed by English smugglers in Spain's American colonies, and claims beyond reason made by the English Government. English trade with Spanish possessions was prohibited, and attacks by corsairs on English vessels were authorized. On this occasion, Spain proved by the swiftness and strength of her armaments and operations, principally naval, that the efforts of those of her rulers who had given their attention to restoring the economic forces of the State and regularizing its administration had borne fruit for national defense. It is also true that public opinion was so roused because of the English procedure from first to last that the nation as a whole was this time completely with the Government and eager to fight.

War was not slow in coming, especially to America where the English squadrons, after a vain effort to capture the port of La Guaira in Venezuela, overpowered Porto Bello and sacked the town (November 22, 1739) ; but that was the only advantage obtained in that part of the Indies. The attack against Cartagena attempted soon afterward by Admiral Vernon (who had felt so sure of success that he had had a victory medal struck beforehand) was repulsed by the Viceroy, Don Sebastián de Eslava, with great losses for the English [George Washington's elder brother took part in this battle and later named the Washington estate in Virginia after Admiral Vernon]. The English were defeated likewise in Panama and Cuba. On the Pacific Coast they won only minor victories at Paita and Acapulco. The Spanish corsairs, on the other hand, were taking many prizes and seriously injuring English trade. The principal events in the European theater of conflict were the siege of Gibraltar and Mahon by the Spanish forces; a Spanish naval expedition to Ireland; and a fruitless attempt by the English to blockade El Ferrol. France was Spain's ally in this war.

Such was the state of affairs when the Emperor Charles VI died in October 1740 and the question of the succession to his imperial throne provoked another war. Several kings and princes alleged their right to a share of his realms; among them Philip V, who, urged on by his Queen, renewed his claim to the Italian duchies and other ancient Spanish possessions. The war that broke out was to last for seven years, chequered with a complexity of alliances and vicissitudes. Spain had to fight against Austria and England, chiefly in Italy and the Mediterranean, and as a rule with France as ally. Spanish fortunes varied, but were usually good in the land engagements. Prolongation of the conflict, however, represented greater sacrifices than Spain could then withstand; and public opinion was against continuing it. The French people were also demanding peace. Negotiations to this end were begun in 1746, but Philip V did not see them through. He died of apoplexy in July of that year.

Philip's son and heir, Isabella Farnese's stepson, Ferdinand VI, a pacifist at heart, continued the negotiations and speeded them up. The peace treaty, signed at Aix-la-Chapelle, or Aquisgram, in October 1748 gave Isabella Farnese's son Philip, son-in-law of Louis XV, the duchies of Parma, Placentia, and Guastalla. Charles was affirmed as King of the Two Sicilies; and the disputes with England were settled by the grant of trade advantages to that country; especially with regard to the monopoly privilege of importing Negro slaves into the American colonies. Two years later, in 1750, the *asiento* was liquidated by Spain's payment to England of 100,000 pounds sterling and reaffirmation of English trade privileges. But in so far as Isabella Farnese was concerned, all her ambitions had been achieved.

Administrative Reform and Enlightened Despotism

To offset these many ills, the fact should be stated that the Bourbon kings felt a concern both deep and sincere (considering the limitations of absolute monarchy) with remedying some of the defects from which the Government of Spain was then suffering, particularly in regard to the Treasury (taxes and expenditures). The Bourbons also helped in great measure to rekindle a literary and scientific activity which in some respects came to be as intense as had been the case in the Golden Age. While at first, because of the lowered morale that the decadence had caused throughout the nation, the Bourbon kings made use of foreign experts and advisers (usually French) in these fields, they soon came to depend upon Spaniards, who were well-equipped for carrying out the program that the monarchs had undertaken.

Such were, for example, Zenón de Somodevilla, Marquis of Ensenada, who greatly enlarged the Spanish navy and sponsored construction of many public works; Roda; Pedro Rodríguez, Count of Campomanes, one of the leading economists of his time, especially in the sphere of labor legislation; Francisco Antonio Miranda, Count of Floridablanca, builder of good roads and liberalizer of commerce by the great decree for free trade; the Count of Aranda, to whose reforms in public works was added his unsleeping watch-dog policy in international affairs (in 1775 he forecast that the Thirteen Colonies would become a world power) ; Baltasar Patiño, economic reformer, developer of trade, upbuilder of the armed forces, a man who is remembered also for the honorable distinction that after years in high public office he died poor; and Gaspar Melchor de Jovellanos, man-of-letters, jurist, and economist, enlightened agrarian reformer and zealous exponent of public education. These men and others—some belonging to the nobility, some to the middle class—"intellectuals" and "practical men"—were responsible for many social, economic and political reforms in Spain under the Bourbons.

The Bourbons devoted considerable attention also to the material progress of the country, to industry, commerce, shipping, and very especially to the interests of the working class—the artisans and mechanics. They tried to raise the status of the worker by showing honor for manual labor, which they looked on as being meritorious in itself as well as essential to the prosperity and welfare of the country. In 1778, Charles III proclaimed the principle of civic responsibility in cases of accident occurring on the job.

These progressive and beneficial measures, accompanied by an absolutist method of exercising the royal authority which in certain aspects was even more rigid and personal than had been that wielded by the House of Austria, constituted the Spanish version of "enlightened despotism," a theory and practice of government characteristic of eighteenth century Europe. It is summed up in the formula, "All for the people but not with the people"; which is to say, "Public welfare must be fostered, but the public must be given no participation in government." Philip V's successors, Ferdinand VI and Charles III, were the kings who applied this theory most notably in Spain. The years of peace which the former maintained for the country from 1746 to 1759 contributed greatly to the nation's industrial and commercial resources.

Charles III and England

Consequently, just as the reign of Philip II (1556-1598) was the high-tide of greatness in all the currents of national life during the rule of the House of Austria, Charles III's reign (1759-1788) represented the high-water mark of the economic and cultural renascence in the eighteenth century.

Except for the Peace of Aquisgram, or Aix-la-Chapelle, which ushered it in, Ferdinand VI's reign offered little of importance in international relations. The King was most discreetly neutral, steering clear of the various wars racking Europe and responding to none of the overtures for alliance made him by France and England. His half-brother Charles—King of the Two Sicilies since 1735—succeeded Ferdinand on the throne in 1759, ceding his own Kingdom to his third son, Ferdinand.

Like his predecessor Ferdinand VI, Charles sincerely loved peace. His Queen Doña Amalia cherished the same sentiment. But upon both King and Queen was imposed the inescapable necessity of defending Spain's New World dominions against the ambitious designs of England. The English Government and the English merchant class desired to possess the greatest possible number of colonies with the object of extending their commerce beyond that of any other nation. A huge barrier in their way was Spain's rich dominion in the Americas, with Spanish colonies including most of the territory there. The new strength of the Spanish navy, brought about during Ferdinand VI's reign, also disquieted England. In consequence, practically every act of the English Government with relation to the Americas was directed toward stirring up difficulties between Spain and the Spanish colonies in the Western Hemisphere and toward occupying Spanish terrain whenever possible, in addition to encouraging contraband trade. These were the causes that led Charles III, despite his innate pacifism, to ally himself with France, and that ultimately produced new wars with England.

One interesting episode of those wars was the financial and military aid given by Spain to the English colonies in America during the Revolution that they fought for their independence. Apart from this, Charles III on two occasions tried to mediate between the Thirteen Colonies and England in the interests of their independence (though not of that of Canada) ; an independence that they themselves achieved in 1783, and which brought into being the United States of America.

The Family Pact and the First War with England

Charles III changed the orientation of international politics by the alliance of Spain and France. The reasons set forth in detail in the following paragraph motivated this change and gave rise to the Franco-Spanish alliance, which was called the Family Pact.

At first, Charles III was a partisan of peace. So, even more decidedly, was Queen Amalia. She had a great deal to do with Charles' rejection of the initial French proposals. But neither she nor her husband could be unaware that at that time England was Spain's strongest enemy, and was seeking every possible occasion for striking at Spanish colonial power and impeding the new development of Spanish shipping and commerce, which had made rapid strides in the thirteen years of Ferdinand VI's reign, as we have seen. In fact, English ambition to possess the greatest colonial empire of the world necessarily found in the Spanish provinces of America a barrier for which the commercial advantages in the recent treaties were not sufficient compensation. Every extension of English dominion and operations in the New World was inevitably at the expense of Spain. Consequently, to undermine Spanish strength was a political and economic necessity for England. The latter's conduct, after 1702, reflected clearly a consciousness of that necessity. Of course, every advance in Spain's naval power and wealth was a fresh obstacle in England's way. Queen Amalia herself, though by natural inclination very friendly toward the English people, recognized the danger that this state of things represented for Spain. "London," she said, "needs to feel a telling blow; otherwise she will be insupportable, deeming herself mistress of the world." Proof of the Queen's discernment was the overbearing arrogance with which the English Government rejected Charles III's offer of mediation, made at the instance of France and Austria, in an effort to end the war. The Queen's death in 1760 freed Charles III, who had an even clearer perception than she of the inherent danger, from the restraining influence that she had exercised as much for her love of peace as for her aversion to France. Meanwhile, the French Government increased its efforts for an alliance with Charles III which was urgently necessary to it because of the defeats suffered in the latest, not yet ended, war with England. The Spanish monarch likewise had very strong reasons, besides those already mentioned, for seeking an ally in prevision of very possible conflicts with the English. As a matter of fact, the latter had seized a piece of territory in peninsular Spain, on the River Tinto, and was very loath to give it up. The English continued their smuggling and acts of aggression in Spain's American colonies; placed difficulties in the way of Spanish fishing off Newfoundland; founded settlements for cutting dyewoods in Honduras, without permission from Spain, and in defiance of Spanish rights; and discriminated against Spanish merchants in the British Isles. Furthermore British vessels harassed our Spanish boats without motive; and there was even a personal element to include in the score, since Charles himself had suffered, and did not forget, British affronts in the Italian wars during his fathers' reign.

However, the actual initiative for the Franco-Spanish alliance was taken by France early in 1761. The Spanish Ambassador Grimaldi opined that "it was helpful to have a defensive alliance obligating France to aid the King of Spain in the event some enemy molested him in the Americas," but without reciprocal aid from Spain for the war which, despite pending peace negotiations, still existed between France and England. In reality, it was Charles III's intention, if he did not obtain satisfaction from the English Government for his claims through diplomatic channels for indemnities, to declare war the following year; and that was the spirit presiding over negotiations for the Family Pact between Grimaldi and the French Minister Choiseul. The first consequence was that France declared to representatives of the English Government with whom she was also negotiating that she supported Spain's claims for indemnities, namely: restoration of Spanish vessels that had been seized despite Spain's neutrality, free access of Spanish fishing boats to Newfoundland waters, and abandonment of English logging camps in Honduras. The English Government refused to include consideration of Spanish petitions in the negotiations with France, though taking occasion to state that there would never be any yielding with regard to Newfoundland fishing rights, and to demand an explanation for Spain's maritime armaments. Such an attitude increased the probabilities of war, so the Family Pact was signed by France and Spain on August 15, 1761. It comprised two treaties, the second bearing the date February 4, 1762. The first treaty was the one of friendship and union, on the basis that "who attacks one, attacks the other." The second was the treaty "of offensive and defensive alliance," directed expressly against England.

The break came very soon. England declared war January 2, 1762, and Spain responded with a like declaration January 16. Louis XV and Charles III asked Portugal to join the alliance but she elected to remain neutral, which was equivalent to aiding the English; so the French and Spanish Ambassadors withdrew from Lisbon. Operations commenced in Portugal in May, with success for the Spanish Army, which captured Almeida and other fortified towns, though later on Anglo-Portuguese troops obtained some minor advantages.

In the Americas the most notable campaigns were the attack on Havana by the British fleet and that city's surrender on August 12, 1762 after heroic resistance; and the Spanish conquest of Sacramento, a Portuguese settlement on the River Plate, with the capture as well of 27 richly laden English vessels; a victory that frustrated a projected Anglo-Portuguese expedition to seize the River Plate territories.

In the Philippines, despite the fact that Manila was taken by the English, the *Oidor* Don Simón de Anda organized resistance in the form of guerrilla warfare, inflicting severe losses on the enemy. But about mid-year peace began to be talked. France hoped for it, because the war was going against her; and that desire was becoming more evident in negotiations with England. In Spain some elements of public opinion were favorable, at least, to strong coastal defenses. The peace treaty finally signed at Paris on February 10, 1763 established the following provisions with respect to Spain: the questions relating to prize-ships taken by England in time of peace were to be submitted to English Admiralty Courts, and England was to demolish "all the fortifications that her subjects may have constructed on the bay of Honduras and other Spanish districts in that part of the world," but on condition that English citizens be permitted to continue to cut and transport logwood, or dyewood; that Spain withdraw all claims to fishing rights off Newfoundland; that England restore the territory which she had conquered in Cuba; and that Spain cede Florida to England, including the Fort of St. Augustine and Pensacola Bay as well as the whole of the Spanish territory east and southeast of the Mississippi River. Sacramento on the River Plate was returned to Portugal, and the Philippines to Spain. Such was the disadvantageous result of that first war, from which Spain obtained nothing more than demolition of the English outposts in Honduras and the cession from France of the Louisiana Territory (November 3, 1762). As a matter of fact, Louisiana—which France had already tried to cede to England in the preliminary peace negotiations—though it comprised a vast expanse of territory, lacked value as a colonial possession for the French. The cession of Louisiana to Spain was not effected until 1764, and as the colonists there refused to accept the new dominion, it was necessary to bring them to terms by force of arms (June, 1769).

The Mutiny of Esquilache and Its Consequences

Charles III had come to Madrid from Naples accompanied as personal secretary by the Marquis de Squillaci who had been his Minister there. One of Charles' first acts as King of Spain was to give Squillaci—whose name Spaniards Hispanicized into "Esquilache"—a Ministerial post. Squillaci enthusiastically set about decreeing reforms and, going beyond reforms as such, decreed also measures regarding public order and compliance with the laws (such as paying taxes, and other matters), and undertook a campaign to rout out malefactors. These measures did not meet with that public approval which he had expected. People viewed him with suspicion because he was a foreigner, since they had no taste for being governed by politicians who came in now from France, now from Italy or elsewhere. The Spanish people remembered perfectly the excellent Spanish officials of Philip V's and Ferdinand VI's reigns. Furthermore, Squillaci's luxurious style of living and lavish household caused the public to suspect him of immorality; and the truth is that his former reputation at the Court of Naples in no wise allayed such suspicions. Above all, it was Squillaci's misfortune that his six years in the Ministry of Finance coincided with an extraordinary drought, which caused the price of bread and other foods to rise; with many of the public unjustly blaming Squillaci's bad administration for the high prices. This was set forth in a document presented to the King toward the close of 1765 by some *"leales vasallos"* —loyal subjects—in which the Finance Minister was blamed for all the public ills and accused of tyranny. The public was consequently ready to demonstrate against Squillaci whenever a propitious occasion should present. It came in the guise of an order, more indiscreet than harmful, relating to dress.

It is a well-known fact that on different occasions in past centuries legislation had tried to prohibit both men and women from covering their faces with shawls or scarfs or cloaks, or hats with turned-down brims. Between 1713 and 1745 several edicts prohibiting such attire, which lent itself easily to disguise, were issued; all to no avail. Because it would be a help in routing out criminals to see their faces clearly, without concealment, Charles III, at Squillaci's instigation, on January 22, 1766 dictated a Royal Order prohibiting soldiers and government employees from wearing the long cape and the broad-brimmed hat; decreeing instead a short cape or riding-coat; a small wig, or peruke, or else no wig at all; and a tricorne, or three-cornered hat. The order was obeyed, as were instructions to the same effect sent by Squillaci in a personal letter to Deputies of the Five Greater Guilds of Madrid; but not content with this, the Minister asked to have the regulation extended from government employees to the general public. In its final form, the order prohibited government employees, members of the middle class, and servants from wearing the long Spanish cape and the broad-brimmed hat, and forbade the poor to wear the latter. The infuriated public replied with lampoons, petitions of protest, and street clashes between bailiffs and the people. Many persons in Madrid were jailed, and groups of citizens in long capes worn in the typical face-concealing manner of tradition paraded defiantly past their prisons. An organization "in defense of King and Country, formed by Spanish zeal to end and throw out the oppression that is attempting to violate these realms" demanded the resignation of Squillaci and his colleague Grimaldi. On March 23, 1766 these protests became an insurrection—the "Mutiny of Esquilache"—which attacked Squillaci's home, stoned Grimaldi, emptied the prisons, fought the Palace guards and especially the hated Walloon infantrymen, several of whom they killed, and obliged the Duke of Medinaceli to present their grievances to Charles III. Squillaci and his family were exiled from Spain in consequence; foreign Ministers were replaced by Spaniards; the order against long cape and broad-brimmed hat was rescinded; and the Count of Aranda was named Premier. In a typically Spanish gesture, the latter achieved Squillaci's original purpose very easily and painlessly: he made the long cape and broad-brimmed hat the official uniform of the public executioner.

The Falkland Islands; the War in Brazil; and the Expeditions against Morocco and Algiers

While the treaty signed at Paris in 1763 had put an end to the war with England which had been commenced the preceding year, it did not settle the disputes between Spain on the one hand and England and Portugal on the other; nor much less did it allay English antipathy and resentment toward Charles III. It was obvious that another clash would not be long in coming.

In truth the English made no effort to avoid it. Hardly had the treaty been signed when they began again to cut and ship the valuable dyewoods from Honduras, giving rise to new Spanish reclamations. At this juncture there occurred what is known as the incident of the Malvinas, or Falkland Islands. The Malvinas (Falklands is their English name) are an island group off the coast of South America, some two hundred and forty miles east of the Strait of Magellan, with a total area of about five thousand square miles. They seem to have been discovered by the first Spanish sailors who rounded Cape Horn in the sixteenth century, who wrote out a detailed description of the isles, under the name of the Isles of Lions, for the Secretariat for the Indies. Later, English, French and Dutch mariners visited the group; and in 1763 the Spanish pilot Santos Mathei again claimed the islands for Spain, but his intention to establish a settlement was forestalled by a French expedition under Bougainville which founded a town on the largest island in 1764. Spain immediately presented her claim to all the islands to the French Government, which in 1766 formally ceded them back to Spain. Meanwhile, ignoring both French and Spanish titles, the English Commodore Byron had occupied one of the small islands of the group, building at Port Egmont not only houses but a fort with a battery of 24 cannon. When the newly appointed Spanish Governor, Felipe Ruíz Puente, demanded that the English withdraw, the English Governor replied that the islands belonged to his own sovereign and gave the Spaniards six months in which to evacuate them. Ruíz Puente reported these facts to Don Francisco Bucareli, Captain-General at Buenos Aires (of which Province the Islands were a dependency). England's position was diplomatically untenable, since in 1748 she had made formal recognition of Spanish right to the Malvinas; but, tenable or not, she held to it. Spain claimed France's assistance under the Family Pact. Meanwhile, Bucareli sent out an expeditionary force from Buenos Aires, which arrived at the Islands in June 1770 and on the tenth of that month forced the surrender of the English garrison, who were returned to England on the gunboat *Favorita* in September. The occurrence produced great excitement there, where the whole affair was regarded as an insult; and there were vociferous demands for an immediate declaration of war against Spain. War would have broken out, in fact (the respective Ambassadors had been recalled), had not the King of France sent word to Charles III that he opposed hostilities and counselled a sacrifice in order to avoid a clash. Thus deserted by his ally, the Spanish King had no recourse but to resume negotiations with England and cede back to that country that portion of the Falkland Islands from which the English troops had been ousted. The specific reservation was made, nevertheless, that this cession in no wise affected Spanish sovereignty over the rest of the Malvinas. The Malvinas—or Falklands—however, remained but briefly in English hands at that time. When the latter abandoned them in 1774, the Spanish repossessed the Islands and continued in undisputed possession, in spite of new wars with the English, until the establishment of Argentine independence. Argentina then occupied the Islands, claiming them by virtue of the fact that they had been a colonial dependency of Buenos Aires. Nevertheless, since 1833 the Falklands have again been in possession of England.

The next incident was with Portugal. The question of the boundary line between Spanish and Portuguese possessions in South America gave rise to endless disputes. Through the influence of his mother, Doña Bárbara de Braganza, and of the English Ambassador Keene, Ferdinand VI had tried to settle those questions by a treaty (January 13, 1750), which gave to Spain the Portuguese colony of Sacramento on the eastern bank of the River Plate, while Portugal acquired certain Spanish territories on the Brazilian frontier. This treaty, however, was strongly opposed by the Marquis of Ensenada, Minister of State and of the Indies; the Governor of Buenos Aires; the Jesuit missionaries who had established large Indian settlements in Paraguay; and the Paraguayan Indians—the Guaraní—who lived in the mission settlements. The opposition of all those elements was united, unquestionably at the more or less direct instigation of the Jesuits. The treaty in truth was highly disadvantageous for Spain; not only because of the loss of colonized territories necessary for the economic existence of the missions in Paraguay, but also, a consideration of even greater force, because by multiplying the points of contact between Portuguese possessions and Spanish, it greatly facilitated smuggling by the former. Resistance to the treaty flamed into war, which the Jesuits alleged that they were unable to prevent, and which the Spanish settlers and the

Guaraní Indians of Paraguay carried on until 1759 against joint forces of the Spanish and Portuguese Governments charged with escorting the commissions who were fixing the boundaries, and with carrying out provisions of the treaty. Finally, in 1761, with José I on the throne of Portugal and Charles III succeeding Ferdinand in Spain, the treaty of 1750 was annulled: which left the question of Sacramento as much a moot point as ever.

José I's Minister Cavalho, better known in history by his later title as Marquis de Pombal, was ambitious to extend Portugal's dominions in South America. Portuguese colonists and officials in Brazil continued to seize Spanish frontier districts, especially along the River Plate and in the Jesuit missions in Paraguay. The Portuguese looted the latter of a half million head of cattle and carried off seven thousand Guaraní families as slaves. All Spanish claims upon that score were answered evasively or negatively by the Portuguese Government which at the same time encouraged the Brazilians in their depredations. In February 1776 several Portuguese warships attacked Spanish vessels at Rio Grande do Sul, and soon afterwards captured the Fort of Santa Tecla. The patience of Charles III and his Ministers was at an end. In November of that year they sent a strong expeditionary force to Brazil. It captured the Island of Santa Catalina, and the town of Sacramento (destroying its fortifications), and was preparing to attack Rio Grande do Sul when a cease fire order arrived; in virtue of a new treaty between Spain and Portugal. The pact had come about because of the death of King José, whose sister María Victoria became regent and promptly dismissed Pombal, prime mover of the conflict with Spain. This Treaty of 1777 returned the Sacramento territory to Spain and afforded other advantages: Portugal's renunciation of any rights that the Treaty of Tordesillas in 1494 might have given her to the Philippines, Falklands, and other islands; and acquisition by Spain of the Portuguese islands of Annobon and Fernando Po off Africa; as well as trading rights in ports and along coasts of the African littoral.

While these questions were being debated with England and with Portugal, Spanish arms were engaged in other undertakings in North Africa, where the Moroccans and the Algerian pirates continued to menace Spain. Ever since 1694 the Moroccans had been laying siege to Ceuta. Hoping to put an end to this situation, in 1720 Spain sent out an expeditionary force of 16,000 troops supported by a fleet, which raised the siege and put the Moroccans to flight. In 1732 another expetionary force of 26,000 troops, 600 sails, and many cannon captured the fortified city of Oran. This African conflict continued in Ferdinand VI's reign as the only exception to his policy of peace; an exception of which the necessity was made clear in a letter from the Marquis of Mina, Viceroy of Catalonia, to Ensenada (November, 1750) : "My post teaches me to be on the alert and keep troops ready to prevent the pirates from defying our coasts, sacking our houses and the settlements on the shore, and surprising wayfarers in lonely places. And all this has happened more than once, and is no figment of panic nor terror nor is it exaggerated zeal." At the initiative of the Marquis of Ensenada, Spain after 1748 kept up a continuous patrol of the Barbary coast, which gave rise to several clashes with the pirates, including some major engagements. In 1767 the Sultan of Morocco sent a peace embassy to Charles III and agreed to abandon piracy and to grant free trade and certain exclusive fishing rights to Spain, along with other advantages; but in 1774 the Sultan notified Charles III of his intention to recover the sites occupied by the Spanish on the African littoral, and forthwith began the siege of Melilla. The Moroccans were unsuccessful in this, as they were likewise at Gomera and Alhucemas. Spain then decided to attack the pirate stronghold of Algiers. In June 1775 the talented Irish adventurer, General Alejandro O'Reilly, with a squadron of 49 warships, 384 transports and 18,000 troops attacked the city; but the expedition, in spite of O'Reilly's military fame and his prestige as reorganizer of the Spanish Army, was a disastrous failure, suffering 5,000 casualties. In 1783 and 1784 Algiers underwent two further bombardments by the Spanish fleet which did not however put an end to piracy. Nevertheless the intensified military preparations by Spain finally decided the Algerians to come to terms, in the Treaty of June 14, 1786, by which they agreed to stop piracy and the enslaving of Spanish captives, and to permit establishment of a Spanish consulate at Algiers with religious freedom for resident Spaniards. There were similar agreements, at earlier and later dates, with Tunis, Tripoli, and Turkey. So ended the aggressions of the Barbary pirates, which had harassed the seas and coasts of Spain ever since the time of Charles I and which had so long and so seriously threatened the nation.

Spanish Intervention in the American Revolutionary War against England

Naturally, the war of 1762-63 with England intensified Spanish enmity toward that country, and it was to be supposed that Charles III and his Ministers would take advantage of a favorable opportunity for revenge. France held similar sentiments. The opportunity came in 1773 with the first uprising of the English colonies in North America. That was the year of the Boston Tea Party, when a British ship's cargo of tea was tossed into Boston Harbor as a gesture of defiance against the tax on tea; and in 1774 the First Continental Congress met. The French Government at once suggested that Spain break off relations with England and aid the American revolutionists as France herself was doing surreptitiously. Both Minister Grimaldi and the Count of Aranda, at that time Spanish Ambassador in Paris, favored these moves; though Grimaldi and Charles III, believing the time unpropitious, opposed giving such ostensible motives for provoking war. Aranda, however, resolute in the matter, had other reasons for concern with respect to the English colonies in America, since he believed (as set forth in his despatch of August, 1775) that whichever way the victory went, for England or for her colonies, it would prove dangerous for Spain. These English colonies, he averred, independent or not, "in the course of time, because of their position and with increase of population, would be our rivals." For their part, the North American colonies sent to Europe representatives commissioned to negotiate for aid from the powers there, without obstacle to other conversations which had been begun in August 1776 with Spanish officials at New Orleans. Benjamin Franklin was appointed on a secret mission to the Spanish Government, but did not make the journey, remaining at Paris and sending Arthur Lee in his stead. The latter, brother of Richard Henry and Francis Lightfoot Lee, had been appointed a secret agent by the Continental Congress the preceding year. He arrived at Madrid early in 1777 but because of the Spanish Government's diplomatic scruples remained a short time only. In fact, Grimaldi had been succeeded in the Ministry by Floridablanca, who, like the King, was unwilling to force an immediate break with England and notified Aranda that he should not agree to any action in common with the French Cabinet since it was to Spain's advantage to act independently, without ceasing to maintain friendly relations with France. This withdrawal was barely in time, if real neutrality were to be maintained, since Grimaldi —with the King's acquiescence— had already been giving undercover aid to the American revolutionists. He had sent them through the French as intermediaries one million *livres tournois* in June 1776, which was followed toward the close of the year by various shipments of arms, munitions and other war materièl. These were sent out from Spanish ports to Havana and transshipped to New Orleans. Lee was promised more assistance of this nature and was given letters of credit to the amount of 50,000 *pesos*. As 1777 drew to its close, with Florida-blanca in the Ministry, Charles III promised the agents of the North American colonies up to six million *pesos* additional, on condition of inviolable secrecy; and authorized the Bilbao merchant Gardoqui to arrange with the banker Grand, who was in the confidence of the American revolutionists, for the importation into Spain of tobacco and other American products in return for Spanish assistance. On March 24, 1778 additional promises were made of supplies to be sent via Havana. Ostentatiously Floridablanca reinforced the naval stations in Spain's American colonies and put the fleet in fighting condition in order to insure the regular remission of treasure from the Spanish colonies and the safe return of the expeditionary force sent to Brazil, as well as to be prepared for any eventuality. At the same time he demanded indemnities from England for attacks by English corsairs on Spanish vessels in American waters.

When matters were at this stage, France, throwing off all reserve, but without forewarning to Spain, in February 1788 concerted a treaty of peace and commerce with the English colonies which by this time already called themselves the United States. This treaty involved recognition of the autonomy of the United States and its immediate consequence was war between France and England. Both countries, with equal insistence and urgency, sought aid of the Spanish Government; but the latter refused both alike, resenting the French Government's concealment of its dealings with the American colonies (though many explanations were proffered) and still undecided as to whether to break with England. As Floridablanca wrote to Aranda, "We neither desire war nor fear it."

Spain felt suspicious of France's good faith, suspecting that the latter would leave her in the lurch whenever it profited French interests to do so (despatch of April, 1778). What Spain finally resolved to do was to advance the idea of acting as mediator for peace, an offer refused by England. As a matter of fact, Charles III did not give up entirely all thought of aid to France, but resolved to intervene at the opportune moment (Floridablanca's despatch to Aranda, August 25, 1778). However, he made, and failed in, a second attempt at mediation. Thereupon Spain proposed that England elect one of the following measures: concession by England to her American colonies of a truce of 25 or 30 years which would give time to decide serenely upon the peace terms; a truce with France, the American colonies being also included; appointment of a joint commission, with representatives of England, France, and the American colonies, to discuss peace terms. The proposal was made January 20, 1779. England delayed reply until March; and this delay—with tension growing all the time because of the incessant attacks of English corsairs on Spanish merchant ships—as well as the form that the answer took, angered Charles III so greatly that he strengthened relations with France, made ready for war, and sent the English Government an ultimatum on April 3 in which he asked for a categorical reply to various questions. A few days later (April 12) a secret treaty with France was signed at Aranjuez in which it was agreed that if England rejected the ultimatum, Spain too would declare war against that country. Special objectives in such event, it was further agreed, would be the restoration to Spain of Gibraltar, Pensacola and the whole of the Florida coast, Minorca, the fort and river of Mobile in Alabama, and the expulsion of the English from Honduras with revocation of the license granted them to cut dyewoods there. This treaty was a victory of the war policy which Aranda had supported consistently and which was now upheld as zealously by Father Osma, the King's Confessor. Nevertheless, Charles III was dilatory in starting hostilities, though now even Floridablanca was urging him on. The English themselves took the initiative, foreseeing the inevitable, and prepared to make two attacks: one on the Philippine Islands and the other on Nicaragua. When the Spanish Government learned of these preparations and received the suave rejection of its ultimatum, the Spanish Ambassador was recalled from London and a formal declaration of war against England was made on June 23, 1779.

Spain was very well prepared this time. One favoring factor was the good relations then existing with Portugal, so that England could not use that country as base of operations as had been done in former conflicts. Helpful too were other alliances and treaties of friendship with European and Asiatic sovereigns. The campaign plans mapped out by Spain and France included, among other things, the invasion of England and the reconquests of Gibraltar and Minorca. The threatened invasion, which caused great alarm in England, was frustrated by the combination of stormy weather which made fleet operations difficult; a violent epidemic of scurvy afflicting both soldiers and sailors; slow movements of the fleet; tactical errors of the French Admiral d'Orvilliers; the great ability of the English Admiral Hardy; and Franco-Spanish bad management. The expedition, which set out in June, had returned to the French coast by September 13 without having accomplished anything worth while beyond keeping the English navy in port, thus insuring safe arrival at Peninsular ports of Spain's American fleet, and preventing England from sending troops against the Revolutionary Army of the Continental Congress. The attack on Gibraltar commenced in July with a blockade; but in January 1780, when the besieged were on starvation rations, an English fleet—which had previously vanquished a Spanish naval force very inferior in numbers at Cape St. Vincent—entered the port with abundant supplies. Though the city was surrounded and bombarded in 1781, neither that action nor further efforts in 1782, nor the employment against it of floating batteries, a recent invention of the Spanish mariner Barceló and the Frenchman D'Arçon, had the expected success (the battery in fact was a gigantic failure) . The siege continued fruitlessly until the war ended. Minorca, however, was reconquered, without great effort, in February 1782. In the Americas the fortunes of war were in general with the Spanish. They reconquered Florida, seized the dyewood establishments in Honduras, and expelled the English from the Bahamas. There was no action in the Philippines.

The war ended in January 1783 with a preliminary treaty to suspend hostilities. So far back as November 1779 England had made direct peace overtures to Spain, offering to return Gibraltar in exchange for Spanish neutrality, and furthermore to hand over Florida to Spain and recognize Spanish fishing rights in Newfoundland waters, if Spain would assist England against the United States. Twice these offers had been renewed, the second time through medium of a regularly appointed commissioner, Mr. R. Cumberland, who in 1780-81 made every effort to create bad feeling between Spain and France, calling the attention of the Spanish Government to the fact that it would approach the peace table in more favorable conditions than France because it had never dealt directly with the American revolutionists. These English efforts all failed for the same reason: England would not yield on what was to Spain an essential point: protection of the honor of France and fidelity to Spanish agreement with that country. Moreover, Cumberland's arguments, while favorable to Spain, were not wholly exact; because the Spanish Government had not only dealt with American revolutionary agents who had come to Spain (John Jay and his secretary, William Carmichael) but had had its own agents in the United States (Miralles and Rendón); besides which Bernardo de Gálvez (one of the most resolute and able of the Spanish Generals in the war in the American zone) at New Orleans gave aid to agents and friends of the Continental Congress.

The failure of Cumberland's mission stimulated France to give a greater degree of assistance toward reconquest of Gibraltar and of Minorca. In 1781 Austria and Russia made new offers of mediation, in which they were joined by Prussia; but England rejected them. Finally the English Government decided to deal directly with France and Spain at Paris, and it was there that the preliminary treaty referred to was signed, because of hasty, ill-considered, and unauthorized action by Aranda in renouncing Spain's demand for the restitution of Gibraltar. Aranda based his decision on the fact that England flatly refused to return the Rock unless she received in exchange Puerto Rico from Spain or Guadeloupe from France—and there was no doubt of France's refusal to sacrifice Guadeloupe for Spain's sake; nor was Spain willing to yield up Puerto Rico. In spite of the very bad impression caused at Court by Aranda's relinquishment of Gibraltar, the preliminary treaty was accepted. The final treaty was signed at Versailles September 3, 1783. One year previous, in November, 1782, England had recognized the independence of the United States. By the Versailles treaty Spain recovered Minorca and the whole territory of Florida; and limited English dyewood privileges in Honduras to a fixed term of years. Spain restored to England the Bahamas and New Providence Island in the Caribbean. A second treaty, on July 14, 1786, fixed the limits of Spain's American possessions. On December 14, 1788, Charles III died and his son Charles IV succeeded him as King of Spain.

Gregorio Hernández: *St. Teresa.*

The Enlightened Despotism of Charles III and His Ministers

Notwithstanding these martial preoccupations, Charles III, as we have noted, was the Bourbon king who interested himself most actively in the development of culture, commerce, and industry. He may therefore be regarded as the prime embodiment, among Spaniards, of that *enlightened despotism* to which we have previously referred. In carrying out its precepts his efforts were ably seconded by his Spanish Ministers, Counts de Aranda and Floridablanca, and by the Marquis of Grimaldi, who was Italian.

The same ideas are represented in the organizations of very distinguished membership called *Sociedades Económicas de Amigos del País*—Economic Societies of Friends of the Country; the first of which was founded at Biscay in 1746. By 1804, seventy-two of these organizations had been created. They established centers for teaching industrial uses of applied science in such technical fields as chemistry, machinery, agriculture, textiles, and draughtsmanship. They likewise made experiments in land cultivation, silk manufacture, and other fields. For its part, the Government built model factories, including those for glass, cabinetry, and tapestries, at Madrid; two for woven stuffs and fine fabrics, at Guadalajara and Segovia; the glass-works at San Ildefonso (La Granja) ; the factories for hats at San Fernando, cotton textiles at Avila, porcelain at Buen Retiro in Madrid; the brass foundry at Alcaraz; and the Model Farm at Aranjuez.

Among the various examples that might be cited to show the productive economic ideas that were typical of Spanish administration at that period, note should be made of Floridablanca's program, which included securing new markets and ports for our shipping in the Mediterranean by taking advantage of the opportunity afforded by peace with Turkey. The commercial importance of the Black Sea at that time was very great. The program of Minister Patiño was a parallel example with respect to the American trade.

Campomanes and Labor Education

It is clear, from what has been said already, that the ends chiefly desired were the revival of industries and the establishment of professional or technical training for the worker; and in consequence, a higher scale of living for him. This is very clearly set forth in *Discurso*

Alonso Berruguete: *Adoration of the Three Kings, or Wise Men from the East.*

sobre el fomento de la industria popular (Address on Fostering Popular Industry) and *Discurso sobre la educación popular de los artesanos y su fomento* (Address on Public Education for Artisans and Its Development) , works published during Charles III's reign and written by the Asturian counselor Don Pedro Rodríguez de Campomanes, then the chief authority on these matters and prime mover in making the industrial revival as complete and effective as possible. Later on, as we shall see, another Asturian, Jovellanos, Charles IV's Minister, voiced the same aspirations.

Agricultural Colonies in Spain

Charles III was deeply interested in agriculture also, and particularly in bringing into production much land that was still uncultivated. The method of achieving this was to establish settlers in underpopulated areas, and to distribute plots of land and help them acquire what they needed for prospering in their labors. The plan, in other words, was to carry out an *internal colonization* of the Peninsula. The best example of such "colonization" undertaken by the Crown in Charles III's time is the project at Sierra Morena. Six thousand German and Flemish laborers were brought in for it, in addition to the Spanish workers, and fifteen new towns were constructed in conformity with principles laid down by Campomanes. Some of these towns survive, among them La Carolina, in Jaen. The example of Sierra Morena inspired several private landholders who likewise established "colonies" on their own properties. The most important of such were the colony on lands close by Orihuela sponsored by Cardinal Belluga, out of which grew the present towns of Dolores, San Felipe Neri, and San Fulgencio; and the one established by Don Felipe Solesco, who on his estates in Andalusia set out 200,000 grapevines and many fruit trees—12,000 mulberries, 5,000 olives, and 580 figs, and numerous others—giving employment to 800 laborers and 12 overseers. Furthermore, the Government ordered all the *Ayuntamientos,* or City Councils, to plant every year in their respective localities a fixed number of trees; a regulation which gave rise to the annual celebration of Arbor Day which has since been adopted in many countries of both hemispheres. At the same time, an effort was made to bring about a revival of stockraising, then greatly on the decline. However, there was restriction of some of the privileges of the *Mesta*, or General Association of Sheep and Cattle Raisers, which were prejudicial to the laborers.

Social Classes and Institutions

Fundamentally there was no legal nor social change affecting Spanish society from 1700 to 1808, except in the case of the rural population of Aragón. The privileges which marked the difference between the nobles and the common people continued practically the same as in the preceding period, as did the hierarchy within the nobility itself. Nevertheless, there was an indefinite but widely diffused democratic sentiment which rarely passed beyond what was then termed "philanthropy," a vague sentimental love of mankind which was translated into a desire for economic and material betterment of the people without ever arriving at the concept of equality before the law which was later to be proclaimed. Nevertheless, it was a sentiment that had an ameliorating and humanizing effect on social relationships. This was evidenced especially by interest in public education, by legislation to foster industry and agriculture, by the foundation of workshops and factories, and by a certain sentimentality that would later fructify into doctrines of true democratic feeling which in the eighteenth century had only legislative expression.

However, the nobility continued in enjoyment of all its ancient legal and economic privileges. The nobles had a pride of birth and a sense of rank that was almost an obsession. In 1754 Ferdinand VI declared that all the Biscayans were nobles by right and so entitled to a hidalgo's privileges. Since there were many petitions from persons who wished to have their *hidalguía*, or rank as *hidalgos*, established, a Royal Order of January 6, 1758 required payment of a large sum when the petitioner's *hidalguía* derived from "the fourth or fifth generation." In 1785 the King ordered that the concession of *hidalguía* should not be requested except in cases where "personal merits should be united to services" to king or country sufficient to compensate for the losses to the State which the hidalgo's financial and other exemptions would involve. There was a similar law regarding titles of Castile. Nevertheless, the kings did their part to stimulate this pride of rank, creating or reviving distinctions and bestowing titles of Castile for services to the Crown. This was the epoch of, for example, the Marquis of the Royal

Transport (*Transporte Real*), the Marquis of the Guarantee (*Garantía*), the Prince of the Peace, and such like. Charles III created the Order that bears his name with 60 Grand Crosses and 200 Knights, which in later years was greatly enlarged and very liberally conceded. Charles IV founded the Order of Noble Dames of María Luisa. Several Equestrian Societies of noblemen—*Maestranzas*—were organized, which, among other privileges, prevented suits for criminal action against the members, their wives, and one of their servants. Even degraded nobles enjoyed the privileges of nobility. For instance, a *Cédula* of 1781 provided that nobles arrested "as vagabonds and evildoers" should be sent to the Army with the qualification of "distinguished soldiers."

The Grandees of Spain and other nobles with seignorial estates continued in possession of their ancient jurisdictional rights, especially that of appointing most municipal officials: in 1787 seignorial rights (in some instances divided between King and Lord) were exerted over 17 cities, 2,358 *villas*, and 8,818 villages and towns. There were also certain monopolies in favor of the Lords, such as those of hunting, fishing, the baking of bread, the milling of flour, rights to streams and forests, and so on; just as in the Middle Ages. Furthermore the Lord had an equally medieval claim to tributes and services from his vassals. While some of the most unjust of these were abolished—Philip V, for example, did away with the dreadful right of life and death over their vassals possessed by Lords of Aragón—the oppressive tributes continued to further impoverish the poor and enrich the wealthy. The Kings did not dare suppress all the privileges, but in a general way modified them, sometimes by subjecting to rigorous proof the legitimacy and title of seignorial rights, again by hindering sales of jurisdiction, or requiring confirmation by the *Cámara* of Castile for officials appointed by the Lords; by appointing a royal trustee for each seignorial holding; and, in general, facilitating the reintegration into the Crown of such holdings and of public offices. The Kings also tried to make the higher nobility subject to paying taxes (the simple *hidalgos* enjoyed few exemptions of this nature) ; and succeeded to some extent by employment of such indirect methods as payments in lieu of military service, and *media anata* (half annats) , a payment required of the heir to landed estates. No Grandee and no noble had his rank recognized without payment of the *media anata*. To be sure, the payment was no heavy burden on them, even though it greatly aided the national Treasury, because the nobility, especially the Grandees, were possessed of vast properties. The Duke of Medinaceli, for example, had 1,000,000 *reales* annually from his fisheries. The yearly income of the Count of Aranda was 1,600,000 *reales*. Most of the nobility lived at Court. Spain was a land of absentee landlords, as much in Catalonia as in Castile. The Grandees were very jealous of their prerogatives. When at the beginning of his reign the francophile Philip V granted to the Peers of France the same rights as those of the Grandees of Spain, the Duke of Argos, in the name of the latter, protested in a document enumerating the special privileges of a Grandee. These included the right to keep on his hat and sit down in the presence of a king; to be called "Cousin" by the monarch; to have a private bodyguard wherever he went; to be visited and saluted by *Ayuntamientos,* deputations, and Viceroys; to have a preferred place indoors and out; to be imprisoned only by the King's decree . . . and so on. Grandee or not, the Duke was exiled for his temerity; and the King did not alter his policy.

The Middle Class, the Laboring Class, and Other Social Classes

The "middle class" in the eighteenth century as in the seventeenth was made up of industrialists, merchants, landowners, and professional literary men, whose wealth or wellbeing distinguished them from the workers who made up the masses of the people, and whose lack of *hidalguía* set them apart from the nobility. Economically many out-of-pocket *hidalgos* belonged to the middle class; and many tradesmen or small landowners to the working class. But the dividing line of aristocratic privileges continued to separate the groups, regardless of wealth or poverty. At attempt to erase this line and to counteract the belief that manual labor was incompatible with nobility occasioned Charles III's *Cédula* of March 23, 1776. It declared that "not only the trade of tanner, but all the other arts and crafts of ironworker, tailor, shoemaker, carpenter, and others of the kind are honest and honorable; that the practice of them lowers neither the family nor the person of him who exercises it, nor incapacitates him for obtaining municipal employment from the Commonwealth [which, as we know, usually went to the noble and the *hidalgo*], wherein is enrolled as citizen the artisans or craftsmen who exercise them; and that likewise practice of arts and trades does not prejudice the enjoyment and prerogatives of *hidalguía* to those who acquired it legitimately . . . even though in their own persons they exercise these arts and trades." The King's desire to favor the non-noble classes was proved also by University scholarships awarded some poor students. However, since the intention was not to do away with any of the laws but simply with class prejudice, the *Cédula* of 1783 was not very effective. This was shown when an attempt was made to interpret it in the sense that it authorized artisans to enter Military Orders reserved for the nobility: a Royal Order stated flatly that it had never been the intention to constitute an "equality that would be chimerical" and "much less should it be understood" that there had been any intent to change the regulations and constitution of the Military Orders "so justly established and founded on the solid principles of the necessity of preserving the lustre of the Nobility."

With the dividing line maintained between it and the aristocracy, the wealthy middle class had to content itself with emulating the latter in building up the entail or in keeping up its predominance in rural life, as was especially the case in Catalonia. As for the working-men in the cities, their condition was pretty much the same as formerly, though somewhat freer from the ancient guild restrictions; and in the country they continued to live bound to the landowners, more or less according to the region: but almost always their living was precarious. The general impression made on travelers over the countryside was that the laborer's existence was wretched. The census of 1787 reckoned the small landholders and share-croppers at 907,197 and the male day-laborers at 964,571. The farmers in the Basque Provinces were the most prosperous. The Castilian farmer's lot was hard; he was oppressed by taxes and had to hold his farm on a short-term lease, always a hazardous arrangement. The Andalusians were worse off still. The Galicians, exploited by the great landowners, emigrated in numbers to the cities to work as carters, and so did the Leonese. The situation of the poorer rural classes in Catalonia was not enviable, though they were hard-working by nature; except in the mountainous northern section, where cattle-raising and communal lands afforded them moderate well-being, according to the testimony of the English traveler, Arthur Young, in 1787. It is true that many of these evils proceeded from backwardness in agricultural methods, enormous expanses of uncultivated land, and entails.

One evidence of tolerance was Charles III's effort in 1783 to raise the status of the gypsies, declaring that "they are not . . . nor do they come from, any infected stock whatever"; and the liberation of the known or presumed descendants of Jews from the legal disabilities that for generations had barred them from many trades and from military service. However, Jews who retained their religion were still prohibited from entering Spain (*Cédula* of 1802). Slavery, while not much in evidence, remained legal in Spain in the eighteenth century, the existent slaves being mostly Moors and Negroes brought to the Peninsula from the Americas. In 1799 a treaty with the Sultan of Morocco abolished the enslavement of prisoners of war (the Moors).

In the colonies the open slavery of Negroes and the disguised slavery of Indians continued. The concession of *asientos,* or contracts, for the importation of slaves into the Americas was sometimes granted by international treaties (such treaties were usually with England). There were various attempts at improving the conditions of slavery during the eighteenth century. In 1784 branding was abolished by law; in 1789 regulations were laid down for the education, treatment, and employment of Negro slaves and methods facilitated for them to purchase their own freedom. But since slavery itself was not abolished—abolition being too radical an idea for the times, though Minister Urquijo launched it toward the century's close—laws were unable to prevent the cruelty and harshness of some slaveowners.

The Family and Property

Legislation relating to the family strengthened the ties between parents and children, which undoubtedly had been slackened somewhat by the increasing sense of individualism and freedom of manners; although even in 1800 the classic type of household was marked by the stern discipline and the corresponding submissiveness reflected in Moratín's *El sí de las niñas* (1806). In 1766 consent of the parents was made a legal requisite for marriage, though recourse was offered in the courts if the parents withheld consent without just reason. In 1801 the Cordovan law depriving married women of sharing in the family income was revoked.

As for property, there were two movements which frequently met and mingled: a tendency to break the entails and share the land, and a decided communal tendency with respect to landholding. The leading theories in the eighteenth century, upheld by such eminent writers as Campomanes, Floridablanca, Castro, Jovellanos, and Sempere, were contrary to entails in every form, lay or ecclesiastical.

Industrial and Social Legislation

In order to increase the effectiveness of the measures taken and to encourage establishment of factories and workshops, a number of very sound laws were enacted, including one giving women the right to work in any industry for which they were physically fitted; several establishing new standards for woolen, silk, linen and hempen textiles; one exempting the soap, silk thread, and bitumen industries from taxation; one authorizing weavers to set up as many workshops as they wished; and various others.

The Spanish Renascence and Its Paralyzation

With all these progressive steps, and many more which it would take too long to enumerate, some industries again became flourishing, and not a few Spanish districts and cities grew prosperous; among them Catalonia (and especially Barcelona and Reus), the Basque provinces, Asturias, the district of Almadén (in metal industries and in mines), Valencia (especially in manufacture of silks and of linen and hempen textiles), Segovia (in woolen and cotton textiles); and others in these and other manufactures. Taken as a whole, the wealth of Spain was then greater than that of France and was better distributed among the population; that is, with less inequality of fortune between one social class and another.

The outward manifestations of this new economic well-being took the same forms that we noted in discussing the sixteenth century: abundant industrial activity in small towns where life today has become stagnant in this respect, and the frequent construction of new, privately owned buildings which, along with those of the sixteenth century, are still in many villages and rural districts the most eloquent testimony to the moments of Spain's greatest splendor prior to the nineteenth century. Scrupulously accurate statistics on housing construction during those two periods, the sixteenth century and the eighteenth, would supply us, once the dates were verified, with data for documenting the facts concerning the majority of these urban and rural groups. With respect to eighteenth century industrial life, Larruga's well-known book, *Memorias sobre los frutos, fábricas y minas de España* (Notes on the Products, Factories, and Mines of Spain), and other contemporaneous sources, added to the stories told by old people who still recalled, at the close of the nineteenth century, what they themselves had seen at that century's dawn, and who remembered the things that their own parents had related about the century preceding, provided a rich source of informative detail.

The economic revival, based on the renascence of scientific studies from which are derived inventions with industrial application (such as physics, mechanics, chemistry, and botany) would have gone on increasing, beyond any doubt, if the governmental sponsorship characteristic of Charles III's reign had been prolonged. It is true that under his successor, Charles IV, Campomanes (who was the latter King's Minister also), Jovellanos, and other learned and patriotic men kept on along the same lines as in former years; but this beneficial official activity soon began to be abandoned because questions of internal and international politics claimed most of their attention. Thus the industrial and agricultural renascence was very speedily paralyzed in part. The War of Independence, which we shall discuss further on, and in which many factories were destroyed and other elements of wealth perished, finally stifled that progressive eighteenth century effort.

While the measures previously mentioned favored the development of industry, other means were taken to promote commercial expansion. Noteworthy in this regard were steps for rebuilding the Navy and for introducing into the laws and trade practices relating to the Americas a feeling of more freedom and of less protectionism than had been the rule up to that time. This was the first manifestation of the system of Mercantile Companies having to do with the New World colonies: a system which, much in vogue among the Dutch, English, and French, had not had previous application in Spain. Despite these improvements, in some regions of Spain's American colonies there was increasing dissatisfaction with Spanish mercantile policy, especially as regarded trading with foreigners; and contraband trade was on the increase. England and other European countries desirous of trading freely with Spanish possessions overseas, shrewdly added fuel to this discontent.

THE ECONOMIC PROBLEM

The economic condition of Spain was at lowest ebb at the beginning of the eighteenth century in consequence of the general decadence of the seventeenth. It was the special merit of the statesmen and scientists of the period that they recognized the fact that much of the national weakness was economic at root, and resolved to correct it. They were assisted by the prevailing spirit of the century which was particularly heedful of economic problems. The Spanish statesman most genuinely representative of this economic policy was Campomanes.

Pedro Pérez y Rodríguez, the Count of Campomanes, born of a very humble Asturian family, was a great sponsor of communications and a great promoter of industry, commerce, and technical education, as well as the most convinced regalist of the eighteenth century. He organized the postal service; created a port for despatch-boats at La Coruña; established schools and university chairs to teach the trades and crafts which it was most essential to revive or introduce in Spain; openly fostered the *Sociedades Económicas del País;* encouraged "interior colonization"; and was the most active promoter of social and economic rehabilitation that Spain had in the eighteenth century.

Though educated chiefly in the ideas of the French physiocratic school of thinkers—which looked on agriculture as the principal support of a nation's wealth—Campomanes, while a great land reformer, was well aware of the value of manufacturing industries and worked for their regeneration in the two ways open to him: education of public opinion and enactment of fostering legislation with parallel creation of model institutions.

Gaspar Melchor de Jovellanos, an Asturian like Campomanes and like him a great Finance Minister, was unlike him in being of illustrious family. A man of exceptional talent, deeply cultured, in love with letters and learning and himself an excellent writer, of upright and noble sentiments and stainless honor and integrity, Jovellanos could not bring these multiple gifts fully to bear upon official life because Godoy's hostility soon deprived him of his post. He had time to effect some reforms, however; and his creation of the Asturian

Institute proved that even though agriculture was his chief interest, he realized the necessity of encouraging other elements as well.

The general effect of all this reform policy, together with the periods of peace that the country enjoyed in the eighteenth century, was beneficial and made itself felt in all the branches of production, commerce, and consumption, as well as in a remarkable increase in population. The 5,700,000 inhabitants of Spain at the close of the seventeenth century had become 10,541,221 by 1797.

The following is a comparative table of the trades and professions followed by Spaniards in the year 1787 and 1797, a decade apart:

	1787	1797
Clergy	182,425	168,248
Nobles	480,589	402,059
Government Employees	41,014	31,981
Soldiery	77,884	149,340
Students	50,994	29,812
Small Farmers	907,197	871,937
Day Laborers (agricultural)	964,571	805,235
Factory Workers and Artisans	310,739	533,769
Servants	280,092	174,095
Merchants		25,685

In ten years, therefore, there had been a decrease in numbers of clergy, nobles, government employees, students, servants, farmers who worked their own small farms, and day laborers. In contrast, the number of artisans had increased. In other words, agriculture seems to have been stationary while industry developed. It should however be borne in mind that 1787 was a year of peace and 1797 a war year.

The northern and eastern Provinces were the most densely populated, the density decreasing toward La Mancha and again rising in the Andalusian region. In 1797 the most densely populated districts were Guipúzcoa, with 80 inhabitants a square kilometer; Valencia, with 48; Asturias, 47; Navarre, 43; Biscay, 42. The most sparsely settled were La Mancha and Cuenca, each with only 13 to a square kilometer; Estremadura with 14; Catalonia and Granada each with 34; Seville with 39; Aragón with 21. In 1787 Spain had less than forty cities with as many as 10,000 inhabitants; and 17 of these were in Andalusia. Madrid's population in 1787 was 156,672 civilian residents; in 1797 there were in Madrid 167,607 civil inhabitants, 10,250 soldiers, and 30,000 foreigners. Barcelona had 115,000 population in 1797; Seville, 96,000; Valencia, 80,000; Saragossa, 42,000; Valladolid, 21,000; and Burgos between 8,000 and 9,000.

Economic prosperity did not correspond exactly to these figures, since it depended on other factors also, such as soil and climate, water supply, proximity to the sea. Generally speaking, the seaboard Provinces and those occupying the great river valleys were the most prosperous; but the area that they represented was small compared with the country as a whole. Thus, notwithstanding the richness of the valleys of the Ebro and the Jalón, an Aragonese said of his region in 1783 that there was much land that the plough had never broken; that the wools, silks and other products were exported from Aragón to be processed and shipped in again as yard-goods; that irrigation was scanty; the rivers not navigable; and the villagers wretchedly poor. Old Castile was also impoverished, treeless, waterless; a wheat-growing region that did not produce enough bread to feed its own people. The situation of La Mancha was still worse. Antonio Ponz, the Valencian antiquarian and traveler, said that the Manchegans had nothing but wheat and barley, and when these crops failed, their condition was appalling. Most of the population there were daylaborers with no other source of income than the pittance given for a daily wage in the country. That was also true of Andalusia, though the capital cities and some of the important rural settlements [*villas*] presented a deceptive aspect of wealth and prosperity; deceptive, that is, if taken to represent the state of the country as a whole. In Galicia the enormous emigration from rural districts to urban centers where even the humblest manual labor was eagerly sought is telling evidence as to the prevailing economic condition.

Housing was also an expressive indication of this state of things. Cave dwellings abounded in Castile, as did wretched hovels, cramped huts of clay thatched with straw. In Galicia, said an early nineteenth century traveler, the habitations "offer the dreariest aspect in the world. The walls are of rough stone, often not bound with cement, and they are hardly higher than a man. Light enters only through the door, and through that door and a hole in the roof the smoke escapes. . . . Domestic animals live in with the family." In La Mancha the towns lacked water and consequently were without vegetable and flower gardens. The housing in the Basque Provinces and in Navarre, on the other hand, was very comfortable, with walls of stone, brick and timber; each house usually being supplied with a bake-oven, a fountain, and a garden. The Valencian cabin, or *barraca,* ample, clean, and cool, denoted a population that lived well and comfortably.

However, the Spanish house, as a rule, is very deficient in comfort. In the eighteenth century, French and English and other foreign visitors to Spain almost always complained of the unglazed windows and balconies, the lack of chimneys, and so on. Decoration and furniture, except in the homes of the wealthy and in ancient structures, were poor. Toward the end of the eighteenth century, shops in the towns began to sell painted wallpaper and French furniture, which gave a new aspect to Spanish interiors.

If it is recalled that along with these prevalent living conditions went the ignorance of the masses, resulting in resistance and prejudice against all reform; economic inequality, in consequence of the concentration of property, such as in entails and the churches; the burden of taxes; the difficulty of communications; administrative disorder; frequent wars; and, on the part of not a few people, a persistent repugnance toward manual labor and a traditional attitude of acceptance with respect to charity and beggary: it will be easily understood that except for a few persons and places, the economic situation was deplorable and the economic problem was to the end of the period the most pressing of all. Its obvious manifestations were the beggar and the vagabond. The two together, Campomanes said, comprised an army of 140,000 men, women and children; the majority able to work but not always able to find work. Charles III's Ministers had a project for dealing with the situation by sending the women to hospices where they could work, the aged and the invalid to hospitals and poorhouses, the able-bodied men to the armed forces. But the plan fell through: the national treasury had not the funds to carry it out.

Agriculture

In order to form a clear idea of the state of agriculture in the eighteenth century, and more especially of the economic situation of the farmers, it is necessary to note the distribution and methods of land ownership. Distribution was more or less the same in all regions. The rule was vast holdings in a few hands. At the beginning of the nineteenth century the Spanish Church possessed 9,093,400 *fanegas* (a *fanega* being about 1.59 acres); the nobility 28,306,700 *fanegas;* and the commoners, 17,599,000. However, most of the land of nobles and commoners alike was entailed, and therefore accumulated and not susceptible to sale or division; a fact that barred the way to increase of the number of small landholders. Few indeed were the localities where these latter were in the majority. An English economist, Arthur Young, who traveled through Catalonia in 1787, noted that the best cultivated fields belonged to small farmers who bought untilled plots of land from the municipalities; but that most of the landowners were gentlemen who lived in Barcelona and rented out their properties. In fact, the proportion was one small-farm proprietor to every 40 inhabitants. In Catalonia it was 1 to 13, but the population was sparse and the cultivated acreage small. In the Province of Toledo, 1,541,688 *fanegas* belonged to the nobles, only 657,000 to the commoners; in Estremadura, 2,149,898 to the former and 741,610 to the latter. In Avila 157,092 *fanegas* were entailed, 239,591 belonged to the Church, and a mere 8,160 were cultivated by farmers who lived in the locality. In Asturias, wrote Jovellanos, "the entails and the monasteries and churches are almost the only proprietors." And so it was, all over Spain.

This unequal distribution of land gave rise to differing practices as to length of lease, terms of payment, and system of cultivation. Fundamentally, the methods were three: that of a small farm which the owner worked himself; that of rental in various forms; and that of *latifundio*—the property of an absentee landlord cultivated by groups of day-laborers who hired themselves out in the work season. The first method was infrequent; most of the small farmers lived in northern Spain and on the Spanish Levant. The second method—rental—was general in Castile and also in North Spain and on the Mediterranean littoral. The absentee landlord was typical of the Andalusian Provinces, where the result of the system was a numerous proletariat which during the greater part of the year had no work and consequently starved or begged. In Estremadura this condition was somewhat tempered by the usage of communal lands.

However, as we have said, the well-being of even the best organized districts was only comparative, and few localities and families were really well-off. The poverty in Andalusia was so great in 1750 that the rural population thought of emigrating en masse. The Government had to send the Provincial Governor 10,000,000 *reales* to avert a general exodus. The Governors tried to improve the rental system by prolonging the time period for leases and requiring the owners to take part of the rent in produce, since raising ready cash was extremely difficult for the small farmers. Jovellanos revived a law of 1768 preventing a proprietor from evicting a renter without just cause; and legislation in 1785 and 1794 forbade a landlord to evict the tenant farmer except to live on his land and cultivate it himself. The abusive privileges of the *Mesta,* or stock-breeders corporation, came under direct attack. Flocks and herds constituted one of Spain's chief sources of income. Statistics at the end of the eighteenth century showed 2,521,702 goats; 1,266,918 swine; 1,650,073 head of cattle; 236,522 horses and 1,200,000 mules. The 1797 census reported 107,790 persons engaged in caring for these flocks and herds. In 1795 the separate jurisdiction of the Mesta was abolished, but as the law did not clearly authorize the fencing of cultivable land, the relief to agriculture was not very great. The farmers declared with perfect logic that unless they could make their crops secure, neither irrigation nor cultivation counted for much.

The principal agricultural products of the Peninsula during the seventeenth century were wheat; grapes, from which excellent wine was made (Rioja, Aragón, Catalonia, Mallorca, Valencia, Valdepeñas, Alicante, Málaga, and Jérez, or sherry); figs, oranges and lemons; almonds and hazelnuts; and olives. Among legumes chickpeas, string-beans, lima beans, and black-eyed peas were abundant. Neither hemp nor flax were produced in quantities sufficient to meet the home demand. Rush (esparto grass), salt wort (*barilla*), saffron and many other industrial plants flourished in some localities and were much utilized. Sugarcane, plentiful in the early years of the century in southern and eastern Spain, had almost, but not quite, ceased to be cultivated there by its close, in view of the extensive production in Spain's American colonies. In industrial agriculture, the most important products were honey and silk. Wool was still exported but, generally speaking, it was of inferior quality.

Freedom of Labor

Spain was rather early in adopting some of the social modifications that have most influenced present-day economic life. Among these were the abolition of the Guilds, and establishment instead of the principle of freedom of labor; and the prohibition of great accumulations of real estate (lands and houses) in a few hands.

In the eighteenth century the Guilds had intensified their exclusionist policy, making it difficult for workers and industrialists who were non-guild-members to join, and stressing the social distinctions among master workmen, craftsmen, and apprentices. At the same time, the Government was intervening more and more in regulation of the Guilds and in unification of ordinances concerning the crafts. All this was creating an unfavorable atmosphere for the Guild groups, and successive laws or royal orders further facilitated free establishment in their trades of workers who were not members of a Guild: by declaring examinations not requisite for workmen of proved ability and by dissolving various guilds, such as that of the silk-twisters (1793). These measures were completed in the nineteenth century; whereupon the ancient institution of the Guilds disappeared completely.

Entail and Accumulation of Landed Property

In the eighteenth century property in land and houses was, generally speaking, cumulative. There were various reasons for this. For one thing the nobility for generations had owned vast country estates. Likewise the churches, ancient monasteries, and convents possessed considerable amounts of wealth of this kind derived from the gifts of kings and rich members of the congregation and from the system of resettlement adopted during the Reconquest. Moreover, the middle class itself, in proportion as it became wealthier, in order to maintain the family's property and prestige had adopted the custom of not dividing the estate among all the children, or other relatives, upon death of the parents, but of leaving the total landed property to a single heir, with prohibition against selling any part of it; and so availing themselves of the institution of entail, legally introduced, as we have noted, by the Laws of Toro. The nobility followed the same practice. Thus huge fortunes were amassed in lands and houses. When two entailed estates were united by a marriage, wealth was very much increased, but not all members of the families concerned were benefited on that account.

Because of these things, the number of small landowners was relatively few, and the majority of the farm-workers were renters; who paid the owners in theoretical proportion to what the soil produced. In this respect the situation of the agricultural laborers in Castile, Galicia, Andalusia, and even Catalonia, was wretched. Only in the Basque provinces did they live with some comfort.

Breaking the Entail

The cure for such a state of things was to divide and distribute the land, and this was attempted by means of the "internal colonizations" already discussed; but in order for large numbers of persons to share in the distribution, free lands had to be available. The inevitable con-sequence was decision to prohibit entailed estates and to force existing entails to be converted into cash or other property so that the land involved might pass into hands of workers who would agree to cultivate it. That process was called breaking the entail, or *desamortazación*. All eighteenth century intellectuals favored it, and through their influ-ence many new laws were passed prohibiting establishment of new entails, authorizing the sale of lands and houses included in entails already existing, and denying permission for churches and convents to continue accumulating real estate. As regards these ecclesiastical properties, in 1805 King Charles IV obtained the Pope's authorization to sell part of them; and this was done to the amount of 1,600,000 *duros*. Moreover, since the *Ayuntamientos,* or City Councils, also possessed lands adapted to cultivation and pasturage, which had been rendered inalienable by reason of municipal ownership, it was ordered that a goodly portion of them should be divided among laborers who had no land to till.

Internal Administrative Reform

These many measures, so far-reaching in economic and social fields, were companioned by a sense of austerity and justice with regard to government administration in general. It was first felt, and practiced, in connection with the Public Treasury, and in the reign of Philip V, as we have said. It spread later to every branch of the administration,

A. Sánchez Coello: *Portrait of Father Sigüenza.*

and in the reigns of Ferdinand VI and Charles III took on a general aspect of security and of regard for the interests of the public which, in this respect, impressed upon the Spanish State a special stamp typical of the period. It was observable in the functioning of public office and in the appearance of reforms and new guarantees for carrying out the Government's good intentions. That policy reached as far as the colonies, and brought about in the Americas an era of good feeling which is rightly termed "the epoch of the good Viceroys." In America those Viceroys, and in Spain such Prime Ministers as Campomanes and Jovellanos, are embodiment of the praiseworthy desire for just and upright administration which was for some time a guiding star in our eighteenth century. At its close, in the time of Charles IV and his favorite, the Minister Godoy, the morale that had sustained that policy broke down; and all the selfishness, neglect, and disregard of the public interest which had marked the second half of the rule of the House of Austria again held sway. Although the good tradition was not wholly lost, its scope on the Peninsula was definitely limited by interposition of measures proceeding from the highest levels of the Administration, just as in the Americas it was stopped short at times by the passive resistance of some public officials. The episodic continuation of that tradition which Campomanes and Jovellanos represented in industrial relations during Charles IV's reign, itself proves how deeply those governmental procedures had taken root in enlightened public opinion.

At the same time, the vicious system of government by the King's boon companions, or favorites, which seventeenth century arbitrariness had put in the saddle, gave way to government by a group or cabinet of Spanish Ministers, one for each branch of the Administration; a system that was prelude to the constitutional government of the nineteenth century and replaced that of the Councils.

The legislation expressive of these policies, as well as of policies relating to other spheres of State action, may be found in great part in the *Novísima Recopilación,* or Latest Code, which conforms in type to the Code published in Philip II's time. The *Novísima Recopilación* contains the legislation still in effect in 1800, the date of issue, which had been included in the most recent editions of the Code of 1567, in addition to eighteenth century enactments. However, while extremely interesting historically, as a juridical source it is deficient and sometimes misleading.

A new, revised edition of the *Recopilación de las leyes de Indias—*
Code of the Laws of the Indies—was likewise planned but not completed.

Modifications of Colonial Policy

The administrative reforms were also extended, as we have said, to
the colonial territories. Strictly speaking, not all the changes and
innovations made in this field can be attributed to the same spirit that
produced those effects in Spain. Undoubtedly in the Americas part
of them resulted from the dual determination to reduce corruption,
abuses, and negligence in government of the colonies, and to regularize
the functioning of the colonial Treasury and the utilization of income
from the colonies. Another factor was the natural effect of the change
that had been brought about in Europe, with increasingly favorable
auguries, in economic ideas relative to the wealth of nations and to
trade. Some of the changes in colonial policy were due to the development of colonization itself, which made necessary new services and
organisms of government, and to the effects already produced by two
centuries of Spanish emigration to the New World and by exploitation
of the natural resources there.

To this last group of reforms belongs creation of two additional
Vice-royalties: the Vice-royalty of New Granada, in 1718, composed
in part of the northern territory of the South American mainland and
of part of Central America, plus the regions of Santa Fe de Bogotá
and Quito; and the River Plate, or Río de la Plata, Vice-royalty in
1777, composed, generally speaking, of almost all of what are today
the Republics of Argentina, Uruguay, and Paraguay, together with
the regional governments of Charcas and Cuyo. At the same time
Caracas (Venezuela), Chile, Puerto Rico, and Louisiana were raised
to the status of Captaincies-General. Those facts demonstrate that
the fundamental bases of the administrative organizations implanted
in the sixteenth century did not undergo modification in form. But
toward the close of the eighteenth century a new organization, that
of the *Intendencias*—Administrations—and Sub-delegations, came to
be superimposed upon them. The primary legislation in this field
dates from 1782, and after various changes in text, arrived at its final
general form in 1803. The *intendentes*, or administrators, had jurisdiction in matters of justice, policy, public funds (to a very great

Velázquez: *Self-Portrait*. Detail of the painting called *Las Meninas*.

degree), and war; so that they intervened in almost every sphere of government which theretofore had been the province of the Viceroys, Governors, and *Audiencias* or Courts of Judicature. As for the Sub-delegates, they took the place of the *Corregidores*, or Town Magistrates, and the *Alcaldes Mayores*, or Mayors.

Prior to this new arrangement, the institution of the *Visitadores*, or Occasional Judges, which had existed formerly in principle and had functioned from the time of the Catholic Kings with respect to the municipalities, had been extended and intensified in all Spain's American colonies. Those *Visitadores* were charged with inspecting public administration, reporting on its deficiencies, and trying to remedy them. Their work was very effective; and on several occasions the best from among their ranks were chosen as heads of government in Vice-Royalties and other incorporated territories. With the high personnel of government and some of the subordinate ranks thus specialized and, in natural consequence, improved, the period of able administration—"the epoch of the Good Viceroys"—came into being. Especially notable among these "good Viceroys" were Vértiz, Ceballos, Arredondo, Amat, Manso, Bucareli, Gálvez, Azanza, O'Higgins, the Marquis de Croix, and the Marquis de Revillagigedo.

At the same time new measures favored emigration and the establishment in America of suitable colonists. This policy is exemplified by Captain-General Manso's introduction into Chile of Biscayans and Frenchmen, and of the bringing of German miners to Santa Fe de Bogotá, an undertaking by Charles III in response to the petition of Don Antonio Caballero, Viceroy of New Granada and Archbishop of Bogotá. Moreover, abuses were corrected in the *repartimientos* (territories given as fiefs to the Conquistadors), and the *encomiendas* (feudal estates in the Americas assigned or granted by the Spanish Crown), which were finally suppressed altogether. Thus Las Casas' idea triumphed fully, though in practice it was not always possible to avoid illegal abuses by some *patrones*, or landowners. The Secretariat of Overseas Colonies—*Secretaría de Indias*—was created in 1714, with some of the attributes formerly pertaining to the Council, the Royal Funds (*Cajas Reales*), and the Deposits of Overseas Colonies, or *Depositaría de Indias*. Regular postal service was inaugurated in 1764. The *Casa de Contratación*—House of Trade—was discontinued at Seville and transferred to Cádiz in 1777, part of its functions being assigned to the Consulates, the number of which was increased in the Americas. Great public works were constructed in the various colonies (aqueducts, highways, cutwaters, irrigation canals, ports, public buildings, et cetera) ; a system was begun for distributing plots of land to the Indians in order to afford an economic basis making abolition of the *repartimientos* practical; and, in general, colonial administration was regularized and cleaned up; so that it reached a level of zeal and of technical effectiveness—within the bureaucratic pattern that was the rule then and now—to which numerous administrative archives of the colonial period bear witness.

In the field of economic and commercial expansion, there was, as we have noted, experimentation with the system of Mercantile Companies. Among those established were the Royal Guipuzcoan Company of Caracas and those of Havana, Ezcaray, Burgos, and the Philippines, some of them producing beneficial results in production and trade. Likewise the system of merchant fleets was changed to that of free voyages; first, under special permit (1735-78) ; then, as a general practice (1778). The trading monopoly of the port of Seville gave way to freedom to trade directly with the Americas; a concession made first to the ports of Catalonia (1765 and subsequently) and later to 13 ports at different points of the Peninsula. Beginning with 1789, Spanish trade with all colonial territories was permitted. Freedom for international trade also, previously restricted, was allowed in 1774; and other measures were taken along the same line.

The results justified the efforts, and were demonstrated by increase in national income, trade, agricultural production, and the economic well-being of the colonial population; as well as by the high technical achievements in development of some national resources. Witness was borne to all this during the eighteenth century by several foreign visitors to the New World, the German scientist and traveler Humboldt in particular, whose eulogiums, based on very concrete facts observed at first hand, are the best evidence of the success of Spanish colonization at the close of the period of our colonial domination. Had it not been for the revival at that time of contraband trade (to which we have had occasion to refer several times) , the national economy as a whole and the income of the Spanish Government would have benefited to much greater extent than it was able to do, through other factors, from advantages derived in the Americas.

All these advances in the administrative and economic spheres were paralleled by others in the realm of culture. The principal achievements in the fields of scientific theory and applied science will be discussed further on; but mention should be made here of such supplementary activities as the creation of new institutes of learning, especially in scientific branches; the publication of professional and learned journals; and the sending out of men of science to the Americas. These things also are all reported extensively not only in official documents but in the writings of travelers of the period.

The Economic Life of the Spanish Colonies

Naturally enough, the vast territories of the Spanish colonial world had a much larger population than Spain itself, although exact statistics for the former are lacking. Alexander von Humboldt's figures, gathered during his American travels, are generally taken as the most reliable. He said that there were 18,802,000 inhabitants in the Spanish colonies, of which number 1,900,000 were in the Philippines. The figures for the American possessions were broken down as follows: 7,530,000 Indians; 5,310,000 *Mestizos;* 3,276,000 whites; and 786,000 Negroes. A later calculation, by the economist Canga Argüelles, fixed the total at approximately 14 millions. Whichever of these figures are accepted, the lands were obviously underpopulated and the Spaniards and their children were in the minority.

Most of the wealth was in Spanish hands, however, and came principally—varying with the region—from farming, stock-raising, or mining. Round about the city of Buenos Aires in the Argentine, for example, was a broad belt of great estates which produced a powerful middle class, the mainstay of political control and economic life. However, the Spaniards cared little for agriculture in comparsion with exploitation of the mines of precious metals; and it was to the latter that they dedicated their efforts most zealously, except in the River Plate region where the lack of deposits to be mined forced them into country life and cattle breeding. In the American colonies it was illegal to cultivate flax, hemp, olive orchards, vineyards (except in Peru), or to raise silkworms. To be sure, these prohibitions were not observed, not even by the Viceroys. Thus von Humboldt found large and profitable olive orchards and vineyards.

The Spaniards in the eighteenth century continued the practice begun with Columbus of introducing into their American colonies, with such plants and trees as produced dyes, textiles and medicaments; known in the Western Hemisphere. Wheat rendered a 25 to 100% yield instead of the 5% that it gave in Spain. The fields of the Jesuit missions in Paraguay were an enviable example of what skilled cultivation could produce.

In the vegetable kingdom the Spaniards were concerned principally with such plants and trees as produced dyes, textiles and medicaments; such as dyewood, Brazilwood, rubber trees, indigo, quinine. Indigo was cultivated extensively in Guatemala and Cumaná. In 1802 cochineal to the value of 67,000,000 *reales* was exported from Vera Cruz. Cocoa was the principal product of both Caracas and Quito. Toward the close of the eighteenth century more than 615,000 pounds of quinine were sold. Sugarcane came to be the leading crop in Cuba, and Mexico and Peru cultivated it also; but transportation difficulties retarded development of the industry. Coffee began to be cultivated commercially in Cuba in 1769, and by 1809 the port of Havana exported 320,000 arrobas. In Peru maté and a variety of tea were grown for export, and maté was (and is) also an important crop in Paraguay. Tobacco was a variable factor because of restrictive legislation and the competition of Brazil. Mexico exported vanilla, sarsaparilla, and jalap. The fieldhand at first was the aboriginal Indian, later almost always a Negro. The white day laborer, in consequence, had to struggle against the almost invincible competition of slave labor. The best he could do was to rent a plot from the great landowners; but high rates and other obstacles usually kept his nose to the grindstone.

While the best grazing lands were in the Viceroyalty of Buenos Aires, where there were 12,000,000 head of cattle and 3,000,000 horses, Mexico also had large herds of horses and mules. New Granada (Colombia) shipped 30,000 mules annually to the islands of the Antilles. In the River Plate region, cattle were raised principally for the hides.

The mining industry was developed to a remarkable degree in the American colonies; though it was limited for the most part to precious metals. Mexico produced some 56,000 ounces of gold annually (a figure rising in 1806 to 80,064 ounces). From 1753 to 1792 the average annual production in Peru was 27,200 ounces; in Chile, 97,696 ounces; in Buenos Aires, 17,600 ounces; in New Granada, 164,040 ounces.

There were some 3,000 silver mines in Mexico, employing 30,000 free miners and producing 19,704,000 ounces annually. Alexander von Humboldt calculated that in 110 years Mexico had put in circulation more than 1,192,000,000 ounces of silver, representing upwards of 5,069,000,000 *reales.* The mines of Peru and Chile, which were difficult to work because of the high altitude, and in which the Indians toiled under the *mita,* or law of forced labor, afforded annually more than 8,975,360 ounces of silver. In comparison with this enormous production of gold and silver the iron of Mexico, the copper of Chile, the zinc, antimony and arsenic of Mexico and Peru, and the tin of Mexico (Guadalajara), were relatively of small value. Mexico also had mines of mercury, but they were not worked regularly. Platinum, discovered in 1735 and brought to Spain by Ulloa, was not highly valued. For the rest, industrial life in the colonies was limited. If the laws had favored the establishment of workshops and factories—instead of restricting them for the benefit of Peninsular industry—beyond question the development of colonial economic life along these lines would have been very great.

It was in commerce that the effect of the new economic ideas of freedom, and the sense of reform which was dominant in government after the middle of the eighteenth century, were most evident. Private individuals were permitted to ship goods in their own boats, but registry for these vessels was not only expensive but bound up in red tape. Usually several boats made the voyage together, under convoy. In 1764 Spain established postal service with Cuba, Puerto Rico and the River Plate region; soon extending it to the other colonies. In 1774 free trade was authorized between the Peninsula and New Spain, Guatemala, New Granada, and Peru. The Cataláns were authorized to trade with the Antilles (1765), South America (1775), and Mexico (1789); with the result that commerce increased by leaps and bounds through the ports of Barcelona, Reus, and especially Arenys de Mar, which at the beginning of the nineteenth century had under registry 42 ships for carrying on the American trade. Finally, in 1788 the system of Government merchant fleets was abolished and free trade was authorized between some dozen leading Spanish ports and twenty in the American colonies; tariffs on Spanish imports into the colonies were lowered; various colonial products with a Spanish market were relieved of all duty; and other relief measures were taken. The result was an immediate and extraordinary increase in both export and import trade. In 1788 Spain shipped her American colonies goods to the value of 158,000,000 *reales* and America sent to Spain more than 804,000,000 *reales* worth of colonial products: a trade balance obviously far more favorable to the colonies than to the Peninsula. At the beginning of the nineteenth century, Mexico's imports from Spain valued 20,000,000 *reales;* her exports to Spain, 27,000,000. In 1765 boats carrying on the Cuban trade were few and far between; by 1778 the number was 200.

In order to stimulate commerce still further, much thought was given to the project of a canal that would unite the Atlantic and the Pacific. The idea had been first discussed during Charles I's reign. Among several proposals presented was one drawn up in 1533 by Gaspar de Espinosa for a Panama canal; a proposal which the King approved in a letter of 1534. The plan was not carried out because of the many matters closer home then requiring the attention of the State, and also because of the opposition of various supporters of other sites for the suggested canal: Nicaragua or Colombia or Mexico. Several routes were outlined; and in 1788 the Frenchman, La Bastide, presented a project for an interoceanic canal making use of the Lake of Nicaragua. A silken fan of the period depicting the plan complete is still preserved.

The *Casa de Contratación,* or House of Trade, was suppressed in 1790, since its principal functions had been transferred to the Consulates of the Sea (*Consulados del Mar*). *Consulados* analogous to those in Spain were created in the Americas, and played a leading part in economic life. The one at Buenos Aires, for instance, waged a successful campaign to abolish oppressive duties which made inland trade difficult, planned and built new roads, introduced new types of machinery, improved harbors, constructed lighthouses, and facilitated the spread of techniques and knowledge. The creation of Mercantile Companies with special privileges, on the foreign pattern, was also fostered. Among those established were the Royal Guipuzcoan Company of Caracas (1728); that of Havana (1740); of Barcelona (1751) for trading with Puerto Rico, Cumaná and Margarita; those of Ezcaray and Burgos; that of the Philippines (1733 and 1783); and two for the traffic in Negro slaves. The Company of the Five Greater Guilds of Madrid, a corporation which in 1777 numbered 375 merchants and had a capital of 210,000,000 *reales*, as well as that of the *Lonja* (or Exchange) and others, were dedicated to the American trade, with special ships assigned for the purpose. The most important of all these Mercantile Companies were those of Caracas and the Philippines. The former became a veritable power in Venezuela, and its abuses of that power caused armed uprisings. It was constituted with 100 shares of 7,500 *reales* for which the merchants of the Province subscribed, and 200 that were taken by the King. The former were increased to 300 in 1753, and the Company, which dealt principally in cocoa, established huge plantations, founded cities, and constructed or improved ports. It obtained the monopoly of all the trade of Caracas in 1742 and of all that of Maracaibo ten years later. Proof of the scope of its operations and their success is in the export figures. Venezuela exported 643,215 *fanegas* of cocoa from 1700 to 1730. With the Company functioning, 1,448,746 *fanegas* were exported from 1730 to 1756, and the price fell in consequence from 80 *pesos* a *fanega* in 1728 to 45 *pesos* in 1735. During three-quarters of a century, the history of this Company is the history of Venezuela, which it ruled like a master. In 1783 the Company was suppressed in Venezuela and incorporated in the Company of the Philippines. The latter, after an initial attempt in 1733 which was unsuccessful because of foreign sabotage, was created by Royal *Cédula* in 1785 with a 25-years monopoly of "all the expeditions that are made to the Philippines and other parts of Asia and for the return shipments of products and goods to the qualified ports of this Peninsula," into which it was authorized to introduce freely "all the fruits and merchandise of Asia." The efforts of this Company resulted in a noteworthy development of the commerce of the Philippine Islands and stimulated the cultivation there of indigo, sugarcane, cotton, pepper, and other industrial crops. In spite of all these favorable measures, which enriched many persons and produced a powerful merchant class in Caracas, Mexico, Vera Cruz, Buenos Aires, and other towns, the colonial trade did not prosper to the extent promised by its initial energy. Among the reasons for this were smuggling and foreign competition, prejudicial taxation, monopolies, private control of commodities, and the misgivings of the State with regard to formation of a rich Creole class. Sometimes there was a high export tax (on cereals, for instance) in order to keep the Peninsula itself supplied with enough for its needs. Again, in the colonies, in order to prevent the rich merchants there from cornering the market on articles of prime necessity as well as on imported products, the Viceroys established price control or prohibited export or import of wheat and flour. But in any case, the final result was always detrimental to both producer and consumer. As for monopolies, there were many: on fish, gunpowder, tobacco, Cordovan leather, tin, lead, playing cards, quicksilver, salt, vicuña wool, et cetera. It can therefore be understood that foreign propaganda in favor of absolute freedom found a ready echo in Spain's American colonies and was a strong motive for independence.

The public works constructed by Spain in order to improve public health and raise the standard of living in the colonies included during the period under consideration the several aqueducts built in Mexico, especially those at Querétaro and Xalpan; the highways built or reconstructed by Manso, Ortíz de Rozas, and O'Higgins in Chile; the breakwaters also constructed in Chile by O'Higgins; the Maipo Canal, irrigating the central Chilean valley; many public buildings, such as the Mints in Chile and Mexico; and the roads and waterways opened up in the River Plate region.

Foreigners in the Economic Life of Spain and the Colonies

The problem of the intervention of foreigners in the economic life of Spain, which had begun to be felt in the seventeenth century, became more pressing in the eighteenth. Among the reasons for this were the industrial decline of the seventeenth century, which favored the importation of foreign goods; the official efforts in the eighteenth century to restore economic prosperity, which naturally caused foreign models as well as trained foreign personnel to be introduced; the dynastic change from Hapsburgs to Bourbons, which brought about a French influx; and the defeats suffered in the War of the Spanish Succession, which forced Spain to yield to many economic exactions and usurpations by her enemies. As a result of all this the number of foreign merchants who established themselves in Spain and the Spanish colonies increased greatly; as did the legal facilities for their doing so. Cádiz was the principal center of French mercantile negotiations, which were of very considerable scope. In 1743 Ensenada declared that it was "necessary to see who is master of Spain, the King or the French merchants." Next in importance were the Italians—mostly Genoese—of whom some 5,018 were resident in Cádiz. The English were also numerous and were a great power in Spanish trade. Twenty English commercial houses were functioning at Cádiz in 1712. The silver mines of Güadalcanal in Spain, abandoned in the seventeenth century, were successfully reopened by English industrialists in 1728. Cobalt mines in the Gistán valley in Aragón, and those of Almadén, were managed by Germans.

In colonial economic life the problem acquired a special character because of the intentions with respect to the Americas which were cherished by France, England, and Holland. At bottom, one and the same desire inspired the men and the Governments of those countries: the desire to capture the American trade. French, English and Dutch censured the monopoly maintained by Spain on trade with her colonies; but French, English and Dutch were very far from favoring a policy of worldwide free trade.

In considering the political history, we have seen how the Spanish Government was forced by hard circumstance to act contrary to its traditional American policy: for example, in the cession of New World territories—Florida, Louisiana, and others. It is true that in 1750 the *asiento* permitting the English to import Negro slaves was abolished, but the English acquired in exchange license to cut dyewoods in Honduras (from which region they carried on an enormous contraband trade with Mexico), and in 1797 they acquired also the Island of Trinidad, which served as a base for smuggling with Venezuela.

All this contraband trade by foreigners was carried on, directly or indirectly, with the connivance of Spanish merchants. Statistics in 1790 showed that of 800,000,000 *reales* worth of merchandise imported in Spain's American colonies during that year, only 70,000,000 *reales* worth came from Spain. Humboldt estimated contraband to be one-fourth of the total trade; in Mexico alone, he set the value of smuggled goods at 280,000,000 *reales*. Later calculations fix at approximately $13\frac{1}{2}\%$ the imports into Mexico of Spanish and American products from the other colonies; at 43%, Spanish products brought directly from the Peninsula; and at $43\frac{1}{2}\%$, foreign products. Such figures—even allowing for some inexactitude—indicate the enormous proportions of contraband trade and the extent of foreign participation in the colonial markets.

Military Occurrences in the Americas and the Philippines

Several times in these pages, in the relation of the military events of the eighteenth century, we have alluded to operations in the American theatre of action in order not to break the uniformity of those events; but there are still other occurrences, not as yet noted but deserving of attention, and those we group together here.

Though the violence of the War of the Spanish Succession was felt most forcibly in Europe, it had its impact on Spain's American colonies as well, resulting principally in sea-fights and attacks on ports. At the beginning (1702-1704) the English tried to take St. Augustine in Florida, Arecibo in Puerto Rico, Antioquía and the mines of Santa Cruz de la Cana in Darien (eastern Panama), the Island of Trinidad in the Caribbean, and Tabasco and Apalache in New Spain (Mexico). All these attacks failed except at Trinidad where the settlement was sacked. The French and Spanish revenged themselves by a landing party in the Bahamas which took prisoners and captured armaments and shipping. Nor were the English successful in an attempt against Havana in March 1707; though in June of the following year they overpowered first the man-of-war *Gobierno,* with a cargo of silver, and then the *San Joaquin,* though merchant vessels escaped. In the Pacific area there were various raids by privateers, which sacked the city of Guayaquil, Ecuador in 1709 and captured a vessel on the Philippine run in 1710. After the War of the Succession had ended, there was still fighting in the Caribbean and in the Pacific against English pirates and smugglers whom it was necessary to pursue with boats of the Royal Navy and with privateers; a pursuit in which the mariner Don Blas de Lezo distinguished himself.

The war with France in 1719 resulted in loss of the colony of Pensacola in Florida—which, later recovered, was again taken by the French —and in a victory off Punta Maldonado in South America (Uruguay), which dislodged the enemy from positions that they had won. During this period hand-to-hand fighting continued with English, Dutch, and French smugglers who were bent on carrying out contraband trade with Spanish colonies in America and who were pursued by Spanish coastguards with varying success. In 1726 an official expedition under Admiral Hosier, sent out from London by the English Government, was frustrated in its effort to conquer, or at least to block, the Spanish fleet. Operations arising from the war of 1739 have been noted hitherto.

The disputes with Portugal along the Brazilian frontier caused many complications, the later developments of which were mentioned in connection with the wars of 1762 and 1766. Here is a brief sketch of the antecedents: In the seventeenth century, a group of deportees sent out by the Portuguese Government to settle Brazil founded the colony of São Paulo. From that base the settlers carried on continual expeditions into territories of the Paraná River, which belonged to the Government of Buenos Aires—smuggling, sacking the towns, and trying to extend the Portuguese dominions. These raids, which were not merely tolerated but encouraged by the authorities at Rio de Janeiro and Lisbon, kept reaching farther and farther south; and in 1679 they resulted in the foundation on the eastern shore of the River Plate of a stronghold called the colony of Sacramento.

When the Governor of Buenos Aires learned of this, he sent out troops that captured the fort, destroyed it, and took the garrison prisoners (August, 1680). This victory was rendered ineffective by the provisional treaty of May 7, 1681 between Portugal and Spain, which returned the Sacramento territory to Portugal, though with a prohibition against constructing works of defense there and of founding any kind of establishment until the boundaries should be fixed. Philip V, by the treaty of mutual alliance with Portugal which he signed June 18, 1701, settled the question by declaring (Article 14) that he ceded and renounced "any and every right that he might have in the lands concerned in the provisional treaty . . . of May 7, 1681, in which is situated the colony of Sacramento; the which treaty shall be without effect and the dominion of the said colony and use of the country shall pertain to the Crown of Portugal as it does at present." The War of the Spanish Succession interrupted the carrying out of this treaty, and the Spaniards recaptured Sacramento; but the Peace of Utrecht again handed the colony over to the Portuguese.

This did not settle border problems. The Portuguese at Sacramento revived them by an attempt in 1723 to capture Montevideo, from which city they were driven out the following year. Such barefaced smuggling was carried on from Sacramento that the Spanish Government decided to destroy the colony; but the diplomatic intervention of several powers detained the blow. Nevertheless, it was urgently necessary to do away with that center of contraband trade. As the best means of achieving this, a compensation was agreed upon in a treaty January 31, 1750, regarding the general fixing of boundary lines between Spanish and Portuguese possessions in America and in Asia. By this treaty

Portugal ceded to Spain "the colony of Sacramento and all adjacent territory on the northern bank of the River Plate . . . and also navigation of the said river"; and Spain in exchange ceded to Portugal "all and any towns and establishments which have been built . . . in the angle of the land included between the northern bank of the Ibicuí River and the eastern of the River Uruguay, and those that may have been founded on the eastern shore of the Pepirí River, and the town of Santa Rosa and any others that may have been established by Spain on the western shore of the Guaporé River." Part of the lands thus ceded by Spain were the Jesuit missions of Paraguay; namely, the settlements of San Juan, San Miguel, San Lorenzo, San Luis, San Nicolás, El Angel and San Borja, inhabited by Guaraní Indians. With respect to them, the treaty provided that "the missionaries shall go forth with the furnishings and effects, taking the Indians with them to settle them in other terrain of Spain, and the said Indians may likewise take their movable property and livestock and the arms, powder and munitions which they possess." From the first this treaty had its critics, chief among whom, as we have seen, was the Marquis of Ensenada. He reported its contents to Charles, King of Naples, heir presumptive to the throne of Spain, who tried to keep it from going into effect. Another obstacle, also noted, was the opposition of the Guaraní Indians, roused by the missionaries who objected to the cession, and who presented reports and petitions against it, alleging that it was prejudicial to hand over to the Portuguese districts colonized by the Society of Jesus. It availed nothing that the General of the Order had written beforehand to the Provincial of Paraguay, suggesting that he try to persuade the Indians "to leave without the least resistance"; nor did it avail that the same General sent Father Luis Altamirano to Paraguay for the same purpose and with full power. The Indians—regarding whom the missionaries said that they had lost all authority and could convince them of nothing—threatened Altamirano himself, who had to flee, and made ready to repel with arms the Commissioners of Spain and Portugal. Meanwhile, the missionaries multiplied their statements and petitions and tried to interest persons of influence against the treaty, including the King's confessor, Father Rábago, who at first approved the cession and later upheld resistance to it. The Guaranís did not falter in their opposition and had to be overcome by force of arms, which was done in 1756. After their defeat, the Indians abandoned the disputed localities, first burning some towns; which circumstance the Portuguese seized on as a pretext for declaring that the treaty had not been complied with and refusing to hand over Sacramento, though they held on to the missions. A new treaty, on February 12, 1761, by which Charles III annulled the treaty of 1750 was not conclusive, since the Portuguese continued in possession of both Sacramento and the missions. That was the background for the Spanish campaigns, in 1762 and later, to take Sacramento.

Spain's last war with England gave rise to an important episode in the River Plate region. Toward the end of 1805, the English despatched to the Brazilian coasts a powerful fleet with the primary objective of attacking the Dutch colony at the Cape of Good Hope in South Africa. Notified of the proximity of this expeditionary force, Viceroy Sobremonte of Buenos Aires, fearing an attack on Montevideo, sent forces to that city, leaving Buenos Aires itself without a garrison. But it was Buenos Aires that the British attacked in June, 1806, returning from the Cape. They took the capital with great ease. Sobremonte had abandoned it, withdrawing to Luján, an inland town. But if the Viceroy could not or dared not fight the invaders, the residents of Buenos Aires refused to resign themselves to foreign domination and organized conspiracies for a country-wide uprising. They lacked a military leader, but one soon presented himself in the person of Don Santiago Liniers, a Frenchman by birth who had been in the service of Spain since 1775. At the time, Liniers was commander of the fleet protecting the coastline of the Viceroyalty. On the pretext of visiting his family, who resided at Buenos Aires, he entered Buenos Aires and established contacts with the conspirators. What he learned determined him to go to Montevideo and demand the aid of the Governor there, Don Pascual Ruíz Huidobro, and of his troops, to reconquer Buenos Aires. He found things ready and waiting at Montevideo, since not only the Governor but all the people (in representation of whom the *Cabildo* had of its own initiative named Huidobro military chief of the River Plate in substitution for the pusillanimous and vacillating Viceroy), were resolved on military action. A plan of operations had been drawn up by several Spanish officers (Concha, Michelena, Córdoba, and others). When it was communicated to Liniers and approved by him, he was given command of an expedition to attack the English in Buenos Aires, which was made up of troops from the Montevideo garrison and volunteers, the latter including a group of Catalán light infantrymen and 73 French sailors. With this exceedingly small army, which began to increase in size by new adhesions as soon as it landed at the port of Las Conchas, eighteen miles from Buenos Aires (August 4, 1806), Liniers attacked the capital; and in spite of the valiant resistance of the English under command of General Beresford, he conquered the city and forced the enemy to capitulate on August 12.

In an open session of the *Cabildo* on August 14, the public had its way and Liniers was named civil and military chief of the vice-royalty; an appointment that Sobremonte had to recognize, confirming Liniers in his command of the Army and entrusting the political government to the Audiencia while he himself retired to Montevideo.

That victory did not end the war. When the English Government was apprised of the taking of Buenos Aires, it fitted out a formidable expeditionary force to conquer the colony. Its first successful action was the taking of Montevideo (February 3, 1807), after defeating Sobremonte on the outskirts of the city. This produced such excitement in Buenos Aires that the leading citizens and the city officials in a meeting specially called on February 10, decreed the deposition of Sobremonte, his imprisonment and return to Spain, with the exercise of provisional government by the *Audiencia* until the King should take action. However, the Viceroy was really Liniers, who was recognized as such *de facto* by the *Cabildo* on August 14, 1806. Liniers, seconded in all his plans by the Ayuntamiento and the citizenry, enthusiastically set about making the city ready for defense, and instructing and drilling the inhabitants—Spaniards, Creoles, Negroes, Mulattos and Indians—forming them into several·battalions.

The English did not keep them waiting for the attack, after failure of an expedition under the Spanish Colonel Elio. The English troops, commanded by General Whitelocke and numbering 10,000, presented themselves before Buenos Aires 'at the end of June. At first Liniers was defeated on the city's outskirts (partly because Colonel Elio had not taken the position assigned him), but the citizens were not downcast by this fact. Under direction of the Mayor, Don Martín Alzaga, they prepared for strong resistance with Liniers, who had reentered the city, in command. Success crowned their efforts. The English were defeated utterly and had to surrender, July 6, 1807, promising to evacuate the entire River Plate region within two months; a promise that they kept.

Liniers was confirmed by the King of Spain in the post of Viceroy which the people had conferred upon him. That was the state of affairs when the events of Bayonne occurred and the Second of May uprising at Madrid; events that were to have a far-reaching influence on the American colonies of Spain.

Finally, in the Philippines, ever since the beginning of the eighteenth century there had been repeated attacks on Spanish towns by the Moros of Mindinao, Jolo, and Borneo. These attacks, suspended in 1726 by a treaty of peace, were soon renewed and occasioned complications with the Dutch (1731-35), who intervened in the conflict between Malinog, King of Jolo, and the Sultan Diafar, whom the Spaniards supported.

Mention should also be made of the embassies which the Spanish Governor of the Philippines sent to the Kings of Siam and Tongking in 1719. They resulted in fruitful treaties of friendship and trade and the cession to Spain of lands for establishing factories to facilitate commerce.

Eighteenth Century Uprisings and Political Conspiracies in the Americas

Along with the international questions enumerated, which brought war to the Spanish colonies in the Americas, there were internal disturbances, not exempt from seriousness in themselves, but some of them still more serious because of clashes in ideology which they represented. These disturbances consisted of a series of uprisings of differing character, which occurred in almost all Spain's New World possessions, and which had had precedents in former centuries. These American insurrections during the eighteenth century and at the commencement of the nineteenth (until 1808) may be classified in two groups: one comprising revolts provoked simply by ambition to rule on the part of some individuals, but without separatist motivation, and those made in protest against certain acts of the Governors and the Companies, or against the imposition of some tax; the other, uprisings that evidently had political independence as their purpose.

The earliest of the first group was the insurrection in Paraguay in 1721 called the revolt of the *Comuneros* (in memory of the rebellion of the *Comuneros* in Castile). It was started by an Investigating Magistrate (*juez pesquisador*), Don José de Antequera, who had been sent to Asunción by the *Audiencia* of Charcas, and who took possession of the government and refused to hand it over, on the pretext that all the orders to that effect presented to him were false. The rebellion lasted for some years, until Antequera was taken prisoner and executed in July 1731; but this did not end anarchy in Paraguay. Energetic attempts to repress it were countered by Antequera's followers with a new uprising and assassination of the Governor. The country, pacified in 1735, was drowned in blood in 1741 by another insurrection, in which some priests took part.

In 1724 the cities of Salta and Jujuy in the Argentine mutinied against Governor Ortiz de Oro who had to take refuge in flight. Not long after in Peru, while Don Juan Antonio de Mendoza was Viceroy, the Indians of the missions of Chanchamayo revolted and assassinated several religious. In 1749 Captain Juan Francisco de León led an insurrection which had nothing to do with independence but was against abuses by the Guipuzcoan Company; and which recurred in 1751, ending in León's surrender and trial. In 1752 the militia at Rioja and Catamarca in the Argentine revolted against the periodical obligation of military service; and in 1754 the cities of San Miguel del Tucumán, Catamarca and Rioja revolted against their Governor Martínez Tineo. In 1755 there was an Indian uprising at Quito in Ecuador because of taxes; it was promptly put down through the Archbishop's mediation and an amnesty. In 1767 Salta and Jujuy rebelled again, this time against Governor Campero.

In Mexico (in addition to the mutinies because of the expulsion of the Jesuits to which we shall refer later on in more detail) there was an important uprising at Guanajuato in protest against the administrative and especially the financial changes made by the Occasional Judge Gálvez—new taxes, tobacco monopoly, et cetera; and another of the miners of Pachuca against the mine-owner, Don Pedro Terrero. There were also two Indian rebellions, at Izúcar in 1781 and in Yucatán in 1765, the latter costing many lives before it was suppressed. It was stirred up by a baker named Jacinto Canek who was proclaimed King of the Mayas. Canek aroused the Indians by preaching against taxes, against the severities of the courts, and against the neglectfulness of the clergy.

The second, and much more important, group of uprisings includes the following: In 1742, the savage Chuncho Indians in Peru rebelled. In 1748 there was a similar rebellion in Cauta and Huarochirí Provinces in Peru, with participation of several Indian tribes and of Negro slaves; the intention being to cast out the Spaniards and restore the Inca empire. Though six of the principal agitators were hanged, another succeeded in bringing about an insurrection of the Province of Huarochirí, which resulted in assassination of the Lieutenant General, the *Corregidor,* and other persons, and caused great property damage until conquered by armed force.

A rebellion of utmost gravity occurred in 1780-81 in territories of the Vice-royalties of Peru and Buenos Aires. In Peru, after several attacks and riots in previous years at Chuco, Sisaticia, Pacages, Chunvivilcas, Urubamba, Cuzco, and other points, the rebellion was prepared and led by a descendant of the Incas called José Gabriel Condorcanqui, *cacique* of Tungasuca in the Province of Tinta. Condorcanqui took the name of his ancestor Tupac-Amaru and presented himself as liberator of Indians and *Mestizos,* who were always exasperated over oppressions suffered by the colonists, notwithstanding the numerous protective laws and efforts of the Viceroys on their behalf. It cost much sweat and blood to subdue this rebellion, which for some time mastered not only the Province of Huarochirí but Cuzco as well, where the capital city of the same name was besieged by the Indians and came near to falling into their hands. Tupac-Amaru and six of his associates were executed May 18, 1781; but a brother of his and other followers, among them the brothers Catasí, continued the war, chiefly in the Province of Cuzco and of La Paz in Bolivia, so that troops had to be sent from Buenos Aires to Upper Peru. There, in combination with Peruvian forces they succeeded after great effort in conquering and subjecting the rebel leaders who were springing up on every side throughout those regions and who among other feats of arms, several times besieged La Paz. Not until 1782 was this rebellion definitely suppressed; and a relative of Tupac-Amaru even made an unsuccessful attempt to renew it in June 1783.

In the same period there was an insurrection in the mountain village of Socorro in New Granada (Colombia). It was a revolt of *Mestizos* who took the name *Comuneros* (like the rebels in Paraguay). It is believed that the seed for it might have been sown by the liberal sentiments of the Viceroy Don Manuel Antonio Flórez. However, it did not break out during his rule. When Flórez was recalled to Spain, the severity of the Royal Delegate (*comisario regio*) Piñeres, who took his place, and the discontent over taxes, caused an uprising of the town of Socorro March 16, 1781. The movement spread rapidly, and some 2,000 insurgents started out against Bogotá. The authorities there capitulated, decreeing amnesty and abolishing the taxes. But as soon as troops arrived in sufficient numbers to put down the rebellion, these concessions were revoked and the leaders of the *comuneros* were condemned to death and executed—José Antonio Galán, Lorenzo Alcantuy, Isidro Molina, and Manuel Ortiz. (In contemporary American literature, Archibald MacLeish's radio play *Socorro, When Your Stones Forget!* deals with this uprising).

In 1780 a conspiracy that matched in gravity the one in Peru was discovered at Santiago, Chile. Its purpose was to free the country from Spanish rule; and its leaders, two Frenchmen, Antonio Gramosset and Antonio Berney, were taken prisoner and shipped to Spain with utmost secrecy. Their accomplices among Chilean Creoles and *Mestizos* included Don José Antonio Rojas, a man of means, imbued with the ideas of the Encyclopedists.

There were several uprisings in Mexico: that of the Indians of the northern border, in Chihuahua and Sonora, during Bucareli's governorship (1777-79), a movement inspired and clandestinely armed by the English; and the insurrection which was led by the Indian Mariano in 1802 in the Tepic Sierra, with the object of restoring the kingdom of Montezuma, and which was soon suppressed. There was also a conspiracy discovered while still brewing (November, 1799), stirred up by Don Pedro de la Portilla and others at Mexico City and aspiring to proclaim Mexican independence and declare war on Spain: proposals that were somewhat academic for revolutionists who had a cash capital of one thousand pesos, two guns, and fifty machetes. The Viceroy assigned slight importance to the affair in itself but kept the conspirators in prison for several years.

Separatist doctrines were preached in Colombia during the closing years of the eighteenth century, the leading propagandists being Antonio Nariño and Francisco Zea. The Viceroy sought to suppress the movement by arresting its leaders, some of whom were deported to the Peninsula

Venezuela witnessed similar reckless ventures. The first of these, occurring in 1797, was headed by a retired captain of the veteran battalion of Caracas, Don Manuel Gual, and the Chief Justice of Macuto, Don José María España. It is probable that the Spanish Republicans Picornell, Cortés, and Andrés were involved in it. They had been exiled from the Peninsula in 1796 and imprisoned at La Guaira; escaping the following year. Gual and España had a small army of Creoles and *Mestizos* and a few troops, and they proposed to proclaim the Republic of Venezuela. When the plot was discovered, 89 persons were tried, including two Franciscan friars. Picornell and Cortés succeeded in fleeing to the Island of Curaçao. España was beheaded and quartered. It became apparent during the trial that the germ of that plot had been disseminated with ideas of the French Revolutionists, and that encouragement by the English Governor of Trinidad had been a fostering element. In May 1799 another attempt at Maracaibo was likewise frustrated. About that time, a major revolutionary project was being plotted by Don Francisco de Miranda who had served in the Spanish Army, with Washington and Lafayette in the American War of Independence, and with the French as one of Napoleon's Marshals. A native son of Caracas, Miranda travelled widely. In 1790 he had negotiated with the English Prime Minister William Pitt for aid in organizing an expeditionary force, presenting to him the draft of a Constitution which would create an independent State of all South America (except Brazil and Guiana) together with Cuba. Fifteen years later Miranda was promised by the English Government the aid that he sought, and obtained additional assistance in the United States. Sailing from New York with 200 men, his expedition was a failure before its landing in April 1806 on the Venezuelan coast. The second expedition that he led failed likewise in August of the same year.

The lack of success of all these conspiracies was due chiefly to the indifference of the majority of the colonial population, especially of the so-called *"pardos'*—or Mulattoes— and to the opposition of the Creole aristocracy and wealthier bourgeoisie who at that time sup· ported the Spanish Government and repudiated foreign aid which would result only in a geographical change of the center of government.

The French, for their part, in various ways tried to provoke a general uprising of Spain's American colonies. The National Assembly attempted this, and warning of the plot was communicated to the Count

Cathedral of Santiago de Compostela.

of Floridablanca by the Spanish Ambassador at Paris, Count Fernan-Nuñez. He had been assured, he said, by "a reliable source" that "some members of the National Assembly, among them one called M. Cotein," had proposed "to have introduced into the Americas a seditious Manifesto in order to arouse . . . the inhabitants . . . to throw off the yoke of Spanish rule, following the example of France." That propaganda seems not to have had any effect evident at the time. Napoleon later resumed the separatist campaign, sending to America emissaries who, together with citizens of the United States, contributed powerfully toward forming that state of opinion in the Spanish colonies of the New World which not long after was to produce the decisive movement for Independence. Louisiana was one of the great centers of the conspiracy against Spain, which irradiated principally, however, from Mexico.

Finally, there were several uprisings of native peoples in the Philippines: at Malaveg and Ticao (Cagayán) and at Ilo-Ilo (1718).

The Regalism and the Religious Tolerance of the Bourbon Kings

The Bourbon dynasty reigning in Spain inherited from the House of Austria, and firmly maintained, regalism with respect to its relations with the Church. This led to a struggle, fundamentally jurisdictional, with the *Curia,* or ecclesiastical court, at Rome, and with its representatives in Spain (including the *Tribunal de la Nunciatura,* or Tribunal of the Nunciature, and the *Tribunal de la Cruzada,* or Tribunal of the Crusade) , which exercised considerable intervention in affairs of the national Church. The first episode of that struggle on political grounds was motivated by the fact that in the War of the Spanish Succession the Pope took the part of the Archduke of Austria, and thereby occasioned the immediate closure of the Tribunal of the Nunciature, the exile of the Papal Nuncio, and the breaking off of relations with Rome. This jurisdictional dispute was ended in Ferdinand VI's reign by the Treaty, or Concordat, of 1753 between the Spanish Monarchy and the Holy See; but it was renewed for other reasons in the reigns of Charles III and Charles IV. The Concordat satisfied many of the Crown's jurisdictional aspirations.

Questions arose also between the State and the Inquisition, principally in relation to that Tribunal's overstepping its jurisdiction, and

Juan Cariño de Miranda: *Charles II as a Boy.*

o the obstacles that it frequently placed in the way of civil suits. Therein lay the origin of the proposal to limit and regulate the Inquisition's sphere of action; a proposal initiated in Philip V's reign and achieved under Charles III and Charles IV. In practice, in so far as touches upon repression of heresy, the Inquisition of the eighteenth century was much less harsh and exigent than it had been formerly. There was a prevailing spirit of tolerance among eminent men of the period and the kings themselves. Moreover, the Spanish State had been forced to yield to this spirit in several peace treaties contracted with Protestant Countries such as England. Besides instances of this with regard to subjects of foreign nations, there are other very significant examples; among them that already cited of the German miners sent by Charles I to Bogotá, who were permitted to bring in their Bibles and practice their religion freely in New Granada.

Closely related to the jurisdictional questions already cited, but in a way more political than juridical (analogous to the effect, produced in the time of the House of Austria, by the State's punishment of several clerics who from the pulpit censured Government measures) was occurrence of an event amazing for that period, the expulsion of the Jesuits. It took place in the reign of Charles III (1767), and was the result chiefly of the King's conviction that in Spain the Jesuits constituted an element prejudicial to public tranquillity and to the Monarchy. Among the known facts that seem to have contributed to this belief was the conduct of the Jesuits in relation to questions of the territorial limits for Paraguay then agreed on by Spain and Portugal; the attempts against the lives of the Kings of France and Portugal which some attributed to the Company of Jesus; and the resolute Jesuit opposition to canonization of the Spanish cleric Palafox, seventeenth century Bishop of Puebla de los Angeles in New Spain, author of a history of the Tartar conquest of China, and unremitting polemist with the Jesuits in the Americas; and the reputed intervention of the Company of Jesus in the preparation and outbreak of a widely publicized mutiny against the King's Minister, Squilacci. To these reasons, which the King and his Ministers deemed just, was added the widespread unpopularity of the Jesuits among other religious orders and the priesthood. Because of all these things together, the expulsion of the Jesuits was viewed with either approbation or indifference by the Spanish

INTERIOR DIVISIONS
IN INTENDENCIAS OF
VICEROYALTIES OF
PERU É RÍO DE LA PLATA
EIGHTEENTH CENTURY

clergy in general; although protests were not lacking, such as those from the Bishops of Burgos and Cuenca and the Archbishop of Toledo. The expulsion was effected not only in Spain but in the Spanish colonies of America, where the Company of Jesus had many important missions. Years later (August 17, 1773), it was followed by a Papal Bull ordaining dissolution of the Order, in consequence of reiterated efforts to that end made by the Kings of Spain and France. Clement XIV was Pope at the time. In commemoration of the event a medal was coined at Rome. The Order was re-established in 1814 by Pope Pius VII.

Revival of Culture

The intellectual and artistic decadence of the late seventeenth century soon ended, largely as a result of the renewed encouragement given Spanish cultural life by the kings; of the foundation (already mentioned) of primary schools, workshops, technical schools for workers, factories, and scholarships for foreign study; and of widespread university reform. Taken as a whole, all this brought about a notable revival, although it did not in general, nor specifically in most of the arts and sciences and certainly not in literature, recover the glory of the past. The eighteenth century renascence was especially marked in the physical and natural sciences, with Spanish workers in those fields emulating in the number and value of their contributions sixteenth and seventeenth century scientific pioneers; in some industrial arts (ceramics, tapestries, silks); and in painting and other plastic arts. All this, occurring in the space of a very few years, demonstrates not only the effectiveness of the means employed for stimulating such activities, but also the persistence in the national mentality of the same innate qualities which it had been revealing ever since the fifteenth century, and before. There is no other credible explanation than natural Spanish ability for the speedy appearance on the scene in eighteenth century Spain of so large a group of illustrious men in many of whom was observable the spirit of criticism which characterized the period. What might be called the popular expression of that spirit, up to the point that it could be felt by a liberal-minded Catholic, is exemplified in the Benedictine, Father Benito Feijoo, whose reasoned critical approach to philosophic material and to the supersti-

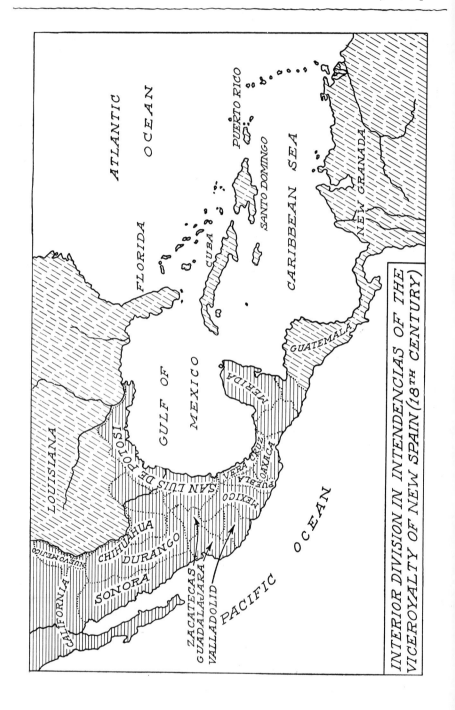

INTERIOR DIVISION IN INTENDENCIAS OF THE
VICEROYALTY OF NEW SPAIN (18TH CENTURY)

tions and prejudices of the masses are to be found in a kind of diary or running commentary that he called *Teatro Crítico* (Critical Theatre; 1726-39), and in its continuation, *Cartas eruditas* (Learned Letters; 1742 and thereafter). These are of a lasting importance far beyond the positive effect produced in their own time, notwithstanding the fact that they then ran to many editions. Much the same could be said of José de Cadalso, army officer and man-of-letters, at one and the same time a great patriot and a man of his century, whose *Cartas marruecas* (Moroccan Letters, 1789) is an interesting essay on the psychology of the Spanish people and a criticism of its backwardness which was vitalized by faith in its future. From another point of view, Juan Pablo Forner, magistrate and author, in his *Apología* written to counteract the Hispanophobia shown by many foreigners of the time, stated similar problems, perhaps with more equanimity in his patriotic approach. Diego de Torres Villaroel, a free and inquiring mind, while inferior to Feijoo, still affords good reading in his satirical sketches of the customs and institutions of his day. Also worthy of note because of the solid content of his book, *Gobierno político de los pueblos de España*—Political Government of the Towns of Spain; 1769—is Lorenzo de Santayana Bustillo, ancestor of the present-day philosopher George Santayana, whose fame, though he is a Spaniard, has come from his writings in English.

The renascence affected the arts also, though less extensively than in the case of history and the sciences. However, in the special field of painting and allied *genres* towered the overwhelming personality of Goya, whose genius was multiple as Shakespeare's, and who was not only one of the world's greatest and most vigorous painters, but also a profound observer of the contemporary scene, a thinker of very independent mind in some respects far in advance of his age, and a critic of society and politics to a degree that is seldom attained by artists of any century, and that was particularly infrequent in his own.

Spanish architecture of the eighteenth century includes some good examples of construction still in use today, such as the Prado Museum, the Ministry of Finance (formerly the Custom House), the Royal Palace at Madrid, the Palace of Prince Luis (Luis I) at Arenas de San Pedro, the Puerta de Alcalá, and many more, both ecclesiastical and governmental, in various towns; all of them Renaissance or classic, which style had again become paramount after the interlude of Churrigurism, lasting for some years. The sculptures of the period were likewise Renaissance in type, examples being the Statue of the Cybeles, the Fountain of the Four Seasons at the Prado in Madrid, the Fountain of Neptune, the sacred sculptures of Salcillo (showing Italian influence) , and others. Ceramics (Retiro, Alcora, Talavera) either followed foreign styles, such as the English, or revived the Spanish tradition. Etching was reborn and revitalized because of the work of Goya himself and of several other such artists as Carmona and Galván. The weaving and embroidery of tapestry was revived likewise, principally by the Royal Factory of Tapestries (1721) to which we have made previous reference. Goya painted many cartoons (which are still extant) for its tapestry designs. Along with drapes of silk and damask (there was a famous factory for the latter at Talavera) , tapestry became the characteristic decoration of Spanish interiors, which were further adorned with mirrors of the cornucopia type, of which there is a large and choice collection in the Cathedral of Segovia; and other art objects and fine furniture.

In literature, notwithstanding the widespread influence then exercised by French writers, who were extremely popular throughout Europe—an influence so intensive as even to affect the purity of the Spanish of many of our writers,—the great tradition of Spanish literature was maintained by some authors, few but important, whose characteristic independence and originality opened up new paths in the world of letters. The persistence of that tradition was shown by the important series of Spanish classics then reissued in new editions; and by the sound knowledge of these classics evidenced by various eighteenth century authors (such as Cadalso) and literary critics. In the theatre, where the works of Lope de Vega and other dramatists of the Golden Age continued to be represented, the struggle between French modes and Spanish—Gallicism and Hispanism—was more intense than it was in other *genres*. The *sainetes*, or brief dramatic farces, of Don Ramón de la Cruz, an accomplished stylist, and those of Don Juan del Castillo (dealing with the local customs of Cádiz) were the most vigorous Hispanist expressions of the time. In music, much influenced at this period by the Italian schools, the same thing was true for a while of the *tonadillas*, or musical interludes. Leandro Fernández de Moratín, a follower of Molière, completes the picture—with comedies truly Spanish in style and substance (*El café* and *El sí de las niñas*) —of that end-of-the-eighteenth-century society when the first stirrings began to be felt of the spirit of liberty which was soon to transform Spanish life. In this sense, and making allowance for the considerable differences, it may be said that Moratín was our Spanish Beaumarchais. The writings on art history and art criticism were also important, both in general, and in particular with respect to Music. Toward the close of the century, in Germany especially, there was much enthusiasm for the classics of Spanish literature.

Of far greater importance were Spain's contributions at that time to both national and general historiography. The culminating work of national historiography was Juan Francisco Masdeu's *Historia crítica de España y de la cultura española*—Critical History of Spain and Spanish Culture; 1783—which for the first time added to the old type of a purely political history an historical study of Spanish civilization, even though the latter is confined in Masdeu's book to culture in the usual limited acceptance of that term. The book marks a notable advance over such works as Father Juan de Mariana's old-style History of Spain. General historiography—literary and in other fields—was cultivated also, in many phases with great originality, by the Jesuits who upon their expulsion emigrated to Italy; and in Spain by Father Enrique Florez with his *España Sagrada* (Sacred Spain), a copious collection of documents, and his *Medallas de las colonias, municipios, y pueblos antiguos de España* (Medals of the Colonies, Municipalities, and Ancient Peoples of Spain) ; Antonio Capmany, with his *Memorias históricas sobre la marina, comercio y artes de la antigua ciudad de Barcelona* (Historical Records of the Shipping, Commerce, and Arts of the Ancient City of Barcelona; 1799), which—from another standpoint than Masdeu's—is also a history of civilization; Asso y de Manuel, author of *Economía política de Aragón*; Juan Sempere; Juan Antonio Llorente; Father Andrés Marcos Burriel; and many others, besides Francisco Martínez Marina whose *Ensayo crítico histórico sobre la antigua legislación de los reinos de León y Castilla* (Essay in Historical Criticism on the Ancient Legislation of the Kingdoms of León and Castile; 1808) closes the period under discussion. Mention should be made also of the reprintings of our sixteenth and seventeenth century literary classics and of the numerous works dealing with the history of Spanish literature and language, of which we cite individually only those of Father Martín Sarmiento (1775), Luis José Velázquez (1749) —

which was translated into German—Gregorio Mayans, Father Garcés, the monumental *Catálogo de las lenguas de las naciones conocidas* (Catalogue of the Languages of Known Nations; 1800-1805), by the Jesuit Hervás y Panduro who made important studies in other fields also; and the *Historia literaria de España* (Literary History of Spain; 1776 and later) written by the Mohedanos Fathers.

The cultured Spaniard of the eighteenth century was keenly aware that the need for public education was a national problem. He was as conscious of the decadence of learning as he was of the economic decadence. He knew that the majority of the Spanish people could not read and write, and that they were beset by superstition and dread. Almost as soon as Queen Amalia, wife of Charles III, reached her kingdom of Spain, she described conditions in a letter to Tanucci (1766) : "This nation has never been completely conquered, and I believe that its total conquest is reserved for the King. In everything here there is somewhat of barbarism. . . . One does not know what to talk about with the women," she added: "their ignorance is incredible."

And yet, in spite of this harsh judgment by the new-come Queen, one of the signs of the times in eighteenth century Spain was the widespread desire of the women for education. It was analogous to the devotion to learning so frequently shown by Spanish women during the reign of the Catholic Kings, and in the period of greatest splendor of the House of Austria. Ladies of the nobility at Madrid formed a Commission—the *Junta de Damas*—which was devoted to establishing primary schools. Some of these women of noble birth—the Duchess de Huéscar y de Arcos, the Marquesa of Santa Cruz, one of the daughters of the Count of Oñate, and the Marquesa of Guadalcazar—were received into the Royal Academy as honorary members. The Marquesa de San Millán, devoting herself to the study of astronomy, constructed an observatory at her house in Victoria. The Marquesa de Tolosa translated educational and devotional works from the French. Doña Josefa Amor y Borbón, honorary member of the Aragonese Royal Society and a member of the *Junta de Damas,* published a treatise on the Physical and Moral Education of Women (*Discurso sobre la educación física y moral de las mujeres;* 1790). Doña María Reguera y Mondragón read papers on teachers' training and other educational problems before the Royal Society of Lugo. Doña Joaquina Tomaseti, of Cádiz, wrote a politico-sociological study of The Spirit of the Spanish Nation. Queen Doña Bárbara de Braganza founded a young women's seminary in the Visitation Convent. Many other examples could be adduced to show how the example set by the *préciuses* of the Marquise de Rambouillet's salon at Paris, together with the Spanish tradition in these matters, made the Spanish woman a working ally of the Spanish man in the great task of reeducating the nation.

Public Works

The revival extended also to public works of utilitarian character, in such form and measure as to amount to a third period marking administrative attention to and satisfaction for the human necessities bound up in natural conditions of soil and climate. The first and the second period in which these pressing needs were given due consideration were, as we know, the epoch of Roman domination and Philip II's reign.

The eighteenth century rulers devoted much thought to increasing and improving means of communication, which were greatly needed all over the country. Some highways were improved or reconstructed at the end of the eighteenth century, and mile-posts were erected, with stone bridges, and, at the entrance to the principal cities, stone benches, many of which are still in use. As for irrigation, the canals of Castile and Huesca, and the Imperial—or Pignatelli—Canal of Aragón were constructed, as were the reservoirs of Val del Infierno and Puentes; besides such public works as necessarily were built in connection with "internal colonizations."

Dissemination of Revolutionary Ideas

The political and social ideas of the French Encyclopedists in the first place and of the French Revolution later had trickled into Spain and, though at first affecting only a small minority, had begun to produce results. Among the many evidences of this were the increasingly widespread dissemination among the educated classes of French books and pamphlets, including the Encyclopedia itself, which had numerous subscribers, especially in the Basque Provinces. Some French reformers maintained close contacts with such Spanish statesmen as Aranda and Azara. There was also extensive correspondence between

the Duke of Alba and Rousseau; the Duke of Villahermosa and Beaumarchais; Galiani and D'Alembert; the Marquis of Miranda and
Voltaire. Many young Spaniards were sent to France to be educated;
and French revolutionary agents as well as French teachers and master-
craftsmen took up residence in Spain. On the shelves of the libraries
of the *Sociedades de Amigos del País* were to be found the works of
Voltaire, Rousseau, Mirabeau, Bayle, D'Alembert, Montesquieu,
Hobbe, Locke, Hume, and many other foreigners.

Chapter XII

The New Liberal Ideas and the First Crisis of the Bourbon Monarchy

BY THE end of the eighteenth century the political ideas of eminent men were very different from what they had been at the century's beginning and in the time of the House of Austria. The thinking of the time was opposed to the absolutist and patrimonial pattern of European monarchies. The right of peoples to govern themselves and human rights—the rights of the individual—defined and enlarged upon in contemporaneous writings of very wide circulation, achieved their first legal determination in the War of Independence fought by the English colonies of North America, who proclaimed those principles as self-evident in their Declaration of Independence (July 4, 1776). The French Revolution, which in 1789 overthrew the monarchy and established the system of constitutional and parliamentary government on the continent of Europe, made the same affirmation in the Old World.

These ideas had repercussion in Spain; in part, and principally, as already noted, through influence of the Encyclopedia published 1751-65: expression, condensed and classified by subject matter, of the philosophic spirit of the French eighteenth century, applied to politics, religion, history, science, letters, and art in the attempt to find a rational explanation of the universe. The personal influence of Rousseau was also deeply felt in Spain, especially through his book *The Social Contract,* which was translated into Spanish; and the effect of the French Revolution itself was very great, and was augmented by the writing of some English and Italian philosophers and critics. We have shown that even among the Spanish nobility there were persons who maintained relations of friendship and corresponded with several of the most advanced French writers. In addition to all this, there was a Republican conspiracy in 1795 which, since it had little backing, was ended by the police almost as soon as discovered. The fact is that nothing in the atmosphere of Spain at that time favored a radical political change; but there was a strong sentiment for the constitutional and liberal reforms of the State which were soon to be effected.

The new political ideas were widespread also throughout the Spanish possessions in the Americas, and produced there a mobilization of opinion toward the example of independence that had been set by the English colonies in North America.

Charles IV, the King of Spain contemporaneous with the French Revolution, tried to keep its fiery seed from taking root in Spanish soil. He even went so far as to declare war on the French Republicans when he learned that the National Convention had decreed the trial and execution of Louis XVI and Marie Antoinette in 1793. This initial attitude of the Spanish Crown, however, was followed by an amicable relationship in 1795 when the Reign of Terror gave way to the Directorate, a government of moderate Republicans who replaced Robespierre's Jacobins. That understanding materialized in the Treaty of San Ildefonso (1796). One reason for it was the bad faith and contemptuous attitude shown by England in dealing with Spain, notwithstanding the fact (already mentioned) that the English and the Spanish had been allies during the War of 1793-95. It is probable that Charles IV was influenced also by the hope—fostered by French diplomacy—of obtaining the throne of France himself by reason of his being a Bourbon, if and when the Republic should cease to survive, as he expected it to do. A coalition was formed against the Directorate, with England, Russia, Naples, Tuscany, Turkey, and Austria entering into it. Charles IV and his Government, which was now in the hands of his Ministerial favorite Godoy, tried to dissuade Portugal from joining, but was unsuccessful in the effort. Spain continued to abide by the Treaty of San Ildefonso, notwithstanding the disrespectful manner in which she was treated by the Directorate during its new conflict with the Coalition, and in spite of the alternate threats and cajoleries which Russia and England employed as arguments to convince Charles IV.

Spain and the French Revolution

As the revolutionary movement in France, however, increased in popular strength and in menace to the monarchy, it confronted Charles IV's Government immediately as a new political problem, in some ways more serious than those that had gone before. It was important to the Spanish King and his Ministers in two aspects: because of the propaganda of revolutionary ideas all over the Peninsula, and because of the family solidarity of the Spanish ruling house and the French. The propaganda was a grave cause of alarm. Floridablanca, who was Charles IV's Minister as he had been Charles III's, was a man of liberal mind but a sincere royalist and consequently an enemy to everything that would undermine the throne, as absolutists then envisaged it. It is not strange therefore that he tried to prevent the introduction into Spain of the ideas that the frontier revolutionists were constantly trying to convey across the border by means of books and pamphlets. Suspicion of such propaganda cut short the efforts at reforms made by some members of the *Cortes* which, after years without session, was convoked by Charles IV on September 23, 1789. The frontier was narrowly watched to prevent the contagion from spreading into Spain. Furthermore, when Louis XVI's situation in France became increasingly difficult as the final tragedy was brewing, Floridablanca made public statements criticizing the conduct of the National Assembly and the state of things in France; so that the French revolutionists naturally regarded the Spanish Premier as an enemy. However, a turn in international affairs forced a change in Floridablanca's policy. In May 1789 a Spanish naval expedition was sent out from Mexico to visit the western coast of North America and destroy the foreign establishments that had been set up on territory belonging to Spain. Off Vancouver, in Nootka Bay, which had been discovered in 1774 and named the Bay of San Lorenzo by the commander of the Spanish frigate *Santiago,* the expedition found and seized two English vessels which, along with others, had been trading there and preparing to establish a factory. When the Viceroy of Mexico learned of the affair, he had the English boats released, dis-

authorizing the capture; but he made the English give bail for their appearance in court when the case of the attempted usurpation of Spanish property at Nootka should come up for trial. In January 1790 Floridablanca communicated these facts to the English Government, complaining of the frequent usurpations of Spanish colonial territories by British subjects, and asking for recognition of Spanish ownership of the Island and Bay of Nootka. The English Government refused until Spain should give satisfaction for the supposed insult to the British flag, the prompt action of the Mexican Viceroy being held insufficient in this respect. Floridablanca for his part refused to make any further amends, and war seemed imminent. In preparation for it, the Spanish Minister turned to the French Government, invoking the Family Pact, while at the same time reinforcing Spain's naval strength so that it might withstand England's great navy. The French National Assembly acknowledged the obligation and ordered a strong squadron to be armed, but hedged about its proffered aid with such unfavorable conditions that Floridablanca and Charles IV finally decided to settle the dispute with England pacifically. By the convention of October 28, 1790, it was agreed that subjects of either of the two contracting nations could fish freely, without molestation from the other, in waters of the Pacific Ocean and the South Seas and could land in unoccupied territory on the adjacent coasts to trade with the natives or to form establishments. However the English obligated themselves not to fish within ten leagues of coasts occupied by Spain nor to establish themselves in such areas. Two other conventions followed, by which Spain paid an indemnity for seizure of an English vessel at Nootka, and Nootka was declared an open port, England and Spain alike pledging themselves not to form a permanent establishment there nor to claim sovereignty.

On June 18, 1790, four months before the signing of the first of these treaties, a Frenchman had tried to assassinate Floridablanca, stabbing him twice. This attempt, which was attributed to French revolutionists, gave Charles IV's Minister a certain authority in approaching the European powers, as he did, in favor of concerted, energetic action to save Louis XVI from the dangers enmeshing him. It should be stated that in October 1789 the French King had written to his kinsman Charles IV to protest before him "against all acts contrary to the Royal authority, which has been taken from me by force since July 15 of this year," and to ask also that this protest be kept secret "until occasion make its publication needful." Such a step by Louis XVI was a strong basis for the anti-revolutionary policy of the Spanish Government. The note to the French National Assembly which the Spanish Ambassador presented in consequence was measured in tone but threatening at bottom since it declared that the friendship and esteem of His Catholic Majesty were "worth more [to the Assembly], from any point of view, than any other consideration." The note was received indignantly, and the Assembly tabled it without discussion.

In continuation of this policy, after detention of the French royal family at Varennes in June 1791, regarding which Charles IV issued a statement on July 1, Floridablanca ordered that a census be taken of all foreigners resident in Spain, and that they swear fidelity to the King, laws, and religion of the Peninsula—which was equivalent to renouncing the citizenship of their native country. In September of the same year Floridablanca prohibited rigorously the entry into Spain of all revolutionary literature (of which there was much in circulation along the frontier) and even of letters to foreign subjects. Finally, when Louis XVI's acceptance of the Constitution voted by the Assembly was communicated to Floridablanca, the latter replied that the King of Spain declined to acknowledge that the French monarch had made such acceptance of his own free will, and requested that, in proof of his pretended freedom, Louis XVI and his family be permitted to depart from France to a neutral country. War again seemed imminent. If the previous communication and the above-cited orders of the Spanish Government had caused indignation, this last message kindled positive fury, since it was an open defiance of the Revolution. However, instead of breaking off relations, the Assembly procured the fall of Floridablanca. To that end it sent an agent, M. de Bourgoing, to Spain, who, in union with the French Ambassador, tried to convince Charles IV of the dangers inherent, even for Louis XVI, in Floridablanca's policy. Their arguments were reinforced by the Prime Minister's political enemies and probably by the Queen, with the result that in February 1792 Charles yielded, and Aranda replaced Floridablanca in the Ministry.

The latter, not merely because of sympathy with the Revolution, as has been supposed, but also from a sense of caution and a realization of the need for relieving the tension caused by his predecessor's attitude toward France, did much to improve relations. However, Aranda did not for the time being give up conferring with European sovereigns as to a concerted plan of action for saving Louis XVI and aiding French Princes in exile; though he failed to foresee the extremes of violence which were so swift in coming. The excesses of the summer of 1792, with the storming of the Tuileries in August, alarmed Aranda to the point of changing his policy. On August 24 he consulted the Council on the advisability of declaring war on France, in a joint military action with Austria, Prussia, and Sardinia. The Council voted for war, and Aranda ordered the necessary preparations, although for reasons of prudence he delayed the formal declaration. With matters in this state, the French Government itself took the initiative, proposing to Spain the alternative of alliance or war. Aranda and Charles IV hesitated, fearing that if extreme measures were taken, it would be the worse for Louis XVI who was now a prisoner in the Temple. Aranda therefore proposed a treaty of neutrality, but the conditions imposed by France—beginning with recognition of the French Republic, which had now been proclaimed—were inacceptable to the Spanish monarch. Negotiations continued, however, until suddenly, on November 15, 1792, Aranda was relieved of his post.

This fall from power was not due to any political motive but to palace intrigue, instigated by Queen María Luisa who wanted her lover Manuel Godoy to be Prime Minister. Godoy, a former soldier of the Royal Guard belonging to the lesser nobility of Estremadura, was twenty-five years old when he was thus elevated to the most influential position in Spain. He was a favorite with Charles IV, who had made him Duke of Alcudía, and had considerable natural talents which he tried to polish and develop in the hope of achieving an important career with royal sponsorship. The effect of his talents and studies will be revealed as his story unfolds. Meanwhile, the appointment of this young adventurer to the Ministry, especially in view of the attendant murmurs of scandal, caused profound public indignation and prepared the way for the strife that was soon to divide not only Spaniards as a whole but the royal family itself.

Godoy's French policy—doubtless in accord with Charles IV's—was to save the life of Louis XVI without going to war with France nor forming an alliance with that country. To begin with, he tried to bribe some members of the French Convention; and he presented to that body a timid petition in favor of the imprisoned King along with the bases for the treaty of neutrality, which included recognition of the Republic. But the intransigents in the Convention succeeded in carrying the majority with them: the petition regarding Louis XVI was rejected, and the treaty was modified with terms more favorable to France and returned to Spain for signature. When a further attempt to save Louis also failed, Spain refused to sign the modified treaty and on March 7, 1793 France declared war. Charles IV made the corresponding declaration of war against France on March 23. Six days later he signed a treaty of alliance with England.

The War of 1793-1795

The execution of Louis XVI on January 21, 1793, not only caused a deep and painful impression in Spain, but roused Charles IV to demand vengeance for the offense against the House of Bourbon. Spain joined the first coalition against France but the campaign, which was fought mainly in Rousillon, was a failure. The Spaniards were driven from the fortresses guarding the Pyrenees, and the French advance neared the Ebro. Following Prussia's example, Spain decided to make peace. The terms were agreed on at Basle in July 1795, and ratified in August: the French evacuated all the territories that they were controlling in Spain, and Spain ceded to France that portion of the Island of Española, or Santo Domingo, still belonging to her; which gave France possession of the entire Island. France was also given a six-years license to take stallions and brood mares and sheep from Andalusia; and Charles IV agreed not to prosecute any of the Basques who had been won over to French ideas.

Though there was much discussion of the peace pro and con, and some censure of Godoy for its terms, public opinion in general rejoiced that the war was over and attached no importance to the loss of Santo Domingo. To Godoy the settlement brought the title Prince of the Peace.

The Alliance with the Directory and the New War with England

The Treaty of Basle annoyed the British Government extremely by depriving it abruptly of an ally in the struggle against France in which she was engaged. The truth is that even as an ally England had not been friendly toward Spain, nor loyal. On one occasion the Spanish treasure ship *Santiago* which had been captured by the French was recovered by the English with the cargo of about one billion *pesos,* and retained as a British prize in spite of their treaty with Spain. English smuggling continued in the Peninsula, as did English encouragement of separatist ideas in the Spanish colonies of America; while England refused to grant Spain any subsidy for the campaign of 1795. Such controversial actions were multiplied after the peace of Basle. Godoy, for his part, was inclined to convert that document into a treaty of alliance with France. All the French politicians cherished the same idea, obsessed as they were by the war with England and illusioned by hope of the possible aid of the Spanish Navy. Nevertheless, Godoy hesitated for some time until his hesitation was overborne by the Francophile tradition of the Spanish Government, greatly aided in this instance by the error of the English in employing threats against such an alliance, an attitude which caused a hostile reaction at the Spanish Court. The Council voted in favor of the French alliance, which took form in the Treaty of San Ildefonso on August 18, 1796. If, as some historians believe, there was some wishful thinking (possibly fostered by French intrigue) that an imminent fall of the French Republic might seat a Spanish Bourbon on the throne of France, nothing of the sort appears in the minutes of the Council. Its deliberations centered about the many complaints against England and the desire to reduce her power. This is also expressed in a manifesto against England published in the Royal *Cédula* of October 7, 1796, after preparations had been made for the war on the Peninsula and in the Americas. When hostilities broke out, the principal engagements were at Cape St. Vincent (February 14, 1797) resulting in a Spanish defeat with loss of five vessels; the attacks by the English, all successfully repulsed, on Cádiz in Spain, Tenerife in the Canary Islands, Puerto Rico in the Caribbean, and on Central America; and the conquest by the English of the Spanish Island of Trinidad, off Venezuela.

In this same year England, where the general public, wearied of the strife and isolation of war, yearned for peace, initiated negotiations with the Directory, at Lille. Logically, Spain would have taken part; but this was not the case, since the English proposed that representatives of the allied powers should not participate but that their respective claims should be presented by the only two nations carrying on the negotiations. The French agreed, unfaithful to their Spanish allies at Lille as they had been in the Austrian peace conference at Udina. Furthermore, far from presenting Spain's demands to England, France herself rejected some and paid little heed to others. This, as was natural, chilled the relations between Charles IV and the Directory, but his anger reached its height when French troops dispossessed Charles' relative, the Duke of Parma, of his territories.

The Directory, suspicious of Godoy, who was thought to incline toward the English and to have cooperated reluctantly in French policy (suspicion was based chiefly on his failure to oblige Portugal to deny British vessels the right of asylum in Portuguese ports), sent Citizen Turguet to Madrid to plot Godoy's downfall. Turguet exerted such pressure on Charles IV that the latter, by a decree of March 28, 1797, relieved Godoy of his Ministry, though continuing all "honors, emoluments and income" that he possessed. He was succeeded by Saavedra, Godoy's own former appointee as Finance Minister. However this was all merely a surface change for France's benefit. Godoy neither left the Court nor ceased to exercise influence. Saavedra as Premier and his colleague Jovellanos as Minister of Grace and Justice, suffered compulsions from Godoy, whose complete overthrow they dared not attempt lest they incur the active hostility of Queen María Luisa, but who meanwhile was working to overthrow them. Occasion for another change soon arose when Saavedra and Jovellanos became too ill to attend their offices—quite possibly because in some way poison had been administered to both. They were dismissed from their posts because of the serious nature of their illness, and replaced in August, 1798 by Mariano Luis de Urquijo (who introduced vaccination into Spain) and Soler, respectively. While they continued the policy of acquiescence toward the Directory, both Urquijo and Soler did what they could, without any moral support from the King, to resist French impositions.

Meanwhile, a new coalition against France had been formed, consisting of England, Russia, Naples, Tuscany, Turkey, and, finally, Austria. Portugal, though Charles IV had labored to reconcile that Government with the Directory, also made frank adherence to the coalition. Spanish diplomacy exerted every effort to keep war from breaking out, striving to further an agreement between the Directory and the Coalition. Agreement was impossible. The French, attacked

by Neapolitan troops in November, 1798, had vanquished the latter
and captured Naples on January 23, 1799. Charles IV, not showing
concern now about the flight of his relative the King from the conquered city, presented through the Spanish Ambassador at Paris a
demand for recognition of his rights, as the last Bourbon on a throne,
to the Kingdom of Naples. The powers of the Coalition—particularly
Russia, urged on by England who also made direct offers of financial
assistance to Spain if she would break with France—tried to dissuade
the Spanish King from friendly relations with the French. The Czar
first offered him ships and money and then threatened him with war;
all without effect, in spite of the fact that as recently as November,
1798, Spain had suffered a new blow in the loss of Minorca to the
English without aid for its reconquest from the Directory, although
the latter made continuous demands on Spain for warships which were
never used to Spain's advantage but rather the contrary, since Spanish
squadrons were maintained inactive in the port of Brest. Because Azara
warned his Government of the dangers inherent in this, and for other
acts of patriotism, the Directory obliged Urquijo to recall the Ambassador. Meanwhile Naples had been reconquered by its King and
the French troops driven out.

What were the reasons for Charles IV's submission to the Directory
and his consequent refusal to break relations with it? It has been supposed that he was motivated by the persistent hope of occupying the
throne of France when the French crisis was settled. While it is true
that Charles IV was ingenuous enough to hug such an illusion, it is
more probable that his attitude was due to his pusillanimity in the
face of the Directory's strategems and threats. The history of Charles
IV affords repeated proofs of the ease with which he could be intimidated and cowed. If, however, he did have hopes for the Crown of
France, they were shattered by Napoleon's *coup d'etat* of 18 Brumaire
(November 10, 1799) in destroying the Directory and naming himself
First Consul.

Napoleon and Godoy

Napoleon's first act was an unsuccessful effort to make peace with
England and Austria. He did however succeed in separating Russia
from the Coalition. The change of Government in France was welcome

news in Spain, where it was assumed that the new regime would be less tyrannical and more considerate of its ally. But this assumption proved false. Following the policy of his predecessors, Napoleon tried primarily to make use of the Spanish squadron anchored at Brest for his special purposes of succouring the Island of Malta, which was blockaded by the English, and reembarking the French Army in Egypt. He therefore communicated with the Spanish Admiral Mazarredo indicating this plan of campaign, which Mazarredo disapproved. After an increasingly acrimonious interchange of despatches, Napoleon prevailed, and stressed the reconquest of Minorca as a principal objective. At the same time, he promised to aid the Duke of Parma (restored to his duchy) in enlarging his realm, and sent General Berthier to Madrid to draw up the proposals that would be "most agreeable to his Majesty the King of Spain in favor of the Duke of Parma." Berthier's mission was wholly successful and materialized in the new Treaty of San Ildefonso (October 1, 1800), by which the French Republic pledged itself to procure extension of the Duchy of Parma in exchange for Louisiana and six warships.

The war of nerves between Napoleon and Mazarredo continued, the latter insisting on his own views regarding the expeditions to Malta and Egypt, and refusing to give in to the egolatry of the First Consul. Napoleon tried to win over the second in command but Mazarredo, apprised of this, ordered the latter to remain at Brest. The Spanish Government upheld the conduct of its Admiral, instructing him in a Royal Order of November 18, 1800, that he should return with the squadron to Cádiz, but in such manner as "to avoid, at least in appearance, any indication of resentment toward that [French] Government." This order angered Napoleon and he made up his mind to bring about the downfall of Urquijo's Government as the Directory had of Godoy's. It was not difficult to overthrow Urquijo, whose radical ideas had won him the hostility of the Catholic element. Urquijo further injured himself by opposing the appointment of Lucien Bonaparte as Envoy Extraordinary to Spain, though that opposition was well-grounded. Lucien arrived at San Ildefonso early in December 1800, however, and a few days later Urquijo was replaced as Minister by Pedro Ceballos, and Mazarredo was relieved of his command of the squadron at Brest.

Soon after (February 9, 1801), Napoleon achieved an advantageous peace with all the allies except England. The treaty signed then gave the territory of Tuscany to Parma, forming a new kingdom called Etruria with Florence as its capital, but on condition that the Duke of Parma renounce his own rights so that Prince Don Luis, married to Charles IV's daughter María Luisa, should occupy the new throne. Negotiations between Spain and France on that point were incorporated in the Treaty of March 21, 1801, which provided further that in case of a lack of succession of the reigning House of Etruria, a Prince of the Spanish royal family should inherit the throne which would be "property of Spain for all time." An earlier treaty (January 29, 1801) obligated Charles IV to send an ultimatum to Portugal demanding abandonment of the English alliance, on pain of war with Spain in alliance with France. A third treaty, of February 13, established formation of four Franco-Spanish fleets: one to set out for Brazil or India; another to threaten Ireland; a third to reconquer Trinidad and other West Indian Islands; and the fourth to operate in the Mediterranean.

This Treaty and that of March 21 bear the signature of Godoy (Prince of the Peace since 1795) as Plenipotentiary. Godoy in fact, though out of office, had never ceased to wield influence at Court and intervene in negotiations. There had hardly been a matter of importance on which his counsel had not been sought, as is proved by the files of his correspondence. Even Urquijo agreed to having Godoy called in at the difficult moment of Lucien Bonaparte's arrival at Madrid. The courtiers were aware of Godoy's power, which they had believed they toppled in 1797, but though they murmured against it, they could not put an end to it. It is not surprising therefore that Godoy was placed in command of the Army to invade Portugal on that country's rejection of the Spanish ultimatum. Napoleon did not oppose the appointment, though he considered it purely decorative, commenting in a despatch to General Berthier "The Prince of the Peace . . . is not a military man." The war, while victorious for the Spaniards, was as brief as it was insignificant. French troops, maintained as rear guard, scarcely took part in the action. After a series of conquests in May and June 1801, treaties of peace were signed in the latter month. Portugal agreed to close her ports to England in return for Spain's promise to guarantee Portuguese territorial integrity. The victory was celebrated with pomp and ceremony at Badajoz, with a military review attended by the King and Queen, the latter being presented with golden-fruited boughs of orange trees cut for her in Portuguese orchards. The war in consequence was called "The War of the Oranges." Godoy was rewarded with the title of Generalissimo of the Armies afloat and ashore.

Napoleon, astounded and indignant at the rapid termination of a campaign which he had intended to be more productive, threatened that if Spain did not continue the war with Portugal and ignore Godoy's counsels, "the last hour of the Spanish monarchy" would strike. However Azara managed to calm the ire of the First Consul who agreed to sign a second treaty by which Portugal increased the amount of the war indemnity to be paid France.

Meanwhile the war against the English continued, an important episode being the naval battle of Algeciras on July 6, 1801. The English fleet was routed by the combined forces of French vessels, Spanish gunboats, and the batteries of Algeciras. The growing desire for peace on the part of both Napoleon and the English, from different motivations, led to a provisional convention, the Preliminaries of London, ratified in the Peace Treaty of Amiens (March 27, 1802) by which Spain recovered Minorca from England but ceded the Island of Trinidad to that country.

Fourth War with England, and the Results

This peace between England and France was not long enduring. In May 1803 hostilities began again. Napoleon again had recourse to threats and promises to win Spanish support. He accused Godoy of attempting to thwart that monarch's sovereignty and of underhand plotting with England. Napoleon at the same time was carrying on hidden dealings of his own. He had decided to raise money for the war by selling Louisiana to the United States. Negotiations were carried forward in secret, since the Treaty of 1800, by virtue of which France had recovered Louisiana, expressly prohibited that the territory should ever again be relinquished to any other country than Spain. When the fact of the sale was made public, the Spanish Government at first protested but later acquiesced, alleging as the reason Spain's friendship and goodwill toward the United States; but the real motive for acceptance of the *fait accompli* was the desire to avoid a war with the United States, which was determined to possess Louisiana, and with Napoleon, especially since an English alliance was very uncertain. Napoleon also imposed a new treaty on Spain, obliging payment of six millions monthly to France. England protested energetically, and refused to be appeased by Godoy's various concessions. That the English were determined to fight it out became apparent with the attack, without previous declaration of war, by four English vessels on four Spanish frigates at Cape Santa María, Portugal, October 5, 1804. This unexpected peacetime aggression resulted in the capture of three of the Spanish boats. Similar attacks followed on Spanish merchant shipping and on a transport taking troops from the Peninsula to the Balearic Isles. Although all Europe and the British press itself censured the action of October 5, stigmatizing it as shameful, the British Government refused any satisfaction, declaring that it did not regard the captured vessels as war prizes but as deposits for and guarantee of Spanish neutrality. In view of such intransigency, Spain issued a very logical Manifesto on December 12, followed by a Patriotic Proclamation by Godoy. United by common interests once more, France and Spain ratified their alliance January 4, 1805.

Military operations began with a Franco-Spanish expedition to the Antilles, in accordance with Napoleon's previous plan of combined naval effort. The expedition was planned in great secrecy, but many divergent rumors were set afloat purposely in order to mislead the English Admiral Nelson. The latter at the time was scouring the Mediterranean, and he learned of the true plans from the King of Naples to whom they had been revealed by the Princess of Asturias, disloyal to her rank and her native land. By the time that Nelson had been so advised, however, the Franco-Spanish fleet was already at Martinique in the Caribbean; whither the English Admiral sailed after it. This was what Napoleon desired, since he purposed to distract Nelson's attention toward the Americas, and then, by a rapid return of the allied fleet to attack England on its own ground. The indecisiveness of the French Admiral Villeneuve when he learned in June that Nelson was in Antillean waters delayed the execution of the plan; so that Nelson had time to return to Europe (Gibraltar) almost as soon as the allied fleet.

Villeneuve, attacked off Cape Finisterre (July 22) by another English squadron—with which Spanish vessels fought heroically, losing two ships but rendering useless three of the English—took refuge at Vigo instead of proceeding to Brest as Napoleon ordered, or following up the English squadron in withdrawal, as his own officers demanded. Later he returned to Cádiz where he remained inactive and practically blockaded by the English from August to October. Discontent reigned among the allied forces. Spanish mariners made no secret of their disgust, and asked that Villeneuve be relieved of his command because of notorious incompetence. Time and again Napoleon despatched orders that his Admiral should sally forth from Cádiz, but his Admiral did not dare. The Spanish officers were opposed to this plan also because of the English superiority in numbers and the insufficiency of Spanish armaments as well as troops; factors which would mean defeat on the high seas but might be less advantageous in a defensive engagement fought out in the bay. Such was the decision reached by the Council of War held October 8, 1805.

But Napoleon, in a towering rage, called Villeneuve a coward and declared that he would be replaced; whereupon the Admiral decided to risk everything on a single throw, and give battle. The Spanish, fearing that they might be deemed cowards and much against their better judgment, resigned themselves to follow the leader that France had imposed upon them. The Franco-Spanish fleet consisting of 33 men-of-war (15 of them Spanish), five frigates and two brigantines, sailed out from Cádiz on October 20 and the following day encountered Nelson's fleet of 29 men-of-war, four frigates and six smaller vessels, off Trafalgar. An ill-advised maneuver ordered by Villeneuve, upsetting the plan of battle that had been agreed upon beforehand, permitted Nelson to break through the Franco-Spanish line with ease at several places. This converted the battle into a series of separate engagements, isolating the vessels one from another when they should have fought group to group. To this initial disadvantage was added lack of assistance from the French vanguard, which held aloof from the battle. The Spanish vessels and the French (the majority) which entered into the firing fought with great ardor; but victory went to the English who destroyed the allied fleet totally, though at the cost of many vessels and many lives, including Lord Nelson's. Among the Spanish slain were the Admiral Gravina and Commanders Alcalá Galiano, Churruca, and Alcedo, as well as numerous other officers; while practically all survivors suffered wounds. Three Spanish vessels were sunk, three captured by the English, four lost on the rocks in a tempest that followed the battle; and the other five, which managed to save themselves, were greatly damaged.

That defeat was the destruction—although a glorious destruction—of the Spanish navy. Its effect on Spanish morale was terrific, and was not relieved in the least by victories later on over the English on the River Plate. Two English attacks on Buenos Aires were repulsed (August 1806 and July 1807), and the English at Montevideo were forced to capitulate and give up the city, thanks to the intrepidity of Captain Liniers of the Spanish Navy, seconded enthusiastically by the citizens of Buenos Aires and of Montevideo; as already related.

Godoy and Ferdinand

At the Spanish Court in the year 1801 the animosity between Manuel Godoy and the Crown Prince Ferdinand, Charles IV's eldest son, was an open secret. It was rooted in mutual distrust and ambition for power and for influence with the Throne. (Ferdinand was the son of King Charles IV and Queen María Luisa; Godoy was the King's favorite and the Queen's lover.) Rivalry between Crown Prince and Minister was intensified by Ferdinand's marriage to María Antonia, Princess of Naples, an alliance which Godoy had opposed. After her marriage, the new Crown Princess, whose influence over her husband was always great, was the center of the political opposition to Godoy, which was composed of the latter's critics and his personal enemies. This group was the origin of the Fernandista party—the party of Ferdinand—which from the first had the support of Napoleon who not only held Godoy in contempt but was apprehensive about his influence over the King and Queen.

In 1805, the moral effect of Trafalgar was to arouse the spirit of Spain and cause Godoy to change his policy; that is, to oppose Napoleon, who in 1804 had proclaimed himself Emperor of France. Though Godoy started secret negotiations with the English Government (October, 1806), the highly important Napoleonic victory at Jena (October 14, 1806) caused him once again to become subservient to Napoleon. The latter, without permitting it to be evident that he was aware of the political instability of Charles IV's favorite, had already decided upon Charles' overthrow, and with him, that of the Bourbon monarchy of Spain. The natural point of support for such a plan, if it were to succeed, was the Fernandista party, which Napoleon found very receptive. In July 1807, in fact, Prince Ferdinand himself appeared before the Emperor to request the latter's "paternal protection" and permission to marry a princess of the Bonaparte family. (Ferdinand's wife María Antonia had died the previous year.) This request was formalized in a letter of October 11, 1807, which made transparent allusion to the Queen's adulterous relations with Godoy. The Prince thus sacrificed to rancor and ambition the good name of his own mother.

Not suspecting this accord between Napoleon and his enemies at home, Godoy made every effort to curry favor with the former. Consequently, he agreed to send 1500 Spanish soldiers to the aid of the French troops in Germany; and he persuaded Charles IV to sign two new conventions (at Fontainebleau, November 27, 1806) which involved the fate of the Spanish monarchy even more deeply in Napoleonic schemes. One of these conventions decided upon the conquest of Portugal (which was always inclined to favor England) by the combined armies of France and Spain. Portuguese territory after the conquest was to be carved into three parts, from which would be formed a new kingdom for Charles IV's son-in-law, the King of Etruria; a principality for Godoy; and a territory to be held as a bargaining reserve and exchanged, if possible, for Gibraltar, the Island of Trinidad, and other Spanish territories captured by the English. The preparations for military cooperation began with the entry into Spain of a strong French army under General Junot, days before the signing of the conventions at Fontainebleau. Each of the two rival parties at the Spanish Court (Godoy's followers and the Fernandistas) saw in those incoming French troops an effective ally against the other. Neither Godoy nor Ferdinand, nor the henchmen of either, had the slightest inkling of the truth: that Napoleon's forces would be utilized not only against Portugal but also against Spain. Blissfully unaware, both parties continued to pin their hopes on Napoleon and to confide their plans to him, while they kept up the bitter struggle with each other. One of its episodes in 1807 was Ferdinand's conspiracy against Godoy ("the plot of the Escorial") and, apparently, against Charles IV himself; which proved to be the first step along the path that led to the Crown Prince's speedy imprisonment and trial. The intervention of Napoleon, and possibly that of the Queen, caused the affair to end in a verdict of Not Guilty (January 1808). While this was going on, one French army after another continued to pour into Spain. The allied Franco-Spanish forces, commanded by Junot, invaded Portugal, capturing Lisbon on November 30, 1808. Meanwhile the Portuguese royal family and many nobles and persons of importance embarked on English ships for Brazil.

March 19 and Its Results

Finally, the Spanish public began to worry about the movements of the French troops who under one pretext or another were seizing the fortified towns of northern Spain from Guipúzcoa to Catalonia. Godoy himself, at last coming to see Napoleon's intrigues for what they were, proposed to the Royal Council that it demand the withdrawal of French military forces and declare war on France. But the Council and the King, always timorous when it was a question of opposing Napoleon, rejected Godoy's suggestion. The latter thereupon asked to be relieved of his post as Minister, but this request also was denied.

Disillusionment speedily became general when the Spanish Ambassador at Paris informed Madrid of a new demand by Napoleon. The Emperor was now asking that he be ceded certain Spanish provinces in north Spain down to the Ebro, or that his title to the whole of Portugal be recognized, together with concession of a military road across Spain from Irún to that country. The only way out of the difficulty which occurred to Charles IV (it was advised by Godoy and the Ambassador) was to set out for the south of Spain with the intention of following the example of the Portuguese royal family and embarking for America. With that purpose in view, the King and Queen hastened to Aranjuez, as the first stage of their journey; but they got no further. On the night of March 17, 1808 an insurrection broke out there, organized and led by the Fernandista party. The consequences were the downfall, imprisonment, and forced retirement of Godoy on March 18, and abdication of the throne by Charles IV on March 19. Rejoicing became general throughout Spain as the news spread. This was partly because of relief that the extremely unpopular Godoy was now out of the picture, and partly because of a confident expectation that the new broom of King Ferdinand would sweep clean. But public opinion on this point failed to take into account Napoleon's determination, although, as we have said, many Spaniards were increasingly suspicious of the intentions of the French troops.

It would have simplified matters for Napoleon if the royal family had carried out their project of sailing for America. When that plan fell through, Napoleon, while ordering French forces under General Murat to occupy Madrid, instructed them to maintain a prudent reserve with regard to recognizing the new King. Charles IV himself played into Napoleon's hands by entering upon negotiations with Murat, withdrawing his abdication of March 19, and humbly seeking Napoleon's support. The latter, by threats and by deceptions, succeeded in getting the new King Ferdinand VII to leave Madrid. The pretext was that Ferdinand was to meet the Emperor, who sent word that he greatly desired to confer with Ferdinand and was on his way to Spain for that purpose. That this was untrue became clear as soon as Ferdinand and his entourage arrived at Vitoria, the appointed meeting place, only to be informed that Napoleon was not there but awaited them at Bayonne, on French territory. Although the citizens of Vitoria clamored against Ferdinand's leaving Spain for any such purpose, and even cut the traces of the horses drawing the royal coach, the advice of the Ministerial favorite, the canon Escóiquiz, as well as his own trusting nature, impelled Ferdinand to continue the journey. On April 20 he reached Bayonne, and ten days later his royal parents arrived there also. There Napoleon obtained Ferdinand's abdication of the Crown in favor of Charles IV; and immediately thereafter, Charles IV's abdication in favor of Napoleon was obtained also (the Treaty of May 5) on two conditions: first, that the integrity and independence of the Kingdom of Spain should be maintained, with whatever Prince Napoleon should decide to name as its ruler (in his own mind he had already fixed on his brother Joseph Bonaparte, then King of Holland) ; and second, that the Catholic religion should be respected as the only religion in Spain. By a further treaty (May 10) Ferdinand, in exchange for preservation of his rank as Prince dignitary of the French Empire and an annual income of one million francs in addition to some territorial possessions, agreed to the cession of the Crown made by his father to Napoleon.

May 2 and the War of Independence

While these humiliating scenes were taking place at Bayonne, there

Lewis Michael Van Loo: Philip V and the Royal Family.

Madrid: Prado Museum

was a reaction in Spain upon which Napoleon had not counted. Popular opinion, supported by the ardent patriotism of some officers of the Spanish army, not so blind to the facts as the courtiers were, viewed with alarm increasing momentarily the successive departure from Madrid of the members of the royal family. They witnessed at the same time the conduct of French military leaders who were conducting themselves in the Spanish capital as though they were in a vanquished country. The growing resentment against all this was augmented by sight of the passiveness with which Spanish officials permitted Napoleon's intentions to be carried out. Tension increased at Madrid and at Toledo when news arrived of Charles IV's protest against the abdication forced upon him at Aranjuez and of Napoleon's refusal to recognize Ferdinand as King of Spain. Several riots and insurrections at Toledo, Burgos, and other cities soon showed that public indignation was running high. The decisive outbreak occurred at Madrid on May 2, 1808, with departure of the little Prince Francisco de Paula (aged thirteen) from the Palace to journey to Bayonne in company of Prince Don Antonio, chairman of the Junta of Government appointed by Ferdinand on leaving Madrid. The crowd that had gathered in the Plaza de Oriente to see this last member of the royal family take leave waited with growing excitement. This increased when word came that at the last moment the young Prince, bursting into tears, had refused to depart from the Palace and Madrid. The smouldering wrath of the people needed only this to touch off the flame. The crowd set upon one of Murat's aides and cut the leather thongs of the coaches. Such was the seemingly slight circumstance that sparked the beginning of the uprising of the Spanish people against Napoleon.

During that same day, May 2, a heroic struggle was staged in Madrid by the populace, who had few weapons, no organization, and only the aid of some artillery and infantry soldiers and officers (Captains Velarde and Daoiz, Lieutenant Ruiz, and others) against the numerous and well-equipped forces of the French garrison. News of this uprising and of the executions that followed (immortalized in Goya's art) caused the revolution of the whole of Spain and initiated the War of Independence: the first instance of a nation's daring to do such a thing as oppose Napoleon's power and prestige though it had no king and no officials of government and no army, since Spanish armed forces were

Vicente López: *Portrait of Goya.*   *Madrid: Prado Museum*

for the time being immobilized by order of the Junta representing Ferdinand VII.

Therewith began a new era in the history of Spain. That war was also one of the first manifestations in Europe of the political movement of nationalities which was to characterize the nineteenth century. The extraordinary vigor and scope of Spanish nationalism, and the unique example that it afforded, in the political life of the period, of a collective determination pursuing its own course, with neither monarch nor political leader to inspire and direct it, claimed the immediate attention of the world. A German patriot, the philosopher Fichte, who was at the time, by his *Addresses to the German Nation* instilling into the youth of his country a patriotic sentiment of rebellion against Napoleon's imperialism, pointed out as an example for them to follow the impassioned resistance of Spain to the impositions of a war-lord.

Chapter XIII

The Struggle for Constitutionalism and the Economic and Cultural Renascence

I. FROM 1808 TO 1874

The War of Independence

The Spanish War of Independence lasted six years, from 1808 to 1814, and in itself was a great surprise to Napoleon. Like the rest of Europe, he had believed that the only opposition to him in Spain would come from the courtiers and the army. Through his own dealings with Godoy and Ferdinand VII, he had learned to despise the former. With regard to the army, he knew his ground and felt no anxiety. But to his astonishment, he found himself confronted by a nation in arms. Nothing in his experience had taught him how to measure such a force as that. Nor did he realize that this uprising of the Spanish people expressed not merely the idealistic but the practical determination of a country that would not tolerate having an alien power decide its fate, but was resolved to settle its own destiny. Rejection of the patrimonial monarchy stirred underneath that determination, although many Spaniards were not yet thinking about this consequence implicit in their act of rebellion against Napoleon and against the abdications at Bayonne. On the contrary, adherence to the patrimonial theory was what caused some army officers who were loyal to the principle of traditional monarchy to join the group of King Joseph Bonaparte's adherents; but the mass of the Spanish people would have no part in such hidebound royalism. And so the people on their own initiative fought the French armies, with no king nor any other national leader to be their guide and example; but fired by those two mighty determinants in mass psychology: love of freedom and love of country. These two sentiments were translated at the moment into hatred for Napoleon the Emperor who had deceived them and disposed of the Crown of Spain arbitrarily without regard for the opinion of the country, and into love and hope for Ferdinand VII their King whom they longed and expected to see restored to his throne. It was this devotion, very general among Spaniards at that time, that caused the people to call Ferdinand *"el Deseado,"* the Desired. And while the people of Spain poured out their blood to maintain the independence of Spanish earth and the Spanish throne, Ferdinand himself was adulating Napoleon and congratulating him on his victories in Spain.

Ignorant of that fact, the Spanish nation with intrepid confidence, defying Napoleon's power and military genius, kept on fighting; at first, alone and unaided; later (1809) with the assistance of English troops that came to join forces on the Peninsula against the Emperor. All Spaniards—merchants, laborers, artisans, students, physicians, lawyers, some members of the nobility, priests, some of the parish clergy, and many women— snatched up what arms they could lay hand on, and began fighting; some in ranks of the regular army, which also rose in rebellion, and others in independent or guerrilla groups, and also in beleaguered cities, as happened during the sieges of Saragossa and Gerona. A moving example of patriotism was the impassioned violence with which the Spanish troops that had been sent to Germany years before, now confined under very strict French vigilance on the islands of Langeland and Fionia and on the peninsula of Jutland, broke through the blockade hemming them in and made their way back to Spain to join the fighting forces. Led by the Marquis of Romana, 9,000 men managed to sail to Sweden and thence to Spain, where they arrived October 9, 1808. The only exceptions to this wellnigh universal patriotism of the Spanish people were the group of Spanish radicals (called the *afrancesados,* or "Frenchified Spaniards") , of whom we shall have more to say, and the Catalán aristocrats, clergy, and bourgeoisie, who in the number of some 40,000 emigrated to Mallorca, thereby moving out of range of the sacrifices that the war entailed.

With that improvised fighting force—and before any help came from England—the Spaniards inflicted on Napoleon's troops their two first defeats: the battle of Bailén, July 19, 1808, and the battle of Bruch in Catalonia in the same year. The French Emperor had to come to Spain in person to direct the fighting and repair the disaster. During the six years of warfare, the Spaniards continued to show great endurance and high courage. The two sieges of Saragossa (1808 and 1809) and the siege of Gerona (1809), exemplifying the heroism of a whole people, amazed and confounded the French themselves, just as the siege of Numantia had astonished the Romans. In other countries dominated by Napoleon where also the spirit of independence was stirring, the valiant action of the Spaniards was esteemed at its just value as the dynamic example of a people who fought to establish the right of nations to rule themselves.

Joseph Bonaparte and the Constitution of Bayonne

The stoutheartedness of the Spanish masses was the more praiseworthy because it meant a break with their own deeprooted feeling of respect for the person and the words of kings; and because it opposed at one and the same time the conduct of the government officials representing Ferdinand VII and that of a great part of the nobility, the bureaucracy, and the higher clergy. According to the ideology of these social and political elements, the acts of abdication by the Kings had to be accepted unquestioningly. Taking the same position,—although, as we have said, for different reasons—was a small but important group of Spaniards well versed in and much influenced by the doctrines of the French Revolution, to whom France, in spite of the Empire and its absolutism, continued to mean the triumph of liberal principles. Consequently, they viewed the replacement of the Spanish Bourbons by a French Emperor as a progressive step beneficial for Spain. These were the *afrancesados* already mentioned, men whose patriotism, though wholly different in orientation, was no less sincere than that of those who revolted against Napoleon.

The latter, as soon as he had obtained the abdications at Bayonne, had renounced the Crown of Spain for himself in favor of his brother Joseph Bonaparte. This decision was made public by a decree of June 6, 1808; and on the following day Joseph Bonaparte received the felicitation of Spanish personages who were then at Bayonne: grandees, members of the Councils of Castile, the Indies, Finance, and the Inquisition; and army officers. Their congratulatory letters were intercepted and revised by Napoleon, who suspected that they might convey sentiments which would incline the newly-named King against adopting his own point of view; since at that moment it was by no means certain that Joseph Bonaparte would accept the proffered Crown of Spain. The Emperor's suspicions were not without foundation, as was proved by the text of the message of felicitation sent to Joseph by the Grandees of Spain: "The laws of Spain do not permit us to offer another thing (congratulations) to Your Majesty. We hope that the nation will explain itself and permit us to enlarge at greater length on our sentiments." Napoleon ordered that this paragraph be modified, and he was obeyed. Joseph Bonaparte, letting himself be persuaded, accepted the Crown and proceeded to prepare for the meeting of a kind of *Cortes* which was to be held at Bayonne on General Murat's advice seconded by Napoleon, and to which was confided the task of drawing up and adopting a Constitution for the new Spanish monarchy.

Ninety-one of the 150 deputies who were to compose this *Cortes* attended the meeting. Twenty of them had been elected by vote in the Spanish provinces that were dominated by Napoleon's forces and therefore were utterly lacking in electoral guarantees. In representation of Spain's dominions in the Americas, the *Junta* of Madrid, by agreement with Murat, appointed six Spanish Americans then resident in Spain. The *Cortes* deliberated on the basis of a draft constitution supplied by Napoleon himself, the text of which was read at the *junta*, or session, of June 20, 1808. The result was the adoption by the *Cortes* of what is called the Constitution of Bayonne, with which the constitutional system of government was inaugurated in Spain. But neither this lip-service to new liberal ideas, nor the promises of good government emanating from Joseph Bonaparte, weakened in the slightest the revolt of the immense majority of Spaniards nor dimmed the flame of independence burning within them. That majority refused to recognize the Napoleonic King and continued to regard Ferdinand VII as their legitimate ruler, and to expect a victory that would redeem him from captivity by the usurper. The arrival in Spain of King Joseph I and the Ministry of his Government (which, generally speaking, was very superior to that of Charles IV's epoch) did not alter the problem at all. Spanish patriots not only kept up the war, but proceeded to organize the country politically on their own account, with no assistance whatever from the royal family—the Bourbons—nor from foreign sources. It was the first time that such a thing had ever occurred in a European monarchy. Despite initial reverses, by 1814 Spain was in possession of the Spaniards.

The Constitutional Regime: A New Political and Social Program

In 1808 when the Bourbon monarchy was working toward its own destruction, the political and social situation of Spain might have been summed up as follows: An aristocracy, especially the courtiers, which had lost respect for the kings; rotten politics, ruled by personal animosities and reciprocal fears; absolute lack of patriotism among the upper classes, who subordinated everything else to passions and greed; the delirious hope of the masses, centered upon a Prince—Ferdinand— who had already shown himself to be both false and vengeful; and, finally, the profound influence in intellectual circles of the ideas of the Encyclopedists and of the French Revolution, which represented a mixture of doctrines very characteristic of the moment, notwithstanding the disagreements among the Encyclopedists and the Revolutionists of 1789 and 1793 on purely political matters. Out of that situation— unfavorable in one aspect and dangerous in another—the Spanish people knew how to produce organizing government action, the fundamental need of the hour, which brought into the open without reserve all the political and social aspirations that had been retarded or brushed aside by the absolutism of the preceding regime. In accordance with their natural tendency, the different regions of Spain constituted themselves into distinct centers of action, each with its own ample *Junta* of government; and they aspired to restore the ancient *Cortes* as a general governing body that would represent them all and would duly respect the needs and wishes of the nation during enforced absence of the King. What was desired, therefore, was not a separate *Cortes* for each region, as had been formerly the case, but one *Cortes* common to all the Spanish State: the first collective, popular affirmation of national unity. And so it was that there met in Cádiz (1809-1813) an Assembly made up of four classes of Deputies: from those cities that had had a vote in the previous *Cortes;* from the newly organized Provincial *Juntas;* from the people by direct vote, with one representative for each group of 50,000 persons; and from the American colonies, with one vote for each 100,000 white inhabitants.

A large number of the Deputies, especially those representing the *Juntas,* brought with them a spirit of reform (voiced already in petitions from their *Juntas*) which came to be infused conjointly with the philanthropic and liberal program of the eighteenth century and the more recent influences of the French Revolution. It should be noted that the group of reformers was being made up principally of middle class intellectuals, some members of the provincial nobility, and numerous Liberal priests, such as Diego Muñoz Torrero, José Antonio Ruiz de Padrón, and Francisco Martínez Marina. It was, in fact, Muñoz Torrero who explained in the first Parliamentary address of our history the program of reforms that these men sought. Along with implantation of the reforms to the extent that we shall soon consider, the same thing occurred in Spain that had characterized the triumph of constitutionalism in France, from the social standpoint; namely, the complete entry of the middle class into political life, with the intellectuals, as we have seen, taking the first step. As the century grew older, the middle class came to be the political class *par excellence.*

With the *Cortes* constituted as an extraordinary and sovereign body in its legislative function, it began its task by swearing in the Deputies by a fourfold oath to maintain the Catholic religion, the national integrity, and the faithful observance of the laws, and by proclaiming Ferdinand VII as King. Successive decrees and resolutions (which were included for the most part in the so-called Constitution of 1812) developed the new Liberal program. Its fundamental planks were: sovereignty of the nation, conjointly with the King; constitutional monarchy; separation of the powers of the State; personal inviolability of the Deputies and prohibition against their holding public office; equality of rights between Peninsular Spaniards and Spanish subjects in the Americas; abolition of laws abusive of the rights of the Indians, of which laws some were still extant; political freedom of the press, which, however, remained subject to the former censorship in religious matters; submission of the King to the *Cortes* with respect to his marriage, and to whatever international pacts he had made during his captivity; abolition of torture; formalization of a national budget, with requirement that the clergy pay war-taxes; abolition of feudal jurisdiction, which still existed, and of seignorial rights and rights of vassalage; inauguration of freedom for negro slaves, and abolition of punishment by lash and by imprisonment for Indians who refused to be baptized; recognition of human rights (civil liberty, ownership of property, capacity to hold public office, equality before the law, et cetera) ; means of amending the Constitution; responsible King's Ministers; municipalities with elective *Ayuntamiento,* or City Council; a national militia and a permanent army; accelerated development of public education; abolition of the Tribunal of the Inquisition, with religious offences to be punishable in the Bishop's Courts as had been the case before the Inquisition was established; restriction of the number of religious communities; distribution of uncultivated and of communal lands to the poor and to pensioned soldiers; abolition of flogging in the schools; establishment of a direct single tax; and other analogous innovations.

Reaction against the New Program; and the Struggle for Constitutionalism

Although the great majority of the Deputies voted for all these measures, they represented in reality only the opinion of those whose thinking had been shaped and influenced by the epoch's spirit of reform. On the other hand, the new enactments had many enemies, beginning with King Ferdinand, who saw with displeasure that they trimmed down his absolutist faculties. All the social classes and organisms whose ancient privileges were sacrificed on the altars of juridical equality (and, in especial, many of the clergy) stirred up public opinion against the political and social reforms. The masses, indifferent in the matter because they failed to understand the new ideas, could be inclined much more easily toward familiar tradition than toward things new and strange. Thus it was possible, on Ferdinand VII's return to Spain (March 22, 1814), to abolish—lock, stock and barrel—all the work of the *Cortes,* instead of adopting the regime of compromises followed by the French Bourbons when, after Napoleon's dethronement, they returned to rule France and granted a Constitution (the Charter of 1814) that was much more liberal than Napoleon's government had been. Fernandist reaction went very far. It not only persecuted the Liberals unrelentingly, declaring null and void all decrees issued during the King's absence, reestablishing the Inquisition, and so on (proclaiming the principle that it should be as if the years between 1808 and 1813 had never existed) ; but Ferdinand himself also grew more stubbornly absolutist in conviction, and went back to a system more restrictive than the eighteenth century at its worst. This was true in the fields of culture and religion as well as of politics. The Jesuits were readmitted (the Company of Jesus having been reestablished by the Holy See in August, 1814) ; the number of convents of nuns and of monks was greatly increased; universities and theatres were closed; the publication of any other newspaper than the official gazette —*Gazeta Oficial*—was prohibited; and all open advocacy of the material or the moral improvement of the country was prevented. The Ministry of Finance once more fell into utter disorganization; public wealth decreased; the number of Government employees was augmented beyond reason; and again there was a hungry people and an impoverished Army that did not receive its pay.

Those Liberals who could, fled the persecution; emigrating for the most part to France and England, countries where the contact with more progressive civilizations, the spectacle of peoples better governed, the desire for vengeance and the bitterness of exile, worked in their different ways to strengthen the political convictions of the expatriates, quickening their determination to apply these convictions anew in their own country. Some sought refuge in the Americas.

This duality of irreducible tendencies blazed the inevitable trail of national history throughout almost the whole of the nineteenth century. The problem consisted in determining what men and what ideas should govern Spain, whether liberals or reactionaries. Therefore the struggle necessarily had to be in the political arena, for the purposes of obtaining power and limiting absolutism, so that the aspirations of the reformers and of the people as a whole could be freely expressed; or else definitely stifled. The tenaciousness on both sides; the resistance, always strong, of the reaction, which was resolved not to yield a jot to the "Year-Twelvers" (the *Doceañistas,* nickname of the supporters of the Constitution of 1812) ; the cruelty with which these men were persecuted; and the resultant hatred that rankled in both parties: all this together, in the period between Ferdinand's return in 1814 and his death in 1833, combined to bring about an uninterrupted series of conspiracies, revolts, and plots by one party or the other which consumed the attention and the strength of the nation. The Liberals made different attempts to restore the Constitutional regime, but were successful only in the military insurrection led by Rafael del Riego, Commander of the Regiment of Asturias, and Colonel Antonio Quiroga.

As we have said, the intellectuals—though a minority—were for the most part Liberals, whether Year-Twelvers or "Frenchified"; and Liberal ranks were increased by many members of the middle class. In Cádiz most of the population was Liberal, perhaps because that city had been the site of the *Cortes*. In such regions as Asturias, where resistance to the French had been strongly organized, the Liberal element was strong, though ceding some ground to the Conservative. The Army officers whom the French had imprisoned during the War of Spanish Independence and who had returned to Spain, were in themselves a force for Liberalism; and some of them, such as Riego himself, were Freemasons, or members of other foreign secret societies.

Freemasonry had existed in Spain since about 1750; first depending on centers established in other countries, later with a separate Spanish organization. Not all Masons were revolutionists; but all aided one another; and the radical elements used the lodges as a cloak for conspiracy. Alcalá Galiano says that while Spanish Freemasonry in 1817 "had not yet decided to take direct and vigorous action against the Government," most of the Liberal converts and the other opponents of the existing regime were becoming Masons.

In 1819 the Andalusian Masons, especially those at Seville and at Cádiz, where an expeditionary force was being assembled to send to the Americas, decided to further the Revolution. They were aided by the fact that the Army and the Navy heartily disliked the American project; a repugnance justified by the mismanagement of the expedition from the first, and by such incidents as recent scandals in connection with the purchase of Russian warships at an excessive valuation by Ferdinand's government. Colonel Quiroga was appointed military leader of the insurrection, but a storm delayed him; and it was Rafael del Riego who on the day fixed—January 1, 1820—with the force under his command, in the town of Cabezas de San Juan proclaimed the Constitution of 1812. In doing so, he acted in contradiction to plans of the civilian leaders of the movement whose aims went far beyond those of 1812. Initial skirmishes were followed on February 21 by the revolt of Corunna, and then in swift succession of Galicia, Asturias, Saragossa, Barcelona, and Pamplona; while the Government remained strangely inactive. On March 4, with the revolutionary strength increasing by leaps and bounds, a royal decree ordered reorganization of the Council of State and consultation of Council and Judges with the King as to "what they deemed expedient for good government of the kingdom." On March 6, a Royal Order announced convocation of the *Cortes;* and on the day following—March 7,—an extraordinary number of the Official Gazette announced that the *Cortes* would meet at once and that Ferdinand "in accordance with the general will of the people had decided to swear adhesion to the Constitution of 1812." And so the Revolution of 1820 triumphed, with almost no bloodshed.

Ramón Mesonero Romanos, an eye-witness to these events, says that the rejoicing was on the part of the middle class and the aristocracy, but not of the working class which in general evinced little interest in constitutional government, whether from ignorance of its nature or from adherence to absolutist tradition. The intellectual character of the revolution, partly aristocratic and partly bourgeois, was evident at the Madrid mass-meeting on March 7 when the new municipal government was chosen by acclamation. In Cádiz, however, the military element was still strong. When an order came requiring the troops to swear to the Constitution, Riego and Quiroga sent messages of congratulation to Ferdinand VII and offered him the submission of the "Liberating Army." Both were raised to the rank of General, an honor which Riego—who was at once impulsive, brave, unselfish, easily offended, and childish—was unwilling to accept; partly from real reluctance, partly because he felt that there should be a difference made between him and Quiroga. No excesses were committed by the Government against the Constitutionalists. Ferdinand took oath on March 9 and on the following day issued a Royal Proclamation containing a phrase that became famous, "Let us advance frankly, myself leading the way, along the constitutional path." We shall soon see into what byways Ferdinand strayed from that path.

All the proscribed persons and refugees of 1814 flocked back to Spain. Some were included in the first constitutional Government. During the four months before the *Cortes* met, there was a strange period when the new Ministry and the provincial revolutionary *Juntas,* which did not disband, conducted a kind of joint administration. One such *Junta* even continued to sit in Madrid. Moreover, another power was forming, unofficial but far-reaching: that of the clubs of "patriotic societies," such as wielded influence in France. The majority of these groups were radical in tendency. The most famous of them in Madrid were the "Patriotic Society of the Friends of Liberty"; the "Friends of Order," more commonly called the *Fontana de Oro* because it met in the basement of the inn of that name; and another similar group that congregated at the Café Gran Cruz de Malta. These were discussion centers, and their politics was characterized by florid oratory, much patriotic and topical verse, and such songs as the Hymn of Riego— *Himno de Riego*—and *Trágala,* so called from its refrain, which means "Swallow it!" and referred to the Constitution of 1812. Several rival claimants disputed the authorship of the Hymn of Riego; and, for that matter, several different songs disputed the title, until one of them was adopted, and for a half century prevailed, as the Liberal anthem.

However, the new Liberal administration was brief, enduring only from 1820 to 1823. It resumed in that period the task of legislative reforms; including division of the country into Provinces (that same political division exists in Spain today) ; the organic law of the Navy; public welfare legislation; customs duties; penal code; new curriculum for the schools. But these measures were highly unpopular. They were too moderate for the Radicals, and too radical for the Moderates. The latent dissension among the Liberals themselves grew pronounced; and so in the very year of the Liberal triumph, Liberal forces were not only divided but embittered and weakened by internal differences, of which Ferdinand and his followers took full advantage.

It hardly needs saying that Ferdinand VII had never sincerely accepted the Revolution. He had hardly sworn to the Constitution before he began to connive against it. Now far from being the beloved monarch, "the Desired," Ferdinand complained bitterly to the *Cortes* in 1821 about insults proffered him in the clubs and on the streets. Moreover, he had been making for several months appeals to foreign sovereigns for help in overthrowing the Liberals. In a letter to Louis XVIII of France, Ferdinand declared that he himself was a captive and Spain was on the verge of anarchy. Czar Alexander of Russia, alarmed by success of the Spanish Revolution, had on his own account presented to the Allied Powers a proposal for armed intervention in Spain. Austria, Prussia, and England, however, fearing any implantation of Russian or French influence on the Peninsula, at first opposed intervention, as, for that matter did Louis XVIII, who was kept busy at home; but at length Ferdinand's appeals were listened to, with France,

Russia, Austria and Prussia joining together to restore the pre-Revolutionary situation of 1820. Great Britain, influenced by a strong popular sentiment at home favoring the Spanish Liberals, tried to obtain from the Liberal Ministry a compromise with Ferdinand that might prevent intervention. The Liberals refused to compromise, and they were right. In the first place the strong Liberal sentiment then dominant in Spain prohibited the Spanish Government from making concessions. In the second, the proposed concessions were presented in the guise of pressure by foreign nations on the internal affairs of Spain; in the third, there was the wholly practical consideration that even if the concessions had been granted they would hardly have checked action by the Holy Alliance which was actuated by enmity toward constitutional principles. The British Government, despite Liberal sympathies, had declared that it would be neutral in case of war.

In 1823 the Ambassadors of France, Russia, Austria, and Prussia presented a note to the Spanish Government making these demands in common: abolition of the Constitution of 1812; liberation of the King whom they regarded as "a prisoner of the Liberals"; and cessation of the anarchy which they apparently believed to be prevailing in the country. The Spanish Ministry replied by declining to displace the Constitution, repudiating intervention as contrary to the law of nations, and indignantly refuting the charges brought against the Liberals. The respective Ambassadors were recalled from Spain, as was the French Ambassador soon after. Louis XVIII told the French Chamber that because of the intransigence of the Spanish Government, he was ready to send a hundred thousand Frenchmen into Spain. In April 1823 French troops did cross the border and on May 23 entered Madrid. No effective resistance was offered; a fact which is proof in itself that the Revolution of 1820 was not, like the Revolution of 1808, a movement of the masses. A capitulation was soon arranged, stipulating that Ferdinand VII be released from "captivity"—which was to say, Liberal control. On October 1 the King of Spain passed over to the French camp, after first promising a general amnesty and formation of a moderate Government—promises that it is improbable he ever meant to keep.

Thus the second period of constitutional government came to an end in Spain. It perished not so much on account of its mistakes, which have been excessively commented upon, as of the indifference of the majority of the Spanish people to its principles, and of the reactionary movement then prevalent in Europe which led to intervention against Liberalism in Spain. If this period is judged only by its political action, as such, it would seem to represent a mania for liberty leading to lawlessness; but if its legislative achievement is examined, it becomes clear that much was done for the educational progress of the country and foundations were laid for basic juridical institutions. The establishment of the General Direction of Studies (1821), the reform of the College of San Isidro and of the Seminary of Nobles (1822), the establishment of the National Academy (on the model of the French), of the original *Ateneo,* or Athenaeum (1820) which was to influence later cultural life profoundly, and of the famous *Colegio de San Mateo* which was in a sense the cradle of Spanish Romanticism: all these movements of the period built toward the widening educational horizons of the Spanish people.

This intellectual movement was smothered for the time being by a reaction more violent, blind, and cruel than that of 1814. No sooner had Ferdinand recovered his liberty than a new order decreed death for the supporters of the Constitution, and even for those who had shouted *Viva Riego* or *Mueran los serviles—*"Long live Riego!" or "Death to the servile!" Until the end of 1829, the political history of Spain alternated between terrorism and a relaxation of coercive measures, depending on the King's advisers or his desires to conciliate one group or another.

The ameliorating influence in 1829 was that of María Cristina, Ferdinand's new bride. His third wife, Maria Amalia of Saxony, had died in May of that year. Since Ferdinand was childless and frail, the hope that his brother, Prince Don Carlos, might succeed him grew stronger. Ferdinand, however, had decided to marry again; and his decision brought an open and shameless conflict of ambitions in the royal family. One faction was led by María Francesca, who was the wife of Don Carlos and was always influential with Ferdinand; the other by Maria Carlota of Naples, wife of another brother of Ferdinand's, Prince Don Francisco. The enmity between the two women was such that it became a political factor, since the Liberals looked on Doña Carlota as being their friend at Court although she was in fact no whit less royalist than Doña Francesca. That delusion of the Liberals, however, gave the question of the new marriage a bearing which affected the history of Spain. Doña Carlota preferred as candidate for the royal marriage her sister Princess Maria Cristina of Naples; and so did Ferdinand, for the Neapolitan Princess was beautiful and charming. The partisans of Don Carlos attempted to discredit Maria Cristina by declaring far and wide that she was a thorough-going Liberal in her politics, which she was not. They failed to convince Ferdinand, but they did convince the Liberals, who in any case felt a natural affinity for anybody who weakened Carlist influence at Court. The new Queen, in spite of innate reactionary instincts, did feel inclined to favor Liberals for the same reason, a desire to combat the Carlists; but she had no liberal convictions.

When it was known that María Cristina was about to give birth to a child, the political tension was heightened. If María Cristina should bear a son, that would put an end to Don Carlos' hopes of the throne, then and there; if she bore a daughter, the problem would become very complicated. Contrary to medieval law and custom in the Spanish kingdoms, Philip V in 1713, it will be recalled, had published an Act which by always giving preference of succession to the male line, was designed to prevent any union of the Spanish and French Crowns in one person. (This Act has been called the Spanish Salic Law.) With passing of the international situation that called it into being, the Act had been abrogated in 1789 by Charles IV, who restored the ancient law of the *Siete Partidas* which permitted a woman to succeed to the throne. However, this reform—while wholly consonant with Spanish tradition—was not published at the time but kept secret, though duly recorded in the Archives of both Charles IV and the *Cortes*. In order to meet every contingency, María Cristina, when apprised of these facts, induced Ferdinand to publish on May 19, 1830 the law of 1789. Don Carlos was thunderstruck, all the more so when María Cristina gave birth to a girl on October 30, 1830. She was named Isabella and at once proclaimed Princess of Asturias; which was to say, heiress to the throne. Thenceforward the struggle between Queen María Cristina and Don Carlos was over the Law of 1789: Should it be maintained or abrogated?

In the final year of Ferdinand VII's reign (he died in 1833), royal policy toward the Liberals was somewhat softened through influence of María Cristina who needed Liberal support to defend the Princess Isabella's right to the throne. Amnesty was given many of the emigrés;

the universities were reopened; and other ameliorative measures were adopted. The reactionary program came to be defended in its entirety by Don Carlos, aspirant to the Crown. Thus was born the *Carlista,* or Carlist, Party. The Liberals decisively became partisans of Isabella and of Cristina, while the Carlistas were the Absolutists.

If María Cristina, who was Regent during Isabella II's minority, had been sincere in adherence to the Liberal cause, the Spanish political problem would have reduced itself simply to a struggle between Absolutists and Constitutionalists which would have enabled the latter to organize a legitimate party in consonance with the general development of ideas in Europe. But this was not to be. After María Cristina's initial triumph—the assembly of the Liberal *Cortes* in the ancient Spanish manner to recognize Isabella as heiress to the throne—she became increasingly wary of reform, unable to realize that public opinion was more enlightened than it had been in 1814 and 1823, and that constitutional and liberal principles had gained much ground among the masses of the people. When Doña Isabella became Queen, she made the same mistake. The result was that while other nations were finding surer and swifter methods of solving internal problems, the political conflict in Spain was disastrously prolonged. Liberalism's struggle was twofold: first, with the Carlists, in the *civil wars;* secondly, with the Crown, in *government.* The latter phase was the effort to induce María Cristina, Isabella, and the courtiers to accept the Liberal program sincerely, instead of trying to prevent its reforms by subterfuge and confusionism. Added to this was the continued existence of many of the factors that had caused previous dissensions between moderate and extremist sections of the Liberals, together with a certain indefiniteness as to aims. The Spaniards who had emigrated to France and England in the decade 1824-1833 had been exposed to the influence either of Doctrinaires and Radicals in the one country, or of English institutions and customs in the other; and in neither case did they preserve an unquestioning reverence for the Constitution of 1812 such as was felt by many Liberals who had stayed at home. Meanwhile the Absolutists, though the spread of Liberalism was making great inroads upon them, long were in the majority in some districts and in rural areas. The Carlist cause was identified, not always either logically or justly, with maintenance of the ancient *fueros,* and with sentiments handed down from the Middle Ages of regional independence. Carlist resistance continued to be formidable, and costly in life and treasure, almost until our own day.

Don Carlos had strong Conservative support, as well as armed aid of the Basques, who feared for their *fueros,* and of the hardy mountaineers of Navarre, Aragón, Catalonia and Valencia. María Cristina, although she had the support of the Army and controlled the mechanism of Government, found that these of themselves were insufficient against the impassioned force of the Carlist troops in the field and the skilled maneuvers of their clerical allies at Court. Driven to seek reinforcements, she made a successful bid for Liberal assistance by accepting their demand for parliamentary institutions.

It should be noted that, apart from the defense of the individual— that is, of human rights—the political problem then most discussed was that of municipal autonomy. It was chiefly a question as to whether municipal officers should be elected, or appointed by the central Government.

Loss of the Spanish Dominions on the American Mainland

A political event of far-reaching importance for Spain and for the Americas occurred during Ferdinand VII's reign: the independence of the dominions on the American continent which Spain had won during the fifteenth and the sixteenth centuries.

Except for the losses or cessions of Florida, the Mississippi territories (Louisiana), Santo Domingo (Española), and Trinidad, to which successive reference has been made already, in 1808 the Spanish Crown still possessed the greater part of the territory of the Americas. Spanish colonies in the Western Hemisphere at that time included the southwestern portion of the present United States (including California and Texas), Mexico, all of Central America, and all of South America except Brazil and the small holdings of European Powers in the Guianas. In Oceania the Spanish colonies included the Philippines and other island groups—the Marianas, the Carolines, and the Palaus.

As always happens in all colonies as they progress in prosperity and education (and in this latter field Spain had shown as much concern for inhabitants of her possessions in America as for the Peninsular population, except as regards restrictions imposed for political reasons in the final years of the eighteenth century), an anti-Spanish party, or

SPANISH DOMINIONS
OF THE AMERICAS, 1810

at least one permeated with distrust of Spain, was forming in the American colonies. This party was made up of descendants of the colonizers with unmixed Spanish blood and of *mestizos* with varying degrees of Indian admixture; who had been led, the one group and the other, to adopt that attitude of hostility not only because the psychology of colonial and mixed peoples inclines that way, but also because of frequent mistakes, abuses, and political anachronisms commmitted by Spanish officials and clerics. During the eighteenth century there had been some manifestations of a similar attitude, and a few of the Ministers of the Bourbon Kings had given warning, pointing out the inherent dangers and even going so far as to suggest a change in the system of colonial government. In fact, as we have seen, something was done about it; but not enough.

The example of the former English colonies in North America, which toward the close of the eighteenth century, in 1783, emancipated themselves and laid the foundations of what is now the United States of America, encouraged the Hispanic American separatists, making new converts for them and adding fresh fuel to the desire for independence.

Premature outbreaks took place at Caracas and Quito and in Alto Peru in 1809. The first real uprising came in 1810 in Venezuela, and was followed in swift succession by others in Buenos Aires, New Granada, Chile, Quito, and Mexico. Nevertheless, American Deputies from all the Vice-Royalties and other units of Government appeared at the sessions of the *Cortes* of Cádiz; and perhaps the separation from Spain of the New World colonies would not have come about if the political doctrine of the Spanish Liberals had been more flexible on this point. As a matter of fact, the Liberals had begun by saying that Spain's territorial possessions in the Americas should not be regarded as regions for foreign trade, nor as colonies, but simply as "an essential or integral part of the Spanish monarchy"; for which reason the American territories were to be governed in exactly the same manner as the Peninsular territories and called "overseas provinces"—*provincias ultramarinas* —and the absolute juridical equality of Spaniards and Spanish Americans was to be proclaimed. But when this doctrine was incorporated in the Convocation and the Constitution of the *Cortes*, all inhabitants of the American colonies who were not free and white ("descendants of Spaniards on both sides") were excluded from citizenship and denied the vote; and an unequal proportional representation by Deputies in the *Cortes* was established for the Peninsula and the American colonies. The American Deputies forcefully denounced these differences, and their polemic with the Spaniards "produced a series of verbal clashes and wounded feelings, . . . the Peninsular Deputies resentful because they were accused of being illiberal, and the American Deputies indignant because in theory and in fact they were assigned a lower place."

Rebellion in America spread. It was led by Bolívar in the northern part of South America; at first by Belgrano and Artigas and later by San Martín in the region of the River Plate and Chile, with O'Higgins joining in in the latter sector; by Hidalgo and Morelos in Mexico. Of these regions, independence *de facto* had been achieved by 1813 by Buenos Aires, Uruguay, Paraguay, Chile, and a considerable portion of New Granada. The first reactionary Bourbon Government (1814) rekindled the conflict by employing terrorism in some of the territories still dominated by Spanish troops or Spanish partisans; a proceeding which served only to stir up greater hatred on the part of the American colonies. The strength of the revolt, together with the lack of Spanish troops—for, as we have seen, the expeditionary force that had been readied to sail in 1830 had joined the Peninsular insurrection under Riego and Quiroga—helped on the victory of the Revolutionists in the Americas; and the Independence of the whole of South America was consummated in 1824. Mexico had achieved independence in 1821, Guatemala and Venezuela in the same year, and Ecuador in 1823. Consequently, the only remaining possessions of Spain in the New World were the Greater Antillean islands of Cuba and Puerto Rico in the Caribbean and the large, dispersed island groups of Oceania. Thus Spain had lost in a very few years almost one million square miles of territory inhabited by about 12,000,000 persons—Indians, whites, Negroes, and mestizos—the largest single group being the Indians, who numbered some 6,000,000. Of the emancipated mainland colonies in the Western Hemisphere were born the new Republics of Argentina, Uruguay, Paraguay, Chile, Peru, Bolivia, New Granada (later Colombia), Ecuador, Venezuela, the United Provinces of Central America (afterwards divided into the five Central American Republics), and Mexico: all of which have inherited and are perpetuating the Spanish civilization and the Spanish language. The monarchy of Spain had lost many of its vast colonial possessions, but the spirit of Spain was part of their being and has burgeoned continuously in fresh shoots that will

Mengs: *King Charles III.*

Madrid: Prado Museum

grow ever stronger and more fruitful, enriching the heritage of the Spanish mind, whatever be the material future of Spain.

The Spanish Government, lacking any prevision of coming events, held out for some years, under different Ministries and for different reasons, against recognizing the independence of those Spanish American States; and thus they failed to bridge the great gulf of misunderstanding naturally created by the Wars of Independence. Official cognizance of the new Republics was initiated finally in 1836 with recognition of Mexico in conformity with a bill of the Spanish *Cortes* (the Law of December 4, 1836) which authorized the Government to "conclude Treaties of Peace and Friendship with the new States of Spanish America on the basis of recognition of their independence"; but even so there were further clashes, including the war with Peru and Chile, 1864-66.

By the end of the nineteenth century, cordial relations had been fully established between Spain and her former colonies on the American mainland. In 1892, the celebration of the four hundredth anniversary of the Discovery of America, and the conferences and congresses held at Madrid in commemoration of that event, with delegates attending from all the Hispanic American countries, was a vibrant demonstration of that friendly relationship; and it marked the origin of the current of inalienable kinship and amity flowing through the Spanish-speaking world called Hispano-Americanism—*Hispanoamericanismo*—which has grown constantly stronger from that time to this, with its course ever more definitely mapped out and its goals of understanding and cooperation already within sight of attainment.

Isabella II and the Civil War

María Cristina's principal motive for supporting the Liberal cause was, as we have seen, the fact that her brother-in-law Prince Don Carlos insisted that he had a preferential right to the throne, notwithstanding Ferdinand VII's express desire that it should be inherited by his daughter Isabella, who at the time of Ferdinand's death in 1832 was a child of two years.

Don Carlos based his claim to the Crown on the presumption that there was still in effect the Act which Philip V had published reluctantly more than a century previous and which declared that the pre-

Mengs: *Queen Maria Amalia, Wife of Charles III.*

ferred succession to the throne of Spain should always be in the male line (so to circumvent possible union of the Spanish and French Crowns in one person). But when the international crisis responsible for this Act had passed, Charles IV abrogated it, since it was contrary to the tradition of Spain, in whose long history there have been many Queens. It was to leave no legal loophole that Ferdinand VII ratified the abrogation before the birth of his daughter Isabella. Don Carlos, who did not therefor renounce his claims, let himself be guided rather by his ambition and by his concept of monarchy as absolute power than by the obligation incumbent upon him to acknowledge the right (within the patrimonial idea of monarchy) which clearly pertained to Ferdinand as King to bequeath his Crown where he willed.

Civil War then broke out between the adherents of Isabella—who was proclaimed Queen as Isabella II—and Don Carlos' partisans. The conflict, which was both dynastical and political, was extraordinarily violent, and abounded in acts of cruelty expressive of the blind passions that had unleashed them. Soon after Ferdinand's death the war was begun by the Carlists, who organized as soldiers in Navarre and the Basque Provinces. For a half-dozen years, Carlism constituted a real danger; but the year 1839 was to be fatal to the Carlist cause which in the meantime had been profoundly undermined. Among the mixed reasons for this were Don Carlos' own lack of personality, his departure from his army, the group of boon-companions who roused his suspicions of his best generals, his ingratitude toward those generals, and a budget which augmented the expenses of his Court without providing for the needs of his soldiers. The result was formation among the Carlists of a Court party and a Military party. The latter prevailed; and the Carlist General Rafael Maroto—a man of great energy and courage, and the idol of his men—himself advocated the making of peace, both because of disillusionment concerning the capabilities of the Pretender and of weariness caused by a conflict for which no end was discernible. General Baldomero Espartero for the Crown and General Maroto for the Carlists signed a peace pact at Vergara on August 31, 1839. Espartero undertook to recommend to the *Cortes* confirmation or modification of the *fueros;* and it was agreed that the military grades and civil posts of the Carlists who submitted were to be recognized by the Government.

The Convention of Vergara was an expression of weariness on both sides, as well as of Carlist disillusionment with the administrative ability and the character of the Pretender Don Carlos. General Ramón Cabrera, who commanded the Carlist forces in Valencia and Catalonia, did not wish to accept the Convention and kept on fighting until June 1840. Civil war broke out afresh in 1847 but lasted only a short time, until April 1849. After that Isabella II was recognized as Queen by all Spaniards except for a small group of partisans who continued loyal to the family of Don Carlos.

Moderates and Progressives

But this did not bring peace to Spain. Among Isabella II's adherents were many Liberals who desired an ample Constitution, either the one of 1812 or one like it; and there were others who, without daring to break with the constitutional principle, tried in every possible way to loosen the restraints placed by the Constitution on the Crown and to reduce the freedoms inherent in what were then called *individual rights* —human rights, the rights of the human being in everyday living and in the world of politics. Partisans of this latter doctrine were called Moderates, and the Queen and her mother were always inclined to favor them. Hence there ensued a series of fluctuations in government and a frequent change of Constitutions which in some instances were liberal and in others restrictive. The first of these, in 1832, was really, rather than a constitution, a law providing for convocation of the *Cortes* and regulation of its forms and faculties. It was called the Royal Statute—*Estatuto Real*—and differed essentially from the French Charter of 1814. After the Statute, Spain was ruled more or less, in succession, by the Constitution of 1812 (restored for a short time), and those of 1837 and 1845, and by the Law of July 17, 1857 which reformed the Constitution of 1845.

The Constitution of 1837, which agreed with that of 1812 in some principles, especially national sovereignty, differed from it by establishing two Chambers for the *Cortes*, giving the Crown an absolute veto, and restricting the suffrage. Yet even these provisions had their progressive aspect: the Upper House or Senate was made elective, the *Cortes* was given the right to meet of itself if not convoked by the King before December 1 in any year; and so on. The influence of the English Reform Bill of 1832 appeared in the Constitution of 1837 and, along with that of other English institutions, was otherwise strong upon Spanish politicians of the nineteenth century. While neither the Moderates nor the Twelve-Yearers welcomed the Constitution of 1837, it was for a long time the militant standard of Progressive Liberals and it had a lasting importance that was twofold: it assured the constitutional principle, never thereafter denied in Spain, and it put an end to the almost idolatrous attitude toward the Constitution of 1812.

All the Progressive reforms were abrogated along with the Constitution of 1837. The latter was replaced by a new Constitution on May 23, 1845, a doctrinary pact between sovereign and people (as its preamble has it). The Constitution of 1845 denied by implication the principle of popular sovereignty, gave back to the Crown the power of appointing the Senate, retired the right of the *Cortes* to spontaneous assembly, abolished trial by jury in the case of offences committed by the Press, kept significantly silent on the principle of uniformity of codes and *fueros,* and converted "judicial power" into simple "administration of justice."

During all this time, which is to say until 1868, the persistent and at times blood-stained conflict continued between Moderates and Liberals, who took the name of Progressives—*Progresistas.* This conflict occasioned numerous insurrections, violent changes of Government, and every kind of disturbance. In substance, it produced a practice according very ill with constitutional principles which, moreover, were not very well understood by the Liberal masses who were lacking in political education.

Military Leaders

Although many men eminent in civil life were to be found in both parties, both, time and again, had recourse to the Army in order to gain power by force. As a result, political leadership finally came to be consolidated in Generals who disputed among themselves not only the post of commander-in-chief but the portfolios of the Ministries of Government. The chief exponents of this attitude were, among the Moderates, General Ramón M. Narváez and General José Enrique O'Donnell (who was less impervious to constitutional principles) ; and, among the Progressives, first General Baldomero Espartero and later General Juan Prim.

Espartero, whose popularity and influence were first kindled by a victory over the Carlists at Bilbao in 1835, was appointed Prime Minister in 1837, succeeding José María Calatrava whose Government earlier in the same year had shaped the Constitution of 1837. That year was otherwise marked by the Carlist war and by a fresh predominance of Moderate influence in Government, with appearance on the scene as popular Moderate leaders of General Córdoba and General Narváez. The latter, who like Espartero, had distinguished himself fighting the Carlists, showed such an inclination for dictatorship as to alarm the Liberals, while his overweening ambition, soon clashing with Espartero's, produced a personal enmity between the two men which affected events as much as did their political differences. In 1837 Narváez was banished on Espartero's accusation. After the Convention of Vergara in 1839, which added greatly to Espartero's popularity, María Cristina tried to persuade the latter to overthrow the Constitution of 1837, to which as Minister he had sworn allegiance. He refused to accede to the Regent's wishes and at the same time tried to persuade her to refuse sanction to a new Municipal Law which was exceedingly unpopular, since it involved almost absolute centralization, with consequent loss of most of the municipal political and administrative independence. María Cristina made fair promises but sanctioned the law nevertheless, whereupon an outbreak against it occurred at Barcelona (July 18, 1840). As a measure of appeasement, María Cristina appointed a Progressive Ministry but soon replaced it by Moderates. Then an outbreak came at Madrid, spreading rapidly to the Provinces, and forcing María Cristina to appoint a new Ministry suggested by the Revolutionists with Espartero Prime Minister once more. To this humiliation and the irksomeness of the new Ministry's Progressive program, which displeased María Cristina to the utmost, were added personal attacks on her private life in an anonymous pamphlet attributed to the reactionary journalist Luis González Bravo, who years later would be Prime Minister. The attacks were motivated by María Cristina's second marriage, a morganatic alliance with the young guardsman Fernando Muñoz, who was ennobled as Duke of Riansares; an alliance which she had persistently denied in order to retain the Regency. Apparently however her desire to be Regent could not withstand so many perturbations. On October 12, 1840, against all the advice and entreaties of her Ministers, María Cristina abdicated. In her address on that occasion, she asked the *Cortes* to name her successor as Regent and stated that her abdication was due to differences with her Ministers regarding certain political measures, especially the Municipal Law. Thus ended the Regency of María Cristina, which began auspiciously and which her own insincerity and wilfulness had clouded and marred. When not playing politics without much regard for the rules, she liked to be a patroness of art and literature. Her name is closely associated with the Romantic movement in Spain, and there was a decided cult for María Cristina among Romantic writers of her day.

María Cristina's brief regency of six years had three well-defined periods: 1843-45, a period of hesitant reform, characterized in legislation by the Royal Statute; 1836-37, a period of Radical policy and substantial reforms, with a brief restoration of the Constitution of 1812, soon replaced by the Constitution of 1837; and finally, 1838-40, a period of return to Moderation which brought on revolutionary outbreaks and resulted in María Cristina's abdicating.

In October 1840 began a new Progressive period, which was the high-water mark both of Progressive policy as mapped by the 1820 and 1836 Liberals, and of Espartero's popularity. It was characterized, nevertheless, by the open appearance of tendencies that had not theretofore developed into violent opposition. At Barcelona in 1842 it took Espartero's presence and a bombardment of the city to put down a violent insurrection which was partly republican in motivation and partly due to resentment against measures taken for suppressing contraband trade. It was not such outbreaks, however, so much as Espartero's political inexperience which laid pitfalls for his Government. He was an honest man and a sincere Liberal, frank, loyal, and courageous; but his education and experience were those of a military leader. By no means dictatorial in nature, he found himself drawn by training and by ambition into the ways of dictatorship. His success and his popularity were, in the circumstances, merely two pitfalls more. His Ministry, from October, 1840 through June, 1843, was a protracted three-year struggle against the Moderates, against the ex-Regent María Cristina, and against dissatisfied Liberals. María Cristina's opposition was voiced forthwith by a Proclamation from retirement in Marseilles which condemned the Progressive Ministry and declared that her abdication had been forced. This Proclamation became a rallying-cry for Espartero's opponents and gave all the European Governments—except England, consistently friendly to Espartero—a pretext for hostility toward the existing regime in Spain. In May 1841 the Cortes nominated Espartero as Regent; and in the same year Augustín Argüelles, silver-tongued orator who had been in the first constitutional Ministry, was appointed guardian of the eleven-year-old Queen Isabella. María Cristina, who claimed that tutorial charge as her maternal right, again protested bitterly. Surrounded in France by Moderate supporters, the ex-Regent's expatriate court became a center of conspiracy. This brought on an outbreak at Madrid on October 7, 1841, when Generals Manuel de la Concha and Diego León led an attack on the Royal Palace in order to "rescue" the little Queen, who was—they averred—the prisoner of the Esparterists. The attempt failed, but new outbreaks took place in 1843, with the support of Liberal malcontents. First, Brigadier General Juan Prim revolted at Reus and declared that Isabella II was of age. Though this was contrary to the Constitution, Isabella was consequently considered to be of age in November 1843, when she was thirteen. The mutiny of other troops followed, led by Espartero's personal enemies, such as Generals Ramón Narváez, Manual de la Concha, Juan de la Pezuela, Francisco Serrano. The counter-revolution grew in strength, and Espartero, abandoned by most of his troops, fled to England. The end of his Regency meant the end of the Progressive Party's control. Those of its members who had joined the counter-revolution because of dissatisfaction with Espartero's Ministry were given short shrift, although the first Moderate Ministry did include one Progressive. This marked the beginning of the preponderance of military leaders—of generals especially, though there were officials of lower rank as well—in Spanish political life; a preponderance that reached its peak in the second decade of the present century during the reign of the last Bourbon king, Alfonso XIII.

From 1843 to 1845 the leader of the Moderates was General Narváez. Dictatorial, inflexible, and cruel, he was reputed never to spare the life of an enemy who fell into his hands. The reactionary Constitution of 1845 was his creation. And yet in spite of that reactionary document and in spite of Narváez' own intolerant nature, the permanent progress made by tolerance in Spain is demonstrated by the fact that despite the victory of the Moderates, no check was placed on Protestant propaganda which had made much headway under the Progressives.

In English literature. George Borrow's *The Bible in Spain* gives a vivid, more or less fictional picture, from a foreigner's point of view, of the period from 1835 to 1840, during which Borrow was colporteur for the British and Foreign Bible Society.

For a quarter of a century—from her accession in 1843 to her expulsion in 1868—Isabella II's reign was merely a continuation of her mother's regency. It was a continuous struggle between her own instinct (and the desire of her Court) to rule autocratically, and the increasing demand of the Spanish people for the honest and efficient government which they believed a strong constitutional *Cortes* would ensure. It was a quarter of a century of kaleidoscopic political changes, revolutions, constitutional amendments—and misrule. The Party leaders were Generals for the most part: Espartero, Narváez (who headed the conservative, *quasi*-absolutist group which called itself the Moderates), O'Donnell, Prim.

In 1846 Isabella was forced by her mother and by Louis Philippe of France—who was eager for a new alliance between Bourbon France and Bourbon Spain—into marriage with her cousin Don Francisco d'Assis. It was a notorious fact that the latter could not be expected to father an heir; so, in perfection of Louis Philippe's scheme, Isabella's younger sister was married to Louis Philippe's son, the Duke of Montpensier. Both weddings took place on the same day and they were the climax of the plots and counterplots by Spanish, French and British which are usually referred to as "the Spanish marriages," and of which Isabella, who was married on her sixteenth birthday, October 10, 1846, was the pawn. Louis Philippe's first plan had been that Isabella should marry his son the Duke d'Aumale; and the British and French Premiers—Lord Aberdeen and Guizot—conferred at length on the subject, the former registering Great Britain's objection. Louis Philippe then agreed to Isabella's marriage to Don Francisco d'Assis, provided her younger sister marry the Duke de Montpensier. To this Lord Aberdeen agreed, but with the proviso that the latter marriage should take place only after Isabella had borne a child. The double wedding on the same day was Louis Philippe's triumph over this diplomatic pledge. It was not a long-lived triumph. On November 28, 1857, Isabella confuted expectations by giving birth to a son who was to become Alfonso XII.

The Revolution of 1868 and Its Consequences

Both the regency of María Cristina and the reign of Isabella II were successful in thwarting—because the Crown held that it was to its interest to do so—the full and sincere practice of constitutional Liberalism; but neither could keep out of Spain and away from the Spanish people the ideas which the evolution of liberal thought itself, and the scientific examination of politics and society, was impressing upon the contemporary world. These ideas reached Spain in various ways. They were brought in by the returning emigrés who had been forced to flee because of their connection with the Constitutions of 1812 and 1814. They emanated from the influence of political events in France and in England. They came from the frequent presence in Spain of foreign agitators, especially Frenchmen and Italians; and from the contact with the English and the German schools of philosophy. The Spanish translation of these philosophic works began in 1820, growing in importance during the next twenty years because of the significance of the work translated; and the widespread popularization of these philosophies from 1860 to 1868 reflected the increasing flow of translation. The net result of all these factors was the revolutionary movement of 1868.

The friends of General José Enrique O'Donnell, Count of La Bisbal, an Irishman by birth, were at odds with the Queen because of the arbitrary and violent proceedings of the latest Moderate Ministry. The Progressives allied themselves with this group and with the Republicans—a party that had already begun to take shape in 1854. These combined political elements furthered a revolution in which the majority of the Army joined (1868). When the Revolutionaries had triumphed and had exiled Isabella II, a new dynasty was sought because General Juan Prim, and most of the other insurrectionists, continued to be monarchists. Amadeo, Duke of Aosta, a Prince of the House of Savoy, the royal house of Italy, accepted the Crown of Spain in 1870 when it was proffered him by the *Cortes*. He was the second son of Victor Emmanuel II. On the day when the new King, Amadeo I, arrived at Cartagena, General Prim was assassinated. Amadeo's pitiful and episodic reign lasted only two years. He was regarded by Monarchists and Republicans alike as an interloper; Carlist forces began gathering in the mountains, while republican feeling ran high in the towns. Nevertheless, Amadeo's liberal and democratic character won him the nickname of the Knightly King—*el Rey Caballero*—and the esteem of a portion of the Spanish people. Amadeo abdicated in 1872, however, finding it an impossible task to dominate the opposing cliques among the Liberals. The Republic was proclaimed without a revolution and by vote of the *Cortes* in 1873.

This new regime (the First Republic) also held power very briefly. In the first place, it had to contend with the divisions in the ranks of its own party-members, among whom were prominent Emilio Castelar, Nicolás Salmerón, Estanislao Figueras, and Francisco Pí y Margall; each striving for the triumph of his own respective program, while the unitary or federal system of government caused frequent changes in Ministries and in the Presidency. But this was not all: the Republic had to contend also with a new Carlist civil war; with the Monarchists who schemed for the return of the Bourbons; and with a rebellion on the Island of Cuba, which at that time still belonged to Spain. In the end the Monarchists triumphed by means of a military insurrection of December 1874 which proclaimed Isabella II's son, Don Alfonso, as King of Spain. As Alfonso XII, he disembarked on the Peninsula in January 1875. This event has been called the *Restoration*. It marked the definite end of the Carlist Wars; and Spain entered upon a period of internal peace which endured for many years but did not put an end to the political struggle between the two fundamental ideologies of the national mind: the conservative and the liberal. The latter, since the Revolution, had itself split into two large factions: Monarchic Liberalism (which held that the fundamental principles of liberal constitutionalism were compatible with the monarchy) and the Republican Party.

Initiation of a Renascence in National Economic and Cultural Life

The War of Independence, first and foremost, then the Fernandist reaction from 1814 to 1833, followed by the half-dozen years of the Carlist War (1833-39), were weighty and effective reasons why the Spanish public did not take part as soon as the other European countries did in continuation into the nineteenth century of the economic and cultural renascence achieved in the eighteenth, and of its progressive and successful development to meet the needs of everyday life. In Spain the renascence not only stagnated but lost ground. Little attention was given material and intellectual progress, and the nation lacked the means to restore its wealth, which had been drained off by the wars and the political conflicts dividing the country. It is no exaggeration to say that it was well-nigh a miracle that during those thirty-one years from 1808 to 1839 the energies of the Spanish people were not totally exhausted. Its formidable resistance and its latent vitality were sufficient not only to prevent exhaustion but to achieve some progress, beginning with 1833 and broadening after the first Civil War. But by that time the world as a whole had made great advances, and the conditions of material civilization which affected the economic life of peoples were very different from what they had been at the end of the eighteenth century.

Mechanized Industrial Inventions

That change, with regard to activities relating to industry, commerce, communications, commodities, and the like, was characterized by the abundance of industrial inventions and the rapidity with which they appeared and were adopted.

In 1768 the work of the Englishmen John and Robert Kay and Sir Richard Arkwright had produced water-powered machinery for weaving cotton textiles; and at the beginning of the nineteenth century the Frenchman Joseph Marie Jacquard perfected similar machinery for silk-weaving. Both inventions had reduced the time that had been required for handweaving and consequently had greatly increased and cheapened production. They also brought about the disappearance of the old-fashioned home industries. Their place was taken by factories in which there were many looms and many workers, because each industrialist wished to produce more in less time than his competitors so that he could outsell them. Not long after Kay and Arkwright, another Englishman, James Watt, in 1775 made the first successful steam-engine, which the North American Robert Fulton applied, building the first workable steamboat in 1807. The first steamboat crossing of the Atlantic was in 1818, the vessel being owned by an Englishman. In 1818 George Stephenson, another Englishman, constructed the first locomotive to run on rails, and out of that invention grew the world's railroads, which, until 1821 used only to move coal, have carried passengers ever since 1830. From these initial inventions came the applications of steam, in ever greater degree of perfection, to propel other machinery than that of ships and trains; with consequent stimulation of industry. The immediate consequence of these inventions was development of coalmining, since machines required coal; and thus originated one of the chief industries of our time. Then when in 1824 English workers indirectly obtained the right to organize, this step brought with it a greatly increased use of machines. Therewith modern capitalism with all its social consequences came into being.

From 1833 to 1838 the first electric telegraphs were produced, and in 1850 they came into frequent use; and the outgrowth was the increasing application of electricity to machinery, the electric light, and a host of other inventions. In many fields electricity has replaced steam, and it has brought about a profound change in living conditions.

Spain was slow in adopting all these inventions, both generally speaking and for the specific reasons noted; and was even slower in popularizing them—that is, in using them to any great extent. Therein lies the reason for the backwardness of our industry and of our system of communications, and consequently of our trade in comparison with that of other European and of American countries which adopted them and swiftly multiplied their use. Only at the end of the nineteenth century, as we shall see, Spain began to make up for lost time, though always with the disadvantage of being a latecomer. For the same reason, the unionization of great numbers of workers has been slower here than in other nations, and is not yet an achieved fact except in certain regions —such as Catalonia, Biscay, Asturias—and in a few cities.

Nevertheless, economic life began to improve, even though slightly, toward the end of Ferdinand VII's reign. The Government throughout María Cristina's regency, and later during the two reigns of Isabella II, fostered both public works and culture. In 1834 the School of Highway Engineers—*Escuela de Ingenieros de Caminos*—which had already functioned previously in the eighteenth century, reopened its doors. The system of roads, the total mileage of which in 1807 did not exceed 2,250 miles, was greatly extended. The first lighthouse with convex lens was inaugurated at Santander in 1839, and by 1856 forty others had been built and nineteen more were under construction. Canals had been dug or were under way along various rivers (the Guadalquivir, the Tagus, the Ebro, the Alcocer, the Lozaya, and others) ; these were the first canals to be constructed in Spain since the time of Philip II except, as we have seen, for the works undertaken in the eighteenth century more in the interest of securing water for irrigation than for use as ship canals. The first Spanish railroads were planned early in 1829, from Jerez to Portal, and the trains began running in 1848 and in 1851. The Spanish telegraph system, first the old-fashioned signal method and later the electrical, dates from the same period. Industries, such as the textile factories in Catalonia, were founded or reestablished. Commerce expanded to a considerable extent in consequence of the natural increase of the nation's wealth, which permitted the Government to acquire through taxes the means of improving public services.

As much as by the things just enumerated, Spain's economic restoration was influenced by the laws of 1833 and 1855 which completed preceding measures for disentailment, or breaking the entail on real property, toward which numerous steps had been taken in the eighteenth century, as we have noted. These new laws, which were due to the initiative of Prime Minister Juan Alvarez Mendizábal, included the entails on property of the nobility and of the middle class and on the properties of churches, convents, and *Ayuntamientos*. Although the method of breaking the entail was less successful than occasion demanded and so did not do as much as was expected of it, nevertheless the number of small landowners increased all over Spain. Entails have never since been reestablished and as the nineteenth century advanced, the tendency toward distribution of land from the vast estates was strengthened, even though in some regions there were still considerable absentee holdings and uncultivated lands. On the other hand much of the communal land, or commons—the lands belonging to a community as a whole and supplying the elemental needs of a considerable portion of the rural population—passed into private ownership.

Cultural Progress

During Isabella II's reign public education and cultural media were also extended and improved, thanks to promulgation of the first special law with that end in view (1859), and to the foundation of primary schools and many learned institutions. These included the Prado Museum, the Conservatory of Music, the Lyceum, the College of Medical Surgery, the Government High Commission of Medicine and Surgery, the Corps of Military Sanitation, the Corps of Physicians of Medicinal

Springs, the Normal Schools, the School of Engineering, the School of Veterinary Science, the Diplomatic School, the Academy of Science; and other artistic and scientific institutions. The universities were reorganized in 1845. There was further progress along the same line. Some of the advancement in the field of medicine was due to the initiative of Doctor Castelló, Ferdinand VII's physician. Though Castelló was an unrepentant Liberal and had been persecuted up to the time that his services came to be considered essential for the King's health, he had a great influence over Ferdinand.

All this served to intensify the thirst for knowledge; and once again Spain produced a crop of scientists, writers, and artists, in great number and worth as compared with former scarcity; but still not so many as the times demanded. The *Ateneo* of Madrid—the Athenaeum; but the English word does not begin to express what the Spanish fact represents in the intellectual history of the nation—which had been created in 1820 by private initiative and had been stopped short in its work of tolerance and culture by absolutism, reopened in 1835 and has been ever since a powerful influence on the cultural life of Spain.

A strong contribution was made to the literary renascence by those Liberals who had emigrated after 1833 and whose contact with such nations as France, Italy, and Germany acquainted them with the great literary movement then afoot in Europe, reviving interest in aesthetics. This literary renascence was deeply, intrinsically Spanish, even in those of its aspects that reflected foreign trends. It was especially so in the theatre, where the rhetorical doctrine of freedom proclaimed by the Romantics who broke with the three unities had had long since its precedent and its model in Spain, well exemplified in the comedies of the Golden Age. This inherent Spanish quality is to be seen in the Romantic works of the Duke of Rivas (*Don Alvaro o la fuerza del destino*); of García Gutiérrez (*El Trovador*); of Juan Eugenio Hartzenbusch (*Los Amantes de Teruel*) and José Zorrilla (*Don Juan Tenorio*); as well as in the poems of some of these same dramatists and of Espronceda. Campoamor, Ruíz Aguilera, Pastor Díaz, Gil, Piferrer, García Tassara, Gertrudis de Avellaneda, Florencio Sanz, Ayala, and Selgas, among others. Their work showed that the weight of the New French, English and German schools was not enough to impede the upward flow of the native sap. The principle representative at that time of the group unaffected by Romanticism was the lyric poet Manuel

José Quintana. To the same period belongs creation of the first choral groups—the Orpheons—which were formed by the Catalán musician José Anselmo Clavé. He established the first Orpheon at Barcelona in 1850; and by 1864 the number had grown to fifty-seven and the example had spread to other Provinces, with great benefit to the culture of the people. Literary criticism and criticism of manners found their leading exponents in the greatly gifted writer José de Larra (*Figaro*) and in Ramón Mesonero Romanos.

What has been said of literature and the fine arts did not hold true of the social and political sciences nor of philosophy. With respect to these, and viewing the intellectual configuration of Spain as a whole, we may say that a gulf had opened wide between Spanish thinking of that period and what had been loftiest, finest, and most original in the Spanish thought of past centuries. In the early years of the nineteenth century this situation could not be changed for the better, because of reasons that we have noted. Rather, it was aggravated; since many Spaniards who shared the new political ideas looked on all Spanish history anterior to constitutionalism, and particularly the centuries of absolute monarchy, as a period offering absolutely nothing that could serve any purpose in modern life and for the spiritual needs of today. When new channels for our Spanish culture were being considered, the adoption of modern ideas and systems much in vogue in other countries was discussed; but not with the intention of making them conform to our national character nor to our lost tradition. Nevertheless, in the beginnings of constitutional life, some intellectuals (the historian Martínez Marina in particular) had upheld the thesis that a substantial bond existed between the new political ideology and Spanish governmental legislation and practice during the Middle Ages. Apart from some few exceptions such as this, no one, until many years of the nineteenth century had passed, believed it necessary—but rather, in fact, thought it would be prejudicial—to look into what had been said and done by our philosophers, jurists, historians and other savants of time long past. In consequence, one of the fundamental problems that the nineteenth century Spaniard had to solve was that of breaking down these prejudices and, while taking advantage of every intellectual achievement made by nations more favored by circumstance than ours, of seeking out once more the veritably Spanish method and tradition, in order to link them up with the new needs of the spirit; thus to recover confidence in

568 A History of Spain

our own strength and in the worth of the Spanish cultural heritage amassed through the centuries. Such ideas as these were growing stronger day by day among a large number of patriotic intellectuals in both political parties, the Constitutional and the Doctrinaire; but the Liberal and Democratic masses continued for a long time to feel that already deeprooted scorn of the national past, unable to discern therein any historic value worthy of preservation.

This problem, although it was presented practically—that is, with the idea of applying wisdom gained from past experience to pressing immediate needs—in the reign of Isabella II by some enlightened minds (including the philosopher Balmes) was not solved then, nor until the end of the nineteenth century.

Neither such problems, which then preoccupied a minority of intellectuals and of fervent patriots, nor the political persecutions which so often disturbed the nation between 1808 and 1833, and to a lesser degree from 1833 to 1868, hindered, during those sixty years, full and fruitful and sound production in historical, juridical, political and economic fields; as is proved by many works published between 1808 and 1868. The authors of some of them had already become well-known by 1800; while others, still young at that time, did their work during the first half of the nineteenth century and even later. It is enough to note here merely a few names. León Bermúdez in 1800 published his *Diccionario de Bellas Artes* (Dictionary of Fine Arts). The studies on political economy by Alvaro Flórez Estrada, who died in 1852, embody theories and observations that shed a new light on that science. Antonio Capmany, philologist, antiquarian, and man-of-letters, in 1821 added to the erudite work of his already cited his interesting history of the Courts of Aragón, Catalonia, and Valencia. The Count of Toreno was author of the *Historia de la sublevación, guerra y revolución de España* (History of the Uprising, War, and Revolution of Spain)—which is to say, of the War of Independence against Napoleon and of the first period of liberal constitutionalism of the Spanish people. Martínez Marina, already mentioned, in his *Teoría de los Cortes* (Theory of the *Cortes*) set out to prove that the *Cortes* of 1812 at Cádiz was merely a resurrection of the ancient *Cortes* of the Middle Ages and of the transition to modern times. Not to prolong citation from what is a lengthy list,[1] let me mention merely the names of his-

---

* Discussed fully in my specialized *Historia de la Civilización Española*. Author's note.

torians of politics, literature, plastic arts, music, medicine, and other branches of knowledge: Félix Torres Amat, Bishop of Astorga, translator of and commentator on the Bible; Pascual de Gayangos, Academician, critic, author of erudite studies on medieval Spanish literature; Vicente Boix, Valencian chronicler; Tejada y Ramírez; A. de Castro and Uzoz y Río (historians both, and publishers of the works of Spanish Protestants of the sixteenth and seventeenth centuries) ; Juan Antonio Llorente, historian of the Inquisition and of other related matters, who in 1822 was still writing about the influence of twelfth-century kings on the division of the Peninsular bishoprics; Janer; Godoy; Alcántara; Pedro José, Marquis of Pidal (statesman and man-of-letters) ; Yanguas; Caveda Villanueva, with his twenty-two volumes of *Viajes* (Travels) —the whole of that voluminous tour being among the churches of Spain (1803-1852) ; Pons, author of another *Viaje* no less interesting and useful than Villanueva's; Nicolás de Azara, (Aragonese diplomat, translator, and editor) ; Martín Fernández de Navarrete (mariner and bibliophile) , to whom we owe the monumental Collection of documents of the Spanish discoverers of the Americas and of Oceania (1829-1859) ; the musician Saldoni; Juan Sempere y Guarinos, who wrote steadily from 1822 to 1847 on Spanish juridical institutions and bibliography; Morejón, to whom we owe the first *Biblioteca* of Medicine, or Medical Library. And there were others. A few years later (1840) one of Isabel's Ministers, and by that token a Conservative, sent the Spanish professor Julián Sanz del Río to Germany to study German philosophy in order to acquaint Spain with its tenets. The result of this travel-grant was that under the appearance of a school directed by the German Krause, there was produced among a considerable number of the cultured Spaniards of the second half of the nineteenth century a movement, not of acceptance of Krausism (which was little lasting and had few disciples) , but of a freedom of philosophic thought that thenceforward directed the formation of Spanish thinking. If the old-school scholastics had then felt less intransigence and more patriotic awareness, instead of persecuting the Krausists as they did they would have formed an alliance with them to counteract the agnostic and materialistic influence that soon began to be in evidence, proceeding from Comte and Herbert Spencer. That error of conservative Spaniards was to be repeated in 1933, as we shall see, in the field of politics.

Progress, 1868-1874

The Revolutionary Period, far from paralyzing the progress achieved between 1833 and 1868, augmented it, notwithstanding continuous political agitation, in all three of its stages: the Provisional Government (1868-1870) ; Amadeo I's reign (1870-1872) ; and the First Republic (1873-1874) .

In the field of legislation (and not alone in that affecting the constitutional problem) , one evidence of accelerated progress was the Constitution of 1869, which was the clear and resolute expression of the program of nineteenth century Liberalism. Others were the reorganization of the administration of justice, beginning with establishment of the principle that Judges could not be removed; modification of the colonial policy by making it more liberal and less subject to corruption; the restoration to Puerto Rico of that colony's right to elect Deputies to the Spanish *Cortes;* the introduction of abolitionist measures with regard to negro slavery in the Antilles; reform of the penal Code; the institution, for the first time in Europe (by Decree of July 24, 1873) of the mixed juries, or boards of arbitration, composed of both employers and workers, to settle labor disputes; the creation of the Bank of Spain, an institution that was fundamentally the work of the engineer and dramatist Don José Echegaray; the Civil Registry Law; the marriage law; and others of lesser importance.

In the field of culture, and aside from the progress already mentioned in educational administration and methodology, the Revolutionary period with its atmosphere of freedom which invited the expanding wings of the mind, witnessed appearance of some of the men of letters and of science who were to lend lustre to the closing years of the century; garnered grain from European culture in translations of numerous significant books; and published magazines, newspapers, and other vehicles of general information. The first novel by Benito Pérez Galdós appeared in 1870; and from early in 1873 to the end of 1874 appeared almost the whole of the first of the five series of his *Episodios nacionales* (National Episodes) , a factual and realistic but highly dramatic evocation of Spanish history—civil, martial, and political—from 1808 to 1878. In 1874 appeared also Juan Valera's *Pepita Jiménez,* Pedro Antonio Alarcón's *El Sombrero de Tres Picos* (The Three-Cornered Hat) , and José Echegaray's first dramatic efforts. In 1870

Concepción Arenal, jurist, criminologist, educator, and sociologist, began her admirable contributions to *La Voz de la Claridad* and wrote her pacifist book, *Cuadros de la guerra* (War Pictures), one of the first works of the kind to be published in Europe, if not the very first. To the same period belong the first book and the early articles by Francisco Giner de los Ríos, Professor of the Philosophy of Law at the University of Madrid, founder of the Free Institution for Teaching (*Institución Libre de Enseñanza*), and of the Commission for Educational Extension, or *Junta para Ampliación de Estudios*. These few representative names are sufficient in themselves to indicate the intellectual ferment during those years, which was likewise evident in Catalonia and other regions. The solid educational foundation that had been given the generation that made this period illustrious was incontrovertible proof of the vitality with which, amid the most hindering political conditions, had germinated the new aspirations which not only made possible the Revolution of 1868 but imbued it with idealism that made it into something more than just a political episode.

After the Revolution of 1868 there was also notable progress in the economic field, upon the details of which we shall not enter.

II. FROM 1875 TO 1902

The Policy of the Restoration

The Bourbon Restoration of 1875 was not absolutist in political principle, as Ferdinand VII's Restoration had been. It was constitutional, although ushered in by a brief period of persecutions and by the derogation or suspension of some of the revolutionary laws, such as the one establishing civil marriage. Alfonso XII's first Prime Minister, Antonio Cánovas del Castillo, triumphantly obtained from the *Cortes* a Constitution—the Constitution of 1876—which, while not so progressive as the one given by the Revolutionary Government of 1869, included some of the fundamental Liberal tenets. Years later that Constitution was rounded out by laws establishing universal suffrage and other institutions then already existing in most of the countries of Europe and the Americas.

For their part, the Republicans made several revolutionary attempts during the early years of the Restoration (until 1892); but some were discovered and brought down punitive measures and others faded out.

Republican political forces had their right to public action again recognized as lawful after a period during which they were proscribed, and then sent to the *Cortes* a delegation which, while not numerous, was picked and able—it included some of the great leaders of the First Republic, such as Emilio Castelar, Nicolás Salmerón, and Francisco Pí y Margall—and which constituted the only real parliamentary opposition; except for the Cataláns, to whom we shall return. Not long afterwards a Socialist minority joined the Republican group.

Thus the regime continued, despite the premature death in 1885, at the age of twenty-eight, of Alfonso XII. In 1878 he had married, for love, his cousin Mercedes, daughter of the Duke and Duchess of Montpensier. She died five months later of gastric fever; in English both Madame Calderón de la Barca and James Russell Lowell, then United States Minister at Madrid, wrote touching accounts of the young King's grief. His second marriage, in 1879, had been to the Archduchess María Cristina, niece of the Austrian Emperor Franz Joseph.

Alfonso XII's posthumous son, Alfonso XIII, born May 1, 1886, was not old enough to occupy his throne until he attained his sixteenth year in 1902. In the interim his widowed mother, Queen María Cristina, ruled the country as Regent without any constitutional change being effected. This period from 1885 to 1902 has been denominated the *Regency*. Alfonso attained his majority in the latter year at the age of sixteen. In 1905 he married Princess Victoria Eugenia, granddaughter of Queen Victoria of England.

During the regency of María Cristina and the preceding decade from 1875 to 1885, the years of Alfonso XII's reign, the constituent problem—achievement and maintenance of a basic constitutional law—was no longer the central point of political conflict, though previously it had been so ever since 1808. Now, however, discussion centered rather about the problem of complying efficiently with political and administrative norms and of the more or less ample, more or less sincere, interpretation by the Executive Power of constitutional precepts. On the one hand, the Conservative Party (to which Cánovas himself gave the name Conservative-Liberal—*Conservador-Liberal*), and on the other the Liberals (called the *Fusionista* or Fusion Party, and formed by Praxedes Mateo Sagasta, Amadeo I's ex-Prime Minister), represented during those periods the alternating currents of the two policies of government, even under the Constitution itself. The Lib-

Madrid: Prado Museum

Goya: *The Family of Charles IV.*

eral Party, logically enough, spurred on by Republican opposition, was responsible for the laws cited which established universal suffrage and for others deemed compatible with the Constitution of 1876 but not included in the Restoration's initial program. The man who represented that ideal of cooperation in favor of liberalization of the monarchy was the Republican Emilio Castelar (1832-1899), President of the Spanish Republic in 1873 and later collaborator in the monarchical liberalism of the Restoration.

But the fact that such laws were on the books did not mean necessarily that they were in force. Nor did it give any real guarantee that parliamentary representation was the free and authentic expression of the political opinion of the country. The majority of the voting population was not taking part spontaneously in the elections nor in efficient discharge of the obligations of citizenship. Moreover, the flexibility or the indefiniteness of certain Articles in the Constitution of 1876 (among them Article 11, relating to religious freedom) —qualities which had been esteemed by some politicians as favorable to the progress of political ideas and to making the text of the Constitution permanent—resulted in fact in making insecure the juridical status of the Constitution itself, and favored the restrictive interpretations, which were both more frequent and more rigid than were the ampler interpretations. In proportion as modern political ideas, progressively more radical, were spreading over Spain, the aspiration for a really liberal government and for honesty in use of the vote and sincerity in constitutional principles was felt more pressingly by progressive groups. Consequently the gulf was growing wider between the opposition and the monarchical parties, now that the Liberal Party itself had come to be very little differentiated from the Conservative in practical politics. Every passing day brought fresh evidence of this, as many Liberals themselves openly admitted. The Crown, for its part, made no effort whatever to mend matters.

The Question of the Antilles

Those overseas possessions remaining to Spain after 1824, Cuba and Puerto Rico in the Caribbean and the island groups of Oceania, were still very important. The latter included more than 14,640 square leagues, according to the unit of measurement then in use (some 43,820

Vicente López: *Homage Paid by the University of Valencia to King Charles IV and Queen María Luisa.*

square miles), with a population of 1,300,000. In the Americas, Cuba measured 44,000 square miles, in 1818 had 700,000 inhabitants; Puerto Rico, with an area of 3,670 square miles, had a population of 100,000. The attention of Peninsular Spain as well as commercial development were centered principally on the two Antillean islands, whose wealth and population alike increased very rapidly. Thus Havana, which in 1800 had had only 60,000 inhabitants, by the end of the century (1900) counted 236,000. Santiago de Cuba during the same period increased from 20,000 to 43,000; Matanzas from 7,000 to 36,000. The last Spanish census of the islands showed Cuba with a population of 1,500,000; Puerto Rico, 800,000. Many of these Cubans and Puerto Ricans were Spanish-born, and the majority were of Spanish descent.

But on both islands surged up the same aspirations for Independence that had brought into being the mainland Republics; aspirations that were quickened by the successful rebellions of 1810-1824 in South America, Mexico, and Central America. Two special factors in Cuba and Puerto Rico further complicated the problem: the negro slave population, an element of continuous disturbance, and the desire of the northern Republic, the United States, which from a very early period in its history aspired to control the Antilles and tried repeatedly to do so by purchase or intervention, while at the same time favoring Antillean conspiracies against Spain and the landing in Cuba of partisans of that island's independence. The several Spanish Governments either failed to realize the gravity of this danger or were powerless to forestall it. Nor did they have the wisdom to calm separatist turbulence by political and administrative reforms, notwithstanding the good intentions of some of the Governors of the Islands and of Señor Cánovas del Castillo who in 1865 was Minister for the Colonies—*Ministro de Ultramar*. The example of what had occurred in the case of Spain's possessions on the American mainland availed nothing. The Peninsular Government went on curtailing the rights of the Cubans and the Puerto Ricans, viewing every liberal movement with distrust, and employing armed force whenever the situation grew more serious. In spite of all this, the separatist movement continued to grow until at last it brought on a war in Cuba which began in 1868 with the insurrection at Jara and did not end until 1878 with the Peace of Zanjón.

The Spanish revolutionary Governments (1868-1873) modified the old colonial policy to some degree. They restored to Puerto Rico the right to elect Deputies to the *Cortes* (1869), as has been mentioned; abolished not a few of the measures enacted against Cuban insurrectionists and suspects, which in some instances had given rise to serious abuses; limited the excessive authority of the Captains-General; and passed laws on immigration, colonization, tribunals of justice, et cetera, tending to benefit the Antilles. But all sentiment for reform was set at naught by the unquestionable strength of the intransigents, who were numerous on the Peninsula as well as in Cuba, where most of them were "armed volunteers" and time and again forced the Captains-General to do their bidding; and who by such acts as the execution of the rebel leader Arango, the shooting of some University of Havana students accused of separatist plotting (1871), and the insubordination shown to Spanish officials who tried to keep the intransigent passions and stubbornness in check, added fresh fuel to the hatred and despair that were blazing into war.

Autonomy and Empire

The Peace of Zanjón in 1878 obligated the Spanish administrations to make an effective change of policy. Many Cubans took heart from this—those who, desiring liberties for their country, desired peace also and had no wish to break completely with the Peninsula. The right and natural thing would have been to set up an autonomous insular government which, while maintaining the dependence of the two islands upon Spain, would have given them a certain freedom in directing and administering their own affairs. This idea, shared by many Peninsular republican and some monarchical elements, was voiced in Spain by the Autonomist Party which issued its first statement in 1872 but was not formally constituted until 1879, after publication of its Manifesto-program in August 1878. As was to be feared, the intransigents, who continued numerous on the Peninsula and in the Antilles, bitterly opposed autonomy, dubbing its defenders disguised filibusters and disloyal citizens. The dominant doctrine was to consider Cuba and Puerto Rico not as *colonies* but as *overseas provinces*, but with application of a system of special laws rather than of pure assimilation. For this reason, although the right of electing Deputies to the *Cortes* was restored to Cuba in 1878, with concession of the Municipal Law, the insular right of suffrage was made much more restrictive than the peninsular. The same thing was true of Puerto Rico, although that island had enjoyed universal suffrage ever since the Revolution. Likewise—that is to say, generally speaking, with some modifications—the Spanish Penal Code was applied to Cuba in 1879; the mortgage loan legislation in 1880; the Constitution of 1876, in 1881; the law for trial courts in 1885; the Commercial Code in 1886. These measures were not enough. The aspiration for autonomy was growing steadily stronger, and in the *Cortes* it was voiced repeatedly by the Deputies from Cuba and Puerto Rico who spoke but were not heard. In 1882 the law of trade relations between Cuba and Spain, although making several general concessions, afforded grounds for the increasing discontent on the Island. In 1893, hope was revived by a project presented by the Conservative politician, Don Antonio Maura, for political and administrative reform in the direction of fuller autonomy, but other politicians turned thumbs down on the proposal; and the very deficient Law of 1895 which was substituted for it never even went into effect.

As regards negro slavery, the remedy was swift and effective. The abolitionist movement, which was initiated at the *Cortes* of Cádiz, by Orense, Nicolás María Rivero, Castelar, and other democrats, had solidified by 1865 into an Abolitionist Society that met with very strong opposition but nevertheless year by year gained adherents. In 1868 the slave trade was definitely suppressed; that is, the importation of new slaves was prohibited. In 1870 a law was enacted to free existing slaves, and a further law in 1873 (despite strong opposition from the pro-slavery element) freed the slaves in Puerto Rico. The Peace of Zanjón with Cuba had recognized the freedom of all negroes who had taken part in the insurrection; but, although justice and logic with even greater reason would have ordained likewise the freedom of those slaves who had not rebelled against Spain, these latter were not emancipated until 1880, and even then they were left subject to their masters for another eight years. Finally, however, in 1886 a law advanced the date and made their freedom immediately effective.

The abolition of negro slavery had had its Spanish apostles as early as the sixteenth century (Bartolomé de Albornoz and others), as we saw. The Constitution of the United States of America, adopted in 1787, left the question of slavery unanswered, and a fierce Civil War had to be fought—the War between the States, 1861-1865—in order to abolish it. In Europe the suppression of the slave trade, in the case of most States possessing colonies, preceded by many years the liberation of slaves already owned; but the abolition of slavery in general was prior to the Spanish Law to that effect enacted in 1870.

The Colonial Disaster

Disillusionment with regard to the reforms attempted in 1893 and 1895, united to complaints against the Spanish administration and to the lack of zeal regarding everything that tended to foster the wealth and culture of the colony, strengthened the radical stand of the separatists; and again there was war, its outbreak announced by what is called the "Cry of Baire"—*grito de Baire*—in 1895; a war that was backed by a strong body of public opinion in the United States. At that time many Spanish politicians again advocated the granting of autonomy as an honorable measure of compromise; but the majority, represented in this instance by the leader of the Conservative Party, Cánovas del Castillo, shut their ears to reason, chose rather to "fight fire with fire," and demanded surrender of the rebels as a necessary preliminary to concession of reforms. That attitude fanned the flames of insurrection in Cuba, though some of the island Autonomists remained loyal to Spain. Puerto Rico held aloof from the conflict, as she had done previously.

But the United States, deeming that the moment had arrived to take a decisive policy step, precipitated the end; alleging, as reasons for intervention in the war, the prolongation of conflict; the military proceedings of the Spanish commander-in-chief in Cuba, General Weyler (harsh measures of repression, concentration camps, et cetera); the blowing-up of the U. S. battleship *Maine* while at anchor in Havana Bay (an act unjustly attributed to the Spaniards); and the necessity of protecting the lives and property of United States citizens residing in Cuba or having Cuban investments. Though none of these reasons was fully established by proved facts, nor much less had valid justification in international law, there is no question that, taken all together, they had weight. Because of that, and of the awareness (already sensed by many Liberal political leaders) that it was essential to cut the rebellion short by granting reforms, the reform legislation of November 25, 1897 was enacted by the *Cortes* and went into effect in January 1898. It represented a much enlarged autonomy; but the remedy came too late. The action of the United States neither gave the reforms time to produce results nor facilitated application of the new law, in the way of which the Separatists too placed every kind of obstacle. Consequently we have no way of judging whether or not autonomy would have taken root in Cuba and Puerto Rico and have satisfied the revolutionists. Nor was time allowed for the experiment to bear fruit.

In view of the exaggerated demands of the Government of the United States, which Spain found wholly unacceptable, war between the two countries broke out in April, 1898, with results unfavorable to us, whose economic and military resources were vastly inferior to those of the United States. The heroic but useless sacrifice of our Navy at Santiago de Cuba and at Manila Bay, and the strong resistance of that part of our Army which participated in the fighting, did not change the situation.

The Spanish-American War ended officially with the Treaty of Paris on December 10, 1898, by which Cuba obtained her independence and Puerto Rico came to be a possession of the United States. The same thing happened with respect to the Philippines, whose inhabitants had also revolted against the Spaniards (1896) and also obtained assistance from the United States (1898). By the Treaty of Paris Spain not only renounced unconditionally all sovereignty over the two islands in the Caribbean, but ceded the Philippines and the Sulu Islands and the largest of the Marianas to the United States in consideration of the payment therefor of twenty million dollars. There remained as Spanish possessions in the Pacific only the Carolines and a few other scattered islands which were sold to Germany in 1899 for forty million dollars, and two small islands unaccountably omitted in the delineation of the Paris Treaty which Spain sold to the United States in 1900.

New Possessions in Africa

Between the first and the second Cuban wars—which is to say, from 1884 to 1886—Spain established dominion over that part of northwestern Africa south of Morocco known as the *Río de Oro;* and also established a protectorate over the neighboring region of Adrad-et-Tamarr. That was the first step in an African policy proclaimed (but in the nature of a guardianship and therefore of pacific penetration) by the great jurist and tribune of the people, Joaquín Costa, and adopted,

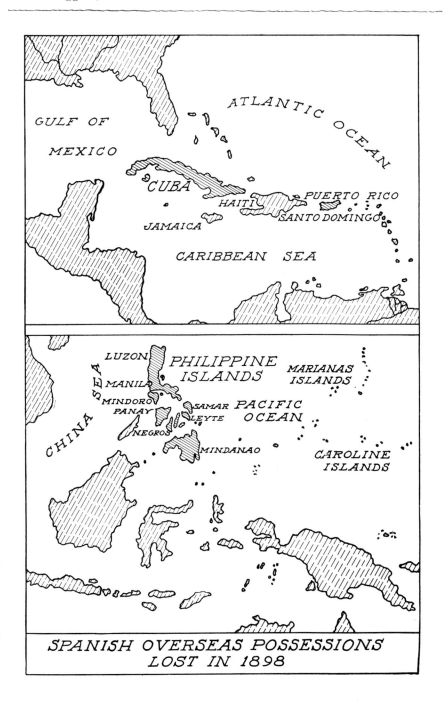

GULF OF MEXICO

ATLANTIC OCEAN

CUBA

HAITI

JAMAICA

PUERTO RICO

SANTO DOMINGO

CARIBBEAN SEA

LUZON

PHILIPPINE ISLANDS

CHINA SEA

MANILA

MINDORO

PANAY

NEGROS

SAMAR

LEYTE

MARIANAS ISLANDS

PACIFIC OCEAN

MINDANAO

CAROLINE ISLANDS

SPANISH OVERSEAS POSSESSIONS LOST IN 1898

though not in its entirety, by Cánovas and the Liberals. In 1900, by the Treaty of Paris of June 27, we obtained on the littoral of the Gulf of Guinea what was called the Muni territory (25,000 kilometers of the 200,000 that Spain claimed) which belonged to us by ancient rights in connection with the islands acquired in 1778 (Fernando Po, Annobón, and Corisco).

The Pessimism of 1898

The loss of the last American dominions caused a spiritual depression in Spain analogous to the lowered morale caused by the defeats of the seventeenth century, beginning with the battle of Rocroy. There was a period of general dejection; and at the same time there was a growing feeling against every enterprise of conquest or domination abroad. The Spanish people wished to withdraw into itself and to work out internal improvement and prosperity; and at the same time it felt lack of confidence in its own strength and circumstances. Joaquín Costa was also an illustrious representative of this doctrine. A new reason for anxiety contributed to prolongation of this prevailing state of mind; the question of Morocco.

The Moroccan Question

The possession, for centuries past, of cities and territories on the north coast of Morocco (Ceuta, Melilla, the Rock of Gomera, Alhucemas) and the strategic importance of that zone with relation to the closely neighboring maritime zone of Andalusia, were facts that forced Spain to give particular attention to the future prospects of this Moslem empire, which at the end of the nineteenth century was in complete decadence. Except for the episode of 1859 (the "war with Africa," as it is commonly called), an artificial and romantic stimulant of the sentiment that characterized some phases of the Peninsular Reconquest, the Spanish public had no appetite for Moroccan expansion, nor was it in the policy of Spanish Administrations during the nineteenth century. The loss of the Antilles and of the Philippine Islands narrowed still further the national interest in foreign enterprises. But the colonial policy of other European States, especially of France; the success of that country in establishing a predominant influence in the closing years of the century; the ever more obvious impossibility of effective duration of the Moroccan empire with its internal anarchy: all these things together forced Spain to lay aside indifference. A first French proposal (1902) to divide Morocco between France and Spain was rejected by the Spanish Government. But a secret treaty between France and England (1904) made us face the issue directly because of a clause to the effect that, taking into consideration Spanish interests resulting from geographical position and territorial possessions on the Mediterranean coasts, France obligated herself to come to an understanding with Spain.

There was undoubtedly the political possibility that Spain continue to refuse to share in the division and distribution of Morocco, a result which was implicit in the Anglo-French convention of 1904 and of others celebrated by France; and which reduced itself to assuring and guaranteeing the integrity and strategic value of ancient Spanish coastal possessions (Melilla, Ceuta, et cetera). The Spanish Government believed, nevertheless, that national interest and security demanded something more, and signed a treaty with France by which Spain accepted a zone in northern Morocco; that is, in the geographical continuity of Spanish coastal possessions toward the south and east.

A brusk intervention in Moroccan affairs by Emperor Wilhelm II of Germany (1905) made necessary the meeting of an international Conference, which was held at Algeciras in 1906 and resulted in an Act by which the signatory States confided to Spain and France the guardianship and policing of Morocco. Soon after, the insurrection of the native inhabitants began, in the Spanish zone and in the French. In the former, the uprising of 1909 on the outskirts of Melilla was especially serious and cost Spain much loss of life.

The downfall of the Ministry headed by Antonio Maura was an ultimate result of the Moroccan crisis. In July, 1909 Rif tribesmen attacked work-crews who were building a railroad to connect Melilla with mines in the hills which were held by Spanish concessionaires. The Minister of War proposed to reinforce the inadequate Spanish military strength in Morocco by calling up the reserves. The tragic recollection of other overseas expeditions was more than the public could bear. A general strike was proclaimed at Barcelona on July 26. Directed at first against conscription, it speedily became a revolutionary insurrection, which spread from the city over the Province. After three days of street-fighting, the uprising at Barcelona was suppressed on July 29, but martial law was declared throughout Spain and a two-months reign of terror ensued.

In the fortress of Montjuich at Barcelona not only insurrectionists but political prisoners (especially newspapermen) were incarcerated. The most sensational arrest was that of Francisco Ferrer, a theoretical anarchist whose anti-clerical educational work was widely known abroad, and who had founded many lay schools in Spain. Ferrer was arrested in August 1909, and tried by court-martial and shot in October. His execution had repercussions throughout Europe, and many Spanish embassies and legations were picketed in protest. In Spain it produced a ministerial crisis. The Cortes, opening that same month, heard Deputy Moret's furious attacks on Premier Maura and de la Cierva, Minister of the Interior, who were accused of having cravenly sacrificed Ferrer. On September 30 the Spanish forces in Morocco had suffered grave losses. The combination of circumstances was too much for Maura's Ministry. He resigned October 21, 1909 and the formation of a new Ministry under Moret was announced October 22.

Finally, a new treaty with France was arrived at in 1912, which ostensibly established the Spanish "zone of influence" in Morocco, bordering the French protectorate on the south, and comprising almost exactly the same territory as had been agreed upon in 1904. But the security of that zone and the development of the policy that the different Spanish Administrations considered advisable, initiated a fresh period of warfare against the native Moroccans, which was more or less continuous and grew increasingly violent and ever more burdensome to the Spanish people in general.

Spanish Literature in the Late Nineteenth Century

After the Romantic period, the Spanish theatre continued to present notable work by Adelardo López de Ayala, Manuel Tamayo, José Echagaray (who in 1904 received the Nobel Prize for Literature), José Feliú y Codina, and Benito Pérez Galdós; the first play by the latter, *Realidad* (1891), being followed by *La loca de la casa* (1892) and *La de San Quentín* (1893). It is due principally to these dramatists that our Spanish theatre at the end of the nineteenth century was one of the most inspired and inspiring in Europe. During the same period the Spanish novel added to its sixteenth and seventeenth century glory great works interpretative of modern manners and of Spanish history. Among these should be mentioned again Pérez Galdós' *Episodios Nacionales* and his companion series, *Novelas contemporáneas.* The regional novels, and those dealing with manners in general, or with special social and psychological problems, were also remarkable. Among the authors of such works were José María de Pereda, Pedro Antonio de Alarcón, Armando Palacio Valdés, Emilia Pardo Bazán, Juan Valera, Leopoldo Alas (whose pen-name was *Clarín*), Vicente Blasco Ibañez, and Gabriel Miró. Collectively, their work expresses the diverse new concepts of the novel which were vying for supremacy in end-of-the-century European literature. Lyric poetry, although on the whole in decadence, was producing nevertheless the lovely singing lyrics of Gustavo Adolfo Bécquer, the sonorous utterances of Gaspar Nuñez de Arce, the experimental harmonies of Salvador Rueda, the rural simplicities evoked by José María Gabriel y Galán, and memorable work also by Vicente Wenceslao Querol, Teodoro Llorente (who rendered exceptionally worthy service as translator of French, English, and German poets), Manuel del Palacio, Federico Balart, and Joaquín María Bartrina. At the same time there was a rebirth in Spain of non-Castilian literature—regional works written in Catalán, Valencian, Galician: languages that though they had not been cultivated for centuries, now shone forth anew, especially in poetry and the drama. The regional literary movement had begun in Catalonia in 1839, with publication in the Catalán language of an Ode to the Fatherland by Carlos Aribau, who later on (1846), in partnership with Manuel de Rivadeneyra, was to establish and edit the comprehensive and important series of works (not in Catalán, but only in Spanish) titled inclusively *Biblioteca de autores españoles desde la formación del lenguaje hasta nuestros días—* Library of Spanish Authors from the Formation of the Language to Our Own Time. In 1859 the *Jochs Florals,* or Floral Games, were revived at Barcelona. These are poetry competitions which contributed to cultivation of the regional language and which later were reestablished at Valencia also.

To that revival of the languages of Spain other than Castilian—the latter being what the rest of the world means when it says "Spanish"—belong, in Catalonia, the names of Mosén Jacinto Verdaguer, Angel Guimará, Juan Maragall, Iglesias, Costa Lloveras, Oller, Santiago Rusiñol, and others; in Galicia, of Rosalía de Castro, Eduardo Pondal, and many more; in Valencia, of Teodoro Llorente, Labaila, Baldoví, Escalante; and here too the list could be extended.

Among the excellent Spanish prose stylists of the period who deserve to be remembered are Alfredo Calderón, Mariano de Cavia, and Antonio Zozaya, who, while best known as journalists, were all three (particularly Calderón and Zozaya) endowed with a wide knowledge of both Law and Philosophy. We owe to Zozaya a *Biblioteca Filosófica,* or Philosophical Library, of Spanish and foreign philosophers (including the Greek and Roman). In another field, Spanish prose suffered a great loss in the premature death of Francisco Navarro Ledesma, who bequeathed us only his biography of Cervantes, *El ingenioso hidalgo Miguel Cervantes Saavedra,* and his edition of Angel Ganivet's *Epistolario.*

Currents in Scientific Knowledge

The restoration of scientific studies (philosophy, anthropology and allied branches, and the natural and physical sciences), undertaken energetically by the Ministries of Ferdinand VI and Charles III, but, as we have seen, paralyzed at the beginning of the nineteenth century, was the slowest in again getting under way. It may well be said that until the early years of the twentieth century the study of these subjects and the scientific production consequent thereupon remained decidedly in the minority as compared to other fields of research and experimentation, although within the scanted field there were scientists of great merit. Above the rest towered the work of the histologist, Santiago Ramón y Cajal, whose theory of nerve-cells was recognized in 1889 as one of the great histological discoveries, while his experimental methods were adopted everywhere. Since the number of Spaniards who devoted themselves to such scientific research was few, the contribution of Spain to experimental science in the nineteenth century has been slight in some fields and wholly lacking in others. However, in spite of this fact, there was in the earlier years of the century a very estimable group of naturalists, chemists, and physicians, many of whom continued their work into the subsequent period, where we shall take note of them.

Something of the sort was true of philosophy as well: a truly Spanish school of philosophy was not formed, in spite of the renascence of Catholic scholasticism through Jaime Balmes (1810-1847), and of the diversified influences of foreign thought, which made themselves felt very early—British (Scottish in particular) and German influences chiefly, both directly and through the medium of Belgian writers. The principle representative of the Scottish influence was the Catalán Llorens, and, as already mentioned, of the German, Julian Sanz del Río (1817-1869), Professor of Metaphysics at the University of Madrid, whose classroom was speedily thronged with liberal youth from among whom would emerge the leading figures of the Revolution of 1868. The influence of Sanz del Río, however, was not due to the widespread popularization of German ideologies, nor even of the specific ideology of Karl Frederick Krause whose disciple in some sort he was, but to the scientific discipline that he himself communicated to his pupils along with the desire for a free investigation of problems not of metaphysics only but of every branch of learning. The special field in which Kraustian doctrine produced its most important scientific results in Spain was Jurisprudence.

Professor Nicolás Salmerón (University professor and statesman), at first a metaphysician in the manner of Sanz del Río—building, therefore, on a Krausist basis—tended later, after returning from exile during the years immediately following the Bourbon restoration, to bring his ideology more into line with the thinking of Comte and other modern philosophers. Marcelino Menéndez y Pelayo did not cultivate pure metaphysics but engaged in various controversial discussions, especially with traditionalists of the type of Juan Donoso Cortés (Marquis of Valdegamas, politician, orator, and publicist), in Isabella II's reign, and later with Alejandro Pidal; but his principal contribution in this field of investigation was as historian of our classic philosophers, recording both their prescience respecting certain philosophic problems that some foreign metaphysicians later on were to study intensively and their indulgence throughout the course of our history in polemics, which were usually on religious questions (Menéndez y Pelayo's work, *Los heterodoxos españoles*, deals with these) and which in the nineteenth century were largely directed against the rationalist trend of the time.

The principal concrete development achieved in Spain by the Kraustian doctrine was, as I have said, in the juridical sciences, and was due chiefly to German and Belgian professors of Krause's school (Röder,

Ahrens, Tiberghien). The Spanish jurists who cultivated this field most successfully (Francisco Giner de los Ríos, Gumersindo de Azcárate, Joaquín Costa, Maranges, and some others) were not however mere imitators of these foreign savants, with whose ideas they not infrequently took issue. The Spanish intellectuals worked independently, outside the limitations of Krausist theory and with the dual consciousness of immediate and pressing Spanish problems and of a Spanish tradition that had not lost vitality.

Among those cited here, Francisco Giner de los Ríos had the greatest genius and the broadest vision. He was Professor of the Philosophy of Law at the University of Madrid throughout his teaching career and we shall have more to say of his constructive work as educator. Azcárate occupied the chair of General History of Ancient and Modern Juridical Institutions. In the field of both Penal and International Law at that time, Doña Concepción Arenal, whom we have already mentioned, was eminent. Here too Nicolás Salmerón, an excellent advocate, merits consideration as a stylist as well as for his forensic skill and professional integrity, qualities which were responsible, among others, for his being called upon to act as executor of Queen María Cristina's will notwithstanding his own Republican ideas. In this same general field, mention should be made of Manresa (commentator on the new Code), Reus, Cepeda, Pérez Pujol, Eduardo Soler, Montero Ríos (authority on canon law), Antonio Maura, Sánchez Román, Juan de la Cierva (brother of the inventor of the gyroscope), and Bergamín. In the field of Political Law, Santamaría and A. Posada distinguished themselves.

Among geologists and geographers who did valuable work in the second half of the nineteenth century were General Carlos Ibañez of the Engineers, renowned at home and abroad for his contributions to geodetics; Mallada, author of the geological map of Spain published in five volumes from 1895 to 1904; Macpherson, father of modern Spanish mineralogy and geology; Salvador Calderón; Botella; Gómez Arteche, who wrote among other things an historico-military geography of the Peninsula; and Rafael Torres Campo, geographer and historian.

The names of the anthropologists Oloriz, Salillas, Hoyos and Aranzadi deserve to be remembered. The list of notable historians is too long for inclusion here even if only as a roll call without notation, because Spaniards have always loved history's difficult discipline with its twofold aspect of art and of science. Among the most eminent prehistorians, besides Aranzadi, were Mélida, Cañal, Font y Sagué, Castilla López, and Father Marcelino de Santuola, discoverer in 1879 of the Caves of Altamira in northern Spain, where the famous Stone Age relics and Cromagnon drawings were found. The historiography of various other aspects of Spanish life was developed by such writers of the period as Lafuente, Fernández Guerra, Zangroniz, Botet y Sisó, Rodríguez de Berlanga, Saavedra, Amador de los Ríos, Cárdenas, Codera, Eguilaz, F. Fernández y González, Riaño, Ribera, Pons, Simonet, the archaeologist Velázquez, Insué, Llabrés, Catalina y García, López Ferreiro, Colmeiro, Pérez de Guzmán, Rodríguez Villa, Father Serrano, Muñoz, Father Fita, Sangrador, the Marquis de Cerralbo, Leguía, Gómez Moreno, Ramón Menéndez Pidal, Valmar, Milá y Fontanals (historian of medieval epic poetry), the two Bofarulls, Giménez Soler, Vicente de la Fuente, Dánvila, Balari, Carreras y Candi, Tomic, Coroleu, Pella y Fargas, Oliver, Sempere y Miguel, Puig y Cadafalch, Teixidor, Quadrado, C. Echegaray, Gorozabel, A. Paz, Barado, La Iglesia, Suárez Inclán, Villaurrutia, Father Antonio Astrain, Father Mir, Father Getino, Father Blanco García, Manuel B. Cossío, Pérez Pastor, Father Ricardo Cappa, Serrano Sanz, Reparaz, Rico Sinobas, Alzola, Gestoso, Maffey y Rúa Figueroa, Sentenach, Valencia de Don Juan y Osma. Francisco Rodríguez Marín was notable for his studies on Cervantes' novels and his magnificent annotated edition of *Don Quixote,* rich with commentary on sixteenth and seventeenth century personages and manners; and he edited also an extensive collection of Spanish proverbs. The Sevillan canon José María Sbarbi, philologist and member of the Spanish Academy, gathered and published a similar collection. Like Navarrete, Jiménez de la Espada was an eminent Americanist; perhaps the most profound and scientific worker in that field.

Fine Arts in the Nineteenth Century

In painting and sculpture, the example of Goya and of his pupil Vicente López (a good late eighteenth century portrait painter) did not produce immediate results since for a period of some years foreign influences were superimposed; French for the most part. But even within the sphere of these influences there were works of original merit by the painters Eduardo Rosales, José Mariano Fortuny, José de Madrazo and his son Federico, and Francisco Pradilla, who in 1878 won a first prize at the Paris Exposition. In the late nineteenth and early twentieth century, our Spanish painters, finding themselves, have created work that has won international recognition. Francisco Domingo, Rico, Joaquin Sorolla, Pinazo, Aureliano de Beruete, Regoyos, Casimiro Sainz, Antonio Muñoz Degrain, Urgell, Santiago Rusiñol (poet and dramatist in Catalán, as well as artist), Ramón Casas, Utrillo, Nonell, and some others were the initiators of this revival of art, which in our own time is exemplified by names known the world over.

With regard to sculpture the story is much the same. Among the most distinguished nineteenth century sculptors in Spain were first Jerónimo Suñol and José Bellver, and later on Inurria, Valera Coullant, Julio Antonio, and Llimona. The musicians of the period were even more widely famed: the modern Spanish school is one of the great contemporary schools of music by virtue of the work of such composers as Albéniz, Granados, Bretón, Pedrell, Chapí, Malats, Manuel de Falla, Usandizaga, Guridi, and others.

The Return to the Spiritual Tradition of Spain

Meanwhile a solution was being arrived at for the spiritual problem of Spain which, as we have said, was implanted in the middle years of the nineteenth century. Little by little tireless and devoted scholarship was bringing to light the great store of our Medieval and Renaissance Spanish culture, which won ever increasing appreciation in other countries—England, Germany—especially in the fields of art and literature; an appreciation first voiced by some eighteenth century critics. Romanticism, particularly in the theater, helped in establishment of cultural contacts, as we have seen.

Marcelino Menéndez y Pelayo and Joaquín Costa (and also Francisco Giner de los Ríos, not sufficiently remembered today), representatives of two viewpoints which were perhaps much less opposed to each other philosophically and politically than might appear at first glance (though their contemporaries would not have admitted as much) are beyond question the most characteristic figures—and characteristic precisely because of their respective differences, which, taken together, embrace the movement in its totality—in the great task of the revindication of Spain's ancient learning and of Spanish literature. In the terrain of fine arts a similar task had already been undertaken by

Madrid: Prado Museum

Goya: *Prince Don Carlos Maria Isidro* (later to be Pretender to the Throne of Spain). Sketch for a painting.

Piferrer, Quadrado, Madrazo, Riaño, Giner de los Ríos, Pedrell, and others; and in the realm of literature and history there were such contributions as the first planned and completed collections of the works of Spanish writers (Ochoa; Milá; what is known as the Rivadeneyra Collection) and of unpublished documents, as well as other valuable source material. Following the same trend, intensified research was carried out on the history of Spain and of Spanish America, in addition to the great literary and philosophic studies among which Menéndez y Pelayo's work outsoars the rest. Together with Laverde Ruíz and others, he not only brought to light a forgotten part of our classic production in the field of science along the same lines of revindication as were pursued by Balmes, but also adduced proofs of his firm conviction that—as indeed some few nineteenth century thinkers in other countries had been well aware—our great ancient writers could still contribute much of worth in shaping our modern culture. This same criterion was expressed and upheld at the turn of the century, in 1898, by the University of Oviedo.

In this connection the formation of the school of Spanish Arabists should be mentioned. It was initiated by Codera and continued by Ribera and Miguel Asín, and to it is due a reinterpretation of medieval history with respect to the different activities of Moslem factors on the Peninsula. As regards the history of Spanish Law, the research and publications of Professor Eduardo Hinojosa are invaluable.

Educational Progress

A combination of intensest national feeling with frankest acceptance of new ideas characterizing world culture from the late nineteenth century to the time of the present writing, made some of these men the real creators and proponents of the Spanish intellectual movement as it is today. Among this group, to which Joaquín Costa belonged, loomed Francisco Giner de los Ríos, philosopher, jurist, and teacher, and animating spirit of the *Institución Libre de Enseñanza* (Free Institution of Teaching) , the famous educational center created in 1876. He was remarkable for the complete moral and intellectual integrity of his work, especially in his defense of culture as the only real and enduring foundation for the progress of a nation as a whole. Without Giner de los Ríos and his pupils, and the *Institución Libre de Enseñanza* which developed and applied his research, there would be

Goya: *Don Leandro Fernández Moratín.*

no explanation for the appearance and success of some of the scientific and educational institutions which during the present century have mapped most effectively the country's intellectual and moral renascence. The present generation of Spanish intellectuals, who give meaning to its contemporary cultural life, was likewise formed amid the fervor of this group and especially under the personal influence of Giner de los Ríos.

However, it should be stated that the historical significance of the *Institución Libre de Enseñanza* in Spanish culture does not reside, as has been said and believed on occasion, in the existence and dissemination of a common and homogeneous doctrine more or less radical. The men of the *Institución Libre,* those who made up the founding group as well as their pupils and successors, maintained the independence of their respective thinking; and no set formula of social, philosophic, or political doctrine of any kind was ever drawn up nor imposed in that Institution, except pedagogical doctrine as such, since teaching was its one and only aim. That purpose, as well as the force and effectiveness that it manifested as it was extended, had a dual basis. First, the *Institución Libre* was an educational center which applied honestly, enthusiastically, and intensively to a picked and carefully graded student body the soundest teaching methods, without regard for formal examinations nor for the time that any given course might require. Second, *the Institución Libre* afforded an example (the only one extant at that time, it may be) of a corps of educators of the highest rank in the academic world, that of the university faculty, who did not consider it beneath their dignity to teach children in the primary grades. And within all this and over it was the unchallenged intellectual and moral authority of Francisco Giner de los Ríos, pilot of that spiritual adventure.

Unification of the Laws

The nineteenth century in Spain was marked also by a social achievement of far-reaching importance: the completion of the unification of the laws which had been begun by Philip V in relation to those regions that had special *Fueros.* Liberalism contributed in part to this unification, by proclaiming in an Article of the Constitution of 1812 that the Civil, Criminal, and Commercial Codes "were one and the same for all the Kingdom," and by making the administration of justice likewise uniform. These were ideas then dominant in Europe that had taken root in all countries. They responded to the belief that the same rational laws could and should be applied to all regions and all peoples. Such ideas were influenced also by the desire for *equality,* typical of the democratic liberalism propagated by the French Revolution. There was united to this in Spain, in the early years of the nineteenth century, the sentiment for political unity represented by the *Cortes* of Cádiz and the War of Spanish Independence, and inherited by Liberals and Moderates alike, with the public opinion of most of the nation upholding it as well.

In virtue of those ideas, common laws in almost every field were being published and applied throughout Spain; while some still-existing *fueros,* such as those of the Basque Provinces, were suppressed. The question of these *fueros* was posed in the Peace Treaty of Vergara with the Carlists in 1839, and was solved—by their abolition—by the Law of July 21, 1876, after the close of the civil war and at the height of the Bourbon Restoration.

Juridical unification, however, never reached the point among us in Spain that it attained in other European countries (France and Italy, for example). In civil matters—with respect, that is, to marriage, property, and other affairs of private right—there were, and are still, maintained and legally respected the special forms pertaining to Catalonia, Aragón, the Balearic Isles and the Basque Provinces. For the rest, common law was drawing all Spaniards closer together and has given juridical homogeneity to the nation as a whole. The Civil Code of 1888, which was the project of Prime Minister Alonso Martínez and which he succeeded in putting through, was the legal expression of this conciliatory formula. Catalonia, notwithstanding Philip V's great political reforms, preserved until well into the nineteenth century her penal legislation and court procedure, her own money, her own taxation, her exemption from military service, and the right to draw up contracts in the Catalán language and to employ Catalán as the language of instruction in the primary schools: all of which things Philip V's reforms had left strictly untouched in conformity with the advice of the Catalán Don Francisco Ametller. Later on, the current of unification was to wear down these special laws.

Aspirations toward Self-Government

But at the same time, and in reaction against the excessive centralization from which political life suffered, especially in its administrative aspects, the close of the nineteenth century saw the awakening of the aspiration for regional autonomy. At first limited to certain fields of public life, the demand later was for self-government complete; and it evinced itself in some of the regions that in the Middle Ages had constituted sovereign kingdoms, or entities within a kingdom (Castile, Aragón, Navarre) with—as we have seen—complete or partial maintenance of their own *fueros* and privileges. That general, theoretical aspiration, expressed by jurists from different regions, including Castile and Andalusia, was transformed into a question of practical politics in some parts of the country which possessed what may be called a strongly regional personality, and it gave birth to special political parties such as the Regionalist, later the *Catalanista* or National, Party in Catalonia, and the *Bizcaitarra* Party in the Basque Provinces, especially in Biscay.

It was in Catalonia that this autonomous nationalist movement was most solidly organized and most strongly supported by public opinion. The Catalán literary renascence, to which we have made previous reference, became staunchly patriotic after publication of Aribau's Ode—expressing what was called for many years the sentiment for *patria chica,* a "little motherland"—with a patriotism strengthening steadily until it became a nationalism assertive of Catalán population and culture as things apart, utterly distinct from the rest of Spain. As early as 1888 that affirmation found its expression and political instrument in the Message which the Regionalists presented to the Queen Regent and in which the autonomist plan for Catalonia was outlined. In 1892 the program was set forth in precise detail in the so-called Bases of Manresa, outcome of the deliberations of a Regionalist Assembly. In 1899 one of the leaders of the Autonomist Party, Dr. Robert, was appointed Mayor of Barcelona; and a Catalán jurist, Durán y Bas, became Minister of Grace and Justice in a Conservative Cabinet in which the Prime Minister inclined toward decentralization of government. Four months later, Durán y Bas resigned his portfolio because of his conviction that the decentralization glimpsed through Government eyes did not satisfy Regionalist aspirations. In 1901 the Regionalists were represented in the *Cortes* for the first time.

In succeeding years, the conflict was intensified, especially in Barcelona, between *Catalanistas* and non-*Catalanistas*. At a critical moment of the struggle, the officers of the Army corps garrisoned at Barcelona assaulted the editorial offices of two newspapers. This posed a very grave juridical problem, settled early in 1906 when the *Cortes* passed and promulgated the measure commonly called "the Law of Jurisdictions," which handed over to the military courts trial and punishment of offenses against the fatherland and the Army. But that was not the last of the Catalán question. Its representation in the *Cortes* during the reign of Alfonso XIII was a highly important factor and unquestionably had weight in political events that we shall consider later on. The man who did most to shape the *Catalanista* program was Prat de la Riba. Within Catalanism, as within all contemporary Spanish political movements, two divergent groups were formed, both as regards the maximum limit of the common autonomist aspiration and as regards the criteria brought to bear on political problems in general. Of those two groups, the one that had the representation in the *Cortes* was the more conservative and also the more moderate in its demands for juridical expression of the Catalán national personality. This was the Regionalist League, or *Lliga Regionalista,* which consistently won the regional elections until 1923.

In the course of time the problem of juridical diversity and autonomy came to be viewed not as a question special to certain regions but as a national problem of autonomies that aspired to transform the ancient centralism of government into a State: a State which some wanted to be semi-federal and which others would have completely federal, the only internal differences being those of administration merely, with some advocacy of political differentiation as well. Thus was implanted once again the problem of federalism, which had caused such deep division among the Republicans of 1873 and which, years after the disappearance of the First Republic, was defined and explained by Pí y Margall in his book *Las Nacionalidades* (The Nationalities; 1877). The title was possibly more exact than the author himself realized, since in reality regionalisms are a phenomenon of the European nationalist movement, the origins of which we have already indicated.

Labor Legislation

Another important trend in the nineteenth century was toward protective legislation for the manual laborer—labor legislation.

As the use of machinery spread, and great manufacturing and mining industries expanded, the precarious and unjust living conditions of the workers became more apparent. They themselves saw their own situation clearly and began demanding that it be improved. In 1844 Karl Marx commenced his preachments against capitalism and in favor of the union of all the workers of the world; and not long afterwards (in 1866) the First International, or International Association of Workers, was formed. In Spain, the measures in favor of the laborers were initiated during the Republic of 1873, as we have seen. In 1879 the first Spanish labor party was organized: it was called the Socialist Party, and thirty-one years later, in 1910, succeeded in electing Deputies to the *Cortes*. In 1888 the *Unión General de Trabajadores,* or General Labor Union (the U. G. T.) , was born; while the non-labor parties, the Conservative and the Liberal, of the Restoration and the Regency passed increasingly ample and progressive laws respecting the daily wage, the hours and conditions of work, and similar problems. The creation in 1903, through Canalejas' initiative, of the *Instituto de Reformas Sociales,* or Institute of Social Reform, marks an important advance in formation and development of that social legislation of which Spain had until 1939 one of the most complete and progressive codes in the world.

The Problem of the Land

The Revolution in its brief trajectory (1868-1873) could not detain its course to consider the great problem of the land, which, viewed from one angle, was dependent on juridical concepts; and from another, on the general policy of modifying the geographical environment to bring about better living conditions; a policy that had been resumed only in some aspects, and even so in scant measure, between 1833 and 1868. The Restoration gave no thought at all to the land problem. An administration by and for the wealthy and conservative classes, it was incapable of interesting itself in anything that did not fit into the pattern of its own needs. The rural middle class and the proletariat of the countryside, while well aware of their own ills, lacked education in the ways and means of remedying them, and kept drudging away with the age-old methods of cultivating the soil or wearing out strength in the heroic and bitter effort to grow crops without water. Joaquín Costa, whom we have had occasion to mention in several different connections, lifted his voice amid that silence to advocate an agrarian policy and in particular what he termed a *hydraulic policy,* which, in view of the climatic conditions of our Peninsula, is a matter of urgent necessity. His famous slogan, *Despensa y Escuela*—Provisions and Schools (or, literally, Larder and School), which meant improvement in the standards of living and of education in Spain, roused great enthusiasm among all forward-looking citizens as well as among the needy who would be the ones immediately benefited; but Costa received slight Government support. The little that was done after 1902 (or, more accurately, the little that was attempted) in the agrarian line, originated with Costa, as did also the programs for sharing the land, for adoption of property laws in line with Spanish realities, and for a colonial policy of peace and education, already noted.

III. FROM 1902 TO 1923

The First Twelve Years of the Reign of Alfonso XIII

Alfonso XIII's accession to the throne when he reached his majority in 1902 at the age of sixteen, did not change outwardly the political and social problems posed during the Regency. Such problems were numerous, and very serious. In the political sphere alone, it is sufficient to mention those arising from the Law of Jurisdictions; from the so-called Military *Juntas,* regarding which we shall have more to say; from the regulation of religious congregations; from Catalonia and its regional autonomy; and from Morocco, the principal steps in relation to which we have already outlined. About 1920 there was added to these the problem of the *latifundios,* or absentee landowners; a problem stated first by a Liberal political leader and bound up in Costa's program; and the problem of the internal dissension in the political parties, which we shall discuss in detail later on.

At the beginning of the new reign, the two oldtime parties, Conservative and Liberal, which almost from the commencement of the Restoration had been alternating in power, followed the same pattern for some years longer, though under new leadership in consequence of the deaths of Cánovas and Sagasta. The former, after ephemeral party presidencies, was succeeded by Antonio Maura (who had already headed the Government during the Regency), Eduardo Dato, and Sánchez Guerra. The most eminent of Sagasta's successors after 1909 were first Canalejas and later the Count of Romanones. But with the progress of the years the political phenomenon was produced—not only in Spain, of course—of the breaking up of the great parties and, to a lesser degree, of the other parties as well, those too small ever to be in control of government and so perpetually in the Opposition. One of the reasons for this splitting of traditional groups in Spain was the emergence and the increasing political activity of the regionalist parties and of the labor party, the former of which acted deliberately and persistently to that end. But there were other, deeper causes that had a profound influence; causes linked with exhaustion of the ancient ideals and failure to replace them by any program capable of capturing the popular imagination.

The most prominent effect of that phenomenon consisted in making the constitution of more or less heterogeneous parliamentary majorities very difficult and the stabilization of Government, the carrying out of definite programs, and even the solution of serious social conflicts and public disturbances, almost impossible. Then the crisis began to shape; not merely the crisis of political parties and of the parliamentary system, but of the whole liberal and constitutional regime; a crisis that was to reach such an unexpected climax in 1923, and that was already extremely acute in 1917, considering its close connection with the weakening of the principle of authority, then already incapable of dominating the lawlessness of those governed, and the appearance on the political scene of a military element that no one dared eliminate or control.

In the election of 1901, as we have noted, the Catalán Regionalist Party had obtained a minority representation in both Houses, and from the first it presented in both the program of autonomy as a primary and urgent necessity. "There can be no political peace in Spain," declared the Catalán Deputies and Senators, "until our problem is settled; which is to say, until Catalonia's claim to self-government is satisfied." The immense majority of non-Catalán politicians (and of some Catalans as well) were willing to grant at most only a degree of decentralization of government, suspecting separatism in the guise of autonomy. By way of compromise, the Conservative Party led by Don Antonio Maura offered ample concessions. At the end of 1913, Catalanism obtained one of these concessions, in the authorization (not by law but by Royal Decree) for the Provincial Deputations to federate themselves into *Mancomunidades,* or Commonwealths, of several Provinces, to which were transferred certain services and functions pertaining to them and until then attributed in principle to the country's central Government. In virtue of that authorization, the four Catalán Provinces constituted a Commonwealth (April, 1914) endowed with sufficient authority, which soon developed in the region a vast administrative program that reached into most areas of public life. But this compromise did not stop Autonomist activities; and the struggle between *Catalanistas* and non-*Catalanistas* followed, impassioned and sometimes violent, notwithstanding the fact that the Regionalist Party had Ministers in several national Administrations, which succeeded one another in power with extraordinary rapidity.

Finally, the Spanish people in general grew wearied of contemplating the uselessness of Administrations that with their frequent changes and heterogeneous composition could not develop substantial programs of policy and government; and felt sceptical or apathetic about the life of the State. The definite improvements that were achieved or initiated in some branches of public life were not enough to overcome these mental attitudes. Some of the improvements were insufficient to meet the country's real needs, because the passive resistance of the majority of the politicians paralyzed them or whittled them down; while others withered in the bud. However, real benefits were obtained, for instance, in fields such as public education, public works, hydraulic policy, rural land ownership. Taking public education as a typical case, because of its profound influence on a people's life, we may mention the following reforms and experiments which reached full development: the establishment of the Chair of Education at the University of Madrid (1904); of the *Junta para ampliación de estudios,* or Commission for Extension of Studies (1907); of the *Escuela Superior del Magisterio* (Normal High School) and the scholarships for students and teachers (1908) ; of the *Residencia de Estudiantes,* or Students Residence, at the University of Madrid (1910) ; of the *Instituto Escuela* or School Institute (1918) ; of the *Inspección escolar femenina* or Girls School Inspection (1913) ; of the first circulating libraries for teachers and students (1912) ; of the salary increase and advancement in grade of many teachers (1907 and 1911) ; of the systematic progression by classes in primary schools (1911 and later) ; the transfer to the State of responsibility for public school teachers in the Basque Provinces, which were the last to fall in line in this respect, since all other Provinces had taken the same step in 1901; the creation in the Graduate School of Law of the University of Madrid of a chair of *Political and Civil Institutions of the Americas,* the first such course to be established; the project for the University City at Madrid, which began to achieve realization soon after 1923; and so on. As indicative of progress made in the university sphere in particular, mention should be made of the creation at the University of Oviedo in 1898 of extension work similar to that of Toynbee Hall at Oxford but much ampler in scope, and much more effective among the working classes, than its English prototype

In the strictly political field, the question of the religious Congregations and of Catalanism had been the chief agencies in dividing Spanish public opinion and had stirred up deep rancor on both sides. The war in Morocco, marked by such dire disasters as that of Anual in 1921, intensified scepticism and unrest.

From the Beginning of the First World War to 1923

In 1914 an event of universal importance, the World War between the Central Powers of Europe and the Allies (France, England, Belgium, in the beginning; with later, Italy and the United States) , seemed likely to produce a hiatus in our internal life in Spain, but in fact, complicated the pending conflicts within our borders both politically and socially. Spanish public opinion in the overwhelming majority, seconding the criterion of the Conservative Party then in power, expressed itself in favor of neutrality. This decision, however, as well as the interpretation and practice of that neutrality, divided national political forces even more than formerly, and produced great unrest throughout the country. Nevertheless, neutrality was declared officially. By reason of this, Spain was not involved in the catastrophes of the War, which swept into its vortex almost the whole of Europe and a considerable part of Asia, Africa, and the Americas. Besides permitting Spain to be of use to friendly countries, this neutrality was the cause of a noteworthy increase in national wealth and in national production.

What remained without remedy was the increasing rottenness and consequent impotence of political forces, with 1917 as the year of crisis. The State was being deprived of the efficient elements necessary for governing the country and subduing the lawlessness that had been gaining ascendancy in some localities and in some public agencies. A leader of the one-time large Monarchist Party declared about this time that a period had come to an end, and with it the function of the great political groups creating strong, homogeneous parliamentary majorities, and that even the empery and necessity of general programs of administration was over; and that these should be replaced by occasional pronouncements on urgent problems as they presented themselves, with the solutions therefor variable in substance and method according to circumstance.

Moreover there was a change of attitude on the part of King Alfonso XIII. At one time (1910) he had shown an inclination toward the frankly liberal and even democratic party programs. There were then high hopes that the throne might come into closer relationship with those forces of republican coloration or tradition which were much more deeply concerned with solving the nation's political problems than with the form of government; that is, with whether Spain became a republic or continued as a monarchy. But with Alfonso's change of heart, he showed a decided preference for the conservative parties and depended on the strength of the Army to maintain him in power, deeming that it would and could support him. The result was a revival of the anti-monarchical feeling which had for the most part been dying out (great militant parties were no longer being formed); and which, in so far as it still existed, had of late years been mostly sporadic and unorganized.

Chapter XIV

The Dictatorship and the Second Republic

The 1923 Coup d'État and the Dictatorial Government

A MILITARY uprising brought this state of things to an unexpected conclusion. It was set off at Barcelona on September 13, 1923 by the Captain-General of that region, Miguel Primo de Rivera. The swift triumphant onsweep of the insurrection, without the firing of a shot, and King Alfonso's acceptance of the *fait accompli* (of which it seems certain that he had prior knowledge) resulted in establishment of a dictatorial regime with suspension of the Constitution of 1876 and of civil rights. During the seven years of the Dictatorship, therefore, the Spanish State found itself in what was, properly speaking, a formative condition; that is to say, there had been cancelled overnight all the results of the effort of one hundred years to achieve political stability on a firm foundation of constitutional law, which is the basic guarantee of individual rights and governmental procedure. The Dictatorship held that this suspension of Spanish constitutional life was a necessary remedial measure for the country's grave political ills during years past; but itself contradicted that theory by preparing a new Constitution through a group called the "National Assembly," all of whose members were Governmental appointees.

The first Government under the Dictatorship consisted of a military Directorate; it was succeeded by a so-called Civil Government, the reason for this designation being that some of its members did not belong to the Army. In both regimes, as a matter of fact, there was only one Minister, the Premier Primo de Rivera, whose relation to and dependence upon the King as Chief of State was never clearly defined. Although the Dictatorship declared repeatedly that one of its principal objects was to bring about the disintegration of the old political parties, annulling their power so that the future constitutional reestablishment could function efficiently, its only achievement in this connection was to render the parties impotent for seven years by suspension of the political rights that enabled them to take action and by rigid censorship of the press. The fact is that the problems implanted in the years preceding the Dictatorship were still unsolved: the old-time political organizations neither disappeared (even though they were mute and inactive) nor were replaced—as a foundation for future majorities capable of governing efficiently—by any new group with a strong organization and a sizable membership.

Growing civil discontent with the dictatorial regime, together with sporadic but recurrent military outbreaks, rendered Primo de Rivera's position increasingly insecure toward the end of 1928. There was continuous dissension between the Minister and Alfonso XIII; student riots in the universities and protests from Spanish intellectuals because of abuses of civil rights became a commonplace; and the fall of the peseta was a painful economic reality which brought about the resignation of Calvo Sotelo, Minister of Finance. When in January 1930 the Dictatorship came to an end as sudden as its emergence had been, the situation of Spain with respect to the pressing political problems proved to be just what it had been from 1917 to 1923, with the general situation unchanged.

The Dictatorship settled two problems only: Morocco and public order. Concretely, the Moroccan solution consisted in terminating simultaneously the tragic, daily waste of lives and money which was an overwhelming, ever-present anguish for the nation and an exhausting drain on the Treasury. The Dictator's personal action brought solution here where it had seemed none could be found. Primo de Rivera arranged with the French Government for a combined offensive against the common enemy, the Moroccan leader Abd-el-Krim. The Spanish attack was carried out in the Rif and followed up by a bold and successful operation at Alhucemas (September, 1926) which led soon to pacification. As a result, the greatest part of the Army was brought home and tax-payers were relieved of the enormous war budget which the Public Treasury had been supporting up to that time. There was nation-wide rejoicing that the long nightmare had come to an end.

As for problems of public order, these were solved automatically by suspension of constitutional guarantees, press censorship, and the untrammeled strong-arm action which is inherent politically in any dictatorial regime. This was, for the seven years of Primo de Rivera's dictatorship, practically equivalent to inflexible and unlimited imposition of Governmental compulsions that made impossible the expression by word or act of any manifestation whatsoever which the Government deemed to be disturbing to the public peace; though that did not mean that the underlying, and perhaps not always anti-juridical, reasons for such manifestations had necessarily disappeared.

But the Dictatorship could not prevent the resurgence of republican ideas. The advocates of a Republic included a large part of what was called "neutral mass opinion"; also the Socialists, who finally decided to cooperate against the anti-constitutional regime; and likewise some political leaders proceeding from the Liberal and Conservative Parties of the Monarchy, who detested the dictatorial Government and had come to the conclusion that a Republic was the only way out of the political maze implanted in 1923. From these differing elements, and from the Catalán separatists, emanated several revolutionary attempts. The most notable was the abortive uprising of Army officers and civilians led by the one-time chief of the monarchical Conservatives, Don José Sánchez Guerra, in January 1929. Nor could the Dictatorship keep the Army from taking sides, with one sector of its officers in favor of a change.

The Dictatorship's principal accomplishments in the way of administrative improvements were in the field of communications, by building roads, and some other public works, such as drainage systems; beginning construction of the physical plant of the University City at Madrid; encouraging tourism and erecting inns and lodging-houses; restoring in part the ancient University of Alcalá; and sending a scientific expedition to Morocco to make a study of the flora and the fauna (1929). On the debit side, the Dictatorship wrecked the Treasury.

The Final Monarchical Ministries

The Dictatorship was followed by a Government with General Damaso Berenguer as Prime Minister which was made up of representatives of the conservative parties. Although its announced purpose was to reestablish "constitutional normality," months went by with

José María Esquivel: *A Reading by Zorrilla.* A gathering, in the artist's studio, of the most eminent poets of the time.

*Madrid: **Prado Museum***

nothing done in the way of restoring political guarantees. The press continued to be subjected to Governmental censorship for about a year.

Unexpectedly, in mid-December 1929 (from December 12 to 15) a republican revolutionary movement burst out. Its two centers were the town of Jaca in Aragón and the Cuatro Vientos Airfield near Madrid. At Jaca the movement was mixed, military and civilian; at Cuatro Vientos it was largely directed by officers of the air corps. They are said to have counted on the cooperation of other military forces and of the working class. But with the exception of small sporadic outbreaks occurring simultaneously in some localities, the rebels at Jaca and Cuatro Vientos were not seconded in their attempt. The Government speedily took command of the situation, and two officers of the Jaca garrison were shot. Copies of a revolutionary proclamation that had been launched by a certain Republican Committee led by Niceto Alcalá-Zamora, one-time Monarchical Prime Minister, were discovered by the police. Those of the signers who did not make good their escape were imprisoned, as were other Republicans and Socialists and many students. The censorship of the press, which had been abolished a few days previous, again went into effect.

As counterpart to the preceding events, the Government issued a call for an election to constitute the *Cortes;* but not one for a constituent convention of the *Cortes* itself, such as was demanded by Republicans and Socialists and also by several Liberal and Conservative monarchical leaders, including Sánchez Guerra, Villanueva, Bergamín, Burgos, and the leader of the old "Reformist" Republicans, Don Melquiades Alvarez. This lack of accord with the Government, further complicated by the fact that the parties of the Left had no confidence whatever in the Cabinet's sincerity in this matter of the elections, produced a very tense situation. Indeed, the leftists, as well as the "Constitutionalists" led by Sánchez Guerra and Alvarez, announced that they would stay away from the polls. The Count of Romanones and the Marquis of Alhucemas, Liberal leaders both, then declared that they would participate only conditionally in the elections and the resultant *Cortes.* The Berenguer Government had failed. It resigned February 14, 1931 and the convocation for the election was cancelled.

Obviously the governmental crisis was a hard nut to crack. One attempt at a "Constitutionalist" and another at a "Reformist" Cabinet fell through in quick succession on February 16 and February 17.

Then, to the great surprise of the public in general, on February 18 a Government of concentrated monarchical tendency was formed, with inclusion of both Conservatives and Liberals, among the latter the Count of Romanones and the Marquis of Alhucemas. Cambó, head of the Catalán Regionalist Party, also lent his support.

The program of this Government set the municipal elections for April 12 (1931). These were to be followed by the election of Provincial Deputies, and later by elections to constitute the *Cortes*. That *Cortes* was to have limited powers for undertaking the reform of certain articles in the Constitution of 1876, which had been suspended and violated by the Dictatorship. Constitutional guarantees remained largely in abeyance until close on the time for the municipal elections (Decree of February 19, promulgated February 22, 1931). But the Republicans, the Socialists, and the so-called "Constitutionalists" continued to demand a real constituent *Cortes*. At the same time, a considerable part of the public, aroused by the executions at Jaca and by the jailings in December 1930, protested against these events and demanded a general amnesty. Feeling ran high because of the trial of the outlawed Jaca survivors and of Señor Alcalá-Zamora and his friends. Many students who had already organized several protests against the Dictatorship and the Governments that had succeeded it, and who had had frequent fierce clashes with the police, joined the demand for amnesty; and there were outbreaks of violence at the University of Madrid between student groups of opposite political camps and between students and police henchmen.

The trial at Jaca began on March 13 and the other trial—Alcalá Zamora's—followed soon. On March 23 it was learned that the Supreme Council of the Army and the Navy, before which Señor Alcalá-Zamora and his associates had been haled, had condemned them to six months imprisonment with sentence suspended. At the same time the extremely severe sentences passed by the Council at Jaca were lightened considerably. But this was not enough to satisfy the public, who persisted in demanding an amnesty.

The Elections of April 12, 1931 and Their Political Consequences

As the April 12 elections drew near, all parties made ready for the contest. All over Spain the Socialists and the Republicans had joined their voting strength. It was thought that the coming elections would

Leonardo Alenza: *Satire on Romanticism.*

show beyond a doubt whether Spaniards in the majority were for or against a monarchy. Most of the Monarchists felt a blind confidence that victory would be theirs. But the voting on April 12 surprised not only the Monarchists but many Republicans as well. Except for four or five of the smaller Provincial capitals, the voters (beginning with those of Madrid, Barcelona, Valencia, Seville and San Sebastian) gave the majority of the ballots cast to the Republican and Socialist alliance. In spite of the fact that in totalling country-wide results from all the municipalities of Spain, the Monarchical Councilmen elected exceeded the Republican in number, the moral effect of the Republican victory in the great population centers was so enormous that the Monarchists, demoralized by its unexpectedness, were too hesitant or too apprehensive to react immediately and energetically. This demoralization was due to the generally recognized fact that, because of the bad electoral policy which had been followed by Monarchical administrations, public opinion for the whole country was shaped in the large cities. The rural populations consequently did not figure greatly in forming political decisions, since as a rule they had neither the civic consciousness nor the independent spirit of the city-dwellers.

Events followed rapidly one upon another. The Republicans interpreted their electoral triumph as a sufficient reason for seizing power. Basing their action on this supposition, they did not even wait for the final scrutiny of the ballots (which in accordance with the law would take place on April 16), but took possession of the *Ayuntamientos* in many towns, proclaimed the Republic on April 14, and requested the King to leave the country. Some eminent Monarchists were at one with the Republicans in deeming it impossible to deny the national will as expressed in the election.

The Ministers of the King's Government conferred with Señor Alcalá-Zamora, who demanded unequivocally King Alfonso's abdication and the immediate transference of power to the Revolutionary Committee. The Count of Romanones made several different proposals to the Republican leader, one of them being to await the elections for the *Cortes*. The Republicans, sure at that moment of their strength, refused to entertain any compromise. King Alfonso XIII thereupon decided to depart from Spain, but without formal abdication. He left Madrid on the afternoon of April 14, 1931; and stated, in a Manifesto written that same day and made public on April 15 by

Admiral Aznar, head of the last Monarchical Ministry, that he was leaving in order to prevent bloodshed. This was the same argument that the Republicans themselves used to show that Don Alfonso's departure was an urgent, immediate necessity. With the situation respecting the Republicans thus regularized, the administrative authority was transmitted to them in a wholly peaceful manner. The great mass of the people remained serene and orderly, without indulging in any of the tumultuous outbursts usual in such circumstances. The Government that took over the direction of public affairs was, with slight differences, the same which the revolutionists of December 1930 had planned to put in power. It was made up of representatives of the different republican Parties, of both the Right and the Left, and of the Socialists.

At the same time, the Catalán extremists, led by Colonel Maciá, proclaimed at Barcelona the regional Republic of Catalonia. This action was said to be the result of a prior pact by which republicans from other regions of Spain had accepted the federal regime—a system of federated States—as the most fitting for the newborn Spanish Republic, with a certain amount of autonomy for Catalonia within that regime.

The Provisional Government

The Spanish people were full of enthusiasm and confidence in the days immediately following the April 12 election, and that was the prevailing state of mind for some weeks. It resulted from a sense of satisfaction because the political problem that had afflicted so many Spaniards was now solved, and because the country had emerged from the uneasy interlude of Dictatorship without bloodshed, and by a single act of citizenship in which not only Republicans had taken part but also, and especially in the large cities, that important group of borderline public opinion called the "neutral mass." The fact is that this was all a natural consequence of the healthy reaction of the Spanish spirit against the pessimism of 1898 and subsequent years; a reaction that materialized in the early part of the nineteenth century, waveringly at first but ever more strongly, into a nation-wide confidence in Spain's future and respect for Spain's past, and into an intense desire to revive the glorious period of Spanish creative genius so that our country might march abreast of the most progressive nations in the modern world.

There had been for a long time a gulf between the State and the people in Spain. Inefficiency in government was largely due to the fact that public opinion expected inefficiency in government. An almost instinctive popular tendency had developed to operate independent of official action, looking to private agencies as the surest means of developing national strength and of improving those conditions both material and spiritual to which the State paid little attention or which it considered beneath its notice. At the commencement of Alfonso XIII's reign, and, of course, much before 1923, the fruits of such efforts carried out by private initiative were already visible, and they included some institutions more or less dependent upon State support which had resolved to help themselves by their own resourcefulness. That hope and that determination were stimulated by the progress made in the economic field. In 1870 Spanish exports had brought 312,500,000 *pesetas*. In 1880 the total rose to more than 507,000,000 and in 1913 to more than 1,000,000,000 *pesetas*. The population of Spain increased from 15,500,000 inhabitants in 1860 to around 20,000,000 in 1910; with the proportional increase continuing to the present time. With the advent of the Republic, many Spaniards felt that they could count thenceforward on the cooperation of the State in bringing about renascence of the national vitality, with all the requisite breadth of vision regarding the problems that previous regimes had passed over in neglect or had considered only intermittently, as well as with respect to the other, newer problems awaiting consideration.

That was the favorable atmosphere in which the Provisional Government of the Second Republic began to organize the new State. In a statement signed by all the Cabinet, and made public on April 15, 1931, the Government laid down the rules that would control it until the *Cortes* should be constituted; rules that would form what was called the "Provisional Statute of the Republic." Immediately thereafter, through a series of Decrees and Decree-Laws it made provision for the most urgent questions: among them, the electoral method by which the future parliament would be chosen. It likewise set about clarifying and settling the situation of Catalonia in relation to the rest of Spain, which had been very clouded since the proclamation of the "Catalán Republic" made by Maciá on April 14 and the qualification of "Catalán State" given that Republic by its President. A discreet and friendly personal approach to Maciá a few days later resulted in agreement by the Cataláns to renounce both terms—"Catalán Republic" and "Catalán State"—which in themselves prejudged the question, and in a pledge by the Provisional Government to prepare a Statute for Catalonia which, after it should have been approved by the four Basque Provinces and put to the further test of a popular referendum, would be presented to the Spanish *Cortes*. Accordingly, the final provisions of the Statute, as to the desirable general content, on which Republican opinion was very divided, remained dependent on the sovereignty of the *Cortes*.

Enumeration of the measures taken by the Provisional Government would be too long for the present volume. Moreover, these things are too close to us in time not to be familiar in general outline to all readers of these pages. We note only that some laws of the monarchical regime were abolished radically, including the Law of Jurisdictions, the scope of which we have indicated already, and more especially the laws established by the Dictatorship, including the Penal Code of 1928. The organization of the Army was reformed substantially and its size decreased, both the officers corps and the ranks; by which measures it was believed that the question of the military *Juntas* was solved implicitly. The appropriation for the Army was much reduced.

The Constituent Cortes

Elections for the constituent *Cortes* of a single House were convoked for June 28 by a Decree of June 3, 1931. These elections when held not only ratified but very markedly extended the April 12 results by giving a resounding victory to the Republican-Socialist alliance and, within that coalition, to the leftist parties integrating it. The largest of the several minorities taking part in these elections was the Socialist; so that when their votes were joined to those of the other allied minority groups (Radical Socialists, Republican Action, et cetera), all together totalled a majority vote more than sufficient to control the pending action on a new Constitution. Nevertheless, the *Cortes* thus elected ratified the powers of the existing Provisional Government, in which figured Rightist-Republicans, beginning with its President, Alcalá-Zamora.

The Constitution voted into being by that *Cortes,* and promulgated December 9, 1931, was notwithstanding a leftist Constitution marked by liberal, democratic, autonomous, and laical conviction and by a broad social and pacifist program. It was the first Constitution in the world's history to renounce war as an instrument of national policy. The debate over Article 26, which established the separation of Church and State and guaranteed complete religious freedom, made all religious creeds (this was the problem of the Law of Congregations which had been so disturbing during the Restoration) subject to a special law; and decreed further the dissolution and nationalization of the property of religious Orders whose rules included other than the three canonical vows (the latter provision was aimed directly at the Society of Jesus). This Article 26 occasioned the first governmental crisis of the new regime, which consisted of the resignation of Alcalá-Zamora, head of the Provisional Government, and of the Premier, Antonio Maura. The Government was reorganized under the premiership of the leader of the Republican Action Party (*Acción Republicana*), Manuel Azaña. Some months later the Constitution was voted into effect, and on December 10, 1931 the former President of the Provisional Government, Niceto Alcalá-Zamora, was elected President of the Republic, notwithstanding his opposition to Article 26 and his recent resignation in protest. The reason for this action, which surprised a large part of the public, was not convincing to many Spaniards since the motive then adduced by the politicians seemed to lack solid foundation. The Azaña Cabinet resigned their portfolios and formed anew under the same Premiership, but this time without the collaboration of Señor Lerroux' Radical Party and of the so-called "Progressives"—"*Progresistas*"—who recognized Señor Alcalá-Zamora as their leader. Automatically, therefore, the Government found itself inclined further toward the left than toward the right.

Thenceforward political life in the parliamentary sphere was divided between debate over the laws complementing the Constitution and others materially important in construction of the Republican State, and the persistent efforts of the "Radicals" and several rightist groups (more or less republican) to provoke a crisis that would throw the Socialists out of Government posts and would open the way to revising certain laws, including some Articles of the Constitution.

Added to these attempts was one later on to dissolve the constituent *Cortes* and hold new elections.

Supported by the parliamentary majority, which was integrated by union of the minorities of the leftist coalition, the Government maintained itself in power, in spite of the opposition noted, throughout 1932 and for nine months of 1933. During that considerable period, in which the *Cortes* met continuously with only the briefest occasional recesses, many important laws on the program of the left and in fulfilment of the Constitution were enacted. Chief among them were the laws on divorce, civil marriage, forced labor on the land, collective rentals, revision of rural rental contracts, mixed arbitration boards of employers and workers, minimum wage, labor contracts, agrarian reform, religious congregations, new Penal Code, recruiting and promoting of army officers, income tax, defense of the Republic; and other additional laws dealing with labor and social welfare. As steps toward equal rights, before the law, women were granted more extended legal powers with relation to the family than they had possessed before, and they were given the vote. In international affairs, the Constitution adopted as a norm of conduct the pacifist principles enunciated by the League of Nations and pacts of like orientation which complemented them. Also, there were resumed, through important public works completed and projected, the policy of communications, the hydraulic policy, and, in general, the policy of modifying the physical environment in such way as to improve the national economy. Public education was made wholly laical; and numerous new schools were built (primary, secondary, and research centers) , in accordance with the traditional practice of every period of liberal government in Spain, beginning with 1810. In 1931 the principal educational problems confronting Spain, which were the high degree of illiteracy and the necessity of making secondary instruction available to all the people— questions of obvious and unchallenged importance for this as for every other country—were almost entirely problems of pitch and of rhythm; that is to say, of augmenting considerably the number of teaching centers, giving them a sufficient appropriation, and doing these things as soon as possible. The constituent *Cortes*, with regard to the portion of this task which devolved upon it, and the Ministry of Public Instruction for its part, tried to carry out the program in full by creating some thousands of schools, increasing the number of existent graduate institutions, establishing a country-wide extension service (the Pedagogical Missions, or *Misiones Pedagógicas*), and taking other similar measures with respect to higher education and to scientific research. Without entering upon details of the reforms, we may say that, by and large, the *Cortes* and the Republican Government remade, with their complementary measures, the legislation in every juridical aspect of Spanish life, the preponderant tendency of these new laws being leftist.

The constituent *Cortes* was dissolved, for the second time, at the beginning of October, 1933, and a coalition Ministry was formed (including representatives of all the Republican parties but not of the Socialist) for the purpose of convoking and holding a new election of Deputies. The election was set for November 19. The Socialists and the Leftist Republicans (the latter very much divided among themselves) went to the polls independently, on separate tickets; and in consequence of all these splits, the election was won by the Right, who thereupon governed with different combinations of the stronger parliamentary elements. When the new *Cortes* was dissolved in its turn, the elections of February 1936 again gave a very large majority to the Left, principally the Socialist group and Azaña's Republican Action Party. The Government constituted as a result of that victory at the polls was composed, nevertheless, only of Republicans, though it had the goodwill and the parliamentary support of Socialists, Syndicalists, and Communists, and pledged itself to carry out while in power a minimum program of political and social reforms asked by the three last-named Parties, the coalition of which was called the *Frente Popular,* or Popular Front. I shall consider these events in greater detail in a later paragraph.

The Structure of the Spanish State, and the Catalán Question

In fulfilment of the pact agreed upon at Barcelona, the Cataláns drew up their Statute, the text of which, ratified on August 2, 1931, by more than a half million regional votes, was presented to the *Cortes* on August 18; and while much debated in that body, was adopted, with some modifications, on September 9. That Statute, as well as the Articles of the Constitution relating to regional autonomy, with the provisions of which no autonomous organization could conflict, was the subject of prolonged and determined debate during 19 daily sessions of the *Cortes,* since there was an anti-autonomy current of opinion based on a concept of national and political unity at variance with the proposed organization of the Spanish State. The parliamentary majority, however, voted for the Constitutional Articles cited and the text of the Statute with some amendments; and thus the solution for the Catalán question was arrived at, ending what ever since 1888, and very actively since 1892, had been a strong irritant in national politics. The intellectual vacillation which that solution underwent and the opposing doctrines that clashed over it are reflected in the quite obvious contradictions in the text of the Constitution of 1931, especially in the inconsistent employment therein of the terms "Nation" and "State."

Catalán autonomy was not granted by special enactment. Its legal basis is inherent in the structure of the Spanish State which is established in the Constitution (first section). That structure, which it was proposed to define by a phrase characterizing the Constitution of 1931 as not a federal but a "federable" Constitution (which meant that it admitted possibility of a future federation of autonomous regions, in case all other Spanish regions should decide to organize themselves on the Catalonian pattern or in some similar fashion), is literally that of a single State—the Spanish State—within which, "if one or various contiguous Provinces with common historical, cultural and economic characteristics decide to organize themselves into an autonomous region in order to form a politico-administrative nucleus, they shall present their Statute in accordance with the conditions set forth in Article 12 [of the Constitution] . . . Once the Statute has been approved, it should be the basic law of the politico-administrative organization of the autonomous region, and the Spanish State shall recognize it and support it as an integrating part of its juridical ordinance."

Up to that time, public opinion had shown itself to be more or less favorable to adoption of an autonomous Statute, in the Basque, Galician, and Valencian regions. As we shall soon see, the Basque autonomists obtained a little later the approval of their own Statute.

The Political Crisis, 1933-1936

Let us retrace our steps now to tell the story of the Second Republic from another point of view.

Besides the legislative reforms of constitutional type, the Republican Government had to give careful consideration to public order, which was imperilled by movements of diverse origin and scope. Some acts of violence, apparently spontaneous popular demonstrations, broke out in Madrid and other cities. Whatever their motivation, such ill-judged outbursts broke the pattern of tolerance and goodwill with which the Second Republic inaugurated its triumph. Several convents and churches were thus victimized. When the Ministry of Government was queried with regard to these things and to a certain negligence in punishing them, it was alleged that such acts might have been reprisals by the people against unjustifiable and insolent aggressions committed by enemies of the Republic. This explanation by no means satisfied those Republican elements that were truly liberal in sentiment; which is to say, the tolerant element that opposed every kind of private reprisal, since the State, and the State alone, had the right to put down and punish aggression.

At the same time, there were typically revolutionary uprisings in Catalonia and Andalusia, as well as a military sedition in Madrid and Málaga that was promptly repressed. Moreover, the parliamentary debates grew more violent every day, and were complicated by internal dissensions of the parties comprising the majority in the *Cortes*. These dissensions were responsible for the step taken in October, 1933, by Alcalá-Zamora, President of the Republic, who dissolved the *Cortes* in accordance with Article 81 of the Constitution, which permitted the Chief of State to dissolve the *Cortes* twice (but only twice) during each term of office. Thereupon a Coalition Government was formed, made up of representatives of the several Republican parties, plus the Socialists, in order to make possible the legal election of new Deputies. Those elections were held on November 12, and gave the victory, as we have seen already, to the rightist parties which had never explicitly declared themselves to be in favor of a Republic and which were at that time in coalition with some minorities that were in open and decided opposition to the constitutional system of government. In consequence, the leftist Republicans, the Socialists, and other parties of the extreme labor left, came to constitute the parliamentary minority. Accordingly, the political struggle was intensified day by day. The victors in November were not republicans, nor did it ever occur to them to act as such; so that again in modern Spanish history the opportunity was lost of forming a Conservative Party (a **republican** Right) which might have been able to prevent the anti-**Republican** uprising of 1936. Patriotism for bringing such an idea to fruition was lacking, though the need was evident.

The result was that in 1934 there was an uprising of the people in Asturias. It was brought about by Socialists, for the most part, and some other leftist labor groups. That revolution had minor repercussions in Madrid and in other cities, mostly of the Basque country. It was extinguished very violently by a system of police persecutions that were cruelly prolonged for months afterwards in some districts and that were carried out by Government troops, some Moslem troops brought in from Morocco, and the International troops, or *tercios,* garrisioned in North Africa up to that time. Notwithstanding this military success, the political situation grew increasingly confused; so much so that because of the concurrence of several very alarming events—such as assassinations and personal attacks made by both friends and enemies of the Republic—the President had to make use again of his right to dissolve the *Cortes* (1936) and issue a call for another election of Deputies. This time (February of the same year) the Union of all the republican parties—consisting of Socialists, Syndicalists, Communists, and Anarchists (the *Frente Popular*) —obtained an overwhelming majority. It is an interesting fact that the Communists did not obtain a single post in the first elections of the Republic (1931), nor in those of 1933; and that in the 1936 elections, in spite of the support of the *Frente Popular,* obtained only an extremely small minority.

This radical change of policy, with the natural consequence that many leftist politicians whom the preceding Administration had jailed were immediately released, produced mob attacks and reprisals on the part of the populace in many towns and regions which until 1934 had kept apart from any such disorders. There was repetition, in greatly intensified degree, of assaulting and burning religious houses; and bloodshed became increasingly frequent in the streets, as did murder and other violence on both sides.

The War of 1936-1939: Origin and Preparation

After February, 1936, or perhaps even before that time, the majority of the commanders and other officers of the regular Army, in connivance with the Monarchists who had been defeated at the polls in 1931, together with the oldtime Carlists, the higher clergy, and other groups adhering to rightist opinions, were at work under cover to organize a revolutionary movement that would overthrow not only the Popular Front Government but the Republic itself. Divergent reasons were alleged in justification of such a revolution. A large number of the Monarchists did not believe that they had been defeated legally in the 1931 elections, since the sum total of the votes that brought about King Alfonso XIII's fall had not amounted to an anti-monarchical majority in Spain as a whole, but only in the large capital cities. Many of those who adduced this argument forgot that they themselves had voted against the King. They also overlooked the fact that the majority obtained in the elections of 1931 (which were for municipal posts, and not to choose delegates to the *Cortes*) was given by the rural communities and some of the smaller cities, where it was customary to falsify both the ballots themselves and the tabulations of the voting; so that these did not express the real intention of the voters as adequately as did the electoral figures from the large capital cities. This, by the way, was the point of view of Alfonso XIII's Ministers; who, if that fictitious nation-wide majority had been real, would certainly have availed themselves of the support in "the will of the people" for continuation of the monarchical regime.

Other supporters of Alfonso (perhaps the majority of them) based their adherence to the Army, which was preparing for revolutionary action, upon the acts of mob violence against the clergy, upon the importance acquired by the extremist popular parties, and upon the fear—which, as we have seen, was not substantiated by the results of the elections—of possible influence by Communists with a Russian leaning. A statement issued by the conspirators, which might be regarded as their official declaration, gave a concrete circumstantial explanation for the act precipitating the revolution, asserting that it responded to "the urgent necessity of preventing the explosion, in the summer of that same year 1936, of an extremist uprising analogous to that of 1934." In reality, the common purpose of the conspirators as such, whatever may have been their respective individual motives, was to overthrow the Second Spanish Republic and restore the Monarchy. The assassination of the rightist Deputy Calvo Sotelo (one of those whose attacks in the *Cortes* on the Popular Front Government had been most violently expressed) by a group of Shock Police—*guardias de asalto*— (a crime preceded by an attack against Jiménez Asúa, Republican Deputy in the *Cortes,* and by the assassination of Lieutenant Cas-

tillo of the *guardias de asalto,* also Republican) , afforded strong provo-
cation to the conspirators, who condoned only those acts of violence
committed by their partisans. Among the Liberals who supported the
Republic, the assassination of Calvo Sotelo produced, on the other
hand, a reaction of moral indignation. His murder never received the
punishment it deserved.

In spite of the number of elements implicated in the revolution that
was being planned, its leaders must have realized that by their own
unaided efforts they could not achieve a swift, decisive victory; and in
order to make that victory sure, they sought the military and political
aid of the totalitarian Governments of Europe: Italy and Germany.
Both Governments promised such aid and kept their promises, sending
into Spain regular troops of their respective armies, especially of their
air corps, of which latter arm the Spanish Republic had a very small
force. This appeal for foreign intervention brought about repetition
of what has become a type-action in our history: the settlement of a
question of internal politics by external help which always ends either
in the conquest of Spain by the helping hand or in its overweening
influence, prejudicial to the very life of those who had besought it.
There were instances enough of this before 1936: the Arabs in the
eighth century; the French in 1640 in Catalonia; and again in 1808
and 1824 the French, in support of the Spanish Throne.

The revolution against the Republic broke out on July 17, 1936,
in Morocco and on July 18 in the Peninsula. The Republican Government, notwithstanding the warnings given by some persons who had
been fearful that what did occur would occur, or who had had concrete
reasons for believing that it might, took no precautionary measures
whatever, except the ingenuous one of telephoning the Captains-
General to receive verbal assurance by long distance of their loyalty to
the legal Government. Naturally, every answer was reassuring on this
point; so that the rebellion on July 18 came both as a surprise and a
bitter disillusionment. The uprising included almost all the regular
Army, the Navy, the volunteer Militia which the anti-Republican
parties (Carlist *Requetés,* Falangists, and so on) had previously mobil-
ized, and the existing troops in Morocco (Spaniards, foreign volunteers,
and native Moslems) . Thanks to the support given by those forces, the
rebels overpowered the whole of Spain except for Madrid, Barcelona
and the other Catalán Provinces, Valencia and all its ancient Kingdom,

Gallés: *Portrait of Jaime Balmes.*

Málaga, Almería, Albacete, and other populations of the Southeast, of
Southern Andalusia, and of New Castile, as well as of the Asturian,
Cantrabrian, and Basque zones up to the French frontier; regions in
which the insurrection was controlled by the mass of the people and
by some elements of the Army loyal to the Government.

It is worthwhile to state, as a psychological factor of great importance, that on the night of July 17 the existing Republican Government resigned and another one was formed with Martínez Barrio as
Premier. While the revolution had broken out in Morocco some
hours earlier, the Peninsular Army had not yet actively revolted. Señor
Martínez Barrio lost no time in putting through long distance tele-
phone calls to three Generals who for one reason or another were his
personal friends. He informed them that his acceptance of the presidency of the new Ministry was motivated primarily by his intense desire
to prevent a civil war, which would be disastrous for all Spain; and
that accordingly he was asking for their help if, as he believed to be
the fact, they shared his point of view. Two of the Generals expressed
displeasure at not having been informed beforehand that Señor Martínez Barrio was going to take over the Republican Government, adding that it was no longer within their own power to make such a
decision as he proposed; and they insisted that he take up the matter
with the third General. The latter, after expressing regret that he had
been kept in ignorance of Señor Martínez Barrio's rise to power and
laudable efforts in behalf of peace, declared that it was now too late to
check the rising tide of rebellion.

The "Civil War" in Spain

What no one seems to have realized at the time (except the
Republican Government and its initiates), neither in most of Spain
nor in other countries, was what is now the obvious fact that the
German-Italian assistance would convert the Spanish armed conflict
into an international European war. Whether or not they foresaw
this inevitable result, the French and the British Governments aggravated the *de facto* situation in this respect by creation of an international Commission on Non-Intervention in the Spanish War, with
the apparent purpose of preventng the conflict from spreading to
other European countries. The practical result of that "non-intervention" was that it affected adversely only the Republican Govern-

ment, since, contrary to the impartial-sounding title of the Commission, the States represented upon it consented tactily to large scale and unhampered Italian and German intervention. What most certainly neither Great Britain nor France then understood was that the Spanish-Italian-German war was, on the part of the two totalitarian States, merely a try-out, a military experiment and a testing-ground, in preparation for the great War which they were preparing for the near future against the French, the British, and many other peoples of Europe. When France and Great Britain came to see this at last, and said as much, it was already far too late to prevent the premeditated aggression against themselves.

It is certain that intervention of Russia in favor of the Spanish Republic was very slight, although the contrary was stated at the time by the July rebels in their insistent and persistent propaganda broadcast and distributed to the rest of the world, and designed to mislead public opinion in all countries by raising the bogy of "the Communist danger." Whether through excess of credulity or because of a perverse determination not to hear both sides, the idea that there was the real menace of having Communists take possession of Spain won ready credence among different social classes in most of the European States (and even in the Americas). But the truth is that the Soviet Union did not send regular troops to Spain, as Germany and Italy did, nor were there any large numbers of Russian volunteers. The Republican combatants of Russian origin were very few, even when there are included in the total some aviation experts serving as instructors of the Spaniards who knew little about aviation techniques. As for the war materiél which the Russian Government consented to sell the Spanish Republic for cash on the board, the amount was likewise small. Meanwhile the totalitarian countries—and some others —supplied the rebels abundantly with weapons of modern warfare.

As yet it is still too soon to write with scientific detachment the history of the war in Spain from 1936 to 1939. We know only a small part of the dual documentation which must be taken fully into account in order to arrive at the whole truth. That truth can never be revealed if the documentation of only one of the opposing bands is utilized. In any case, research must include not military aspects merely, since other social and political factors influenced the course of events in very great degree; and sometimes influenced even military

Manuel de Falla.

operations themselves. I limit myself, therefore, to saying that after many national and international vicissitudes, the war in Spain ended in the month of April, 1939, with the inevitable victory of the rebels of July, 1936, and their auxiliaries. The inclusive official name which they then adopted for themselves was "Nationalists;" a term that may cause some confusion in the mind of the foreign reader since it is also employed self-descriptively by the Basque autonomists, who during the war in Spain were allied with the Spanish Republicans in gratitude for the Statute that had been granted them by the Spanish Republic, and who were for the most part devout practising Catholics, with a considerable number of priests among them, of whom many were shot by General Franco's troops when the latter and their foreign auxiliaries conquered the Basque country.

The personal Dictatorship of General Francisco Franco, when it replaced the earlier *Junta* of Burgos which had been the first rebel Military Government, took the name of *Franquistas*—Franquists, or "Francoists." The political and economical structure of the Dictatorship was formed on the pattern of a totalitarian government in accordance with the characteristic tenets of Italian Fascism and German Nazism; and although outwardly "neutral" during the Second World War, it repeatedly manifested its adherence to those two regimes and its expectancy of their ultimate victory. Soon after the Franquist Dictatorship's assumption of power, it used the pretext of prevention of the presumptive social triumph in Europe of the Russian Communists as an excuse for sending to the German front contingents of its regular Army (the famous "Blue Shirts," or *Camisas Azules*) under command of Generals and other officers who were likewise regulars and who fought in German uniforms (with only a Spanish beret to distinguish them from the rest of Hitler's forces) against one of the Allied Nations (Russia), while the Franquist Government at home vociferated loudly against the others, especially England. This political and military spectacle was observed repeatedly by the French people and by Spanish refugees in the Bas-Pyrenees.

The Twentieth Century Renascence in Spain

The contemporary renascence of Spanish life, in its cultural and economic aspects, had its first roots—still very tenuous—in 1833, once there had passed the two arid periods represented by the War of

Spanish Independence and the reign of Ferdinand VII. The first Carlist Civil War did not offer much encouragement in strengthening the slender beginning; but as soon as that conflict ended, the struggling growth received a new impulse.

We have already noted, in the relevant connection, the most important details of the progress made during Isabella II's reign and the revolutionary period.

An examination of Spanish bibliography after 1833—and to some extent, even prior to that date—shows the literary production to be a continuation of that of the eighteenth century, particularly as regards the attention devoted to studies on the national history in all its divers aspects, and the vindicatory revaluation, which had been initiated in that century, of our Spanish literary classics, of our colonization of the Americas (regarding which misinformation and misinterpretation were widespread), and of other factors pertaining to our past and even to our present. At the same time, as already mentioned, there began a new flowering in Spain of art and literature admirably simple and clear in style, and of education and culture in general.

Nevertheless, all this was relatively little in comparison to the dazzling advance of modern civilization in other countries, so that it can readily be understood why some true patriots felt discouraged, with their discouragement finding propitious occasion for expressing itself (and doing so with obvious exaggeration) in 1898; and no less comprehensible was the contemptuous opinion prevalent abroad with regard to the new "Spanish decadence."

As we have already said, the reaction against that state of mind, and, what is of more value, the mobilization of the nation's productive energy, speedily became evident; and neither the uncertainty and political malaise which lasted from 1917 to 1928, nor the "benevolent dictatorship" of General Primo de Rivera, nor the reappearance when that regime ended of the problems of 1923 with others that had originated in the regime itself, were sufficient to paralyze this energy. In proportion as the Spanish spirit of self-confidence grew stronger, the practical evidences of its capacity for action were multiplied: a movement that increased with great rapidity (as compared to the stagnation of former years) and that was already plain to be seen in visible and palpable proofs by any observer at home or abroad.

It was recognized by foreigners in especial during the years immediately preceding 1914.

In its economic aspect, this movement—which, as we have said, had been intensified by the immediate consequences of the First World War, 1914-1918—continued to expand regardless of the greater or lesser degree of support received from the State, and notwithstanding neglectfulness, and at times even obstaculization, by government officials. It is within the scope of the historian to observe that, in spite of the fact that there were not nearly enough public schools in 1936, and of the continuing illiteracy of the masses (a condition that could not be remedied overnight), the general culture of the country and its creative capacity in this sphere have developed greatly, and justify the cultural prestige newly won by Spain throughout the world.

The possibility of the coexistence of that progress and of a large percentage of the illiterate and the uneducated among the masses of the people, such as there were then in Spain, is a fact of history which often repeats itself. Spain, indeed, gave conspicuous proof of it during the sixteenth and seventeenth centuries, as Russia, for example, did in the nineteenth. The danger from illiteracy lies in another direction, far removed from any considerations regarding scientific and literary production: for example, in public morale in general, in political matters in which the people as a whole intervene, and in social problems. Illiteracy is still more grievous because of the putative number of trained minds which, in many cases, are permanently denied opportunity of development, so that creative intellectual responsibility devolves upon a small minority. Moreover, and particularly with respect to the Spanish public, especially among the poorer classes (and of course this is even more true of those living in rural communities than in urban centers), there exists the fact of a culture, in part self-taught, in part traditional, which finds expression in the proverbs, pithy sayings, and maxims which everybody knows and everybody applies with complete appositeness when occasion presents. That is the knowledge of life, the shrewd insight and deepheld wisdom, which has been observed and commented upon time and again by foreigners who have come to Spain, studied our people at firsthand, and perceived in their philosophy of life an inherent originality of the Spanish mind. This did not pass unnoted by Cervantes, nor could it possibly have done so. He was well acquainted with his country and his compatriots: Cervantes did not put into Sancho's mouth the tangy savor of proverbs wise with knowledge of the world merely as a simple technical device nor as a foil to the madness of the cultured Don; but rather because if he talked in any other way, Sancho would not represent realistically and fully his own social class.

Citation here of that interesting fact, in order to show more clearly that a high degree of culture such as Spain's in the sixteenth and seventeenth centuries can coexist naturally with a seemingly ignorant illiterate mass, by no means implies—such a conclusion would be erroneous—that it does not matter whether or no illiteracy is reduced in Spain or any other nation. The solid advantage of wiping out illiteracy is something else, and was stated above.

A situation somewhat similar to that described after Ferdinand VII's death again held in the economic activities, which were greatly developed and improved in comparison with previous conditions, though for a long while there were undeveloped natural resources: problems, such as agriculture, that remained unsolved in some sections; industries that could live only under the umbrella of high tariff or that were dependent upon machinery, plans, models, and even products from other countries; the aching need to carry out the program of public works in all its ramifications, especially with regard to irrigation, communications, the mechanical utilization of water-power in itself and as a source of electricity; the need to adapt crops to varying local conditions of soil and climate; and so forth.

No less important was the remedy for one of the major ills from which our land was suffering, and with which in spite of the annual Arbor Day (a festival nowadays fallen into neglect), no one tried to deal fundamentally: that is, the problem of deforestation. It is not a natural thing for Spain to lack trees—except in a few districts—but is the result of man's shortsightedness and greed. In Alfonso the Sage's *Libro de Montería,* written in the thirteenth century and repeatedly copied and widely read thereafter, are descriptions of the great spreading Spanish forests which covered regions almost treeless today, such as, for example, a good part of Castile and La Mancha. In the late fifteenth century a foreign Ambassador who crossed the Peninsula from north to south could write: "From the frontier to

Santa Fe (in Granada) I have not emerged from an unending woodland." At the beginning of the nineteenth century, La Mancha and southeastern Spain possessed vast forests of live oak and pine, the existence of which can be divined today only from a few spindling groves here and there or isolated trees such as one comes upon often in old Castile. These drastic physiographic changes have meant no proportional advantage for agriculture comparable to the loss sustained and all the consequences thereof. According to the experts, Spain has 100,000 square kilometers—about 62,137 square miles—devoid of vegetation: that means one-fifth of the total area of the country; or, in other terms of comparison, a territory larger than the whole of Portugal. Clearly, the work of modifying and improving the physical environment which conditions the history of Spain, a work to the pressing need for which we have alluded repeatedly, includes reforestation as a prime factor, a first essential for many others.

These things are deficiencies that cry out for remedy. However, notwithstanding them, the outlines were being drawn, before the Spanish War of 1936-1939, of a future full of hope, with a justified feeling of confidence and optimistic faith in the present. This optimism was based on the effective increase in natural income; the innumerable industrial opportunities awaiting Spanish capital investment, Spanish intelligence, and Spanish labor; the ever-increasing participation of Spaniards in international scientific progress; and the heartening evidence of present achievement as an augur of greater future creativeness and development. The full realization of that future rests on the fact that every individual Spaniard whose mind or whose muscle is capable of cooperating and enlarging the national life must come to feel an intense desire to do his part, an ambition to make himself ever worthier, and a burning desire to be recognized rightfully—and to have his country recognized—as a useful factor in human civilization.

The paralyzation of many social activities both spiritual and economic, which was one fatal result of the recent Spanish War, is only a hiatus, which, once it is over, will not hinder Spain from taking up again the road to greatness through development of her natural resources and her innate qualities and through extension of her culture. Plain proof of this was afforded even during the War itself, by the continuation of not a few scientific labors of research and in other fields which were unrelated to military requirement; and proof continues to be afforded, in proportions a hundred times greater, by the enormous activity in foreign lands, in every field of culture, of the thousands of Spaniards who, as yet unable to return to their own country, find their work appreciated in those nations where they now dwell.

Contemporary Spanish Science

If it were within the scope of historiography to make categorical statements, we could say that the differential characteristic between the Spanish culture of the nineteenth century and that of the twentieth, consists in the fact that the former distinguished itself chiefly by cultivation of arts and letters and the latter by cultivation of science. An explanation of that difference has been stated already under the subheading *Currents in Scientific Knowledge* in Chapter XIII. What is said there does not imply the negation of an important literary culture in the twentieth century so far; nor much less of the artistic. It means merely that, along with them, scientific research and applied and creative science have struck a new and highly important note in our cultural history since 1808. Scientific culture, which long went by default after its eighteenth century renascence, has become again in the twentieth century abundant and valuable.

Before setting down some pertinent facts along these lines, I should say that most of the scientists mentioned in the section cited carried over from the nineteenth century well into the first third of the twentieth. Many of them therefore are deceased at the present writing. Most of those still alive were born after 1900 and much is yet to be expected from them.

Beginning with the physical and natural sciences, the histologist Ramón y Cajal continued to amass the fruits of his research and of his creative mind, and by 1900 was already internationally known. In the same general field, though not in biology alone, distinguished work has been done by Calderón, Linares, Lázaro, Simarro, Torres Quevedo, Oloriz and, more recently, Bolívar, Cabrera, De Buen, and others. In the special field of Medicine, mention should be made of Recasens, Sanmartín, Novoa Santos, Achúcarro (who died prematurely), Alonso, Gómez Ocaña, Tolosa Latour, Calatraveño,

Madinaveita, Santiago de los Albitos, Azúa, García Calderón; and in ophthalmology, which has a long and honored history in Spain—as we saw in the seventeenth century—there are Calvo Martín (who belongs to the mid-nineteenth century); Rafael Cervera, Delgado Jugo (to whom we owe the creation in 1872 of the Ophthalmological Institute—*Instituto Oftálmico*—which had Queen María Victoria de Aosta as its patron), López Ocaña, Santa Cruz, Cisneros, García Mansilla, Barraquer, Covisa (whose death is recent at this writing), Cayetano del Toro, Muñoz Urra, Manacho (initiator of the "Ophthalmological Archives"—*Archivos Oftalmológicos*), Castillo, and, very especially, Dr. Manuel Márquez, whose fame is worldwide and who for the greater glory of science still lives. In the field of anthropology, using the term in its utmost range from anthropology strictly so called to human history, the most important nineteenth century names have been noted earlier in these pages. Among those best known in the twentieth century are Miguel de Unamuno, philologist, philosopher, historian of certain aspects of Spanish thought, prose stylist and poet; Manuel Cossío, teacher, critic, historian of the plastic arts and of philosophy; Buylla, the economist; Sela, internationalist and educator; Posada, political scientist; Bonilla, historian of philosophy and of Spanish literature; the Rubiós, father and son, historians both; Pella y Forgas, likewise a historian; Chabás, who carried out intensive research into Valencian history; Ureña, editor of several medieval *fueros,* especially those of Cuenca; López Ferreiro, already mentioned, historian of Galicia, especially of Santiago de Compostela and its diocese; Riaza, whose premature death deprived us of one of the most learned jurists and authorities on the history of Spanish Law; Father Garci Villada, S.J., a specialist in Spanish ecclesiastical history; Aramburu, the noted penologist; Asín y Palacios, the most productive and most eminent historian of Spanish Moslem philosophy; Méndez Bejarano, historian of the *Afrancesados* of 1808-1815; Ibarra, whose principal field is the history of Aragón; Villamil, devoting himself by preference to the history of art; Béker, Reparaz, Fernández Duro (we owe to the last-named masterly research on the ancient Greek merchant fleet); and others whose fame is in the making.

Modern Spanish historiography has distinguished itself, and continues to do so, principally in its methods; in amplification of what is held to be historical content, casting aside the traditional restriction to purely political history; in making detailed and critical research into sources, both documental and monumental, with greatly increased attention given archeology and archeological excavations; in tending to specialize on periods and themes, thus permitting intensified research on both; and in editing conscientiously prepared texts in excellent formats.

Twentieth Century Literature

Literature, and Spanish literature in particular, is, with the one exception of philosophy, the cultural field in which there is most noticeable a radical change expressive of the evolution it has undergone; for literature has entered as fully as the plastic arts, if not to even greater degree, into twentieth century ideology. That change began to take shape late in the nineteenth century, and was a transformation of both form and substance in prose and poetry alike. As regards poetic style, the fountainhead of the new technique—*Modernismo,* or Modernism—was the Nicaraguan poet Rubén Darío, who lived for some years in Spain and whose influence was very great on the poets who were young at the turn of the century. The Modernists continued to enrich their technique and adopt new modalities which came to affect not only poetry in its every aspect but even the vocabulary of prose. In the field of the novel, schools still newer than the Modernist—Realism, and others—brought about some remarkable transformations, even in the case of writers whose earlier work had been stylistically very different. Antonio Machado is a typical example: the greater (and possibly the superior) part of his poems differ greatly in ideology and in technique from what he produced under the pen-names Abel Martín and Juan de Mairena. To the latter fictitious personage we owe not only a considerable amount of Machado's poetry, but most of his prose. Another poet, an Andalusian like Machado, Federico García Lorca,—whom some critics hold to be the greatest of his generation (1899-1936) —likewise evidences in some of his poems the new literary influences.

As for the content of these poems, Castilian and the rest, it changed less than did the form; though the theories of aesthetics were changed in themselves, and inevitably weighed upon both elements, so organically interrelated. Thus, there are clearly discernible in many

Miguel de Unamuno.

lyric poets much deeper traces than they themselves are probably aware of, of the sentimental romanticism of the preceding generation.

Among contemporary poets of great worth, Juan Ramón Jiménez is internationally recognized; and there are too Valle, Rosales, De Diego, Pedro Salinas, Jorge Guillén, Prados, Altolaguirre, Rafael Alberti, in their present mid-twentieth century manner and mood. These names by no means exhaust the list.

Prose, and especially the novel and the drama, was not so much influenced as poetry by the new literary doctrines; but time and again. in both point of view and choice of theme, every novel that Benito Pérez Galdós—for instance—published from 1900 until his death in 1920 revealed successive modifications. This was perhaps even more true of his dramatic work, which, beginning toward the close of the nineteenth century with *Realidad,* produced in the space of a few years a variety of plays, with *Electra* as representative of his later style.

Also in the field of the novel, to which the nineteenth century novelists who won fame continued to make contributions so long as they lived (Alas, Palacio Valdés, et cetera), new literary figures appeared: Gabriel Miró; Ramón del Valle Inclán; Manuel Azaña (who in the sober, classic Castilian style was as good a writer as he was an orator) ; Pío Baroja, whose first book appeared about 1895 and whom many critics give first place among contemporary Spanish novelists: Ramón Pérez de Ayala; Azorín; Ferrandiz; and some others. There were new dramatists: Jacinto Benavente, the most accomplished dramaturgist among them, in spite of his tendency to become doctrinaire and his sometimes excessive lyricism (he was awarded the Nobel Prize for Literature) ; Manuel Linares Rivas; Gregorio Martínez Sierra; Eduardo Marquina; Casona; Federico García Lorca; and others. The Alvarez Quintero brothers, Serafín and Joaquín, deserve special mention, since they wrote not only *sainetes* (short dramatic pieces) and comedies of manners with Andalusian setting, but also because they brought to the stage emotional and intellectual problems new in our literature, and produced dramas of great interest and range. Francisco Villaespesa should also be named, and, as prose-writers and journalists of great merit, Castrovido, Zozaya and Villanueva.

Besides the novelists, and in various fields of prose, the leading writers were—and many are still writing—Ramón Menéndez Pidal,

Juan Ramón Jiménez

Francisco Rodríguez Marín, Asín, Maura, Américo Castro, Alonso, and a pleiad more of brilliant authors now (1949) so scattered in many different countries that it is difficult to keep in touch with their work, though their names should be borne in mind. One of them, who died but recently, was Enrique Díez Canedo. Because of his services to the history of Spanish literature we should recall Sánchez Moguel, teacher of some of the contemporary Hispanists, though inferior as historian to his colleague Marcelino Menéndez Pelayo. We should also cite, for they deserve it, Balbuena, historian of Castilian literature; Aznar Casanova, and Deleito Piñuela. Aznar is preparing a new and complete edition of Luis Vives for which there has long been need; Deleito is working on the history of the theatre in Madrid in the nineteenth and early twentieth century.

Catalán literature, in full flowering during the present century, presents numerous writers in various *genres;* including Santiago Rusiñol, Iglesias, Sagarra, Montoliu, Riba, Fabra, d'Ors, Carner, Alomar, López Picó, Folguera, Lloreno, Riber, Pons, Corominas, Bertrana, Puig y Ferrater, Valls Tabernar, Pla, Soldevila, Puig y Cadafalch, D'Ollwer, and, in some of his historical works, Bosch Gimpera. There are doubtless others whose work has not come to my attention.

Music and the Plastic Arts

Considered as a whole, the Spanish plastic arts of the present century offer new forms and approaches, just as literature does, but with scope at times more universal.

To begin with painting, the majority of the artists whose works are given most serious critical consideration are still alive. We do not know what they may yet achieve. There is a single exception: a living artist whose work is of weight both because it has won international recognition and because it shows in its own progression the evolution of modern art from Cubism to Surrealism. That artist is Pablo Picasso.

Among the moderns who have died (1949), most of them belonging to the nineteenth century, I shall cite Regoyos, Aurelio Asteto, Aureliano Beruete, García Lesmer, Gonzalo Bilbao, López y Mezquita, the Pinazos father and sons, Martínez Cubells, Sotomayor, Santiago

Rusiñol, Casas, Urgell, Nonell, Romero de Torres, and Chicharro. Most of them continued to paint in the traditional manner. But modern art also had its representatives, other than Picasso; for example, Souto, and others of whose merits time as judge will, we doubt not, crown more than one with praise, whatever new schools of painting there may be. As critic and historiographer, Juan de la Encina— the pseudonym of Gutiérrez Abarcal—is notable.

The case of sculpture is similar. All the sculptors who were more or less known at the close of the nineteenth century have died. Since their names were mentioned in the opportune connection it is unnecessary to repeat them here, but we should take note of the following, not hitherto mentioned, principally because their work has been done since 1900. In general, this is true of Querol, Folgueras, Inurria, Llimona, Clará, Julio Antonio (who before his premature death executed memorable busts representative of the Spanish people), Bañuls, Baurón Mateu, Julio Vicent, Navarro, Gangallo, Blay (one of the finest sculptors of this century), Mateo Hernández, Victorio Macho, Santamaría, Ortells, Capuz, Barvel and Manolo.

Needless to say, the more recent in date the work of these artists, the more it shows the new techniques and the new concept of sculpture which in that art as in painting embodies the modern aesthetic.

As to music, it will suffice to say that the composers who have succeeded those already cited are still living, for the most part, and it may be that their best work is still in the future. Contemporary Spanish music is heard round the world, because of the genius of Isaac Albéniz, Enrique Granados, Manuel de Falla, Esplá (at this writing still composing), and other great artists, whose compositions are often heard in the international centers of the musical world. We may cherish the hope that this will be true also of the younger men just appearing on the scene, whose fame is even now being achieved. It is their responsibility as it will be their glory to see that the Spanish school of music maintains or improves that place it won toward the close of the nineteenth century. With regard to the documentation of musical history and popular art, in which Pedrell, Rafael Mitjana, and Torres did valuable work, the musicologist Subirá has distinguished himself in the present century, and is editor of a rich collection of eighteenth century music (*tonadillas,* and the like) which the Spanish Academy has published.

The Two Generations

In this heading I am using the term "generation" in its amplest sense, which corresponds in Castilian Spanish to the fourth Academy definition of the word: "the sum total of all those living contemporaneously." I interpret it, historically, as applicable not only to those who are living as I write (which is to say, in the year 1949), but also to all those contemporaneous with my own life, even though many of them have died already. That is to say, chronologically I consider my generation to include most of the second half of the nineteenth century plus the twentieth to date. In short, what I wish to say and what my length of days authorizes, is that my own generation is the sum of all the men (and their deeds) that I have known during the more than eighty years of my existence and of those respecting whom I bear direct witness either as to what was seen by my own eyes, or heard by my own ears from my elders, of the Spanish history related in this book. This direct personal acquaintance has also enabled me to observe the men and events concerned with an intensiveness that mere documentation could not have supplied, and that goes deeper in cultural interpretation than would be possible if one had to depend wholly on their spoken and written words. All of this, then, enables me to fill in some gaps in the information given under preceding subheadings (beginning with *The Spanish Renascence in the Twentieth Century*) ; and in some respects it also makes it possible for me to go beyond what they said of themselves in their own works. There can be no doubt, in fact, that however much transcend from the books, speeches, conversations, letters, and outward acts of that select minority of Spaniards, such testimony does not give—not by much—the sum total of the Spanish people. Within that minority itself, the differential notes between the later nineteenth century and the twentieth to date are indicated only by scattered individual manifestations not always in accord with one another, while what is desirable and needful for the integral history of nations is to know the corresponding differential in thought and action of the masses, or of the majority. Therefore, alongside the diversities deriving from the specialized histories of every cultural field, it is necessary to know the *collective differentials* which are characteristic in general of the men of each particular epoch or century.

Ramón Casas: *Portrait of Alfonso XIII.*

The differentials of men of the nineteenth century (even when they survived into the twentieth) and those of men of the twentieth century, are more numerous than might be deduced from what was said in the immediately preceding section. Each of these groups has its own differential which, in the inmost recesses of the spirit, separates them in much, however great the flexibility with which the nineteenth century survivors try to assimilate twentieth century characteristics. In this field of our thought and action a difference does exist between the two generations, which perhaps completes their respective histories.

Of course that fact—which has been observed and hitherto commented upon by some of our contemporaries—must necessarily be included in this relation, not for itself but for its historiography. Among the expressions of it which in my judgment reflect the truth of our history I find one, very recent, which because of its clarity of form I cull with grateful appreciation. I reproduce its most expressive phrases, omitting personal references (though they are very pertinent in the original text) because to repeat these here would diminish the very definite value of the comments as generalizations which, in reality, are common to the immense majority of the two generations.

The world of the men of the nineteenth century was "a world of life and of hope in a possible social, historical and human harmony contained within the generous dream" of that century: in other terms, the firm belief in the intellectual and moral progress of humankind, which across a trajectory with neither deviation nor retrogression needs must achieve the creation of a more perfect society, in which the great defects from which we yet suffer would be extirpated as have been— or as it was then believed had been—human slavery, intolerance, and like evils. Those beliefs nourished the roots of the optimism characteristic of the men of the nineteenth century, and give the clue to their spirit and conduct.

The world that the twentieth century man sees is on the contrary "the organic world of an existentialism which, while meditating upon the profound of the human being and his yearning for the absolute, finds itself at the threshold of nothingness and death." At the same time, that man bears within himself, in natural consequence, "the cold metaphysical passion of pessimistic intellectualism . . . proceeding in great part from the disillusionment that seizes upon the contemporary man facing the break-down of that ingenuous faith of the Eighties."

Those two opposing spiritual positions represent "the two maximum experiences through which man has passed in the last two hundred years: that of an ideal of communion with other men, which restores to his life an ultrapersonal meaning; and the desperation of intellectual individualism, of the man in solitude, thirsting for the absolute."

But while that delineation of difference is exact for most of the years since 1901, it still remains to be seen whether the Spaniards who are living today, those who are still here after 1936 and are therefore most genuinely men of the present century, will continue to be anchored in the disillusionment and despair of those contemporaries of theirs (the majority of whom have already vanished from the scene) who suffered from a pessimism as dark as the optimism of the Eighties was bright; or whether they will instead seek an optimistic solution. At the same time, it would be well for us to ascertain whether all who survive from the previous century retain the characteristic beliefs of their period or whether they are converts to the new way of thinking, which they may have adopted in the transition from nineteenth century to twentieth. Only after we are sure of these two facts shall we be able to say what is the present intellectual position of the Spaniard in the light of his history. Of course, while neither group can be excluded from the historic reality to which both belong, there is the possibility that in the one or the other (or in some individuals of either or both), there has been or is being produced a third position more or less removed from the two just examined, or there may be a mixture of their elements with others derived from the fluid and variable experience of late years, which is already an experience completely beyond anything known to those who died before the years 1936-1939.

I shall conclude this book by answering that question briefly in so far as I can.

The Present Universality of the Real Spain

Two important facts dominate and characterize the present existence of the Spanish people. The first is that that people is split into two parts which neither live together nor desire to do so. The

Prado Museum, Madrid.

"two Spains" of which Maragall wrote long since in conciliatory accents and with sincere conciliatory intent, have again emerged, the divergences aggravated threefold and fivefold, and with no moral possibility of the two parts being welded into one. Whether we deem that a good thing or a bad, it is a fact imposed upon us all, and no one (not even with the most able and well-meaning diplomacy) would be capable, were such a thing proposed, of ignoring or undoing it.

The other fact is that these two Spains are now living as far apart in space as in the spirit. One continues to reside on the Peninsular territory which it does not own exclusively and which none will be able to adjudicate justly as a legal heritage. The other Spain lives scattered fragmentarily in population groups more or less dense, in several countries of Europe, Africa, and the Americas. And ninety-five per cent of it (if not more) represents a considerable mass of Spanish intellectualism; is possessor not only of the innate faculties inherent in what is termed "race" (though the term is a misnomer), but of the creative faculty as well, working day by day to enrich the universal treasurehouse of culture. To give one concrete example, sixty per cent of Spanish university faculties are today expatriates.

The ideologies of these two Spains are very different and cannot be fused. The expatriates, by force of circumstance, inevitably have that advantage (there had to be some advantage, by way of compensation) which twice in the nineteenth century had belonged to Spaniards who loved both freedom and the culture of the mind. Those whose lives today follow that earlier pattern enjoy greater and more varied opportunities for work and for acquaintance with the progress of the most cultured modern peoples, each with its own original contribution complemented by the others and each with its own experience of life, attained at times through suffering and tragedy.

What orientation of the spirit will be the result, what is already taking place, among the mass of the expatriates? Will it overcome the excesses which characterized all nineteenth century orientations and some in the twentieth? Will it ratify the discerning judgment of some one of them with all the sowing of new seed and uprooting of past error which time and a strong and multiple vision of life may impose or counsel?

It is still too soon to answer these questions. Perhaps also an answer is impossible because there does not yet exist the necessary information as to the degree with which every fragment of expatriate Spain has been impregnated with the lessons being learned at firsthand. Furthermore, those expatriate fragmentations, besides being necessarily varied, are far removed one from another. Moreover there are as yet lacking sufficient means of communication to tell us whether or not the Spaniards scattered over the world are arriving at identical conclusions with regard to their own and their country's future.

But however this may be, that expatriate Spain, taken as a whole, is gathering up in utmost universality—a universality far beyond any that could ever have been achieved in the scanty trial attempts of the old-time educational bureaucracy with its travel-grants for visiting and studying in other countries—the human sense of the highest individual and collective minds striving alike to find the formula and the method for a future of peace, of justice, and of truth, which will make life on this earth good to live.

A Selected Bibliography on Spanish History

Since it is designed for the English-speaking reader, the listing here is primarily of works in English, whether translations or original texts. Spanish titles are indicated, however, when no comparable treatment in English is available.

The present work, which has been translated and arranged in accordance with Dr. Rafael Altamira's planning and with his tireless cooperation, is the English version of his *Manual de Historia de España* (2nd edition, Buenos Aires, 1946), together with much additional material supplied by Dr. Altamira himself, both in manuscript and from published work, especially, but not wholly, from his *Historia de España y la civilización española* in four volumes, the fourth edition of which was published in Barcelona in 1929. The present is the first English translation of Dr. Altamira's *Manual*. His four-volume History has never been translated into English. C. E. Chapman's one-volume *History of Spain founded on the 'Historia . . .' of Rafael Altamira* (New York, 1918), is, as the title indicates, not a translation. A translation of Dr. Altamira's brief *Historia de la civilización española* by P. Volkov was published in London and New York in 1930.

GENERAL

Aguado Bleye, Pedro, *Compendio de Historia de España*, 2 volumes, 3rd edition, Madrid, 1932.

Atkinson, William C., *Spain, a Brief History*, London, 1934.

Ballesteros y Beretta, Antonio, *Historia de España y su influencia en la historia universal*, 9 volumes, Barcelona, 1918-41.

Fernández de Navarrete, M., *Colección de documentos sobre la historia de España*, 5 volumes, Madrid, 1842-44.

Hannay, David, *Spain*, London, 1917.

Hume, Martin A. S., *The Spanish People, Their Origin, Growth and Influence*, London, 1901; New York, 1914.

Peers, E. Allison (editor), *Spain: a Companion to Spanish Studies*, New York and London, 1929.

CHAPTER I

Sánchez, Alonso B., *Fuentes de la historia española e hispanoamericana,* 3 volumes, 2nd edition, Madrid, 1927.
Trend, J. B., *The Civilization of Spain,* London, 1944; New York, 1946.
Bosch-Gimpera, Pedro, *El poblamiento antiguo y la formación de los pueblos de España,* Mexico, 1944.
Breuil, Henri and Hugo Obermaier, *The Cave of Altamira at Santillana del Mar, Spain,* Translated by Mary E. Boyle, New York, 1935.
Mélida, Jose Ramón, *Arqueología española,* Barcelona and Buenos Aires, 1929.
Menendez Pidal, Ramón (editor), *Historia de España,* Vol. 1, *España prehistorica,* by Eduardo Hernández-Pacheco [*et al.*], 1935-
Obermaier, Hugo, *Fossil Man in Spain,* Translated by Christine D. Matthew, New Haven, 1924.
Péricot, L., *La prehistoria de la Peninsula ibérica,* Barcelona, 1923.

CHAPTER II

Carpenter, Rhys, *The Greeks in Spain,* New York, London, 1925.
Dixon, Pierson, *The Iberians in Spain,* Oxford, 1940.
Fernández y González, F., *Primitivos pobladores históricos* de la Peninsula, Madrid, 1890.
Hübner, E., *La Arqueología de España,* Barcelona, 1898.
Humboldt, G. de, *Los primitivos habitantes de España,* Madrid, 1879.

CHAPTERS III AND IV

Castillejo, José, *Wars of Ideas in Spain: Philosophy, Politics and Education,* London, 1937.
Frank Tenney, *Economic Survey of Ancient Rome,* Vol. II, Baltimore, 1938, pp. 119-224, *Roman Spain.*
López Mendizábal, I., *Cantabria y la guerra cantábrica,* Tolosa, 1899.
Mélida, J. R., *Excavaciones de Numancia,* Madrid, 1908.
Menéndez Pidal, Ramón (editor), *Historia de España,* Vol. 2, *España romana,* by Pedro Bosch Gimpera [*et al.*], *Madrid, 1935-* .
Menéndez y Pelayo, Marcelino, *Historia de los Heterodoxos españoles,* Madrid, 1884.
Sutherland, E. H. V., *The Romans in Spain,* London, 1939.
Van Nostrand, John James, *The Reorganization of Spain by Augustus,* Berkeley, 1916.

CHAPTER V

Blázquez, A., *La hitación de Wamba,* Madrid, 1907.
Cañal, C., *San Isidoro,* Madrid, 1897.

Fernández Guerra, A., *Historia de España desde la invasión de los pueblos germanos hasta la ruina de la monarquía visigoda,* 2 volumes, Madrid, 1890.

Férotin, D. M., *El Liber Ordinum de la Edad visigoda,* Paris, 1904.

Menéndez Pidal, J., *Leyendas del último rey godo,* Madrid, 1906.

Menéndez Pidal, Ramón (editor), *Historia de España,* Vol. 3, *España visigoda,* by Manuel Torres [*et al.*], Madrid, 1935- .

Pérez Pujol, E., *Historia de las instituciones sociales de la España goda,* 4 volumes, Valencia, 1896.

Ureña, R. de, *La legislación gótico-hispana,* Madrid, 1905.

CHAPTERS VI AND VII

Aben-Adhari de Marruecos, *España árabe. Historia de Alandalus,* Translated by F. Fernández y González, Granada, 1862.

Coppée, Henry, *History of the Conquest of Spain by the Arab-Moors,* 2 volumes, Boston, 1881.

Dozy, Reinhart Pieter Anne, *Spanish Islam: a History of the Moslems in Spain,* London, 1913.

Dunham, Samuel Astley, *Spain and Portugal,* London, 1833.

González Palencia, A., *Historia de la España musulmana,* 2nd edition, Barcelona, 1929.

Ibn 'Abd al-Hakām, *Ibn Abd-el-Hakem's History of the Conquest of Spain,* Göttingen, 1858.

Lane-Poole, Stanley, *The Moors in Spain,* 2nd edition, New York, 1911.

Makkarī, Ahmed 'ibn Mohammed al, *The History of the Mohammedan Dynasties in Spain,* 2 volumes, London, 1840-43.

Sanchez-Albornoz y Menduina, Claudio, *España y el Islam,* Buenos Aires, 1943.

Scott, Samuel Parsons, *History of the Moorish Empire in Europe,* 3 volumes, Philadelphia and London, 1904.

Whishew, Bernhard and Ellen M., *Arabic Spain, Sidelights on Her History and Art,* London, 1912.

CHAPTER VIII

Amador de los Ríos, J., *Historia social, política y religiosa de los judíos de España y Portugal,* 3 volumes, Madrid, 1875-96.

Ballester, Rafael, *Las fuentes narrativas de la Historia de España durante la Edad Media (417-1474),* Palma de Mallorca, 1903.

Beazley, Charles Raymond, *James the First of Aragon,* Oxford, 1890.

Castro y Ross, Adolfo de, *The History of the Jews in Spain from the Time of Their Settlement in that Country till the Commencement of the Present Century,* Translated by D. G. M. Kirwan, Cambridge and London, 1851.

Chaytor, H. J., *A History of Aragon and Catalonia,* London, 1933.

Clarke, Henry Butler, *The Cid Campeador, and the Waning of the Crescent in the West*, New York and London, 1902.

Drane, Augusta Theodosia, *The History of St. Dominic, Founder of the Friars Preachers*, New York and London, 1891.

Hamilton, Earl J., *Money, Prices and Wages in Valencia, Aragon and Navarre, 1351-1500*, Cambridge (Mass.), 1936.

de Macanaz, Melchor, *Regalías de los Señores Reyes de Aragón*, Madrid, 1879.

Manuel Rodríguez, M. de, *Memorias para la vida del santo rey Don Fernando III*, Madrid, 1800.

Markham, Sir Clements R., *The Story of Majorca and Minorca*, London, 1908.

Menéndez Pidal, Ramón, *The Cid and His Spain*, Translated by Harold Sunderland, London, 1934.

Merriman, R. B., *The Rise of the Spanish Empire in the Old World and the New*, Vol. I—The Middle Ages, New York, 1918.

Miron, E. L., *The Queens of Aragon, Their Lives and Times*, London, 1913.

Swift, Francis Darwin, *Life and Times of James I, the Conqueror, King of Aragon, Valencia and Majorca*, Oxford, 1894.

Watts, Henry Edward, *The Christian Recovery of Spain, Being the Story of Spain from the Moorish Conquest to the Fall of Granada*, New York, 1918.

CHAPTER IX

Acosta, Father José de, *The Natural and Moral History of the Indies*, Reprinted from Edward Grimston's translation [1604], London, 1880.

Fernández de Navarrete, M., *Colección de viajes y descubrimientos*, 5 volumes, Madrid, 1829.

Fernández de Oviedo, Gonzalo, *Historia general y natural de las Indias* [*circa 1520*], 4 volumes, Madrid, 1851-55.

Hare, Christopher, *A Queen of Queens and the Making of Spain*, New York, 1906.

Herrera y Tordesillas, Antonio de, *The General History of the Vast Continent and Islands of America . . .*, Translated by Capt. John Stevens, 6 volumes, London, 1725-26.

Hume, Martin A. S., *Queens of Old Spain*, New York, 1906, London, 1911; also *Spain: Its Greatness and Decay, 1479-1788*, 3rd edition, Cambridge, 1913.

Irving, Washington, *The Conquest of Granada*, new edition, New York, 1910.

Jane, Cecil (editor), *Select Documents Illustrating the Four Voyages of Columbus*, London, 1933.

Junco, Alfonso, *Inquisición sobre la Inquisición*, Santander, 1938.

Lea, Charles Henry, *Chapters from the Religious History of Spain Connected with the Inquisition*, Philadelphia, 1890; *A History of the Inquisition of Spain*, 4 volumes, New York and London, 1906-07; *The Moriscos of Spain: Their Conversion and Their Expulsion*, Philadelphia, 1901.

Llorente, Juan Antonio, *The History of the Inquisition in Spain*, Abridged and translated by an American, New York, 1826.

Marcu, Valeriu, *The Expulsion of the Jews from Spain*, London, 1935.

Martyr, Peter, *De Orbe Novo*, Translated by Francis Augustus MacNutt, New York, 1912.

Plunkett, Ierne L., *Isabel of Castile, and the Making of the Spanish Nation, 1451-1504*, New York and London, 1915.

Prescott, W. H., *History of the Reign of Ferdinand and Isabella the Catholic*, 3 volumes, new edition, Philadelphia, 1902.

Rodríguez Vila, A., *Crónicas del Gran Capitán*, Madrid, 1908.

Sala, G., *Política internacional de los Reyes Católicos*, Madrid, 1905.

Seaver, H. L., *The Great Revolt in Castile*, Cambridge (Mass.) and London, 1929.

Serrano y Sanz, M., *Orígenes de la dominación española*, Madrid, 1918.

Starkie, Walter: *Grand Inquisitor, Being an Account of Cardinal Ximenez de Cisneros and His Times*, London, 1940.

Walsh, William T., *Isabella of Spain, the Last Crusader*, New York, 1930.

CHAPTER X

Armstrong, Edward, *The Emperor Charles V*, 2 volumes, 2nd edition, London, 1910.

Bourne, Edward Gaylord, *Spain in America, 1450-1580*, New York and London, 1904.

Brandi, Karl, *The Emperor Charles V*, Translated by C. V. Wedgewood, New York, 1929.

Cánovas del Castillo, Antonio, *Bosquejo histórico de la casa de Austria en España*, Madrid, 1911.

Carande, Ramón, *Carlos V y sus Banqueros*, Madrid, 1944.

Cortés, Hernán, *Five Letters, 1519-1526*, Translated by J. Bayard Morris, New York, 1929.

Cunningham Grahame, Robert B., *Pedro de Valdivia, Conqueror of Chile*, London, 1926.

Davies, R. Trevor, *The Golden Century of Spain, 1501-1621*, London, 1937.

Díaz del Castillo, Bernal, *The True History of the Conquest of New Spain*, Translated by Alfred Percival Maudslay, 2 vols., London, 1908-16.

Gardiner, Samuel Rawson, *Prince Charles and the Spanish Marriage*, 2 volumes, London, 1869.

Griffin, Charles (editor), *Concerning Latin American Culture*, New York, 1940.

Hamilton, Earl J., *American Treasure and the Price Revolution in Spain, 1501-1650*, Cambridge (Mass.), 1934.

Haring, Clarence H., *Trade and Navigation Between Spain and the Indies in the Time of the Hapsburgs*, Cambridge (Mass.), 1918; also *The Spanish Empire in America*, New York, 1947.

Hume, Martin A. S., *The Court of Philip IV. Spain in Decadence,* New York, 1907; also *Spain, Its Greatness and Decay, 1479-1780,* Cambridge, 1897.

Las Casas, Bartolomé, *A Brief Narrative of the Destruction of the Indies by the Spanish,* Translated in Volume XVIII of *Purchas His Pilgrims,* new edition, 20 volumes, Glasgow, 1906.

Lea, Henry Charles, *History of the Inquisition in Spain,* 4 volumes, New York and London, 1906-07.

López de Gómara, Francisco, *Annals of the Emperor Charles V,* Translated by Roger Bigelow Merriman, Oxford, 1912; also *The Conquest of the West India,* facsimile of T. N.'s translation (1578) edited by Herbert Ingram Priestley, New York, 1940.

Lyon, F. H., *Diego de Sarmiento de Acuña, conde de Gondomar,* Oxford, 1910.

McCrie, Thomas, *History of the Progress and Suppression of the Reformation in Spain in the Sixteenth Century,* Edinburgh, 1829.

Means, Philip Ainsworth, *The Spanish Main,* New York, 1935.

Madariaga, Salvador de, *The Rise of the Spanish American Empire,* New York and London, 1947.

Merriman, Roger Bigelow, *The Rise of the Spanish Empire in the Old World and the New,* Vol. I—The Middle Ages, Vol. II—The Catholic Kings, Vol. III—The Emperor, Vol. IV—Philip the Prudent, New York and London, 1918-34.

Parry, J. H., *The Spanish Theory of Empire in the 16th Century,* Cambridge, 1940.

Rose, Stewart, *Ignatius Loyola and the Early Jesuits,* 2nd edition, London, 1891.

Santa Cruz, Alonso de, *Crónica del Emperador Carlos V,* 5 volumes, Madrid, 1920-25.

Tuberville, A. S., *The Spanish Inquisition,* New York and London, 1932.

Vásquez, Alberto and R. Selden Rose (editors), *Algunas Cartas de Don Diego Hurtado de Mendoza, escritas 1538-1552,* New Haven, 1935.

Walsh, William T., *Philip II,* New York and London, 1937.

Zavala, Silvio Arturo, *La Encomienda Indiana,* Madrid, 1935; also *Las Instituciones Jurídicas en la Conquista de América,* Madrid, 1935.

CHAPTER XI

Addison, Joseph, *Charles the Third of Spain,* Oxford, 1900.

Armstrong, Edward, *Elizabeth Farnese, "the Termagant of Spain,"* London, 1892.

D'Auvergne, Edmund B., *Godoy, the Queen's Favorite,* Boston, 1913.

Basterra, Ramón de, *Una empresa del siglo XVIII; los navíos de la Ilustración,* Caracas, 1925.

Blanco, Tomás, *Prontuario histórico de Puerto Rico*, 2nd edition, San Juan, 1943.

Danvila y Collado, M., *El reinado de Carlos III*, Madrid, 1891-94.

Gómez de Arteche, José, *El reinado de Carlos IV*, 3 volumes, Madrid, 1890-92.

Hamilton, Earl J., *War and Prices in Spain, 1651-1800*, Cambridge (Mass.), 1947.

Hill, Constance, *Story of the Princess des Ursins in Spain*, New York, 1899.

Kany, Charles E., *Life and Manners in Madrid, 1750-1800*, Berkeley, 1932.

Madariaga, Salvador de, *The Fall of the Spanish American Empire*, New York and London, 1948.

Parnell, Arthur, *The War of the Succession in Spain During the Reign of Queen Anne, 1702-1711*, London, 1888.

CHAPTER XII

D'Auvergne, Edmund B., *A Queen at Bay: the Story of Christina and Don Carlos*, London, 1910.

Bollaert, William, *Wars of Succession of Portugal and Spain, from 1826-1840: with Resumé of the Political History . . . to the Present Time*, 2 volumes, London, 1870.

Bolos y Saderra, Joaquín de, *La guerra civil en Cataluña, 1872-1876*, Madrid, 1898.

Brandt, Joseph A., *Towards the New Spain*, Chicago, 1933.

Carrión, Pascula, *Los latifundios de España*, Madrid, 1932.

Clarke, Henry Butler, *Modern Spain, 1815-1898*, Cambridge, 1906.

Doblado, Leucadio [Blanco White], *Letters from Spain*, London, 1822.

Eza, Vizconde de, *El problema agrario de España*, Madrid, 1915.

Ford, Richard, *Handbook for Travellers in Spain and Readers at Home*, 2 volumes, London, 1869.

González Posada, Adolfo, *Estudios sobre el régimen parlamentario en España*, Madrid, 1891; also *Evolución legislativa del régimen local en España de 1812 a 1909*, Madrid, 1910.

Hannay, David, *Don Emilio Castelar*, London, 1896.

Hume, Martin A. S., *Modern Spain, 1788-1898*, New York and London, 1900.

Jarnés, Benjamin, *Castelar, Hombre de Sinai*, Madrid, 1935.

Madariaga, Salvador de, *Spain*, 2nd edition, London, 1942.

Millis, Walter, *The Road to War*, New York, 1935.

Oman, Charles William Chadwick, *A History of the Peninsular War*, 5 volumes, Oxford, 1902-14.

Parry, E. Jones, *The Spanish Marriages, 1841-46*, London, 1936.

Pi y Margall, Francisco, *La República de 1873. Apuntes para escribir su historia*, Madrid, 1874.

Pirola, Antonio, *Historia Contemporánea [1843-79]*, 6 volumes, Madrid, 1875-80.

Quin, H. J., *Visit to Spain in 1822 and 1823,* London, 1824.

Romanones, Conde de, *Notas de una vida, 1862-1912,* 2 volumes, 2nd edition, Madrid, 1934; also *Las responsabilidades políticas del antiguo régimen de 1875 a 1923,* Madrid, 1924.

Ruíz Castillo, J., *Antonio Maura. 35 años de vida pública,* 2 volumes, Madrid, 1917.

Strobel, Edward Henry, *Spanish Revolution, 1868-1875,* Boston, 1898.

Tirado y Rojas, M., *La Masonería en España,* Madrid, 1892-3.

Whitaker, Arthur P., *The United States and the Independence of Latin America, 1800-1830,* Baltimore, 1941.

White, George F., *A Century of Spain and Portugal (1788-1898),* London, 1909.

Whitehouse, Henry R., *The Sacrifice of a Throne, Being an Account of the Life of Amadeus, Duke of Aosta, Sometime King of Spain,* New York, 1897.

Wylie, James Aitken, *Daybreak in Spain,* London and New York, 1870.

Young, Arthur, *Travels During the Years 1787, 1788 and 1789 . . . to which is added the Register of a Tour into Spain,* 2 volumes, Dublin, 1793.

CHAPTERS XIII AND XIV

Azaña Manuel, *Mi Rebelión en Barcelona,* Madrid, 1935.

Beneyto Pérez, Juan, *El nuevo estado español,* Madrid and Cádiz, 1939.

Borkenau, F., *The Spanish Cockpit,* London, 1937.

Brenan, Gerald, *The Spanish Labyrinth,* New York and Cambridge, 1943.

Buckley, Henry W., *Life and Death of the Spanish Republic,* London, 1940.

Cambó, Francisco, *Las Dictaduras,* Madrid, 1929; also *Por la Concordia,* Madrid, 1930.

Caravaca, F. and A. Orts-Ramos, *Historia ilustrada de la Revolución Española, 1870-1931,* 2 parts, Barcelona, 1931.

Espinosa, A. M., *The Second Spanish Republic and the Causes of the Counter Revolution,* San Francisco, 1937.

Fernández Almagro, M., *Historia del reinado de Alfonso XIII,* Barcelona, 1933.

Fonteriz, L. de., *The Red Terror in Madrid,* London, 1937.

Francos Rodríguez, José, *La vida de Canalejas,* Madrid, 1917.

George, Robert Esmond Gordon, *King Alfonso, a Biography,* London, 1942.

Godden, G. M., *Conflict in Spain, 1920-1937,* London, 1937.

Gómez, C. A., *La guerra de España, 1936-39,* 2 volumes, Buenos Aires, 1939.

Hayes, Carlton J. H., *Wartime Mission in Spain, 1942-45,* New York, 1945.

Jiménez de Asúa, Luis, *Proceso histórico de la Constitución de la República Española,* Madrid, 1932.

Leval, Gastón, *Problemas económicos de la revolución española,* Rosario, 1931.

López Ochoa, Eduardo, *De la dictadura a la República,* Madrid, 1930.

Maura y Gamazo, Gabriel, *Bosquejo histórico de la dictadura,* 2 volumes, Madrid, 1930.

Mendizábal Villalba, Alfredo, *The Martryrdom of Spain: Origins of a Civil War,* Translated by Charles Hope Lumley, New York and London, 1938.

Ortega y Gasset, José, *Rectificaciones de la República,* Madrid, 1931.

Ossorio y Gallardo, Angel, *Orígenes próximas de la España actual,* Buenos Aires, 1940.

Peers, E. Allison, *The Spanish Dilemma,* London, 1940; also *The Spanish Tragedy, 1930-1936,* New York, 1936.

Pemartín, José, *Qué es 'Lo Nuevo': Consideraciones sobre el momento español presente,* 3rd edition, Madrid, 1940.

Prieto, Carlos, *Spanish Front,* London, New York, and Toronto, 1936.

Santillán, Diego Abad de, *After the Revolution,* Translated by Louis Frank, New York and London, 1937.

Sencourt, Robt. E. [pseudonym of Robt. E. G. George], *Spain's Ordeal: a documented survey of recent events,* London and New York, 1938.

Smith, Rhea Marsh, *The Day of the Liberals in Spain,* Philadelphia, 1938.

Trend, J. B., *The Origins of Modern Spain,* Cambridge, 1934.

WORKS ON SPECIALIZED SUBJECTS

Belaúnde, Victor Andrés, *Bolivar and the Political Thought of the Spanish-American Revolution,* Baltimore, 1938.

Beneyto Pérez, Juan, *España y el problema de Europa,* Madrid, 1942.

Cannon, Dorothy F., *Cajal (1852-1934),* New York, 1949.

Costa, Joaquín, *Colecticismo agrario en España,* Madrid, 1938; also *Oligarquía y Caciquismo como la forma actual del Gobierno de España,* Madrid, 1902.

Cunninghame Grahame, Robert, *A Vanished Arcadia; being some account of the Jesuits in Paraguay, 1607 to 1707,* London, 1907, New York, 1924.

Diffie, Bailey W., *Latin-American Civilization: Colonial Period,* Harrisburg, 1945.

Eza, Vizconde de, *El problema agrario en España,* Madrid, 1915.

Fernández Duro, Cesáreo, *Armada Española desde la Unión de los Reinos de Castilla y de León,* 9 volumes, Madrid, 1895-1903.

Fisher, L. E., *Viceregal Administration in Spanish America,* Berkeley, 1926.

Humboldt, Alexander von and Aimé Bonpland: *Political Essay on the Kingdom of New Spain,* Translated by John Black, London, 1811-22.

Klein, J. G., *The Mesta, a Study in Spanish Economic History (1273-1836),* Cambridge (Mass.), 1920.

Mackay, John A., *The Other Spanish Christ,* London, 1932.

MacLeish, Archibald, *The American Story,* New York, 1944.

Yela Utrilla, Juan F., *España ante la guerra de independencia de los Estados Unidos,* Lérida, 1925.

Wilgus, Alva Curtis (editor), *Colonial Hispanic America,* Washington, 1936.

Viñas y May, Carmelo, *La Política Social y la Política Criminal en las Leyes de Indias,* Madrid, 1922; also *España y los Orígenes de la Política Social,* Madrid, 1930.

Martín Echeverría, L., *España. El país y sus habitantes,* Mexico, 1940.

McLachlan, J. O., *Trade and Peace with Old Spain, 1667-1750,* Cambridge, 1940.

Menéndez y Pelayo, Marcelino, *La Ciencia española,* Vols. XX and XXI of *Obras Completas,* Madrid, 1933.

Ots Capdequí, José María, *Instituciones Sociales de la América española en el período colonial,* La Plata, 1934.

Pattee, Richard, *Introduction to Hispanic America,* New York, 1949.

Scott, James Brown, *The Spanish Origin of International Law,* Washington, 1928; Oxford, 1934.

Smith, Robert S., *The Spanish Guild Merchant: a History of the Consulado, 1250-1700,* Durham, 1940.

Torre Revello, José, *Orígenes de la Imprenta en España y su desarrollo en América Española,* Buenos Aires, 1940.

Wright, Irene A., *Documents Concerning English Voyages to the Spanish Main, 1569-1580,* London, 1932. *Spanish Narratives of the English Attack on Santo Domingo, 1655,* London, 1926. *Spanish Policy Toward Virginia, 1606-1612,* New York, 1920.

Principal Dates in the History of Spain

TABLE 1

Dates in Political and Social History

B.C.

?	Probable foundation of Cádiz by the Phoenicians
Eleventh century	Arrival in Spain of first Cromagnon men
Tenth century	First Celtic invasion
Sixth century	Arrival of the Greeks and establishment of their first colonies
Sixth century	Second and more important Celtic invasion
Sixth century	Arrival of the Carthaginians
Sixth to third century	Carthaginian domination
219	Taking of Saguntum by Hannibal
218	Arrival of the first Roman troops
205	Final defeat of the Carthaginians and their expulsion from Spain
133	Destruction of Numantia

B.C.

Second century B.C.   Conquest of Spain by the Romans
to first century A.D.

35   Beginning of what is termed the Spanish Era
(first day of the first in accordance with which time was counted for
month)   several centuries (until 1384)

A.D.   (Christian Era)

Close of the first   Preaching of Christianity in Spain
century or begin-
ning of the second

From the first cen-   Pacific Roman domination
tury to the begin-
ning of the fifth

314   Council of Iliberis

400   First Council of Toledo

409   The first Germanic peoples (Suevians, Vandals,
                        and Alans) enter Spain

476   Destruction of the Roman Empire in western
                        Europe by the Germanic tribes

476-484   Conquest of a large part of Spain by Euric

?   Establishment of the Visigothic capital at
                        Toledo

549   The troops of Emperor Justinian overpower
                        southeastern Spain

587   Reccared's conversion to Christianity

622   The preachings of Mohammed result in the
                        birth of the Moslem religion

711   Defeat of the Visigothic army at Janda Lake
                        (the Battle of the Guadalate)

712-718   Conquest of Spain by the Moslems

A.D.

Probably between 718 and 725	Battle of Covodonga which began the War of Reconquest
756	Foundation of the independent Emirate of Córdova by Abd-er-Rahman I
780	Charlemagne's expedition to Saragossa Battle of Roncesvalles
785	The Franks conquer Gerona
785-792	Foundation of the Spanish March
801	Taking of Barcelona by the Franks
Middle of the ninth century	The Kings of Asturias cross the cordillera and advance through territory of León
860	Probable birth of the Kingdom of Pamplona, later Navarre
Close of the ninth century	The Counts of the Spanish March make themselves independent of the Frankish Kings
905	Sancho Garcés I, first historically authenticated King of Navarre, begins to rule
914?	Ordoño II establishes the capital of his kingdom in the city of León and assumes the title "Leonese King"
929	Abd-er-Rahman III assumes the title of Caliph and as such founds the Caliphate of Córdova
931-951	Ramiro II in his conquests reaches the Duero in the region of Castile, the Tormes on the southwest, and Madrid
Middle of the tenth century	Count Fernán González in Castile makes himself independent of the Kings of León
950	Fernán González is first cited as King of Castile
981-1002	Period of Almansor's victories

A.D.

1000	Beginning of the reign of Sancho Garcés III, called the Greater, in whose time (1000-1035) Navarre was the most powerful Christian kingdom of Spain, and included not only the Navarrese territory itself but also part of the zone of the Pyrenees to the Spanish March, and the County of Castile
1031	Destruction of the Caliphate of Córdova
1035	Sancho Garcés on his death leaves his kingdom divided among his sons: Navarre is given to García, Castile to Ferdinand, Aragón to Ramiro, and the districts of Sobrarbe and Ribagorza to Gonzalo
1035-1065	Reign of Ferdinand I of Castile and of León
1076	The Counts of Barcelona are already masters of the Counties of Gerona, Manresa and Ausona, and have extended their conquests on the south to Barbastro and the Ebro
1085	Conquest of Toledo. The Tagus becomes the southern boundary of León and of Castile
1086	Entry of the Almoravides
1094	The Cid conquers Valencia. In 1102 the Moslems reconquer it
1096	Conquest of Huesca by Pedro I of Aragón
1118	Conquest of Saragossa by King Alfonso I of Aragón
1137	Union of Aragón and Catalonia by the marriage of the Aragonese Princess Petronilla and Ramón Berenguer IV, Count of Barcelona
1143	Independence of the County of Portugal which soon becomes a kingdom

A.D.

1146	Entry of the Almohades
1188	The sessions of what is believed to be first *Cortes* are held at León
1200	The Province of Guipúzcoa recognizes Alfonso VIII of Castile as king
1212	Battle of Navas de Tolosa
1229-1238	Conquest of Mallorca and Valencia by Jaime I Creation of the Kingdom of Valencia
1230	Definite union of León and Castile
1234	The French Count Theobald of Champagne ascends the throne of Navarre and the period of French influence in that kingdom begins
1236-1247	Conquest of Andújar, Córdoba, Jaén, and Seville by Ferdinand III
1238	Foundation of the Moorish Kingdom of Granada
1266	Conquest of Murcia
1276	Creation of the Kingdom of Mallorca, which in 1349 again became definitely a part of the Crown of Aragón
1282-1284	Conquest of Sicily by Pedro III of Aragón
1283	Concession by Pedro III of the General Privilege of Aragón
1288	Concession of the Privilege of the Union by Alfonso III
1303-1324	Expeditionary force of Cataláns, Aragonese, and Navarrese to the Near East
1323-1324	Conquest of Sardinia
1326	Foundation of the Duchy of Athens, which lasted until 1387

A.D.

1332	Incorporation of the Province of Alava in the Crown of Castile
1340	Battle of the Salado, won by Alfonso XI of Castile. This victory definitely checked Moslem invasions from Morocco
1348	Pedro IV abolishes the Privilege of the Union
1370	The Province of Vizcaya (or Biscay) is incorporated by inheritance into the Crown of Castile
1412	The Compromise of Caspe, which gave the Crown to a Castilian Prince, Ferdinand I
1442-1443	Conquest of Naples by Alfonso V of Aragón
1474	Isabel I the Catholic ascends the throne of Castile
1476	Creation of the *Santa Hermandad* (the Holy Fraternity), the rural constabulary
1477	The Canary Islands are incorporated into the Crown of Castile
1479	Ferdinand II the Catholic begins his reign in Aragón
1481	Creation of the new Inquisition in Castile
1492	Conquest of Granada and end of the Reconquest
October 12, 1492	Columbus discovers America
1492	Expulsion of the Jews
1495-1503	New conquest of Naples by Spanish troops
1500	Isabella the Catholic declares that all the Indians of America are free
1505	Columbus dies at Valladolid
1509-1510	Cisneros conquers the fortified town of Oran and others in Argelia, Tripoli, and Morocco

A.D.

1512	Incorporation of Navarre into the Crown of Castile
1516	Charles I inherits the Kingdom of Aragón
1517	Charles I assumes the title of King of Castile
1519	Charles I is elected Emperor of Germany
1519-1521	Uprising and War of the *Comuneros*
1519-1521	Conquest of Mexico by Hernán Cortés
1525	Battle of Pavia, in which King Francis I of France is taken prisoner
1526	Decree of Charles I laying down rules for the protection of the Indians and their freedom
1532-1534	Conquest of Peru by Pizarro
1535	Conquest of Tunis
1535-1537	Diego de Almagro begins the conquest of Chile, which is completed by Pedro de Valdivia
1536	Mendoza's expedition to the territory of what is now Argentina, and foundation of the city of Buenos Aires
1556	Charles I abdicates the throne of Spain in favor of his son Philip II
1558	Charles I dies and his brother Ferdinand inherits the Empire
1571	Battle of Lepanto
1581	Philip II is elected King of Portugal
1588	The Invincible Armada
1597	Philip II cedes the Low Countries to his daughter Isabel Clara Eugenia and her husband Archduke Albert of Austria

A.D.

1609	Expulsion of the *Moriscos*
1640	Insurrection of Portugal. In 1668 the Spanish Crown recognizes that kingdom's independence
1643	Battle of Rocroy
1648-1661	Definite loss of the Low Countries of the North
1659	Peace of the Pyrenees, by which Spain cedes to France Roussillon, Cerdagne, Artois, Luxembourg and various fortified towns in Flanders
1700	The Crown of Spain passed to the French House of Bourbon. Philip V becomes the first Bourbon King of Spain
1702-1713	The War of the Spanish Succession results from Bourbon inheritance of the Spanish throne
1704	The English take Gibraltar
1713	Peace of Utrecht. Philip V cedes what is left of Flanders to the Elector of Bavaria, from whom it passes into possession of the Emperor of Austria
1716	Abolition of the political *fueros* of Aragón, Valencia, and Mallorca
1767	Expulsion of the Jesuits
1773	Dissolution of the Society of Jesus. (Reestablished by Pope Pius VII, 1814)
1805	Naval battle of Trafalgar
March, 1808	Mutiny at Aranjuez which gives the Crown to Ferdinand VII
May 2, 1808	The Spanish people fight the French soldiery in the streets of Madrid and the War of Spanish Independence is begun

A.D.

June 4, 1808	Battle of the Bruch
July 19, 1808	Battle of Bailén
1808	Constitution of Bayonne
1808	First siege of Saragossa
1808-1809	Second siege of Saragossa
1809	Third siege of Gerona
1810	Beginning of the parliamentary constitutional regime
1812	Constitution of Cádiz
1813	Battle of Vitoria and expulsion of the French troops
1814	Ferdinand VII returns to Spain. Derogation of the Constitution of Cádiz
1820	Uprising led by Riego and Quiroga. New constitutional period lasting three years
1824	The remaining Spanish colonies on the American mainland win their struggle for independence, begun in 1810
1830	Decree of Ferdinand VII publishing and ratifying Charles IV's action in abolishing the so-called Salic Law in 1789
1833	Death of Ferdinand VII. His daughter Isabel II succeeds him
1833-1840	First Carlist Civil War
1834	First Constitution granted by Isabel II (The Royal Statute)
1834	Mendizábal's Law abolishing entail

A.D.

1836	Relations with the Hispanic American countries are resumed as Spain recognizes their independence
1859	War against the Empire of Morocco
1868	The September Revolution and expulsion of Isabel II
1869	Democratic Constitution
1870	Preparatory law for freedom of Negro slaves
1871	Amadeo I is elected King of Spain
1872	The Negro slaves in Puerto Rico are emancipated
1872	Amadeo abdicates
1873	Proclamation in the *Cortes* of the First Republic
July 24, 1873	Creation of mixed arbitration boards of employers and workers, the first such commissions in Europe
January 3, 1874	Fall of the First Republic
December 29, 1874	Alfonso XII, son of Isabel II, is proclaimed King of Spain by the troops of General Martínez Campos
February, 1876	End of the Third and last Carlist Civil War
1876	New Spanish Constitution
1878	Peace of Zanjón, ending the war in Cuba
1879	Constitution of the Cuban autonomist party
1880	International Conference on Morocco
1885	Death of Alfonso XII
1885	Birth of Alfonso XIII. During his minority, his mother, Queen María Cristina, governs as regent

A.D.

1886	Emancipation of all slaves in Cuba
1888	First public manifestation of Catalán regionalism
1888	Publication of the Civil Code which unifies Spanish Private Law except as regards the special legislation in the regional *fueros* and privileges
1893	First draft of a law giving autonomy to the Overseas Provinces (Maura's Draft)
1895	New uprising of the Separatists in Cuba
1897	Law of Autonomy for the Antilles, going into effect January, 1898
1898	Loss of Cuba, Puerto Rico, and the Philippines
1901	The Catalán Regionalists send their first Deputies to the *Cortes*
1902	Alfonso XIII commences his reign
1910	The Socialist Party sends its first Deputies to the *Cortes*
1912	Acquisition of right to the zone of Morocco
1914	First World War, not ending until 1918. Spain remains neutral
September, 1923	General Primo de Rivera proclaims the Dictatorship and suspends the Convention of 1876
January 29, 1930	End of the Dictatorship
April 14, 1931	The Second Republic is proclaimed
December, 1931	The Republican Constitution is promulgated
October, 1933	The constituent *Cortes* is dissolved and general elections convoked

A.D.

February, 1936   The second *Cortes* is dissolved, new elections
                  are convoked, and the Popular Front wins by
                  a large majority

July, 1936   On July 17 the Army garrisoned in Morocco
                  rebels against the Second Republic. On July 18
                  the greater part of the Peninsular Army joins
                  the rebellion

1936-1939   International war on Spanish territory because
                  of the declared military intervention by Italy
                  and Germany in favor of the rebels. The war
                  ends with victory for the latter, with the two
                  totalitarian Powers each claiming a principal
                  part in its success

1939-1948   A dictatorial political regime of totalitarian pat-
                  tern is constituted in Spain and continues to the
                  present writing (1949). Great emigration of
                  Spanish liberals

TABLE II

*Dates of Inventions, Events, Works, and Persons Notable
in Science, Arts, and Letters*

Approximate dates for the discoveries and inventions made by pre-historic man are not known: the shaping and polishing of stone, confection of clothes, cultivation of crops, domestication of animals, use of copper and other metals, construction of dolmens, the wheel and the axle, et cetera.

B.C.

Fifteenth century?	Paintings in the Cave of Altamira and other caves of Northern Spain
?	Paintings in Eastern Spain
Eleventh or tenth century	Introduction of the Phoenician written alphabet
Sixth century	Arrival of the Greeks and introduction of their arts and industries
Fifth to third century	Flowering of the Tartessian, Mastienien, Iberian and Celt-Iberian civilizations
Second and subsequent centuries	Romanization of Spain; especially after the beginning of the first century A.D.
Year 2, 3, or 4 of the first century A.D.	Seneca, author of the *Moral Epistles,* is born at Córdova

A.D.

First to third centuries	Construction of some of the great Roman edifices on the Peninsula
Second and third centuries	Expansion of Christianity. First Christian martyrs

A.D.

Seventh century	Formation of the First Code of Laws common to Spaniards and Visigoths
785	Construction of the Mosque of Córdova on the foundation of the (Visigothic) Christian Church of St. Vincent
929-1031	Flowering of the Cordovan Moslem civilization
Ninth century	Appearance in the Christian kingdoms of Mozárabic architecture which continued to be constructed there into the eleventh century
Eleventh century	Romanic art appears and continues until the thirteenth century
Eleventh to fifteenth centuries	Principal Period of Mudéjar art
Eleventh century	Flowering in León and Castile of sculpture in ivory and in stone
Eleventh century	During this century lived the famous Catalán poet Ots Moncada, whose works have been lost
Eleventh century	Foundation at Toledo by Alfonso VI of the School for Translators of Moslem and Jewish works, an institution continued by Alfonso VII
1126	The Moslem philosopher Averroes is born at Córdova
1193?	Construction of the Giralda at Seville
Twelfth century	This century marks the triumph over Latin of the Romance languages which began to make headway in the tenth century. About the middle of the eleventh century Castilian suffered a temporary paralyzation but became dominant in the twelfth. Catalán was already being used in juridical documents in the eleventh century

A.D.

End of the twelfth century	First known work in Catalán literature: *Homilies d'Organya*
Twelfth and thirteenth century	Period of flowering of Moslem and Jewish philosophy and science in both the Taifa and the Christian kingdoms
Thirteenth century	Appearance of Gothic art and its gradual displacement of the Romanic
1212 or 1214	Foundation of the University of Palencia
1215	Foundation of the University of Salamanca
1226	The cornerstone is laid for the Cathedral of Toledo
1252	Publication of the *Astronomical Tables* of Alfonso X (Alfonso the Sage)
1256-1263	The Code of the *Siete Partidas* is written under Alfonso X's sponsorship
1275-1315	The Mallorcan philosopher Ramon Lull (or Raymund Lully) writes his famous *Arte Magna* and many other works
1283	Creation at Valencia of the first Consulate of the Sea. In the same year, or shortly before, the Code or Book of the Consulate of the Sea was published at Barcelona
Thirteenth to fifteenth centuries	Flourishing period of the port of Barcelona and Catalán commerce
Thirteenth to fifteenth centuries	The great Gothic edifices are built: the Cathedrals of León, Cuenca, Burgos, Toledo, Barcelona, et cetera
Second half of the thirteenth century	A new Spanish school of sculpture in stone flourishes (Burgos, León, Toledo)

A.D.

1330 or 1343	The Archpriest of Hita completes his poem, *Libro de buen amor*, the first book of poetry in Castilian
1384	Abolition of the "Spanish Era" and official substitution for it of the "Christian Era"
1412-1454	Intensive cultivation of letters, principally poetry, at Juan II's Court in Castile
1443-1458	Alfonso V of Aragón converts his Court at Naples into a cultural center of the arts and sciences
Fourteenth and fifteenth centuries	Flowering of the schools of cartographers—Cataláns, Mallorcans, and some Jews
1474	The first printing press is established at Valencia
1483	Probable date of the birth of Father Francisco de Vitoria, whose doctrines on International Law opened the way toward the United Nations
1492-1540	These years comprise the life of the Valencian philosopher, Luis Vives
1499	Publication of *La Celestina,* attributed to Fernando de Rojas
1499-1688	Epoch of the great Spanish voyages of discovery in the Americas and in Oceania
End of the fifteenth century	Epoch of Isabeline architecture and of the beginning of the Plateresque style
1508	Foundation by Cisneros of the University of Alcalá
1510	Birth of Lope de Rueda, known as the first dramatic author of truly popular style and inspiration in the Castilian language

1514	At Alcalá printing is begun of the Complutensian Polyglot Bible
1515?	Bartolomé de Las Casas begins his preaching and activity in favor of the Indians
1515	The great mystic writer St. Teresa is born
1519 to 1522	First circumnavigation of the globe is made by the Spanish mariner Sebastián Elcano
1525	Invention of the compass with variation by Felipe Guillén
1537-1539	St. Ignatius de Loyola founds the Society of Jesus
?	Invention of the "nonius" [a mathematical device for infinitesimal measurements] named after its inventor, Juan Nuñez
?	Discovery by Miguel Servet of the circulation of the blood
1547	Miguel de Cervantes is born at Alcalá
Before 1554	Publication of the first picaresque novel, *El Lazarillo de Tormes*
1557	Philip II arranges for construction of the Monastery of El Escorial
1569	Publication of the second Polyglot Bible is begun at Antwerp under direction of Arias Montano
1570	Voyage of Dr. Hernández to Mexico and Peru; the most important scientific voyage of the epoch
1574-1635	Lope de Vega writes his comedies
1605	Cervantes publishes the first part of *Don Quixote*
1615	Publication in Mexico of a part of the botanical work of Dr. Hernández, recording more than 14,000 species

A.D.

1615	Publication of the second part of *Don Quixote*
1622 to 1659	During this period Velázquez paints his famous pictures
1626	Francisco de Quevedo publishes one of his greatest works, *Historia de la vida del Buscón*
1629-1680	Between these dates Calderón de la Barca wrote his dramatic works
1648	Production of the first Spanish *zarzuela*, with music written for a libretto by Calderón
1660	First opera by Spanish authors, *La Púrpura de la rosa*, libretto by Calderón, music by Delgado
1680	The *Código de las Leyes Indias* (Code of Indian Laws) is published
1713 to 1744	Philip V creates the Spanish Academy of the Language, the Spanish Academy of History, and the Spanish Academy of Fine Arts
1738-1764	The Royal Palace of Madrid is erected
1746 to 1788	This period, which includes the reigns of Ferdinand VI and Charles III, is also that of the greatest renaissance of Spanish scientific culture
1746 to 1804	The *Sociedades Económicas de Amigos del País* (Economic Societies of Friends of the Country) are created
1746	Francisco de Goya is born at Fuente de Todos
1757 to the close of the century	The *tonadilla*, genuinely Spanish folk music, flourishes throughout Spain
1760	The porcelain factory of El Retiro is established
1775	Campomanes publishes his book on *Educación popular de los artesanos* (Popular Education of Artisans)

A.D.

1780	Foundation of the first Normal School, the *Colegio Académico de Primeras Letras*
1786-1791	The collection of *Sainetes* by Ramón de la Cruz is published
End of the eighteenth century	The sculptor Francisco Gutiérrez, in collaboration with Robert Michel, executes the Fountain of the Cybeles
1804-1808	Bartolomé Sureda invents the new ceramic paste called Madrid porcelain which during this period was used in manufacturing articles at El Retiro factory
1810	The philosopher Jaime Balmes is born at Vich
1819	The Prado Museum is inaugurated in the building constructed by the architect Villanueva for the Museum of Natural History
1814 and 1824	Emigrations of Spanish Liberals to various European nations, many of whom were greatly influenced by resultant scientific and cultural contacts and laid the foundations of the Spanish cultural renascence of 1833
1820	The great writer Concepción Arenal was born at El Ferrol
1820	The *Ateneo* (Athenaeum) is founded at Madrid
1829-1888	Epoch of publication of the first codes of laws common to all Spain. The first was the Code of Commerce in 1829
1830	The Conservatory of Music and Declamation is founded
1833	The universities closed by Ferdinand VII in 1830 are reopened

A.D.

1835	The Duke of Rivas' drama *Don Alvaro* is presented for the first time
1835	Mesonero Romanos publishes his *Panorama Matritense*, sketches of Madrid life and manners
1839	The first lenticular lighthouse is inaugurated at Santander
1839	Birth of Francisco Giner de los Ríos at Ronda
1844	Zorrilla's *Don Juan Tenorio* is presented for the first time
1845	The Universities are reformed, becoming government institutions, and the *Institutos de segunda enseñanza* are created
1845	The great Catalán poet Verdaguer is born
1846	Foundation of the Astronomical Observatory, already projected in Charles III's time, for which a building was constructed in 1790 by the architect Villanueva
1846	Birth of the jurist and historian Joaquín Costa
1848	The first train runs on the railway between Barcelona and Mataró. Before this there were several similar projects in 1827 and 1833. In 1850 the railway from Madrid to Aranjuez was inaugurated and later extended to Alicante
1849-1850	The new type of Spanish *zarzuela* appears
1850	Clavé organizes in Catalonia the first popular Orpheon
1856	Birth of the great writer Marcelino Menéndez y Pelayo

A.D.

1857	The general law of Public Education is published
1859	The Floral Games are initiated in Catalonia
1864	Rosales paints his picture, *The Testament of Isabel the Catholic*
1865-1867	The frigate *Numancia* makes the first circumnavigation of the world effected by a steamboat
1873	Benito Pérez Galdós begins to publish *Episodios Nacionales*
1874	José Echegaray presents his first play
1876	Foundation at Madrid of the *Institución Libre de Enseñanza*
1878	Pradilla's picture, *Doña Juana la Loca*, is awarded the first prize for painting at the Paris Exposition
1888	First Spanish World's Fair at Barcelona
1889	Congress of the Anatomical Society of Germany in which official recognition is given to Cajal's theory of nerve-cells, basis of this Spanish scientist's world-wide prestige
1890-1910	Granados writes his *Danzas españolas* and his *Goyescas*
1896	Albéniz presents for the first time his opera *Pepita Jiménez*, which inaugurates his music on Spanish folk-motives
1901	Primary teachers become Government employees. This change is completed in 1912 by incorporation in the official system of the teachers in the Basque Provinces
1901	For the first time scholarships for foreign study by teachers and students are established

A.D.

1903	Creation of the Institute of Social Reform, which exercised great influence on labor legislation
1907	Foundation by the State of the *Junta para ampliación de estudios*
1909	Establishment of the *Escuela Superior del Magisterio* for training Normal teachers
1910	The first Residence for Students is established at Madrid
1912	Establishment of the first circulating school libraries for teachers and pupils in primary schools
1912	Death of Marcelino Menéndez y Pelayo
1913	The Girls' School Inspection is established
February, 1915	Death of Francisco Giner de los Ríos
1918	Creation of the first School-Institute
1919 and subsequent years	Construction of the first trimotor and invention of the autogyro by the engineer Juan de la Cierva
1920	Death of the great novelist Benito Pérez Galdós
1929	World's Fair at Barcelona and Hispanic American-Portuguese Exhibition at Seville
1931-1934	Development of primary and secondary instruction and creation of new centers of scientific research
1934	Death of Julián Ribera, creator, on the basis of the initiative of Professor Codera, of the school of Spanish Arabists
1934	Death of Santiago Ramón y Cajal

Chart of Parallel Events in the History of Spanish Civilization and That of Other Countries

Prehistoric Times (B.C.)

The chronology of prehistoric times is not certainly known. Various dates are still under dispute and subject to possible correction. The chronology hereinafter adopted in this respect is in general that of Obermaier. Some classifications are likewise indecisive.

Epoch	Spain	Other Countries
I. THE PALEO-LITHIC OR OLD STONE AGE. THE PLEISTOCENE PE-RIOD (From its beginning in the Eolithic Age about 25,000 B.C.)	Of the first period of this Age (the pre-Chellean) no trace of human remains nor of human industry has been found in Spain. (In general, the names of these periods, as employed here, are derived from French localities in which character-istic remains have been found.)	Fragments and flakes of stone seemingly shaped by human hands have been found in central Europe, as has also a human lower jawbone (*Homo eidelber-gensis,* or H e i d e l b e r g man) .
	Of the second period (the Chellean) , character-ized by the stone axe, there are deposits in Spain: at San Isidro, Torralba, vicin-ity of Janda, Auronches, Alentajol, M e a l h a d a (north of Coimbra) .	Human remains possibly corresponding to this pe-riod have been found in E n g l a n d (*Eoanthropus dawsoni,* or P i l t d o w n man) .

Epoch	*Spain*	*Other Countries*
I. THE PALEO-LITHIC OR OLD STONE AGE. THE PLEISTOCENE PE-RIOD (From its beginning in the Eolithic Age about 25,000 B.C.) (*Continued*)	The third period (Acheulan) was character-ized by perfecting the stone axe (a new type of flint in-dustry) which perhaps came from Africa, passing through Spain to France and Britain.	This culture does not appear in central Europe where remains are found of a culture still more ancient, lacking the hand axe but possessing flake-tools.
	In the fourth period (Mousterian) there was a temperate climate in Spain. Fauna of warm zones. Small, delicate uten-sils and hand axes. Both types, together or alternat-ing, are found in deposits in the Manzanares basin, at Gibraltar, and in San-tander Province (Castillo and Morin Caves). Human remains (skulls and jaw-bones) at Gibraltar and Bañolas in Gerona. The mingling or interposition of stone instruments noted above gives rise to the pre-sumption that in this pe-riod there were various in-vasions into Spain of differ-ent peoples, and various communal changes of resi-dence.	Central Europe had a cold climate and glacial fauna. The most complete human remains of the pe-riod have been found at Neanderthal, north of Co-logne (*Homo neanderta-lensis*, or Neanderthal man).
II. EARLY PALEO-LITHIC	First period (Aurigna-cian) 25,000 B.C. Deposits in Caves of Castillo, San-tander. ("The stratigraphic succession found here is one of the most complete known among deposits with direct superposition of various industries," ac-	Traces of the culture of this period are found like-wise in France, northern Italy, southern England, and eastern Europe to the Ukraine; exceptionally, in southern Germany. In Italy burial sites appear. Skeletons have been discov-

Epoch	Spain	Other Countries
II. EARLY PALE-OLITHIC (*Continued*)	cording to Obermaier; and, again "The most complete paleolithic deposit of Europe"); t h e M o r i n Cave; Hornos de la Peña: all three localities in Santander.	ered revealing the existence of races unknown with respect to previous periods and types; akin to modern man. The most representative of t h e s e races is the Cromagnon (France), which also existed in Spain.

Second p e r i o d (Solutrean). About 20,000 B.C. Remains are found in the Cantabrian region (Caves of Castillo, Morín, Altamira, Cueto de la Mina, Balmori, Riera) and in the Mediterranean Zone, from Catalonia to Valencia inclusive. T h e Valencian Cave of Parpalló affords deftly shaped long, slender lanceheads or darts, with c e n t r a l   s t e m , lateral f l a n g e s , and sometimes finely wrought indented edges.

This culture is believed to have originated in western Europe, toward Hungary. Human remains in lower Bavaria and western France.

Third period (Magdalenian), 15,000 to 10,000 B.C. The principal deposit is at Cueto de la Mina in Asturias. Great development of q u a r t z implements, long and slender, and of those fashioned from bone and flint. Harpoons and sceptres with ornamentation. S c u l p t u r e s a n d pictures (Altamira, Basondo, Candamo, Castillo, etc.) The zone of this culture extended to the same regions as the Solutrean.

The point of origin of this culture seems to have been western France (Charente) and the watershed of the Pyrenees. It advanced to Belgium, Britain, Switzerland, central Germany, Poland, Moravia and Austria. Burial grounds are f o u n d in France and eastern Germany. Cromagnon anthropological type in some respects is similar to the Eskimo of our time.

Epoch	*Spain*	*Other Countries*
II. EARLY PALE-OLITHIC (*Continued*)	Capsian period. In its first p h a s e s exclusively Spanish in Europe, and contemporaneous with the three periods noted immediately above. This culture came from Africa, spreading through southern, central a n d north central Spain until it encountered the Aurignacian, S o l u - trean, and Magdalenian; all of which it penetrated at times. It was distinguished by its extraordinary geometric stone implements, large bone needles, and spirited human and animal silhouettes engraved on stone plaques. Also pictures of animals. Toward the close of the period these latter became geometrically stylized (Sierra Morena).	The final phases of the Capsian culture extended northward through France, Belgium, Britain, and possibly central Europe. In France it is called the Tardenoisian culture.
III. LATE PALE-OLITHIC, OR EPI-PALEOLITHIC. Be-T W E E N 10,000 AND 5000 B.C.	The first period (Azilian) culture flourished in northwestern S p a i n all a l o n g the Cantabrian coast and was contemporaneous with the final phases of Capsian culture.	Azilian s t a t i o n s are found in the British Isles, and in France and Belgium to the Alps and the Rhine. It was followed in these regions by the Tardenoisian culture which also spread through Germany.
IV. INTERMEDI-ARY PERIODS BE-TWEEN THE PA-LEOLITHIC A N D THE NEOLITHIC	Between the last phase of Capsian culture and the Neolithic p r o p e r l y so called, some intermediate steps or periods are generally recognized. A m o n g these should be noted the Asturian culture (the only Protoneolithic phase	Almost everywhere in Europe there were two intermediary periods: (1) the Campignian culture (from C a m p i g n y, in France), characterized by artificial pits or depressions that served for primitive human habitation; by ru-

Epoch	Spain	Other Countries
IV. INTERMEDIARY PERIODS BETWEEN THE PALEOLITHIC AND THE NEOLITHIC (*Continued*)	known in Spain) which, beginning in the region of the Miño, embraced all the Cantabrian littoral a n d Gerona Province. It is found most abundantly in Asturias. Characteristic remains a r e skull-mounds composed chiefly of edible marine mollusks (limpets, oysters, mussels, cockles, conches, etc.) ; and pointed picks formed from worn, flat, more or less oval, quartzite pebbles sharpened to a rather long point at one end.	d i m e n t a r y agriculture (barley) ; and by coarse pottery with line decoration; and (2) the Kjökkenmödding culture, especially in Scandinavia.

V. THE POLISHED STONE, OR NEOLITHIC AGE. FIRST PERIOD: NEOLITHIC PROPERLY SO CALLED (From 5000 to 2000 B.C., Approximately)

Spain

The Neolithic Age properly so called produced in Spain the general culture of the period, but with certain distinctive characteristics: great development of the megalithic sepulchres (dolmens) and a remarkable ceramic art. At the same time, this culture in Spain apparently lacked pile-built lake dwellings, of which no Spanish examples have been found. In the region of Almería have been discovered sites with walls and houses of stone belonging to this period. Copper was worked in the southern part of the Peninsula.

Other Countries

While Spain and the rest of Europe lived in the Neolithic Age, with an elemental tribal social organization, inhabiting crude huts, fortified hamlets, and lake dwellings built on piles; quarrying quartz for implements and mining and working copper (toward the close of this culture) ; building monumental sepulchres (with cremation in some regions) ; and practising a rudimentary agriculture; advanced cultures were produced in Asia and northeastern Africa on the bases of important States (empires) such as the Sumerian which flourished in Mesopotamia before 4000 B.C.; and the Egyptian (about the same period) , where after the two first dynasties, the Pharaoh Menes ruled the Delta and Upper Nile jointly. The Semites appeared in the UpperEuphrates Valley about the same time, and Abraham may have been the contemporary of the great Babylonian king Hammurabi (twenty-fourth century B.C. according to some archeologists, seventeenth according to others) who inspired a code of laws indicating a very advanced juridical organization. About 3000 B.C., it is believed, the Phoenicians were already occupying Syria. The primitive chronology of China corresponds also to this period: it begins, according to some authorities, with the law-giver Shen-Nung (2737 B.C.) and according to others with the Emperor Huang Ti (2698 B.C.). Imposing monuments of the epoch are, in Egypt, the great Pyramids which still astound us today, the Sphinx at Gizeh and the statue of Khefru (from the Fourth Dynasty which reigned, as some Egyptologists hold, in the fourth—though others opine in the second—millennium B.C.) The Pharaoh Rameses II belonged to the fourteenth century B.C.

Copper was known in the Orient earlier than in Europe (from 5000 B.C.)

NEOLITHIC: SECOND PERIOD: THE BRONZE AGE (From 2000 to 1000 B.C.)

Spain

Talayots (megalithic monuments), jars and burial urns from the Balearic Isles. Rock paintings and stylized drawings of men and animals or of geometric figures (northern Portugal and Galicia). The so-called culture of El Argar (Almería) appeared in this period, with burial in tiled tombs and in urns. Copper, tin and silver were worked, and there was foreign trade in these metals. After a temporary decadence, that trade started up again with regions of the western Mediterranean and with France.

Other Countries

It is believed that by this time the Celts, originating in central Europe, were already inhabiting France. About 1500—or in the fifteenth century— B.C. the Etruscans were inhabiting *Misia* or Lydia (Asia Minor), and about 1000 B.C. the first Etruscan invasion reached Italy, giving rise to an important State, enemy of Rome, and to a characteristic culture. Upon their arrival, the Etruscans found the Italiots already in Italy. In Asia Minor the Hittites, of whose culture a code is known dating from the fourteenth century B.C., likewise created a powerful State. During the same period there flourished in Crete a culture (Aegean or Cretan) remarkable for its art; later, in the Peloponnesus (Greece) came the so-called Mycenean culture (from 1650 to 1200 B.C.). Toward the close of this period (1015 or at latest 975 to 970 B.C.) Solomon began his reign at Jerusalem.

VI. THE IRON AGE

Its beginning, in so far as it refers to Europe, can be determined, for we have learned that iron was known in southwestern Europe in 1200 B.C., but a terminal date for the Iron Age can only be arbitrary, since iron continued during many centuries to be the metal from which were forged arms of offense and defense as well as tools; as indeed is still true in our own time with regard to both iron and steel. Nevertheless, most authorities set the end of this Age at the close of the first millennium B.C. (which in Roman history means the Age of Augustus), and divide it into two periods: one, from 1000 to 5000 B.C.; the other, from 500 to 1 B.C.

Spain

This is the age in which the Tartessian culture flourished in Spain (western Andalusia) as did the so-called Iberian culture which was already perceptible in the sixth century B.C. and reached its climax in the fifth and fourth, to flourish again in central Spain, invaded by Iberian tribes, in the third century B.C. This was the period also of Phoenician and Greek colonizations; of Carthaginian supremacy; of Celtic invasions; and of Roman conquest, with the beginning of Romanization in the Peninsula in the first century B.C.

Other Countries

In the rest of Europe, this age was characterized by the following events: In Italy, the founding of Rome (eighth century, 753 B.C.) and its primary expansion through victories over the Etruscans and the Carthaginians. In Greece, military supremacy and the defeat of Persian attempts at invasion (Marathon, Thermopylae, Salamis, Platea) and the flowering of Greek culture (Age of Pericles) with great creative talent in literature, philosophy, and art (fifth and part of fourth century B.C.). Soon thereafter, loss of Greek independence at the hands of Philip, King of Macedonia, whose son was Alexander the Great (336 to 323 or 324 B.C.).—Asia and Africa witnessed the apogee and the decline of the Phoenicians, and the founding and rise to power of Carthage (ninth to second centuries B.C.).—Buddha, the religious reformer of southern Asia, belonged to the sixth century B.C., in which period the Chinese moralists Confucius and Lao-Tse died.—In the Near East, the Persian Empire of Cyrus was destroyed by Alexander the Great. Northeast Africa saw the Hellenization of Egypt, whose native dynasties were displaced by that of the successors of Alexander the Great (the Ptolemies) with renascence in their reign of Greek culture. In 214 B.C. construction of the Great Wall of China began. In 222, shortly before the commencement of the Punic War, the Romans were masters of the whole of the Italian Peninsula; they had seized Sicily, driving the Carthaginians from that island, as a result of the First Punic War (264-241 B.C.). Victorious also in the Third Punic War (149-146 B.C.), the Romans destroyed Carthage and so put an end to Carthaginian power in Africa. By the middle of the first century B.C. Rome dominated Macedonia and Greece; and conquered all Asia Minor, Syria and Egypt, and, later on, eastern Europe north of the Danube. Gaul (which included the present territories of northern

Italy, France, Belgium and Switzerland, was wholly conquered up to the
Rhine by Julius Caesar (58-51 B.C.). Ever since 510 B.C. Rome had been a
Republic but it ceased to be so after 88 B.C., when the Civil War among the
Generals began. One of them, Octavius, vanquishing his rivals, assumed the
titles of Augustus and Emperor (27 B.C.). During the reign of Octavius
Augustus Jesus Christ was born (some authorities think in the year 4, others
in the year 7, A.D.). The Christian era is counted, effectively, from January
1 of the Roman year 754.—In this period the Roman conquest of Spain was
completed.

CHRISTIAN ERA (A.D.)

ROMAN DOMINATION (From the First to the Beginning of the Fifth Century)

Spain

The Romanization of the Spanish population groups created on the
Iberian Peninsula a culture of Latin type, with Spaniards contributing to its
literary and scientific production their own distinctive characteristics. Spain
was filled with splendid monuments of architecture, constructed by the
Roman administration. For the first time the Peninsula was a single State—
Hispania—comprehending the whole area, though as a part of and under
dominion of the Roman Empire. The Visigoths entered Spain for the first
time in 414. By 409 the Suevians, Vandals, and Alans had entered.

Other Countries

At the beginning of the Fourth century A.D., in order to prevent strife
between aspirants to the Imperial Throne, it was agreed that there should
be two Emperors: one in the West, at Rome; and the other in the East. In
311 A.D. the Emperor Galerius put an end to persecution of the Christians,
great numbers of whom had been martyrized theretofore. The Emperor
Constantine in 326 constructed a city—first called Byzantium and later Constantinople—to be capital of the Eastern Empire. In 323 Constantine presided over the Council of Nicaea which was important in fixing the Catholic
creed. In 337 Constantine was baptized on his deathbed.—In the second century the Germanic peoples began to invade the Empire from the East. One
of these, the Visigoths, under their king, Alaric, invaded Italy in the fourth
century and conquered Rome in 409-410. The Romans forced the Goths to
withdraw from Italy and settle in southern Gaul as allies of Rome (412).—
The Frankish Germans occupied northern and western Gaul, and the Burgundians, eastern Gaul.—A new Germanic invasion (the *Hérulis*) again
conquered Rome and ended the Western Empire (476).

Visigothic Domination (414-711)

Spain

The conquest of Spain by the Visigoths began in the northeastern regions and was completed (468-476) by Euric, except for the northwestern portion which the Suevians occupied until 585. During this period flourished a Hispano-Roman Visigoth culture which later influenced France.

Other Countries

After destruction of the Western Empire, its territories were dominated by various Germanic peoples, forming divers kingdoms. The Ostrogoths— apart from those occupying Gaul—settled in Italy (489-554). Following Justinian's brief rule (554-568), the Longobards entered Italy and established a kingdom in the Po valley, leaving Ravenna and Rome for Byzantine domination. The Saxons, summoned by the Britons, entered Britain (which the Romans had abandoned in 410) and constituted a kingdom in the southern part of the island (477-495). Soon after (500), the Angles arrived, proceeding from the Danish peninsula.—The Eastern Empire, which included present territories of Greece, Turkey, the Balkan States, Asia Minor and Egypt, continued independent. Its culminating period was the sixth century reign of Justinian, compiler of Roman Law (the Code, *Pandects* or Digest, and *Institutes,* or Compendium of Civil Law).—The splendid Basilica of St. Sophia, prototype of Byzantine art in both its architecture and its decoration, belongs to this period.—The Moslem era began in 622, date of the *hegira,* or flight, of Mohammed, founder of Mohammedanism, who was born in 570, died in 632.

Emirate and Caliphate of Cordoba (711 to 1031)

Spain

This is the culminating period of Moslem domination. Under Abderrahman I, Moslem Spain became an independent Emirate, separate from the Eastern caliphate.—The movement of the Christian Spaniards for Reconquest resulted in splitting the former Visigothic States into four Christian kingdoms and one principate or marquisate (Catalonia). A later dismemberment of territories of León and Castile produced the Kingdom of Portugal (1139). Feudalism did not strike deep root in Spain except in Catalonia and part of Aragón. However, although in general the posts held by nobles as governors of frontiers and provinces were neither hereditary nor possessed of sovereignty in law, they tended in actual practise to operate as independently of the Crown as possible. Consequently the kings in Spain strove as much as kings in other countries to obtain fulness of functions for the Throne and to control the rebellious spirit of the landed and titulary nobility.

Other Countries

Although the Moslem invaders of Spain tried also to conquer Gaul, which was dominated by the Franks, they were routed at the battle of Poitiers (732) and fell back. Not long after (752) the Frankish King Pepin inaugurated the Carlovingian dynasty, named for Pepin's son, Charlemagne (771-814), who formed a great empire by conquests in Germany, Italy, eastern Europe and northeastern Spain. He was crowned Emperor in 800, and fostered development of culture. Soon after his death, his grandchildren divided the Empire into three kingdoms (France, Germany, and Italy), with consequent loss of force by the royal authority. Governors of provinces (dukes and counts) asserted their own independence ever more energetically, until they came to be veritable lords of their own territories, demanding that their rule be made an hereditary right, with the attributes of sovereignty. Nevertheless, they did not break the bond of dependence on the king, whose vassals they were, and to whom they swore an oath of fealty. This political system, called Feudalism, was characterized by the hierarchy from king to lowliest vassal—the land being divided into feuds, or fiefs, each held by the tenant, or vassal, so long as he rendered certain services to his immediately superior lord, who in turn might be vassal of a greater lord or of the king—and by the participation of all the lords in the functions pertaining to sovereignty. Feudalism spread all over Europe, undermining authority of the kings, until centuries later there began a movement of reaction toward monarchy, in the sense of obtaining for the Throne the totality of sovereignty and of destroying the power of the dukes and counts.— Between 1139 and 1150 the monk Gratianus (presumably an Italian) wrote the collection of canon law entitled *Decretum* (Gratianus' Decree), of great importance in its own field, which reveals a strong influence of the doctrine of St. Isidore of Seville.

GREAT PROGRESS OF THE RECONQUEST. BEGINNING OF PENINSULA LITERATURE
(1031-1284)

Spain

Soon after the fall of the Caliphate began the great advance of the Reconquest as regards Castile (the taking of Toledo, 1085), Aragón and Catalonia. In 1035 the Kingdom of Aragón was created. In 1137 it united with Catalonia. León and Castile were joined in a single monarchy in 1230.—Literature began to be written in the Castilian, Galician, and Catalán tongues.— It was the period of the jongleurs and the troubadours; of epic poetry (*Poema del mío Cid* and others), and of devotional writings (Berceo and other authors).—Castilian prose is the luminous vehicle of *La Crónica General, La Grande y General Historia* (1270), *Las Siete Partidas*, and other works of Alfonso X's reign,—The flourishing period of municipal life and of the

Cortes likewise began, with strengthening of the local legislation—*fueros*—by which were initiated guarantees of the people's freedoms and recognition of what later centuries call "human rights."

Other Countries

This period was the apogee of feudalism in France. To counteract the system, the kings sought support from the free municipalities: Philip the Fair, who began to reign in 1285, had the plebeians (bourgeois) regularly attend the States General (1302), assemblies of the whole kingdom or of provinces which theretofore had been composed only of nobles and clerics, although there are some evidences of previous bourgeois intervention; but the States General were not deliberative nor did they enjoy any initiative. The king's will was still the final authority.—In Britain a single monarchy had been formed in 827; a new Danish invasion took place in 1014. In 1066 Norman invasion under William the Conqueror resulted in establishment of a Norman monarchy in England, and French Normandy was thereby incorporated into the English Crown. William introduced feudalism into his new State.—In 1215 the nobles and the people obtained the Magna Charta (a document analogous in part to the General Privilege of the Union, of Aragón), in which for the first time limitations were set on the royal power and general guarantees were established for the rights of individuals (for the most part, of individuals belonging to the upper classes) and for municipal autonomy.—In 1258 Parliament was formed, an assembly of nobles and of representative commoners.—The Crusades were begun in 1099 and ended in 1270. In the former year Godfrey de Bouillon took Jerusalem which Saladin, Kurdish-born Sultan of Egypt, reconquered in 1187.—This age witnessed also the jurisdictional conflict (Guelphs and Ghibellines) between the Papacy and the Empire which had been reborn under Otto I in 962.—It was the period when the *chanson de geste* flourished in France, and the *Lemoisin* and Provençal literatures attained their height.—In 1226 St. Francis of Assisi, founder of the Franciscan Order, died.—From 1271 to 1295 Marco Polo was on his famous voyage to Asia.—To the same century belonged St. Thomas Aquinas (1226-1274), author of the *Summa Totius Theologiae,* the harmony of faith and reason, a synthesis of medieval thought and thenceforward a basic document in Catholic philosophy.

END OF THE MIDDLE AGES AND BEGINNING OF SPANISH POLITICAL UNITY
(Fourteenth and Fifteenth Centuries)

Spain

In Aragón the monarchy under Pedro IV subdued the oligarchy of nobles.—The Aragonese Crown made conquests in Italy.—There was a military expedition to the Near East manned by Aragonese, Catalans, and Navarrese. —In Castile, notwithstanding the strength of some kings, the nobility asserted itself, humiliating the monarchs. The Catholic Kings put an end to this situation.—The Reconquest was completed with the taking of Granada.— Discovery of America, and beginning of New World colonization.—Period of great creative literature in Castile, Catalonia, and Valencia: the Arch-priest of Hita, Don Juan Manuel, *La Celestina*, etc.—Appearance of the first artists veritably Spanish, freed from subjection to foreign influences.—A splendid Mudéjar architecture, with appearance of Plateresque and Isabeline styles.— Beginning of Renaissance literary influence and of humanism properly so termed.

Other Countries

The first League or Confederation of the three Swiss cantons was established (1291), followed by that of the eight cantons (1353), origin of the independence achieved by Switzerland in 1476 (battles of Granson and Morat, in which Swiss infantry destroyed the cavalry of Austrian and Burgundian nobles).—The Hundred Years War between England and France (from the mid-fourteenth to the mid-fifteenth century) ended with victory for the French monarchy.—Joan of Arc, heroine of this war, was burned at the stake by the English (1431).—Louis XI of France (1461-1483) dominated the nobles and affirmed the royal authority.—War of the Roses (1455-1485) between the noble families of York and Lancaster for the English Throne.—Division of Italy and Germany into a number of principalities and republics, although with continuance of the institution of Empire; the Emperor being elected by the Diet, an assembly of the upper nobility.—The Turks, who in the eleventh century had seized the Caliphate of Bagdad and other territories of western Asia (Palestine among them) repeatedly attacked the Byzantine Empire, in 1453 conquering Constantinople, which became thereupon capital of the Turkish Empire.

Period of the Renaissance, the great revival of art and letters on the classical model which, originating in Italy in the fourteenth century, was extended throughout Europe, continuing into the fifteenth and sixteenth centuries and marking the transition from mediaeval to modern times. Great representative early figures were Dante (1265-1321), Barberino (1264-1348), Petrarch (1304-1374), Boccaccio (1313-1375), Salutato Coluccio (1330-1406). Period of great Italian and Flemish art, and of Renaissance architecture, with Primitive school of painters: Giotto, Orcagna, Tignarelli, Mantegna, da Vinci.—Invention of the printing press. The first book was printed at Haarlem in Holland by Coster (1446).—The era of geographical discoveries in Africa, Asia, and America began: In 1445 the Portuguese discovered Cape Verde; in 1486 the Portuguese Díaz discovered and doubled the Cape of Good Hope; in 1492 Columbus discovered America; in 1498 Vasco da Gama reached Hindustan.

HEGEMONY OF SPAIN IN EUROPE. THE GOLDEN AGE IN SPANISH
ART AND SCIENCE (Sixteenth and seventeenth centuries)

Spain

The political unity from the time of Charles I, the territorial heritage of
the House of Burgundy, the conquests of Italy and of America, together
with the elevation of Charles I and later of his brother to the throne of
Emperor, gave hegemony to the Spanish monarchy, natural ally of the
Austrian. That situation continued until the middle of the seventeenth century. In consequence, the Spanish State intervened in all international
questions. Spain's decline in international affairs came after Philip II's
death. In internal affairs, the Spanish State was a personal union, maintaining in great part the autonomies of the ancient kingdoms:—Struggle against
Protestantism.—The Counter-Reformation (Society of Jesus).—The new
Inquisition, created at the close of the fifteenth century by the Catholic
Kings.—Loss of municipal liberties and of the *Cortes* in Castile.—Blossoming
in all the fields of culture, and affirmation of the distinctive quality of the
Spanish mind; a period including the sixteenth and much of the seventeenth
century (Lope de Vega died in 1635; Calderón de la Barca in 1681; Tirso de
Molina in 1648). Valásquez painted in Philip IV's reign (1621-1665).

Other Countries

Intensification of cosmographical and geographical discoveries.—Extension of the Renaissance and enrichment of its content.—Schism of the Christian world in consequence of the Reformation and Protestantism.—Religious
wars and persecutions.—Council of Trent and Counter-Reformation.—
Strengthening of the powerful monarchies (France, England) and appearance of new Powers (the Netherlands, Russia, the Scandinavian States).—
In the middle of the seventeenth century, hegemony of Europe passed to
France (Louis XIV).—Civil War in England (1642) resulted in establishment of the Commonwealth (Cromwell).—Revolution of 1688; Bill of
Rights adopted by the Convention Parliament of 1689 at the beginning of
the Dutch dynasty on the English Throne (William of Orange).—Dawn of
the Russian Empire.—Union of the Marquisate of Brandenburg and the
Duchy of Prussia in the person of a Hohenzollern (1617). This gave rise in
1701 to creation of the Kingdom of Prussia, later to exercise great influence
in Germany. In 1609 the Dutch achieved independence, and in 1648 the
Peace of Westphalia officially recognized the Dutch and the Swiss Republics.
—Colonization was greatly developed, with seizure of territories in the Americas, Asia, and Africa by the Portuguese, Dutch, English, and French. Foundation in 1606 of the Virginia Company, beginning of English colonization
on the eastern coast of North America. Arrival of the Puritans at Plymouth
in 1620 (the *Mayflower*).—Creation of the English Navy, Britain's chief
armed force for more than three centuries.—Blossoming of Italian art (Ra-

phael, Michael Angelo, Giorgione, Titian, Veronese, Correggio) and likewise of Flemish and Dutch painting (Rubens, Jordaens, Rembrandt and
Franz Hals).—Age of greatness in English literature. Shakespeare (1564-
1616) was the contemporary of Cervantes (1547-1616), of Rembrandt (1606-
1669) and of Velázquez (1599-1660).—The French classic theatre was born
in the seventeenth century (Corneille, Molière, Racine), under Spanish
influence.—Previously, France had produced notable Renaissance writers,
with Rabelais pre-eminent (1490 or '95-1553).—At the same time flourished
the great French prose writers (Bossuet, Bourdaloue, Fénelon, Descartes,
Montaigne, etc.) and the poets (period of Louis XIV).—The seventeenth
was the century of critical and independent philosophers represented by
Descartes, Malebranche, Spinoza, Leibnitz, Locke, and Bolingbroke, among
others. Some dealt with the problems of political liberty and religious tolerance, thus preparing the way for eighteenth century philosophy.—In 1532
Machiavelli published *The Prince,* which had a practical influence in Spain
though it was contradictory to the national doctrine which opposed dictatorship and was also in substantial opposition to the Empire international and
political policy based on so-called "reasons of State." Consequently Spain
offered the contrast of philosophers and juridical theologians maintaining
that national doctrine while kings and politicians were more inclined toward
Machiavellian practise.—Ideological opposition was also manifested between
the Dutchman Grotius (1583-1645), long held to be the father of the science of International Law, and the Spaniard Francisco de Vitoria and his
followers, with regard to the very bases of International Law and the concept of international political society. The Spanish doctrine was closer to
modern juridical ideas than was that of Grotius.

The Eighteenth Century and the Intellectual and Economic Renaissance

Spain

The French House of Bourbon was seated on the Throne of Spain. There
were frustrated efforts to recover Spain's political position in Europe.—
Renascence of culture and industry, fostered principally by Ferdinand VI
and Charles III.—Political decadence once more at the close of the century.—
Financial and administrative reform on the Peninsula and in the Spanish
possessions in the Americas.—Change in economic orientation with respect
to trade and the concept of wealth, in conformity with new ideas in those
fields—Renascence in scientific thought and research.—"Enlightened despotism" of democratic and economic type.

Other Countries

A century of immense political change.—The political power of Switzerland, Holland and Spain was in decadence; with affirmation of France, Eng-

land, Prussia and Russia as great Powers.—Austria, though conquered in the War of Succession, acquired new force because of having driven out the Turks from part of Austrian territory (Hungary).—While all these States were absolute monarchies, some practised "enlightened despotism," the principal exponents of which were Emperor Joseph II of Austria, Catherine the Great of Russia, and Charles III of Spain.—The social and economic organization of Russia was based on the assignment of the land of the peasant farmers, or *mujiks*, to the service of the nobles as proprietors.—Prussia soon showed itself to be a militaristic State. Its civil model was the France of Louis XIV; its militia was patterned on the Ordinances of the Spanish Army. Its royal organizer was Frederick the Great (1712-1786) whose military talent raised Prussia to a powerful position, as had been the case of Russia under Peter the Great (1672-1725).—England extended her colonial possessions by the conquest of Canada, formerly a French colony, and of Hindustan.—At the close of the century the 13 English colonies in North America rebelled successfully, their independence as the United States being recognized in 1783.—The French Revolution (1789) overthrew the absolute monarchy and established the Republic.—Liberal democratic and constitutional regimes appeared, with the United States Constitution and the Bill of Rights (1797) and with the French revolutionary Constitution of 1791 followed by the more radical document of 1793.—The European monarchies, including England, notwithstanding that country's reform of 1688 and its parliamentarianism, strove against this new form of government.—France confronted them all, but failed to implant liberal constitutionalism and the republican form of government except temporarily in some foreign territories it conquered and dominated. In France itself, by the closing years of the century the Republic was such in name only, and it gave way in 1799 to the Consulate under Napoleon who in 1804 was to proclaim himself Emperor.—Italy continued to be partitioned under the power of foreign rulers (Austrian Empire, Bourbons of Naples, Kingdoms of Tuscany, Sardinia, and Lombardy-Venice, as well as the Papal States).—Germany too was still divided, with no State stronger than Prussia.—Poland suffered its first partition, among Russia, Prussia, and Austria, in 1772.—The legislative union of Ireland and England, agreed upon in 1800, was ratified in 1801.— In the sphere of political economy, the eighteenth century was likewise the century of reform. The so-called Mercantile or Monopoly System, followed in previous centuries by all States, was to some extent modified by the theories of the Physiocrats, who maintained that the soil is the sole source of wealth, and proclaimed economic freedom on the basis of no intervention by the State (*laissez faire, laissez passer*). The physiocratic doctrine was modified and supplemented by the English economist Adam Smith (his book, *An Enquiry into the Nature and Causes of the Wealth of Nations*, appeared in 1776), who held the labor of a nation to be the source of its means of life and the standard of value; with wages, profit and rent entering into price determination.—There was a generally changing attitude toward taxes and the public treasury.—At the end of the century, certain mechanical inventions (looms, steam engines, etc.) produced a considerable increase in manufacturing industries.—In the field of philosophy, the ideas of seventeenth century English writers had repercussions in France, giving rise to two currents: (1) in the first half of the eighteenth century, with Voltaire and Montesquieu as principal figures; (2) toward the close of the century, with Rousseau and the Encyclopedists. Both groups gave especial attention to the political and the religious problem; the first current was not revolutionary; the second in general was, though not all participating in it could be described as revolutionists. The doctrines of the latter group were set forth in the *Encyclopédie,* which in 35 volumes (1759-1772) attempted to give a rational explanation of the universe and which with Rousseau's *Contrat Social* largely inspired the French Revolution of 1789 and was widely read throughout Europe and the Americas.—It was the age of blossoming in German literature (Schlegel, Lessing, Klopstock, Wieland, Schiller, Goethe) and of its influence in other countries. To this period belongs Kant (1724-1804), father of modern metaphysics. The German writers of the time knew and admired sixteenth and seventeenth century Spanish classics, then forgotten in other countries and to some extent in Spain itself.—Sir Isaac Newton, discoverer of the law of gravity, died in 1727.

THE NINETEENTH CENTURY

Spain

Constitutional government appeared in Spain (1810-1812), and almost the whole of the century was marked by the subsequent struggle to have it definitely implanted and strictly applied.—War of Spanish Independence and civil wars.—Loss of the American colonies and the Philippines.—Formation of a group of colonies and a sphere of influence in west Africa.—For Spain most of the nineteenth century was marked by the nation's withdrawal from international life.—Economic and cultural renascence was delayed in comparison with the rest of Europe.—The end of the century was a period of both national pessimism and of reaction against that attitude.

Other Countries

The Napoleonic Empire (1804) inaugurated the century, along with the wars engendered by Napoleon's political ambition. After being conquered by him, the European monarchies combined to eradicate every trace of the liberalism of the French Revolution, and shared among themselves some of Napoleon's acquisitions and some French territory (Congress of Vienna and Holy Alliance).—The consequent reaction produced in all countries except England revolutions and continuous unrest. In 1830 constitutionalists in various countries began to make some gains though these were very rudimentary. In 1832 the British Parliament passed the First Reform Bill, which provided for widening the parliamentary franchise and removing inequalities and abuses in the system of representation.—In 1848 a new revolution brought about the Second Republic in France and won universal manhood suffrage; but the regime was of brief duration. In 1851 Napoleon III, nephew of Napoleon I, re-established the Empire. In the other countries, absolutism followed until about 1860 when some kings decided to grant Constitutions (Austria, 1861; Hungary, 1867).—Russian serfs were declared free in 1863.—Negro slaves were emancipated by the British about 1830, by France in 1848, and somewhat later by other European countries. In the United States emancipation cost a long and bitter civil war (1861-1865).— Several new European States were born: Greece in 1827, after a war of independence (to cast off Turkish domination) in which the Greeks were aided by the British, French and Russians; Belgium in 1830, in consequence of a revolution removing her from under the Crown of Holland; Italy in 1861, through initiative of the Kings of Piedmont (House of Savoy), aided by the French.—Italian political unification was effected with the acquisition of Venice (1866) and the entry into Rome (1870) which ended the temporal dominion of the Holy See.—The unification of Germany was arrived at differently. Austria formed part of the Germanic Confederation, ceasing to belong thereto, however, in 1860, because of having been conquered in the war promoted by Prussia. With the latter kingdom as core, there was formed the Confederation of the North, dominated by the Prussian King, whom the southern German States were pledged to aid in case of war. With Germany victorious in the Franco-Prussian conflict (1870-71), the King of Prussia was enabled to constitute, under his own leadership, the German Empire, of which all the other German States formed part except Austria and the German-speaking Swiss cantons.—Switzerland completed its own Confederation in 1815, with entrance into it of Valais, Neuchatel, Geneva, and the Archbishopric of Basle. The Constitution of 1848 converted the Confederation into a Federal State.—Hungary, subject to the Austrian Empire, achieved the category of kingdom, with independent parliament and government, in 1867.—Norway, which in 1814 belonged to Denmark, in that year became a dominion of the Swedes.—The defeat of Napoleon III by the Germans resulted in proclamation of the Third Republic (still existent) in France.— Turkey lost Egypt in 1808; Serbia separated from Greece in 1817; England occupied Egypt in 1883.—In 1886 the first bill for Home Rule in Ireland was passed under Gladstone's sponsorship. In the continental Americas, the nineteenth was the century of independence for all former Spanish and Portuguese colonies (except the Guianas) and for some of the island colonies; and for organization of these former colonial possessions into republics. It was likewise a century of colossal expansion for the United States, in consequence of European immigration and of occupation and cultivation of vast territories from the Alleghanies to the Pacific, and this territorial expansion was accompanied by achievements denoting the apogee of material and modern mechanized civilization and of capitalism.

In the sphere of religion the nineteenth century was marked by two great events: (1) publication of the Syllabus (Encyclical *Quanta cura,* December 8, 1864) in which the Holy See set forth the index or summary "of the principal errors of our time" with respect to philosophy, social doctrine, politics, relations between Church and State, morals, etc., with corresponding condemnation; and (2) the doctrine of the infallibility of the Pope when speaking *ex cathedra* (Constitution *Pastor aeternus,* July 18, 1870) which was the culmination of the Council of the Vatican (1868-1870). The doctrine of infallibility then set forth refers to the Pope's utterances on *faith* and *customs* and formulates and teaches *what should and what should not be believed* by Catholics.

The nineteenth was the century of mechanical, electrical, and chemical inventions and discoveries which profoundly altered the aspect of modern civilization, and thereby contributed substantially to development of the machine age in industry and agriculture; and at the same time created the apex of capitalism. One inevitable result was to increase the numbers making up the mass of workers. Another consequence, in reaction against the abuses to which labor was subjected in the questions of hours and wages, was formation of the doctrines and of the political parties of Socialism and of the Workers International (1866), with "the class-struggle" as theme. This new political force quickly acquired influence, exercised throughout the second half of the nineteenth, which was augmented in volume and energy in the twentieth. Pope Leo XIII confronted this labor socialism with his Encyclical *Rerum novarum,* issued not in opposition to but in favor of what was humane and just in its aspirations (though in a sense very distinct from that of the Marxist formula) and created what was called "Christian socialism," consisting of middle class elements and some Catholic scientists.

The nineteenth century was a period of great progress also in medicine, a progress continuing to the present and accelerated considerably by developments in surgery and other fields brought about by war conditions.

From the point of view of civilization in the widest sense, the end of the nineteenth century implanted, as a result of all that had gone before, the struggle between guidances that may be termed *material* and *spiritual,* represented respectively by the modern liberal and the religious tradition. For the upper and the wealthy middle classes, whose existence was based on the increase of industry and amassing of riches, the new materialism signified mankind's fundamental civilization. In natural consequence the masses of the people placed themselves in opposition to this concept which was oppressive in its means and materialistic in its ends. Thus the class struggle increased in accordance with the Marxist idea which in turn engendered another economic *materialism* with social consequences plain to be seen in the twentieth century. For their part, the educated and liberal elements in all countries refused to conform to a mechanized pattern or to make money and power their primary aims. Accordingly, the social unity of many countries was fractured; and in the present century totalitarian dictatorships were on the verge of victory in the Second World War waged in Europe by German Nazism, Italian Fascism, and their imitators among the Spaniards. The Japanese allied themselves with these forces; while Soviet Russia, transformed into a Communist nation, threatened practically all other countries in various ways. Hence there were splits in Leftist elements of not a few nations; a situation which, in spite of the 1945 victory in favor of the peoples substantially democratic and liberal, continues to menace mankind with threat of a Third World War.

The Twentieth Century

Spain

The first 33 years of the twentieth century were marked in Spain by the following events: *politically,* the change from *constitutional monarchy* (Alfonso XIII) to a *dictatorship* (1923) which was provoked by the King himself; and in consequence of this change, the great reaction that brought about the alliance of the Leftist political parties with the majority of the Monarchists, and subsequently the dethronement of Alfonso XIII (1930).

Prior to this, Spanish territorial possessions had been expanded by the acquisition, with France's conformity, of a zone of influence in Morocco. This expansion brought wars in its train, occurring for the most part in the period of the Dictatorship, against the Moroccan chief Abd-el-Krim, and terminating with the latter's defeat at Alhucemas (September 1926).

Socially and *culturally,* the period from 1898 to 1932 was characterized by reawakening of the nation's confidence in its own strength and faculties, and by the increase and development of cultural media and of intellectual production. *Economically* also conditions showed considerable improvement; a fact particularly favorable to Spain's neutral position during World War I (1914-18). Thus Spain once more began to figure in European international life, politically as well as in scientific, artistic, and literary activities. Nevertheless, the Dictatorship of 1923-30 engendered the internal political divisionism already noted, which placed the liberal masses, and almost all those who until then had been monarchists, in open hostility to Alfonso XIII; the eventual result being disappearance of the Monarchy and advent of the Republic.

During the Republic, the mixture of elements that had produced the new regime, and the concurrent adoption by Rightist parties of Italian Fascism and even to a certain extent of German Nazism, split the Spanish people into two totally different groups, with, finally, the emigration of one group to various countries of Europe and the Americas.

To complete the picture of the psychology of the Spanish people, both the liberals in all the modalities of liberalism and the non-liberals, it must be borne in mind that they all succeeded in dwelling together in remarkable harmony under the monarchy (as it is only just to recognize) to a degree unusual among peoples naturally stubborn in their determination and violent in their emotions; characteristics attributed often, and sometimes exclusively, to the Spanish. Until 1936, there was, indeed, the frankest and fullest cooperation in the fields of science and art as well as the most fraternal friendship among men of utterly different political and religious ideologies. Only the civil war that enveloped Spain thereafter was capable of destroying this highly civilized manner of life, during the course of which it was exacted of none as price of his participation in its benefits that he belong to any particular race, nor embrace any particular creed, nor adhere to any particular political ideology.

Other Countries

Especially in Europe, the first 33 years of the twentieth century brought great changes, most of these being posterior to World War I (1914-1918). Prior to the War had come the independence of Norway, pacifically achieved in 1905; the granting of a constitutional regime in Russia (1905), and soon thereafter in Turkey (1908). Portugal became a republic in 1910. The separate States of the Irish Free State and Northern Ireland came into being in 1921. World War I, which ended with the Treaty of Versailles (1919) greatly altered the political map of Europe by creation of new nationalities with republican regimes and by conversion of some ancient monarchies into republics (Germany, Austria, Hungary, Russia, Greece, etc.). A similar transformation took place in China; while Japan quickly became a great power with modern cultural orientation. Within this general framework, there should be noted in particular, the rise to power in some of these nations, and in Great Britain, of a Socialist party, either alone or in coalition with bourgeois parties, and the formation of a Communist State in the ancient Russian Empire (U.S.S.R., 1917).—Other nations, however, among them Italy, Germany, and Portugal (some after having passed through a republican regime), were converted more or less openly into dictatorships.—In 1922 Turkey recovered part of the territories that she had lost shortly before in the Balkan War of 1913, and was organized into a republic of modern pattern, with abolition of many traditional Turkish customs.—Egypt again became independent, and the long-term British intervention was ended.

World War I produced not only the foregoing political results but also a great economic crisis arising from the debts contracted by many States during the conflict or from the reparations exacted by the Treaty of Versailles. Concomitant in some cases with the crisis was diminished production, with a considerable mass of workers unemployed; while in other cases over-production found insufficient markets and brought about the destruction of products.

In the sphere of ideologies and morals, mankind's state was one of doubt and insecurity, precursor perhaps of a profound change in the social and political structure in individual relationships. The horror consequent upon the destruction and suffering of the War caused the majority of the countries of the world—59 States and nations—to create the League of Nations (1920), which had as its principal purpose the prevention of another armed conflict. After having rendered great service to the cause of peace, and after having created various efficient organs such as the International Labor Office and the International Tribunal of Justice, the League of Nations underwent a series of crises, principally on account of the withdrawal of important States, including Germany and Japan. The U.S.S.R. refused to participate in the League until 1934. The United States never joined, in spite of President Wilson's sponsorship and advocacy of the Pact of 1919. The policy of isolation and refusal to join the League caused a rift for some years between the United States and the European nations, as well as some Hispanic American States; weakening the League and so making possible World War II. That conflict lasted for five years, 1940-45, and many peoples are still suffering politically and economically from its consequences, including hundreds of thousands who are homeless and hungering.

The victory in 1945 saved the democracies of both hemispheres, but as yet (1949) that victory has not eliminated all dictatorships in Europe and in the Americas, still existing as remains, and in some instances as resurrections, of despotic government with anti-democracy and violence as their organs.

Index